INTRODUCTION TO CRIMINAL LAW

A Contemporary Approach

RUSSELL L. WEAVER
Professor of Law & Distinguished University Scholar
University of Louisville, Louis D. Brandeis School of Law

JOHN M. BURKOFF
Professor of Law Emeritus
University of Pittsburgh School of Law

CATHERINE HANCOCK
Geoffrey C. Bible & Murray H. Bring Professor of Constitutional Law
Tulane University Law School

JAMES D. DIAMOND
Visiting Professor
Roger Williams University School of Law

The publisher is not engaged in rendering legal or other professional advice, and this publication is not a substitute for the advice of an attorney. If you require legal or other expert advice, you should seek the services of a competent attorney or other professional.

© 2021 LEG, Inc. d/b/a West Academic
    444 Cedar Street, Suite 700
    St. Paul, MN 55101
    1-877-888-1330

West, West Academic Publishing, and West Academic are trademarks of West Publishing Corporation, used under license.

Printed in the United States of America

ISBN: 978-1-64020-063-0

To Ben, Kate and Laurence, with love, **RLW**

To Nancy, Amy & Sean, David & Emmy, Emma, Molly, Hannah, and Cyrus, with love, **JMB**

To Peter, Elizabeth, Caitlin, and Margaret, with love, **CH**

To Marian, Aaron, Evelyn, Isabelle and Reuben with love, **JDD**

Preface

This textbook continues the traditions of Weaver, Burkoff, Hancock's Criminal Law, A Contemporary Approach. After teaching several law classes at The University of Arizona, including an introductory criminal law class, James came to the realization that the choices in the marketplace for law textbooks catering to either masters or undergraduate students studying law was imperfect. Masters In Legal Studies programs have become quite commonplace in the United States, and, additionally there are colleges, like the University of Arizona, experimenting with new undergraduate law programs. Faculty teaching in those programs, however, typically have three imperfect choices if they want to use the case method of teaching law: 1) they use a Juris Doctor level casebook but assign substantially less material from the book; 2) they use an undergraduate or high school level text-book; or 3) they develop their own materials.

This textbook, then, is based on the third edition of Russell, John and Catherine's interactive casebook. James took that book, reorganized it, substantially shortened it and added new material which will, hopefully be of interest to students. Our goal is that this approach will be appealing to masters and undergraduate students studying law who still desire to learn criminal law cases while also learning black letter law.

As with the prior Interactive casebooks, the primary goal was to create a "teacher's book"—a book that contains thought provoking problems (referred to as "hypos") designed to stimulate thought and produce interesting classroom discussion. The hypos are woven throughout the chapters and are designed to help students learn doctrine, illuminate trends in the law, and ultimately produce better learning. A secondary goal was to include a focus on teaching "skills." Some of the problems place students in practical situations that they are likely to encounter in a criminal justice career, and therefore encourage students to think about how they might handle those situations in real-life. Each chapter begins with an overview of the law on the subject covered in the chapter for simple and easy access by students. In order to prevent the book from being unduly long, we have chosen not to include encyclopedic notes and references like those found in other books. In the criminal law area students have numerous high-quality secondary sources available to them, and students can consult those sources for expanded discussions of the law. By limiting the scope of notes, we were able to include hypotheticals and to provide greater opportunity for critical thinking. We have included "food for thought" questions that will help students understand how to address the more complex questions that arise in the "points for discussion" material and in the hypotheticals.

We welcome input and feedback on this book.

RLW, JMB, CH, & JDD

Acknowledgment

I am much indebted to Joel Brodfuehrer, my Teaching Assistant, whose help was indispensable. My students Kayla Batt, Megan Irgans, Allison Kahn, Nicolette Malinoff and Sofia Nuno all contributed to the additions. If not for the vision of Brent White, Marc Miller, Robert A. Williams Jr. and Najwa Nabti at the University of Arizona James E. Rogers College of Law for envisioning and designing the groundbreaking undergraduate program, the lightbulb above my head never would have lit. I'm appreciative they allowed me to flourish there. I'm grateful to the team at West Academic Publishing for encouraging the project to go forward, and to Russell L. Weaver, John M. Burkoff and Catherine Hancock for the opportunity to benefit from the years toiled developing the Interactive Casebook.

JDD

Features of This Textbook

Throughout the book you will find various text boxes on either side of the page. These boxes provide information that will help you to understand a case or cause you to think more deeply about an issue. Each chapter begins with a brief overview of the law summarizing the law covered in the chapter.

Food for Thought These boxes point you to resources to consult for more information on a subject	**Take Note** Here you will be prompted to take special notice of something that deserves further thought or attention.
FYI A self-explanatory category that shares useful or simply interesting information relevant to material in the text.	**Hear It** These boxes point you to an audio file that is relevant to the material in the text.
It's Latin to Me The law is fond of Latin terms and phrases; when you encounter these for the first time, this box will explain their meaning.	**Major Themes** A discussion of some of the deeper themes and issues pertaining to the topic covered in that chapter.
Make the Connection When concepts or discussions that pertain to information covered in other law school courses appear in a case or elsewhere in this text, often you will find this text box to indicate the course in which you can study those topics. Here you may also be prompted to connect information in the current case to material that you have covered elsewhere in this course.	**Hypos** These boxes offer relevant hypothetical problems for you to work through, many of which are based on actual cases, with citations to the cases.

Table of Contents

Preface V
Acknowledgment VII
Features of This Textbook IX

Chapter 1. The Purposes of the Criminal Law 1
A. Overview of the Law 1
B. Case Study 2
    Regina v. Dudley & Stephens 2
    Points for Discussion 6
        a. Imposing Punishment 6
        b. Customs & Public Opinion 7
        c. Selection of Victim 7
        d. *Holmes* Case 8
C. Purposes of Punishment 8
    United States v. Bergman 9
    Points for Discussion 14
        a. Social Condemnation 14
        b. Retribution 15
        c. Rehabilitation 15
        d. Deterrence 15
        e. Restraint 16
        f. Economic Efficiency 16

Chapter 2. The Requirement of a "Voluntary Act" 21
A. Overview of the Law 21
B. The Act Requirement 22
    Martin v. State 22
    Points for Discussion 23
        a. Model Penal Code 23
        b. Carried Away 24
        c. When Brakes Fail 24
        d. Possession as Voluntary Act 24
    Fulcher v. State 24
    Points for Discussion 29
        a. Traumatic Amnesia 29
        b. Reflex Shock Reaction 30
    Robinson v. State of California 31
    Points for Discussion 36
        a. Being Drunk in Public 36
        b. Felon Registration Statutes 38
C. Omissions 39
    Jones v. United States 39

	Point for Discussion	42
	Taking Responsibility	42
	Points for Discussion	43
	a. Termination of Life Support	43
	b. Prayer Without Medical Care	44

Chapter 3. *Mens Rea* 49
A. Overview of the Law 49
B. Levels of Criminal Intention 50
   Regina v. Faulkner 50
   Points for Discussion 53
      a. Model Penal Code 53
      b. Jurisdictional Variation in *Mens Rea* Definitions 55
      c. The Difference Between *Intent* & *Motive* 56
C. Strict Liability 58
   Staples v. United States 58
   Points for Discussion 67
      a. *Morissette* Facts 67
      b. *Balint* Facts 67
D. Intoxication & Drugged Condition 68
   People v. Atkins 68
E. Mistake of Fact 74
   Iowa v. Freeman 74
   Points for Discussion 76
      a. Sale of Controlled Substances 76
      b. Attempted Sale of Controlled Substances 76
F. Mistake of Law 76
   Kipp v. Delaware 76
   Points for Discussion 79
      a. Ignorance of the Law Is No Excuse 79
      b. Mistake of Law Exceptions 79

Chapter 4. Causation 81
A. Overview of the Law 81
   Stephenson v. State 82
   Points for Discussion 84
      a. Year and a Day Rule 84
      b. Model Penal Code 85
      c. "But for" Test 86
      d. Causation & Participation 86
   People v. Acosta 86
   Commonwealth v. Root 94
   Point for Discussion 98
        Suicide & Causation 98
   Commonwealth v. Michelle Carter 98

Chapter 5. Complicity 107
A. Overview of the Law 107

B. Accomplice Liability 109
    1. Principals & Accessories 109
        a. Merger of Principals & Accessories 109
            Standefer v. United States 109
            Points for Discussion 111
                a. Merger 111
                b. Acquittal of Principal 111
                c. Significance of the Merger of Principals & Accessories 111
    2. The Act of Aiding or Encouraging 111
        Lane v. Texas 112
        Points for Discussion 113
            a. Model Penal Code 113
            b. Mere Presence 115
            c. Convicted Accomplice 115
    3. Intent to Promote or Facilitate a Crime 115
        Hawaii v. Soares 116
        Point for Discussion 117
            Proper Instruction 117
        New York v. Kaplan 117
        Point for Discussion 120
            Specific Intent 120
C. Vicarious Liability 120
    United States v. Park 120
    Point for Discussion 124
        Model Penal Code 124

Chapter 6. Inchoate Offenses: Attempt & Conspiracy 131
A. Overview of the Law 131
B. Attempt 134
    1. *Mens Rea* 135
        State v. Maestas 135
        Point for Discussion 137
            Model Penal Code 137
    2. *Actus Reus* 137
        Commonwealth v. Peaslee 138
        Points for Discussion 139
            a. Common Law Definitions 139
            b. Model Penal Code 140
        People v. Rizzo 141
    3. Abandonment 143
        State v. Workman 143
        Point for Discussion 145
            Model Penal Code 145
    4. Impossibility 145
        State v. Curtis 146
        Point for Discussion 147
            The *Jaffe* Rule 147
        People v. Dlugash 147

C. Conspiracy 155
   1. Unilateral-Bilateral Jurisdictions 155
      State v. Huff 156
      Points for Discussion 160
         a. New Legislation 160
         b. Coverage 160
         c. Use of Undercover Agents 160
   2. *Mens Rea* 160
      Palmer v. Colorado 161
      Points for Discussion 164
         a. Other Conspiracies? 164
         b. Conspiracies to Commit Negligent Crimes 165
         c. Charging Conspiracy vs. Substantive Offenses 165
         d. Knowledge vs. Intent 165
   3. *Actus Reus*: Agreement 165
      State v. Rosado 166
      Points for Discussion 173
         a. Co-Conspirator Hearsay Exception 173
         b. Wheels & Chains 173
         c. Scouts & Steerers 173
   4. Overt Act 174
      State v. Garcia 174
      Points for Discussion 177
         a. Venue 177
         b. How Much Is Enough for an Overt Act? 177
   5. Renunciation or Withdrawal 178
      New Jersey v. Hughes 178
   6. Merger 179
      State v. Hardison 180
      Point for Discussion 186
         Multiple Inchoate Offenses 186
   7. Culpability of Co-Conspirators 186
      Pinkerton v. United States 187
      Snowden v. United States 192

Chapter 7. Homicide 197
A. Overview of the Law 197
B. Intentional Killings 199
   1. Murder by Degrees 199
      State v. Ramirez 200
      Points for Discussion 203
         a. Model Penal Code 203
         b. Capital Punishment 204
         c. Deterrence & Premeditation 204
   2. Voluntary Manslaughter 205
      a. Provocation or Heat of Passion Defense 205
         Point for Discussion 205
            Model Penal Code 205
         Suprenant v. State 205

Table of Contents

			Points for Discussion	208
		a.	Proving Lack of Provocation	208
		b.	Extreme Emotional Disturbance	209
		c.	Imperfect Defense	209
C.	Unintentional Killings			209
	1.	Unpremeditated Murder		210
		State v. Burley		210
	2.	Felony-Murder		212
		Points for Discussion		213
		a.	Model Penal Code	213
		b.	Independent Felony Required	213
		c.	Triggering Felonies	213
		d.	Acquittal of Underlying Felony	214
		e.	Misdemeanor Manslaughter	214
		f.	*Faulkner*'s Logic	214
	3.	Involuntary Manslaughter		214
		Noakes v. Virginia		215
		State v. Brooks		219
		Point for Discussion		223
			Model Penal Code	223
		State v. Powell		224
		Point for Discussion		227
			Vehicular Homicide Offenses	227

Chapter 8. Assault & Battery 235

A.	Overview of the Law			236
B.	Battery			237
	1.	Offensive Touching Battery		237
		Adams v. Commonwealth		238
		Points for Discussion		241
		a.	*Actus Reus* for Offensive Touching Battery	241
		b.	*Mens Rea* for Offensive Touching Battery	242
		c.	New Crimes for Harms to Law Enforcement Officers	243
	2.	Bodily Injury Battery		243
		Points for Discussion		243
		a.	*Actus Reus* & *Mens Rea* of Bodily Injury Battery	243
		b.	Aggravated vs. Simple Battery	244
		c.	Model Penal Code Approach	244
		d.	Rare Consent Defense	245
	3.	Exposure to Life-Threatening Disease		245
		State v. Richardson		245
C.	Assault			249
	1.	Attempted Battery Assault		249
		Commonwealth v. Henson		249
		Points for Discussion		251
		a.	*Actus Reus* & *Mens Rea* of Attempted Battery Assault	251
		b.	Actual or Apparent Ability to Commit Battery	252
	2.	Frightening Assault		253
		Carter v. Commonwealth		253

		Points for Discussion 256
		a. Attempt Crime or Result Crime 256
		b. Proof Requirements 258
		c. Aggravated vs. Simple Assault 259
D.	Modern Crimes Beyond Assault & Battery 259
	1.	Reckless Endangerment 259
	2.	Stalking 260
		State v. Simone 260
		Points for Discussion 263
		a. Original Elements of Stalking Crime 263
		b. Modern Trends 264
		c. Enforcement of Stalking Laws 265
	3.	Domestic Violence 266
		a. State Crimes 266
		b. Federal Crimes 267
		c. Domestic Violence in Indian Country 268
	4.	Civil Rights 270

Chapter 9. Rape & Sexual Assault 277

A.	Overview of the Law 278
B.	Forcible Rape 280
	1. Force, Threat, or Fear 280
	People v. Iniguez 281
	Points for Discussion 287
	a. Reasons for Rape Law Reforms 287
	b. Jury Attitudes 288
	c. Model Penal Code Proposals 288
	d. Definitions of Force 289
	i. Force as Threat That Overcomes Will to Resist 289
	ii. Force as Psychological Pressure 289
	iii. Force as the Act of Penetration 290
	e. Non-Consensual Sex Without Force 290
	2. Lack of Consent 290
	Points for Discussion 291
	a. Reforms Regarding Lack of Consent Element 291
	b. Definitions of Lack of Consent 292
	i. Lack of Consent as Resistance 292
	ii. Lack of Consent as Manifested Unwillingness 293
	iii. Lack of Consent as Absence of Affirmative Agreement 293
	c. Uses of Resistance Evidence 293
	d. Withdrawal of Consent 294
	3. Consent as an Affirmative Defense 294
	State v. Koperski 294
	Points for Discussion 297
	a. Recognition of the Consent Defense 297
	b. Consent Evidence Needed for Acquittal 298
	4. *Mens Rea* & Mistake of Fact 298
	a. General Intent 298
	b. Recognition of Mistake of Fact Defense 299

			c.	Refusal to Recognize Mistake of Fact Defense	300
				Point for Discussion	300
				Limitations on Mistake Instruction	300
	5.	Marital Rape Exemption			301
	6.	Death Penalty for Rape			302
C.	Rape by Deception				304
D.	Rape of Drugged or Intoxicated Victim				304
E.	Statutory Rape				306
	Points for Discussion				306
		a.	Evolution of "Romeo and Juliet" Statutes		306
		b.	Reasonable Mistake of Fact as to Age		306
F.	Internet Crimes				307
G.	Evidence Rules for Rape Prosecutions				308
	1.	Rape Trauma Syndrome Evidence			308
		Point for Discussion			308
			"Syndrome" Evidence		308
	2.	Rape Shield Laws			308
		a.	Goals of Rape Shield Laws		309
		b.	Exclusions & Exceptions		310
		c.	Prior Sexual Conduct		310

Chapter 10. Property Crimes 315

A.	Overview of the Law				316
B.	Defining "Property"				317
	United States v. Farraj				317
	Points for Discussion				320
		a.	Common Law Limitations on "Property"		320
		b.	Updating "Property" Definitions		321
		c.	Model Penal Code Approach		322
		d.	Intangible Information as "Goods"		322
C.	Larceny & Embezzlement (Theft by Unlawful Taking or Disposition)				323
	1.	Larceny			323
		United States v. Mafnas			324
		Points for Discussion			325
			a.	Origins of Trespass Element in Larceny	325
			b.	Taking & "Carrying Away"	326
			c.	"Trespassory Taking from Possession"	326
			d.	Larceny by Trick	327
			e.	Gaps in the Larceny Rules	328
			f.	Claim of Right Defense	329
	2.	Embezzlement			329
		Batin v. State			329
		Points for Discussion			333
			a.	Charging the Wrong Crime	333
			b.	Entrustment	333
			c.	MPC Fusion of Larceny & Embezzlement Crimes	333
D.	False Pretenses (Theft by Deception)				334

E.	Receiving Stolen Property	334
	Point for Discussion	334
	Elements of Receiving Stolen Property	334
F.	Robbery & Carjacking	335
	United States v. Lake	335
	Points for Discussion	339
	a. Elements of Carjacking	339
	b. Defining Presence	340
	c. Other Elements	340
G.	Burglary	340
	In the Matter of T.J.E.	341
	Points for Discussion	344
	a. Burglary in the Colonies	344
	b. Who Is a Burglar?	344
	c. Limiting the Expansion of Burglary	346
	d. Legislative Exemptions	346
	e. Responses to *T.J.E.* Decision	346

Chapter 11. Justification Defenses 351

A.	Overview of the Law	351
B.	Self-Defense	352
	1. Necessity & Duty to Retreat	352
	Brown v. United States	353
	Points for Discussion	354
	a. Rejection of the Duty to Retreat	354
	b. Preservation of the Duty to Retreat	355
	c. Defense of Others	355
	d. Original Castle Doctrine	356
	e. Aggressor Rule	356
	f. Model Penal Code Approach	357
	2. Reasonable Belief & Imperfect Self-Defense	357
	Points for Discussion	357
	a. Comparing Mistake & Imperfect Self-Defense	357
	b. Objections to the Subjective Standard	358
	c. Measuring Reasonableness	358
	3. Battered Defendants	358
	Bechtel v. State	359
	Points for Discussion	369
	a. Evidence of Battering "Effects" & "Experiences"	369
	b. Retreat from Batterer's Castle	369
	c. Reconsideration of Judgments	370
C.	Defense of Dwelling	370
D.	Expanding the Right to Use Deadly Force	371
	Points for Discussion	371
	a. New "Castle" Laws	371
	b. "Stand Your Ground" Laws	372
E.	Law Enforcement Defense	372

F.	Necessity or Choice of Evils Defense		372
	Points for Discussion		373
	a.	Model Penal Code Approach	373
	b.	Factor Tests for Necessity	373
	c.	Rarely Successful Defense	373

Chapter 12. Excuses ... 379

A.	Overview of the Law			379
B.	Duress			381
	Point for Discussion			382
	Model Penal Code			382
C.	Insanity			382
	1.	*M'Naghten* & Irresistible Impulse Tests		383
		M'Naghten's Case		383
		Points for Discussion		385
		a.	*M'Naghten* & Insane Delusions	385
		b.	Irresistible Impulse Test	385
		Clark v. Arizona		386
		Points for Discussion		397
		a.	Indefinite Commitment	397
		b.	Pleading Insanity	397
		c.	Imposing the Defense	398
		d.	Drugs & Competency	399
		e.	Evaluation by State Psychiatrists	400
		f.	Consequences of NGI Verdict	400
		g.	Jury's Awareness of Drugs	401
		h.	Bifurcation of Guilt & Sanity	402
		i.	Guilty but Mentally Ill	402
		j.	Lay Witnesses	402
		k.	*Yates* Case	402
		l.	Multiple Personalities and the Billy Milligan Case	403
	2.	Effect of Insanity Acquittal		404
		Jones v. United States		404
		Points for Discussion		411
		a.	Civil Commitment	411
		b.	Medical Treatment	411
D.	Infancy & Mental Retardation			411
	In re Devon T.			412

Chapter 13. Sentencing ... 427

A.	Overview of the Law		428
B.	Judge vs. Jury		428
	United States v. Booker		429
	Points for Discussion		434
	a.	Guilty Pleas	434
	b.	"Sentencing Factors"	434
	c.	Mandatory Minimum Sentences	435
	d.	Aggravating Circumstances for Death Penalty	435
C.	Capital Punishment		435
	California v. Brown		436

	Points for Discussion 441
	a. Mandatory Death Sentences 441
	b. Aggravating & Mitigating Circumstances 442
	c. Discriminatory Application 442
	d. Method of Execution 443
D.	Proportionality 443
	Graham v. Florida 444
	Point for Discussion 457
	Geriatric Release 457
	Miller v. Alabama 457

INDEX 465

INTRODUCTION TO CRIMINAL LAW

A Contemporary Approach

CHAPTER 1

The Purposes of the Criminal Law

The criminal law is unique because it is premised on the idea of punishing those who violate legal norms. Permissible punishments can include fines, imprisonment, or, in extreme cases, capital punishment. In this chapter, we explore the underlying justifications for imposing punitive sanctions, and the appropriateness (and defensibility) of such sanctions. What function does the penalty of punishment serve? Moreover, how does that function differ from the purposes served by the law of tort?

A. OVERVIEW OF THE LAW

Deterrence. Although general deterrence is accepted as a purpose for imposing punishment, the existence of a deterrent effect for particular punishments may be contested. Such an effect may be difficult to demonstrate empirically, especially for particular types of crimes. Similarly, the expectation that punishment will achieve "specific deterrence" of individual wrongdoers, with regard to their criminal conduct in the future, may be defeated for many reasons. Yet crime prevention is viewed as the "major goal" or "dominant theme" of modern criminal law, according to the Model Penal Code.

Restraint. The function of punishment as a form of restraint, through the incapacitation of wrongdoers achieved through confinement, may be viewed as a necessity for serious offenses. But the discretion of sentencing and corrections authorities, as well as the dictates of the legislature, will influence the terms and conditions of such confinement. The economic costs of modern systems of restraint have created incentives for experimentation with alternative punishment methods.

Rehabilitation. The rehabilitative function of punishment has been a longstanding ideal in the criminal law, but support for that ideal has waxed and waned during the decades after the Model Penal Code was proposed. Although concerns about the inherent difficulties of achieving rehabilitative goals has led to the abandonment of those goals in some contexts, the achievement of rehabilitative goals in other context remains a priority with regard to some defendants and some crimes.

Retribution. Support for the retributive function of punishment is deeply rooted in history. This perspective on punishment may be viewed as a source of such modern concerns as the avoidance of disproportionate or arbitrary sentences, and the effort to make distinctions among offenders with regard to the "grading" of their crimes and their punishments.

Necessity Defense. Rejection of the necessity defense in *Dudley & Stephens* embodied the principle that the criminal law must enforce the moral duty to refrain from killing another, even when necessary to save lives. Even so, the sentence of six months for the crime of murder illustrated how the British used their sentencing discretion to give weight to the same mitigating circumstances that might have justified an acquittal on grounds of necessity.

B. CASE STUDY

REGINA V. DUDLEY & STEPHENS
14 Q.B.D. 273 [1884].

LORD COLERIDGE, C.J. The two prisoners, Thomas Dudley and Edwin Stephens, were indicted for the murder of Richard Parker on the high seas on the 25th day of July in the present year. They were tried before my brother Huddleston at Exeter on the 6th of November, and, under the direction of my learned Brother, the jury returned a special verdict, the legal effect of which has been argued before us, and on which we are now to pronounce judgment.

On July 5, 1884, the prisoners, Thomas Dudley and Edward Stephens, with one Brooks, all able-bodied English seamen, and the deceased an English boy, between seventeen and eighteen years of age, the crew of an English yacht, were cast away in a storm on the high seas 16,000 miles from the Cape of Good Hope, and were compelled to put into an open boat. They had no supply of water and no supply of food, except two 1 lb. tins of turnips, and for three days they had nothing else to subsist upon. On the fourth day they caught a small turtle, upon which they subsisted for a few days, and this was the only food they had up to the twentieth day when the act now in question was committed. On the twelfth day the remains of the turtle were entirely consumed, and for the next eight days they had nothing to eat. They had no fresh water, except such rain as they from time

The Purposes of the Criminal Law 3

to time caught in their oilskin capes. The boat was drifting on the ocean, and was probably more than 1,000 miles away from land. On the eighteenth day, when they had been seven days without food and five without water, the prisoners spoke to Brooks as to what should be done if no succor came, and suggested that someone should be sacrificed to save the rest, but Brooks dissented, and the boy, to whom they were understood to refer, was not consulted. On the 24th of July, the day before the act now in question, the prisoner Dudley proposed to Stephens and Brooks that lots should be cast to determine who should be put to death to save the rest, but Brooks refused to consent, and it was not put to the boy, and in point of fact there was no drawing of lots. The prisoners spoke of their families, and suggested it would be better to kill the boy that their lives should be saved, and Dudley proposed that if there was no vessel in sight by the morrow morning, the boy should be killed. Next day, the 25th of July, no vessel appearing, Dudley told Brooks that he had better go and have a sleep, and made signs to Stephens and Brooks that the boy had better be killed. The prisoner Stephens agreed to the act, but Brooks dissented. The boy was then lying at the bottom of the boat quite helpless and extremely weakened by famine and by drinking sea water, and unable to make any resistance, nor did he ever assent to being killed. The prisoner Dudley offered a prayer asking forgiveness for them all if either of them should be tempted to commit a rash act, and that their souls might be saved. Dudley, with the assent of Stephens, went to the boy, and telling him that his time was come, put a knife unto his throat and killed him then and there; the three men fed upon the body and blood of the boy for four days; On the fourth day after the act had been committed the boat was picked up by a passing vessel, and the prisoners were rescued, still alive, but in the lowest state of prostration. They were carried to the port of Falmouth, and committed for trial at Exeter. If the men had not fed upon the body of the boy they would probably not have survived to be so picked up and rescued, but would within the four days have died of famine. The boy, being in a much weaker condition, was likely to have died before them. At the time of the act in question there was no sail in sight, nor any reasonable prospect of relief. Under these circumstances there appeared to the prisoners every probability that unless they then fed or very soon fed upon the boy or one of themselves they would die of starvation. There was no appreciable chance of saving life except by killing someone for the others to eat. Assuming any necessity to kill anybody, there was no greater necessity for killing the boy than any of the other three men. But whether upon the whole matter by the jurors found the killing of Richard Parker by Dudley and Stephens be felony and murder the jurors are ignorant, and pray the advice of the Court thereupon, and if upon the whole matter the Court shall be of opinion that the killing of Richard Parker be felony and murder, then the jurors say that Dudley and Stephens were each guilty of felony and murder as alleged on the indictment."

From these facts, it appears that the prisoners were subject to terrible temptation, to sufferings which might break down the bodily power of the strongest man, and try the conscience of the best. Other details yet more harrowing, facts still more loathsome and appalling, were presented to the jury, and are to be found recorded in my learned Brother's notes. But nevertheless this is clear, that the prisoners put to death a weak and unoffending boy upon the chance of preserving their own lives by feeding upon his flesh and blood after he was killed, and with the certainty of depriving him of any possible chance of survival. The verdict finds in terms that "if the men had not fed upon the body of the boy they would *probably* not have survived," and that "the boy being in a much weaker condition was *likely* to have died before them." They might possibly have been picked up next day by a passing ship; they might possibly not have been picked up at all; in either case it is obvious that the killing of the boy would have been an unnecessary and profitless act. It is found by the verdict that the boy was incapable of resistance, and, in fact, made none; and it is not even suggested that his death was due to any violence on his part attempted against, or even so much as feared by, those who killed him. Under these circumstances the jury say that they are ignorant whether those who killed him were guilty of murder, and have referred it to this Court to determine what is the legal consequence which follows from the facts which they have found.

The question is whether killing under the circumstances set forth in the verdict be or not be murder. The contention that it could be anything else was, to the minds of us all, both new and strange, and we stopped the Attorney General in his negative argument in order that we might hear what could be said in support of a proposition which appeared to us to be at once dangerous, immoral, and opposed to all legal principle and analogy. It is said that it follows from various definitions of murder in books of authority, that in order to save your own life you may lawfully take away the life of another, when that other is neither attempting nor threatening yours, nor is guilty of any illegal act whatever towards you or anyone else. But if these definitions be looked at they will not be found to sustain this contention.

The doctrine contended for receives no support from the great authority of Lord Hale. It is plain that in his view the necessity which justified homicide is that only which has always been and is now considered a justification. Lord Hale regarded the private necessity which justified, and alone justified, the taking the life of another for the safeguard of one's own to be, what is commonly called "self-defence."

We are dealing with a case of private homicide, not one imposed upon men in the service of their Sovereign and in the defence of their country. It is admitted that the deliberate killing of this unoffending and unresisting boy was clearly murder, unless the killing can be justified by some well-recognised excuse admitted by the law. It is further admitted that there was in this case no such excuse, unless the killing was justified by what has been called "necessity." But the temptation to the act which existed here was not what the law has ever called necessity. Nor is this to be regretted. Though law and morality are not the same, and many things may be immoral which are not necessarily illegal, yet the absolute divorce of law from morality would be of fatal consequence; and such divorce would follow if the temptation to murder in this case were to be held by law and absolute defence of it. It is not so. To preserve one's life is generally speaking a duty, but it may be the plainest and the highest duty to sacrifice it. War is full of instances in which it is a man's duty not to live, but to die. The duty, in case of shipwreck, of a captain to his crew, of the crew to the passengers, of soldiers to women and children, as in the noble case of the *Birkenhead*; these duties impose on men the moral necessity, not of the preservation, but of the sacrifice of their lives for others, for which there is no country, least of all, it is to be hoped, in England, will men ever shrink, as indeed, they have not shrunk. It is not correct, therefore, to say that there is any absolute or unqualified necessity to preserve one's life. "Necesse est ut eam, non ut vivam," is a saying of a Roman office quoted by Lord Bacon. It would be a very easy and cheap display of commonplace learning to quote from Cicero, from Euripides, passage after passage, in which the duty of dying for others has been laid down in glowing and emphatic language as resulting from the principles of heathen ethics; it is enough in a Christian country to remind ourselves of the Great Example whom we profess to follow. It is not needful to point out the awful danger of admitting the principle which has been contended for. Who is to be the judge of this sort of necessity? By what measure is the comparative value of lives to be measured? Is it to be strength, or intellect, or what? It is plain that the principle leaves to him who is to profit by it to determine the necessity which will justify him in deliberately taking another's life to save his own. In this case the weakest, the youngest, the most unresisting, was chosen. Was it more necessary to kill him than one of the grown men? The answer must be "No"—

So spake the Fiend, and with necessity The Tyrant's plea, excused his devilish deeds.

It is not suggested that in this particular case the deeds were "devilish," but it is quite plain that such a principle once admitted might be made the legal cloak for unbridled passion and atrocious crime. There is no safe path for judges to tread but to ascertain the law to the best of their ability and to declare it according to their judgment; and if in any case the law appears to be too severe on individuals, to leave it to the Sovereign to exercise that prerogative of mercy which the Constitution has intrusted to the hands fittest to dispense it.

It must not be supposed that in refusing to admit temptation to be an excuse for crime it is forgotten how terrible the temptation was; how awful the suffering; how hard in such trials to keep the judgment straight and the conduct pure. We are often compelled to set up standards we cannot reach ourselves, and to lay down rules which we could not ourselves satisfy. But a man has no right to declare temptation to be an excuse, though he might have yielded to it, nor allow compassion for the criminal to change or weaken in any manner the legal definition of the crime. It is therefore our duty to declare that the prisoners' act in this case was willful murder, that the facts as stated in the verdict are no legal justification of the homicide; and to say that in our unanimous opinion the prisoners are upon this special verdict guilty of murder.

> **Major Themes**
>
> **a. Morality vs. Custom**—The treatment of the *Dudley & Stephens* defendants illustrates the operation of competing punishment goals. Their conviction and sentence upheld the value of life against the custom of the sea, whereas the commutation of their sentence illustrated a compassionate judgment regarding their failure to live up to an "unreachable standard" of conduct.
>
> **b. Multiple Punishment Purposes**—The varied justifications for punishment sometimes produce conflicting results when applied in particular cases. Both legislatures and courts are vested with the responsibility of choosing among such justifications, when establishing or interpreting the elements of crimes and the criminal defenses.

[The Court then proceeded to pass sentence of death upon the prisoners].

POINTS FOR DISCUSSION

a. Imposing Punishment

Given the circumstances that they were facing, should Dudley & Stephens have been subjected to punishment at all? Why? Why not? If punishment was appropriate, given the circumstances, what punishment should have been imposed? Was the capital punishment sentence (that the House of Lords purported to impose, but which was not imposed) appropriate? Was it appropriate to later commute the sentence to six months in prison?

b. Customs & Public Opinion

Should a court consider customs, practices, and public opinion, when deciding upon a criminal sentence? Historical evidence suggests that there was widespread acceptance of maritime cannibalism at the time this case was decided: In most instances, when a ship floundered, the crew drowned. J.R. Spencer, *Book Review*, Cannibalism and the Common Law, 51 U. Chi. L. Rev. 1265 (1984). Those who were fortunate enough to make it into a life boat were likely to die of hunger and thirst, and it was not uncommon for them to resort to cannibalism in order to survive. *Id.* Indeed, there were "were a number of well-authenticated instances of survivors actually killing one of their number in order to eat him." *Id.* By and large, the public was oblivious to the plight of seaman. *Id.* Indeed, public acceptance of cannibalism was so widespread that Dudley "frankly described the whole ordeal to his rescuers and, on arriving in England, to government officials. Clearly, Captain Dudley's attitude was that such things happen." Robert C. Berring, *Book Review*, Cannibalism and the Common Law, 73 Calif. L. Rev. 252 (1985). Should the public's acceptance of cannibalism, and the public's opinion of the case, have had any bearing on the result?

c. Selection of Victim

Should it matter how Parker was chosen as the victim? Although cannibalism was accepted at the time of the case, it was generally accepted that the stranded sailors should draw straws to determine who would be put to death rather than simply choosing a victim. John Friedl, *Book Review*, A.W. Brian Simpson, Cannibalism and the Common Law: The Story of the Tragic Last Voyage of the Mignonette and the Strange Legal Proceedings to Which it Gave Rise, 83 Mich. L. Rev. 702 (1985). However, in the actual case, the evidence showed that Parker was near death anyway, and the decision to kill him was made in order "to save as much blood as possible to drink." *Id.* Indeed, Dudley actually suggested that the stranded sailors draw straws, but abandoned that idea since they believed that Parker would die anyway, as well as because two of the others were "family men whose death would condemn their wives and children to a lifetime of destitution." *Id.* Even if the law accepts the defense of necessity in this context, should Dudley and Stephens have been condemned for deciding to kill Parker rather than drawing straws to determine who should die?

d. *Holmes* Case

In an American case, *United States v. Holmes*, 26 F. Cas. 360 (C.C.E.D.Pa. 1842), a ship struck an iceberg off Newfoundland and immediately foundered. The first mate, 8 seamen, of whom the prisoner was one (these 9 being the entire remainder of the crew), and 32 passengers, in all 41 persons, scrambled indiscriminately into the long-boat. The remaining 31 passengers were left behind to drown. When the long-boat began to leak, and the passengers were deemed to be in great jeopardy, the crew decided to throw 14 passengers overboard. The court held that:

> The passenger stands in a position different from that of the officers and seamen. It is the sailor who must encounter the hardships and perils of the voyage. Nor can this relation be changed when the ship is lost by tempest or other danger of the sea, and all on board have betaken themselves, for safety, to the small boats; for imminence of danger can not absolve from duty. The sailor is bound, as before, to undergo whatever hazard is necessary to preserve the boat and the passengers. Should the emergency become so extreme as to call for the sacrifice of life, there can be no reason why the law does not still remain the same. The passenger, not being bound either to labour or to incur the risk of life, cannot be bound to sacrifice his existence to preserve the sailor's. If the source of the danger have been obvious, and destruction ascertained to be certainly about to arrive, though at a future time, there should be consultation, and some mode of selection fixed, by which those in equal relations may have equal chance for their life. When the selection has been made by lots, the victim yields of course to his fate, or, if he resist, force may be employed to coerce submission.

The convicted crew member was sentenced to imprisonment at hard labour for six months, and ordered to pay a fine of $20. The appellate court affirmed the conviction noting that: "Considerable sympathy having been excited in favour of Holmes, by the popular press, an effort was made by several persons, and particularly by the Seamen's Friend Society, to obtain a pardon from the executive. President Tyler refused, however, to grant any pardon. The penalty was subsequently remitted."

C. PURPOSES OF PUNISHMENT

Individuals who violate the norms established by the criminal law can be subjected to fines, imprisonment and possibly capital punishment. In addition, a criminal conviction carries a moral stigma that can have a variety of other damaging effects upon the convicted person. In this respect, the criminal law differs from tort law. Although tort law can also impose consequences for the purpose of punishment (*e.g.*, sometimes, it imposes punitive damages), and criminal law can be like tort law in requiring compensation to those who have been injured (*e.g.*, some laws require the payment of restitution), criminal law differs from tort because it generally imposes punishment rather than compensation to achieve its objectives.

In imposing punishment, a rational system of criminal justice might attempt to accomplish a number of different objectives, including retribution, deterrence (which includes both "specific deterrence" and "general deterrence"), restraint (or "incapacitation") and rehabilitation. In this section, we think about these objectives and consider whether they provide sufficient justification for imposing punishment.

UNITED STATES V. BERGMAN
416 F.Supp. 496, 499 (S.D.N.Y.1976).

FRANKEL, DISTRICT JUDGE. Defendant is being sentenced upon his plea of guilty to two counts of an 11-count indictment. Defendant appeared until the last couple of years to be a man of unimpeachably high character, attainments, and distinction. A doctor of divinity and an ordained rabbi, he has been acclaimed by people around the world for his works of public philanthropy, private charity, and leadership in educational enterprises. Scores of letters have come to the court from across this and other countries reporting debts of personal gratitude to him for numerous acts of extraordinary generosity. (The court has also received a kind of petition, with fifty-odd signatures, in which the signers, based upon learning acquired as newspaper readers, denounce the defendant and urge a severe sentence.) In addition to his good works, defendant has managed to amass considerable wealth in the ownership and operation of nursing homes, in real estate ventures, and in a course of substantial investments. Beginning about two years ago, investigations of nursing homes in this area, including questions of fraudulent claims for Medicaid funds, drew to a focus upon this defendant among several others. The results that concern us were the present indictment and two state indictments. After extensive pretrial proceedings, defendant embarked upon elaborate plea negotiations with both state and federal prosecutors. As part of the detailed plea arrangements, it is expected that the prison sentence imposed by this court will comprise the total covering the state as well as the federal convictions.

The plea on Count One (carrying a maximum of five years in prison and a $10,000 fine) confesses defendant's knowing and willful participation in a scheme to defraud the United States in various ways, including the presentation of wrongfully padded claims for payments under the Medicaid program to defendant's nursing homes. Count Three, for which the guilty plea carries a theoretical maximum of three more years in prison and another $5,000 fine, is a somewhat more "technical" charge. Here, defendant admits to having participated in the filing of a partnership return which was false and fraudulent in failing to list people who had bought partnership interests from him in one of his nursing homes, had paid for such interests, and had made certain capital withdrawals. The conspiracy to defraud is by no means the worst of its kind; it is by no means as flagrant or extensive as has been portrayed in the press; it is evidently less grave than other nursing-home wrongs for which others have been convicted or publicized. At the same time, the sentence, as defendant has acknowledged, is imposed for two federal felonies including, as the more important, a knowing and purposeful conspiracy to mislead and defraud the Federal Government.

This court agrees that this defendant should not be sent to prison for "rehabilitation." This court shares the growing understanding that no one should ever be sent to prison for rehabilitation. Imprisonment is punishment. If someone must be imprisoned for other, valid reasons we should seek to make rehabilitative resources available to him or her. But the goal of rehabilitation cannot fairly serve in itself as grounds for the sentence to confinement.

Equally clearly, this defendant should not be confined to incapacitate him. He is not dangerous. It is most improbable that he will commit similar, or any, offenses in the future. There is no need for "specific deterrence."

Two sentencing considerations demand a prison sentence in this case: First, the aim of general deterrence, the effort to discourage similar wrongdoing by others through a reminder that the law's warnings are real and that the grim consequence of imprisonment is likely to follow from crimes of deception for gain like those defendant has admitted. Second, the related, but not identical, concern that any lesser penalty would, in the words of the Model Penal Code, s 7.01(1)(c), "depreciate the seriousness of the defendant's crime."

Resisting the first of these propositions, defense counsel invoke Immanuel Kant's axiom that "one man ought never to be dealt with merely as a means subservient to the purposes of another." In a more novel effort, counsel urge that a sentence for general deterrence "would violate the Eighth Amendment proscription against cruel and unusual punishment." Treating the latter point first,

The Purposes of the Criminal Law

if general deterrence as a sentencing purpose were now to be outlawed, as against a near unanimity of views among state and federal jurists, the bolt would have to come from a place higher than this. As for Dr. Kant, a criminal punished in the interest of general deterrence is not being employed "merely as a means." Reading Kant to mean that every man must be deemed more than the instrument of others, and must "always be treated as an end in himself," the humane principle is not offended here. Each of us is served by the enforcement of the law not least a person like the defendant in this case, whose wealth and privileges, so long enjoyed, are so much founded upon law. More broadly, we are driven regularly in our ultimate interests as members of the community to use ourselves and each other, in war and in peace, for social ends. One who has transgressed against the criminal laws is certainly among the more fitting candidates for a role of this nature. This is no arbitrary selection. Warned in advance of the prospect, the transgressor has chosen, in the law's premises, "between keeping the law required for society's protection or paying the penalty."

But the whole business, defendant argues further, is guesswork; we are by no means certain that deterrence "works." The position is somewhat overstated; there is, in fact, some reasonably "scientific" evidence for the efficacy of criminal sanctions as deterrents, at least as against some kinds of crimes. Moreover, the time is not yet here when all we can "know" must be quantifiable and digestible by computers. The shared wisdom of generations teaches meaningfully, if somewhat amorphously, that the utilitarians have a point; we do, indeed, lapse often into rationality and act to seek pleasure and avoid pain. It would be better, to be sure, if we had more certainty and precision. Lacking these comforts, we continue to include among our working hypotheses a belief (with some concrete evidence in its support) that crimes like those in this case deliberate, purposeful, continuing, non-impulsive, and committed for profit are among those most likely to be generally deterrable by sanctions most shunned by those exposed to temptation.

The idea of avoiding depreciation of the seriousness of the offense implicates two or three thoughts, not always perfectly clear or universally agreed upon, beyond the idea of deterrence. It should be proclaimed by the court's judgment that the offenses are grave, not minor or purely technical. Some attention must be paid to the demand for equal justice; it will not do to leave the penalty of imprisonment a dead letter as against "privileged" violators while it is employed regularly, and with vigor, against others. There probably is in these conceptions an element of retributiveness. Retribution, so denominated, is in some disfavor as a reason for punishment. It remains a factor, however, as Holmes perceived, and as is known to anyone who talks to judges, lawyers, defendants, or people generally. It may become more palatable, and probably more humanely understood, under the rubric of "deserts" or "just deserts." However the concept is formulated, we have not yet reached a state, supposing we ever should, in which the infliction of punishments for crime may be divorced generally from ideas of blameworthiness, recompense, and proportionality.

Resisting prison above all else, defense counsel make proposals for what they call a "constructive," and therefore a "preferable" form of "behavioral sanction." One is a plan for Dr. Bergman to create and run a program of Jewish vocational and religious high school training. The other is for him to take charge of a "Committee on Holocaust Studies," again concerned with education at the secondary school level. A third suggestion was that Dr. Bergman might be ordered to work as a volunteer in some established agency as a visitor and aide to the sick and the otherwise incapacitated. The proposal was that he could read, provide various forms of physical assistance, and otherwise give comfort to afflicted people.

No one can doubt either the worthiness of these proposals or Dr. Bergman's ability to make successes of them. But both of the carefully formulated "sanctions" involve work of an honorific nature, not unlike that done in other projects to which the defendant has devoted himself in the past. It is difficult to conceive of them as "punishments" at all. The more recent proposal is somewhat more suitable in character, but it is still an insufficient penalty. The seriousness of the crimes to which Dr. Bergman has pled guilty demands something more than "requiring" him to lend his talents and efforts to further philanthropic enterprises. It remains open to him, of course, to pursue the interesting suggestions later on as a matter of unforced personal choice.

In cases like this, the decision of greatest moment is whether to imprison or not. As reflected in the submissions for defendant, the prospect of the closing prison doors is the most appalling concern; the feeling is that the length of the sojourn is a lesser question once that threshold is passed. Nevertheless, the setting of a term remains to be accomplished. In some respects it is a subject even more perplexing, unregulated, and unprincipled. Days and months and years are countable with a sound of exactitude. But there can be no exactitude in the deliberations from which a number emerges. Without pretending to a nonexistent precision, the court notes at least the major factors.

The criminal behavior is blatant in character and unmitigated by any suggestion of necessitous circumstance or other pressures difficult to resist.

However metaphysicians may conjure with issues about free will, it is a fundamental premise of our efforts to do criminal justice that competent people, possessed of their faculties, make choices and are accountable for them. In this sometimes harsh light, the case of this defendant is among the clearest and least relieved. Viewed against the maxima Congress ordained, and against the run of sentences in other federal criminal cases, it calls for more than a token sentence.

Defendant's illustrious public life and works are in his favor, though diminished, of course, by what this case discloses. This is a first, probably a last, conviction. Defendant is 64 years old and in imperfect health, though by no means so ill, that he could be expected to suffer inordinately more than many others of advanced years who go to prison.

Defendant says others involved in recent nursing home fraud cases have received relatively light sentences for behavior more culpable than his. He lays special emphasis upon one defendant whose frauds appear indeed to have involved larger amounts and who was sentenced to a maximum of six months' incarceration, to be confined for that time only on week nights, not on week days or weekends. This court has examined the minutes of that sentencing proceeding and finds the case distinguishable in material respects. But even if there were a threat of such disparity as defendant warns against, it could not be a major weight on the scales. Our sentencing system, deeply flawed, is characterized by disparity. We are to seek to "individualize" sentences, but no clear or clearly agreed standards govern the individualization. The lack of meaningful criteria does indeed leave sentencing judges far too much at large. But the result, with its nagging burdens on conscience, cannot be meaningfully alleviated by allowing any handful of sentences in a short series to fetter later judgments. The point is easy, of course, where Sentence No. 1 or Sentences 1–5 are notably harsh. It cannot be that a later judge, disposed to more leniency, should feel in any degree "bound." The converse is not identical, but it is not totally different. The net of this is that this court has considered and has given some weight to the trend of the cited sentences (though strict logic might call for none), but without treating them as forceful "precedents" in any familiar sense.

How, then, the particular sentence adjudged in this case? The case calls for a sentence that is more than nominal. Given the other circumstances, including that this is a first offense, by a man no longer young and not perfectly well, where danger of recidivism is not a concern it verges on cruelty to think of confinement for a term of years. We sit in a nation where prison sentences of extravagant length are more common than they are almost anywhere else. By that light, the term imposed today is not notably long. For this sentencing court, however, for a nonviolent first offense involving no direct assaults or invasions of others' security (as in bank robbery, narcotics, etc.), it is a stern sentence. For people like Dr. Bergman, who might be disposed to engage in similar wrongdoing, it should be sufficiently frightening to serve the major end of general deterrence. For all but the profoundly vengeful, it should not depreciate the seriousness of his offenses.

Writing about a particular sentence concentrates the mind with possibly special force upon the experience of the sentencer as well as the person sentenced. Consigning someone to prison, this defendant or any other, "is a sad necessity." There are impulses of avoidance from time to time toward a personally gratifying leniency or toward an opposite extreme. But there is, obviously, no place for private impulse in the judgment of the court. The course of justice must be sought with such objective rationality as we can muster, tempered with mercy, but obedient to the law, which, we do well to remember, is all that empowers a judge to make other people suffer.

The motion to postpone surrender is granted. Defendant will surrender to begin service of his sentence at 10:30 a. m. on July 7, 1976.

It is so ordered.

POINTS FOR DISCUSSION

a. Social Condemnation

There is debate regarding the role of "social condemnation" in the criminal law. For example, Henry M. Hart, Jr., in *The Aims of the Criminal Law*, 23 Law & Contemp. Probs. 401, 405 (1958), argues that criminal conviction brings with it the "moral condemnation of the community." While society may also impose other punishments (*e.g.*, imprisonment, fines or deprivation of life), he believes that these other punishments "take their character as punishment from the condemnation which precedes them and serves as the warrant for their infliction." Louis Michael Seidman, in *Soldiers, Martyrs, and Criminals: Utilitarian Theory and the Problem of Crime Control*, 94 Yale L.J. 315, 337–38 (1984), argues that moral condemnation imposes a unique type of penalty and provides "a kind of deterrence that other punishment cannot achieve," and may deter even criminals who attach particular value to the prohibited conduct: "the condemnation is moral in character precisely because we are blaming an individual for preferring pleasure to pain in a situation where he should be obeying a categorical imperative."

b. Retribution

Many regard "retribution" as one of the principal justifications for imposing punishment. The concept of retribution is revealed in such sayings as "an eye for an eye and a tooth for a tooth." Those who endorse this theory believe that society is morally justified in taking retribution against individuals who violate societal norms, especially when they commit heinous crimes. But is retribution a justifiable objective? Herbert Wechsler, in *The Challenge of a Model Penal Code*, 65 Harv. L. Rev. 1097 (1952), argues that the focus of the criminal law should be on deterrence: "while invocation of a penal sanction necessarily depends on past behavior, the object is control of harmful conduct in the future."

c. Rehabilitation

Should punishment focus on rehabilitation? The concept of "rehabilitation" is particularly appealing in the criminal context. Of course, we have all heard of extraordinary cases in which criminals have rehabilitated themselves and gone on to live useful and productive lives. For example, there is the story of a former bank robber who became a "jailhouse" lawyer during his time in prison, and achieved the extraordinary feat of having two petitions for certiorari granted by the U.S. Supreme Court. He graduated from law school, and accepted a clerkship with the D.C. Circuit of the U.S. Court of Appeals. *See* Mark Memmott, *The Incredible Case of the Bank Robber Who's Now a Law Clerk*, National Public Radio, All Things Considered (Sept. 5, 2013). To the extent that society can work similar magic with other criminals, is it better for these individual, their families and (ultimately) for society to pursue rehabilitation?

Henry M. Hart, Jr., in *The Aims of the Criminal Law*, 23 Law & Contemp. Probs. 401 (1958), asks whether "people who behave badly should simply be treated as sick people to be cured," and questions whether it is good for society to return individuals to society (following punishment) with the "negative vacuum of punishment-induced fear." Would it not be better to return them with the "affirmative and constructive equipment—physical, mental and morality—for law-abidingness"? Would the latter approach not provide a better way to protect society against anti-social conduct?

d. Deterrence

"Deterrence" is often regarded as one of the primary justifications for imposing criminal punishment. Deterrence is often divided into "specific deterrence" and "general deterrence." With specific deterrence, the goal is to deter this particular defendant from committing future similar crimes. With general deterrence, the goal is to deter others from committing similar crimes. In theory, the concept of deterrence might help explain the outcome in *Dudley & Stephens*. While there may be no specific deterrent in that case (what is the likelihood that either of them will ever find themselves in a similar situation, or that they would kill someone else?), the judges might have hoped to provide a general deterrent that would discourage other sailors from killing under similar circumstances. However, is the deterrent likely to be a strong one? Faced with similar circumstances, is a sailor likely to be deterred from killing for fear of eventual conviction in England?

e. Restraint

Another justification for punishment is the concept of "restraint." When individuals have committed particularly heinous crimes, there is a desire to "restrain" those individuals (*e.g.*, put them in prison) and separate them from society so that they cannot commit similar crimes in the future. For example, there was a recent case in Cleveland involving an individual who had held several women captive for a decade and repeatedly raped them during their detention. Likewise, there have been individuals who have committed particularly heinous crimes, or serial murders. With such individuals, there are often clamors to "lock them up" and "throw away the key" in order to ensure that they never do such things again. The Cleveland man was given life plus 1,000 years in order to ensure that he would never re-enter society (and, as a matter of fact, he ended up committing suicide shortly after sentencing). Of course, capital punishment is the ultimate form of restraint. However, even shorter detentions can serve a restraint function by removing criminals from society. One would hope that restraint also includes rehabilitation for those who will re-enter society, especially for those that have the potential to become productive members of society and avoid return to their former criminal ways.

f. Economic Efficiency

Should the Criminal Law be based on economic efficiency? Richard A. Posner, in *An Economic Theory of the Criminal Law*, 85 Colum. L. Rev. 1193 (1985), argues that many criminal law doctrines "can be given an economic meaning and can indeed be shown to promote efficiency," and he regards markets as the "the most efficient method of allocating resources." For example, he explains that if A wishes to own B's car, it is more efficient to force A to bargain with B regarding the price, instead of allowing A to take the car and then face judicial action to compel A's payment. A coerced transfer cannot improve the allocation of resources since "value is a function of willingness to pay." Since a coerced transfer would force A to spend resources trying to take the vehicle, and would encourage

B to spend money to prevent A from doing so, these expenditures would "yield no social product." Therefore, the sanction for such a coerced transfer should be higher than B's loss to reflect the possibility "that the thief may place a higher subjective value on the object than does the victim." Likewise, for violent crimes, since it is not easy to place an economic value on such crimes (given that the damages for some violent crimes (*e.g.*, death) will be quite high), it may be beyond the ability of some individuals to pay for such damages. As a result, Posner argues that criminal sanctions are generally reserved for individuals who suffer from solvency issues because the "affluent are kept in line, for the most part, by tort law." The possibility of moral condemnation and imprisonment may deter even the impecunious. Even when the criminal law imposes only fines, the criminal penalty bears a social stigma. Heavy prison terms often help deter crime when there are "low probabilities of apprehension and conviction."

A contrasting view is provided by Louis Michael Seidman, in *Soldiers, Martyrs, and Criminals: Utilitarian Theory and the Problem of Crime Control*, 94 Yale L.J. 315, 315–17, 323, 325–26, 329 (1984). He indicates that law and economics literature suggests that society could have as little crime as it desires to have if it is willing to spend sufficient resources on "police, court, jails and so on to make probabilities of arrest very, very high for most crimes."

Now, let's think about how the justifications for punishment might apply in particular contexts, and the results that they might suggest or dictate in a particular case. Although this can be done with any type of crime, for convenience let's focus on homicide. Given the purposes of the criminal law, should different homicides be treated differently for purposes of punishment? Do the principal justifications for punishment (retribution, restraint, rehabilitation, general deterrence and special deterrence) justify different sentences based on factual differences? Think about these issues as you consider the following hypotheticals.

> ### Hypo 1: *The Cheating Spouse*
>
> Defendant, who is feeling sick, comes home early from work to find his or her spouse in bed with another person. In a fit of rage, defendant kills the other person. Is punishment appropriate under such circumstances? If so, what punishment should be imposed?

> **Hypo 2: *Compassionate Euthanasia***
>
> Defendant's husband is suffering from a severe, painful, debilitating fatal disease. Day-after-day, the husband begs the wife to help him end his life and thereby end his suffering. The wife repeatedly refuses. Finally, unable to deal with her husband's desperate plight, she administers poison to him. Is punishment appropriate under these circumstances? If so, what punishment should be imposed?

> **Hypo 3: *Absent-Minded Father***
>
> On a hot day in mid-summer, a father is supposed to take his infant child to day care on the way to work. The father, being absent-minded, forgets about the child and leaves the child in the rear car seat (buckled into his seat). Since no one happens to notice, the baby dies of suffocation. The father, who truly loved the child despite his appalling level of absent-mindedness, is devastated by the child's death and falls into a deep depression. The mother, unable to forgive the father, divorces him. Suppose that you are the prosecutor, and must decide how to handle the case. Of course, the father can be prosecuted for manslaughter. Is a criminal prosecution appropriate? If so, what purpose(s) would it serve? If you decide to prosecute, what punishment would you seek?

> **Hypo 4: *Loan Shark's Threat***
>
> Defendant is charged with illegally selling narcotics. The facts reveal that defendant was not regularly engaged in the sale of narcotics. However, he borrowed money from a loan shark at an exorbitant interest rate. When defendant was unable to repay the money, the loan shark ordered defendant to "handle" a narcotic transaction for him. With a gun lying on his lap, the loan shark threatened to harm the defendant and his family. Because of this threat, defendant agreed to "handle" the drug transaction. Unfortunately for defendant, the police "got wind" of the transaction and arrested him. Given the purposes of the criminal law, does it make sense to punish defendant? Explain.

> **Hypo 5: *Reconsidering* Dudley & Stephens**
>
> Now, reconsider the facts in *Regina v. Dudley & Stephens*. What punishment did the defendants deserve? What is the function of the punishment? Did they need rehabilitation? Was there a risk that they or others would commit similar acts in the future, and can society hope to deter them or others by imposing punishment on them? Did they need to be "restrained" or "incapacitated" lest they run around killing others? Did they need to be punished in order for society to exact retribution for the death of Parker?

CHAPTER 2

The Requirement of a "Voluntary Act"

An essential element of just punishment is the requirement of a voluntary "act" or an "omission" to act when an appropriate duty to act exists (the "*actus reus*" requirement). If the alleged act was involuntary, there may be no justification for imposing punishment. For example, if "one person physically forces another person into bodily movement, as where A by force causes B's body to strike C; under these circumstances, there is no voluntary act by B." WAYNE R. LAFAVE & AUSTIN W. SCOTT, JR., CRIMINAL LAW § 6.1(c), at 324 (5th ed. 2010).

A. OVERVIEW OF THE LAW

Voluntary Act Requirement. The requirement of a voluntary act is a prerequisite for criminal liability. The MPC recognizes particular acts as involuntary, including reflexes or convulsions, a bodily movement during unconsciousness or sleep, and conduct during hypnosis or resulting from hypnotic suggestion. The MPC also endorses an all-purpose definition to provide recognition for other involuntary acts, namely those bodily movements that are not "a product of the effort or determination of the actor, either conscious or habitual." However, if defendant foresaw the danger (*e.g.*, she became drowsy while driving, but kept driving), unconsciousness or sleep may not provide a defense.

Unconsciousness Defense. Courts have recognized the availability of the unconsciousness defense in cases in which a concussion or gunshot wound caused symptoms of unconscious behavior that could be diagnosed by expert witnesses and supported with sufficient evidence.

Other Involuntary Act Defenses. Some other types of conduct have been recognized as justifying an instruction on the involuntary act defense, such as conduct during an epileptic seizure or an episode of somnambulism. When such conduct allegedly occurs during a hypnotic state, however, courts have been reluctant to grant a jury instruction.

Status Crime. The Supreme Court relied on the Eighth Amendment to invalidate a statute that made it a crime "to be addicted to the use of narcotics." This law created a "status crime" because it punished an illness and required no proof of an act, such as the use or possession of drugs. This ruling provided some constitutional recognition of the fundamental nature of the voluntary act requirement. However, the Court limited the scope of this ruling by later upholding a statute that made it a crime to be "found in a state of intoxication in a public place," reasoning that this statute did not penalize a "status crime" because it required an act.

Omissions to Act. Even though criminal liability must be based on a voluntary act, the term "act" is defined broadly enough to include an "omission" to act. For example, the Model Penal Code provides that liability may be based on an "omission to perform an act of which a person is physically capable."

Legal Duty to Act. Courts have established a narrow set of legal duties to act, so that the failure to act in accordance with that duty may lead to criminal liability based on omission. Such legal duties arise in these contexts: 1) when a statute imposes a duty to care for another; 2) when a person has a particular status relationship with another that gives rise to the duty of care; 3) when a person has assumed a contractual duty to care for another; and 4) when a person voluntarily assumed the care of another and then secluded the other person in a way that prevented others from rendering aid.

Duty to Rescue. Although not recognized at common law, the duty to provide assistance at the scene of an emergency has been imposed by statute in some states.

B. THE ACT REQUIREMENT

MARTIN V. STATE
17 So.2d 427 (Ala. App. 1944).

SIMPSON, JUDGE.

Appellant was convicted of being drunk on a public highway, and appeals. Officers of the law arrested him at his home and took him onto the highway, where he allegedly committed the proscribed acts, viz., manifested a drunken condition by using loud and profane language.

The Requirement of a "Voluntary Act"

The pertinent provisions of our statute are: "Any person who, while intoxicated or drunk, appears in any public place where one or more persons are present, and manifests a drunken condition by boisterous or indecent conduct, or loud and profane discourse, shall, on conviction, be fined."

Under the plain terms of this statute, a voluntary appearance is presupposed. The rule has been declared, and we think it sound, that an accusation of drunkenness in a designated public place cannot be established by proof that the accused, while in an intoxicated condition, was involuntarily and forcibly carried to that place by the arresting officer.

Conviction of appellant was contrary to this announced principle and, in our view, erroneous. It appears that no legal conviction can be sustained under the evidence, so the judgment of the trial court is reversed and one here rendered discharging appellant.

Reversed and rendered.

POINTS FOR DISCUSSION

a. Model Penal Code

The MPC Commentary for § 2.01 states:

"The law cannot hope to deter involuntary movement or to stimulate action that cannot physically be performed; the sense of personal security would be undermined in a society where such movement or inactivity could lead to formal social condemnation of the sort that a conviction necessarily entails." These ideas are codified as follows:

§ 2.01. Requirement of Voluntary Act; Omission as Basis of Liability; Possession as an Act.

(1) A person is not guilty of an offense unless his liability is based on conduct that includes a voluntary act or the omission to perform an act of which he is physically capable.

(2) The following are not voluntary acts within the meaning of this Section:

(a) a reflex or convulsion;

(b) a bodily movement during unconsciousness or sleep;

(c) conduct during hypnosis or resulting from hypnotic suggestion;

(d) a bodily movement that otherwise is not a product of the effort or determination of the actor, either conscious or habitual.

b. Carried Away

In *State v. Boleyn*, 328 So.2d 95 (La. 1976), a prisoner was subjected to a sodomous rape. Afterwards, he voluntarily intoxicated himself with pills and beer. While in an unconscious drugged condition, defendant was "carried away" from the prison by another prisoner. The court concluded that "evidence of the state of consciousness of defendant and of his intoxicated or drugged condition should have been submitted to the jury." Likewise, in *People v. Shaughnessy*, 66 Misc. 2d 19, 319 N.Y.S.2d 626 (1971), defendant was found not guilty of violating an ordinance prohibiting entry upon private property. The state's evidence failed to show an overt voluntary act by the defendant who was merely a passenger in a trespassing car.

c. When Brakes Fail

In *State v. Kremer*, 262 Minn. 190, 114 N.W.2d 88 (1962), the court held that a defendant could not be guilty of violating a city ordinance requiring all traffic to stop at a flashing red light when the evidence showed that his brakes failed with no prior warning. However, in *Kettering v. Greene*, 9 Ohio St.2d 26, 222 N.E.2d 638 (1966), the Ohio Supreme Court reached the opposite result even though defendant had no prior warning of any defect in the brakes. The court concluded that the statutory requirement to stop at a stop sign is mandatory and brake failure is not a legal excuse.

d. Possession as Voluntary Act

A voluntary act can include "possession" of an item. MPC § 2.01(4) provides: "Possession is an act, within the meaning of this Section, if the possessor knowingly procured or received the thing possessed or was aware of his control thereof for a sufficient period to have been able to terminate his possession."

FULCHER V. STATE
633 P.2d 142 (Wyo. 1981).

BROWN, JUSTICE.

Appellant consumed seven or eight shots of whiskey over a period of four hours in a Torrington bar, and had previously had a drink at home. Appellant claims he got in a fight in the bar restroom, then left the bar to find a friend. According to his testimony, the last thing he remembers until awakening in jail, is going out of the door at the bar.

Appellant and his friend were found lying in the alley behind the bar by a police officer who noted abrasions on their fists and faces. Appellant and his

The Requirement of a "Voluntary Act"

friend swore, were uncooperative, and combative. They were subsequently booked for public intoxication and disturbing the peace. During booking appellant continued to swear, and said he and his friend were jumped by a "bunch of Mexicans." Although his speech was slurred, he was able to verbally count his money, roughly $500 to $600 in increments of $20, and was able to walk to his cell without assistance.

Appellant was placed in a cell with one Martin Hernandez who was lying unconscious on the floor of the cell. After the jailer left the cell, he heard something that sounded like someone being kicked. He ran back to the cell and saw appellant standing by Hernandez. When the jailer started to leave again, the kicking sound resumed, and he observed appellant kicking and stomping on Hernandez's head. Appellant told the officer Hernandez had fallen out of bed. Hernandez was bleeding profusely and was taken to the hospital for some 52 stitches in his head and mouth. He had lost two or three teeth as a result of the kicking.

Appellant testified that the doctor diagnosed him with a concussion, although there is no evidence of medical treatment. Appellant entered a plea of not guilty. In preparation for trial, appellant was examined by Dr. Breck LeBegue, a forensic psychiatrist. The doctor reviewed the police report and conducted a number of tests. At the trial Dr. LeBegue testified that in his expert medical opinion appellant suffered brain injury and was in a state of traumatic automatism at the time of his attack on Hernandez. Dr. LeBegue defined traumatic automatism as the state of mind in which a person does not have conscious and willful control over his actions, and lacks the ability to be aware of and to perceive his external environment. Dr. LeBegue further testified that another possible symptom is an inability to remember what occurred while in a state of traumatic automatism.

Dr. LeBegue was unable to state positively whether or not appellant had the requisite mental state for aggravated assault and battery, but thought appellant did not because of his altered state of mind. He could not state, however, that the character of an act is devoid of criminal intent because of mind alteration.

We hold that the trial court properly received and considered evidence of unconsciousness absent a plea of "not guilty by reason of mental illness or deficiency." The defense of unconsciousness perhaps should be more precisely denominated as the defense of automatism. Automatism is the state of a person who, though capable of action, is not conscious of what he is doing. While in an automatistic state, an individual performs complex actions without an exercise of will. Because these actions are performed in a state of unconsciousness, they are involuntary. Automatistic behavior may be followed by complete or partial inability to recall the actions performed while unconscious. Thus, a person who acts automatically does so without intent, exercise of free will, or knowledge of the act.

Automatism may be caused by an abnormal condition of the mind capable of being designated a mental illness or deficiency. Automatism may also be manifest in a person with a perfectly healthy mind. In this opinion we are concerned with the defense of automatism occurring in a person with a healthy mind. In this case, we are concerned with alleged automatism caused by concussion.

The defense of automatism, while not an entirely new development in the criminal law, has been discussed in relatively few decisions by American appellate courts, most of these being in California where the defense is statutory. Some courts have held that insanity and automatism are separate and distinct defenses, and that evidence of automatism may be presented under a plea of not guilty. Some states have made this distinction by statute. In other states the distinction is made by case law.

> "A defense related to but different from the defense of insanity is that of unconsciousness, often referred to as automatism: one who engages in what would otherwise be criminal conduct is not guilty of a crime if he does so in a state of unconsciousness or semi-consciousness." LAFAVE & SCOTT, CRIMINAL LAW, § 44, p. 337 (1972).

> "The defenses of insanity and unconsciousness are not the same in nature, for unconsciousness at the time of the alleged criminal act need not be the result of a disease or defect of the mind. As a consequence, the two defenses are not the same in effect, for a defendant found not guilty by reason of unconsciousness, as distinct from insanity, is not subject to commitment to a hospital for the mentally ill." *State v. Caddell*, 287 N.C. 266, 215 S.E.2d 348, 360 (1975).

The principal reason for making a distinction between the defense of unconsciousness and insanity is that the consequences which follow an acquittal, will differ. The defense of unconsciousness is usually a complete defense. That is, there are no follow-up consequences after an acquittal; all action against a defendant is concluded. In the case of a finding of not guilty by reason of insanity, the defendant is ordinarily committed to a mental institution.

The mental illness or deficiency plea does not adequately cover automatic behavior. Unless the plea of automatism is allowed, certain anomalies will result. For example, if the court determines that the automatistic defendant is sane, but refuses to recognize automatism, the defendant has no defense to the crime with which he is charged. If found guilty, he faces a prison term. The rehabilitative value of imprisonment for the automatistic offender who has committed the offense unconsciously is nonexistent. The cause of the act was an uncontrollable physical disorder that may never recur and is not a moral deficiency.

If, however, the court treats automatism as insanity and then determines that the defendant is insane, he will be found not guilty. He then will be committed to a mental institution for an indefinite period. The commitment of an automatistic individual to a mental institution for rehabilitation has absolutely no value. Mental hospitals generally treat people with psychiatric or psychological problems. This form of treatment is not suited to unconscious behavior resulting from a bump on the head.

It may be argued that evidence of unconsciousness cannot be received unless a plea of not guilty by reason of mental illness or deficiency is made pursuant to Rule 15, W.R.Cr.P. We believe this approach to be illogical.

It does not seem that the definition of "mental deficiency" in § 7–11–301(a)(iii), which includes "brain damage," encompasses simple brain trauma with no permanent after effects. The "brain damage" contemplated in the statute is some serious and irreversible condition having an impact upon the ability of the person to function. It is undoubtedly something far more significant than a temporary and transitory condition. The two defenses are merged, in effect, if a plea of "not guilty by reason of mental illness or deficiency" is a prerequisite for using the defense of unconsciousness.

The committee that drafted Wyoming Pattern Jury Instructions Criminal, apparently recognized mental illness or deficiency and unconsciousness as separate and distinct defenses. Admittedly the instructions in Wyo. P.J.I.Cr. are not authoritative, because they were not approved by the Wyoming Supreme Court, and this was a matter of design. Still they are the product of a distinguished group of legal scholars, including judges, attorneys and teachers of the law. The comment to this pattern jury instruction notes that it is limited to persons of sound mind, and the comment distinguishes persons suffering from "mental deficiency or illness." In this respect, it tracks the case law from other jurisdictions, which authorities hold that unconsciousness and insanity are completely separate grounds of exemption from criminal responsibility.

Although courts hold that unconsciousness and insanity are separate and distinct defenses, there has been some uncertainty concerning the burden of proof. We believe the better rule to be that stated in *State v. Caddell, supra*, at 363, 215 S.E.2d 348:

> "Unconsciousness, or automatism, is a complete defense to the criminal charge, separate and apart from the defense of insanity; that it is an affirmative defense; and that the burden rests upon the defendant to establish this defense, unless it arises out of the State's own evidence, to the satisfaction of the jury."

The rationale for this rule is that the defendant is the only person who knows his actual state of consciousness.

Our ruling on the facts of this case is that the defense of unconsciousness resulting from a concussion with no permanent brain damage is an affirmative defense and is a defense separate from the defense of not guilty by reason of mental illness or deficiency.

Appellant's conviction must, nevertheless, be affirmed. Dr. LeBegue was unable to state positively whether or not appellant had the requisite mental state for aggravated assault. He could not state that the character of the act was devoid of criminal intent because of the mind alteration. The presumption of mental competency was never overcome by appellant and the evidence presented formed a reasonable basis on which the trial judge could find and did find that the State had met the required burden of proof.

Further, the trial judge was not bound to follow Dr. LeBegue's opinion. The trier of the facts is not bound to accept expert opinion evidence in the face of other substantial and credible evidence to the contrary. There was an abundance of other credible evidence that appellant was not unconscious at the time of the assault and battery for which he was convicted.

Affirmed.

RAPER, JUSTICE, specially concurring, with whom ROONEY, JUSTICE, joins.

The majority has taken the mistaken view that a little old bump on the head is not serious. We do not know from the record how much of a blow on the head causing concussion and brain damage was received by appellant. Wyoming did not adopt that part of the ALI Model Penal Code which would consider automatism as a separate defense:

The Requirement of a "Voluntary Act"

Section 2.01.

"(1) A person is not guilty of an offense unless his liability is based on conduct which includes a voluntary act or the omission to perform an act of which he is physically capable."

Wyoming adopted language which embraced the alternative suggested in the comments to § 2.01, supra:

Any definition must exclude a reflex or convulsion. The case of unconsciousness is equally clear when unconsciousness implies collapse or coma, as perhaps it does in ordinary usage of the term. There are, however, states of physical activity where self-awareness is grossly impaired or even absent, as in epileptic fugue, amnesia, extreme confusion and equivalent conditions. How far these active states of automatism should be assimilated to coma for this legal purpose presents a difficult issue. There is judicial authority supporting the assimilation. An alternative approach, however, is to view these cases as appropriate for exculpation on the ground of mental disease or defect excluding responsibility. This view has also had support in the decisions. It offers the advantage that it may facilitate commitment when the individual is dangerous to the community because the condition is recurrent. By the same token, however, it bears more harshly on the individual whose condition is non-recurrent, as in the case where an extraordinary reaction follows the administration of a therapeutic drug. And there may be a difficulty in regarding some of these conditions as " 'mental disease or defect,' within the meaning of section 4.01 of the draft or as 'insanity' under prevailing law, although cognition is sufficiently impaired to satisfy that aspect of the test." (Emphasis added.)

The Wyoming legislature clearly defined "mental deficiency" to unquestionably include appellant's alleged condition (brain damage).

POINTS FOR DISCUSSION

a. Traumatic Amnesia

In *People v. Cox*, 67 Cal. App. 2d 166, 153 P.2d 362 (1944), defendant was charged with homicide. He claimed that he was hit over the head with a bottle and was unconscious when he committed the crime. The evidence showed that he suffered from traumatic amnesia. Defendant had cuts on his forehead, had bled from the right ear, and had suffered superficial bruises on his abdomen, and some type of brain injury. One witness testified that defendant had suffered a "loss of memory or traumatic amnesia caused by a blow on the head." The Court held that, because there was evidence suggesting that defendant's "conscious mind has ceased to operate and his actions are controlled by the subconscious or subjective mind," it was error not to instruct the jury regarding the legal effect of unconsciousness. *See also State v. Mercer*, 275 N.C. 108, 165 S.E.2d 328 (1969).

b.   Reflex Shock Reaction

In accord is *People v. Newton*, 8 Cal. App. 3d 359, 87 Cal. Rptr. 394 (1970), in which defendant was shot by a police officer, and later shot and killed the officer. At his trial, defendant claimed that he was unconscious during the killing. Defense witnesses testified that "defendant's recollections were 'compatible' with the gunshot wound he had received; and that 'a gunshot wound which penetrates in a body cavity, the abdominal cavity or the thoracic cavity is very likely to produce a profound reflex shock reaction, that is quite different than a gunshot wound which penetrates only skin and muscle and it is not at all uncommon for a person shot in the abdomen to lose consciousness and go into this reflex shock condition for short periods of time up to half an hour or so.'" The court concluded that defendant was entitled to an instruction on unconsciousness, and discussed the distinction between "diminished capacity" and "unconsciousness:

> A trial court is under a duty to instruct upon diminished capacity, in the absence of a request and upon its own motion, where the evidence so indicates. The difference between the two states—of diminished capacity and unconsciousness—is one of degree only: where the former provides a "partial defense" by negating a specific mental state essential to a particular crime, the latter is a "complete defense" because it negates capacity to commit any crime at all. Moreover, evidence of both states is not antithetical; jury instructions on the effect of both will be required where the evidence supports a finding of either. We hold, therefore, that the trial court should have given appropriate unconsciousness instructions upon its own motion in the present case, and that its omission to do so was prejudicial error.

ROBINSON V. STATE OF CALIFORNIA
370 U.S. 660 (1962).

MR. JUSTICE STEWART delivered the opinion of the Court.

A California statute makes it a criminal offense for a person to "be addicted to the use of narcotics." Appellant was convicted after a jury trial in the Municipal Court of Los Angeles. The evidence against him was given by two Los Angeles police officers. Officer Brown testified that he had occasion to examine the appellant's arms one evening on a street in Los Angeles, and he observed "scar tissue and discoloration on the inside" of the appellant's right arm, and "what appeared to be numerous needle marks and a scab which was approximately three inches below the crook of the elbow" on the appellant's left arm. The officer also testified that the appellant had admitted to the occasional use of narcotics.

Officer Lindquist testified that he examined appellant the following morning in the Central Jail in Los Angeles. At that time he observed discolorations and scabs on appellant's arms, and he identified photographs which had been taken of appellant's arms shortly after his arrest the night before. Based upon more than ten years of experience as a member of the Narcotic Division of the Los Angeles Police Department, the witness gave his opinion that "these marks and the discoloration were the result of the injection of hypodermic needles into the tissue into the vein that was not sterile." He stated that the scabs were several days old at the time of his examination, and that appellant was neither under the influence of narcotics nor suffering withdrawal symptoms at the time he saw him. This witness also testified that appellant admitted using narcotics in the past.

The trial judge instructed the jury that the statute made it a misdemeanor for a person "either to use narcotics, or to be addicted to the use of narcotics. That portion of the statute referring to the 'use' of narcotics is based upon the 'act' of using. That portion of the statute referring to 'addicted to the use' of narcotics is based upon a condition or status. They are not identical. To be addicted to the use of narcotics is said to be a status or condition and not an act. It is a continuing offense and differs from most other offenses in the fact that it is chronic rather than acute; that it continues after it is complete and subjects the offender to arrest at any time before he reforms. The existence of such a chronic condition may be ascertained from a single examination, if the characteristic reactions of that condition be found present." The judge further instructed the jury that appellant could be convicted under a general verdict if the jury agreed either that he was of the "status" or had committed the "act" denounced by the statute. "All that the People must show is either that the defendant did use a narcotic in Los Angeles

County, or that while in the City of Los Angeles he was addicted to the use of narcotics." The jury returned a verdict finding the appellant "guilty of the offense charged.".

It would be possible to construe the statute under which appellant was convicted as one which is operative only upon proof of the actual use of narcotics within the State's jurisdiction. But the California courts have not so construed this law. Although there was evidence that appellant had used narcotics in Los Angeles, the jury were instructed that they could convict him if they found simply that the appellant's "status" or "chronic condition" was that of being "addicted to the use of narcotics." It is impossible to know from the jury's verdict that defendant was not convicted upon precisely such a finding.

This statute, therefore, is not one which punishes a person for the use of narcotics, for their purchase, sale or possession, or for antisocial or disorderly behavior resulting from their administration. It is not a law which even purports to provide or require medical treatment. Rather, we deal with a statute which makes the "status" of narcotic addiction a criminal offense, for which the offender may be prosecuted "at any time before he reforms." California has said that a person can be continuously guilty of this offense, whether or not he has ever used or possessed any narcotics within the State, and whether or not he has been guilty of any antisocial behavior there.

It is unlikely that any State at this moment in history would attempt to make it a criminal offense for a person to be mentally ill, or a leper, or to be afflicted with a venereal disease. A State might determine that the general health and welfare require that the victims of these and other human afflictions be dealt with by compulsory treatment, involving quarantine, confinement, or sequestration. But, in the light of contemporary human knowledge, a law which made a criminal offense of such a disease would doubtless be universally thought to be an infliction of cruel and unusual punishment in violation of the Eighth and Fourteenth Amendments.

We cannot but consider the statute before us as of the same category. In this Court counsel for the State recognized that narcotic addiction is an illness. Indeed, it is apparently an illness which may be contracted innocently or involuntarily.[9] We hold that a state law which imprisons a person thus afflicted as a criminal, even though he has never touched any narcotic drug within the State or been guilty of any irregular behavior there, inflicts a cruel and unusual punishment in violation

---

[9] Not only may addiction innocently result from the use of medically prescribed narcotics, but a person may even be a narcotics addict from the moment of his birth.

of the Fourteenth Amendment. To be sure, imprisonment" for ninety days is not, in the abstract, a punishment which is either cruel or unusual. But the question cannot be considered in the abstract. Even one day in prison would be a cruel and unusual punishment for the "crime" of having a common cold.

We are not unmindful that the vicious evils of the narcotics traffic have occasioned the grave concern of government. There are countless fronts on which those evils may be legitimately attacked. We deal in this case only with an individual provision of a particularized local law as it has so far been interpreted by the California courts.

Reversed.

MR. JUSTICE DOUGLAS, concurring.

The first step toward drug addiction may be as innocent as a boy's puff on a cigarette in an alleyway. It may come from medical prescriptions. Addiction may even be present at birth. Earl Ubell recently wrote: "In Bellevue Hospital's nurseries, Dr. Saul Krugman, head of pediatrics, has been discovering babies minutes old who are heroin addicts. More than 100 such infants have turned up in the last two years, and they show all the signs of drug withdrawal: irritability, jitters, loss of appetite, vomiting, diarrhea, sometimes convulsions and death. Of course, they get the drug while in the womb from their mothers who are addicts.' "

The addict is under compulsions not capable of management without outside help. Some say the addict has a disease. Others say addiction is not a disease but "a symptom of a mental or psychiatric disorder." Some States punish addiction, though most do not. Nor does the Uniform Narcotic Drug Act, first approved in 1932 and now in effect in most of the States.

We know that there is "a hard core" of "chronic and incurable drug addicts who, in reality, have lost their power of self-control." The impact that an addict has on a community causes alarm and often leads to punitive measures. Those measures are justified when they relate to acts of transgression. But I do not see how under our system being an addict can be punished as a crime. If addicts can be punished for their addiction, then the insane can also be punished for their insanity. Each has a disease and each must be treated as a sick person.

The command of the Eighth Amendment, banning "cruel and unusual punishments," stems from the Bill of Rights of 1688. And it is applicable to the States by reason of the Due Process Clause of the Fourteenth Amendment. The historic punishments that were cruel and unusual included "burning at the stake, crucifixion, breaking on the wheel", quartering, the rack and thumbscrew, and in some circumstances even solitary confinement.

The Eighth Amendment expresses the revulsion of civilized man against barbarous acts—the "cry of horror" against man's inhumanity to his fellow man. By the time of Coke, enlightenment was coming as respects the insane. Coke said that the execution of a madman "should be a miserable spectacle, both against law, and of extreme inhumanity and cruelty, and can be no example to others." Blackstone endorsed this view of Coke.

We should show the same discernment respecting drug addiction. The addict is a sick person. He may, of course, be confined for treatment or for the protection of society. Cruel and unusual punishment results not from confinement, but from convicting the addict of a crime. The purpose of § 11721 is not to cure, but to penalize. Were the purpose to cure, there would be no need for a mandatory jail term of not less than 90 days. A prosecution for addiction, with its resulting stigma and irreparable damage to the good name of the accused, cannot be justified as a means of protecting society, where a civil commitment would do as well. This age of enlightenment cannot tolerate such barbarous action.

MR. JUSTICE HARLAN, concurring.

Insofar as addiction may be identified with the use or possession of narcotics within the State (or, I would suppose, without the State), in violation of local statutes prohibiting such acts, it may surely be reached by the State's criminal law. But in this case the trial court's instructions permitted the jury to find the appellant guilty on no more proof than that he was present in California while he was addicted to narcotics. Since addiction alone cannot reasonably be thought to amount to more than a compelling propensity to use narcotics, the effect of this instruction was to authorize criminal punishment for a bare desire to commit a criminal act. The statute is an arbitrary imposition which exceeds the power that a State may exercise in enacting its criminal law. Accordingly, I agree that the application of the California statute was unconstitutional in this case and join the judgment of reversal.

MR. JUSTICE CLARK, dissenting.

The majority acknowledges that a State can punish persons who purchase, possess or use narcotics. Although none of these acts are harmful to society in themselves, the State constitutionally may attempt to deter and prevent them through punishment because of the grave threat of future harmful conduct which they pose. Narcotics addiction—including the incipient, volitional addiction to which this provision speaks—is no different. California courts have taken judicial notice that "the inordinate use of a narcotic drug tends to create an irresistible craving and forms a habit for its continued use until one becomes an addict, and he respects no convention or obligation and will lie, steal, or use any other base means to gratify his passion for the drug, being lost to all considerations of duty or social position." Can this Court deny the legislative and judicial judgment of California that incipient, volitional narcotic addiction poses a threat of serious crime similar to the threat inherent in the purchase or possession of narcotics? If such a threat is inherent in addiction, can this Court say that California is powerless to deter it by punishment?

It is no answer to suggest that we are dealing with an involuntary status and thus penal sanctions will be ineffective and unfair. The section at issue applies only to persons who use narcotics often or even daily but not to the point of losing self-control. When dealing with involuntary addicts California moves only through § 5355 of its Welfare Institutions Code which clearly is not penal. Even if it could be argued that § 11721 may not be limited to volitional addicts, petitioner undeniably retained the power of self-control and thus to him the statute would be constitutional. Nor is the conjecture relevant that petitioner may have acquired his habit under lawful circumstances. There was no suggestion by him to this effect at trial, and surely the State need not rebut all possible lawful sources of addiction as part of its prima facie case.

Properly construed, the statute provides a treatment rather than a punishment. But even if interpreted as penal, the sanction of incarceration for 3 to 12 months is not unreasonable when applied to a person who has voluntarily placed himself in a condition posing a serious threat to the State. Under either theory, its provisions for 3 to 12 months' confinement can hardly be deemed unreasonable when compared to the provisions for 3 to 24 months' confinement under § 5355 which the majority approves. I would affirm.

Mr. Justice White, dissenting.

I do not consider appellant's conviction to be a punishment for having an illness or for simply being in some status or condition, but rather a conviction for the regular, repeated or habitual use of narcotics immediately prior to his arrest and in violation of California law. Addiction is the regular use of narcotics and can be proved only by evidence of such use. To find addiction in this case the jury had to believe that appellant had frequently used narcotics in the recent past. Nor do I find any indications that California would apply § 11721 to the case of the helpless addict. I agree that there was no evidence at all that appellant had lost the power to control his acts.

The Court does not rest its decision upon the narrow ground that the jury was not expressly instructed not to convict if it believed appellant's use of narcotics was beyond his control. The Court recognizes no degrees of addiction. The Fourteenth Amendment is today held to bar any prosecution for addiction regardless of the degree or frequency of use, and the Court's opinion bristles with indications of further consequences. If it is "cruel and unusual punishment" to convict appellant for addiction, it is difficult to understand why it would be any less offensive to the Fourteenth Amendment to convict him for use on the same evidence of use which proved he was an addict. The Court has not merely tidied up California's law by removing some irritating vestige of an outmoded approach to the control of narcotics. It has effectively removed California's power to deal effectively with the recurring case under the statute where there is ample evidence of use but no evidence of the precise location of use. Beyond this it has cast serious doubt upon the power of any State to forbid the use of narcotics under threat of criminal punishment.

POINTS FOR DISCUSSION

a. Being Drunk in Public

What if a chronic alcoholic is convicted of the crime of "being found in a state of intoxication in a public place"? In *Powell v. Texas*, 392 U.S. 514 (1968), appellant contended that he was "afflicted with the disease of chronic alcoholism," that "his appearance in public while drunk was not of his own volition," and therefore "that to punish him criminally for that conduct would be cruel and unusual, in violation of the Eighth and Fourteenth Amendments to the United States Constitution." The Court disagreed:

> The present case does not fall within *Robinson's* holding, since appellant was convicted, not for being a chronic alcoholic, but for being in public while drunk on a particular occasion. The State of Texas thus has not sought to punish a mere status, nor has it attempted to regulate appellant's behavior in the privacy of his own home. Rather, it has imposed upon appellant a criminal sanction for public behavior which may create substantial health and safety hazards, both for appellant and for members of the general public, and which offends the moral and esthetic sensibilities of a large segment of the community. This seems a far cry from convicting one for being an addict, being a chronic alcoholic, being "mentally ill, or a leper."

The Requirement of a "Voluntary Act"

It is suggested in dissent that *Robinson* stands for the "simple" but "subtle" principle that "criminal penalties may not be inflicted upon a person for being in a condition he is powerless to change." The thrust of *Robinson's* interpretation of the Cruel and Unusual Punishment Clause is that criminal penalties may be inflicted only if the accused has committed some act, has engaged in some behavior, which society has an interest in preventing, or perhaps in historical common law terms, has committed some *actus reus*. It thus does not deal with the question of whether certain conduct cannot constitutionally be punished because it is, in some sense, "involuntary" or "occasioned by a compulsion." We are unable to conclude that chronic alcoholics in general, and Leroy Powell in particular, suffer from such an irresistible compulsion to drink and to get drunk in public that they are utterly unable to control their performance of either or both of these acts and thus cannot be deterred at all from public intoxication.

Mr. Justice Black concurred: "Punishment of such a defendant can clearly be justified in terms of deterrence, isolation, and treatment." "Even if we were to limit any holding in this field to 'compulsions' that are 'symptomatic' of a 'disease,' the sweep of that holding would still be startling. Such a ruling would make it clear beyond any doubt that a narcotics addict could not be punished for 'being' in possession of drugs or, for that matter, for 'being' guilty of using them. A wide variety of sex offenders would be immune from punishment if they could show that their conduct was not voluntary but part of the pattern of a disease." Mr. Justice White also concurred: "Powell's conviction was for the different crime of being drunk in a public place. Many chronic alcoholics drink at home and are never seen drunk in public. The alcoholic is like a person with smallpox, who could be convicted for being on the street but not for being ill, or, like the epileptic, who would be punished for driving a car but not for his disease." Mr. Justice Fortas dissented:

> This case does not raise any question as to the right of the police to stop and detain those who are intoxicated in public, whether as a result of the disease or otherwise; or as to the State's power to commit chronic alcoholics for treatment. Nor does it concern the responsibility of an alcoholic for criminal acts. We deal here with the mere condition of being intoxicated in public.
>
> The essential constitutional defect here is the same as in *Robinson*, for in both cases the particular defendant was accused of being in a condition which he had no capacity to change or avoid. Powell is a "chronic

alcoholic" which is "a disease which destroys the afflicted person's will power to resist the constant, excessive consumption of alcohol," and, therefore, "a chronic alcoholic does not appear in public by his own volition but under a compulsion symptomatic of the disease of chronic alcoholism." I read these findings to mean that appellant was powerless to avoid drinking; that having taken his first drink, he had "an uncontrollable compulsion to drink" to the point of intoxication; and that, once intoxicated, he could not prevent himself from appearing in public places. The findings of the trial judge call into play the principle that a person may not be punished if the condition essential to constitute the defined crime is part of the pattern of his disease and is occasioned by a compulsion symptomatic of the disease. This principle, narrow in scope and applicability, is implemented by the Eighth Amendment's prohibition of "cruel and unusual punishment," as we construed that command in *Robinson*.

b. Felon Registration Statutes

In *Lambert v. People*, 355 U.S. 225 (1957), a Los Angeles ordinance required "any convicted person" to register with the police within five days of arriving in the city. Defendant failed to register and was charged for her failure. The Court overturned her conviction because the ordinance punished passive behavior (the "mere failure to register") and there was nothing that would alert the felon to the obligation to register. Although the Court recognized the importance of the idea that "ignorance of the law will not excuse," the Court held that notice of the obligation is required under these circumstances:

> The present ordinance is entirely different. Violation of its provisions is unaccompanied by any activity whatever, mere presence in the city being the test. Moreover, circumstances which might move one to inquire as to the necessity of registration are completely lacking. At most the ordinance is but a law enforcement technique designed for the convenience of law enforcement agencies through which a list of the names and addresses of felons then residing in a given community is compiled. Appellant on first becoming aware of her duty to register was given no opportunity to comply with the law and avoid its penalty, even though her default was entirely innocent. She could but suffer the consequences of the ordinance, namely, conviction with the imposition of heavy criminal penalties there under. We believe that actual knowledge of the duty to register or proof of the probability of such

knowledge and subsequent failure to comply are necessary before a conviction under the ordinance can stand.

Mr. Justice Frankfurter dissented: "The present laws of the United States and of the forty-eight States are thick with provisions that command that some things not be done and others be done, although persons convicted under such provisions may have had no awareness of what the law required or that what they did was wrongdoing."

C. OMISSIONS

Even though criminal liability must be based on a voluntary act, the term "act" is defined broadly enough to include an "omission" to act. For example, MPC § 2.01 provides that liability can be based on an "omission to perform an act of which he is physically capable."

JONES V. UNITED STATES
308 F.2d 307, 113 U.S. App. D.C. 352 (D.C.Cir. 1962).

WRIGHT, CIRCUIT JUDGE.

Appellant, together with Shirley Green, was tried on an indictment charging them jointly with involuntary manslaughter through failure to perform their legal duty of care for Anthony Lee Green, which failure resulted in his death. Appellant was also convicted of involuntary manslaughter. Shirley Green was found not guilty. Appellant argues that there was insufficient evidence as a matter of law to warrant a jury finding of breach of duty in the care she rendered Anthony Lee. Alternatively, she argues that the trial court committed plain error in failing to instruct the jury that it must first find that appellant was under a legal obligation to provide food and necessities to Anthony Lee before finding her guilty of manslaughter in failing to provide them. The first argument is without merit. Upon the latter we reverse.

In late 1957, Shirley Green became pregnant, out of wedlock, with a child, Robert Lee, subsequently born August 17, 1958. Apparently to avoid the embarrassment of the presence of the child in the Green home, it was arranged that appellant, a family friend, would take the child to her home after birth. Appellant did so, and the child remained there continuously until removed by the police on August 5, 1960. Initially appellant made some motions toward the adoption of Robert Lee, but these came to nought, and shortly thereafter it was agreed that Shirley Green was to pay appellant $72 a month for his care. According to appellant, these payments were made for only five months. According to Shirley Green, they were made up to July, 1960.

Early in 1959 Shirley Green again became pregnant, this time with the child Anthony Lee, whose death is the basis of appellant's conviction. Soon after birth, Anthony Lee developed a mild jaundice condition, attributed to a blood income with his mother. The jaundice resulted in his retention in the hospital for three days beyond the usual time, when Anthony Lee was released to appellant's custody. Shirley Green, after a two or three day stay in the hospital, also lived with appellant for three weeks, after which she returned to her parents' home, leaving the children with appellant. She testified she did not see them again, except for one visit in March, until August 5, 1960. Consequently, though there does not seem to have been any specific monetary agreement with Shirley Green covering Anthony Lee's support,[5] appellant had complete custody of both children until they were rescued by the police.

With regard to medical care, the evidence is undisputed. In March, 1960, appellant called a Dr. Turner to her home to treat Anthony Lee for a bronchial condition. Appellant also telephoned the doctor at various times to consult with him concerning Anthony Lee's diet and health. In early July, 1960, appellant took Anthony Lee to Dr. Turner's office where he was treated for "simple diarrhea." At this time the doctor noted the "wizened" appearance of the child and told appellant to tell the mother of the child that he should be taken to a hospital. This was not done.

On August 2, 1960, two collectors for the local gas company had occasion to go to the basement of appellant's home, and there saw the two children. Robert Lee and Anthony Lee at this time were age two years and ten months respectively. Robert Lee was in a "crib" consisting of a framework of wood, covered with a fine wire screening, including the top which was hinged. The "crib" was lined with newspaper, which was stained, apparently with feces, and crawling with roaches. Anthony Lee was lying in a bassinet and was described as having the appearance of a "small baby monkey." One collector testified to seeing roaches on Anthony Lee.

Three days later, the collectors returned to appellant's home in the company of several police officers and personnel of the Women's Bureau. At this time, Anthony Lee was upstairs in the dining room in the bassinet, but Robert Lee was still downstairs in his "crib." The officers removed the children to the D.C.

---

[5] During the entire period the children were in appellant's home, appellant had ample means to provide food and medical care.

The Requirement of a "Voluntary Act"

General Hospital where Anthony Lee was diagnosed as suffering from severe malnutrition and lesions over large portions of his body, apparently caused by severe diaper rash. Following admission, he was fed repeatedly, apparently with no difficulty, and was described as being very hungry. His death, 34 hours after admission, was attributed without dispute to malnutrition. At birth, Anthony Lee weighed six pounds, fifteen ounces—at death at age ten months, he weighed seven pounds, thirteen ounces. Normal weight at this age would have been approximately 14 pounds.

Appellant argues that nothing in the evidence establishes that she failed to provide food to Anthony Lee. She cites her own testimony and the testimony of a lodger, Mr. Wills, that she did in fact feed the baby regularly. At trial, the defense made repeated attempts to extract from the medical witnesses opinions that the jaundice, or the condition which caused it, might have prevented the baby from assimilating food. The doctors conceded this was possible but not probable since the autopsy revealed no condition which would support the defense theory. It was also shown by the disinterested medical witnesses that the child had no difficulty in ingesting food immediately after birth, and that Anthony Lee, in the last hours before his death, was able to take several bottles, apparently without difficulty, and seemed very hungry. This evidence, combined with the absence of any physical cause for nonassimilation, taken in the context of the condition in which these children were kept, presents a jury question on the feeding issue.

There is substantial evidence from which the jury could have found that appellant failed to obtain proper medical care for the child. Appellant relies upon the evidence showing that on one occasion she summoned a doctor for the child, on another took the child to the doctor's office, and that she telephoned the doctor on several occasions about the baby's formula. However, the last time a doctor saw the child was a month before his death, and appellant admitted that on that occasion the doctor recommended hospitalization. Appellant did not hospitalize the child, nor did she take any other steps to obtain medical care in the last crucial month. Thus there was sufficient evidence to go to the jury on the issue of medical care, as well as failure to feed.

Appellant also takes exception to the failure of the trial court to charge that the jury must find beyond a reasonable doubt, as an element of the crime, that appellant was under a legal duty to supply food and necessities to Anthony Lee. The problem of establishing the duty to take action which would preserve the life of another has not often arisen in the case law of this country. The most commonly cited statement of the rule is found in *People v. Beardsley*, 150 Mich. 206, 113 N.W. 1128, 1129: "The law recognizes that under some circumstances the omission of a duty owed by one individual to another, where such omission results in the death of the one to whom the duty is owing, will make the other chargeable with manslaughter. This rule of law is always based upon the proposition that the duty neglected must be a legal duty, and not a mere moral obligation. It must be a duty imposed by law or by contract, and the omission to perform the duty must be the immediate and direct cause of death."

There are at least four situations in which the failure to act may constitute breach of a legal duty. One can be held criminally liable: first, where a statute imposes a duty to care for another; second, where one stands in a certain status relationship to another; third, where one has assumed a contractual duty to care for another; and fourth, where one has voluntarily assumed the care of another and so secluded the helpless person as to prevent others from rendering aid.

It is the contention of the Government that either the third or the fourth ground is applicable here. However, the instructions given in the case failed even to suggest the necessity for finding a legal duty of care. The only reference to duty in the instructions was the reading of the indictment which charged, inter alia, that the defendants "failed to perform their legal duty." A finding of legal duty is the critical element of the crime charged and failure to instruct the jury concerning it was plain error.

Reversed and remanded.

POINT FOR DISCUSSION

Taking Responsibility

In *Commonwealth v. Pestinikas*, 421 Pa. Super. 371, 617 A.2d 1339 (1992), Joseph Kly was hospitalized with a serious illness, and subsequently chose to live with the Pestinikas in their home. When the Pestinikas took Kly from the hospital to their home, medical personnel instructed them regarding his care and gave them a prescription to fill. The prescription was never filled. Instead of giving Kly a room in their home, appellants placed him in a rural house which had no insulation, no refrigeration, no bathroom, no sink and no telephone. The walls contained cracks which exposed the room to outside weather conditions. Kly's predicament was compounded by defendants' affirmative efforts to conceal his whereabouts. They gave misleading information in response to inquiries, telling members of Kly's family that they did not know where he had gone and others that he was living in their home. At some point, appellants had their names added to Kly's savings account, and they subsequently withdrew $300 dollars per month which Kly had agreed to pay for his care. After a while, the Pestinikas withdrew much larger sums (amounting to a total of $30,000) so that only $55 dollars remained when Kly died. When Kly died, emergency personnel found that he was emaciated and that his ribs and sternum were greatly pronounced. Mrs. Pestinikas told police that she had given him cookies and orange juice on the morning of his death. A subsequent autopsy, however, revealed that Kly had been dead at that time and may have been dead for as many as thirty-nine (39) hours before his body was found. The cause of death was determined to be starvation and dehydration. The Court affirmed the Pestinikas' conviction for murder, concluding that there was evidence suggesting that they failed to provide him with food and medical care: "The jury was required to find that appellants, by virtue of contract, had undertaken responsibility for providing necessary care for Kly to the exclusion of the members of Kly's family. This would impose upon them a legal duty to act to preserve Kly's life. If they maliciously set upon a course of withholding food and medicine and thereby caused Kly's death, appellants could be found guilty of murder." *See also People v. Montecino*, 66 Cal. App. 2d 85, 152 P.2d 5 (1944).

POINTS FOR DISCUSSION

a. **Termination of Life Support**

In *Barber v. Superior Court*, 147 Cal. App. 3d 1006, 195 Cal. Rptr. 484 (1983), a doctor was charged with murder for terminating life support to a patient in a persistent vegetative state. The court treated the act as an "omission," but concluded that the doctor acted permissibly:

> There is no criminal liability for failure to act unless there is a legal duty to act. Thus the critical issue becomes one of determining the duties owed by a physician to a patient who has been reliably diagnosed as in a comatose state from which any meaningful recovery of cognitive brain function is exceedingly unlikely. A physician has no duty to continue treatment, once it has proved to be ineffective. Although there may be a duty to provide life-sustaining machinery in the immediate aftermath of a cardio-respiratory arrest, there is no duty to continue its use once it has become futile in the opinion of qualified medical personnel.
>
> If it is not possible to ascertain the choice the patient would have made, the surrogate ought to be guided in his decision by the patient's best interests. Under this standard, such factors as the relief of suffering, the preservation or restoration of functioning and the quality as well as the

extent of life sustained may be considered. Finally, since most people are concerned about the well-being of their loved ones, the surrogate may take into account the impact of the decision on those people closest to the patient.

> ### Make the Connection
>
> In Chapter 1, we examined the justifications for imposing punishment under the criminal law: retribution; restraint; deterrence (both specific and general); & rehabilitation. If the defendant committed what would otherwise be a criminal act, but lacked voluntariness, none of the justifications for imposing punishment would be served by imposing criminal sanctions. Of course, the critical issue to be determined is which acts are truly involuntary.
>
> As we shall see, some crimes (*e.g.*, murder) are "result" crimes in that a conviction requires that defendant "cause" a particular result (with the required *mens rea*). Other crimes are "conduct" crimes in that conviction requires that defendant engage in prohibited conduct with the required *mens rea*. In most instances, there must be "concurrence" between the *actus reus* and the *mens rea* when defendant engages in the conduct (as well as when defendant causes a particular result). The notions of *mens rea*, concurrence, causation and result will be explored in later chapters.

b. **Prayer Without Medical Care**

In *Walker v. Superior Court*, 222 Cal. Rptr. 87 (Cal. App. 1986), defendant's daughter died of acute purulent meningitis which had been present in her body for at least two weeks at the time of death. Defendant knew that her daughter was ill, but chose to treat her daughter by spiritual healing rather than the use of medical specialists or practitioners. The court upheld a conviction for manslaughter: "The point at which parents may incur liability for substituting prayer treatment for medical care for their child is clear—when the lack of medical attention places the child in a situation endangering its person or health."

> ### Hypo 1: *Reconsidering* Martin
>
> Was *Martin* correctly decided? Although Martin was involuntarily placed in the street, did he commit the act of being loud and boisterous? Under the circumstances, is that "act" sufficient for conviction under the relevant statute?

The Requirement of a "Voluntary Act"

> ### Hypo 2: *Sleeping Driver*
>
> Defendant, a shuttle operator, was dispatched to pick up some passengers at the local airport. On the way, she became drowsy. She opened the windows for a breeze to combat the feeling, and drove on. At some point, she fell asleep, ran off the road, and killed a pedestrian. She is charged with involuntary manslaughter. Since the driver was asleep when she killed the pedestrian, did she commit a voluntary act? *See State v. Olsen*, 108 Utah 377, 160 P.2d 427 (1945).

> ### Hypo 3: *Voluntariness and Multiple Personalities*
>
> Defendant was charged with driving under the influence of alcohol. At the time of the offense, she was dissociated from her primary personality (Robin) and in the state of consciousness of a secondary personality (Jennifer). She claims that she was suffering from psychological trauma (report of a lump on her breast) which caused her to dissociate into the personality of Jennifer, who is impulsive, angry, fearful and anxious. Jennifer has a drinking problem. Defendant contends that when she is Jennifer, Robin is unaware of what is going on, has no control over Jennifer's actions, and no memory of what Jennifer did later on when she is restored to the primary personality of Robin. As a result, Robin argues that "she" did not commit the "act" of driving under the influence. Do you agree with defendant? Are the actions of a person with a multiple personality disorder voluntary when she is dissociated from her primary personality and in the state of consciousness of a secondary personality? *State v. Grimsley*, 3 Ohio App. 3d 265, 444 N.E.2d 1071 (1982).

> ### Hypo 4: *Analyzing* Robinson
>
> How far does *Robinson*'s logic extend? Suppose that Robinson had been convicted of using narcotics in the State of California and is now on probation. Following his release, a narcotics detective notices that Robinson has extensive needle marks on his arms (indicative of drug use). Rather than charging Robinson with "being addicted to the use of narcotics" (as Robinson was charged), the officer seeks to charge Robinson with actually using narcotics in California. The officer seeks to use Robinson's past history, and the recent needle marks, to infer the recent drug use. Is a conviction appropriate under these circumstances?

> ### Hypo 5: *Should the Law Impose a "Duty" to Rescue Others?*
>
> Rhode Island requires those present at the scene of an emergency to render assistance to those exposed to "grave physical harm" if he/she can do so "without danger or peril to himself or herself or to others." Vermont has a similar law.
>
> **12 V.S.A. § 519. Emergency Medical Care**
>
> (a) A person who knows that another is exposed to grave physical harm shall, to the extent that the same can be rendered without danger or peril to himself or without interference with important duties owed to others, give reasonable assistance to the exposed person unless that assistance or care is being provided by others.
>
> (b) A person who provides reasonable assistance in compliance with subsection (a) of this section shall not be liable in civil damages unless his acts constitute gross negligence or unless he will receive or expects to receive remuneration. Nothing contained in this subsection shall alter existing law with respect to tort liability of a practitioner of the healing arts for acts committed in the ordinary course of his practice.
>
> (c) A person who willfully violates subsection (a) of this section shall be fined not more than $100.00.
>
> Other states have comparable laws including Wisconsin and California. In the *Jones* case, should appellant be responsible without regard to the existence of a "duty?" Do these laws go far enough in imposing a duty to help? Do they go too far?

> ### Hypo 6: *The Kitty Genovese Case*
>
> Consider the murder of Kitty Genovese which was described in *Moseley v. Scully*, 908 F. Supp. 1120 (E.D.N.Y. 1995), as follows:
>
> > This case involves one of the most infamous and brutal murders committed this century, which shocked the nation when it was committed in 1964, and continues to trouble the public today. The 1964 murder of Katherine "Kitty" Genovese ("Genovese") in Queens, New York "symbolized urban apathy since 38 people heard her screams but did nothing." Defendant left his house in the early morning hours with a hunting knife for the purpose of "finding a

woman and killing her." About 3:00 a.m., he spotted a red car, driven by Genovese, which he followed for approximately ten blocks. When Genovese exited her car, Moseley "stabbed her twice in the back." Because someone had called out from an open window, Moseley returned to his car and moved it, but he "could see that Genovese had gotten up and that she wasn't dead." Since he "did not think that the person that called would come down to help Genovese regardless of the fact that she had screamed, he came back and looked for her in the Long Island railroad station." Not finding her there, Moseley looked in some nearby apartment buildings, where he found her in a hallway. "As soon as she saw me, she started screaming, so I stabbed her a few times to stop her from screaming, and I stabbed her once in the neck. She only moaned after that."

During this brutal attack, Moseley could hear that he had awakened residents of the apartment building. He heard a door open "at least twice, maybe three times, but when he looked up, there was nobody up there." Since he "didn't feel that these people were coming down the stairs," he decided to rape Genovese and left Genovese dead.

Can the state bring homicide prosecutions against those who overheard the incident, but who did nothing to help? If not, should the law be changed to allow prosecution of those who overheard? If so, how would you formulate the new law?

Hypo 7: *The Rapist and His Victim*

Defendant attacked and raped Edith Barton. Immediately afterwards, as she was in great distress of mind and body, she fell into a stream called Sugar Creek. Defendant made no attempt to rescue her even though he could have done so easily with no risk to himself. Edith Barton drowned. Did defendant have a legal obligation to rescue Barton? *See Jones v. State*, 220 Ind. 384, 43 N.E.2d 1017 (1942).

Hypo 8: *The Gateman*

Defendant was employed by a railroad company as a crossing gateman. Although a train was approaching, defendant failed to lower the crossing gate. Dan Goble, not realizing that a train was coming, drove across the tracks in his automobile and was hit by the train. Goble was killed. Did defendant have a legal duty to lower the gate so that he can be prosecuted criminally for his failure to do so? *See State v. Harrison*, 107 N.J.L. 213, 152 A. 867 (1931).

Hypo 9: *The Engineer and the Locomotive*

The engineer of a locomotive moved to the side track of a railroad yard, and was returning the locomotive to the roundhouse when he realized that the incoming track was "spiked" (in other words, it had been nailed up and put out of service). In violation of company rules, the engineer continued inward on the outgoing track. The locomotive had gone a little over a quarter of a mile, perhaps half a mile, on the wrong track, when it collided with an oncoming train. Two railroad employees were killed. Under company rules, the locomotive's foreman is responsible for insuring that the train is on the right track. Can the foreman be convicted of manslaughter if he failed to realize that the engineer had the train on the wrong track? *See State v. Irvine*, 126 La. 434, 52 So. 567 (1910).

CHAPTER 3

Mens Rea

Traditionally, the criminal law looked to a person's mental state (his or her "*mens rea*") and the associated notion of that person's presumed "blameworthiness" in assessing the existence or absence of criminal culpability. From this perspective, intentional criminal conduct has classically been viewed as more serious—more wicked, more immoral, more blameworthy—than unintentional criminal conduct. Indeed, Oliver Wendell Holmes made this same point more than a century ago when he observed that "even a dog distinguishes between being stumbled over and being kicked." OLIVER WENDELL HOLMES, JR., THE COMMON LAW 3 (1881).

A. OVERVIEW OF THE LAW

Proof of Specific *Mens Rea*. The prosecution must prove the specific *mens rea* elements of crimes beyond a reasonable doubt. A showing of general wickedness is never enough to satisfy the *mens rea* requirement.

Model Penal Code. The Model Penal Code established four levels of intentionality to be used as standard *mens rea* elements: purpose; knowledge; recklessness; and negligence. Many jurisdictions have followed all or part of this MPC approach, although there is still great variation between jurisdictions with respect to *mens rea* terms used, and their definitions.

***Mens Rea* Application.** The key to determining to which other elements of a crime a particular *mens rea* term applies is the intention of the legislature.

Strict Liability. Where a criminal statute does not contain an explicit *mens rea* element, it is still not necessarily a strict liability statute. A felonious criminal offense with common law roots is presumed to have an implicit *mens rea* element, unless there is a clear legislative intent to the contrary. The legislature has the power to decide whether a particular crime is or is not strict liability. Courts are only to interpret the legislature's intent.

Intoxication Defense. Intoxication or drugged condition is a good defense in most jurisdictions if crime is a specific intent crime only. It is not a good defense if the crime is a general intent or strict liability crime. Where intoxication is recognized as a tenable defense, it must be proved to have been so profound that the accused did not possess the required *mens rea*.

Mistake of Fact. A defendant's honest but mistaken belief that factual circumstances existed that would have made his or her actions *not* criminal due to the absence of the required *mens rea* is a good defense to a criminal charge. But often jurisdictions require that such an honest belief (subjective focus) also be a reasonable belief (objective focus) in order to make out a good defense to some specified crimes. Mistake of fact is never, however, a defense to strict liability crimes as it is a *mens rea* defense only.

Mistake of Law. A defendant's mistaken belief in the lawfulness of his or her otherwise criminal conduct is not a good defense unless the accused was told—officially—that such conduct was not criminal or where the criminal statute specifically makes knowledge of illegality an element of the crime.

B. LEVELS OF CRIMINAL INTENTION

At common law, a number of different mental states were used as elements of different crimes. In addition to the mental state used in the following case ("maliciously"), courts often referred to other types of criminal intentions, such as "fraudulently," "corruptly," "willfully," "feloniously" and "intent to steal."

REGINA V. FAULKNER
13 Cox Crim. Cas. 550 (1877).

[The prisoner was indicted for setting fire to the ship Zemindar, on the high seas, on June 26, 1876. The indictment charged that he "feloniously, unlawfully, and maliciously" burned a ship with the intent "to prejudice the owner of the ship and the owners of certain goods and chattels then laden, and being on board said ship." The ship was carrying a cargo of rum, sugar, and cotton, worth £50,000. The facts showed that the prisoner, a seaman on the ship, went into the bulk head, and forecastle hold, opened the sliding door in the bulk head, to steal rum. The facts further showed that he bored a hole in the cask with a gimlet, that the rum ran out, that when trying to put a spile in the hole out of which the rum was running, he had a lighted match in his hand; that the rum caught fire; that he was burned on the arms and neck; and that the ship caught fire and was completely destroyed. At the close of the Crown's case, counsel for the prisoner asked for a direction of an acquittal on the ground that on the facts proved the indictment was not sustained, nor the allegation that the prisoner had unlawfully and maliciously set fire to the ship proved. The Crown contended that inasmuch as the prisoner was at the time engaged in the commission of a felony, the indictment was sustained, and the allegation of intent was immaterial].

At the second hearing of the case before the Court for Crown Cases Reserved, the learned judge made the addition of the following paragraph to the case stated by him for the court.

"It was conceded that the prisoner had no actual intention of burning the vessel, and I was not asked to leave any question as to the jury as to the prisoner's knowing the probable consequences his act, or as to his reckless conduct."

The learned judge told the jury that although the prisoner had no actual intention of burning the vessel, still if they found he was engaged in stealing the rum, and that the fire took place in the manner above stated, they ought to find him guilty. The jury found the prisoner guilty on both counts, and he was sentenced to seven years penal servitude. The question for the court was whether the direction of the learned judge was right, if not, the conviction should be quashed.

Dowse, B., gave judgment to the effect that the conviction should be quashed.

BARRY, J.—A very broad proposition has been contended for by the Crown, namely, that if, while a person is engaged in committing a felony, or, having committed it, is endeavouring to conceal his act, or prevent or spoil waste consequent on that act, he accidently does some collateral act which if done wilfully would be another felony either at common law or by statute, he is guilty of the latter felony. I am by no means anxious to throw any doubt upon, or limit in any way, the legal responsibility of those who engage in the commission of felony, or acts *mala in se*; but I am not prepared without more consideration to give my assent to so wide a proposition. No express authority either by way of decision or dictum from judge or text writer has been cited in support of it. I consider myself bound by the authority of *Reg. v. Pembliton* (12 Cox C. C. 607). That case must be taken as deciding that to constitute an offence under the Malicious Injuries to Property Act, sect. 51, the act done must be in fact intentional and wilful, although the intention and will may

> **It's Latin to Me**
>
> *Malum in se.* A crime or an act that is inherently immoral, such as murder, arson, or rape.

(perhaps) be held to exist in, or be proved by, the fact that the accused knew that the injury would be the probable result of his unlawful act, and yet did the act reckless of such consequences. The present indictment charges the offence to be under the 42nd section of the same Act, and it is not disputed that the same construction must be applied to both sections. The jury was directed to give a verdict of guilty upon the simple ground that the firing of the ship, though accidental, was caused by an act done in the course of, or immediately consequent upon, a felonious operation, and no question of the prisoner's malice, constructive or otherwise, was left to the jury. I am of opinion that, according to *Reg. v. Pembliton*, that direction was erroneous, and that the conviction should be quashed.

FITZGERALD, J.—I concur in opinion with my brother Barry, and for the reasons he has given, that the direction of the learned judge cannot be sustained in law, and that therefore the conviction should be quashed. [In] order to establish the charge of felony under sect. 42, the intention of the accused forms an element in the crime to the extent that it should appear that the defendant intended to do the very act with which he is charged, or that it was the necessary consequence of some other felonious or criminal act in which he was engaged, or that having a probable result which the defendant foresaw, or ought to have foreseen, he, nevertheless, persevered in such other felonious or criminal act. The prisoner did not intend to set fire to the ship; the fire was not the necessary result of the felony he was attempting; and if it was a probable result, which he ought to have foreseen, of the felonious transaction on which he was engaged, and from which a malicious design to commit the injurious act with which he is charged might have been fairly imputed to him, that view of the case was not submitted to the jury. Counsel for the prosecution in effect insisted that the defendant, being engaged in the commission of, or in an attempt to commit a felony, was criminally responsible for every result that was occasioned thereby, even though it was not a probable consequence of his act or such as he could have reasonably foreseen or intended. No authority has been cited for a proposition so extensive, and I am of opinion that it is not warranted by law.

O'BRIEN, J.—I am also [of the] opinion that the conviction should be quashed. At the trial, the Crown's counsel conceded that the prisoner had no intention of burning the vessel, or of igniting the rum; and raised no questions as to prisoner's imagining or having any ground for supposing that the fire would be the result or consequence of his act in stealing the rum. The reasonable inference from the evidence is that the prisoner lighted the match for the purpose of putting the spile in the hole to stop the further running of the rum, and that while he was attempting to do so the rum came in contact with the lighted match and took fire.

KEOGH, J.—I have the misfortune to differ from the other members of the Court. I am of the opinion, that the conviction should stand, as I consider all questions of intention and malice are closed by the finding of the jury, that the prisoner committed the act with which he was charged whilst engaged in the commission of a substantive felony.

PALLES, C.B.—I concur in the opinion of the majority of the Court. The Lord Chief Justice of the Common Pleas, who, in consequence of illness, has been unable to preside to-day, has authorized me to state that he considers that the case before us is concluded by *Reg. v. Pembliton*.

DEASY, B., and LAWSON, J., concurred.

Conviction quashed.

POINTS FOR DISCUSSION

a. **Model Penal Code**

The drafters of the Model Penal Code chose to abandon most of the common law mental states, and to focus upon only four standard *mens rea* terms:

§ 2.02. General Requirements of Culpability.

(1) **Minimum Requirements of Culpability.** Except as provided in Section 2.05, a person is not guilty of an offense unless he acted purposely, knowingly, recklessly or negligently, as the law may require, with respect to each material element of the offense.

(2) Kinds of Culpability Defined.

(a) **Purposely.** A person acts purposely with respect to a material element of an offense when:

(i) if the element involves the nature of his conduct or a result thereof, it is his conscious object to engage in conduct of that nature or to cause such a result; and

(ii) if the element involves the attendant circumstances, he is aware of the existence of such circumstances or he believes or hopes that they exist.

(b) **Knowingly.** A person acts knowingly with respect to a material element of an offense when:

(i) if the element involves the nature of his conduct or the attendant circumstances, he is aware that his conduct is of that nature or that such circumstances exist; and

(ii) if the element involves a result of his conduct, he is aware that it is practically certain that his conduct will cause such a result.

(c) **Recklessly.** A person acts recklessly with respect to a material element of an offense when he consciously disregards a substantial and unjustifiable risk that the material element exists or will result from his conduct. The risk must be of such a nature and degree that, considering the nature and purpose of the actor's conduct and the circumstances known to him, its disregard involves a gross deviation from the standard of conduct that a law-abiding person would observe in the actor's situation.

(d) **Negligently.** A person acts negligently with respect to a material element of an offense when he should be aware of a substantial and unjustifiable risk that the material element exists or will result from his conduct. The risk must be of such a nature and degree that the actor's failure to perceive it, considering the nature and purpose of his conduct and the circumstances known to him, involves a gross deviation from the standard of care that a reasonable person would observe in the actor's situation.

(3) **Culpability Required Unless Otherwise Provided.** When the culpability sufficient to establish a material element of an offense is not prescribed by law, such element is established if a person acts purposely, knowingly or recklessly with respect thereto.

(4) **Prescribed Culpability Requirement Applies to All Material Elements.** When the law defining an offense prescribes the kind of culpability that is sufficient for the commission of an offense, without distinguishing among the material elements thereof, such provision shall apply to all the material elements of the offense, unless a contrary purpose plainly appears.

(5) **Substitutes for Negligence, Recklessness and Knowledge.** When the law provides that negligence suffices to establish an element of an offense, such element also is established if a person acts purposely, knowingly or recklessly. When recklessness suffices to establish an element, such element also is established if a person acts purposely or knowingly. When

acting knowingly suffices to establish an element, such element also is established if a person acts purposely.

(6) **Requirement of Purpose Satisfied if Purpose Is Conditional.** When a particular purpose is an element of an offense, the element is established although such purpose is conditional, unless the condition negatives the harm or evil sought to be prevented by the law defining the offense.

(7) **Requirement of Knowledge Satisfied by Knowledge of High Probability.** When knowledge of the existence of a particular fact is an element of an offense, such knowledge is established if a person is aware of a high probability of its existence, unless he actually believes that it does not exist.

(8) **Requirement of Wilfulness Satisfied by Acting Knowingly.** A requirement that an offense be committed wilfully is satisfied if a person acts knowingly with respect to the material elements of the offense, unless a purpose to impose further requirements appears.

(9) **Culpability as to Illegality of Conduct.** Neither knowledge nor recklessness or negligence as to whether conduct constitutes an offense or as to the existence, meaning or application of the law determining the elements of an offense is an element of such offense, unless the definition of the offense or the Code so provides.

(10) **Culpability as Determinant of Grade of Offense.** When the grade or degree of an offense depends on whether the offense is committed purposely, knowingly, recklessly or negligently, its grade or degree shall be the lowest for which the determinative kind of culpability is established with respect to any material element of the offense.

b. **Jurisdictional Variation in *Mens Rea* Definitions**

Although there are often similarities between the definitions of various *mens rea* terms in different jurisdictions and, sometimes these terms were borrowed (at least initially) from the Model Penal Code, it is nonetheless important for criminal law practitioners to discern the precise meaning—and judicial interpretation—of each *mens rea* term for each criminal offense in the Crimes Code in his or her jurisdiction. There is great—and often significant—variation in the definition of the same *mens rea* term of art in different jurisdictions. *See, e.g.,* Jerome Hall, General Principles of Criminal Law 142 (2d ed. 1960) ("there must be as many mentes reae as there are crimes").

c. **The Difference Between *Intent* & *Motive***

"Intent" and "motive" are two very different things. Intent focuses on the mental state of the offender and is of critical importance to criminal liability. When discussing intent, we ask, "what was the desired result of the defendant's actions?" "Intent to deprive a person of property," for example, the *mens rea* required for larceny, and "intent to cause death of a human being," the *mens rea* required for murder, are two examples of criminal intent. Motive, on the other hand, while occasionally relevant in a criminal trial, is of far greater concern to law enforcement in their attempt to solve or prevent crimes from occurring. It is of greater concern to psychologists, sociologists and criminologists who treat offenders or study why offenders commit crimes. When discussing motive, we ask "why did the offender commit the offense?" Motive may be of concern to prosecutors when contemplating whether to prosecute a case, or what sentence to recommend, and it may be of concern to a judge when sentencing a defendant.

Justice Samuel Alito summed up the difference between intent and motive in his concurrence in *Rosemond v. United States*, 572 U.S. 65 (2014):

> The Court confuses two fundamentally distinct concepts: intent and *motive*. It seems to assume that, if a defendant's motive in aiding a criminal venture is to avoid some greater evil, he does not have the *intent* that the venture succeed. But the intent to undertake some act is of course perfectly consistent with the motive of avoiding adverse consequences which would otherwise occur. We can all testify to this from our daily experience. People wake up, go to work, balance their checkbooks, shop for groceries—and yes, commit crimes—because they believe something bad will happen if they do not do these things, not because the deepest desire of their heart is to do them. A person may only go to work in the morning to keep his or her family from destitution; that does not mean he or she does not intend to put in a full day's work. In the same way, the fact that a defendant carries out a crime because he feels he must do so on pain of terrible consequences does not mean he does not intend to carry out the crime. When Jean Valjean stole a loaf of bread to feed his starving family, he certainly intended to commit theft; the fact that, had he been living in America today, he may have pleaded necessity as a defense does not change that fact. See V. Hugo, Les Misérables 54 (Fall River Press ed. 2012).
>
> Common-law commentators recognized this elementary distinction between intent and motive. As Sir James FitzJames Stephen

explains, if "A puts a loaded pistol to B's temple and shoots B through the head deliberately, ... [i]t is obvious that in every such case the intention of A must be to kill B." 2 A History of the Criminal Law of England 110–111 (1883). This fact "throws no light whatever on A's motives for killing B. They may have been infinitely various.... The motive may have been a desire for revenge, or a desire for plunder, or a wish on A's part to defend himself against an attack by B, ... or to put a man already mortally wounded out of his agony." *Id.*, at 111. "In all these cases the intention is the same, but the motives are different, and in all the intention may remain unchanged from first to last whilst the motives may vary from moment to moment." *Ibid.*

Here is another set of examples:

1. Frank lives next door to a house filled with gang members. The gang members have destroyed Frank's property. One day he sees the gang leader in front of the house. He points a gun at him and shoots the gang leader, killing him. Frank's motive was revenge for the damage to his property.

2. Bill and Tony get into an argument over a parking spot at the mall. Tony comes at Bill with a gun. Bill pulls out a gun and shoots Tony, killing him. Bill's motive was self-defense.

3. Susan is very jealous of Julia, as Julia flaunts her wealth and Susan works three jobs to make ends meet. Susan sees Julia walking on the street wearing an expensive diamond ring. Susan shoots Julia and steals the diamond ring. Susan was motivated by jealousy and a desire to gain something of monetary value.

All three people, Frank, Bill and Susan had different motives. All three of them had the same intent, the intent to cause death.

Hypo 1: *Running over "Leaves"*

Cinthya was driving home when she decided to run over a pile of leaves on the side of the readjust for fun. She felt a bump when the passenger-side tire ran over the leaves, later saying that it felt "[l]ike if I went [over] a pothole." Tragically, Cinthya had run over and killed a little girl who had been playing in the leaf pile. Do you think that Cinthya acted purposely, knowingly, recklessly, or negligently in causing the death of the little girl? *Cf. State v. Garcia-Cisneros*, 285 Or. App. 252, 397 P.3d 49 (2017).

> **Hypo 2: *Real or Virtual Porn***
>
> Orlando was prosecuted under a state statute that criminalizes possession of images of children other than that person's own children in "a state of nudity including a lewd exhibition or a graphic focus on the genitals." Orlando claims that he thought that the graphic images of naked children engaging in sexual activity that were found on his computer were not images of real children, but rather were images of virtual children. If a jury believes Orlando's claim, can he be found guilty of purposely, knowingly, recklessly, or negligently possessing such images in violation of this statute? *Cf. State v. Videen*, 990 N.E. 2d 173 (Ohio Ct. App. 2 Dist. 2013).

C. STRICT LIABILITY

STAPLES V. UNITED STATES
511 U.S. 600 (1994).

JUSTICE THOMAS delivered the opinion of the Court.

The National Firearms Act (Act), 26 U.S.C. §§ 5801–5872, imposes strict registration requirements on statutorily defined "firearms." The Act includes within the term "firearm" a machine gun, and further defines a machine gun as "any weapon which shoots, or can be readily restored to shoot, automatically more than one shot, without manual reloading, by a single function of the trigger," § 5845(b). Thus, any fully automatic weapon is a "firearm" within the meaning of the Act. Under the Act, all firearms must be registered in the National Firearms Registration and Transfer Record maintained by the Secretary of the Treasury. Section 5861(d) makes it a crime, punishable by up to 10 years in prison for any person to possess a firearm that is not properly registered.

Upon executing a search warrant at petitioner's home, local police and agents of the Bureau of Alcohol, Tobacco and Firearms (BATF) recovered, among other things, an AR-15 rifle. The AR-15 is the civilian version of the military's M-16 rifle, and is, unless modified, a semiautomatic weapon. The M-16, in contrast, is a selective fire rifle that allows the operator, by rotating a selector switch, to choose semiautomatic or automatic fire. Many M-16 parts are interchangeable with those in the AR-15 and can be used to convert the AR-15 into an automatic weapon. No doubt to inhibit such conversions, the AR-15 is manufactured with a metal stop on its receiver that will prevent an M-16 selector switch, if installed, from rotating to the fully automatic position. The metal stop on petitioner's rifle, however, had been filed away, and the rifle had been assembled with an M-16 selector switch and several other M-16 internal parts, including a hammer, disconnector, and trigger. Suspecting that the AR-15 had been modified to be capable of fully automatic fire, BATF agents seized the weapon. Petitioner subsequently was indicted for unlawful possession of an unregistered machine gun in violation of § 5861(d).

At trial, BATF agents testified that when the AR-15 was tested, it fired more than one shot with a single pull of the trigger. It was undisputed that the weapon was not registered as required by § 5861(d). Petitioner testified that the rifle had never fired automatically when it was in his possession. He insisted that the AR-15 had operated only semiautomatically, and even then imperfectly, often requiring manual ejection of the spent casing and chambering of the next round. According to petitioner, his alleged ignorance of any automatic firing capability should have shielded him from criminal liability for his failure to register the weapon. He requested the District Court to instruct the jury that, to establish a violation of § 5861(d), the Government must prove beyond a reasonable doubt that the defendant "knew that the gun would fire fully automatically."

The District Court rejected petitioner's proposed instruction and instead charged the jury as follows: "The Government need not prove the defendant knows he's dealing with a weapon possessing every last characteristic which subjects it to the regulation. It would be enough to prove he knows that he is dealing with a dangerous device of a type as would alert one to the likelihood of regulation."

Petitioner was convicted and sentenced to five years' probation and a $5,000 fine. The Court of Appeals affirmed. The court concluded that the Government need not prove a defendant's knowledge of a weapon's physical properties to obtain a conviction under § 5861(d). We granted certiorari to resolve a conflict in the Courts of Appeals concerning the *mens rea* required under § 5861(d).

Whether or not § 5861(d) requires proof that a defendant knew of the characteristics of his weapon that made it a "firearm" under the Act is a question of statutory construction. As we observed in *Liparota v. United States*, 471 U.S. 419 (1985), "[t]he definition of the elements of a criminal offense is entrusted to the legislature, particularly in the case of federal crimes, which are solely creatures of statute." Thus, we have long recognized that determining the mental state required for commission of a federal crime requires "construction of the statute and ... inference of the intent of Congress." *United States v. Balint*, 258 U.S. 250, 253 (1922).

The language of the statute, the starting place in our inquiry, provides little explicit guidance in this case. Section 5861(d) is silent concerning the *mens rea* required for a violation. It states simply that "[i]t shall be unlawful for any person . . . to receive or possess a firearm which is not registered to him in the National Firearms Registration and Transfer Record." 26 U.S.C. § 5861(d). Nevertheless, silence on this point by itself does not necessarily suggest that Congress intended to dispense with a conventional *mens rea* element, which would require that the defendant know the facts that make his conduct illegal. On the contrary, we must construe the statute in light of the background rules of the common law, in which the requirement of some *mens rea* for a crime is firmly embedded. As we have observed, "[t]he existence of a *mens rea* is the rule of, rather than the exception to, the principles of Anglo-American criminal jurisprudence."

There can be no doubt that this established concept has influenced our interpretation of criminal statutes. Indeed, we have noted that the common-law rule requiring *mens rea* has been "followed in regard to statutory crimes even where the statutory definition did not in terms include it." Relying on the strength of the traditional rule, we have stated that offenses that require no *mens rea* generally are disfavored, and have suggested that some indication of congressional intent, express or implied, is required to dispense with *mens rea* as an element of a crime. *Morissette v. United States*, 342 U.S. 246, 250 (1952).

According to the Government, the nature and purpose of the Act suggest that the presumption favoring *mens rea* does not apply to this case. The Government argues that Congress intended the Act to regulate and restrict the circulation of dangerous weapons. Consequently, in the Government's view, this case fits in a line of precedent concerning what we have termed "public welfare" or "regulatory" offenses, in which we have understood Congress to impose a form of strict criminal liability through statutes that do not require the defendant to know the facts that make his conduct illegal. In construing such statutes, we have inferred from silence that Congress did not intend to require proof of *mens rea* to establish an offense.

For example, in *Balint*, we concluded that the Narcotic Act of 1914, which was intended in part to minimize the spread of addictive drugs by criminalizing undocumented sales of certain narcotics, required proof only that the defendant knew that he was selling drugs, not that he knew the specific items he had sold were "narcotics" within the ambit of the statute. Cf. *United States v. Dotterweich*, 320 U.S. 277, 281 (1943) (stating in dicta that a statute criminalizing the shipment of adulterated or misbranded drugs did not require knowledge that the items were misbranded or adulterated). As we explained in *Dotterweich, Balint* dealt with "a now familiar type of legislation whereby penalties serve as effective means of regulation. Such legislation dispenses with the conventional requirement for criminal conduct—awareness of some wrongdoing."

Such public welfare offenses have been created by Congress, and recognized by this Court, in "limited circumstances." Typically, our cases recognizing such offenses involve statutes that regulate potentially harmful or injurious items. In such situations, we have reasoned that as long as a defendant knows that he is dealing with a dangerous device of a character that places him "in responsible relation to a public danger," he should be alerted to the probability of strict regulation, and we have assumed that in such cases Congress intended to place the burden on the defendant to "ascertain at his peril whether his conduct comes within the inhibition of the statute." Thus, we essentially have relied on the nature of the statute and the particular character of the items regulated to determine whether congressional silence concerning the mental element of the offense should be interpreted as dispensing with conventional *mens rea* requirements.

The Government argues that § 5861(d) defines precisely the sort of regulatory offense described in *Balint*. In this view, all guns, whether or not they are statutory "firearms," are dangerous devices that put gun owners on notice that they must determine at their hazard whether their weapons come within the scope of the Act. On this understanding, the District Court's instruction in this case was correct, because a conviction can rest simply on proof that a defendant knew he possessed a "firearm" in the ordinary sense of the term.

The Government seeks support for its position from our decision in *United States v. Freed*, 401 U.S. 601 (1971), which involved a prosecution for possession of unregistered grenades under § 5861(d). The defendant knew that the items in his possession were grenades, and we concluded that § 5861(d) did not require the Government to prove the defendant also knew that the grenades were unregistered. To be sure, in deciding that *mens rea* was not required with respect to that element of the offense, we suggested that the Act "is a regulatory measure in the interest of the public safety, which may well be premised on the theory that one would hardly be surprised to learn that possession of hand grenades is not an innocent act." Grenades, we explained, "are highly dangerous offensive weapons, no less dangerous than the narcotics involved in *United States v. Balint*." But that reasoning provides little support for dispensing with *mens rea* in this case.

If we were to accept as a general rule the Government's suggestion that dangerous and regulated items place their owners under an obligation to inquire at their peril into compliance with regulations, we would undoubtedly reach some untoward results. Automobiles, for example, might also be termed "dangerous" devices and are highly regulated at both the state and federal levels. Congress might see fit to criminalize the violation of certain regulations concerning automobiles, and thus might make it a crime to operate a vehicle without a properly functioning emission control system. But we probably would hesitate to conclude on the basis of silence that Congress intended a prison term to apply to a car owner whose vehicle's emissions levels, wholly unbeknownst to him, began to exceed legal limits between regular inspection dates.

Here, there can be little doubt that, as in *Liparota*, the Government's construction of the statute potentially would impose criminal sanctions on a class of persons whose mental state—ignorance of the characteristics of weapons in their possession—makes their actions entirely innocent. The Government does not dispute the contention that virtually any semiautomatic weapon may be converted, either by internal modification or, in some cases, simply by wear and tear, into a machinegun within the meaning of the Act. But in the Government's view, any person who has purchased what he believes to be a semiautomatic rifle or handgun, or who simply has inherited a gun from a relative and left it untouched in an attic or basement, can be subject to imprisonment, despite absolute ignorance of the gun's firing capabilities, if the gun turns out to be an automatic.

As we noted in *Morissette*, the "purpose and obvious effect of doing away with the requirement of a guilty intent is to ease the prosecution's path to conviction." We are reluctant to impute that purpose to Congress where, as here, it would mean easing the path to convicting persons whose conduct would not even alert them to the probability of strict regulation in the form of a statute such as § 5861(d).

The potentially harsh penalty attached to violation of § 5861(d)—up to 10 years' imprisonment—confirms our reading of the Act. Historically, the penalty imposed under a statute has been a significant consideration in determining whether the statute should be construed as dispensing with *mens rea*. Certainly, the cases that first defined the concept of the public welfare offense almost uniformly involved statutes that provided for only light penalties such as fines or short jail sentences, not imprisonment in the state penitentiary. See, *e.g., Commonwealth v. Raymond*, 97 Mass. 567 (1867) (fine of up to $200 or six months in jail, or both). In rehearsing the characteristics of the public welfare offense, we, too, have included in our consideration the punishments imposed and have noted that "penalties commonly are relatively small, and conviction does no grave damage to an offender's reputation."

Our characterization of the public welfare offense in *Morissette* hardly seems apt, however, for a crime that is a felony, as is violation of § 5861(d). After all, "felony" is, as we noted in distinguishing certain common-law crimes from public welfare offenses, " 'as bad a word as you can give to man or thing.' " Close adherence to the early cases described above might suggest that punishing a violation as a felony is simply incompatible with the theory of the public welfare offense. In this view, absent a clear statement from Congress that *mens rea* is not required, we should not apply the public welfare offense rationale to interpret any statute defining a felony offense as dispensing with *mens rea*.

> **Food for Thought**
>
> Do you agree with the view that—absent a clear statement from the legislature—any felony offense should be presumed to possess a *mens rea* element? What would be the significance of such a rule, for example, for sex offenses?

We need not adopt such a definitive rule of construction to decide this case, however. Instead, we note only that where, as here, dispensing with *mens rea* would require the defendant to have knowledge only of traditionally lawful conduct, a severe penalty is a further factor tending to suggest that Congress did not intend to eliminate a *mens rea* requirement. In such a case, the usual presumption that a defendant must know the facts that make his conduct illegal should apply.

In short, we conclude that the background rule of the common law favoring *mens rea* should govern interpretation of § 5861(d) in this case. Silence does not suggest that Congress dispensed with *mens rea* for the element of § 5861(d) at issue here. Thus, to obtain a conviction, the Government should have been required to prove that petitioner knew of the features of his AR-15 that brought it within the scope of the Act.

We emphasize that our holding is a narrow one. We note that our holding depends critically on our view that if Congress had intended to make outlaws of gun owners who were wholly ignorant of the offending characteristics of their weapons, and to subject them to lengthy prison terms, it would have spoken more clearly to that effect.

Reversed.

JUSTICE GINSBURG, with whom JUSTICE O'CONNOR joins, concurring in the judgment.

Conviction under § 5861(d), the Government concedes, requires proof that Staples "knowingly" possessed the machine gun. The question before us is not *whether* knowledge of possession is required, but what level of knowledge suffices:

(1) knowledge simply of possession of the object; (2) knowledge, in addition, that the object is a dangerous weapon; (3) knowledge, beyond dangerousness, of the characteristics that render the object subject to regulation, for example, awareness that the weapon is a machine gun.

Recognizing that the first reading effectively dispenses with *mens rea*, the Government adopts the second, contending that it avoids criminalizing "apparently innocent conduct," because under the second reading, "a defendant who possessed what he thought was a toy or a violin case, but which in fact was a machinegun, could not be convicted." The Government, however, does not take adequate account of the "widespread lawful gun ownership" Congress and the States have allowed to persist in this country. Given the notable lack of comprehensive regulation, "mere unregistered possession of certain types of regulated weapons—often difficult to distinguish from other, non-regulated types," has been held inadequate to establish the requisite knowledge.

The Nation's legislators chose to place under a registration requirement only a very limited class of firearms, those they considered especially dangerous. The generally "dangerous" character of all guns, the Court therefore observes did not suffice to give individuals in Staples' situation cause to inquire about the need for registration. Only the third reading, then, suits the purpose of the *mens rea* requirement—to shield people against punishment for apparently innocent activity.

I conclude that conviction under § 5861(d) requires proof that the defendant knew he possessed not simply a gun, but a machinegun. The indictment in this case, but not the jury instruction, properly described this knowledge requirement. I therefore concur in the Court's judgment.

JUSTICE STEVENS, with whom JUSTICE BLACKMUN joins, dissenting.

To avoid a slight possibility of injustice to unsophisticated owners of machine guns and sawed-off shotguns, the Court has substituted its views of sound policy for the judgment Congress made when it enacted the National Firearms Act (or Act). Because the Court's addition to the text of 26 U.S.C. § 5861(d) is foreclosed by both the statute and our precedent, I respectfully dissent.

In *Morissette,* Justice Jackson outlined one such interpretive rule: "Congressional silence as to mental elements in an Act merely adopting into federal statutory law a concept of crime already well defined in common law and statutory interpretation by the states may warrant quite contrary inferences than the same silence in creating an offense new to general law, for whose definition the courts have no guidance except the Act."

Although the lack of an express knowledge requirement in § 5861(d) is not dispositive, its absence suggests that Congress did not intend to require proof that the defendant knew all of the facts that made his conduct illegal.

The provision's place in the overall statutory scheme confirms this intention. In 1934, when Congress originally enacted the statute, it limited the coverage of the 1934 Act to a relatively narrow category of weapons such as submachineguns and sawed-off shotguns—weapons characteristically used only by professional gangsters like Al Capone, Pretty Boy Floyd, and their henchmen. At the time, the Act would have had little application to guns used by hunters or guns kept at home as protection against unwelcome intruders. Congress therefore could reasonably presume that a person found in possession of an unregistered machinegun or sawed-off shotgun intended to use it for criminal purposes. The statute as a whole, and particularly the decision to criminalize mere possession, reflected a legislative judgment that the likelihood of innocent possession of such an unregistered weapon was remote, and far less significant than the interest in depriving gangsters of their use.

"Public welfare" offenses share certain characteristics: (1) they regulate "dangerous or deleterious devices or products or obnoxious waste materials," (2) they "heighten the duties of those in control of particular industries, trades, properties or activities that affect public health, safety or welfare," and (3) they "depend on no mental element but consist only of forbidden acts or omissions." Examples of such offenses include Congress' exertion of its power to keep dangerous narcotics, hazardous substances, and impure and adulterated foods and drugs out of the channels of commerce.

Public welfare statutes render criminal "a type of conduct that a reasonable person should know is subject to stringent public regulation and may seriously threaten the community's health or safety." Thus, under such statutes, "a defendant can be convicted even though he was unaware of the circumstances of his conduct that made it illegal." Referring to the strict criminal sanctions for unintended violations of the food and drug laws, Justice Frankfurter wrote:

> "The purposes of this legislation thus touch phases of the lives and health of people which, in the circumstances of modern industrialism, are largely beyond self-protection. Regard for these purposes should infuse construction of the legislation if it is to be treated as a working instrument of government and not merely as a collection of English words. The prosecution is based on a now familiar type of legislation whereby penalties serve as effective means of regulation. Such legislation

dispenses with the conventional requirement for criminal conduct—awareness of some wrongdoing. In the interest of the larger good it puts the burden of acting at hazard upon a person otherwise innocent but standing in responsible relation to a public danger." *United States v. Dotterweich*, 320 U.S. 277, 280–281 (1943).

The National Firearms Act unquestionably is a public welfare statute. Congress fashioned a legislative scheme to regulate the commerce and possession of certain types of dangerous devices, including specific kinds of weapons, to protect the health and welfare of the citizenry. We have read a knowledge requirement into public welfare crimes, but not a requirement that the defendant know all the facts that make his conduct illegal. Although the Court acknowledges this standard, it nevertheless concludes that a gun is not the type of dangerous device that would alert one to the possibility of regulation.

The enforcement of public welfare offenses always entails some possibility of injustice. Congress nevertheless has repeatedly decided that an overriding public interest in health or safety may outweigh that risk when a person is dealing with products that are sufficiently dangerous or deleterious to make it reasonable to presume that he either knows, or should know, whether those products conform to special regulatory requirements. The dangerous character of the product is reasonably presumed to provide sufficient notice of the probability of regulation to justify strict enforcement against those who are merely guilty of negligent, rather than willful, misconduct.

This case presents no dispute about the dangerous character of machine guns and sawed-off shotguns. Anyone in possession of such a weapon is "standing in responsible relation to a public danger." In the National Firearms Act, Congress determined that the serious threat to health and safety posed by the private ownership of such firearms warranted the imposition of a duty on the owners of dangerous weapons to determine whether their possession is lawful. Semiautomatic weapons that are readily convertible into machineguns are sufficiently dangerous to alert persons who knowingly possess them to the probability of stringent public regulation. The jury's finding that petitioner knowingly possessed "a dangerous device of a type as would alert one to the likelihood of regulation" adequately supports the conviction.

Accordingly, I would affirm the judgment of the Court of Appeals.

POINTS FOR DISCUSSION

a. *Morissette* Facts

In *Staples*, the Supreme Court referred extensively to its seminal decision in *Morissette v. United States*, 342 U.S. 246 (1952). The underlying facts in *Morissette* were as follows: On a large tract of uninhabited and untilled land in a wooded and sparsely populated part of Michigan, the federal government established a practice bombing range over which the Air Force dropped simulated bombs at ground targets. These bombs consisted of metal cylinders about forty inches long and eight inches wide filled with sand and enough black powder to cause a smoke puff by which the strikes could be located. Signs read "Danger—Keep Out—Bombing Range." Despite the signs, the range was known as deer country and was extensively hunted. Spent bomb casings were cleared from the targets and thrown into piles "so that they would be out of the way." They were not sacked or piled in any order but were dumped in heaps, some of which had been accumulating for four years or upwards. They were also exposed to the weather and rusting away. Jackson went hunting in this area but did not bag a deer. He decided to meet his expenses by salvaging some of the casings. He loaded three tons of them on his truck and took them to a nearby farm, where they were flattened by a tractor, and then trucked to Flint where he obtained $84 for them. Morissette was indicted under a federal law which provided that:

> Whoever embezzles, steals, purloins, or knowingly converts to his use or the use of another, or without authority, sells, conveys or disposes of any record, voucher, money, or thing of value of the United States or of any department or agency thereof, or any property made or being made under contract for the United States or any department or agency thereof;
>
> Shall be fined not more than $10,000 or imprisoned not more than ten years, or both; but if the value of such property does not exceed the sum of $100, he shall be fined not more than $1,000 or imprisoned not more than one year, or both.

b. *Balint* Facts

In *Staples*, the Supreme Court referred extensively to its decision in *United States v. Balint*, 258 U.S. 250 (1922). The underlying facts in *Balint* were as follows: Congress enacted a law that provided that those dealing in the production, importation, manufacture, compounding, dealing in, dispensing, selling, distributing, or giving away of opium or coca leaves must register with the Internal Revenue Service and pay a tax. The statute read as follows:

> It shall be unlawful for any person to sell, barter, exchange, or give away any opium or cocoa leaves except in pursuance of a written order of the person to whom such article is sold, bartered, exchanged, or given, on a form to be issued in blank for that purpose by the Commissioner of Internal Revenue. Every person who shall accept any such order, and in pursuance thereof shall sell, barter, exchange, or give away any of the aforesaid drugs, shall preserve such order for a period of two years for inspection by any officer, agent, or employee of the Treasury Department duly authorized for that purpose, and the state, territorial, district, municipal, and insular officials who are similarly authorized.

Balint admitted that he sold an opium-based substance, but he denied that he knew its content.

D. INTOXICATION & DRUGGED CONDITION

Criminals often commit criminal acts while they are "high" on alcohol and/or drugs. Where a criminal offense is *not* a strict liability offense, it is easy to imagine situations where such a defendant does not (sometimes, virtually cannot) possess the *mens rea* required for the criminal offense in question. Nonetheless, courts have been extremely reluctant to acquit on this basis. Common law jurisdictions have traditionally taken the position that an intoxication or drugged condition can negative the *mens rea* for a "specific intent" crime, but it does not negative the *mens rea* of a "general intent" crime. Just what general and specific intent mean in this setting has been the subject of considerable controversy.

PEOPLE V. ATKINS
25 Cal. 4th 76, 18 P.3d 660, 104 Cal. Rptr. 2d 738 (2001).

CHIN, J.

Is evidence of voluntary intoxication admissible on the issue of whether defendant formed the required mental state for arson? We conclude that such evidence is not admissible because arson is a general intent crime. Accordingly, we reverse the judgment of the Court of Appeal.

On September 26, 1997, defendant told his friends that he hated Orville Figgs and was going to burn down Figgs's house. On the afternoon of September 27, defendant and his brother David drove by Figgs's home on the Ponderosa Sky Ranch. Defendant "flipped the bird" at Figgs as they passed by.

Later that day, around 5:00 p.m., a neighbor saw David drive a white pickup truck into the Ponderosa Sky Ranch canyon, but could not tell if he had a passenger. Around 9:00 p.m., the same neighbor saw the pickup truck drive out of the canyon at a high rate of speed. A half-hour later, a fire was reported. Shortly after 10:00 p.m., Figgs was awakened by a neighbor. Because the fire was rapidly approaching his house, Figgs set up a fire line. The fire came within 150 feet of his house.

At 9:00 or 9:30 p.m., one of defendant's friends saw defendant at David's apartment. He was angrily throwing things around. When asked if defendant was heavily intoxicated, the friend replied, "Yes. Agitated, very agitated."

The county fire marshall, Alan Carlson, responded to the fire around 1:30 a.m. and saw a large fire rapidly spreading in the canyon below the ranch. He described fire conditions on that night as "extreme." Both the weather and the vegetation were particularly dry. The wind was blowing from 12 to 27 miles per hour, with gusts up to 50 miles per hour. The canyon had heavy brush, trees, grass, and steep sloping grades. The fire could not be controlled for three days and burned an area from 2.5 to 2.8 miles long.

The fire marshall traced the origin of the fire to an approximately 10 foot-square area that was completely burned and smelled of "chainsaw mix," a combination of oil and gasoline. A soil sample taken from that area tested positive for gasoline. About 40 feet away, the marshall found defendant's wallet, which was near a recently opened beer can, and tire tracks. He also found a disposable lighter nearby and two more beer cans in other parts of the canyon. All the cans had the same expiration date.

Several days later, defendant spoke with the fire marshall. After waiving his Miranda rights, defendant told the marshall that he and his brother had spent much of the day drinking. They then drove in David's white pickup to the Ponderosa Sky Ranch canyon, where they drank some more and stayed between three and one-half to five hours. Defendant saw that the area was in poor condition and decided to burn some of the weeds. His family had once lived there. He pulled out the weeds, placed them in a small pile in a cleared area, retrieved a plastic gasoline jug from David's truck, and from the jug poured "chainsaw mix" on the pile of weeds. Defendant put the jug down a few feet away and lit the pile of weeds with a disposable lighter. The fire quickly spread to the jug and got out of hand. He and David tried to put the fire out, unsuccessfully. They panicked and fled while the jug was still burning. Defendant told the marshal that he meant no harm, claimed the fire was an accident, but admitted that he and his family had hard feelings with the Figgs family.

The marshall testified that the fire had not been started in a cleared area. The area was covered with vegetation, and there was no evidence that the fire started accidentally during a debris burn or that someone had tried to put it out. The marshall opined that the fire was intentionally set.

An information charged defendant with arson of forest land. The trial court instructed on arson and on the lesser offenses of arson to property, unlawfully causing a fire of forest land, and misdemeanor unlawfully causing a fire of property. It described arson and all lesser offenses as general intent crimes and further instructed that voluntary intoxication is not a defense to arson and the lesser crimes and does not relieve defendant of responsibility for the crime. The jury found defendant guilty as charged.

Defendant appealed, arguing that evidence of voluntary intoxication was admissible to show that he lacked the requisite mental state for arson. The Court of Appeal agreed. It reasoned that [the] *mens rea* for arson is the intent to set fire to or burn or cause to be burned forest land, a specific mental state, as to which voluntary intoxication evidence is admissible under section 22, subdivision (b). The court reversed because the instruction that voluntary intoxication was not a defense to arson "denied defendant the opportunity to prove he lacked the required mental state."

Section 22 provides, as relevant:

"(a) No act committed by a person while in a state of voluntary intoxication is less criminal by reason of his or her having been in that condition. Evidence of voluntary intoxication shall not be admitted to negate the capacity to form any mental states for the crimes charged, including, but not limited to, purpose, intent, knowledge, premeditation, deliberation, or malice aforethought, with which the accused committed the act.

"(b) Evidence of voluntary intoxication is admissible solely on the issue of whether or not the defendant actually formed a required specific intent, or, when charged with murder, whether the defendant premeditated, deliberated, or harbored express malice aforethought."

Evidence of voluntary intoxication is inadmissible to negate the existence of general criminal intent. In *People v. Hood (1969)* 1 Cal. 3d 444, 82 Cal. Rptr. 618, 462 P.2d 370, we first addressed the question whether to designate a mental state as a general intent, to prohibit consideration of voluntary intoxication or a specific intent, to permit such consideration. There, we held that intoxication was relevant to negate the existence of a specific intent, but not a general intent, and that assault is a general intent crime for this purpose. We stated:

> "The distinction between specific and general intent crimes evolved as a judicial response to the problem of the intoxicated offender. That problem is to reconcile two competing theories of what is just in the treatment of those who commit crimes while intoxicated. On the one hand, the moral culpability of a drunken criminal is frequently less than that of a sober person effecting a like injury. On the other hand, it is commonly felt that a person who voluntarily gets drunk and while in that state commits a crime should not escape the consequences.
>
> "Before the nineteenth century, the common law refused to give any effect to the fact that an accused committed a crime while intoxicated. The judges were apparently troubled by this rigid traditional rule, however, for there were a number of attempts during the early part of the nineteenth century to arrive at a more humane, yet workable, doctrine. The theory that these judges explored was that evidence of intoxication could be considered to negate intent, whenever intent was an element of the crime charged. As Professor Hall notes, however, such an exculpatory doctrine could eventually have undermined the traditional rule entirely, since some form of *mens rea* is a requisite of all but strict liability offenses. To limit the operation of the doctrine and achieve a compromise between the conflicting feelings of sympathy and reprobation for the intoxicated offender, later courts both in England and this country drew a distinction between so-called specific intent and general intent crimes."

Although we noted in *Hood* that specific and general intent have been notoriously difficult terms to define and apply, we set forth a general definition distinguishing the two intents: "When the definition of a crime consists of only the description of a particular act, without reference to intent to do a further

Food for Thought

Does this distinction between general and specific intent crimes make sense to you?

act or achieve a future consequence, we ask whether the defendant intended to do the proscribed act. This intention is deemed to be a general criminal intent. When the definition refers to defendant's intent to do some further act or achieve some additional consequence, the crime is deemed to be one of specific intent." The basic framework that *Hood* established in designating a criminal intent as either specific or general for purposes of determining the admissibility of evidence of voluntary intoxication has survived.

Defendant argues that arson requires the specific intent to burn the relevant structure or forest land, a mental state that may be negated by evidence of voluntary intoxication. The People argue that arson is a general intent crime with a mental state that cannot be negated by such evidence. The Courts of Appeal have disagreed on the intent requirement for arson.

In this case, the [Court of Appeal held] that the *mens rea* for arson, [the] intent to set fire to or burn or cause to be burned forest land—is a "required specific intent" for which evidence of voluntary intoxication is admissible under section 22, subdivision (b).

We agree with the People that arson requires only a general criminal intent and that the specific intent to set fire to or burn or cause to be burned the relevant structure or forest land is not an element of arson. As relevant here, the proscribed acts within the statutory definition of arson are to: (1) set fire to; (2) burn; or (3) cause to be burned, any structure, forest land, or property. Language that typically denotes specific intent crimes, such as "with the intent" to achieve or "for the purpose of" achieving some further act, is absent. "A crime is characterized as a 'general intent' crime when the required mental state entails only an intent to do the act that causes the harm; a crime is characterized as a 'specific intent' crime when the required mental state entails an intent to cause the resulting harm." The statute does not require an additional specific intent to burn a "structure, forest land, or property," but rather requires only an intent to do the act that causes the harm. This interpretation is manifest from the fact that the statute is implicated if a person "causes to be burned . . . any structure, forest land, or property." Thus, the intent requirement for arson fits within the *Hood* definition of general intent, i.e., the description of the proscribed act fails to refer to an intent to do a further act or achieve a future consequence.

Defendant reasons that, since arson is the more serious crime, it should have a more culpable mental state than the recklessness requirement of the lesser offense of recklessly causing a fire. From that premise, he infers that the more culpable mental state of arson must be a specific intent. However, the lesser offense requires mere recklessness; arson requires the general intent to perform the criminal act. This is a continuum that does not support specific intent. The fact that a crime requires a greater mental state than recklessness does not mean that it is a specific intent crime, rather than a general intent crime. The fact that reckless burning is a lesser offense of arson is also not dispositive.

In arson, as with assault, there is generally no complex mental state, but only relatively simple impulsive behavior. A typical arson is almost never the product of pyromania, it often is an angry impulsive act, requiring no tools other than a match or lighter, and possibly a container of gasoline. "Arson is one of the easiest crimes to commit on the spur of the moment . . . it takes only seconds to light a match to a pile of clothes or a curtain."

The apparent legislative policy concerns are consistent with studies that have shown the following: that revenge and vindictiveness are principal motives for; that there is a strong relationship between alcohol intoxication and arson; and that recidivist arsonists committing chronic or repetitive arson have high levels of alcohol. Thus, the motivations for most arsons, the ease of its commission, and the strong connection with alcohol reflect the crime's impulsiveness. "It would therefore be anomalous to allow evidence of intoxication to relieve a man of responsibility for the crime of arson, which is so frequently committed in just such a manner."

We reverse the judgment of the Court of Appeal and remand the cause to the Court of Appeal for further proceedings consistent with this opinion.

Concurring Opinion by MOSK, J.

Although they apparently recognize that "general intent" should be affixed to the crime of arson because arson is itself closely linked to voluntary intoxication in its commission, the majority deny that the mental state required could readily be deemed to be one of specific intent. Their denial is inexplicable. It is also incorrect. They seem to rest on the premise that the perpetrator's intent must be inceptive, aiming to start a fire, and apparently need not be resultative, aiming to burn down an indicated object. Even if their premise is sound, it gives them no aid. For, even if the perpetrator's intent must be inceptive rather than resultative, the required mental state could readily be deemed to be one of specific intent— again, an intent to engage in proscribed conduct involving setting fire to an indicated object, burning it, or causing it to be burned, for the purpose of bringing about, or allowing, a proscribed result involving any other wrong, including vexation, fraud, annoyance, or injury to another person. At the end of the day, all that the majority have to justify their denial seems to be an assumption that the perpetrator's intent must be resultative rather than inceptive. *Hood* itself is plain: "When" a crime "refers to" the perpetrator's "intent to do some further act or achieve some additional consequence" beyond the "description of a particular act," the "crime is deemed to be one of specific intent." The majority's assumption is that, beyond referring to the perpetrator's setting fire to an indicated object, burning it, or causing it to be burned, arson must refer to an intent on his part to achieve a particular additional consequence, that is, to burn the object down, as opposed to doing any other wrong, including vexation, fraud, annoyance, or injury to another person. Their assumption is unsupported. Hence, it falls of its own weight.

E. MISTAKE OF FACT

IOWA V. FREEMAN
450 N.W.2d 826 (Iowa 1990).

MCGIVERIN, CHIEF JUSTICE.

The facts of this case are not disputed. The defendant, Robert Eric Freeman, agreed to sell a controlled substance, cocaine, to Keith Hatcher. Unfortunately for Freeman, Hatcher was cooperating with the government. Hatcher gave Freeman $200, and Freeman gave Hatcher approximately two grams of what was supposed to be cocaine. To everyone's surprise, the "cocaine" turned out to be acetaminophen. Acetaminophen is not a controlled substance.

Freeman was convicted at a bench trial of delivering a simulated controlled substance with respect to a substance represented to be cocaine. The sole question presented by Freeman's appeal is whether he can be convicted of delivering a simulated controlled substance when, in fact, he believed he was delivering and intended to deliver cocaine.

Our review is to determine whether any error of law occurred. Finding no error, we affirm the conviction.

Iowa Code section 204.401(2) provides, in relevant part:

It is unlawful for a person to create, deliver, or possess with intent to deliver a simulated controlled substance.

The term "simulated controlled substance" is defined by Iowa Code section 204.101(27):

"Simulated controlled substance" means a substance which is not a controlled substance but which is expressly represented to be a controlled substance, or a substance which is not a controlled substance but which is impliedly represented to be a controlled substance and which because of its nature, packaging, or appearance would lead a reasonable person to believe it to be a controlled substance.

Our cases indicate that knowledge of the nature of the substance delivered is an imputed element of section 204.401(1) offenses[, offenses involving real, non-simulated controlled substances]. Proof of such knowledge has been required to separate those persons who innocently commit the overt acts of the offense from those persons who commit the overt acts of the offense with *scienter*, or criminal intent. In general, only the latter are criminally responsible for their acts.

Seizing upon the similarity of the statutory prohibitions, Freeman argues that he cannot be convicted of delivering a simulated controlled substance because he mistakenly believed he was delivering and intended to deliver an actual controlled substance.

We disagree. Freeman's construction of section 204.401(2) would convert the offense of delivery of a simulated controlled substance into one requiring knowing misrepresentation of the nature of the substance delivered. The statute clearly does not require knowing misrepresentation of the nature of the substance delivered.

The gist of [the 204.401(2)] offense is knowing representation of a substance to be a controlled substance and delivery of a noncontrolled substance, rather than knowing misrepresentation and delivery.

Freeman's mistaken belief regarding the substance he delivered cannot save him from conviction. Mistake of fact is a defense to a crime of *scienter* or criminal intent only where the mistake precludes the existence of the mental state necessary to commit the crime. In this case, Freeman would not be innocent of wrongdoing had the situation been as he supposed; rather, he would be guilty of delivering a controlled substance. His mistake is no defense. The *scienter* required to hold him criminally responsible for committing the overt acts of the charged offense is present regardless of the mistake. Freeman knowingly represented to Hatcher that the substance he delivered was cocaine.

In conclusion, we hold that a person who delivers a substance that is not a controlled substance, but who knowingly represents the substance to be a controlled substance, commits the offense of delivery of a simulated controlled substance regardless of whether the person believed that the substance was controlled or not controlled.

Freeman attempted and intended to sell cocaine. The fact that Freeman was fooled as much as his customer is no defense to the charge in this case.

AFFIRMED.

> **Hypo 3: *The Homicidal Clown***
>
> As part of a circus act, a clown is supposed to point a gun loaded with blanks at another clown and pull the trigger. One day, unbeknownst to the clown who pulled the trigger, the gun was loaded with real bullets. When he pulled the trigger, he shot and killed the other clown. Does the clown have a good defense to potential homicide charges? Why?

POINTS FOR DISCUSSION

a. Sale of Controlled Substances

After this decision in *Freeman*, can a mistake-of-fact defense be presented where an accused is charged with sale of controlled substances (not *simulated* controlled substances)?

b. Attempted Sale of Controlled Substances

Could Freeman have been convicted of *attempted* sale of a controlled substance? If so, why did the prosecutor not charge that offense?

> **Hypo 4: *He Looked 18***
>
> Defendant William Saponaro, Jr., 49 years old, had consensual sex with a 13 year-old boy that he met on an online site, GrindrX. Subsequently charged with sexual assault and endangering the welfare of a child, he argues that he was reasonably mistaken as to the age of the boy because: the boy told defendant that he was 18 years old; he actually appeared to be 18; and he had used a website that required him to pay with a credit card. Do you think that, if all of these averment are true, Saponaro might have a good defense to these charges? *New Jersey v. Saponaro*, 2017 WL 2348869 (N.J. App. Div. 2017).

F. MISTAKE OF LAW

KIPP V. DELAWARE
704 A.2d 839 (Del. 1998).

HOLLAND, JUSTICE:

This is an appeal following a bench trial in the Superior Court. The defendant-appellant, Hugh A. Kipp, Jr. ("Kipp"), was convicted of three counts of Possession of a Deadly Weapon by a Person Prohibited. The State has confessed error on appeal and submits that Kipp's judgments of conviction should be reversed.

On the morning of September 17, 1995, several police officers went to Kipp's home in Wilmington. They were investigating a "man with a gun" complaint from Kipp's girlfriend, Lisa Zeszut ("Zeszut"). At first, Kipp refused to come out of his house, but eventually surrendered to the police.

The police searched the house for other weapons. The police found a handgun and two unloaded shotguns. The police discovered ammunition for those weapons scattered on the bedroom floor. The police also found two hunting bows, with arrows. Upon checking Kipp's criminal record, police ascertained that he was a person prohibited from possessing deadly weapons.

Kipp was charged with five counts of Possession of a Deadly Weapon by a Person Prohibited.

The only defense offered by Kipp at trial was that he was unaware of his status as a "person prohibited." Kipp was a "person prohibited" as a result of his guilty plea to Assault in the Third Degree in 1990. Kipp testified he was told that he would not be prohibited from possessing weapons as a result of the plea.

The 1990 guilty plea form, which was submitted into evidence, has a space which provides that a guilty plea will result in loss of the right to possess deadly weapons. That portion of the form was marked "N/A." Kipp testified that "N/A" meant the provision did not apply to him. The completed guilty plea form was provided to the judge during the 1990 plea colloquy. Neither the prosecutor nor the judge, however, brought the error on the guilty plea form to Kipp's attention.

After hearing all of the evidence, the Superior Court concluded that the two hunting bows were not deadly weapons. The Superior Court found Kipp guilty of three counts of Possession of a Deadly Weapon by a Person Prohibited in connection with his possession of the three firearms.

Under 11 Del.C. § 1448(b), "any prohibited person who knowingly possesses, purchases, owns or controls a deadly weapon while so prohibited shall be guilty of possession of a deadly weapon by a person prohibited." A person is a "prohibited person" for purposes of § 1448(b) when, inter alia, he or she has "been convicted in this State or elsewhere of a felony or a crime of violence involving physical injury to another." Assault in the Third Degree is a misdemeanor crime of violence involving physical injury to another. A person who has been convicted of a violent misdemeanor is prohibited from possessing a deadly weapon for the five-year period from the date of conviction.

The State has confessed error in Kipp's case on appeal. Under the facts presented, the State concedes that Kipp presented a valid mistake of law defense. This Court has held that, in very narrow circumstances, mistake of law can be a defense to a criminal charge. That defense is cognizable when the defendant: (1) erroneously concludes in good faith that his particular conduct is not subject to the operation of the criminal law; (2) makes a "bona fide, diligent effort, adopting a course and resorting to sources and means at least as appropriate as any afforded or under our legal system, to ascertain and abide by the law;" (3) "acts in good faith reliance upon the results of such effort;" and (4) the conduct constituting the offense is "neither immoral nor anti-social."

Kipp presented evidence that he was misled in connection with his plea to Assault in the Third Degree. His 1990 guilty plea form, which was introduced at trial, and his testimony indicated he was told that the prohibition against possession of a deadly weapon which would result from a guilty plea was "not applicable" to the plea which he was entering. Kipp testified that he was told that prohibition was not applicable to him because he was pleading to a misdemeanor.

Kipp's plea agreement and truth-in-sentencing guilty plea form were submitted to the judge in 1990 at the plea colloquy before his guilty plea to Assault in the Third Degree was accepted. Apparently, the prosecutor and the judge who accepted his guilty plea failed to notice the "not applicable" notation on the guilty plea form. The judge referred to the plea agreement in the plea colloquy, but never informed Kipp that the "not applicable" notation was incorrect with respect to the prohibition against future possession of a deadly weapon which would result from the plea.

Under 11 Del.C. § 1448, a person is guilty of possession of a deadly weapon by a person prohibited when he is: (a) a person prohibited; and (b) knowingly possesses a deadly weapon. Thus, to be guilty of the offense, the defendant need only know that he or she possessed the weapon. Section 1448 does not require the defendant to know that it was criminal to do so.

Ignorance of the law is not a defense to crime. But "a defendant is not charged with knowledge of a penal statute if he is misled concerning whether the statute is not being applied." A mistake of law defense is appropriately recognized where the defendant demonstrates that he has been misled by information received from the State.

Under the unique circumstances of this case, the State concedes on appeal that Kipp presented a proper and complete mistake of law defense. In relying on the advice of counsel, memorialized in an official guilty plea document presented to and not corrected by either the prosecutor or the judge, Kipp had "made a bona fide, diligent effort, adopting a course and resorting to sources and means at least as appropriate as any afforded under our legal system, to ascertain and abide by the law." The State submits that Kipp's three convictions for possession of a deadly weapon by a person prohibited should be reversed.

The mistake of law defense is based upon principles of fundamental fairness. A review of the record and the applicable law supports the State's confession of error. The State's confession of error "is in accordance with the highest tradition of the Delaware Bar and the prosecutor's unique role and duty to seek justice within an adversary system."

The judgments of conviction are reversed.

POINTS FOR DISCUSSION

a. Ignorance of the Law Is No Excuse

In general, the old maxim, "ignorance of the law is no excuse" ("*ignorantia legis neminem excusat*"), is a perfectly accurate statement of the prevailing law, unless the criminal statute in question expressly prescribes that knowledge of the unlawfulness of one's conduct is an element of the offense.

b. Mistake of Law Exceptions

The Hawaii mistake-of-law statute, H.R.S. § 702–220, also contains provisions, not at issue in *DeCastro*, taken from the Model Penal Code, that provide a further mistake-of-law defense where an individual acts in reasonable reliance upon an official (albeit erroneous) statement of the law contained in "(1) a statute or other enactment; or(2)[a judicial decision, opinion, or judgment."

CHAPTER 4

Causation

Some crimes require only an *actus reus* committed with the required *mens rea* in order to gain a conviction. Other crimes are "result" crimes which require that defendant "cause" some result. In some instances, it is not difficult to determine that a defendant caused a particular result, as when a defendant fires bullets into a victim who falls over dead. In other instances, the "cause" of death may be less clear, as when "intervening factors" intrude between the act and the death.

A. OVERVIEW OF THE LAW

Proof of Causation. In order to convict a defendant of a "result" crime (*e.g.*, murder), the prosecution must show that defendant acted with the necessary *mens rea*, and committed any required acts with any necessary attendant circumstances, but also that defendant caused the required result (the death of the victim).

"Year and a Day" Rule. At common law, defendant's conduct could not be deemed to be the "cause" of a homicide unless the victim died within a year and a day following the defendant's acts. Even though defendant might not have been guilty of homicide, if the victim failed to die within a year and a day, defendant might have been convicted of other crimes such as attempted murder, assault or battery.

MPC and Causation. The Model Penal Code provides that causation exists when conduct is the cause of a result, and either "it is an antecedent but for which the result in question would not have occurred," or "the relationship between the conduct and result satisfies any additional causal requirements imposed by the Code or by the law defining the offense." However, subject to some exceptions, when "purposely or knowingly causing a particular result is an element of an offense, the element is not established if the actual result is not within the purpose or the contemplation of the actor." Again, with exceptions, when "recklessly or negligently causing a particular result is an element of an offense, the element is not established if the actual result is not within the risk of which the actor is aware or, in the case of negligence." When "causing a particular result is a material element for which absolute liability is imposed by law, the element is not established unless the actual result is a probable consequence of the actor's conduct."

Actual Cause or Legal Cause. Even though a defendant may be the "actual cause" of a result (as exemplified by the "but for" test), courts also require proof that defendant was the "legal cause" of death. The concept of "legal cause" has been formulated in different ways, including "proximate cause."

Intervening Causes. Many jurisdictions distinguish between different types of "intervening causes." In general, an "independent intervening cause" breaks the chain of causation unless it was "foreseeable." A "dependent intervening cause" does not break the chain of causation unless it is regarded as "abnormal." Different jurisdictions also impose other limitations on whether an independent cause breaks the chain of causation.

MPC Approach to Intervening Causes. The Model Penal Code takes a similar approach, focusing on whether the result is "too remote or accidental in its occurrence to have a just bearing on the actor's liability or on the gravity of his offense." *See* MPC § 2.03(2)(b).

STEPHENSON V. STATE
205 Ind. 141, 179 N.E. 633 (1932).

PER CURIAM.

The victim of this homicide is Miss Madge Oberholtzer, who was a resident of the city of Indianapolis and lived with her father and mother. She was twenty-eight years of age; weighed about 140 pounds, and had always been in good health; was educated in the public primary and high school and Butler College. Just prior to the time of the commission of the alleged acts, she was employed by the state superintendent of public instruction as manager of the Young People's Reading Circle.

Appellant Stephenson kidnapped Miss Oberholtzer, forced her to drink liquor, and then took her to Chicago by train. On the way, appellant took hold of the bottom of her dress and pulled it over her head, against her wishes, and she tried to fight him away, but was weak and unsteady. Then Stephenson took hold of her two hands and held her, but she did not have strength to get away, because what she had drunk was affecting her. Then Stephenson took off all her clothes and pushed her into the lower berth. After the train started, Stephenson got into the berth with her and attacked her. He chewed her all over her body; bit her neck and face; chewed her tongue; chewed her breasts until they bled and chewed her back, her legs, and her ankles, and mutilated her all over her body. At Hammond, Indiana, Stephenson, flourishing a revolver, took her to a hotel. [Later that day, she obtained some poison and ate it. Later, she died from the combined effect of the poison and the wounds. Appellant delayed for many hours before taking Ms. Oberholzer home.]

Appellant earnestly argues that the evidence does not show appellant guilty of murder. He points out that, after they reached the hotel, Madge Oberholtzer left the hotel and purchased a hat and the poison, and voluntarily returned to his room, and at the time she took the poison she was in an adjoining room to him, and that she swallowed the poison without his knowledge, and at a time when he was not present. From these facts he contends that she took her life by committing suicide; that her own act in taking the poison was an intervening responsible agent which broke the causal connection between his acts and the death; that his acts were not the proximate cause of her death, but the taking of the poison was the proximate cause of death. Appellant is charged with having caused the death of Madge Oberholtzer while engaged in the crime of attempted rape. The evidence shows that the deceased was at all times from the time she was entrapped by the appellant at his home on the evening of March 15th till she returned to her home two days later, in the custody and absolute control of appellant. Neither do we think the fact that the deceased took the poison some four hours after they left the drawing-room on the train or after the crime of attempted rape had been committed necessarily prevents it from being a part of the attempted rape. Suppose they had not left the drawing-room on the train, and, instead of the deceased taking poison, she had secured possession of appellant's revolver and shot herself or thrown herself out of the window of the car and died from the fall. We see no vital difference. At the very moment Madge Oberholtzer swallowed the poison she was subject to the passion, desire, and will of appellant. She knew not what moment she would be subjected to the same demands that she was while in the drawing-room on the train. What would have prevented appellant from compelling her to submit to him at any moment? The same forces, the same impulses, that would impel her to shoot herself during the actual attack or throw herself out of the car window after the attack had ceased, was pressing and overwhelming her at the time she swallowed the poison. The evidence shows that she was so weak that she staggered as she left the elevator to go to the room in the hotel, and was assisted by appellant and Gentry. That she was very ill, so much so that she could not eat, all of which was the direct and proximate result of the treatment accorded her by appellant. To say that there is no causal connection between the acts of appellant and the death of Madge Oberholtzer, and that the treatment accorded her by appellant had no causal connection with the death of Madge Oberholtzer would be a travesty of justice. The whole criminal program was so closely connected that it should be treated as one transaction. We conclude that the evidence was sufficient and justified the jury in finding that appellant by his acts and conduct rendered the deceased distracted and mentally irresponsible, and that such was the natural and probable consequence of such unlawful and criminal treatment, and that the appellant was guilty of murder in the second degree as charged in the first count of the indictment.

We think the evidence justified the court in submitting the question to the jury, as there was evidence that the deceased died from the joint effect of the injuries inflicted on her, which, through natural cause and effect, contributed mediately to the death. We think the proposition of law stated in this instruction is well supported by authority. "The general rule, both of law and reason, is, that whenever a man contributes to a particular result, brought about, either by sole volition of another, or by such volition added to his own, he is to be held responsible for the result, the same as if his own unaided hand had produced it. The contribution, however, must be of such magnitude and so near the result that sustaining to it the relation of cause and effect, the law takes it within its cognizance. Now, these propositions conduct us to the doctrine, that whenever a blow is inflicted under circumstances to render the party inflicting it criminally responsible, if death follows, he will be holden for murder or manslaughter, though the person beaten would have died from other causes, or would not have died from this one, had not others operated with it; provided, that the blow really contributed mediately or immediately to the death as it actually took place in a degree sufficient for the law's notice." BISHOP ON CRIMINAL LAW, § 653.

We have examined all of appellant's alleged errors, and find none that would justify a reversal of this cause.

Judgment affirmed.

POINTS FOR DISCUSSION

a. Year and a Day Rule

At common law, defendant's conduct could not be deemed to be the "cause" of a homicide unless the victim died within a year and a day following the defendant's acts.

Causation

b. **Model Penal Code**

§ 2.03 Causation.

Causal Relationship Between Conduct and Result; Divergence Between Result Designed or Contemplated and Actual Result or Between Probable and Actual Result

(1) Conduct is the cause of a result when:

(a) it is an antecedent but for which the result in question would not have occurred; and

(b) the relationship between the conduct and result satisfies any additional causal requirements imposed by the Code or by the law defining the offense.

(2) When purposely or knowingly causing a particular result is an element of an offense, the element is not established if the actual result is not within the purpose or the contemplation of the actor unless:

(a) the actual result differs from that designed or contemplated, as the case may be, only in the respect that a different person or different property is injured or affected or that the injury or harm designed or contemplated would have been more serious or more extensive than that caused; or

(b) the actual result involves the same kind of injury or harm as that designed or contemplated and is not too remote or accidental in its occurrence to have a [just] bearing on the actor's liability or on the gravity of his offense.

(3) When recklessly or negligently causing a particular result is an element of an offense, the element is not established if the actual result is not within the risk of which the actor is aware or, in the case of negligence, of which he should have been aware unless:

(a) the actual result differs from the probable result only in the respect that a different person or different property is injured or affected or that the probable injury would have been more serious or more extensive than that caused; or

(b) the actual result involves the same kind of injury or harm as the probable result and is not too remote or accidental in its occurrence to have a [just] bearing on the actor's liability or on the gravity of his offense.

(4) When causing a particular result is a material element for which absolute liability is imposed by law, the element is not established unless the actual result is a probable consequence of the actor's conduct.

c. "But for" Test

Defendant's act may be the "cause" of death even though absent his or her conduct, the death would have occurred anyway. For example, two independent actors simultaneously shoot revolvers at a single victim and each inflicts a wound which would be fatal in and of itself. Neither actor can be the "but for "cause of death because, absent the conduct of either actor, the victim would have died anyway. Nevertheless, both actors are responsible for the victim's death. Otherwise, both defendants would be able to escape liability. *See, e.g., Jones v. Commonwealth*, 281 S.W.2d 920 (Ky. App.1955): "The law will not stop, in such a case, to measure which wound is the more serious, and to speculate upon which actually caused the death."

d. Causation & Participation

In *Commonwealth v. Atencio*, 345 Mass. 627, 189 N.E.2d 223 (1963), defendants and deceased decided to play a game of "Russian roulette." The deceased was the third to play. The cartridge exploded and he fell over dead. The court concluded that defendants "caused" the death: that the defendants participation "in the game of Russian roulette could be found to be a cause and not a mere condition of death. The testimony does not require a ruling that when the deceased took the gun from Atencio it was an independent or intervening act not standing in any relation to the defendants' acts which would render what he did imputable to them. It is an oversimplification to contend that each participated in something that only one could do at a time. There could be found to be a mutual encouragement in a joint enterprise."

PEOPLE V. ACOSTA
284 Cal. Rptr. 117 (Cal. App.1991).

WALLIN, ASSOCIATE JUSTICE.

At 10 p.m. on March 10, 1987, Officers Salceda and Francis of the Santa Ana Police Department's automobile theft detail saw Acosta in Elvira Salazar's stolen Nissan Pulsar parked on the street. The officers approached Acosta and identified themselves. Acosta inched the Pulsar forward, then accelerated rapidly. He led Salceda, Francis and officers from other agencies on a 48-mile chase along numerous surface streets and freeways throughout Orange County. The chase ended near Acosta's residence in Anaheim.

During the chase, Acosta engaged in some of the most egregious driving tactics imaginable. He ran stop signs and red lights, and drove on the wrong side of streets, causing oncoming traffic to scatter or swerve to avoid colliding with him. Once, when all traffic lanes were blocked by vehicles stopped for a red light, he used a dirt shoulder to circumvent stationary vehicles and pass through the intersection. When leaving the freeway in Anaheim, he drove over a cement shoulder.

Throughout the pursuit, Acosta weaved in and out of traffic, cutting in front of other cars and causing them to brake suddenly. At one point on the freeway, he crossed three lanes of traffic, struck another car, jumped the divider between the freeway and a transition lane, and passed a tanker truck, forcing it to swerve suddenly to avoid a collision.

Acosta generally drove at speeds between 60 and 90 miles per hour, slowing only when necessary. During several turns, his wheels lost traction. When an officer was able to drive parallel to the Pulsar for a short distance, Acosta looked in his direction and smiled. Near the end of the chase, one of the Pulsar's front tires blew out, but Acosta continued to drive at 55 to 60 miles per hour, crossing freeway traffic lanes.

Police helicopters from Anaheim, Costa Mesa, Huntington Beach, and Newport Beach assisted in the chase by tracking Acosta. During the early part of the pursuit, the Costa Mesa and Newport Beach craft were used, pinpointing Acosta's location with their high beam spotlights. The Costa Mesa helicopter was leading the pursuit, in front of and below the Newport Beach helicopter. As they flew into Newport Beach, the pilots agreed the Newport Beach craft should take the lead. The normal procedure for such a maneuver is for the lead helicopter to move to the right and swing around clockwise behind the other craft while climbing to an altitude of 1,000 feet. At the same time, the trailing helicopter descends to 500 feet while maintaining a straight course.

At the direction of the Costa Mesa pilot, the Newport Beach helicopter moved forward and descended while the Costa Mesa helicopter banked to the right. Shortly after commencing this procedure, the Costa Mesa helicopter, having terminated radio communication, came up under the Newport Beach helicopter from the right rear and collided with it. Both helicopters fell to the ground. Three occupants in the Costa Mesa helicopter died as a result of the crash.

Menzies Turner, a retired Federal Aviation Administration (FAA) investigator, testified as an expert and concluded the accident occurred because the Costa Mesa helicopter, the faster of the two aircraft, made a 360-degree turn and closed too rapidly on the Newport Beach helicopter. He opined the Costa Mesa helicopter's pilot violated an FAA regulation prohibiting careless and reckless operation of an aircraft by failing to properly clear the area, not maintaining communication with the Newport Beach helicopter, failing to keep the other aircraft in view at all times, and not changing his altitude. He also testified the Costa Mesa pilot violated another FAA regulation prohibiting operation of one aircraft so close to another as to create a collision hazard.

Turner could not think of any reason for the Costa Mesa helicopter's erratic movement. The maneuver was not a difficult one, and was not affected by the ground activity at the time. He had never heard of a midair collision between two police helicopters involved in tracking a ground pursuit, and had never investigated a midair collision involving helicopters.

After his arrest Acosta told the police he knew the Pulsar was stolen and he fled the police to avoid arrest. He also saw two helicopters with spotlights, and turned off the Pulsar's lights to evade them. Acosta knew that his flight was dangerous "to the bone," but he tried to warn other cars by flashing the car lights and by otherwise being "as safe as possible."

Acosta claims there was insufficient evidence that he proximately caused the deaths of the victims. He argues that although a collision between ground vehicles was a foreseeable result of his conduct, one between airborne helicopters was not, noting his expert had never heard of a similar incident. He also contends the Costa Mesa helicopter pilot's violation of FAA regulations was a superseding cause. Because the deaths here were unusual, to say the least, the issue deserves special scrutiny.

Proximate cause in criminal cases is determined by ordinary principles of causation. It is initially a question of fact for the jury to decide. To determine whether Acosta's conduct was not, as a matter of law, a proximate cause of death of the Costa Mesa helicopter's occupants, I enter a legal realm not routinely considered in published California cases.

"Proximate cause" is the term historically used[6] to separate those results for which an actor will be held responsible from those not carrying such responsibility. The term is, in a sense, artificial, serving matters of policy surrounding tort and criminal law and based partly on expediency and partly on concerns of fairness and justice. Because such concerns are sometimes more a matter of "common sense" than pure logic, the line of demarcation is flexible, and

---

[6] The American Law Institute has urged the use of "legal cause" instead. Although there is some merit to its arguments, I abide with the traditional term, "proximate cause."

attempts to lay down uniform tests which apply evenly in all situations have failed. That does not mean general guidelines and approaches to analysis cannot be constructed.

The threshold question in examining causation is whether the defendant's act was an "actual cause" of the victim's injury. It is a *sine qua non* test: But for the defendant's act would the injury have occurred? Unless an act is an actual cause of the injury, it will not be considered a proximate cause.

The next inquiry is whether the defendant's act was a "substantial factor" in the injury. This test excludes those actual causes which, although direct, play only an insignificant role in the ultimate injury.[8] Although there is no strict definition, the RESTATEMENT SECOND OF TORTS, *supra*, section 433, lists considerations in determining whether a factor is "substantial": (1) the number and extent of other factors contributing to the harm; (2) whether the forces created by the actor are continuous in producing the harm or merely create a condition upon which independent forces act; and (3) any lapse of time between the act and the harm.

In California, the substantial factor issue has arisen most often where multiple causes act concurrently, but independently,[9] to produce the harm. The test is one of exclusion only. Unless a cause is a substantial factor in the harm it will not be considered a proximate cause, but some substantial factor causes may not be deemed proximate causes.

A related concept which may lead to a refusal to treat an actual cause as a proximate cause is where a force set in motion by the defendant has "come to rest in a position of apparent safety." Perkins and Boyce give the example of the actor who dislodges a rock which comes to rest against a tree. If the tree bends or breaks six months later, releasing the rock, the original action is not considered the proximate cause of any resulting harm.

To this point I have spoken only of direct causes, "causes which produce a result without the aid of any intervening cause." Because it is tautological, the definition is of little value in identifying a cause in the absence of a working definition of an indirect cause. However, Perkins and Boyce list several examples of direct causation, headed by the observation that, "If sequences follow one

---

[8] An independent intervening cause could be explained by saying it rendered the defendant's act "insubstantial." However, the traditional approach has been to determine only whether the defendant's act is substantial in the abstract or in comparison with a contributory or concurrent cause. If it is not, the analysis goes no further. If it is, the question becomes whether there is an intervening cause which should relieve the defendant of responsibility.

[9] If the actors are acting in concert, both would be culpable using an aiding and abetting theory, even if only one directly caused the death.

another in such a customary order that no other cause would commonly be thought of as intervening, the causal connection is spoken of as direct for juridical purposes even though many intervening causes might be recognized by a physicist."

The critical concept is that a direct cause which is a substantial factor in the ensuing injury is almost always a proximate cause of it. This is so even if the result is exacerbated by a latent condition in the victim or caused by a third party. *People v. Stamp* (1969) 2 Cal. App. 3d 203, 210–211, 82 Cal. Rptr. 598 (defendant triggered heart attack in store clerk during armed robbery). The only exception is where the result is "highly extraordinary" in view of its cause.

However, the defendant is not always the direct cause of the harm. Sometimes forces arise between the act of the defendant and the harm, called "intervening causes." They are of two types, dependent and independent, and include acts of God.

An intervening cause is dependent if it is a normal or involuntary response to, or result of, the defendant's act. These include flight and other voluntary or involuntary responses of victims, as well as defense, rescue and medical treatment by third parties. Even where such responses constitute negligent conduct, they do not supersede the defendant's act; *i.e.*, they are nevertheless considered proximate causes of the harm. *People v. Armitage, supra*, 194 Cal. App. 3d at p. 420, 239 Cal. Rptr. 515 (victim foolishly chose to attempt to swim to shore after defendant capsized the boat).[15]

Conversely, when the defendant's conduct merely places the eventual victim in a position which allows some other action to cause the harm, the other action is termed an independent intervening cause. It usually supersedes the defendant's act; *i.e.*, precludes a finding of proximate cause. 1 LAFAVE & SCOTT, *supra*, at pp. 406–407 (distinguishing matters of "response" from matters of "coincidence"). The issue usually arises when the victim has been subjected to the independent harm after being disabled by the defendant, or is somehow impacted by the defendant's flight. *See People v. Pike, supra*, 197 Cal. App. 3d at pp. 747–748, 243

---

[15] The refusal to allow "contributory negligence" to be a bar to a proximate cause finding need not be the product of any mechanical policy rule. It can be grounded in the notion that it is not "abnormal" for people to react less "reasonably" under stress than if the stress were not present. For purposes of ascribing causal responsibility it may be said that a negligent or foolish response is "normal." To the extent that a dependent intervening cause is thought to "directly" carry through the act of the defendant to a harmful result, this analysis comports well with the rule that a defendant's act is the proximate cause of any harm caused directly by his act unless the result is "highly extraordinary." It also allows the court to find that a negligent, but highly extraordinary response precludes a finding of proximate cause, while a reckless but predictable response does not. The focus is properly on the objective conditions present at the time the defendant perpetrated the causal act and the predictable, albeit sometimes unreasonable, responses of human beings to them.

Cal. Rptr. 54 (one police officer killed when struck by another while pursuing defendant).

An independent intervening variable will not be superseding in three instances: (1) where it is merely a contributing cause to the defendant's direct cause; (2) where the result was intended; or (3) where the resultant harm was reasonably foreseeable when the act was done. As to the third exception, "the consequence need not have been a strong probability; a possible consequence which might reasonably have been contemplated is enough. The precise consequence need not have been foreseen; it is enough that the defendant should have foreseen the possibility of some harm of the kind which might result from his act."

As Perkins and Boyce put it, " 'Foreseeability' is not a 'test' which can be applied without the use of common sense; it presents one of those problems in which 'we must rely on the common sense of the common man as to common things.' It is employed in the sense of 'appreciable probability.' It does not require such a degree of probability that the intervention was more likely to occur than not; and on the other hand it implies more than that someone might have imagined it as a theoretical possibility. It does not require that the defendant himself actually thought of it. For the purposes of proximate cause 'an appreciable probability is one which a reasonable man in ordering his conduct in view of his situation and his knowledge and means of knowledge, should, either consciously or unconsciously, take into account in connection with the other facts and probabilities then apparent.' "

Prosser and Keeton, in an in-depth discussion of the dynamics of foresight, conclude that although it is desirable to exclude extremely remarkable and unusual results from the purview of proximate cause, it is virtually impossible to express a logical verbal formula which will produce uniform results. I agree. The standard should be simply stated, exclude extraordinary results, and allow the trier of fact to determine the issue on the particular facts of the case using "the common sense of the common man as to common things. "As with other ultimate issues, appellate courts must review that determination, giving due deference to the trier of fact.

The "highly extraordinary result" standard serves that purpose. It is consistent with the definition of foreseeability used in California. It does not involve the defendant's state of mind, but focuses upon the objective conditions present when he acts.[19] Like numerous other legal definitions, what it means in practice will be determined as case law develops. Limitations arising from the mental state of the actor can be left to concepts like malice, recklessness and negligence.

Because the highly extraordinary result standard is consistent with the limitation on direct causes, it simplifies the proximate cause inquiry. The analysis is: (1) was the defendant's conduct the actual cause of the harm (but for his actions would it have occurred as it did)? (2) was the result an intended consequence of the act? (3) was the defendant's action a substantial factor in the harm? and (4) was the result highly extraordinary in light of the circumstances?

If the first question is answered no, proximate cause is lacking. If answered yes, the next question must be examined. If the second question is answered yes, proximate cause is established. If answered no, the next question must be examined. If the third question is answered no, proximate cause is lacking. If answered yes, proximate cause is established unless the fourth question is answered yes, in which case it is lacking. The analysis does away with the need to consider the distinction between direct, concurrent, contributory, and dependent and independent intervening causes. It focuses, as it should, upon the role the defendant's act played in the harm, limiting culpability only where the conduct was *de minimis* or the result highly extraordinary.

Here, but for Acosta's conduct of fleeing the police, the helicopters would never have been in position for the crash. However, there was no evidence he intended the harm, so I must examine questions three and four.

Although an extremely close question, Acosta's conduct was a substantial factor in causing the crash. He was fleeing when the accident occurred, and there was no lapse of time between his flight and the crash—his action had not "come to rest." The only other factor operating at the time was the improper flight pattern of the Costa Mesa pilot. Although Acosta's horrendous driving did not cause the helicopter's improper maneuver, his flight undoubtedly infused excitement and tension into the situation, which can be considered to be a substantial factor. No similar case has held otherwise, although the third party collisions all have involved accidents on the ground.

---

[19] The Model Penal Code takes a similar approach, focusing on whether the result is "too remote or accidental in its occurrence to have a just bearing on the actor's liability or on the gravity of his offense." Model Pen.Code, § 2.03(2)(b). LaFave and Scott also appear to look to the extraordinary nature of the result in determining causal responsibility, although they discuss it in terms of foreseeability.

The result was not highly extraordinary. Although a two-helicopter collision was unknown to expert witness Turner and no reported cases describe one, it was "a possible consequence which reasonably might have been contemplated." Given the emotional dynamics of any police pursuit, there is an appreciable probability that one of the pursuers, in the heat of the chase, may act negligently or recklessly to catch the quarry. That no pursuits have ever before resulted in a helicopter crash or midair collision is more a comment on police flying skill and technology than upon the innate probabilities involved.

Justice Crosby's opinion parts company with this analysis, reasoning that "neither the intervening negligent conduct nor the risk of harm was foreseeable." He justifies this conclusion by reference to the well-traveled opinion of Justice Cardozo in *Palsgraf v. Long Island R. Co.* 248 N.Y. 339, 162 N.E. 99, 100 (1928). Reliance on *Palsgraf* reveals the error in the analysis. Justice Cardozo approached the problem from the perspective of duty, concluding that the defendant owed no duty of care to an unforeseeable plaintiff. Although the interesting facts and novel analysis of *Palsgraf*[24] have made it a favorite in law school texts, the four-to-three decision is not the gospel on proximate cause. Because of its confusion between foreseeability as it relates to negligence and as it relates to causation, I have eliminated it from the proximate cause analysis.

Doing so avoids the undesirable risk of completely absolving a defendant of all liability on causation grounds when morally he should suffer some punishment for the consequences. When a defendant is the actual and substantial cause of the harm, the consequences of the act should depend upon the *mens rea* involved.

The undisputed facts of this case mandate the result. Contrary to Justice Moore's assertion, I do not find the result extraordinary, but almost so. I presume he does not dispute that it was extremely unusual. In fact, he cites no similar instances of aircraft colliding during police pursuits. But neither does Justice Crosby cite any case to support his claim the result was highly extraordinary.

Neither concurring opinion offers case law "on all fours," suggesting this case is unique and presents a close question. Partly because this is so, it is appropriate to rely on two compelling factors: the jury found proximate cause based on proper instructions, and the dearth of case law to support a rejection of that finding. Given these circumstances, a finding of proximate cause is appropriate.

---

[24] The defendant's railway attendants accidentally knocked a package of fireworks from a passenger's arms while boarding a train, causing a concussive explosion which overturned scales on the platform which struck the plaintiff.

The judgment is reversed on the murder counts and is affirmed in all other respects.

COMMONWEALTH V. ROOT

403 Pa. 571, 170 A.2d 310 (1961).

CHARLES ALVIN JONES, CHIEF JUSTICE.

Appellant was found guilty of involuntary manslaughter for the death of his competitor in the course of an automobile race between them on a highway. We accepted this appeal to decide the important question as to whether the defendant's unlawful and reckless conduct was a sufficiently direct cause of the death to warrant his being charged with criminal homicide.

The testimony, discloses that, on the night of the fatal accident, the defendant accepted the deceased's challenge to engage in an automobile race; that the racing took place on a rural 3-lane highway; that the night was clear and dry, and traffic light; that the speed limit on the highway was 50 miles per hour; that, immediately prior to the accident, the two automobiles were being operated at varying speeds of from 70 to 90 miles per hour; that the accident occurred in a no-passing zone on the approach to a bridge where the highway narrowed to two directionally-opposite lanes; that, at the time of the accident, the defendant was in the lead and was proceeding in his right hand lane of travel; that the deceased, in an attempt to pass the defendant's automobile, when a truck was closely approaching from the opposite direction, swerved his car to the left, crossed the highway's white dividing line and drove his automobile on the wrong side of the highway head-on into the oncoming truck with resultant fatal effect to himself.

This evidence would of course amply support a conviction of the defendant for speeding, reckless driving and, perhaps, other violations of The Vehicle Code. In fact, it may be noted, a recent Act makes automobile racing on a highway an independent crime punishable by fine or imprisonment or both up to $500 and three years in jail. In any event, unlawful or reckless conduct is only one ingredient of the crime of involuntary manslaughter. Another essential and distinctly separate element of the crime is that the unlawful or reckless conduct charged to the defendant was the direct cause of the death in issue. The first ingredient is obviously present in this case but, just as plainly, the second is not.

While precedent is to be found for application of the tort law concept of "proximate cause" in fixing responsibility for criminal homicide, the want of any rational basis for its use in determining criminal liability can no longer be properly disregarded. When proximate cause was first borrowed from the field of tort law and applied to homicide prosecutions in Pennsylvania, the concept connoted a much more direct causal relation in producing the alleged culpable result than it does today. Proximate cause, as an essential element of a tort founded in negligence, has undergone in recent times, and is still undergoing, a marked extension. More specifically, this area of civil law has been progressively liberalized in favor of claims for damages for personal injuries to which careless conduct of others can in some way be associated. To persist in applying the tort liability concept of proximate cause to prosecutions for criminal homicide after the marked expansion of civil liability of defendants in tort actions for negligence would be to extend possible criminal liability to persons chargeable with unlawful or reckless conduct in circumstances not generally considered to present the likelihood of a resultant death.

Legal theory which makes guilt or innocence of criminal homicide depend upon such accidental and fortuitous circumstances as are now embraced by modern tort law's encompassing concept of proximate cause is too harsh to be just.

Even if the tort liability concept of proximate cause were to be deemed applicable, defendant's conviction of involuntary manslaughter in the instant case could not be sustained under the evidence. The operative effect of a supervening cause would have to be taken into consideration. But, the trial judge refused the defendant's point for charge to such effect and erroneously instructed the jury that "negligence or want of care on the part of the deceased is no defense to the criminal responsibility of the defendant."

The Superior Court, in affirming the defendant's conviction, approved the charge above mentioned, despite a number of decisions in involuntary manslaughter cases holding that the conduct of the deceased victim must be considered in order to determine whether the defendant's reckless acts were the proximate (*i.e.*, sufficiently direct) cause of his death. The Superior Court did so on the ground that there can be more than one proximate cause of death. The point is wholly irrelevant. Of course there can be more than one proximate cause of death just as there can also be more than one direct cause of death. For example, in the so-called "shield" cases where a felon interposes the person of an innocent victim between himself and a pursuing officer, if the officer should fire his gun at the felon to prevent his escape and fatally wound the person used as a shield, the different acts of the policeman and the felon would each be a direct cause of the victim's death.

If the tort liability concept of proximate cause were to be applied in a criminal homicide prosecution, then the conduct of the person whose death is the basis of the indictment would have to be considered, not to prove that it was merely an additional proximate cause of the death, but to determine, under fundamental and long recognized law applicable to proximate cause, whether the subsequent wrongful act superseded the original conduct chargeable to the defendant. If it did in fact supervene, then the original act is so insulated from the ensuing death as not to be its proximate cause.

Under the uncontradicted evidence in this case, the conduct of the defendant was not the proximate cause of the decedent's death as a matter of law. In *Kline v. Moyer and Albert*, 1937, 325 Pa. 357, 364, 191 A. 43, 46, the rule is stated as follows: "Where a second actor has become aware of the existence of a potential danger created by the negligence of an original tortfeasor, and thereafter, by an independent act of negligence, brings about an accident, the first tortfeasor is relieved of liability, because the condition created by him was merely a circumstance of the accident and not its proximate cause."

In the case now before us, the deceased was aware of the dangerous condition created by the defendant's reckless conduct in driving his automobile at an excessive rate of speed along the highway but, despite such knowledge, he recklessly chose to swerve his car to the left and into the path of an oncoming truck, thereby bringing about the head-on collision which caused his own death.

To summarize, the tort liability concept of proximate cause has no proper place in prosecutions for criminal homicide and more direct causal connection is required for conviction. In the instant case, the defendant's reckless conduct was not a sufficiently direct cause of the competing driver's death to make him criminally liable therefore.

The judgment of sentence is reversed and the defendant's motion in arrest of judgment granted.

EAGEN, JUSTICE (dissenting).

Defendant, at the time of the fatal accident, was engaged in an unlawful and reckless course of conduct. Racing an automobile at 90 miles per hour, trying to prevent another automobile going in the same direction from passing him, in a no-passing zone on a two-lane public highway, is certainly all of that. Admittedly, there can be more than one direct cause of an unlawful death. To me, this is self-evident. But, says the majority opinion, the defendant's recklessness was not a direct cause of the death. I cannot agree.

If the defendant did not engage in the unlawful race and so operate his automobile in such a reckless manner, this accident would never have occurred. He helped create the dangerous event. He was a vital part of it. The victim's acts were a natural reaction to the stimulus of the situation. The race, the attempt to pass the other car and forge ahead, the reckless speed, all of these factors the defendant himself helped create. He was part and parcel of them. That the victim's response was normal under the circumstances, that his reaction should have been expected and was clearly foreseeable, is to me beyond argument. That the defendant's recklessness was a substantial factor is obvious. All of this, in my opinion, makes his unlawful conduct a direct cause of the resulting collision.

The majority opinion states, "Legal theory which makes guilt or innocence of criminal homicide depend upon such accidental and fortuitous circumstances as are now embraced by modern tort law's encompassing concept is too harsh to be just." If the resulting death had been dependent upon "accidental and fortuitous circumstances" or, as the majority also say, "in circumstances not generally considered to present the likelihood of a resultant death," we would agree that the defendant is not criminally responsible. However, acts should be judged by their tendency under the known circumstances, not by the actual intent which accompanies their performance. Every day of the year, we read that some teen-agers, or young adults, somewhere in this country, have been killed or have killed others, while racing their automobiles. Hair-raising, death-defying, law-breaking rides, which encompass "racing" are the rule rather than the exception, and endanger not only the participants, but also every motorist and passenger on the road. To call such resulting accidents "accidental and fortuitous," or unlikely to result in death, is to ignore the cold and harsh reality of everyday occurrences. Root's actions were as direct a cause of Hall's death as those in the 'shield' cases. Root's shield was his high speed and any approaching traffic in his quest to prevent Hall from passing, which he knew Hall would undertake to do, the first time he thought he had the least opportunity.

While the victim's foolhardiness in this case contributed to his own death, he was not the only one responsible and it is not he alone with whom we are concerned. It is the people of the Commonwealth who are harmed by the kind of conduct the defendant pursued. Their interests must be kept in mind.

I, therefore, dissent and would accordingly affirm the judgment of conviction.

POINT FOR DISCUSSION

Suicide & Causation

Suicide is a controversial subject provoking a wide range of public opinion. Prosecutors, judges, and juries struggle with how to treat suicide from a criminal liability and causation point of view. Is it criminal for a person, by text message, to encourage another person to commit suicide? Are words, alone, without action, enough to justify a criminal conviction?

COMMONWEALTH V. MICHELLE CARTER
474 Mass. 624, 52 N.E.3d 1054 (2016).

Michelle Carter, 17 years old, and Conrad Roy III, 18 years old, lived approximately 35 miles from each other, but their relationship existed almost entirely through phone calls and text messages. Prior to Roy's suicide, Carter discussed Roy's suicidal thoughts over text message over approximately a month-long period. Not only did she fail to seek help for Roy, Carter continued to encourage him to commit suicide in hundreds of text messages. While Carter did not provide Roy with any of the instruments used in his death and was not physically present at the time of his death, were her words sufficient enough to convict her of involuntary manslaughter?

In the state of Massachusetts, involuntary manslaughter is defined as, "An unlawful killing that was unintentionally caused as the result of the defendants' wanton or reckless conduct." *Commonwealth v. Earle*, 458 Mass. 341, 347 (2010). Were Michelle Carter's words so wanton or reckless that they caused the unintentional death of her boyfriend? Massachusetts defines wanton or reckless conduct as "conduct which creates a high degree of likelihood that substantial harm will result to another person." *Commonwealth v. Earle*, 458 Mass. 341, 347 (2010). In the weeks prior to Roy's death, he confided in Carter that he felt depressed, She asked, "Take your life?" Carter then began suggesting methods Roy could employ to commit suicide: "Hang yourself, jump off a building, stab yourself idk there's lots of ways."

On the day of his death, Carter dozens of text messages urging Roy to end his life. "You can't think about it," "you just have to do it." As if that was not enough, Carter proceeded to manipulate Roy with more text messages, saying "I thought you really wanted to die but apparently you dont." There was more to Carter's encouragement. While Roy was sitting in his carbon monoxide-filled truck, he was on the phone with Carter when he started to get scared and exited the vehicle. Carter encouraged Roy to get back into the truck. In Massachusetts, a person has a duty to take reasonable steps to alleviate a risk when that person's actions create a life-threatening risk to another *Commonwealth v. Levesque*, 436 Mass. 443, 449 (2002). Carter was aware that Roy was in an extremely dangerous situation and failed to help him.

Were Carter's actions and her failure to alleviate a life-threatening risk were not only wanton and reckless conduct, but the direct cause of Mr. Roy's death? Did Michelle Carter kill Conrad Roy?

The trial court held there was sufficient evidence that Carter's words were the proximate cause of Roy's death. The court found that but for Carter's explicit order for Roy to get back in his truck, he would not have died. The Massachusetts Supreme Judicial Court, denying a motion to dismiss, held that words can be a sufficient basis for establishing causation, finding that advances in technology during the last century have made it is possible for people to be "virtually present." Were they correct? Is Conrad's conviction likely to be upheld on appeal?

Hypo 1: *Dr. Death and His Suicide Machine*

Marjorie Miller suffered from multiple sclerosis, and her condition had deteriorated to the point that she used a wheelchair and was confined either to bed or the wheelchair, did not have the use of her legs or her right arm, had only limited use of her left arm, and had problems talking and breathing. Miller contacted defendant, a champion of physician-assisted suicide, and he agreed to assist her in taking her life by hooking her up to his "suicide machine." The machine consisted of a needle to be inserted into a blood vessel that could convey various chemicals into the bloodstream. One of the chemicals was methohexital, a fast-acting barbiturate that quickly depresses respiration. A large dose can cause the recipient to stop breathing. After defendant inserted the needle into a vein in Ms. Miller's arm, he tied strings to two of her fingers. The strings were attached to clips on the tubing connected to the needle. Defendant instructed Ms. Miller how to pull the strings so as to allow the drugs to flow into her bloodstream. Ms. Miller followed defendant's instructions and died as a result of a lethal dose of methohexital. Is defendant criminally responsible for "causing" death when he provided deceased with the means by which she killed herself, but she performed the fatal final act? *See People v. Kevorkian*, 205 Mich. App. 180, 517 N.W.2d 293 (1994).

Hypo 2: *The Burglary and the Suicidal Jump*

Jane Munson, the village nurse, lived alone. Late one night, defendant broke into Munson's house. He went upstairs and found the bedroom door locked. Defendant threatened to break the door down if Munson did not let him in. Munson refused. As defendant tried to break-in, Munson jumped out the window falling to her death. Is defendant criminally responsible for Munson's death? *See State v. Lassiter*, 197 N.J.Super. 2, 484 A.2d 13 (1984); *Rex v. Beech* [23 Cox Cr. Law Cas. 181 (1912)].

Hypo 3: *The Detouring Victim*

Wyman is on his way home from work when defendant fires three shots at him. Defendant's shots miss and Wyman escapes unharmed. Wyman, afraid to go home because defendant might be lying in wait for him, decides to spend the night at a friend's house. Changing his route (since he is no longer going home but rather to his friend's house), Wyman is killed on the way to the friend's house. Consider the following scenarios and decide whether defendant "caused" the victim's death: A) The death resulted from lightning which struck and killed Wyman; B) The death resulted from an automobile accident, totally the fault of another driver, and Wyman just "happened" to be in the wrong place at the wrong time; C) The death resulted because Wyman was very upset by defendant's conduct and was paying insufficient attention to his driving. In each instance, argue the case for the state. How might defendant respond? How would you rule?

Hypo 4: *The Doubleparked Truck Driver*

Defendant, a truck driver, double parked his truck blocking a sidewalk in violation of a local ordinance. Because of the double parking, a minor girl was forced to walk in the street to get past the truck. The girl was struck by a car and killed. Did the truck driver cause the girl's death? *See Marchl v. Dowling & Co.*, 157 Pa. Super. 91, 41 A.2d 427 (1945).

Hypo 5: *The Fatally Wounded Victim*

Defendant 1 and John Taylor fought, and defendant fatally wounded Taylor. The wound severed the mesenteric artery, and medical witnesses testified that it was necessarily mortal, and that death would ensue within the hour. Internal hemorrhaging occurred and Taylor was suffering intense pain. While he lay dying, defendant 2 (a long-time enemy) inflicted a knife wound on Taylor. The wound was severe enough that it killed Taylor within five minutes. Medical witnesses testified that, even though death was inevitable from the initial wound, it was accelerated by the knife wound. Which defendant is responsible for the death? Argue the case for defendant 1. Argue the case for defendant 2. How might the state respond to these arguments? *See Henderson v. State*, 11 Ala. App. 37, 65 So. 721 (1914); *People v. Lewis*, 124 Cal. 551, 57 P. 470 (1899).

Hypo 6: *The Driver and the Jogger*

John is a jogger who is trying to cross a busy street when he is struck by defendant's vehicle. John survives the impact, but is thrown into the middle of the northbound lane of traffic with his head pointing toward the curb, and his feet pointing toward the road. A second car was fast approaching. A witness tries to flag the second car down, but is unable to do so. The second car drives over John causing severe internal injuries. John dies two hours later. Expert testimony indicates that both sets of injuries were severe and independently could have resulted in John's death. Who is responsible for his death? *See People v. Tims*, 449 Mich. 83, 534 N.W.2d 675 (1995).

Hypo 7: *The Failure to Rescue*

Defendants went to the home of Pepper armed with revolvers, forcibly took possession of Pepper, bound his arms so as to render him helpless, and in the presence of Pepper avowed their purpose to kill him. Defendants placed Pepper in an automobile and started to drive away. When the car reached the banks of a river, Pepper leaped from the car into the water and drowned. Defendants stood by and made no effort to rescue Pepper. Are defendants responsible for Pepper's death? Argue the case for the state. How might defendant respond? *See State v. Shelledy*, 8 Iowa 477 (1859).

> **Hypo 8: *The KKK Rally***
>
> Defendant, a Ku Klux Klan member, gave a racist speech on a city square. Throughout the speech, defendant was confronted by a large and hostile crowd. As the crowd became more hostile and potentially violent, defendant randomly fired his gun towards the crowd. Although defendant did not hit anyone, Harriett Burnett was killed when a crowd member (Joe Howard) unknown to defendant accidentally discharged his own gun while seeking refuge from defendant's gunfire. Ironically, the victim was Howard's close friend and there was no evidence of any animosity between the two. Upon seeing Harriett on the ground, Howard immediately tried to revive her. When his efforts proved unsuccessful, Howard fired four shots in defendant's direction. Who caused the victim's death? Defendant? Howard? Both? *See Hodges v. State*, 661 So.2d 107 (Fla.App. 1995).

> **Hypo 9: *The Firefighter***
>
> Defendant intentionally set fire to a couch causing a serious fire on the fifth floor of an abandoned building. The fire department, responding to the conflagration, arrived to find the rear portion of the fifth and sixth floors burning. The firemen attempted to bring the situation under control, but were unable to do so and decided to withdraw from the building. At that point, the firemen were suddenly enveloped by a dense smoke, which was later discovered to have arisen from another independent fire that had broken out on the second floor. Although this fire was also determined to have originated in arson, there is virtually no evidence implicating the defendant in its responsibility. However, the combination of the thick smoke and the fifth floor fire made evacuation from the premises extremely hazardous, and one fireman sustained injuries from which he subsequently died. Did defendant "cause" the death of the fireman? How would the state argue that he did cause the death? How might defendant respond? *See People v. Arzon*, 92 Misc. 2d 739, 401 N.Y.S.2d 156 (1978).

Hypo 10: *The Game of Chicken*

Defendant and deceased entered into a suicide pact which was supposed to be carried out by driving a car off a cliff. The "cliff" was on a car turnout on a curve overlooking a 300 to 350-foot precipice on a country road. The two proceeded up the hill past the cliff, turned around and drove down around the curve and over the steep cliff at a speed in excess of 50 mph. No one saw brake lights flash. The impact of the crash killed deceased and caused severe injuries to defendant, resulting in the amputation of a foot. The State has charged defendant with the homicide of deceased. How would the State argue that defendant caused deceased's death? How might defendant respond to these arguments? How should the case be resolved? *See Forden v. Joseph G.*, 34 Cal. 3d 429, 667 P.2d 1176, 194 Cal. Rptr. 163 (In Bank 1983).

Hypo 11: *The Drug Addicts*

David Groleau, who was an alcoholic and who previously had used depressants such as Valium and Percocet, "had been drinking and doing pills" throughout the course of the day. By early evening, Groleau was visibly inebriated. Defendant prepared one "bag" of heroin and injected the heroin into his own arm. Defendant exclaimed that the heroin was "very, very good," which meant that it was particularly potent. Defendant then gave another bag of heroin to Groleau, who injected the heroin into his own arm. Groleau, who was approximately thirty to forty pounds heavier than defendant, injected the same amount of heroin as had defendant. Approximately fifteen seconds later, Groleau lost consciousness, collapsed onto the floor, and died. The evidence revealed that the level of heroin was "potentially life-threatening," and that Groleau would not have died but for the administration of the heroin. Was defendant's conduct the cause of Groleau's death? *See State v. Wassil*, 233 Conn. 174, 658 A.2d 548 (1995); *Shirah v. State*, 555 So.2d 807 (Ala. Crim. App.1989); *People v. Cline*, 270 Cal. App. 2d 328, 75 Cal. Rptr. 459 (1969); *Ureta v. Superior Court*, 199 Cal. App. 2d 672, 18 Cal. Rptr. 873 (1962).

> **Hypo 12: *The Thieves and Their Victim***
>
> Defendants robbed Stafford of his money and car, and forced him to lower his trousers and take off his shoes (to be certain that he had given up all his money), and then threw him out of a car. As he was thrust from the car, Stafford fell onto the shoulder of a rural two-lane highway. His trousers were still around his ankles, his shirt was rolled up towards his chest, and he was shoeless. Before defendants left, they placed Stafford's shoes and jacket on the shoulder of the highway. Although Stafford's eyeglasses were in the vehicle, defendants (perhaps through inadvertence) did not give them to him. The temperature was near zero, visibility was occasionally obscured by heavy winds which intermittently blew previously fallen snow into the air and across the highway, and there was snow on both sides of the road as a result of previous plowing operations. About an hour later, two cars approached from opposite directions. Immediately after passing the other car, a driver of one car saw Stafford sitting in the road in the middle of the northbound lane with his hands up in the air. The driver was operating his truck travelling at 50 miles per hour, and he "didn't have time to react" before his vehicle struck Stafford. After he brought his truck to a stop and returned to try to offer assistance, he observed that the victim's trousers were down around his ankles and his shirt was pulled up around his chest. Stafford was not wearing shoes or a jacket. At trial, the medical examiner testified that death had occurred fairly rapidly from massive head injuries. In addition, he found proof of a high degree of intoxication with a .25%, by weight, of alcohol concentration in the blood. Who is responsible for Stafford's death? The robbers? The passing driver? Both? *See People v. Kibbe*, 35 N.Y.2d 407, 321 N.E.2d 773, 362 N.Y.S.2d 848 (1974).

> **Hypo 13: *The Mother and the Abusive Lover***
>
> Defendant, who had a daughter, moved in with McCue who severely and brutally whipped the child. He would order the child to hold out her hand, and then he would slap her. Then he would say, "Where's your baby doll?" When the child reached for it, there would be a loud slap. A neighbor testified that his tone of voice was "crafty, nauseating." One night, McCue whipped the baby until 11:00pm. Defendant asked McCue to stop, but the whipping continued and he dragged "the baby up and down the hall beating her." Defendant pleaded with the neighbors not to call the police telling them that she loved "Eddie" and that they must have been imagining that the beatings were more

severe than they actually were. Defendant explained that McCue was worried over some difficulty at work and was bothered by the heat. Later, McCue struck the child with blows which ripped the infant's liver and tore the mesentery, a fatty, vascular tissue supporting the colon. Hemorrhaging ensued and the baby began vomiting. Defendant took the baby to the doctor where she died. The child had multiple bruises from head to foot, including both arms, both legs, back, front and face. Defendant stated that she loved the child and was never unkind to her, and, if she had thought McCue's discipline of Terry too severe, she would have left him. Did defendant conduct cause the death? See *Palmer v. State*, 223 Md. 341, 164 A.2d 467 (1960).

Hypo 14: *Negligent Medical Care*

Defendants were charged in the savage beating of Glen "Bear" Albea, a member of a drug ring headed by defendant Bowie in the Bronx. Essentially, defendant beat Albea with a baseball bat for 20–30 minutes, breaking several of his bones and splattering his blood at the scene. Bear later died at the hospital of complications stemming from the beating. Subsequent negligent treatment at the hospital may have contributed to Albea's death. When Albea developed malignant hyperthermia, a "possibly hereditary" reaction to anesthesia, his blood pressure dropped precipitously. Surgeons rushed to open his chest and perform cardiac massage. In doing so, they inadvertently punctured his lung, requiring three sutures to close the wound. Albea never recovered consciousness. The cause of death, four days later, was septicemia, a bacterial infection resulting from "blunt force injuries of the head and extremities with surgical intervention." Was defendant the "cause" of death? Argue the case for the state? How would defendant respond? See *People v. Bowie*, 200 A.D.2d 511, 607 N.Y.S.2d 248 (1994).

CHAPTER 5

Complicity

Whether they are referred to as accomplices, accessories, or aiders-and-abettors, every jurisdiction has statutory provisions that punish actors whose only relationship to a criminal offense is the provision of assistance to the principal offender. Occasionally a person or a corporation may be found guilty of criminal conduct of other persons about which the person or corporation is completely unaware.

A. OVERVIEW OF THE LAW

The Nature of Accomplice Liability. Whether they are referred to as accomplices, accessories, or aiders-and-abettors, every jurisdiction has statutory provisions that punish actors whose only relationship to a criminal offense was the provision of assistance to the principal offender.

Common Law Classifications. At common law, the parties to a crime were divided into four distinct categories: (1) principals in the first degree (who actually perpetrated the crime); (2) principals in the second degree (who were actually or constructively present at the scene of the crime and aided or abetted its commission); (3) accessories before the fact (who aided or abetted the crime, but were not present at its commission); and (4) accessories after the fact (who rendered assistance after the crime was completed). In misdemeanor cases, all accomplices were treated as principals.

Common Law Oddities. In the early common law, all parties to a felony received the death penalty. An accessory to a felony could not be convicted without the prior conviction of the principal offender. As a result, if the principal fled, died or was acquitted, an accomplice could not be convicted. These rules did not apply to accomplices to misdemeanors. Modern rules overturn the common law conviction distinctions.

Merger. The merger of principals and accessories has occurred in all American jurisdictions so that there is only a single crime: complicity. One significant exception, however, is for accessories after the fact. When an actor assists another only after the substantive criminal offense has taken place (*e.g.*, harboring a fugitive after a bank robbery), that offense does not merge with the principal offense, (*e.g.*, bank robbery).

Model Penal Code. Under the Model Penal Code, a defendant is an accomplice to another person in the commission of an offense if either (a) with the purpose of promoting or facilitating the commission of the offense, he (i) solicits such other person to commit it, or (ii) aids or agrees or attempts to aid such other person in planning or committing it, or (iii) having a legal duty to prevent the commission of the offense, fails to make proper effort so to do; or (b) his conduct is expressly declared by law to establish his complicity. Special rules can apply to result crimes, to victims, and to those incapable of committing a crime.

Accomplice Liability and Conspiracy. Related to the crime of complicity is the crime of conspiracy. In general, conspiracy involves an agreement between two or more persons (although an actual agreement between the two may not be required) to commit an unlawful act or a lawful act by unlawful means. One who is complicit in a crime may have explicitly or implicitly engaged in a conspiracy to commit that crime.

***Mens Rea* of Complicity.** The *mens rea* of accomplice liability is often described in the case law as having two separate (and independent) components: (1) the intent to assist a principal actor in committing the target act; and (2) the intent that the principal actually commit that act. In most jurisdictions, this intent can be (and

---

Major Themes

a. ***Actus Reus*** —The modern crime of complicity applies to persons who aid in the commission of a crime, or who provide assistance after the crime is completed. In evaluating whether a person's conduct satisfies the *actus reus* element, courts usually require evidence of tangible assistance or active promotion that goes beyond mere encouragement.

b. ***Mens Rea*** —The mental state for complicity is the purpose of promoting or facilitating the commission of the crime. Such purpose may be inferred from a person's conduct.

c. **Corporate Liability** —Although vicarious liability is disfavored, a corporation may be held liable for the unlawful acts of employees, with additional limitations often imposed by statute. A corporate officer may be held liable for such unlawful acts when serving in a managerial position with the power to correct the criminal conduct.

often is) inferred from a person's actions.

Vicarious Liability. Sometimes, an individual may be found guilty based on vicarious liability, in other words based on the criminal actions of other persons, about which the individual may be unaware. This liability is regarded as unusual and generally inappropriate in the criminal law, and is most commonly employed against corporations and corporate agents. A number of jurisdictions have legislated higher *mens rea* requirements for the imposition of such liability.

Model Penal Code and Corporate Liability. The Model Penal Code provides for the imposition of criminal liability on corporations, and some corporate officials, in limited situations.

B. ACCOMPLICE LIABILITY

1. Principals & Accessories

a. *Merger of Principals & Accessories*

STANDEFER V. UNITED STATES
447 U.S. 10 (1980).

MR. CHIEF JUSTICE BURGER delivered the opinion of the Court.

At common law, the subject of principals and accessories was riddled with "intricate" distinctions. In felony cases, parties to a crime were divided into four distinct categories: (1) principals in the first degree who actually perpetrated the offense; (2) principals in the second degree who were actually or constructively present at the scene of the crime and aided or abetted its commission; (3) accessories before the fact who aided or abetted the crime, but were not present at its commission; and (4) accessories after the fact who rendered assistance after the crime was complete. By contrast, misdemeanor cases "did not admit of accessories [sic] either before or after the fact"; instead, all parties to a misdemeanor, whatever their roles, were principals.

Because at early common law all parties to a felony received the death penalty, certain procedural rules developed tending to shield accessories from punishment. Among them was the rule that an accessory could not be convicted without the prior conviction of the principal offender. Under this rule, the principal's flight, death, or acquittal barred prosecution of the accessory. If the principal were pardoned or his conviction reversed on appeal, the accessory's conviction could not stand. In every way "an accessory followed, like a shadow, his principal."

This procedural bar applied only to the prosecution of accessories in felony cases. In misdemeanor cases, where all participants were deemed principals, a prior acquittal of the actual perpetrator did not prevent the subsequent conviction of a person who rendered assistance. In felony cases a principal in the second degree could be convicted notwithstanding the prior acquittal of the first-degree principal. Not surprisingly, considerable effort was expended in defining the categories—in determining, for instance, when a person was "constructively present" so as to be a second-degree principal. In the process, justice all too frequently was defeated.

To overcome these judge-made rules, statutes were enacted in England and in the United States. In 1848 the Parliament enacted a statute providing that an accessory before the fact could be "indicted, tried, convicted, and punished in all respects like the Principal." As interpreted, the statute permitted an accessory to be convicted "although the principal be acquitted." Several state legislatures followed suit. In 1899, Congress joined this growing reform movement with the enactment of a general penal code for Alaska which abrogated the common-law distinctions and provided that "all persons concerned in the commission of a crime, whether it be felony or misdemeanor, and whether they directly commit the act constituting the crime or aid and abet in its commission, though not present, are principals, and to be tried and punished as such."

The enactment of 18 U.S.C. § 2 in 1909 was part and parcel of this same reform movement. The language of the statute, as enacted, unmistakably demonstrates the point: "Whoever directly commits any act constituting an offense defined in any law of the United States, or aids, abets, counsels, commands, induces, or procures its commission, is a principal."

The statute "abolished the distinction between principals and accessories and made them all principals." Read against its common-law background, the provision evinces a clear intent to permit the conviction of accessories to federal criminal offenses despite the prior acquittal of the actual perpetrator of the offense. It gives general effect to what had always been the rule for second-decree principals and for all misdemeanants.

With the enactment of that section, all participants in conduct violating a federal criminal statute are "principals." As such, they are punishable for their criminal conduct; the fate of other participants is irrelevant.

POINTS FOR DISCUSSION

a. Merger

The merger of principals and accessories has occurred in all American jurisdictions. One significant exception, however, is for accessories after the fact. When an actor assists another *only* after the substantive criminal offense has taken place (*e.g.*, harboring a fugitive after a bank robbery), that offense does *not* merge with the principal offense, bank robbery.

b. Acquittal of Principal

In *Standefer*, the Supreme Court concluded that an aider-and-abettor could be held culpable for a criminal offense (bribery) for which the principal had previously been acquitted. Does this make sense to you? Is it fair? The *Standefer* Court dismissed these concerns, observing that "while symmetry of results may be intellectually satisfying, it is not required."

Is it fair to treat accomplices as if they had actually committed the criminal act in question themselves? Is a "getaway driver" just as culpable as a bank robber? How about the actor who simply arranges to provide the getaway car? Is the conduct of all accomplices (and principals) really equally blameworthy?

c. Significance of the Merger of Principals & Accessories

The merger of principals and accessories has created some significant procedural problems in criminal trials and criminal pretrial procedure. For example, what kind of notice (if any at all) must a defendant receive as to whether or not he or she is going to be tried for his or her principal and/or accessorial acts? And when must or should that notice be received?

2. The Act of Aiding or Encouraging

It is critically important—but often difficult to determine—just how much participatory or encouraging activity on the part of an alleged accomplice is necessary to establish the *actus reus* of aiding or encouraging a principal. It is clear that an individual's "mere presence" at the scene of a crime does not (in and of itself) suffice to make an actor an accomplice. The cases that follow explore what more is required.

LANE V. TEXAS
991 S.W.2d 904 (Tex. Ct. App. 1999).

PER CURIAM.

Appellant James William Lane was convicted of the offense of aggravated robbery of an elderly person, and he appealed. The issue is whether the trial court erred in refusing Lane's request to instruct the jury that a particular witness, Patricia R., was an accomplice as a matter of fact. The State's evidence revealed that Patricia and Kris Shank, who lived together, went to Lane's house. Lane quickly recruited Patricia, Shank and Anna Eason to rob 71-year-old Hillard Doss. Lane drove Shank and Eason to the scene of the robbery. Patricia was a passenger in Lane's truck at the time. Lane and Patricia waited in the truck while Shank and Eason went to commit the crime. At first the pair returned to the truck without having carried out the plan, but after encouragement from Lane, they went back to Doss's home, again gained entrance, committed the robbery, and returned to Lane's truck for their get-a-way.

At trial, both Patricia and Eason testified against Lane. Shank's testimony from a prior hearing was also introduced against Lane. The jury was instructed that Shank and Eason were accomplices as a matter of law. Therefore, the only testimony linking Lane to the crime, except Patricia's, came from accomplices. Because a conviction cannot be had on uncorroborated accomplice testimony, and the only evidence corroborating Lane and Shank's testimony came from Patricia, the issue of whether she is an accomplice is crucial to the case. Were the jury to have found that Patricia was an accomplice, there would be no corroborating evidence upon which a conviction in this case could be upheld against a sufficiency challenge.

The court of criminal appeals set out the general requirements for a finding that a witness is an accomplice witness: "A person who is merely present at the scene of the offense is not an accomplice; an affirmative act or omission is required. An accomplice participates before, during, or after the commission of the crime—presence at the scene of the offense is not required—though one is not an accomplice for knowing about a crime and failing to disclose it, or even concealing it." We have also repeatedly stated that a person is an accomplice if he or she could be prosecuted for the same offense as the defendant, or a lesser included offense.

To make the determination, the entire record is examined for evidence raising the issue of whether or not a particular witness is an accomplice. In doing so, we eliminate from our consideration the evidence from the accomplice witness and examine the remaining evidence to ascertain if there is inculpatory evidence, that is, evidence of incriminating character, which tends to connect defendant with the commission of the offense. An accomplice witness charge is required if raised by the evidence.

Patricia was present when Lane told Shank and Eason that he knew of an old man who carried lots of money in cash. Patricia was present when Lane, Shank and Eason planned the crime. Patricia was a passenger in Lane's truck as he drove Shank and Eason to the scene of the crime and let them out of the truck to commit the crime. Patricia remained present in the truck when Shank and Eason returned the first time without committing the robbery, traveled back to Lane's residence in the truck, and were there encouraged by Lane to begin anew and carry out the robbery plan. Patricia was a passenger in the truck when Lane again drove Shank and Eason to the crime scene. Patricia was present when the pair returned to the truck after committing the robbery, and accompanied the trio back to Lane's residence. At the residence, she was present when the other three divided up the cash taken from Doss. She also saw Shank toss his dirty clothing into the bathtub.

Taking these facts as a whole and measuring them against the criteria espoused by the court of criminal appeals, we do not believe that an issue as to whether Patricia was an accomplice was raised by the evidence. Patricia was present during the entire series of events that night and knew full well what the other three actors were doing. However, Patricia committed no affirmative act in furtherance of the crime. Further, her omission of not stopping the crime and not alerting anyone about the crime was not an omission that our laws have criminalized so that she would become an accomplice by omission. In sum, we disagree with Lane's characterization of the facts. There was simply no accomplice witness fact issue raised for the jury to decide. We therefore hold that the trial judge did not err in denying Lane's request for an instruction on Patricia's status as an accomplice.

The judgment of the trial court is *affirmed*.

POINTS FOR DISCUSSION

a. Model Penal Code

Consider the MPC's provisions relating to accomplice liability. Note that § 2.06(3)(a)(i) punishes the person who solicits another person to commit a crime. Solicitation was a common law inchoate offense. Inchoate offenses are discussed in Chapter 6:

§ 2.06. Liability for Conduct of Another; Complicity.

(1) A person is guilty of an offense if it is committed by his own conduct or by the conduct of another person for which he is legally accountable, or both.

(2) A person is legally accountable for the conduct of another person when:

(a) acting with the kind of culpability that is sufficient for the commission of the offense, he causes an innocent or irresponsible person to engage in such conduct; or

(b) he is made accountable for the conduct of such other person by the Code or by the law defining the offense; or

(c) he is an accomplice of such other person in the commission of the offense.

(3) A person is an accomplice of another person in the commission of an offense if:

(a) with the purpose of promoting or facilitating the commission of the offense, he

(i) solicits such other person to commit it, or

(ii) aids or agrees or attempts to aid such other person in planning or committing it, or

(iii) having a legal duty to prevent the commission of the offense, fails to make proper effort so to do; or

(b) his conduct is expressly declared by law to establish his complicity.

(4) When causing a particular result is an element of an offense, an accomplice in the conduct causing such result is an accomplice in the commission of that offense if he acts with the kind of culpability, if any, with respect to that result that is sufficient for the commission of the offense.

(5) A person who is legally incapable of committing a particular offense himself may be guilty thereof if it is committed by the conduct of another person for which he is legally accountable, unless such liability is inconsistent with the purpose of the provision establishing his incapacity.

(6) Unless otherwise provided by the Code or by the law defining the offense, a person is not an accomplice in an offense committed by another person if:

(a) he is a victim of that offense; or

>> (b) the offense is so defined that his conduct is inevitably incident to its commission; or
>
>> (c) he terminates his complicity prior to the commission of the offense and
>
>>> (i) wholly deprives it of effectiveness in the commission of the offense; or
>
>>> (ii) gives timely warning to the law enforcement authorities or otherwise makes proper effort to prevent the commission of the offense.
>
> (7) An accomplice may be convicted on proof of the commission of the offense and of his complicity therein, though the person claimed to have committed the offense has not been prosecuted or convicted or has been convicted of a different offense or degree of offense or has an immunity to prosecution or conviction or has been acquitted.

b. Mere Presence

Do you agree that there is no evidence that Patricia did *anything* other than be present as the robbery took place? Does it matter that the court acknowledged that Lane "recruited" Patricia to participate in the robbery and that she "went along for the ride?"

c. Convicted Accomplice

Do you think that it made any difference in the disposition of this case that the reason the court was deciding Patricia's accomplice status was only to determine whether her testimony was admissible to uphold Lane's conviction? If Patricia had been charged and convicted as an accomplice, do you think that—on this same evidence—the appellate court would have upheld her conviction?

3. Intent to Promote or Facilitate a Crime

The *mens rea* of accomplice liability is often described in the case law as having two separate (and independent) components: (1) the intent to assist a principal actor in committing the target act; and (2) the intent that the principal actually commit that act. In most jurisdictions, this intent can be (and often is) implied from a person's actions.

HAWAII V. SOARES
72 Haw. 278, 815 P.2d 428 (1991).

LUM, CHIEF JUSTICE.

On August 22, 1989, Holiday Mart store detective Mitchell Tam observed appellants [Ronald Soares and Hollie Suratt] placing several cartons of cigarettes into a shopping cart. Tam then saw Soares place the cigarettes into a large handbag. Appellants left the store, with Suratt carrying the bag, without paying for the cigarettes. Outside the store, Tam approached appellants, identified himself, showed his badge, and told appellants that they were under citizen's arrest for shoplifting. As Soares turned towards him, Tam grabbed Soares. During their struggle, the back of Soares' head hit Tam in the mouth causing Tam to release Soares. Soares then fled. While struggling with Soares, Tam instructed Conway Marks, a Holiday Mart clerk who was assisting Tam, to stop Suratt from leaving the area. Marks blocked Suratt's escape by standing directly in front of her path. After unsuccessfully attempting to push Marks out of her way, Suratt tricked Marks into looking the other direction and then fled with the bag.

We conclude that the court's accomplice jury instruction was a misstatement of Hawaii law. The accomplice instruction provided: All persons who are present and participate in the commission of a crime are responsible for the acts of each other done or made in furtherance of the crime. It is not necessary to prove that each one committed all of the acts of the crime. Each person who does one act which is an ingredient of the crime or immediately connected with it is as guilty as if he or she committed the whole crime with his or her own hands.

Section 702–222 requires that to be guilty as an accomplice, a person must act with the intent of promoting or facilitating the commission of the crime. The court's accomplice instruction clearly does not contain such a *mens rea* element. The court's instruction implies that a person merely needs to be present and participate in an act of the crime to be guilty as an accomplice. Under the court's accomplice instruction, the State is relieved from its burden of proving that appellants acted with the requisite intent.

Accordingly, appellants' convictions are reversed and the cases are remanded for new trials.

POINT FOR DISCUSSION

Proper Instruction

If the jury had been properly instructed on intent, what do you think the result would have been in this case?

NEW YORK V. KAPLAN
76 N.Y.2d 140, 556 N.E.2d 415, 556 N.Y.S.2d 976 (1990).

TITONE, JUDGE.

Defendant Murray Kaplan was convicted of first degree criminal sale of a controlled substance because of his involvement in a narcotics network which operated out of a garment business office located in the Empire State Building. His primary contention on appeal is that although the culpable state required for the commission of this crime is "knowledge," the trial court should have instructed the jury that defendant could not be held liable as an accomplice unless he acted with the specific intent to sell a controlled substance. We conclude that such an instruction is not required and that, accordingly, the conviction should be affirmed.

From 1986 to 1987, the police investigated a cocaine ring which operated out of an office maintained by defendant's cousin, Mike Kaplan, in the Empire State Building. Detective Janis Grasso, posing as a drug courier for "Ronnie" from Atlantic City, engaged in a series of transactions, primarily with Mike Kaplan. The charges against defendant were based on his actions on October 15, 1986, when, pursuant to a prior phone call, Grasso went to Kaplan's office to purchase 10 ounces of cocaine and found Kaplan, Kaplan's brother and defendant present. After introducing Grasso to the other two men, Mike Kaplan told defendant "to take care of the young lady." Defendant got off the couch, walked to a file cabinet in the room, removed a manila envelope from it, and placed it on the desk in front of Grasso. She took out $15,000 in prerecorded buy money and placed it on the table. Defendant picked up the money, took it over to the table and began counting it. At the same time, Grasso opened the manila envelope, took out a ziplock plastic bag, and placed the drugs into her purse remarking that "it looks nice."

Defendant was subsequently charged with, *inter alia*, criminal sale of a controlled substance. Before the case was submitted to the jury, defense counsel asked the court to instruct the jurors that in order to convict defendant as an accomplice they must find that he had "specific intent" to sell a controlled substance, and that he had to "share the intent or purpose of the principal actors."

The court denied defendant's request, noting that the mental culpability required for criminal sale was not "intent" but "knowledge" and, further, that the standard charge for accomplice liability requires proof that the defendant "intentionally aided" the other participants. Following the court's charge, which tracked the language of the applicable statutes, the jury found defendant guilty of criminal sale. The Appellate Division affirmed defendant's conviction, and leave to appeal was granted by a Judge of this court.

Penal Law § 20.00 provides that a person may be held criminally liable as an accomplice when he performs certain acts and does so "with the mental culpability required for the commission" of the substantive crime. Despite this language, defendant argues that even though the substantive crime with which he was charged—criminal sale of a controlled substance—requires only knowledge,[3] the statute should be construed to require proof of a more exacting *mens rea*, namely specific intent to sell.

Under section 2 of the former Penal Law, a person could be convicted as a principal if he "aided and abetted in the commission of a crime". The former Penal Law, however, did not specifically state what type of acts were required for conviction. Consequently, in order to prevent the imposition of criminal liability for the principal's crime on someone who may have been merely present, the courts required proof that the aider or abetter "shared the intent or purpose of the principal actor."

Defendant's argument is that this "shared intent or purpose" test required proof that he acted with the specific intent to sell cocaine. However, any lack of clarity that previously existed under section 2 of the former Penal Law was eliminated by the adoption of section 20.00 of the revised Penal Law, which specifies that an accomplice must have acted with the "mental culpability required for the commission" of the particular crime. Further, we have already construed section 20.00 as not requiring specific intent within the meaning of Penal Law § 15.05(1) when the substantive crime does not involve such intent. Finally, the "shared intent or purpose" language from our earlier cases cannot be read for the proposition, advanced by defendant, that a specific wish to commit the principal's substantive crime is required in all circumstances, including those involving substantive crimes with mental states other than that defined in Penal Law § 15.05(1). Indeed, the "shared intent or purpose" test set forth in the case law

---

[3] Penal Law § 220.43 provides, in pertinent part, that "a person is guilty of criminal sale of a controlled substance in the first degree when he knowingly and unlawfully sells". A person acts knowingly "when he is aware that his conduct is of such nature or that such circumstance exists". In contrast, a person acts intentionally "when his conscious objective is to cause such result or to engage in such conduct."

merely establishes that acts undertaken in relative innocence and without a conscious design to advance the principal's crime will not support a conviction for accomplice liability. The same conclusion, however, is implicit in the specific requirement in Penal Law § 20.00 that the accomplice "solicit, request, command, importune, or intentionally aid" the principal, since all of the delineated acts import goal-directed conduct.

The distinction made here is a subtle, but important, one. It is well illustrated by our holding in *People v. Flayhart*, 72 N.Y.2d 737, 536 N.Y.S.2d 727, 533 N.E.2d 657, in which we concluded that the defendants could be guilty as accomplices to the crime of criminally negligent homicide under Penal Law § 125.10, even though neither defendant had the victim's death as a "conscious object". This result flowed naturally from the fact that both defendants could be found to have "failed to perceive a substantial and unjustifiable risk" of death—the "mental culpability required for the crime"—and that both engaged in deliberate conduct to advance the common enterprise, i.e., the egregious neglect of the victim.

For the same reasons, we reject defendant's alternative argument that the crime of which he was convicted under the court's charge is indistinguishable from second degree criminal facilitation. A person is guilty of second degree criminal facilitation when "believing it probable that he is rendering aid to a person who intends to commit a class A felony, he engages in conduct which provides such person with means or opportunity for the commission thereof and which in fact aids such person to commit such class A felony". This statute was enacted to provide an additional tool in the prosecutorial arsenal for situations where the "facilitator" knowingly aided the commission of a crime but did not possess the mental culpability required for commission of the substantive crime. Additionally an "accomplice" and a "facilitator" are distinguishable in that the accomplice must have intentionally aided the principal in bringing forth a result, while the facilitator need only have provided assistance "believing it probable" that he was rendering aid.

In defendant's case there was sufficient evidence for the jury to find that, knowing the substance in question was cocaine, defendant intentionally aided Mike Kaplan by delivering it to Detective Grasso. The evidence established that after being asked by Mike Kaplan to "take care of" Detective Grasso, defendant immediately went to a file cabinet drawer, retrieved a package containing cocaine, and gave the package to Grasso in exchange for money which defendant immediately began to count. That defendant neither negotiated nor arranged the transactions does not affect his liability as an accomplice, and the court was not required to include specific intent to sell as an element in its charge on accessorial liability. The elements were adequately conveyed when the court told the jury that it must find both that defendant acted with the specific intent required for the substantive offense, i.e., knowledge that the substance was cocaine, and that he "intentionally aided" the sale.

Order *affirmed*.

POINT FOR DISCUSSION

Specific Intent

If the court had ruled differently—if it had held that a specific intent to sell a controlled substance was required in order to support a conviction—was there sufficient evidence on the record to support a jury verdict based upon accomplice culpability? What was that evidence?

C. VICARIOUS LIABILITY

Sometimes, an individual may be found guilty of criminal conduct based on the criminal actions of other persons, about which the individual may be unaware. This "vicarious liability" is most commonly employed against corporations and corporate agents. There are, however, limits to the scope of such culpability.

UNITED STATES V. PARK
421 U.S. 658 (1975).

MR. CHIEF JUSTICE BURGER delivered the opinion of the Court.

Acme Markets, Inc., is a national retail food chain with approximately 36,000 employees, 874 retail outlets, 12 general warehouses, and four special warehouses. Its headquarters, including the office of the president, respondent Park, who is chief executive officer of the corporation, are located in Philadelphia, Pa. In a five-count information filed in the United States District Court for the District of Maryland, the Government charged Acme and respondent with violations of the Federal Food, Drug and Cosmetic Act. Each count of the information alleged that the defendants had received food that had been shipped in interstate commerce and that, while the food was being held for sale in Acme's Baltimore warehouse following shipment in interstate commerce, they caused it to be held in a building accessible to rodents and to be exposed to contamination by rodents.

Acme pleaded guilty to each count of the information. Respondent pleaded not guilty. The evidence demonstrated that in April 1970 the Food and Drug Administration (FDA) advised respondent by letter of insanitary conditions in

Acme's Philadelphia warehouse. In 1971 the FDA found that similar conditions existed in the firm's Baltimore warehouse. An FDA consumer safety officer testified concerning evidence of rodent infestation and other insanitary conditions discovered during a 12-day inspection of the Baltimore warehouse in November and December 1971. A second inspection of the warehouse had been conducted in March 1972. On that occasion the inspectors found that there had been improvement in the sanitary conditions, but that 'there was still evidence of rodent activity in the building and in the warehouses and we found some rodent-contaminated lots of food items.'

At the close of the evidence, respondent's renewed motion for a judgment of acquittal was denied. Respondent's counsel objected to the instructions on the ground that they failed fairly to reflect our decision in *United States v. Dotterweich* and to define "responsible relationship." The trial judge overruled the objection. The jury found respondent guilty on all counts of the information, and he was subsequently sentenced to pay a fine of $50 on each count.

The Court of Appeals reversed the conviction and remanded for a new trial. That court viewed the Government as arguing 'that the conviction may be predicated solely upon a showing that respondent was the President of the offending corporation,' and it stated that as 'a general proposition, some act of commission or omission is an essential element of every crime.'

The question presented in *United States v. Dotterweich* was whether 'the manager of a corporation, as well as the corporation itself, may be prosecuted under the Federal Food, Drug, and Cosmetic Act of 1938 for the introduction of misbranded and adulterated articles into interstate commerce.' In *Dotterweich*, a jury had disagreed as to the corporation, a jobber purchasing drugs from manufacturers and shipping them in interstate commerce under its own label, but had convicted Dotterweich, the corporation's president and general manager. The Court of Appeals reversed the conviction on the ground that only the drug dealer, whether corporation or individual, was subject to the criminal provisions of the Act, and that where the dealer was a corporation, an individual connected therewith might be held personally only if he was operating the corporation 'as his 'alter ego."

In reversing the judgment of the Court of Appeals and reinstating Dotterweich's conviction, this Court looked to the purposes of the Act and noted that they 'touch phases of the lives and health of the people which, in the circumstances of modern industrialism, are largely beyond self-protection.' It observed that the Act is of 'a now familiar type' which 'dispenses with the conventional requirement for criminal conduct—awareness of some wrongdoing. In the interest of the larger good it puts the burden of acting at hazard upon a person otherwise innocent but standing in responsible relation to a public danger.'

Central to the Court's conclusion that individuals other than proprietors are subject to the criminal provisions of the Act was the reality that 'the only way in which a corporation can act is through the individuals who act on its behalf. At the same time, the Court was aware of the concern which was the motivating factor in the Court of Appeals' decision, that literal enforcement 'might operate too harshly by sweeping within its condemnation any person however remotely entangled in the proscribed shipment.' A limiting principle, in the form of 'settled doctrines of criminal law' defining those who 'are responsible for the commission of a misdemeanor,' was available. In this context, the Court concluded, those doctrines dictated that the offense was committed 'by all who have. a responsible share in the furtherance of the transaction which the statute outlaws.'

Thus *Dotterweich* and the cases which have followed reveal that in providing sanctions which reach and touch the individuals who execute the corporate mission—and this is by no means necessarily confined to a single corporate agent or employee—the Act imposes not only a positive duty to seek out and remedy violations when they occur but also, and primarily, a duty to implement measures that will insure that violations will not occur. The requirements of foresight and vigilance imposed on responsible corporate agents are beyond question demanding, and perhaps onerous, but they are no more stringent than the public has a right to expect of those who voluntarily assume positions of authority in business enterprises whose services and products affect the health and well-being of the public that supports them.

The Act does not, as we observed in *Dotterweich*, make criminal liability turn on 'awareness of some wrongdoing' or 'conscious fraud.' The duty imposed by Congress on responsible corporate agents is one that requires the highest standard of foresight and vigilance, but the Act, in its criminal aspect, does not require that which is objectively impossible. The theory upon which responsible corporate agents are held criminally accountable for 'causing' violations of the Act permits a claim that a defendant was 'powerless' to prevent or correct the violation to 'be raised defensively at a trial on the merits.' If such a claim is made, the defendant has the burden of coming forward with evidence, but this does not alter the Government's ultimate burden of proving beyond a reasonable doubt the defendant's guilt, including his power, in light of the duty imposed by the Act, to prevent or correct the prohibited condition.

We cannot agree that it was incumbent upon the District Court to instruct the jury that the Government had the burden of establishing 'wrongful action' in the sense in which the Court of Appeals used that phrase. The concept of a 'responsible relationship' to, or a 'responsible share' in, a violation of the Act indeed imports some measure of blameworthiness; but it is equally clear that the Government establishes a prima facie case when it introduces evidence sufficient to warrant a finding by the trier of the facts that the defendant had, by reason of his position in the corporation, responsibility and authority either to prevent in the first instance, or promptly to correct, the violation complained of, and that he failed to do so. The failure thus to fulfill the duty imposed by the interaction of the corporate agent's authority and the statute furnishes a sufficient causal link. The considerations which prompted the imposition of this duty, and the scope of the duty, provide the measure of culpability.

Turning to the jury charge in this case, it is of arguable that isolated parts can be read as intimating that a finding of guilt could be predicated solely on respondent's corporate position. But this is not the way we review jury instructions, because 'a single instruction to a jury may not be judged in artificial isolation, but must be viewed in the context of the overall charge.' Reading the entire charge satisfies us that the jury's attention was adequately focused on the issue of respondent's authority with respect to the conditions that formed the basis of the alleged violations. Viewed as a whole, the charge did not permit the jury to find guilt solely on the basis of respondent's position in the corporation; rather, it fairly advised the jury that to find guilt it must find respondent 'had a responsible relation to the situation,' and 'by virtue of his position [had] authority and responsibility' to deal with the situation. The situation referred to could only be 'food held in unsanitary conditions in a warehouse with the result that it consisted, in part, of filth or may have been contaminated with filth.'

We conclude that, viewed as a whole and in the context of the trial, the charge was not misleading and contained an adequate statement of the law to guide the jury's determination. Although it would

> **Take Note**
>
> Vicarious liability is unusual in the criminal law. As a general rule, an individual cannot be held liable for the conduct of another absent evidence of complicity. When vicarious liability can be imposed, criminal liability is imposed absent complicity. Why do legislatures and courts sometimes impose vicarious liability?
>
> Note how the Model Penal Code permits the imposition of vicarious liability, not only on corporations, but also on various corporate employees with responsibility over the issues implicated by a statute.

have been better to give an instruction more precisely relating the legal issue to the facts of the case, we cannot say that the failure to provide the amplification requested by respondent was an abuse of discretion.

Reversed.

MR. JUSTICE STEWART, with whom MR. JUSTICE MARSHALL and MR. JUSTICE POWELL join, dissenting.

POINT FOR DISCUSSION

Model Penal Code

Consider the Model Penal Code's provisions relating to corporate liability:

§ 2.07. Liability of Corporations, Unincorporated Associations and Persons Acting, or Under a Duty to Act, in Their Behalf.

(1) A corporation may be convicted of the commission of an offense if:

(a) the offense is a violation or the offense is defined by a statute other than the Code in which a legislative purpose to impose liability on corporations plainly appears and the conduct is performed by an agent of the corporation acting in behalf of the corporation within the scope of his office or employment, except that if the law defining the offense designates the agents for whose conduct the corporation is accountable or the circumstances under which it is accountable, such provisions shall apply; or

(b) the offense consists of an omission to discharge a specific duty of affirmative performance imposed on corporations by law; or

(c) the commission of the offense was authorized, requested, commanded, performed or recklessly tolerated by the board of directors or by a high managerial agent acting in behalf of the corporation within the scope of his office or employment.

(2) When absolute liability is imposed for the commission of an offense, a legislative purpose to impose liability on a corporation shall be assumed, unless the contrary plainly appears.

(3) An unincorporated association may be convicted of the commission of an offense if:

(a) the offense is defined by a statute other than the Code that expressly provides for the liability of such an association and the conduct is performed by an agent of the association acting in behalf of the association within the scope of his office or employment, except that if the law defining the offense designates the agents for whose conduct the association is accountable or the circumstances under which it is accountable, such provisions shall apply; or

(b) the offense consists of an omission to discharge a specific duty of affirmative performance imposed on associations by law.

(4) As used in this Section:

(a) "corporation" does not include an entity organized as or by a governmental agency for the execution of a governmental program;

(b) "agent" means any director, officer, servant, employee or other person authorized to act in behalf of the corporation or association and, in the case of an unincorporated association, a member of such association;

(c) "high managerial agent" means an officer of a corporation or an unincorporated association, or, in the case of a partnership, a partner, or any other agent of a corporation or association having duties of such responsibility that his conduct may fairly be assumed to represent the policy of the corporation or association.

(5) In any prosecution of a corporation or an unincorporated association for the commission of an offense included within the terms of Subsection (1)(a) or Subsection (3)(a) of this Section, other than an offense for which absolute liability has been imposed, it shall be a defense if the defendant proves by a preponderance of evidence that the high managerial agent having supervisory responsibility over the subject matter of the offense employed due diligence to prevent its commission. This paragraph shall not apply if it is plainly inconsistent with the legislative purpose in defining the particular offense.

(a) A person is legally accountable for any conduct he performs or causes to be performed in the name of the corporation or an unincorporated association or in its behalf to the same extent as if it were performed in his own name or behalf.

(b) Whenever a duty to act is imposed by law upon a corporation or an unincorporated association, any agent of the corporation or association having primary responsibility for the discharge of the duty is legally accountable for a reckless omission to perform the required act to the same extent as if the duty were imposed by law directly upon himself.

(c) When a person is convicted of an offense by reason of his legal accountability for the conduct of a corporation or an unincorporated association, he is subject to the sentence authorized by law when a natural person is convicted of an offense of the grade and the degree involved.

> ### Hypo 1: *Scope of Accomplice Responsibility*
>
> Defendant is charged with being an accomplice to murder. The evidence shows that the perpetrator used defendant's shotgun in committing the murder, and that defendant loaned him the shotgun just prior to the murder. Is defendant an accomplice to murder if defendant loaned the gun based on the perpetrator's assertion that he was going duck hunting? Suppose, instead, that defendant knew that the perpetrator was going to commit a murder?

> ### Hypo 2: *Accomplices to Rape*
>
> You are an assistant district attorney in Pittsburgh, and police officers have reported to you that a victim, Jane Roe, was raped in a pool hall by two men: John Smith and Joe Doe. While the rapes were taking place, three other individuals were present: a bartender, Jerry Ames, and two individuals drinking at the bar, Bob Baker and Cathy Cox. Ames watched the rapes take place and yelled at the rapists to "stop," but when they did not listen to him, he did nothing to stop them from committing the crimes nor did he make any attempt to call the police. Baker watched the rapes and yelled at Smith and Doe to encourage them to commit the assaults. Cox watched the rapes and said nothing. Should Ames, Baker and Cox be charged as accomplices in the rape? Why or why not?

> ### Hypo 3: *The Burglary*
>
> David Vaillancourt and a friend, Richard Burhoe, were seen standing on the front porch of a home, ringing the doorbell and conversing with one another for ten minutes. When there was no answer at the door, the pair walked around the side of the house where Burhoe allegedly attempted to break into a basement window. Tipped off by a suspicious neighbor, the police arrived and

arrested Vaillancourt and Burhoe as they were fleeing the scene. Burhoe is charged with attempted burglary. If you are the prosecutor, what kind of proof would you use to show that Vaillancourt was an accomplice? If you are the defense attorney, how might you respond to that evidence? *See New Hampshire v. Vaillancourt*, 122 N.H. 1153, 453 A.2d 1327 (1982).

Hypo 4: *The Housekeeper*

Gudelia Ramirez was found in a residence with a large amount of heroin when police arrived to execute a lawful search warrant for evidence related to a heroin-distribution operation. The State's evidence showed that, although Ramirez was not a "member" of the operation, she was aware of its existence, and she cooked and cleaned for the group that ran it. She was, for example, cooking dinner in the kitchen when heroin was cut and packaged on the kitchen table. However, her wages were those of a housekeeper and a cook. Under these circumstances: a) is there sufficient evidence to establish her culpability as an accomplice to the crime of possession of heroin? b) What if, instead of paying Ramirez an hourly rate, she is paid a percentage of the profits? *See Washington v. Amezola*, 49 Wash. App. 78, 741 P.2d 1024 (1987).

Hypo 5: *The Execution*

Following an all-night dance at which a good deal of whisky was consumed, Rowe and Colvard got into an argument which continued for some time. Twice, Rowe raised his rifle, aimed it at Colvard, and then lowered it. The third time that Rowe raised the rifle, he fired it, killing Colvard. Consider the following facts and decide whether Hicks was complicit in the murder: A) Hicks sat and silently watched the entire series of events; B) Each time Rowe raised the rifle, Hicks laughed; C) Each time Rowe raised the rifle, Hicks not only laughed, but also yelled "Take off your hat and die like a man"; D) Prior to the killing, Hicks yelled to Rowe: "Go ahead and shoot him." *See Hicks v. United States*, 150 U.S. 442 (1893).

Hypo 6: *The Contrived Burglary*

Hayes agreed with Hill to burglarize a store. Hayes raised a store window and helped Hill slide through it. Hill then handed Hayes a 45-pound piece of meat through the window. Both men were captured within a matter of minutes. Hill was not arrested because he was the brother of the store's owner. The facts showed that Hayes had originally proposed the burglary. When Hill agreed to commit the crime, he had no intent to actually burgle the store, but simply wanted to trap Hayes. To this end, Hill alerted his brother, the store's owner, about the plan. Police were waiting to apprehend Hayes, and Hill knew that they were there when he entered the store. Can Hayes be an accomplice to the crime of burglary if Hill had absolutely no intention of actually burglarizing the store and in fact acted with the knowledge and consent of the store owner? *See State v. Hayes*, 105 Mo. 76, 16 S.W. 514 (1891).

Hypo 7: *More on Contrived Burglaries*

Wilson and Pierce agreed to burglarize a drugstore. Pierce helped Wilson enter the store. While Wilson was inside stealing cash, Pierce called the police. Pierce then helped the police track Wilson down. Pierce later testified that the sole reason for his participation in the burglary was to get even with Wilson, and to arrange for the police to "catch Wilson in the act." Can Wilson be convicted of burglary? Can Pierce be convicted as an accomplice? *See Wilson v. People*, 103 Colo. 441, 87 P.2d 5 (1939). Suppose that Wilson told Pierce that he planned to burglarize a store and asked Pierce for help. Pierce responded by giving Wilson a list of tools that would be needed, and by helping Wilson plan the crime. However, before the plan could be executed, Pierce told the police who were lying in wait when Wilson arrived. Wilson is charged with attempted burglary. Can Pierce be convicted as an accomplice?

> **Hypo 8: *Ford Motor Co. and the Exploding Gas Tank***
>
> At one point, the Ford Motor Company (Ford) manufactured the "Pinto," a compact car. The Pinto suffered from a major gas tank defect that could cause the vehicle to explode when it was hit from behind, and lots of people were killed or seriously injured as a result of this defect. There is evidence suggesting that Ford's officers were aware of the problem, and could have remedied the problem rather cheaply, but chose not to spend the money. What would it take to impose criminal liability on Ford or its officers for the deaths or injuries? If you are the prosecutor in the case, what types of proof might you offer against the officers?

CHAPTER 6

Inchoate Offenses: Attempt & Conspiracy

Criminal law punishes conduct society does not condone. It also seeks to prevent crime from occurring. Inchoate offenses, therefore punish those who are preparing to commit a crime. The word inchoate comes from the Latin *inchoare*, which means "to start work on." There are three such offenses: solicitation, attempt, and conspiracy. Solicitation was discussed in Chapter 5.

A. OVERVIEW OF THE LAW

Theory of Attempt Law. Although the criminal law does not punish people merely for "bad thoughts," the State does have an interest in intervening early before a suspect goes so far as to commit a crime. The goal is to prevent defendant from actually causing harm. The law of attempt plays this role in the law. The evidence required for an attempt conviction, both as to the *mens rea* and the *actus reus*, can vary from state to state.

Relationship to Other Crimes. The crimes of solicitation and conspiracy also allow the police to intervene early to prevent the commission of criminal acts. Solicitation was discussed in Chapter 4, in relation to the topic of complicity, and conspiracy is discussed in this chapter.

MPC Definition of *Mens Rea*. The Model Penal Code defines the crime of attempt as occurring when an individual, acting with the kind of culpability otherwise required for commission of the crime, does any of three things: (a) purposely engages in conduct that would constitute the crime if the attendant circumstances were as he believes them to be; or (b) when causing a particular result is an element of the crime, does or omits to do anything with the purpose of causing or with the belief that it will cause such result without further conduct on his part; or (c) purposely does or omits to do anything that, under the circumstances as he believes them to be, is an act or omission constituting a substantial step in a course of conduct planned to culminate in his commission of the crime.

***Actus Reus* Requirement of Attempt.** Even if a defendant has the required *mens rea* for an attempt, the defendant must commit the *actus reus*. At common law, the *actus reus* of the crime of attempt was defined in many different ways, and included the following tests: (1) The "physical proximity" doctrine under which defendant must have committed an overt act that was proximate to the completed crime, or directly tending toward the completion of the crime, or amounting to the commencement of the consumation; (2) The "dangerous proximity" doctrine under which the court considers the gravity and probability of the offense, and the nearness of the act to the crime; (3) The "indispensable element" test (similar to the proximity tests) which emphasizes whether an indispensable aspect of the criminal endeavor remains, over which the actor has not yet acquired control; (4) The "probable desistance" test which focuses on whether, in the ordinary and natural course of events, without interruption from an outside source, defendant's conduct will result in the crime intended; (5) The "abnormal step" approach under which the focus is on whether defendant's conduct has gone beyond the point where the ordinary person would think better of his or her conduct and desist; (6) The "*res ipsa loquitur*" or unequivocality test under which the defendant's conduct must manifest an intent to commit a crime.

MPC Definition of *Actus Reus*. The Model Penal Code defines the crime of attempt as requiring a "substantial step" toward commission of the crime. Various acts can constitute a substantial step, if they are "strongly corroborative of the actor's criminal purpose, including: (a) lying in wait, searching for or following the contemplated victim of the crime; (b) enticing or seeking to entice the contemplated victim of the crime to go to the place contemplated for its commission; (c) reconnoitering the place contemplated for the commission of the crime; (d) unlawful entry of a structure, vehicle or enclosure in which it is contemplated that the crime will be committed; (e) possession of materials to be employed in the commission of the crime, that are specially designed for such unlawful use or that can serve no lawful purpose of the actor under the circumstances; (f) possession, collection or fabrication of materials to be employed in the commission of the crime, at or near the place contemplated for its commission, if such possession, collection or fabrication serves no lawful purpose of the actor under the circumstances; (g) soliciting an innocent agent to engage in conduct constituting an element of the crime."

Attempt and Abandonment. With many crimes, if defendant commits both the *actus reus* and the *mens rea* of the crime, the crime is complete and chargeable.

Inchoate Offenses: Attempt & Conspiracy

By contrast, since attempt can involve something less than the completed crime, abandonment of the criminal enterprise is still possible. The Model Penal Code recognizes the defense of abandonment under certain circumstances.

Impossibility. The crime of Attempt is somewhat unique in that an individual may attempt to commit a crime under circumstances where it is impossible to actually complete the crime (*e.g.*, an individual tries to murder someone who is already dead). The courts, and criminal statutes, recognize the defense of impossibility in some circumstances (although defendant may be guilty of some other crime).

Bilateral vs. Unilateral Conspiracies. In bilateral conspiracy jurisdictions, two or more persons must conspire for a conspiracy to exist. In unilateral jurisdictions, an accused can be found guilty of conspiracy if the accused believes that he or she has agreed to commit a crime with another, whether or not that is true.

Mens Rea. The *mens rea* of conspiracy is the intent to agree with another person to commit a crime and the intent to commit that crime. There is no conspiracy to commit a crime when defendant has only the *mens rea* of recklessness or negligence. And the mere knowledge that someone else intends to commit a crime is not enough to make a person a conspirator.

Actus Reus. The *actus reus* of conspiracy is an agreement with another person to commit a criminal act. A single conspiracy can have multiple criminal objectives. The number of conspiracies that exist is determined by the number of conspiratorial agreements, not by the number of criminal objectives.

Overt Act. Some conspiracy statutes also require proof of an overt act undertaken by one of the co-conspirators in furtherance of the conspiracy. This overt act is separate from the *actus reus* of the conspiracy.

Renunciation or Withdrawal. Some jurisdictions allow for a renunciation or withdrawal defense to the crime of conspiracy if the accused's actions are voluntary and complete and he or she provides assistance in preventing the crime.

Merger. Unless the law expressly provides otherwise, conspiracy convictions do not merge with convictions for crimes which were an object of the conspiracy.

Culpability of Co-Conspirators. Many jurisdictions follow the federal criminal law approach which provides that a conspirator is deemed culpable for the reasonably foreseeable criminal acts of his or her co-conspirators undertaken in furtherance of the conspiracy.

> **Major Themes**
>
> **a. Influence of the MPC**—The MPC's influence led to the simplification and expansion of the attempt crime in most states. That crime, now recognizes attempt liability for the conduct of taking a "substantial step" toward the commission of a crime, when that step is strongly corroborative of criminal purpose. Other popular MPC reforms include elimination of the impossibility defense and imposition of strict limitations on the abandonment defense.
>
> **b. Traditional Approaches**—Some states continue to rely on one of the various common law formulas for the *actus reus* of attempt, which require that a person's conduct must go beyond mere preparation and must come within a close degree of proximity to the completion of the crime. Although these formulas may be more difficult to apply than the "substantial step" test, they usually require evidence of conduct that supplies more unequivocal proof of the required *mens rea* of criminal purpose.
>
> **c. Controversial Crime**—Most (but not all) jurisdictions include a conspiracy offense in their crimes codes. Many jurisdictions do not, however, believing that the conduct covered by that offense is adequately criminalized by other substantive or inchoate offenses. And some commentators have argued that conspiracy no longer serves a useful or sensible function and that the conspiratorial "net" extends too broadly to individuals who were not significantly involved in the supposed criminal enterprise.
>
> **d. Change in Conspiracy Approach**—The traditional "bilateral" conspiracy crime was designed to respond to the supposed special danger to society posed by actual group criminal activity; the modern "unilateral" approach, in contrast, criminalizes the actions of a single individual who is or simply believes that he or she is agreeing with another person to commit a criminal act.

B. ATTEMPT

Although the criminal law does not punish people merely for "bad thoughts," the State does have an interest in intervening early before a suspect actually commits a crime and actually causes harm. The law of attempt plays this role in the law. The evidence required for an attempt conviction, both as to the *mens rea* and the *actus reus*, can vary from state to state.

1. *Mens Rea*

STATE V. MAESTAS
652 P.2d 903 (Utah 1982).

HALL, CHIEF JUSTICE:

Defendant allegedly robbed a bank and attempted to escape in a black van. Sergeant Cecil Throckmorton of the Salt Lake City Police Department had stationed his car on an island in the center of the street and was standing beside the car awaiting defendant's approach. As defendant's van passed, Sergeant Throckmorton fired a shot in an unsuccessful attempt to disable it. As he drove away, defendant allegedly leaned out of the van window holding a 38-caliber revolver and fired it at the officer. Defendant drove several blocks further before crashing into a parked car, at which time he was apprehended by other police officers.

Defendant was found guilty of attempted first degree murder. The court granted defendant's motion to dismiss on the ground that "specific intent to kill could not properly be inferred from the evidence." U.C.A., 1953, 76–5–202(1) describes the elements of first degree murder:

> Criminal homicide constitutes murder in the first degree if the actor intentionally or knowingly causes the death of another under any of the following circumstances:
>
> * * *
>
> (d) The homicide was committed while the actor was engaged in the commission of, or an attempt to commit, or flight after committing or attempting to commit, aggravated robbery, robbery, rape, forcible arson, aggravated burglary, burglary, aggravated kidnapping or kidnapping.
>
> (e) The homicide was committed for the purpose of avoiding or preventing an arrest by a peace officer acting under color of legal authority or for the purpose of effecting an escape from lawful custody.

In order to find defendant guilty of attempted first degree murder, the jury was required to determine beyond a reasonable doubt that he "intentionally or knowingly" attempted to kill Sergeant Throckmorton under one of the circumstances listed above.

Defendant argues that the crime of attempted murder requires a stronger showing of intent than does the crime of murder itself. This theory derives from the common law rule that intent is a necessary element of every "attempt" crime even where the corresponding completed crime does not require intent. As an example, defendant cites cases which discuss the common law rule that there is no crime of "attempted felony murder" because of the fact that felony murder requires no specific intent to kill, while an "attempt" crime must always consist of an intent to commit the corresponding completed crime accompanied by a substantial step toward realization of that crime. Defendant then attempts to carry this rule one step further by asserting that the crime of attempted first degree murder with which he is charged requires a "specific intent" beyond that which would have been required in order to prove first degree murder itself if an actual death had occurred. Defendant does not argue that the evidence concerning intent would have failed to support a first degree murder conviction in the event of actual death, but rather that such evidence fell short of establishing the stronger "specific intent" allegedly required for the crime of attempted first degree murder.

The statute makes clear that regardless of any requirements which the common law may impose concerning "attempt" crimes, Utah law requires only "the kind of culpability otherwise required for the commission of the completed offense." Thus, there can be no difference between the intent required as an element of the crime of attempted first degree murder and that required for first degree murder itself.

Even if the common law rule of attempt governed this Court's interpretation of the elements of that crime, that rule would not require the result urged by defendant. That rule differentiates between the intent requirements for an attempted and a completed crime only where the completed crime may be committed without the intent to commit that crime in particular, as in the case of felony murder. Where an intent to commit the particular crime committed is an element of the completed crime, the same intent requirement applies to the corresponding "attempt" crime, even at common law. Thus, Utah's first degree murder statute, which does contain such an intent requirement, would not fall within the rule cited by defendant even under common law principles.

There was "substantial evidence" from which the jury could have concluded not only that defendant aimed and fired a revolver at Sergeant Throckmorton, but also that he did so "intentionally or knowingly." Because of the near impossibility of proving intent directly, Utah law clearly permits the inference of such intent from the actions of a defendant considered in light of surrounding circumstances.

In order to determine defendant's intent, the jury might have considered further evidence concerning his conduct and the circumstances surrounding the alleged gunshot, including testimony that he had just committed a bank robbery, that he had attempted to avoid capture by throwing money out of the van window and that he had demonstrated an indifference to the safety of others by driving erratically and on the wrong side of the traffic divider in his efforts to elude pursuers. We therefore hold that substantial evidence supported the jury in finding that the state had established both the act and the intent components of attempted first degree murder by defendant.

Reversed.

POINT FOR DISCUSSION

Model Penal Code

Consider the MPC's approach to defining the crime of Attempt:

§ 5.01. Criminal Attempt

(1) *Definition of Attempt.* A person is guilty of an attempt to commit a crime if, acting with the kind of culpability otherwise required for commission of the crime, he:

    (a) purposely engages in conduct that would constitute the crime if the attendant circumstances were as he believes them to be; or

    (b) when causing a particular result is an element of the crime, does or omits to do anything with the purpose of causing or with the belief that it will cause such result without further conduct on his part; or

    (c) purposely does or omits to do anything that, under the circumstances as he believes them to be, is an act or omission constituting a substantial step in a course of conduct planned to culminate in his commission of the crime.

2. *Actus Reus*

Even if defendant has the required *mens rea* for attempt, it may be difficult to prove the *actus reus*. Different jurisdictions define the *actus reus* using a variety of statutory and case law formulas.

COMMONWEALTH V. PEASLEE
177 Mass. 267, 59 N.E. 55 (1901).

HOLMES, C.J.

Defendant was indicted for an attempt to burn a building and certain goods therein, with intent to injure the insurers of the same. The defense is that the overt acts alleged and proved do not amount to an offense.

Defendant constructed and arranged combustibles in the building in such a way that they were ready to be lighted, and if lighted would have set fire to the building and its contents. To be exact, the plan would have required a candle which was standing on a shelf six feet away to be placed on a piece of wood in a pan of turpentine and lighted. The defendant offered to pay a younger man to go to the building, seemingly some miles away, and carry out the plan. This was refused. Later the defendant and the young man drove towards the building, but when within a quarter of a mile the defendant said that he had changed his mind, and drove away. This is as near as he ever came to accomplishing what he had in contemplation.

The question is whether defendant's acts come near enough to the accomplishment of the substantive offense to be punishable. The statute does not punish every act done towards the commission of a crime, but only such acts done in an attempt to commit it. The most common types of an attempt are either an act which is intended to bring about the substantive crime, and which sets in motion natural forces that would bring it about in the expected course of events, but for the unforeseen interruption, as in this case, if the candle had been set in its place and lighted, but had been put out by the police, or an act which is intended to bring about the substantive crime, and would bring it about but for a mistake of judgment in a matter of nice estimate or experiment, as when a pistol is fired at a man, but misses him, or when one tries to pick a pocket which turns out to be empty. In either case the would-be criminal has done his last act.

New considerations come in when further acts on the part of the person who has taken the first steps are necessary before the substantive crime can come to pass. In this class of cases there is still a chance that the would-be criminal may change his mind. In strictness, such first steps cannot be described as an attempt, because that word suggests an act seemingly sufficient to accomplish the end, and has been supposed to have no other meaning. That an overt act, although coupled with an intent to commit the crime, commonly is not punishable if further acts are contemplated as needful, is expressed in the familiar rule that preparation is not an attempt. But some preparations may amount to an attempt. It is a question of degree. If the preparation comes very near to the accomplishment of the act, the intent to complete it renders the crime so probable that the act will be a misdemeanor, although there is still a *locus poenitentiae*, in the need of a further exertion of the will to complete the crime. The degree of proximity held sufficient may vary with circumstances, including, among other things, the apprehension which the particular crime is calculated to excite.

As a further illustration, when the servant of a contractor had delivered short rations by the help of a weight, which he had substituted for the true one, intending to steal the meat left over, it was held by four judges that he could be convicted of an attempt to steal. *Cheeseman's Case*, Leigh & C. 140, 10 Wkly. Rep. 255. So, lighting a match with intent to set fire to a haystack, although the prisoner desisted on discovering that he was watched. So, getting into a stall with a poisoned potato, intending to give it to a horse there, which the prisoner was prevented from doing by his arrest.

In this case, a majority of the court is of opinion that the exceptions must be sustained. A mere collection and preparation of materials in a room for the purpose of setting fire to them, unaccompanied by any present intent to set the fire, would be too remote. If the accused intended to rely upon his own hands to the end, he must be shown to have had a present intent to accomplish the crime without much delay, and to have had this intent at a time and place where he was able to carry it out. We are not aware of any carefully considered case that has gone further than this. The indictment would have been proved if, for instance, the evidence had been that the defendant had been frightened by the police as he was about to light the candle. On the other hand, if the offense is to be made out by showing a preparation of the room, and a solicitation of someone else to set the fire, which solicitation, if successful, would have been the defendant's last act, the solicitation must be alleged as one of the overt acts. If the indictment had been properly drawn, we have no question that the defendant might have been convicted.

Exceptions sustained.

POINTS FOR DISCUSSION

a. Common Law Definitions

At common law, the *actus reus* of the crime of attempt was defined in many different ways. Consider the following common law tests as summarized by the drafters of the MPC:

(1) The "physical proximity" doctrine under which defendant must have committed an overt act that was proximate to the completed crime, or directly tending toward the completion of the crime, or amounting to the commencement of the consummation.

(2) The "dangerous proximity" doctrine under which the court considers the gravity and probability of the offense, and the nearness of the act to the crime.

(3) The "indispensable element" test (similar to the proximity tests) which emphasizes whether an indispensable aspect of the criminal endeavor remains over which the actor has not yet acquired control.

(4) The "probable desistance" test which focuses on whether, in the ordinary and natural course of events, without interruption from an outside source, defendant's conduct will result in the crime intended.

(5) The "abnormal step" approach under which the focus is on whether defendant's conduct has gone beyond the point where the normal citizen would think better of his conduct and desist.

(6) The "*res ipsa* loquitur" or unequivocality test under which the defendant's conduct manifests an intent to commit a crime.

See United States v. Mandujano, 499 F.2d 370, 376 (5th Cir. 1974).

b. **Model Penal Code**

Consider the MPC's definition of a "substantial step":

§ 5.01. Criminal Attempt.

* * *

(2) **Conduct That May Be Held Substantial Step Under Subsection (1)(c).** Conduct shall not be held to constitute a substantial step under Subsection (1)(c) of this Section unless it is strongly corroborative of the actor's criminal purpose. Without negativing the sufficiency of other conduct, the following, if strongly corroborative of the actor's criminal purpose, shall not be held insufficient as a matter of law:

(a) lying in wait, searching for or following the contemplated victim of the crime;

(b) enticing or seeking to entice the contemplated victim of the crime to go to the place contemplated for its commission;

(c) reconnoitering the place contemplated for the commission of the crime;

(d) unlawful entry of a structure, vehicle or enclosure in which it is contemplated that the crime will be committed;

(e) possession of materials to be employed in the commission of the crime, that are specially designed for such unlawful use or that can serve no lawful purpose of the actor under the circumstances;

(f) possession, collection or fabrication of materials to be employed in the commission of the crime, at or near the place contemplated for its commission, if such possession, collection or fabrication serves no lawful purpose of the actor under the circumstances;

(g) soliciting an innocent agent to engage in conduct constituting an element of the crime.

(3) **Conduct Designed to Aid Another in Commission of a Crime.** A person who engages in conduct designed to aid another to commit a crime that would establish his complicity under Section 2.06 if the crime were committed by such other person, is guilty of an attempt to commit the crime, although the crime is not committed or attempted by such other person.

PEOPLE V. RIZZO
246 N.Y. 334, 158 N.E. 888 (1927).

CRANE, J.

Defendant has been convicted of an attempt to commit the crime of robbery in the first degree. There is no doubt that he had the intention to commit robbery, if he got the chance. An examination of the facts is necessary to determine whether his acts were in preparation to commit the crime if the opportunity offered, or constituted a crime in itself, known to our law as an attempt to commit robbery in the first degree. Defendant Rizzo, with three others, planned to rob Charles Rao of a pay roll which he was to carry from the bank for the United Lathing Company. Defendants, two of whom had firearms, started out in an automobile, looking for Rao. They went to the bank from which he was supposed to get the money and to various buildings being constructed by the United Lathing Company. At last they came to One Hundred and Eightieth Street and Morris Park Avenue. By this time, they were being watched and followed by two police officers. As Rizzo jumped out of the car and ran into the building, all four were arrested. The four men intended to rob the pay roll man, whoever he was. They were looking for him, but they had not seen or discovered him up to the time they were arrested.

Does this constitute the crime of an attempt to commit robbery in the first degree? The Penal Law, § 2, prescribes:" An act, done with intent to commit a crime, and tending but failing to effect its commission, is "an attempt to commit that crime."

The word "tending" is very indefinite. "Tending" means to exert activity in a particular direction. Any act in preparation to commit a crime may be said to have a tendency towards its accomplishment. The procuring of the automobile, searching the streets looking for the desired victim, were in reality acts tending toward the commission of the proposed crime. The law, however, had recognized that many acts in the way of preparation are too remote to constitute the crime of attempt. The line has been drawn between those acts which are remote and those which are proximate and near to the consummation. The law must be practical, and therefore considers those acts only as tending to the commission of the crime which are so near to its accomplishment that in all reasonable probability the crime itself would have been committed, but for timely interference. The cases which have been before the courts express this idea in different language, but the idea remains the same. The act or acts must come or advance very near to the accomplishment of the intended crime.

In *Hyde v. U.S.*, 225 U. S. 347, it was stated that the act amounts to an attempt when it is so near to the result that the danger of success is very great. "There must be dangerous proximity to success." Halsbury in his "Laws of England," says:" An act in order to be a criminal attempt must be immediately and not remotely connected with an directly tending to the commission of an offense."

The method of committing or attempting crime varies in each case, so that the difficulty, if any, is not with this rule of law regarding an attempt, which is well understood, but with its application to the facts. As I have said before, minds differ over proximity and the nearness of the approach.

How shall we apply this rule of immediate nearness to this case? To constitute the crime of robbery, the money must have been taken from Rao by means of force or violence, or through fear. The crime of attempt to commit robbery was committed, if these defendants did an act tending to the commission of this robbery. Did the acts above described come dangerously near to the taking of Rao's property? Did the acts come so near the commission of robbery that there was reasonable likelihood of its accomplishment but for the interference? These defendants had planned to commit a crime, and were looking around the city for an opportunity to commit it, but had planned to break into a building and were arrested while they were hunting about the streets for the building not knowing where it was. So here these defendants were not guilty of an attempt to commit robbery in the first degree when they had not found or reached the presence of the person they intended to rob.

For these reasons, the judgment of conviction of this defendant appellant must be reversed and a new trial granted.

3. Abandonment

If a defendant has the necessary *mens rea* for attempt, and commits the *actus reus*, should it matter that defendant subsequently "abandons" the attempt?

STATE V. WORKMAN
90 Wash. 2d 443, 584 P.2d 382 (En Banc 1978).

HOROWITZ, JUSTICE.

Defendants Lawrence Dean Workman and Steven Lynn Hughes spent the evening of July 22, 1976 drinking and dancing with their wives in State Line, Idaho. On the way home to Moses Lake, Washington after the taverns closed, defendants decided to commit a robbery. Taking the freeway exit for Spokane, they spotted the Fill-em' Fast Gas Station and chose it as their target. They parked their car in an alley behind the station. Leaving their wives asleep, they took a .22 caliber rifle from the trunk of the car and loaded it. They also took a gunny sack with holes punched in it for eyeholes, and a stocking cap, both intended for use as masks. Then they walked up the alley to a fence behind the station and waited. This was normally a busy time at the station. After about 15 minutes, they moved to a hiding place just behind the pay booth, where they waited again.

At about 2:30 a.m., when business at the station was slack, the attendant took a short walk to get some fresh air and saw defendants, unmasked, behind the pay booth. He returned to the booth and called the police. Defendant Workman later appeared at the window without a mask or gun and asked for a cigarette and match. The attendant refused, and Workman rejoined defendant Hughes. During this period, according to defendants' testimony, they were trying to summon the "courage" to commit the robbery and decide how to do it.

Sometime after the cigarette episode, an unmarked police car took up a position across the street from the station. The police officer could see both the defendants and a second police car which had turned into the alley behind the station. The first car then pulled into the station.

At that time, defendants, having decided not to go through with their plans, started walking away from the station. They testified at their trials that they had not seen the police before they decided to leave. They were stopped and arrested in the alley behind the station. Defendant Hughes was found to have the sawed-off rifle concealed under his clothes.

Defendants were each charged with attempted first degree robbery while armed with a deadly weapon. At their separate trials, each defendant was found guilty. At trial, defendants tried to show they abandoned their plan before the crime of attempt was committed. They proposed an instruction on abandonment derived essentially from a New York statute which sets up abandonment of criminal purpose as an affirmative defense to the crime of attempt. The trial courts both rejected the proposed instruction and gave an instruction properly based on our attempt statute.

The instruction, given correctly, stated that a person is guilty of attempt if, with intent to commit a specific crime, he does any act which is a substantial step towards the commission of the crime. The instruction qualified the meaning of a "substantial step" by stating that the conduct must be more than mere preparation. Defendants contend, however, that the statutory language, "substantial step," is unconstitutionally vague unless further defined, that an instruction on abandonment is necessary in order to properly define it, and that without the requested instruction, they were precluded from arguing their theory of the case to the jury.

We disagree. The question of what constitutes a "substantial step" under the particular facts of the case is for the trier of fact. The instruction given informed the jury that mere preparation would not be sufficient, that something more must be present in order to constitute a substantial step. When preparation ends and an attempt begins, depends on the facts of the particular case. We cannot agree that the instruction given was unconstitutionally vague.

Furthermore, an instruction relating to abandonment is neither necessary, nor particularly helpful in defining the meaning of a substantial step. Once a substantial step has been taken, and the crime of attempt is accomplished, the crime cannot be abandoned. Defendants' attempt to show they abandoned their plan is thus relevant only if the abandonment occurred before a substantial step was taken. Through arguing their theory at trial, they could only have hoped to show they never took a substantial step toward the specific crime. Abandonment is not, however, a true defense to the crime of attempt under our statute that is, a showing of abandonment does not negate the State's allegation that a substantial step occurred. Thus, pursuing the theory of abandonment could only be a strategy for showing why a substantial step was never taken. Defendants could not thereby show whether such a step was taken. We therefore conclude an instruction on abandonment is not necessary as a matter of law to properly define a "substantial step."

It is so ordered.

POINT FOR DISCUSSION

Model Penal Code

The MPC takes the following position regarding abandonment:

§ 5.01   Criminal Attempt.

* * *

(4) **Renunciation of Criminal Purpose.** When the actor's conduct would otherwise constitute an attempt under Subsection (1)(b) or (1)(c) of this Section, it is an affirmative defense that he abandoned his effort to commit the crime or otherwise prevented its commission, under circumstances manifesting a complete and voluntary renunciation of his criminal purpose. The establishment of such defense does not, however, affect the liability of an accomplice who did not join in such abandonment or prevention.

Within the meaning of this Article, renunciation of criminal purpose is not voluntary if it is motivated, in whole or in part, by circumstances, not present or apparent at the inception of the actor's course of conduct, that increase the probability of detection or apprehension or that make more difficult the accomplishment of the criminal purpose. Renunciation is not complete if it is motivated by a decision to postpone the criminal conduct until a more advantageous time or to transfer the criminal effort to another but similar objective or victim.

4. Impossibility

Suppose a defendant tries to commit a crime which turns out to be impossible to commit. Has the defendant committed attempt? Should defendant be punished?

STATE V. CURTIS
157 Vt. 629, 603 A.2d 356 (1992).

MORSE, JUSTICE.

Defendant shot a deer decoy and was convicted of attempting to take a wild deer out of season under 10 V.S.A. § 4745. His principal argument on appeal is that the defense of legal impossibility precludes a conviction under this statute and under Vermont's attempt statute.

A person is prohibited from taking "a wild deer except specified wild deer during the seasons provided by law." A person is guilty of attempting a crime by doing "an act toward its commission but by reason of being interrupted or prevented fails in the execution of the same." We have held that an "attempt consists not only of an intent to commit a particular crime, but some overt act designed to carry out such intent." Undoubtedly, defendant's behavior demonstrated an intent to take a wild deer out of season. He performed an overt act toward the commission of the intended crime. His conduct went as far as it could in achieving the goal of taking a wild deer out of season. Except for the fact that the "wild deer" in his sights was not real, he would be guilty of the crime prohibited by § 4745.

Defendant was "prevented" from shooting a wild deer because he was tricked into shooting a decoy. We see no meaningful distinction between the infeasible act of putting a bullet-proof protection on a live deer to prevent its demise and the use of a decoy to divert a hunter's attention from a live deer. Either way, live deer are given a measure of protection.

Defendant possessed the specific intent to take a wild deer out of season. Defendant's failure to actually take a live wild deer is of no consequence. This is not a case where defendant's conduct was equivocal. There was no testimony that defendant thought the decoy was not a live deer. Failure to find that defendant's actions amount to a crime would frustrate the goals underlying wildlife protection legislation. A contrary holding would oblige state and local officials to respond to illegal hunting by more cumbersome, dangerous, after-the-fact methods. Prosecution based on a fresh kill defeats the purpose of legislation drafted to preserve wildlife. The difficulties and risks associated with detecting poachers without the benefit of decoys are manifest. As stated by a game warden at trial, there is a serious concern for the safe detection of poachers, and the decoy system was established in response to those concerns.

Affirmed.

POINT FOR DISCUSSION

The *Jaffe* Rule

In *People v. Jaffe*, 185 N.Y. 497, 78 N.E. 169 (1906), defendant was charged with attempting to receive stolen property under a statute providing "that the accused shall have known to have been stolen or wrongfully appropriated in such a manner as to constitute larceny." When the property was sold to defendant, the police and the owner were acting in collaboration so that the goods were not actually stolen. The court reversed the conviction: "The defendant could not know that the property possessed the character of stolen property when it had not in fact been acquired by theft." The *Jaffe* rule was rejected in *People v. Rojas*, 55 Cal. 2d 252, 358 P.2d 921, 10 Cal. Rptr. 465 (1961): "The criminality of the attempt is not destroyed by the fact that the goods, having been recovered by the police had, unknown to defendants, lost their 'stolen' status." *See also People v. Rollino*, 37 Misc. 2d 14, 233 N.Y.S.2d 580 (1962).

PEOPLE V. DLUGASH
41 N.Y.2d 725, 363 N.E.2d 1155, 395 N.Y.S.2d 419 (1977).

JASEN, JUDGE.

The issue is whether an individual's intentions and actions, though failing to achieve a manifest and malevolent criminal purpose, constitute a danger to organized society of sufficient magnitude to warrant the imposition of criminal sanctions. Difficulties in theoretical analysis and concomitant debate over very pragmatic questions of blameworthiness appear dramatically in reference to situations where the criminal attempt failed to achieve its purpose solely because the factual or legal context in which the individual acted was not as the actor supposed them to be. Phrased somewhat differently, the concern centers on whether an individual should be liable for an attempt to commit a crime when, unknown to him, it was impossible to successfully complete the crime attempted. For years, serious studies have been made on the subject in an effort to resolve the continuing controversy when, if at all, the impossibility of successfully completing the criminal act should preclude liability for even making the futile attempt. The 1967 revision of the Penal Law approached the impossibility defense to the inchoate crime of attempt in a novel fashion. The statute provides that, if a person engages in conduct which would otherwise constitute an attempt to commit a crime, "it is no defense to a prosecution for such attempt that the crime charged to have been attempted was, under the attendant circumstances, factually or legally impossible of commission, if such crime could have been committed had the attendant circumstances been as such person believed them to be." This appeal presents to us, for the first time, a case involving the application of the modern statute.

Defendant admitted that, on the night in question, he, Bush and Geller had been out drinking. Bush had been staying at Geller's apartment and during the evening, Geller several times demanded that Bush pay $100 towards the rent on the apartment. Bush told Geller that "you better shut up or you're going to get a bullet." All three returned to Geller's apartment at midnight and continued to drink. When Geller again pressed his demand for rent money, Bush drew his .38 caliber pistol, aimed it at Geller and fired three times. Geller fell to the floor. After the passage of a few minutes, perhaps two, perhaps as much as five, defendant walked over to the fallen Geller, drew his .25 caliber pistol, and fired approximately five shots in the victim's head and face. At the time defendant shot at Geller, Geller was not moving and his eyes were closed.

The jury found the defendant guilty of murder. All three medical expert witnesses testified that they could not, with any degree of medical certainty, state whether the victim had been alive at the time the latter shots were fired by the defendant. Thus, the People failed to prove beyond a reasonable doubt that the victim had been alive at the time he was shot by the defendant. Whatever else it may be, it is not murder to shoot a dead body. Man dies but once.

The most intriguing attempt cases are those where the attempt to commit a crime was unsuccessful due to mistakes of fact or law on the part of the would-be criminal. A general rule developed in most American jurisdictions that legal impossibility is a good defense but factual impossibility is not. An example is Francis Wharton's classic hypothetical involving Lady Eldon and her French lace. Lady Eldon, traveling in Europe, purchased a quantity of French lace at a high price, intending to smuggle it into England without payment of the duty. When discovered in a customs search, the lace turned out to be of English origin, of little value and not subject to duty. The traditional view is that Lady Eldon is not liable for an attempt to smuggle.

On the other hand, factual impossibility was no defense. For example, a man was held liable for attempted murder when he shot into the room in which his target usually slept and, fortuitously, the target was sleeping elsewhere in the house that night. Although one bullet struck the target's customary pillow, attainment of the criminal objective was factually impossible. *State v. Moretti*, 52 N.J. 182, 244 A.2d 499, presents a similar instance of factual impossibility. Defendant agreed to perform an abortion, then a criminal act, upon a female undercover police investigator who was not, in fact, pregnant. The court sustained the conviction, ruling that "when the consequences sought by a defendant are forbidden by the law as criminal, it is no defense that the defendant could not succeed in reaching his goal because of circumstances unknown to him."

The New York cases can be parsed out along similar lines. One of the leading cases on legal impossibility is *People v. Jaffe*, 185 N.Y. 497, 78 N.E. 169, in which we held that there was no liability for the attempted receipt of stolen property when the property received by defendant in the belief that it was stolen was, in fact under the control of the true owner. Similarly, in *People v. Teal*, 196 N.Y. 372, 89 N.E. 1086, a conviction for attempted subornation of perjury was overturned on the theory that the testimony attempted to be suborned was irrelevant to the merits of the case. Since it was not subornation of perjury to solicit false, but irrelevant, testimony, "the person through whose procuration the testimony is given cannot be guilty of subornation of perjury and, by the same rule, an unsuccessful attempt to that which is not a crime when effectuated, cannot be held to be an attempt to commit the crime specified." Factual impossibility, however, was no defense. Thus, a man could be held for attempted grand larceny when he picked an empty pocket.

As can be seen, the distinction between "factual" and "legal" impossibility was a nice one indeed and the courts tended to place a greater value on legal form than on any substantive danger the defendant's actions posed for society. The approach of the draftsmen of the Model Penal Code was to eliminate the defense of impossibility in virtually all situations. Under the code provision, to constitute an attempt, it is still necessary that the result intended or desired by the actor constitute a crime. However, the code suggested a fundamental change to shift the locus of analysis to the actor's mental frame of reference and away from undue dependence upon external considerations. The basic premise of the code provision is that what was in the actor's own mind should be the standard for determining his dangerousness to society and, hence, his liability for attempted criminal conduct.

In the belief that neither of the two branches of the traditional impossibility arguments detracts from the offender's moral culpability, the Legislature substantially carried the code's treatment of impossibility into the 1967 revision of the Penal Law. Thus, a person is guilty of an attempt when, with intent to commit a crime, he engages in conduct which tends to effect the commission of such crime. It is no defense that, under the attendant circumstances, the crime was factually or legally impossible of commission, "if such crime could have been committed had the attendant circumstances been as such person believed them to be." Thus, if defendant believed the victim to be alive at the time of the shooting, it is no defense to the charge of attempted murder that the victim may have been dead.

Turning to the facts of the case before us, the jury could conclude that the defendant believed Geller to be alive at the time defendant fired shots into Geller's head. Defendant admitted firing five shots at a most vital part of the victim's anatomy from virtually point blank range. Although defendant contended that the victim had already been grievously wounded by another, the jury could conclude that the defendant's purpose and intention was to administer the coup de grace.

The jury convicted the defendant of murder. Necessarily, they found that defendant intended to kill a live human being. Subsumed within this finding is the conclusion that defendant acted in the belief that Geller was alive. Thus, there is no need for additional fact findings by a jury. Although it was not established beyond a reasonable doubt that Geller was, in fact, alive, such is no defense to attempted murder since a murder would have been committed "had the attendant circumstances been as (defendant) believed them to be." The jury necessarily found that defendant believed Geller to be alive when defendant shot at him.

The order of the Appellate Division should be modified and the case remitted to the Appellate Division for its review of the facts and for further proceedings with respect to the sentence in the event that the facts are found favorably to the People.

> **Hypo 1: *Love Rival***
>
> In February, 2007, NASA Astronaut Lisa Marie Nowak was charged with attempted murder for an attack on another woman, an Air Force captain. The prosecution alleged that Nowak drove 900 miles from Houston to Florida, and that she carried a wig to disguise her appearance. She brought a steel mallet, a knife, pepper spray, rubber tubing, latex gloves and garbage bags with her. The prosecution also alleged that she wore a diaper during her drive so that she would not have to stop. Nowak claims that she did not intend to murder the captain, or even to hurt her, but only to talk to her and perhaps intimidate her. However, Nowak did approach the captain's car in a parking lot and a minor altercation ensued before Nowak drove off. If you are the prosecutor, how do you go about proving intent to murder?

Inchoate Offenses: Attempt & Conspiracy

> ### Hypo 2: *Attempted Assault?*
>
> Defendant was charged with attempt to commit assault with intent to rape. When Ms. Allen left the "Tiny Diner," she noticed defendant sitting in a truck. According to Allen, as she passed the truck, defendant said something unintelligible, and opened the door. He then followed her down the street until she stopped at a friend's house. By this time, defendant was within two or three feet of her. She waited ten minutes for appellant to pass. When she proceeded, defendant came toward her from behind a telephone pole. When a man unexpectedly emerged from a nearby house, defendant immediately turned and went back to his truck. Defendant gave a different version of the facts. He testified that, on the evening in question, he was carrying a load of junk-iron with a partner, and happened to stop near the diner. When the partner disappeared, defendant walked up the street to look for him. As he did, he saw Ms. Allen. He waited until she had gone, and then walked up the street. When he reached the telephone pole, he remained there for 25 or 30 minutes to see if his partner would arrive. He denied that he followed Allen or made any gesture toward molesting her. Under the circumstances, is there sufficient evidence to conclude that defendant had the *mens rea* for the crime of attempted assault with intent to commit rape? *See McQuirter v. State*, 36 Ala. App. 707, 63 So.2d 388 (1953).

> ### Hypo 3: *An Attempted Attack on the Capitol?*
>
> Police receive information suggesting that a man is planning an attack on the U.S Capitol building and the Pentagon using remote-controlled aircraft armed with explosives. They receive this information from jihadi websites which indicate that the man is "evil," and that he is planning to conduct a "jihad" against the U.S. On those websites, the man indicates that he wants to strike a "psychological blow" against the "enemies of Allah" by striking at the Pentagon and the Capitol.

Hypo 4: *Actus Reus*

Consider the following problems under the various common law tests, and the MPC's substantial step test, to decide whether the *actus reus* of attempt has been committed. As you think about how these tests apply, consider whether one test is preferable to the others. Is one test more consistent with justifications for punishment? Does a particular test encourage the police to intervene too early or too late?

Searching for the Intended Victim. Carrying a firearm and ammunition, the Ortiz brothers leave their apartment in search of Jose Rodriguez. The Ortiz and Rodriguez families were feuding, and the Ortizes believed that Rodriguez had gone to their father's apartment with a gun. The Ortizes drove through Rodriguez's neighborhood six times hoping to find him. When they could not find him, the Ortizes drove to their father's apartment. As the vehicle arrived at the apartment building, the police stopped the brothers, who admitted that they wanted to "hurt" Rodriguez. What tests would allow conviction for attempted assault and battery with a dangerous weapon on Rodriguez? *See Commonwealth v. Ortiz*, 408 Mass. 463, 560 N.E.2d 698 (1990).

Approaching the Intended Victim with a Loaded Weapon. Defendant, who threatened to kill Delbert Jeans for annoying his wife, went to a field where Jeans was working. Carrying a rifle, defendant walked in a direct line toward Jeans who was 250 yards away. When defendant was 100 yards away, he stopped to load his rifle. At no time did he take aim. When Jeans saw defendant, Jeans fled. Defendant started to chase after Jeans, but another man stepped in and took the rifle from Jeans. Defendant was drunk and offered no resistance. The gun was loaded with a .22-caliber long, or high-speed, cartridge. What tests would allow conviction for attempted murder? *See People v. Miller*, 2 Cal. 2d 527, 42 P.2d 308 (1935).

The Men in the Weeds. At 6:15 a.m., the police are informed that two armed men are hiding behind a service station. When a police officer arrives, he sees defendant crouched in the weeds in an empty lot 20 to 30 feet from the station. Defendant jumps up, climbs a fence, and runs down an adjoining street. He throws away a gun before he scales the fence. Minutes later, defendant is found hiding in the weeds behind a company some 200 feet from the service station. He has removed his shirt, and has a black nylon stocking with a knot in the end. Although defendant claims that he went to the gas station to buy cigarettes, he has no money. On these facts, can defendant be convicted of the crime of attempted robbery? How would you argue the case for the State? How might defendant respond? *See People v. Terrell*, 99 Ill. 2d 427, 459 N.E.2d 1337, 77 Ill. Dec. 88 (1984).

Attempted Grand Larceny? Defendant Mahboubian insured his collection of gold and silver Persian antiquities with Lloyd's of London for $18.5 million. He then traveled to New York where he rented a vault at a long-term storage facility, and arranged to have two men steal the art. Although they were expert burglars, when they tried to burglarize the facility, they were apprehended by police. Defendant Mahboubian was charged with staging the theft with the objective of recovering insurance proceeds (*i.e.*, attempted grand larceny). Did he commit the *actus reus* if he never submitted a false claim to his insurer? *See People v. Mahboubian*, 74 N.Y.2d 174, 543 N.E.2d 34, 544 N.Y.S.2d 769 (1989).

Hypo 5: *Attempted Escape?*

Shortly after midnight, a prison guard heard an alarm which indicated that someone was attempting to escape from a prison recreation area. Guards immediately check the prison population, but find no one missing. In the recreation area, they find that a piece of barbed wire has been cut, and they also find a prison laundry bag filled with civilian clothing. The next morning, without prompting, defendant voluntarily tells a guard that, "I was gonna make a break last night, but I changed my mind because I thought of my family, and I got scared of the consequences." Defendant testified that he was depressed because he had been denied a holiday furlough. Defendant is charged with attempted prison escape. On these facts, should defendant be convicted? Under the MPC, did he sufficiently renounce the attempt? What would you argue on defendant's behalf? How might the State respond? *See Commonwealth v. McCloskey*, 234 Pa. Super. 577, 341 A.2d 500 (1975).

Hypo 6: *Attempted Bank Robbery?*

While his wife was away, defendant rented an office directly over the vault of a bank. Defendant placed drilling tools, acetylene gas tanks, a blow torch, a blanket, and a linoleum rug in the office. Subsequently, defendant drilled two groups of holes in the floor above the vault. The holes did not go through the floor. He came back to the office several times to drill down, covering the holes with the linoleum rug. At some point, defendant's landlord became aware of his activities and notified the police. At trial, defendant testified that he had planned to rob the bank, but that he "began to realize that, even if I were to succeed, a fugitive life of living off of stolen money would not give me enjoyment of life. I still had not given up my plan however. I felt I had made a certain investment of time, money, effort and a certain psychological commitment to the concept. I came back several times thinking I might slowly drill down. When my wife came back, my life as bank robber seemed more and more absurd, and I decided not to go through with it." Under the circumstances, should the defense of abandonment be available to defendant? *See People v. Staples*, 6 Cal. App. 3d 61, 85 Cal. Rptr. 589 (1970).

Hypo 7: *The Pickpocket*

Defendant was observed in a crowded market and was seen to thrust his hand into the pocket of a man. Defendant found the pocket empty and withdrew his hand without obtaining anything. A police officer arrested defendant and charged him with attempted theft. Given that the pocket was empty, can defendant be convicted of attempted theft? *See People v. Twiggs*, 223 Cal. App. 2d 455, 35 Cal. Rptr. 859 (1963); *People v. Moran*, 123 N.Y. 254, 25 N.E. 412 (1890).

Hypo 8: *The Ticket Scalper*

Defendant wants to scalp his tickets to the Louisville-Kentucky basketball game outside the Yum Arena in Louisville, Kentucky. Fearing that it is illegal to scalp tickets (in fact, it is not illegal), defendant is extremely furtive as he approaches prospective purchasers. An undercover detective, who happens to notice defendant's unusual behavior, approaches defendant to ask about the tickets. Realizing that defendant believes that it is illegal to scalp tickets, the officer charges defendant with attempted scalping. Can he be convicted?

> **Hypo 9:** *HIV and Attempted Murder*
>
> Defendant was an HIV positive inmate. On several occasions, he had threatened to kill corrections officers by biting or spitting at them. One day, he bit an officer's hand, causing puncture wounds of the skin during a struggle which he had precipitated. Defendant was charged with attempted murder. At trial, defendant claims that his bite could not transmit HIV. If defendant's claim is correct, can he be convicted of attempted murder? Would it matter whether he knew that a bite could not transmit HIV? *See State v. Smith*, 262 N.J. Super. 487, 621 A.2d 493 (1993).

C. CONSPIRACY

Conspiracy statutes respond to the special danger to society posed by group criminal activity. It is more likely, in theory at least, that a group will succeed in its criminal endeavors than will an individual, acting alone. As a result, most (but not all) crimes codes contain a "general" conspiracy offense, a statute that prohibits individuals from agreeing with someone else to commit another criminal offense. A few jurisdictions, however, do not criminalize conspiracies, and some states limit the criminal conspiracy offense to agreements to commit only particular, serious crimes.

Given the increasingly widespread increase in conspiracy prosecutions over the last few decades in some jurisdictions, and given the fact that some conspiracy offenses overlap with the coverage of other inchoate and substantive offenses, and given the fact that most jurisdictions no longer even require an actual agreement between two or more individuals to make out a conspiracy, some commentators have argued that the crime of conspiracy no longer serves a useful or sensible function. *See, e.g.*, Philip E. Johnson, *The Unnecessary Crime of Conspiracy*, 61 Cal. L. Rev. 1137 (1973).

> **Food for Thought**
>
> As you review the cases and materials that follow, you should ask yourself whether there still is an appropriate place for the offense of conspiracy in our criminal justice system. Is it really necessary? Desirable?

1. Unilateral-Bilateral Jurisdictions

At common law, a conspiracy consisted of an agreement between two or more persons to commit, by concerted action, an unlawful act or a lawful act by unlawful means (the "bilateral" approach, i.e. two or more persons must be in actual agreement). Today, in contrast, most jurisdictions follow the approach of

> **Food for Thought**
>
> Does it make sense to criminalize *one person's* actions as a conspiracy when the original rationale for the conspiracy offense was to respond to the special danger to society posed by *group* criminal activity?

the Model Penal Code, and focus on the act of a single individual who is or believes that he or she is agreeing with another person to commit a criminal act (the "unilateral" approach, i.e. one person who is or believes that he or she is agreeing with someone else).

This "unilateral" or "bilateral" distinction is very important. Given the extensive use of undercover agents by law enforcement agencies, the trend toward adoption of a unilateral—broader and more inclusive—conspiracy offense has resulted in harsher punishment for many defendants who are accused and convicted of conspiracy in addition to other inchoate and/or substantive offenses.

> **Make the Connection**
>
> Entrapment is a complete defense to criminal charges. Some jurisdictions use an "objective" entrapment test which focuses upon the question how outrageous the police conduct was in encouraging or assisting the accused criminal conduct. Other jurisdictions (including the federal) use a "subjective" entrapment test focusing instead on the question whether or not the accused was predisposed to commit the crime in question.

STATE V. HUFF
319 Wis. 2d 258, 769 N.W.2d 154 (Ct. App. 2009).

FINE, J.

Garrett L. Huff appeals the judgment convicting him after a jury trial of three counts of conspiracy to commit election bribery in violation of WIS. STAT. §§ 12.11(1m)(a)1 (election bribery) and 156 939.31 (conspiracy). He claims that because the persons with whom he was found to have conspired were undercover law-enforcement officers ineligible to vote in the election involved, it was impossible for him to have committed the crimes. We affirm.

Huff was convicted of conspiring to violate WIS. STAT. § 12.11(1m)(a)1. This statute provides:

Any person who does any of the following violates this chapter:

(a) Offers, gives, lends or promises to give or lend, or endeavors to procure, anything of value, or any office or employment or any privilege or immunity to, or for, any elector, or to or for any other person, in order to induce any elector to:

1. Go to or refrain from going to the polls.

" 'Anything of value' " is defined to "include any amount of money, or any object which has utility independent of any political message it contains and the value of which exceeds $1." Sec. 12.11(1).

This case arose out of a re-call election in the Sixth Aldermanic District in Milwaukee that was held on April 3, 2007. Qualified electors were able to vote before April 3rd by going to the Milwaukee City Hall. A Milwaukee election official testified that a flyer bearing the disclaimer that it was "paid for and authorized by citizens to re-elect Mike McGee, Jr," the Sixth District incumbent, invited people to attend an "election party" that promised "Free! Food/Drinks" and explained that to be admitted a person "must show vote sticker at door." The election official testified that he was concerned that the flyer was promoting a potential violation of the election law, and that as a result, he contacted the City Attorney. This set the stage for the undercover operations by Milwaukee police officers Wardell Dodds and Dwayne Barnes, and Willie Brantley, a special agent with the Wisconsin Department of Justice. The jury's verdicts found Huff guilty of conspiring with Dodds to violate WIS. STAT. § 12.11(1m)(a)1 on March 15, 2007, and of conspiring with Brantley and Barnes to violate § 12.11(1m)(a)1 on March 27, 2007.

Dodds testified that he went with Barnes to the "election party" at a store in Milwaukee on March 15, 2007. He testified that he met with Huff who told him that he would "take me downtown to vote and that he was working for the Mike McGee, Junior, campaign, that he was taking people downtown to City Hall to vote for Mike McGee." Dodds related that Huff drove him to City Hall and that when they arrived Huff told him to " 'go up to the fifth floor and vote,' " and that Huff also told him: " 'They'll give you something after you vote.' " Dodds testified that Huff paid him five dollars "on the return from City Hall," after Dodds showed Huff an "I voted" sticker. Dodds also testified that when they returned to the store Huff told him that if he, Dodds, knew of "anyone else that want[s] to vote in the election, the ballot, to tell them to come see Mr. Huff. Everyone come see Mr. Huff regarding transportation and getting paid to go vote." Dodds did not live in the Sixth Aldermanic District and could not have legally voted.

Brantley testified that he went to the "election party" store with Barnes on March 27th. According to Brantley's testimony, Barnes told Huff that Brantley was there to vote, and Brantley agreed that he would "if my change was right, indicating that I was going to get paid for the services of voting." Brantley told the jury that he got into a car with Huff who indicated in response to Brantley's question whether "my change was going to be right," that Huff "would take care of me when we got back," by paying him five dollars after they returned to the store.

Huff drove Brantley to City Hall and, Brantley testified, told him to go to the place where he could vote. According to Brantley, when he returned to the car, he showed Huff his "I voted" sticker and "the registration papers." Brantley told the jury that Huff gave him five dollars after they returned to the store. Brantley also did not live in the Sixth Aldermanic District and could not, therefore, legally vote in the re-call election.

Brantley also related Huff's interactions with Barnes, telling the jury that Barnes told Huff that he wanted, as phrased by Brantley, "to get paid for bringing people down for voting." Brantley testified that he saw Huff give Barnes five dollars.

Barnes testified that he went to the "election party" store on both March 15th and March 27th. He reiterated Brantley's testimony that he, Barnes, told Huff that he wanted to be paid for bringing people to the store so they could vote and that Huff then paid him five dollars. Barnes wanted to stay at the store and not vote so his cover story was that he "was on probation for a felony and could not vote."

Huff did not call any witnesses and rested his defense after the State presented its evidence.

Huff contends that because none of the law-enforcement officers pretending to be electors with whom he was convicted of conspiring to violate WIS. STAT. § 12.11(1m)(a)1 could lawfully vote in the April 3, 2007, special election in the Sixth Aldermanic District, they were not bona fide electors, and, accordingly, the conspiracy was a legal impossibility. We disagree.

As material here, WIS. STAT. § 939.31 provides:

> whoever, with intent that a crime be committed, agrees or combines with another for the purpose of committing that crime may, if one or more of the parties to the conspiracy does an act to effect its object, be fined or imprisoned or both not to exceed the maximum provided for the completed crime.

This makes unlawful both unilateral and bilateral conspiracies. *State v. Sample*, 215 Wis. 2d 487, 489, 502, 573 N.W.2d 187, 188, 193–194 (1998). *Sample* explained the difference between the two concepts:

Under a unilateral formulation, the crime of conspiracy is committed when a person agrees to proceed in a prohibited manner." The unilateral approach assesses the subjective, individual behavior of a defendant in determining guilt. Under the unilateral approach, criminal conspiracy will lie even where one of two alleged "co-conspirators" is, unknown to the defendant, an undercover police agent or a police informant who merely feigns participation in the conspiracy. "The immateriality of co-conspirators' legal status to defendant's criminal liability is implicit in the unilateral approach." "Under a bilateral formulation, the crime of conspiracy is committed when two or more persons agree to proceed in [a prohibited] manner."

Thus, under a unilateral conspiracy a person who intends to accomplish the objects of the conspiracy is guilty even though "the other members of the conspiracy never intended that a crime be committed." For example, a person would be guilty of unlawfully conspiring to kill a business associate by hiring an undercover law-enforcement officer to commit the murder even though the officer had no intention to fulfill the contract. This same logic applies to the next step: that is, where the fulfillment of the conspiracy is not only highly unlikely, as in *Sample*, a reverse delivery-of-narcotics sting involving a jail inmate and an undercover officer, or our murder-for-hire hypothetical, but is legally impossible, as is the case here.

Indeed, although there is no published Wisconsin authority dealing with the legally-impossible situation, the law elsewhere is consistent with our next-logical-step conclusion, as revealed by a recent analysis and survey by *United States v. Fiander*, 547 F.3d 1036, 1042–1043 (9th Cir. 2008):

> "It is elementary that a conspiracy may exist and be punished whether or not the substantive crime ensues, for the conspiracy is a distinct evil, dangerous to the public, and so punishable in itself." Thus, we have held that a conspiracy conviction may be sustained even where the goal of the conspiracy is impossible. Our sister circuits are in accord.

As *Sample* recognizes, "under the inchoate crime of conspiracy, by definition *no substantive crime is ever needed*. Wisconsin Stat. § 939.31 focuses on the subjective behavior of the individual defendant."

Huff argues, however, that *State v. Crowley*, 41 Wis. 271 (1876), stands for the proposition that "impossibility" is "a defense to the crime of conspiracy." He is wrong. *Crowley* concerned a plan by the defendants to cheat Daniel Burke by purporting to sell Burke counterfeit money that turned out to be merely a box of sawdust. According to *Crowley*, "Burke purchased the counterfeit money for the purpose and with the intention of uttering and passing it as good money." Burke was arrested by a constable, also a defendant in the case, whom he and another of the defendants bribed. After an extensive analysis of conflicting case law from other jurisdictions, Crowley held that the conspiracy charging a plan to cheat Burke would not lie because Burke was not an innocent victim, noting: "Neither the law nor public policy designs the protection of rogues in their dealings with each other, or to insure fair dealing and truthfulness, as between each other, in their dishonest practices." *Crowley* has nothing to do with an alleged impossibility being a defense to a unilateral conspiracy.

Judgment affirmed and cause remanded with directions.

POINTS FOR DISCUSSION

a. **New Legislation**

If you were planning to enact a conspiracy law today, in a jurisdiction which did not already have one, would you make it unilateral or bilateral? Why did you choose the approach that you chose?

b. **Coverage**

Is it really necessary—or even desirable—to punish individuals who have actually acted alone more harshly, just as if they were not acting alone?

c. **Use of Undercover Agents**

Assuming that your answer to the question above is "yes"—*yes*, it is either necessary or desirable to punish individuals who have acted alone more harshly in these circumstances—does that conclusion give the government the opportunity through the use of undercover agents to essentially "entrap" people into engaging in conspiracies, people who otherwise might not be so inclined?

2. *Mens Rea*

The *mens rea* of conspiracy is often described in the case law as having two separate (and independent) components: (1) the intent to agree with another person to commit a criminal act; and (2) the intent to commit the criminal act itself.

PALMER V. COLORADO
964 P.2d 524 (Colo. 1998).

JUSTICE BENDER delivered the Opinion of the Court.

The defendant, Aaron Palmer, was convicted of multiple felonies for having fired gunshots at several victims. The district court sentenced Palmer to the Department of Corrections for a substantial period of time and imposed a concurrent term for the single count of conspiracy to commit reckless manslaughter that is at issue here. On appeal, Palmer argued that conspiracy to commit reckless manslaughter is not a legally cognizable crime in Colorado. Noting that conspiracy is a crime requiring a specific intention to achieve the forbidden result and that reckless manslaughter is a crime requiring recklessness with respect to the result, Palmer argued that it is logically impossible to specifically intend that an unintended death occur.

The court of appeals determined that conspiracy does not require that the conspirator intend to cause a particular result but merely requires that the conspirator know that he or she and another are engaging in criminal conduct. Since it is possible to know that an agreement to engage in conduct creates a substantial and unjustifiable risk of death, and to disregard that risk, the court of appeals concluded that conspiracy to commit reckless manslaughter is a legally cognizable crime.

Conspiracy is a substantive "offense." Thus, the phrase "with the intent" as it appears in the conspiracy statute refers to and relies on the statutory definition of these words for its meaning: the defendant must have the "conscious objective to cause the specific result proscribed by the statute defining the offense." Since the culpable mental state for the crime of conspiracy is "with intent," conspiracy is a specific intent crime.

The crime of conspiracy requires two mental states. First, the defendant must possess the specific intent to agree to commit a particular crime. Second, the defendant must possess the specific intent to cause the result of the crime that is the subject of the agreement. Specific intent is an integral part of the crime and "must be established with the same certainty as any other material element of the crime."

By contrast, a criminal attempt requires that the accused act with the kind of culpability otherwise required for the commission of the underlying offense. If the underlying offense is a specific intent crime, then the culpable mental state for the crime of attempt will be "intentionally;" if the underlying offense is a general intent crime, then the culpable mental state will be "knowingly." Thus, unlike conspiracy, punishment for attempt "is not confined to actors whose conscious purpose is to perform the proscribed acts or to achieve the proscribed results." Instead, it is enough that the accused knowingly engages in the risk producing conduct that could lead to the result. It is possible to be convicted of attempt without the specific intent to obtain the forbidden result.

Unlike attempt and conspiracy, complicity is not a separate and distinct crime under the Colorado Criminal Code. It is not a violation of, or conduct defined by, a statute for which a fine or imprisonment may be imposed. Rather, complicity is a legal theory in which a person who aids, abets, or advises another who commits an offense is liable for that offense as a principal. The complicity statute creates criminal liability only if the defendant acts "with the intent" to promote or facilitate the offense. Unlike conspiracy, however, complicity is not a substantive offense, and therefore the word "intent" in the complicity statute does not mean specific intent but rather retains its plain and ordinary meaning.

To summarize, conspiracy, attempt, and complicity are distinct legal principles with different requirements for mental culpability. Conspiracy is a specific intent crime that requires the defendant to intend to agree, and to intend specifically to achieve the result of the crime. The phrase "with the intent to promote or facilitate the commission of a crime" contained in the conspiracy statute requires construction using the precise statutory definition. The accused must have the conscious objective to achieve the specific result proscribed by an offense. The culpable mental state for attempt is determined by the required mental state of the underlying crime. Hence, it is possible to commit the crime of attempt without possessing a specific intent, provided that the underlying crime does not require a specific intent. Complicity is a legal theory rather than a crime; the phrase "with the intent to promote or facilitate the commission of the offense" contained in the complicity statute retains its ordinary meaning and usage and does not require specific intent as defined by the General Assembly. With these principles in mind, we turn to the issue of whether conspiracy to commit reckless manslaughter is a cognizable crime.

> **Take Note**
>
> Conspiracy, attempt and complicity are entirely separate and distinct criminal offenses. As a result, a conspiracy conviction does not merge with a conviction for the crime which was the object of the conspiracy, i.e. a defendant can be convicted of and sentenced for both. However, in many jurisdictions, by statute, convictions for multiple inchoate offenses, *e.g.*, conspiracy and attempt, arising out of the same criminal conduct do merge.

Inchoate Offenses: Attempt & Conspiracy

The People argue that the crime of conspiracy to commit reckless manslaughter, if recognized, would not require the defendant to specifically intend the death of the victim, and therefore such an offense would not be a logical impossibility. We disagree. Although a superficial reading of the conspiracy statute might support the People's argument, it is necessary to analyze the statute together with the legislative definition of specific intent and with our prior case law interpreting the crime of conspiracy in Colorado. In doing so, we reach the conclusion that a crime of conspiracy to commit reckless manslaughter would indeed pose a legal and logical conflict that is irreconcilable. Thus, we hold that conspiracy to commit reckless manslaughter is not a cognizable crime.

A person commits reckless manslaughter if "he recklessly causes the death of another person." Reckless manslaughter does not require the specific intent to cause the death of another. Rather, it requires that a person knowingly engage in risk producing acts or conduct that create a substantial and unjustifiable risk of causing a death. "One may be guilty of attempting to commit a crime of recklessness if it is shown that he was merely reckless toward the possibility that his conduct might have a certain consequence."

The culpable mental states for conspiracy and for reckless manslaughter are legally and logically inconsistent. The crime of conspiracy to commit reckless manslaughter would require that the defendant have the specific intent to commit reckless manslaughter. Crimes of recklessness are, by definition, crimes that are committed unintentionally, but with a conscious disregard for a substantial and unjustifiable risk that a result will occur. Thus, the state of mind required for reckless manslaughter is irreconcilable with the specific intent required for conspiracy. Logic dictates that one cannot agree in advance to accomplish an unintended result. Thus, we hold that conspiracy to commit reckless manslaughter is not a cognizable offense in Colorado.

In *People v. Thomas*, 729 P.2d 972, 975 (Colo. 1986), the petitioner argued that the crime of attempted reckless manslaughter was a legal impossibility. We noted that the culpable mental state for attempted reckless manslaughter is the mental state required for the commission of the underlying offense, reckless manslaughter, and that attempt liability focuses on conduct rather than results. Reckless manslaughter requires the conscious disregard of a substantial and unjustifiable risk that death will occur. Thus, we held, the culpable mental state for attempted reckless manslaughter is that the accused knowingly engage in conduct while consciously disregarding a substantial and unjustifiable risk of death. Even though death is an element of reckless manslaughter, one may commit the crime of attempted reckless manslaughter without intending that death occur. Since attempt requires the same mental culpability as the underlying crime, we held that there is no inconsistency between the mental culpability requirement for attempt and that for the underlying crime, reckless manslaughter.

> **Food for Thought**
>
> In some jurisdictions, attempt is a specific intent crime. Where that is true, would that change this analysis? How? *See, e.g., Commonwealth v. Griffin*, 310 Pa. Super. 39, 456 A.2d 171, 177 (1983): "Murder of the second or third degree occurs where the killing of the victim is the unintentional result of a criminal act. Thus, an attempt to commit second or third degree murder would seem to require proof that a defendant intended to perpetrate an unintentional killing—which is logically impossible. While a person who only intends to commit a felony may be guilty of second degree murder if a killing results, and a person who only intends to inflict bodily harm may be guilty of third degree murder if a killing results; it does not follow that those persons would be guilty of attempted murder if a killing did not occur. They would not be guilty of attempted murder because they did not intend to commit murder—they only intended to commit a felony or to commit bodily harm."

Here, however, the culpability requirement for conspiracy and that for the crime of reckless manslaughter conflict. Conspiracy is always a specific intent crime, and conspiracy liability focuses on specifically intended results rather than on conduct. Unlike attempted reckless manslaughter, conspiracy to commit reckless manslaughter would require the accused to possess the specific intent to achieve an unintentional death, which we conclude is a legal and logical impossibility.

In summary, we hold that conspiracy to commit reckless manslaughter is not a cognizable crime under Colorado law. Accordingly, we reverse the judgment of the court of appeals on this issue only and remand the case with instructions to vacate the judgment of conviction for the crime of conspiracy to commit reckless manslaughter.

POINTS FOR DISCUSSION

a. Other Conspiracies?

Even though the Colorado Supreme Court held that Palmer cannot be convicted of the crime of conspiracy to commit manslaughter, did he conspire to commit any other crime? If so, what crime?

b. Conspiracies to Commit Negligent Crimes

In Colorado, after the decision in *Palmer*, can a defendant be found guilty of conspiracy to commit an offense which has the *mens rea* element of criminal negligence? Why or why not?

c. Charging Conspiracy vs. Substantive Offenses

There is a well-established legal principle that a "conspiracy to commit a particular substantive offense cannot exist without at least the degree of criminal intent necessary for the substantive offense itself." *United States v. Hassoun*, 2007 WL 4180844 (S.D.Fla. 2007).

> **Take Note**
>
> Some criminal offenses are simply easier to prove than other criminal offenses, even though both offenses are based upon the same conduct. Conspiracy is often easier to prove than attempt, for example, because there is no hearsay exception applicable to attempt prosecutions, and because an overt act (where proof of one is required) is much easier to prove than a substantial step.

d. Knowledge vs. Intent

Should exceptions exist to the proposition that "knowledge is not intent?" What if someone knows that an actor is about to kill his or her spouse? Wouldn't silence be the same as a tacit agreement to assist in the homicide, i.e. assistance by not creating any impediments to the performance of the criminal act?

> **Take Note**
>
> The *mens rea* of conspiracy is not established simply by showing that an accused person was *merely present* while others were conspiring or that the accused *merely knew* that someone else intended to commit a crime.

3. *Actus Reus*: Agreement

Most conspiratorial agreements are clandestine. They are neither made in front of witnesses nor recorded on video or audio surveillance. Moreover, in the absence of a plea agreement, it is not in the self-interest of individual coconspirators to testify to the existence of such incriminating matters. As a result, the *actus reus* element of conspiracy—the conspiratorial "agreement"—often is established only inferentially and/or circumstantially.

In large part due to the inferential and circumstantial nature of the proof, there is an abiding concern, particularly in large conspiracy trials, that some individuals who were not actually part of the conspiracy under scrutiny will be swept into the conspiratorial "net" simply because they have associated previously with one or more of the coconspirators, however innocently. As you read these decisions, you should bear in mind this concern. Short of eliminating the conspiracy offense, how can it be alleviated?

STATE V. ROSADO

2009 WL 3086436 (Conn. Super. Ct. 2009).

JON C. BLUE, JUDGE of the Superior Court.

On a late summer afternoon in 2006, the young life of Aaron McCrae ended in a hail of bullets near the train station in New Haven. Two and a half years later, Geraldo Rosado, the defendant herein, was tried for being a member of the conspiracy that plotted McCrae's death. Examined in the light most favorable to the State, the evidence establishes the following facts. In the early morning hours of September 17, 2006, a man with the street name of "Carlito" was killed in the area of the Church Street South housing project near the train station in New Haven known as the "jungle." "Carlito's" associates blamed McCrae (who had the street name "A-Love") for the killing.

A man with the descriptive street name of "Primo" called a meeting to place a bounty on McCrae. The only evidentiary description of this meeting is contained in a tape-recorded statement that the defendant gave to the police on December 16, 2006. According to the defendant:

> We went to the jungle. Primo put a hit out to kill A-Love. He gave the two guns to Luis Santana and showed him fifteen thousand that once he do what he had to do he'll get the money and from there we went up chilled for a little bit. Went up the hill, they got a call that A-Love was out there and me, this other kid name Juan Nunez, known as Bebe, went up the hill. Louis Santana was in the alleyway, then from there he ran across the street and shot A-Love.

The evidence shows that McCrae was shot in the back by seven to nine bullets (the fragmentation of some bullets makes the exact count uncertain) fired by two different handguns. Two shots resulted in lethal wounds. McCrae died within moments.

The crime occurred on a warm, sunny afternoon in a public area. Within moments, a crowd of approximately 150 people had gathered. In spite of the fact that many people must have seen the shooting, no one came forward. A 911 caller reported that McCrae was shot by "two Spanish guys." The defendant, as mentioned, told the police that McCrae was shot by Luis Santana. No other description of the crime is in evidence.

According to the defendant's December 16, 2006 statement, after the shooting, "We ran up Carlisle and went straight to Bebe house, known as Juan Nunez." The defendant said that he was on the porch when Santana and Nunez went upstairs. Nunez told him that, "He put the guns away for Luis Santana." A few days later, when the guns were recovered at Nunez's residence, Santana called the defendant and told him "they caught his guns."

DNA mixtures of at least three individuals were recovered from the grips of each gun. The defendant could not be eliminated as a possible contributor with respect to either weapon. Subsequently, on two occasions prior to his December 16, 2006 statement, the defendant falsely told the police that he had not been at the scene of the killing.

Defendant was arrested and subsequently convicted for conspiracy to murder McRae. The question presented by the motion now before the court is whether the evidence is sufficient to sustain the defendant's conviction of conspiracy to commit murder.

The standard of review to be employed by the court in reviewing a sufficiency of the evidence claim following a jury verdict finding the defendant guilty of the crime of conspiracy is well settled:

> We apply a two part test. First, we construe the evidence in the light most favorable to sustaining the verdict. Second, we determine whether upon the facts so construed and the inferences reasonably drawn therefrom the jury reasonably could have concluded that the cumulative force of the evidence established guilt beyond a reasonable doubt.

> To establish the crime of conspiracy the state must show that there was an agreement between two or more persons to engage in conduct constituting a crime and that the agreement was followed by an overt act in furtherance of the conspiracy by any one of the conspirators. The state must also show intent on the part of the accused that conduct constituting a crime be performed. The existence of a formal agreement between the parties need not be proved; it is sufficient to show that they are knowingly engaged in a mutual plan to do a forbidden act.

> While the state must prove an agreement the existence of a formal agreement between the coconspirators need not be proved because it is only in rare instances that conspiracy may be established by proof of an

express agreement to unite to accomplish an unlawful purpose. The requisite agreement or confederation may be inferred from proof of the separate acts of the individuals accused as coconspirators and from the circumstances surrounding the commission of these acts. Further, conspiracy can seldom be proved by direct evidence. It may be inferred from the activities of the accused persons.

The sufficiency of the evidence issue presented here focuses on the element of agreement. Conn. Gen.Stat. § 53a–48(a) provides that, "A person is guilty of conspiracy when, with intent that conduct constituting a crime be performed, he *agrees* with one or more persons to engage in the performance of such conduct, and any one of them commits an overt act in pursuance of such conspiracy." Agreement is an element of the crime that must be proven beyond a reasonable doubt, and the jury in this case was instructed accordingly.[5]

The defendant's December 16, 2006 statement firmly establishes the existence of a conspiracy to murder McCrae. Whether the defendant joined with at least one other person in an agreement to commit the murder is an issue of fact. There was no direct evidence that the defendant joined in an agreement. The evidence was, instead, circumstantial. There is, however, nothing wrong with this latter manner of proof. "Because of the secret nature of conspiracies, a conviction usually is based on circumstantial evidence. Consequently, it is not necessary to establish that the defendant and his coconspirators signed papers, shook hands, or uttered the words we have an agreement. The requisite agreement or confederation may be inferred from proof of the separate acts of the individuals

---

[5] With respect to the element of agreement, the jury was instructed that:

The first element that the State must prove beyond a reasonable doubt is that the defendant made an agreement with one or more persons. It is not necessary for the State to prove that there was a formal or express agreement between them. It is sufficient to show that the parties knowingly engaged in a mutual plan to do a criminal act. Conspiracies are often formed in secret. But an agreement, just like any other fact, may be proven by circumstantial evidence. It is not necessary to establish that the persons making the agreement signed papers, shook hands, or uttered the words, "We have an agreement." Rather, a conspiracy can be inferred from the conduct of the persons involved.

A mere knowledge, acquiescence, or approval of the object of the agreement without cooperation or an agreement to cooperate is not, however, sufficient to make someone a party to a conspiracy to commit the criminal act. Mere presence at the scene of the crime, even when coupled with knowledge of the crime, is insufficient to establish a conspiracy.

In order to convict a person of conspiracy, the State need not show that the person had direct communication with all other conspirators. It is not necessary that each conspirator be acquainted with all others or even know their names. It is sufficient that he has come to an understanding with at least one of the others and has come to such understanding with that person to further a criminal purpose. It is also not essential that he know the complete plan of the conspiracy in all of its details. It is enough if he knows that a conspiracy exists or that he is creating one and that he is joining with at least one other person in an agreement to commit a crime, in this case the crime of murder.

Inchoate Offenses: Attempt & Conspiracy

accused as coconspirators and from the circumstances surrounding the commission of these acts."

Circumstantial evidence is sometimes more reliable than direct evidence. "A fact positively sworn to by a single eyewitness of blemished character, is not so satisfactorily proved, as is a fact which is the necessary consequence of a chain of other facts sworn to by many witnesses of undoubted credibility." Conspiracy jurisprudence recognizes this well-known fact. At the same time, however, our jurisprudence also recognizes that, "Mere presence at the scene of the crime, even coupled with knowledge of the crime, is not sufficient to establish guilt of a conspiracy." The purpose of this rule is to require that a defendant cannot be convicted of conspiracy without evidence that he "was more than a mere bystander."

Rosado views the "mere presence" rule as his safe harbor in this case, but, on this evidence, it is not. The evidence establishes much more than Rosado's "mere presence at the scene of the crime." He was, of course, present at the scene of the crime-he claims to have personally witnessed McCrae's execution-but he was present at a great many other places as well. By his own admission, he was present when "Primo" put a bounty on McCrae and gave two guns to Luis Santana. He was present at the scene of the crime, along with Juan Nunez. He subsequently ran-with Nunez-to Nunez's house on Carlisle Street. Nunez's house is the same place to which Santana ran after the shooting and the location at which the murder weapons were subsequently discovered. After the murder weapons were discovered, Santana called Rosado and informed him of this fact. In addition to these facts-all admitted by Rosado-DNA evidence indicates a probability (although not a certainty) that Rosado at some point touched the grip of each of the murder weapons. Rosado also made false statements to the police concerning his whereabouts at the time of the killing.

This scenario involves much more than mere presence at the scene of the crime. It is, instead, an intricate web of circumstantial evidence. Rosado's statement puts him not just at the scene of the crime but at each of three locations associated with the murder-the bounty meeting with "Primo," the murder scene itself, and Nunez's house. In addition, the same statement shows that Rosado had at least some involvement with at least three different conspirators-"Primo," Nunez, and Santana-and the involvement with Santana was on multiple locations. DNA evidence shows a probability that Rosado touched each of the murder weapons. Finally, Rosado made false statements to the police.

Could all of this be a coincidence? The jury was surely entitled to infer that it was not. It might have been a coincidence that Rosado was present at the bounty meeting with "Primo," it might have been a coincidence that he was present at the murder scene, and it might have been a coincidence that he was present at Nunez's house, but the likelihood that all of these personal appearances were coincidental quite safely approaches zero.

A series of decisions of the United States Court of Appeals for the Second Circuit recognizes the common sense decision between mere presence at the scene of the crime, on the one hand, and the more extensive involvement in a series of events that can safely underpin a finding of conspiracy, on the other. That court has long recognized that, "Mere presence at the scene of the crime, even when coupled with knowledge that at that moment a crime is being committed, is insufficient to prove membership in a conspiracy." *United States v. Johnson*, 513 F.2d 819, 823–24 (2d Cir. 1975).

Johnson is a much-cited case applying this rule. Johnson accompanied a boyhood friend in an automobile trip from New Hampshire to Montreal to buy a motorcycle. Unhappily for Johnson, his friend did not restrict his Canadian purchases to motorcycles. One night, while Johnson was asleep, his friend left their motel room to purchase drugs and secreted them behind a door panel in the car. The drugs were discovered by Customs authorities when the two friends returned to the United States, and Johnson was eventually arrested for conspiracy to import the drugs. On appeal, the Second Circuit vacated the conviction, holding this to be a case of "mere presence." Although Johnson had unwisely told the Customs authorities that he was hitchhiking, the Court explained that, "Falsehoods told by a defendant in the hope of extricating himself from suspicious circumstances are insufficient proof on which to convict where other evidence of guilt is weak and the evidence before the court is as hospitable to an interpretation consistent with the defendant's innocence as it is to the Government's theory of guilt."

The Second Circuit has subsequently explained that *Johnson* does not apply to cases involving multiple appearances by a defendant at a variety of places associated with the crime. *United States v. Pedroza*, 750 F.2d 187 (2d Cir. 1984), *cert. denied*, 479 U.S. 842 (1986), is instructive. Pedroza was convicted of membership in a conspiracy to kidnap. The evidence showed that Pedroza was present at the purchase of the van later used in the abduction. Although Pedroza did not participate in the abduction itself, he arrived at the house to which the victim had been taken. He was then present at a number of locations to which the victim was subsequently taken. *Johnson* did not save Pedroza on appeal following his conviction. The Court explained that, while Johnson's presence in his friend's automobile "could have resulted from happenstance," here there was "nothing in the record to suggest that [Pedroza] may have had any purpose in these timely appearances other than to further the goals of the conspiracy."

The dividing line between "mere presence at the scene of the crime," on the one hand, and a series of "timely appearances," must be located by judgment rather than mathematics in any given case. But the common-sense standard articulated by Ian Fleming's memorable villain, Auric Goldfinger, is helpful in this regard. "Mr. Bond, they have a saying in Chicago: 'Once is happenstance. Twice is coincidence. The third time it's enemy action.'" Ian Fleming, Goldfinger 204 (1959).

There was plenty of "enemy action" here. The totality of the evidence-including Rosado's many "timely appearances" at places closely associated with the crime-was sufficient to allow the jury to find that Rosado agreed with one or more of the other conspirators to take part in that action.

The evidence presented was, as mentioned, less than overwhelming on this issue. Different people, hearing and assessing the same evidence, might draw different inferences and come to different factual conclusions. But hearing and assessing the evidence, drawing inferences, and coming to factual conclusions was the job of the jury-a jury chosen by the defendant as well as by the State.

The motion for judgment of acquittal is denied.

Hypo 10: *Taking Messages*

Louis Lauria operated a telephone-answering service which supplied its services to a number of prostitutes. Lauria knew that some of his customers were prostitutes—one of them received 500 calls a month—and he assured her of the utmost confidentiality in message-taking. When three of these prostitutes were arrested, Lauria was indicted along with the three for conspiracy to commit prostitution. Is he guilty of this charge? *People v. Lauria*, 251 Cal. App. 2d 471, 59 Cal. Rptr. 628 (1967). Would or should the result be different if Lauria charged the prostitutes double the fees he charged his other customers? And would it or should it matter whether he provides a special paging service for an additional fee to his prostitute customers that he does not offer to his other customers?

Hypo 11: *Scalping Tickets*

A & B are scalping tickets to a University of Louisville basketball game in Freedom Hall, Louisville, Kentucky. In Kentucky, scalping is illegal. Before the police arrest A & B, they observe them holding up tickets (suggesting that the tickets were for sale), talking with potential customers, and eventually selling tickets above face value. In addition, from time-to-time, A & B conversed with each other and were observed passing something between one another. Is there sufficient evidence of conspiracy to scalp tickets to convict A & B?

Hypo 12: *The Lookout*

Luis Mercado was seen leaning out a third-floor window and observing three different crack cocaine sales (all to undercover police officers) made on three different occasions by Alex Colon. According to the government, Mercado was operating as a "lookout" for Colon. When the apartment was searched, no drugs were found on Mercado, but officers found 23.7 grams of cocaine sitting out in the open on a tabletop, as well as two plastic packets each containing 20 vials of crack cocaine, numerous clear plastic vials, caps, and packets, and a spoon and a razor, each containing white residue (which turned out to be cocaine). Is there sufficient evidence on this record to convict Mercado of conspiring with Colon to engage in the criminal sale of narcotics? *Commonwealth v. Mercado*, 420 Pa. Super. 588, 617 A.2d 342 (1992).

Hypo 13: *Cocaine Buddies*

Would the result in Hypo 3 be any different, do you think, if Mercado and Colon were frequently seen together, and Colon was not viewed looking out the window, but was instead simply found using cocaine in the apartment when the apartment was searched, i.e. could he be convicted of conspiracy in those circumstances? *See, e.g., Commonwealth v. Rodgers*, 410 Pa. Super. 341, 599 A.2d 1329 (1991).

POINTS FOR DISCUSSION

a. **Co-Conspirator Hearsay Exception**

In establishing the existence of a conspiratorial agreement in court, prosecutors may use testimony by one coconspirator about what another coconspirator said, even though such testimony is ordinarily inadmissible as hearsay. The "coconspirator hearsay exception," is justified on the ground that coconspirators are acting as agents of one another. Under that exception, declarations made by one coconspirator during and in furtherance of the conspiracy are admissible in court, assuming that there has been a substantial and independent showing that a conspiracy existed and that the individuals in question were a part of that conspiracy.

b. **Wheels & Chains**

Some courts have used such metaphors as "wheels" and "chains" to describe the operation of common types of conspiratorial arrangements. A "chain" conspiracy is a single conspiracy where individual members (the "links") interact only with the next link in the chain and may not know any of the other links farther up or down the chain. Narcotics importation and distribution schemes are common examples of chain conspiracies. A "wheel" conspiracy, in contrast, involves separate chain conspiracies ("the spokes") linked to each other through a common individual ("the hub"). *See, e.g., Kotteakos v. United States*, 328 U.S. 750 (1946) (no wheel conspiracy where spokes not connected, *e.g.*, through knowledge by the separate conspirators of the existence of other conspirators or conspiracies).

c. **Scouts & Steerers**

Law enforcement agents seeking to eradicate illegal narcotics sales in particular neighborhoods generally hope to arrest not only the street salespersons themselves, but also the various "scouts," "runners," "lookouts," and other individuals who are paid to support the narcotics sales operation by watching for police presence and/or steering potential customers to the sales force. If you are an Assistant District Attorney assigned to support a joint state-federal law enforcement Task Force that has such a mission, how might you explain to the Task Force officers when precisely such "scouts" or "steerers" might be deemed to be coconspirators with the actual salespersons—and when they may not. What conduct or statements should the officers be looking for (or waiting for) in order to make a lawful arrest for conspiracy?

4. Overt Act

Most (but not all) jurisdictions with general conspiracy statutes require as an element of the offense proof of an "overt act" on the part of one of the coconspirators in order to establish the existence of a conspiracy. It does not usually take much, however, to establish the existence of an overt act. Even a relatively insignificant action on the part of one of the coconspirators will generally suffice.

STATE V. GARCIA
376 P.3d 94 (Kan. 2016).

PER CURIAM.

In 2013, the KBI began working with a confidential informant who had been helping the Garden City Police Department and the Finney County Sheriff's Office. When this informant came forward with knowledge of a drug dealer in Dodge City, Kansas, the information was passed along to the KBI. The informant told the KBI that he could buy drugs from Garcia, his dealer. According to the informant, he had recently bought drugs from Garcia. By contacting locals, checking water records, reviewing past investigations, and using information provided by the informant, the KBI was able to find where Garcia lived. Because Garcia's location had been determined, the plan was to set up a drug deal by phone and then execute a search warrant without ever purchasing any drugs.

Instead of calling Garcia, the informant called Garcia's girlfriend, Mickashell Knapp, because an arrangement had been made that he should call Knapp if Garcia was unavailable. The phone call was made from a KBI special agent's phone in the late afternoon of August 13, 2013; Knapp answered. The informant asked for an ounce of methamphetamine, but Knapp replied that she could only get a half an ounce, or about 14 grams. The informant agreed to that amount, and the buy was scheduled for later that evening. Knapp said she could also get some cocaine. When the informant asked about Garcia, Knapp said he was dealing with some problems, and the informant understood that he was trying to stay clean or out of trouble.

The KBI applied for a search warrant and set up surveillance on the house where Garcia was staying. Surveillance units observed a black car pull into the driveway. A male and a female, later identified as Garcia and Knapp, got out of the car. Law enforcement officers then swarmed the house.

As the officers approached the house, several people, including Knapp, were outside, but Garcia was seen entering the house. Everyone had stopped when it was clear that law enforcement officers were pulling up, but Garcia continued into the house. After arresting Knapp, officers knocked on the front door and announced their presence. Garcia was told to come out and was seen coming from the area near the bedroom in the northeast part of the house. As he was being placed under arrest, Garcia said that he no longer lived at the house and that he had moved out or was moving out.

Law enforcement officers then began searching the house. A glass tray, snort tube, digital scale, and black box were found in the northeast bedroom. The glass tray, which had a white powdery substance on it, and the snort tube were found in plain view on a TV stand. The digital scale was also in plain view and was found to the right of the glass tray. A KBI special agent testified that a snort tube is a tube used to snort drugs. The same special agent testified that a digital scale can be evidence of drug distribution. The snort tube was tested, and traces of methadone and oxycodone were found. Methamphetamine, cocaine, and a synthetic cannabinoid, known as K2 or spice, were detected on the digital scale.

Inside the black box, which was found near the rest of the items, was a plastic bag with a crystalline substance and a prescription bottle. Garcia's name was on the prescription, and a white powdery substance was found inside the bottle. The crystalline substance in the plastic bag weighed 18.24 grams and tested positive for methamphetamine and cocaine. The white powdery substance found in the pill bottle weighed 1.48 grams and also tested positive for methamphetamine and cocaine.

As a result of the fruits from the search warrant and the investigation that followed, the State charged Garcia with possession of methamphetamine with intent to distribute within 1,000 feet of school property; conspiracy to distribute at least 3.5 grams of methamphetamine within 1,000 feet of school property; possession of cocaine with intent to distribute within 1,000 feet of school property; distribution of a naphthoylindole-based controlled substance of less than 3.5 grams within 1,000 feet of school property; conspiracy to distribute cocaine of less than 3.5 grams within 1,000 feet of school property; unlawful use of a communication facility; distributing or possessing methamphetamine without a tax stamp; distributing or possessing cocaine without a tax stamp; and two counts of possession of drug paraphernalia. The State later dismissed the distribution of a naphthoylindole-based controlled substance charge.

The jury found Garcia guilty on all counts, except for unlawful use of a communication device. Garcia timely appeals.

Did the State Present Sufficient Evidence to Support Garcia's Convictions of Conspiracy to Distribute?

Garcia claims that his conspiracy to distribute convictions were not supported by sufficient evidence. When the sufficiency of the evidence is challenged in a criminal case, we review "all the evidence in a light most favorable to the prosecution, and must be convinced a rational factfinder could have found the defendant guilty beyond a reasonable doubt." We also will not reweigh the evidence or the credibility of witnesses. Only in rare cases where the testimony is so incredible that no reasonable factfinder could find guilt beyond a reasonable doubt will a guilty verdict be reversed. To support a conspiracy conviction, the prosecution must present evidence that the defendant agreed with another person to commit or assist in committing a crime and that the defendant or the coconspirator committed an overt act to further the conspiracy. See K.S.A.2015 Supp. 21–5302(a).

> "An overt act which completes the crime of conspiracy is something apart from the conspiracy. It is an act to effect the object of the conspiracy but it need be neither a criminal act, nor the crime that is the object of the conspiracy. However, it must accompany or follow agreement and must be done in furtherance of the object of the agreement."

> "Conversations among co-conspirators in forming and planning the conspiracy are not overt acts." The prosecution must show that " 'defendant took a step beyond the mere preparation so that some appreciable fragment of the crime was committed.' "

In this case, the State presented sufficient evidence to prove both elements. First, the evidence showed that Garcia entered into an agreement with Knapp to sell or assist in the sale of drugs. The informant testified that Garcia was his dealer and that an arrangement had been made that if Garcia was not available, was not around, or was indisposed, the informant could deal with Knapp. When asked how recently that arrangement had been made, the informant said Garcia told him to deal with Knapp 2 or 3 weeks before the search warrant was executed. In her KBI interview, Knapp also stated that she had dealt for Garcia while he was in jail. She was also able to provide specific details about the deal with the informant. Although Knapp denied it at trial, she said that Garcia had been with her and told her what to say when she spoke with the informant on the phone and sent the

Inchoate Offenses: Attempt & Conspiracy

text to the KBI special agent's phone. As it was for the jury to determine whether Knapp had been truthful during the interview or at trial, we cannot say as a matter of law that there was not sufficient evidence to support an agreement between Garcia and Knapp.

The State also presented evidence of an overt act: the use of a phone to arrange a time and place to sell drugs. Garcia notes the evidence did not show that he spoke with the informant on the phone and that he was acquitted on a separate charge of using a communication device in a drug transaction. But the overt act does not have to be committed by the defendant in order to convict the defendant of conspiracy—evidence that the defendant's coconspirator committed the overt act is also sufficient. In this case, Garcia's coconspirator was Knapp. And the evidence in support of her using a telephone to arrange a time and place to sell drugs to the informant is overwhelming. In fact, Garcia does not dispute that Knapp used a cell phone to arrange a deal with the informant. Instead, Garcia argues that State failed to present sufficient evidence of an agreement between him and Knapp. But as we have already explained above, the State presented sufficient evidence to establish this agreement.

In conclusion, the State presented evidence that when viewed in its most favorable light was sufficient to show that Garcia and Knapp had an agreement that Knapp would help Garcia sell drugs when Garcia was unavailable. The State also presented evidence showing that Knapp committed the overt act of using a telephone to arrange a time and place to sell drugs, in furtherance of their conspiracy. Thus, a rational factfinder could have found Garcia guilty beyond a reasonable doubt of conspiracy to distribute.

Affirmed.

POINTS FOR DISCUSSION

a. Venue

Venue for a conspiracy trial is typically deemed to be appropriate in any jurisdiction in which an overt act took place, even if that jurisdiction is not the jurisdiction in which most of the conspiratorial acts took place.

b. How Much Is Enough for an Overt Act?

In 2006, federal authorities charged seven men with plotting to blow up the Sears Tower in Chicago. The prosecution claimed that the men adhered to a militant (but vague) form of Islamic ideology, and had attempted to make contact with al Qaeda. The men provided a supposed al Qaeda representative (actually, an undercover federal officer) with a list of needed supplies (*e.g.*, uniforms, boots, machine guns, radios and vehicles), and claimed that their objective was to wage jihad and to "kill all the devils we can" in a 9/11-style mission. In fact, no member of the group ever really made contact with al Qaeda at all, although the men did manage to obtain some boots and uniforms. Eventually, the plot just "petered out." Did these men commit the crime of conspiracy? Did they commit a sufficient overt act?

5. Renunciation or Withdrawal

Unlike acts leading to the commission of completed criminal offenses, acts leading toward the commission of inchoate offenses (like conspiracy, solicitation and attempt) may, in some jurisdictions, under the proper circumstances, be "taken back" by appropriate acts of withdrawal, contrition, and assistance of law enforcement efforts to prevent whatever criminal enterprise may be ongoing.

NEW JERSEY V. HUGHES
215 N.J. Super. 295, 521 A.2d 1295 (App.Div. 1986).

ANTELL, P.J.A.D.

At approximately 7:00 p.m. September 28, 1982 the cashier at the office of the Courier Post in Cherry Hill was robbed at gun point of a large amount of cash by two men. In connection therewith defendant was indicted for robbery, possession of a weapon for an unlawful purpose, and conspiracy to rob. After a trial by jury he was convicted of conspiracy and a jury disagreement was recorded as to the other two charges.

> **It's Latin to Me**
>
> Where a renunciation defense exists in the law, it is often justified by the belief that would-be criminals should have a *locus poenitentiae*. Locus poenitentiae means "a point at which it is not too late for one to change one's legal position; the possibility of withdrawing from a contemplated course of action, esp. a wrong, before being committed to it."

On this appeal defendant first argues that the trial court erred in failing to instruct the jury as to the defense of "renunciation of purpose" as an affirmative defense to the charge of conspiracy.

The evidence upon which defendant rests his claim to the defense of renunciation is found in the testimony of defendant himself and the testimony of Detective Beverly of the City of Camden Police Department. According to defendant, during the period of approximately one month before the robbery he had been approached on a number of occasions by Tyrone Wolley who solicited him to take part in robbing the Courier Post. On each occasion defendant rejected the invitation and answered Wolley that he was not interested in doing armed robberies. Approximately one or two weeks before the Courier Post robbery actually occurred, defendant visited Detective Beverly and told him of Wolley's solicitations. He did not, however, suggest that he had agreed to join the enterprise and, in fact, said that he told Wolley he would not do so. His purpose, he said, in giving Detective Beverly the information was to enable the police to investigate the matter.

The defense of renunciation to a charge of conspiracy is found, N.J.S.A. 2C:5–2e:

> Renunciation of purpose. It is an affirmative defense which the actor must prove by a preponderance of the evidence that he, after conspiring to commit a crime, informed the authority of the existence of the conspiracy and his participation therein, and thwarted or caused to be thwarted the commission of any offense in furtherance of the conspiracy, under circumstances manifesting a complete and voluntary renunciation of criminal purpose.

It is evident that the basic condition of the defense finds no support in the evidence. The statute presupposes an acknowledgment by the actor that he actually conspired to commit a crime and its benefits are conferred only where he informs police authority of the conspiracy's existence "and his participation therein." Where the elements of the defense have been shown by a preponderance of the evidence one can be said to have "renounced" the conspiracy. Renunciation, after all, posits prior participation, and defendant could not renounce a conspiracy he had not joined. The defense was not available to defendant for the reason that, as he testified, he had steadfastly refused to support the criminal undertaking. His testimony to this effect as well as Detective Beverly's was relevant, not to whether he had renounced the conspiracy, but only to whether he had ever joined it in the first place. Once this issue was resolved against defendant there was nothing else in the record to support a finding of renunciation.

Affirmed.

6. Merger

Since the *actus reus* of conspiracy (a conspiratorial agreement) is different from the *actus reus* of the target crime itself, *e.g.*, the illegal sale of narcotics, the rule in most (but not all) jurisdictions is that a conviction for conspiracy to commit a crime does *not* merge with a conviction for that crime itself for purposes of sentencing, i.e. the accused can be sentenced for *both* crimes.

STATE V. HARDISON
99 N.J. 379, 492 A.2d 1009 (1985).

O'HERN, J.

This appeal concerns the circumstances under which a conviction for a criminal conspiracy and a completed offense that was an object of the conspiracy will merge. Specifically, the appeal concerns N.J.S.A. 2C:1–8a(2), which provides that a defendant may not be convicted of more than one offense if "one offense consists only of a conspiracy or other form of preparation to commit the other." We hold that if the conspiracy proven has criminal objectives other than the substantive offense proven, the offenses will not merge. In this case the conviction does not establish that the conspiracy embraced criminal objectives in addition to the offense proven. Hence, we affirm the judgment below that merged the conviction of conspiracy with the completed offense.

The case arises from two incidents, commencing on the evening of November 19, 1980. At approximately 11:30 p.m., four men entered the Lincoln Café in New Brunswick. After about twenty minutes, when the crowd had thinned out, one of the defendants pulled out a gun, pointed the gun at the bartender and forced him to lie face down behind the bar. Two of the men herded the two remaining patrons, a man and a woman, into the bathroom. The four cleaned out the cash register, and took the bartender's watch and the woman's purse. All three victims were then locked in the men's room with a cigarette machine in front of the door. The four fled.

Within minutes the bartender pushed the door open and alerted the New Brunswick police. They came immediately to the scene, gathered information, and obtained identification of the defendants. The police learned that the four men had fled in a red and white Cadillac.

Before they were able to return to the New Brunswick stationhouse, the police heard on the radio that a robbery had taken place at the Edison Motor Lodge, north of New Brunswick on Route 1. Edison officers on patrol had spotted a suspicious car traveling on Route 1 with its lights off. They began to follow the car. They soon heard on the police radio that a robbery had taken place at the Edison Motor Lodge. They learned as well that a red and white Cadillac had been involved in a robbery in New Brunswick. Other police joined the chase. A

Inchoate Offenses: Attempt & Conspiracy

high-speed pursuit took place up Route 1 and onto the Garden State Parkway. The chase ended when the car ran into a cement divider at Parkway Exit 131 in Clark Township.

At the Edison Motor Lodge, the night manager reported that two men had come into the premises and asked about the price of a room. They went out, came back in with a gun, and robbed him at gunpoint of the motel's property. One of the defendants threatened to kill him; the other brutally assaulted him with brass knuckles, shattering his teeth.

Hardison and Jackson were found within close proximity of the car that had crashed in Clark Township. They were taken to the Clark police station. The woman's purse was retrieved from the car as was a key to the Edison motel room. New Brunswick police took the three witnesses from the Lincoln Café to the Clark police station where they were shown Hardison and Jackson alone with a group of police officers. They identified Hardison and Jackson as being involved in the Lincoln Café robbery, although neither was identified as the gunman. The night manager at the Edison motel was shown the defendants later. He identified them as his assailants. Two other suspects were soon apprehended.

The four were charged with conspiracy to commit robbery, four counts of robbery of the three people in the tavern and the night manager at the motel, possession of a gun for an unlawful purpose, aggravated assault of the night manager; and Hardison was charged with possession of brass knuckles for an unlawful purpose. The trial of two co-defendants was severed. Hardison and Jackson went to trial together.

The jury acquitted these two defendants of the robbery of the Lincoln Café, but convicted them on all other charges. Each was sentenced to an aggregate term of twenty years with five years of parole ineligibility. Separate and consecutive sentences were imposed on the conspiracy and robbery counts. On appeal, the Appellate Division, in two separate opinions, affirmed on all issues but merger, concluding that because the illegal agreement included robbery and the jury found defendants guilty of the motel robbery within the ambit of the conspiracy, the convictions for both the conspiracy and the robbery were barred. We granted the State's petition for certification, limited solely to the issue of whether the conviction for conspiracy to commit robbery should have merged with that of armed robbery. We now affirm.

The law of conspiracy serves two independent values. First is the protection of society from the danger of concerted criminal activity. The second aspect is that conspiracy is an inchoate crime. "This is to say, that, although the law generally makes criminal only antisocial conduct, at some point in the continuum between preparation and consummation, the likelihood of a commission of an act is sufficiently great and the criminal intent sufficiently well formed to justify the intervention of the criminal law." Thus, the law of conspiracy identifies the agreement to engage in a criminal venture as an event of sufficient threat to social order, therefore permitting the imposition of criminal sanctions for the agreement alone, regardless of whether the crime agreed upon actually is committed.

In New Jersey, as elsewhere, the law traditionally considered conspiracy and the completed substantive offense to be separate crimes. Accordingly, the conspiracy to commit an offense and the subsequent commission of that crime normally did not merge.

The reason for the rule was the common law's deep distrust for criminal combinations. The group activity was seen as posing a "greater potential threat" to the public than individual crime.

> For two or more to confederate and combine together to commit or cause to be committed a breach of the criminal laws is an offense of the gravest character, sometimes quite outweighing, in injury to the public, the mere commission of the contemplated crime.

Deeply rooted in the fear of criminal political conspiracy, the substantive crime of conspiracy became superimposed on offenses having no such political motivation. The crime took on a life of its own. At common law, and under some statutes, the combination could be a criminal conspiracy even if it contemplated only acts that were not crimes at all when perpetrated by an individual, or by many acting severally, or could result in a conspirator being found guilty not only of the conspiracy but of a completed offense even when the accused did not participate in the substantive offense.

In addition to its substantive overlay, the crime had distinct procedural advantages including the ability to use the statements of a co-conspirator made during and in furtherance of a conspiracy, the ability to try co-conspirators jointly, flexibility in the selection and place of trial, and finally, the ability to establish the existence of such an agreement through circumstantial evidence.

In this setting, there was perceived a danger of punishment for mere criminal intent with juries unable to separate individual guilt from guilt by association. The drafters of the American Law Institute's 1962 Model Penal Code undertook the "difficult task of achieving an appropriate balance between the desire to afford adequate opportunity for early law enforcement efforts and the obligation to safeguard" individual rights.

The drafters of the New Jersey Criminal Code substantially adopted the approach of the Model Penal Code. They undertook, in the words of the drafters, to "meet or mitigate these objections and then go on to develop a basic framework for the development of a law of conspiracy." Our Code recognizes the dual conception of the offense (1) to reach further back into preparatory criminal conduct than attempt, and nip the crime before its inception, and (2) to provide additional means of facilitating prosecutions, striking against the special dangers of group criminal activity. It balances it with fairness thus:

> The Code embraces this conception in some part but rejects it in another. When a conspiracy is declared criminal because its object is a crime, we think it is entirely meaningless to say that the preliminary combination is more dangerous than the forbidden consummation; the measure of its danger is the risk of such a culmination. On the other hand, the combination may and often does have criminal objectives that transcend any particular offenses that have been committed in pursuance of its goals.

The Code's resolution then is to permit cumulative sentences when the combination has criminal objectives beyond any particular offense committed in pursuance of its goals. The Code takes the view that in this sense conspiracy is similar to attempt, which is a lesser-included offense of the completed offense. A conviction of the completed offense will adequately deal with the conduct. The Code's drafters were equally explicit that "this is not true, however, where the conspiracy has as its objective engaging in a course of criminal conduct since that involves a distinct danger in addition to that involved in the actual commission of any specific offense." The Code recognizes the grave dangers that organized criminal activity poses to society. Therefore, the limitation of the Code is confined to the situation in which the completed offense was the sole criminal objective of the conspiracy. "There may be conviction of both a conspiracy and a completed offense committed pursuant to that conspiracy if the prosecution shows that the objective of the conspiracy was the commission of additional offenses."

Turning to the record before us, we must determine whether the judgment of conviction establishes that the conspiracy had additional criminal objectives other than the completed offense. For purposes of analysis, we shall view the indictment as charging two robberies-one at the Lincoln Café and another at the Edison Motor Lodge-and a conspiracy. The jury acquitted the defendants of the incident at the Lincoln Café, but convicted them of robbery and assault at the Motor Lodge and of conspiracy. The question comes down to this: Does the jury verdict establish that Hardison and Jackson conspired to commit the Lincoln Café Robbery?

The State contends that it does, arguing that there was evidence from which the jury could have inferred that the four defendants traveled from Paterson to New Brunswick for the purpose of committing the crime; and that although they were not the triggermen at the café, they were part of the conspiracy. The State points to one aspect of the charge that suggested that unless there was a knowing agreement between the parties to participate in both robberies, the jury should acquit them on the charge of conspiracy. Yet, other provisions of the charge specifically authorize the jury to find the defendants guilty of conspiracy even if it embraced only the incident at the Edison Motor Lodge. In part, the court charged the jury:

> If, however, you found that these defendants did not enter a conspiracy or agreement to commit a crime of robbery at the Lincoln Café, you may then consider whether or not subsequent to that they formed a conspiracy or agreement to commit a crime at the motel.
>
> If there was one overall conspiracy that covered both robberies, then you may find them guilty.
>
> If you found that they formed a conspiracy or agreement to rob only the motel, you may still find them guilty if you are satisfied as to each and all elements of the crime beyond a reasonable doubt.

Of particular significance too is the fact that although conspiracy was the first offense charged in the indictment, it was not the first offense considered by the jury. The court opened its charge by reading the indictment and stated:

> First it simply says that on the day in question these four gentlemen got together and conspired or agreed with one another to commit the crime of robbery later that day.

The court did not address the substance of the offense further at that time, and, after charging generally with respect to the burden of proof, demeanor, identification, reasonable doubt, and circumstantial evidence, addressed the substantive offenses before turning to the liability of the defendants as conspirators or accomplices. It explained generally robbery, theft, and aggravated assault. The court concluded by stating:

> The last charge that I am going to charge you about, but which is the first charge in the indictment, is called conspiracy, and then that is that these persons agreed to commit a criminal act.

Inchoate Offenses: Attempt & Conspiracy

It then discussed the substance of the offense. The defense strategy at trial had focused upon the fact that Hardison and Jackson were the unwitting companions of the real perpetrators in the Lincoln Café incident; that they had been with them but had no intent to rob. The witnesses at the café did not identify Hardison or Jackson as the triggermen. It was the night manager of the Edison Motor Lodge who positively identified Hardison and Jackson as his assailants, describing Jackson as the gunman and Hardison as the one who had struck him with the brass knuckles.

The jury was given nineteen questions to answer dealing with the various counts. Basically, the jury was asked: did the defendants commit robbery of the bartender and the patron at the Lincoln Café; did they commit robbery or assault of the night manager of the Edison Motor Lodge; did they possess a weapon? Finally they were asked to answer a last question "as to the charge of conspiracy to commit robbery," did they find the defendants not guilty or guilty?

Of course, we will not look behind a guilty verdict if there is legally sufficient evidence to sustain it, but in determining the basis of a jury verdict, courts may consider "the manner in which the case was sent to the jury." In this case, the manner is suggestive that the jury's finding of conspiracy did not embrace the Lincoln Café robbery.

First, the jury asked to be recharged only on the question of accomplice liability. It was specifically charged again:

> A person is legally accountable for the conduct of another, if he is an accomplice of such another person in the commission of a crime or he is engaged in a conspiracy with such other person.

> Now, how do we know what is an accomplice? Conspiracy you're going to have to decide. A person is an accomplice of another in a commission of an offense if, with the purpose of promoting or facilitating the offense, he aids, agrees or attempts to aid such another person in the planning or committing of it.

The jury rendered its verdict, not by reference to the counts of the indictment, but by reference to the questions put to them. The jury was polled as to each of the questions. As to the questions of the robbery of the bartender and the patrons at the Lincoln Café, the verdict was "not guilty." Had they conspired to commit that offense, the charge on accomplice liability would have suggested a verdict of guilt. As to the questions concerning the robbery and aggravated assault of the night manager and the unlawful use of a weapon, the verdict was guilty. The next question as to each was:

THE COURT: As to the charge of conspiracy to commit robbery, how do you find the defendant?

THE FOREMAN: We find the defendant guilty.

Based upon this record, we cannot conclude that the judgments establish that the preparatory conduct proven had other or further criminal objectives than the completed robbery. Hence, pursuant to the provisions of N.J.S.A. 2C:1–8a(2), the Appellate Division correctly ordered that the convictions should be merged.

It may be that in another case the proofs will be susceptible to a contrary conclusion. In this case, since we are satisfied that the conviction did not establish such multiple purposes, the judgment of the Appellate Division is affirmed.

POINT FOR DISCUSSION

Multiple Inchoate Offenses

In some jurisdictions, there are statutory provisions mandating that multiple inchoate offenses aimed at the same target offense merge into one another for purposes of sentencing. *See, e.g.,* 18 Pa. C. S. § 906 (1986) ("A person may not be convicted of more than one of the inchoate crimes of criminal attempt, criminal solicitation or criminal conspiracy for conduct designed to commit or to culminate in the commission of the same crime."). Does this approach make sense since each separate inchoate offense is based upon proof of a different *actus reus*?

Compare that Pennsylvania approach (which was taken from the Model Penal Code) to the approach taken by jurisdictions like Maryland, where the Court of Appeals has concluded that the offenses of *conspiracy* to commit armed robbery and *attempted* armed robbery, two inchoate offenses aimed at the same result, do *not* merge, holding that "the attempt to complete the elements of a crime is separate and distinct from the group planning of the crime itself." *Carroll v. State*, 428 Md. 679, 699, 53 A.3d 1159, 1170 (2012).

Which rule of law makes more sense to you? Why?

7. Culpability of Co-Conspirators

To what extent should a conspirator be deemed culpable for the criminal acts of his or her other co-conspirators? Consider the following leading case.

PINKERTON V. UNITED STATES
328 U.S. 640 (1946).

MR. JUSTICE DOUGLAS delivered the opinion of the Court.

Walter and Daniel Pinkerton are brothers who live a short distance from each other on Daniel's farm. They were indicted for violations of the Internal Revenue Code. The indictment contained ten substantive counts and one conspiracy count. The jury found Walter guilty on nine of the substantive counts and on the conspiracy count. It found Daniel guilty on six of the substantive counts and on the conspiracy count. Walter was fined $500 and sentenced generally on the substantive counts to imprisonment for thirty months. On the conspiracy count he was given a two year sentence to run concurrently with the other sentence. Daniel was fined $1,000 and sentenced generally on the substantive counts to imprisonment for thirty months. On the conspiracy count he was fined $500 and given a two year sentence to run concurrently with the other sentence. The judgments of conviction were affirmed by the Circuit Court of Appeals.

A single conspiracy was charged and proved. Some of the overt acts charged in the conspiracy count were the same acts charged in the substantive counts. Each of the substantive offenses found was committed pursuant to the conspiracy. Petitioners therefore contend that the substantive counts became merged in the conspiracy count, and that only a single sentence not exceeding the maximum two-year penalty provided by the conspiracy statute could be imposed. They rely on *Braverman v. United States*, 317 U.S. 49 (1942).

In the *Braverman* case the indictment charged no substantive offense. Each of the several counts charged a conspiracy to violate a different statute. But only one conspiracy was proved. We held that a single conspiracy, charged under the general conspiracy statute, however diverse its objects may be, violates but a single statute and no penalty greater than the maximum provided for one conspiracy may be imposed. That case is not apposite here. For the offenses charged and proved were not only a conspiracy but substantive offenses as well.

Nor can we accept the proposition that the substantive offenses were merged in the conspiracy. There are, of course, instances where a conspiracy charge may not be added to the substantive charge. One is where the agreement of two persons is necessary for the completion of the substantive crime and there is no ingredient in the conspiracy which is not present in the completed crime. Another is where the definition of the substantive offense excludes from punishment for conspiracy one who voluntarily participates in another's crime. But those exceptions are of a limited character. The common law rule that the substantive offense, if a felony, was merged in the conspiracy, has little vitality in this country. It has been long and consistently recognized by the Court that the commission of the substantive offense and a conspiracy to commit it are separate and distinct offenses. The power of Congress to separate the two and to affix to each a different penalty is well established. A conviction for the conspiracy may be had though the substantive offense was completed. And the plea of double jeopardy is no defense to a conviction for both offenses. It is only an identity of offenses which is fatal. A conspiracy is a partnership in crime. It has ingredients, as well as implications, distinct from the completion of the unlawful project. As stated in *United States v. Rabinowich*, 238 U.S. 78, 88 (1915):

> 'For two or more to confederate and combine together to commit or cause to be committed a breach of the criminal laws is an offense of the gravest character, sometimes quite outweighing, in injury to the public, the mere commission of the contemplated crime. It involves deliberate plotting to subvert the laws, educating and preparing the conspirators for further and habitual criminal practices. And it is characterized by secrecy, rendering it difficult of detection, requiring more time for its discovery, and adding to the importance of punishing it when discovered.'

Moreover, it is not material that overt acts charged in the conspiracy counts were also charged and proved as substantive offenses. As stated in *Sneed v. United States*, 298 F. 911 (5th Cir. 1924), 'If the overt act be the offense which was the object of the conspiracy, and is also punished, there is not a double punishment of it.' The agreement to do an unlawful act is even then distinct from the doing of the act.

It is contended that there was insufficient evidence to implicate Daniel in the conspiracy. But we think there was enough evidence for submission of the issue to the jury.

There is, however, no evidence to show that Daniel participated directly in the commission of the substantive offenses on which his conviction has been sustained, although there was evidence to show that these substantive offenses were in fact committed by Walter in furtherance of the unlawful agreement or conspiracy existing between the brothers. The question was submitted to the jury on the theory that each petitioner could be found guilty of the substantive offenses, if it was found at the time those offenses were committed petitioners were parties to an unlawful conspiracy and the substantive offenses charged were in fact committed in furtherance of it.

Daniel relies on *United States v. Sall*, 116 F.2d 745 (3rd Cir. 1940). That case held that participation in the conspiracy was not itself enough to sustain a conviction for the substantive offense even though it was committed in furtherance of the conspiracy. The court held that, in addition to evidence that the offense was in fact committed in furtherance of the conspiracy, evidence of direct participation in the commission of the substantive offense or other evidence from which participation might fairly be inferred was necessary.

We take a different view. We have here a continuous conspiracy. There is here no evidence of the affirmative action on the part of Daniel which is necessary to establish his withdrawal from it. *Hyde v. United States*, 225 U.S. 347, 369 (1912). As stated in that case, 'having joined in an unlawful scheme, having constituted agents for its performance, scheme and agency to be continuous until full fruition be secured, until he does some act to disavow or defeat the purpose he is in no situation to claim the delay of the law. As the offense has not been terminated or accomplished, he is still offending. And we think, consciously offending,—offending as certainly, as we have said, as at the first moment of his confederation, and consciously through every moment of its existence.' And so long as the partnership in crime continues, the partners act for each other in carrying it forward. It is settled that 'an overt act of one partner may be the act of all without any new agreement specifically directed to that act.' Motive or intent may be proved by the acts or declarations of some of the conspirators in furtherance of the common objective. A scheme to use the mails to defraud, which is joined in by more than one person, is a conspiracy. Yet all members are responsible, though only one did the mailing. The governing principle is the same when the substantive offense is committed by one of the conspirators in furtherance of the unlawful project. The criminal intent to do the act is established by the formation of the conspiracy. Each conspirator instigated the commission of the crime. The unlawful agreement contemplated precisely what was done. It was formed for the purpose. The act done was in execution of the enterprise. The rule which holds responsible one who counsels, procures, or commands another to commit a crime is founded on the same principle. That principle is recognized in the law of conspiracy when the overt act of one partner in crime is attributable to all. An overt act is an essential ingredient of the crime of conspiracy. If that can be supplied by the act of one conspirator, we fail to see why the same or other acts in furtherance of the conspiracy are likewise not attributable to the others for the purpose of holding them responsible for the substantive offense.

A different case would arise if the substantive offense committed by one of the conspirators was not in fact done in furtherance of the conspiracy, did not fall within the scope of the unlawful project, or was merely a part of the ramifications of the plan which could not be reasonably foreseen as a necessary or natural consequence of the unlawful agreement. But as we read this record, that is not this case.

Affirmed.

MR. JUSTICE RUTLEDGE, dissenting in part.

The judgment concerning Daniel Pinkerton should be reversed. In my opinion it is without precedent here and is a dangerous precedent to establish.

Daniel and Walter, who were brothers living near each other, were charged in several counts with substantive offenses, and then a conspiracy count was added naming those offenses as overt acts. The proof showed that Walter alone committed the substantive crimes. There was none to establish that Daniel participated in them, aided and abetted Walter in committing them, or knew that he had done so. Daniel in fact was in the penitentiary, under sentence for other crimes, when some of Walter's crimes were done.

There was evidence, however, to show that over several years Daniel and Walter had confederated to commit similar crimes concerned with unlawful possession, transportation, and dealing in whiskey, in fraud of the federal revenues. On this evidence both were convicted of conspiracy. Walter also was convicted on the substantive counts on the proof of his committing the crimes charged. Then, on that evidence without more than the proof of Daniel's criminal agreement with Walter and the latter's overt acts, which were also the substantive offenses charged, the court told the jury they could find Daniel guilty of those substantive offenses. They did so.

I think this ruling violates both the letter and the spirit of what Congress did when it separately defined the three classes of crime, namely, (1) completed substantive offenses; (2) aiding, abetting or counseling another to commit them; and (3) conspiracy to commit them. Not only does this ignore the distinctions Congress has prescribed shall be observed. It either convicts one man for another's crime or punishes the man convicted twice for the same offense.

Daniel has been held guilty of the substantive crimes committed only by Walter on proof that he did no more than conspire with him to commit offenses of the same general character. There was no evidence that he counseled, advised or had knowledge of those particular acts or offenses. There was, therefore, none that he aided, abetted or took part in them. There was only evidence sufficient to show that he had agreed with Walter at some past time to engage in such transactions generally. As to Daniel this was only evidence of conspiracy, not of substantive crime.

The court's theory seems to be that Daniel and Walter became general partners in crime by virtue of their agreement and because of that agreement without more on his part Daniel became criminally responsible as a principal for everything Walter did thereafter in the nature of a criminal offense of the general sort the agreement contemplated, so long as there was not clear evidence that Daniel had withdrawn from or revoked the agreement.

Whether or not his commitment to the penitentiary had that effect, the result is a vicarious criminal responsibility as broad as, or broader than, the vicarious civil liability of a partner for acts done by a co-partner in the course of the firm's business.

Such analogies from private commercial law and the law of torts are dangerous, in my judgment, for transfer to the criminal field. Guilt there with us remains personal, not vicarious, for the more serious offenses. It should be kept so. The effect of Daniel's conviction in this case, to repeat, is either to attribute to him Walter's guilt or to punish him twice for the same offense, namely, agreeing with Walter to engage in crime. Without the agreement Daniel was guilty of no crime on this record. With it and no more, so far as his own conduct is concerned, he was guilty of two.

> ### Hypo 14: *Conspiracy or Duress*
>
> Quinton Alston attempted to hijack a truck by pointing a gun at the driver (actually, it was a BB gun wrapped in a towel). When apprehended, he claimed that he was forced to participate in the hijacking by Bernard Short who told Alston that he would harm Alston's family if Alston didn't assist in the crime. Alston claims that he told the driver that he was being threatened and that the driver should go and call the police. (The driver denies this.) Alston has been charged, *inter alia*, with conspiracy to commit carjacking. Is Alston entitled to a renunciation instruction? *State v. Alston*, 311 N.J. Super. 113, 709 A.2d 310 (App.Div. 1998).

> ### Hypo 15: *Murder and Conspiracy*
>
> Defendant Jones planned with his codefendants, Craft and Moore, to rob Haywood. The three obtained a gun, and waited outside the lounge Haywood frequented until he exited, followed him to a hotel, and waited again. After several hours of stalking him, they then followed Haywood to his home. One of Haywood's neighbors testified that she heard gunfire and looked out her window to see Jones walk from Haywood's car to an older two-door gray Chevrolet, while the victim's car slowly moved forward to rest against a tree. Haywood was found slumped over the steering wheel of his car, dead from multiple gunshot wounds. Jones was convicted of attempted armed robbery, conspiracy to commit armed robbery, and murder. Should any or all of these offenses merge with one another? What do you think? *People v. Jones,* 234 Ill. App. 3d 1082, 176 Ill. Dec. 382, 601 N.E.2d 1080 (1992).

> ### Hypo 16: *The Murdered Bank Teller*
>
> X conspires with Y to rob a bank. Y is designated to "do the job" itself. X provides support and assistance before the fact. During the robbery, Y kills a bank teller. Can X be convicted of murder? Would it make a difference in your analysis if X and Y agreed that no guns were to be used, but where Y (without X's knowledge) did use a gun . . . and ended up killing someone in the course of the robbery?

SNOWDEN V. UNITED STATES
52 A.3d 858 (D.C. 2012).

RUIZ, SENIOR JUDGE.

Appellant was convicted in Superior Court of several offenses related to an armed robbery of a group of individuals: one count of conspiracy to commit armed robbery, one count of armed robbery, four counts of assault with intent to rob while armed (AWIRWA), one count of aggravated assault while armed (AAWA), and two counts of possession of a firearm during a crime of violence (PFCV).

The charges against appellant stemmed from a robbery and shooting on the evening of May 2, 2008, on the 4900 block of Jay Street, Northeast. That evening Lorenzo Ross ("Lorenzo"), his father, Lorenzo Ross, Sr., and his cousins, Derrick Ross, DeAngelo Martino, and Martin Scales, were "hanging by the dumpster in the parking lot" of Lorenzo's apartment complex, celebrating Lorenzo Ross, Sr.'s recent release from prison. At some point during the celebration, Lorenzo saw a girl he knew from the complex, Shaelin Rush, and he left the group to talk with her privately. While Lorenzo and Shaelin were talking, they saw a group of five "boys" in the vicinity. Lorenzo saw Shaelin approach the boys, hug them, and then go inside a nearby apartment building. Lorenzo recognized one of the boys as appellant because he was standing "right underneath" a lamp post. Lorenzo knew appellant because they rode the bus together to school every day, and that appellant went by the name of "Snoop."

Lorenzo testified that after Shaelin went inside, he saw appellant put on a black ski mask and heard him say to the other boys, "y'all ready, let's go." As the group of boys began to move toward Lorenzo's father and cousins, Lorenzo started toward the dumpster to warn his family that he had a "bad feeling" about the boys. Just as Lorenzo got to the dumpster, however, appellant came around the corner with a gun. As appellant rounded the corner and approached the group, Scales was on a cellular phone walking away from the group and, unknowingly, toward appellant. Lorenzo testified that upon rounding the corner appellant said, "give that shit up." Scales testified that appellant said, "you know what it is, let me get that." A second gunman walked behind the group and positioned himself "to the point where if Lorenzo and his group wanted to run he had a perfect angle to shoot them." The second gunman, who had a bandana covering his face and wielded a "big handgun" similar to an Uzi, was aiming the gun at the group, "moving" the gun between "different people."

Appellant ordered Scales to "get on the gate," and then "patted Scales's pockets." Scales responded by giving appellant $20 that he had in his front pocket. Appellant poked the gun into Scales's side, attempted to search Scales's other pockets and "take him down to the dumpsters so he could do a thorough search." Scales reacted by grabbing the gun and trying "to get the gun away from appellant or to get away from him." Scales "was swinging at appellant trying to hit him with everything he had, hoping appellant would drop the gun." Scales shouted for the rest of his group to flee; as Lorenzo and the others ran, the second gunman did not attempt to stop them. Scales and appellant fell to the ground fighting and the gun fired. Lorenzo testified that after he heard the gun discharge, he looked back and saw "them still fighting, wrestling." Scales tussled with appellant for "a long time," while the second gunman stood about twenty feet away with his gun directed toward Scales. Appellant eventually wrestled free of Scales and took off running with his gun.

After appellant fled, the second gunman kept his gun trained on Scales. Scales raised his arms in submission and told the gunman "you got all of the money that

I have." From the porch of a nearby house, Lanette Ross (Lorenzo's mother) and her sister said, "call the police," and yelled at the gunman, "don't shoot him." The gunman paused, raised and lowered his gun three times, and then shot Scales in the right-side of his abdomen.

The jury found appellant guilty of conspiracy to commit armed robbery; AAWA and armed robbery, as to Scales; four counts of AWIRWA, as to Lorenzo, Lorenzo Ross, Sr., Derrick Ross, and Martino; and seven counts of PFCV—one for each of the seven armed predicate offenses.

There was no evidence that appellant shot Scales; indeed, the evidence showed that appellant had fled with the $20 before the second gunman fired the shot. The government's theory of Scales's liability for AAWA was that the shooting was in furtherance of the conspiracy of which appellant was a part. In *Pinkerton v. United States*, 328 U.S. 640 (1946), the Supreme Court held that a defendant may be liable for the acts of his co-conspirator. Appellant argues that his conviction of AAWA must be vacated "because the evidence was insufficient to prove beyond a reasonable doubt that the aggravated assault of Mr. Scales by the second gunman was (1) in furtherance of the conspiracy or (2) a reasonably foreseeable consequence of it." Rather, he argues, what the evidence supports is that the shooting of Scales was a "random act of violence" by the second gunman for which appellant is not criminally responsible. We conclude that the evidence sufficed to permit the jury to find appellant guilty of AAWA under a *Pinkerton* theory of co-conspirator liability.

Appellant contends that there was no evidence that the second gunman's shooting of Scales was necessary to accomplish the objective of the conspiracy—robbery—as appellant had seized the money and run away with it, thus completing the robbery, by the time the shooting occurred. The government counters that the shooting was in furtherance of the conspiracy because it "occurred before all the culprits had escaped and it advanced the conspiracy's goals by assisting the escape and asportation of proceeds, protecting the robbers from Scales, punishing Scales' resistance, and discouraging Scales and others from reporting the offense or testifying against the robbers."

We have not previously considered whether a shooting by one co-conspirator that takes place after another co-conspirator has fled may be deemed to be "in furtherance of" the conspiracy for purposes of co-conspirator liability.

Insofar as the objective of appellant and his co-conspirators was to rob Scales, their goal was not completed until they had successfully made off with the fruits of their criminal endeavor. Although *Pinkerton* co-conspirator liability and accomplice liability are "distinct legal theories that require proof of different elements," we see no meaningful distinction between these theories of liability for the purpose of assessing whether the evidence supports that another's actions were committed "in furtherance of" a criminal enterprise. A shooting by a co-conspirator that is similarly causally linked to completion of the object of the conspiracy is properly charged against other co-conspirators under a theory of conspiracy liability.

Viewing the evidence presented in appellant's trial in the light most favorable to the government, we conclude that it was sufficient to support a determination that the shooting was in furtherance of the conspiracy to commit armed robbery. As noted, the second gunman shot Scales as appellant was fleeing with the money he had taken from Scales. Because the shooting guaranteed a clean escape for the assailants with the proceeds of their crime, the shooting aided in the successful completion of their criminal endeavor. Even if the second gunman appeared to hesitate, it was not a disconnected act, as the shooting occurred at the scene of the robbery and only about fifteen seconds after appellant had broken free from Scales, such that the jury could reasonably find that the shooting and the robbery were "one continuous and unbroken chain of events," rather than a "random act of violence," as appellant contends.

Appellant also argues that the shooting was not a reasonably foreseeable consequence of the robbery because the objective of the conspiracy had already been completed and there was "some appreciable interval of time" between the robbery and the shooting. We disagree. As the government points out, a shooting is quite naturally a reasonably foreseeable consequence of an armed robbery. A defendant who conspires to commit an armed robbery should anticipate that a shooting may occur during the commission of the robbery and is held accountable if a shooting does, in fact, occur. Appellant himself used a weapon to confront Scales and take his money. As we have discussed, the robbery was progressing even as appellant was fleeing the scene because the asportation of the proceeds was continuing at that time. Moreover, appellant's argument about the timing of the shooting (that "some appreciable interval of time" elapsed between the time appellant took the money from Scales and the shooting) is irrelevant because our proper focus is on whether a shooting is reasonably foreseeable at any point during the commission of the armed robbery. His argument is also factually inaccurate. Once Scales decided to fight back, appellant's ability to keep the cash could not be assured until he was able to break free and run away. The shooting took place only fifteen seconds later. Because appellant and at least one of his co-conspirators brought weapons to the scene of the robbery and both employed those weapons to effectuate the robbery, the jury could properly conclude that the shooting of Scales so soon after appellant fled was a reasonably foreseeable consequence of their conspiracy to commit armed robbery.

For the foregoing reasons, appellant's convictions are hereby Affirmed.

CHAPTER 7

Homicide

Homicide, the most serious of all criminal offenses, involves the killing of a human being by another human being. In some jurisdictions, moreover, relatively recent statutory enactments have extended homicide culpability to an actor's unlawful acts causing the death of a fetus.

By the late Common Law period in England, homicide consisted generally of only two constituent offenses, murder and manslaughter, the former crime distinguished from the latter by the presence of "malice aforethought." Despite the terminology, the crime of murder did not actually require either "malice" or "forethought." "Malice aforethought" was a term of art which referred to a homicide committed in any one of four ways: with the intent to cause death or serious bodily injury; with the knowledge that the action will cause death or serious bodily injury; when the killing occurred during the commission of a felony; or when the perpetrator intended to oppose, by force, an officer or justice of the peace in the performance of his or her duties.

Today, the various criminal code provisions relating to homicide found in federal law and in each of the fifty states (and the District of Columbia) are far more nuanced, more complicated and, candidly, more idiosyncratic. Accordingly, the way in which homicide offenses are classified in this Chapter should be viewed simply as a typical—but not a universal—American homicide taxonomy. Do not assume that any particular jurisdiction follows this approach precisely.

A. OVERVIEW OF THE LAW

Murder. All murder requires a showing of malice. Premeditated murder, sometimes termed murder in the first degree, is an intentional killing that also requires proof of premeditated, willful and deliberate conduct on the part of the accused.

Malice. Malice is wickedness of disposition, hardness of heart, wanton conduct, cruelty, recklessness of consequences, and/or a mind without regard to social duty. It is the distinguishing factor between murder and manslaughter in most jurisdictions. It may be proved expressly or it may usually be implied from the defendant's killing act committed with gross recklessness or from his or her actions establishing extreme indifference to the value of human life.

Premeditation and Deliberation. Some jurisdictions require proof of sustained and meaningful deliberation to establish this element, while others require proof only of momentary reflection. In the latter jurisdictions, "no time is too short" for an accused murderer to have been able to premeditate and deliberate sufficiently to justify conviction for first degree murder.

Voluntary Manslaughter. Voluntary manslaughter is mitigated murder. The mitigation usually arises because the defendant was found to have been reasonably provoked and to have acted in the heat of passion, or because the defendant honestly believed he or she needed to kill for protection purposes, but that belief was objectively unreasonable.

Felony Murder. Most jurisdictions have enacted a separate felony murder offense, transferring the necessary intent for murder from the accused person's commission of a specified, triggering felony.

Involuntary Manslaughter. Involuntary manslaughter is an unintentional killing committed without malice. Most jurisdictions use a gross (criminal) negligence *mens rea* as an element of this offense, but others use the *mens rea* element of recklessness instead.

Negligent Homicide. In some jurisdictions where involuntary manslaughter requires proof of recklessness, there is a lesser offense of negligent homicide which applies to criminally negligent killings.

The homicide rate has increased slightly since 2011. It was 5.0 in 2018, down from the rates in 2017 (6.8 percent) and 2009 (1.2 percent), but up 11.6 percent from the 2014 rate. See F.B.I. Uniform Crime Report, https://ucr.fbi.gov/crime-in-the-u.s/2018/crime-in-the-u.s.-2018/topic-pages/murder.

B. INTENTIONAL KILLINGS

In general, and typically, each jurisdiction's homicide provisions can be divided into two distinct categories: intentional and unintentional killings. The most serious form of homicide is an intentional killing.

1. Murder by Degrees

In most states, the crime of murder is divided into degrees. Homicides committed with the specific intention to kill usually are treated as first-degree murders. Consider, for example, California Penal Code § 189, which provides as follows:

> § 189. Murder; degrees
>
> (a) All murder that is perpetrated by means of a destructive device or explosive, a weapon of mass destruction, knowing use of ammunition designed primarily to penetrate metal or armor, poison, lying in wait, torture, or by any other kind of willful, deliberate, and premeditated killing, or that is committed in the perpetration of, or attempt to perpetrate, arson, rape, carjacking, robbery, burglary, mayhem, kidnapping, train wrecking, ... or murder that is perpetrated by means of discharging a firearm from a motor vehicle, intentionally at another person outside of the vehicle with the intent to inflict death, is murder of the first degree.
>
> (b) All other kinds of murders are of the second degree.
>
> [(d)] To prove the killing was "deliberate and premeditated," it is not necessary to prove the defendant maturely and meaningfully reflected upon the gravity of the defendant's act.

Major Themes

a. Change from Common Law—At common law, the presence or absence of "malice aforethought" was the distinguishing factor between murder (requiring malice) and manslaughter (no malice). That distinction tends to remain true today. But a number of additional, statutory homicide offenses also exist in every jurisdiction, criminalizing both intentional and unintentional killings. Unintentional killings are typically treated as less heinous homicide crimes and are punished less severely; intentional killings are typically treated and punished as the most culpable kinds of homicides.

b. Nature of Homicide Offenses—All homicide offenses require proof of a killing act (*actus reus*) committed by the accused which caused the death of a human being. The key distinction between the various homicide crimes is the different *mens rea* required to establish each separate statutory offense. Typically, the more difficult the *mens rea* is to prove, the more serious the homicide offense.

Like California, many states that divide the crime of murder into degrees specifically provide that a "willful," "deliberate" and "premeditated" homicide constitutes first-degree murder. In some of these states, courts have held that "no time is too short" for a wicked person to premeditate and deliberate upon his or her intention to kill. In other states, in contrast, premeditation and deliberation are not established unless it is shown that a cognizable period of reflection has occurred. Are these positions irreconcilable? Which positions most appropriately reflects first-degree murder's status as the most heinous of homicide offenses?

STATE V. RAMIREZ
190 Ariz. 65, 945 P.2d 376 (Ct.App. 1997).

NOYES, PRESIDING JUDGE.

A young man named David knocked on the door of Appellant's girlfriend's townhouse. Appellant opened the door and greeted David with an aggressive handshake, as if trying to overpower him. The two struggled for a moment, then quit. As they walked into the house, Appellant pressed a gun into David's ribs and said, "I could have took you out already." Nothing more happened between them.

About a month later, Appellant walked out of the townhouse and saw David's brother walking towards him. David and his brother looked alike. Appellant went up to the brother and shook hands with him, and greeted him, and then, for no apparent reason, pulled out a gun and shot him three times, killing him. Appellant paused between the second and third shots. There were several witnesses. As Appellant walked away, he pointed the gun at a girl and said, "Later, Vicki." Appellant said to one witness: "He started it. He deserves it." (The victim had done nothing.) Appellant said to another witness: "He showed me a gun. I gave him a bullet." (The victim had no gun.) By some accounts, Appellant appeared to be under the influence of alcohol and methamphetamine at the time. By all accounts, it was a senseless killing. Whether it was also a premeditated killing was the only contested issue in the trial.

The jury found Appellant guilty of first degree murder. Appellant claims that the jury instruction on premeditation "lessened the State's burden of proving premeditation." The statutory definition of premeditation provides:

> "Premeditation" means that the defendant acts with either the intention or the knowledge that he will kill another human being, when such intention or knowledge precedes the killing by a length of time to permit reflection. An act is not done with premeditation if it is the instant effect of a sudden quarrel or heat of passion.

In *Moore v. State*, 65 Ariz. 70, 75, 174 P.2d 282, 285 (1946), [it was] stated that, "deliberation and premeditation may be as instantaneous as successive thoughts of the mind."

Moore also cautioned that, "While the jury may be told that the brain can function rapidly they must not be misled into thinking that an act can at the same time be impulsive, unstudied and premeditated." The jury was so misled in Appellant's case. The court's instruction, as misargued by the State, essentially told the jury that an act could be both impulsive and premeditated.

The instruction given in Appellant's case was as follows:

> "Premeditation" means the defendant's knowledge that he will kill another person existed before the killing long enough to permit reflection. However, the time for reflection must be longer than the time required merely to form the knowledge that conduct will cause death. It may be as instantaneous as successive thoughts in the mind, and it may be proven by circumstantial evidence.
>
> It is this period of reflection, regardless of its length, which distinguishes first degree murder from second degree murder.

This instruction contains two ambiguities which turned into errors when the State misargued the law. First, by failing to be clear that premeditation requires actual reflection, the instruction allowed the State to argue that premeditation is just a period of time. Second, because the instruction commented that this period of time can be "instantaneous as successive thoughts in the mind" but provided no balancing language to the effect that an act cannot be both impulsive and premeditated, it allowed the State to argue, in effect, that premeditation is just an instant of time. The instruction says it can be as instantaneous as two thoughts in the mind.

The State argues that the instruction and the prosecutor were correct in Appellant's case; that premeditation is, in fact, a period of time rather than actual reflection. The State argues that actual reflection was not required after the 1978 enactment of A.R.S. section 13–1101(1).

Defining premeditation as a length of time (which can be instantaneous as successive thoughts in the mind) obliterates any meaningful difference between first and second degree murder—other than the penalties. The legislature has not merged these two offenses; it has prescribed different elements and different penalties for them. The minimum sentence for first degree murder is life in prison with possible release in twenty-five years; the maximum is the death penalty. The minimum sentence for second degree murder is ten years in prison; the maximum is twenty-two years. This significant difference in penalty ranges strongly suggests that the legislature intended there to be an equally significant difference between first and second degree murder; something with more relevance to criminal responsibility than an instant of time.

In Appellant's case, the only difference between first and second degree murder was the element of premeditation. In this case, as in most, after defendant formed the knowledge that he would kill he could not possibly pull the gun, and aim it, and pull the trigger faster than he could form a successive thought in his mind. Therefore, if the State's argument prevails, any murder is premeditated unless defendant acted faster than he could have a second thought. In real life, of course, many persons act without thinking twice, even when they have time to do so. But the State's definition of premeditation would include those unreflecting killers in the first degree murder category, along with those who actually reflected before acting. We conclude that the first degree murder statute has never been aimed at those who had time to reflect but did not; it has always has been aimed at those who actually reflected—and then murdered.

If the difference between first and second degree murder is to be maintained, premeditation has to be understood as reflection. It is fair to talk of the period of time in which reflection might occur; but it is not fair to define reflection as the period of time in which it might occur. To have meaning, the element of premeditation must describe something that defendant actually does. Just as murder requires actual killing, premeditation requires actual reflection. Premeditation can, of course, be proven by circumstantial evidence; like knowledge or intention, it rarely can be proven by any other means. The more time defendant has to reflect, the stronger the inference that he actually did reflect. This is what the statute is getting at—that actual reflection can be inferred from the length of time to permit reflection. That is the way it has always been and nothing we say here changes that. What we reject, however, is the notion that premeditation is just an instant of time.

Because of the premeditation instruction and argument in Appellant's case, however, the verdict merely establishes that an instant of time existed between Appellant's knowledge and his action. The verdict does not establish actual premeditation. Appellant claimed that he acted impulsively, without premeditation. Substantial evidence supports this claim. At sentencing, the trial court stated that defendant "impulsively and for no reason pulled out a gun and shot this person." If a properly-instructed jury viewed the evidence as the trial court did, it might have a reasonable doubt about premeditation; it might convict on second degree murder. On the other hand, if a properly-instructed jury viewed the evidence as our dissenting colleague does, it might convict on first degree murder.

We conclude that the jury instruction on premeditation, as argued by the State, obliterated the distinction between first and second degree murder. Because substantial evidence supports both Appellant's argument for second degree murder and the State's argument for first degree murder, we cannot say beyond a reasonable doubt that the error in the premeditation instruction did not contribute significantly to the first degree murder verdict.

Reversed and remanded for new trial.

RYAN, JUDGE, dissenting.

I disagree with the majority. This disagreement stems from A.R.S section 13–1101(1)'s clarity: "premeditation" is intent or knowledge of killing which precedes the killing "by a length of time to permit reflection." Under this language no actual reflection is required, and the jury decides the factual question of whether adequate time for reflection existed. Except for rare cases, reflection can be proven only by the passage of time. The legislature clearly decided not to require the state to prove actual reflection. Instead, it determined that an objective standard of proof of a passage of some period of time would be adequate. Such a determination is a legitimate legislative prerogative. Further, if the legislature had intended that actual reflection be an element of first-degree murder, it could have readily said so. I appreciate the majority's concern that, under the present statutory definition of premeditation, the line between first and second-degree murder is not entirely clear. While I share the majority's concern, the answer more appropriately rests with the legislature.

POINTS FOR DISCUSSION

a. Model Penal Code

The Model Penal Code does not divide the crime of murder into degrees. Instead, it treats "purposeful" or "knowing" homicides as murder, as well as unpremeditated murder (which is discussed in greater detail in Part B.1, *infra*):

§ 210.2. Murder.

(1) Except as provided in Section 210.3(1)(b), criminal homicide constitutes murder when:

    (a) it is committed purposely or knowingly; or

(b) it is committed recklessly under circumstances manifesting extreme indifference to the value of human life. Such recklessness and indifference are presumed if the actor is engaged or is an accomplice in the commission of, or an at-tempt to commit, or flight after committing or attempting to commit robbery, rape or deviate sexual intercourse by force or threat of force, arson, burglary, kidnapping or felonious escape.

(2) Murder is a felony of the first degree but a person convicted of murder may be sentenced to death, as provided in Section 210.6.

b. Capital Punishment

In many jurisdictions, first-degree murder can be punished by imposition of the death penalty, a sentence that is not available for conviction of any lesser degrees of murder or other homicide offenses. See Chapter 14, Section B (Capital Punishment).

As you review the cases in this Chapter on Homicide, you might consider whether—in your view—the aggravating factor of premeditation—the specific intention to kill—should be the dispositive factor in determining whether or not a convicted killer might be executed. Indeed, does it make sense to aggravate a conviction from second degree murder to first degree murder based solely on the factor of premeditation? What is the logic behind the focus on this factor to the exclusion of other facts, *e.g.*, the brutality of the killing? Is the focus on premeditation as such a significant aggravating factor justified by any of the classic justifications for punishment: retribution, restraint, deterrence, or rehabilitation? See Chapter 1. Is someone who commits a premeditated murder necessarily more deserving of punishment than someone who commits an unpremeditated, but nonetheless intentional murder?

c. Deterrence & Premeditation

Consider the issue of deterrence. Do you think that someone who reflects before committing a crime is more amenable to deterrence? If so, does that fact provide a reason for punishing premeditated homicides more severely? Is the possibility of punishment likely to deter the anguished spouse of a suffering cancer patient who euthanizes his or spouse out of love? See discussion in the preceding section. Does a deterrence rationale provide sufficient—or any—justification to treat that spouse more severely than an accused person who brutally but impulsively beat an old woman or child to death?

2. Voluntary Manslaughter

The offense of voluntary manslaughter is also an intentional killing, but it is an intentional killing which has been mitigated from murder to manslaughter due to the presence of adequate and sufficient provocation or other appropriate sorts of excuses for engaging in a killing act. Or, to put it another way, voluntary manslaughter is an intentional murder which includes additional circumstances that serve to negative the requisite element of malice needed to establish murder.

Given its mitigating status, voluntary manslaughter is usually not charged by the prosecution, but rather it is raised as a defense by the accused, i.e. "I killed the victim but the killing was the result of circumstances which mitigate the severity of the offense from murder to manslaughter." In most (but not all) jurisdictions, there are two distinct types of voluntary manslaughter: (1) provocation or "heat of passion" defenses; and (2) imperfect defenses.

a. *Provocation or Heat of Passion Defense*

One justification for mitigating an intentional homicide to manslaughter is when the defendant acted as a result of adequate "provocation" or in the "heat of passion."

POINT FOR DISCUSSION

Model Penal Code

The Model Penal Code also contains a "heat of passion" provision (although it does not refer to the provision in that way and does not limit the application to "passion" situations). Section 210.3, manslaughter, provides as follows: "Criminal homicide constitutes manslaughter when a homicide which would otherwise be murder is committed under the influence of extreme mental or emotional disturbance for which there is reasonable explanation or excuse. The reasonableness of such explanation or excuse shall be determined from the viewpoint of a person in the actor's situation under the circumstances as he believes them to be." Is this the right approach to this issue?

SUPRENANT V. STATE
925 N.E.2d 1280 (Ind. Ct. App. 2010).

BAILEY, JUDGE.

Jack Edwin Suprenant, Jr. ("Suprenant") appeals his conviction and sixty-year sentence for Murder, a felony. We affirm.

Suprenant, Kerry Bruckman, and Bruckman's three children (two of which [*sic*] were fathered by Suprenant) lived together in Gary, Indiana. On September 16, 2006, after the couple had argued for several days, in part over Bruckman's involvement with a mutual friend, Bruckman stated her intention to leave Suprenant and began gathering her clothes. Suprenant tried to persuade Bruckman to stay; when his efforts failed, Suprenant stabbed Bruckman repeatedly. Bruckman's screams caused the children to run into their mother's bedroom, where they witnessed some of the attack. Suprenant chased the children back to their bedrooms and continued his attack on Bruckman. Ultimately, Suprenant inflicted sixty-one wounds (including forty-nine stab wounds) upon Bruckman and she died.

Suprenant was tried before a jury on the charge of Murder. He was convicted and sentenced to sixty years imprisonment. He now appeals.

Indiana's Voluntary Manslaughter statute provides:

(a) A person who knowingly or intentionally:

  (1) kills another human being; or

  (2) kills a fetus that has attained viability;

while acting under sudden heat commits voluntary manslaughter, a Class B felony. However, the offense is a Class A felony if it is committed by means of a deadly weapon.

(b) The existence of sudden heat is a mitigating factor that reduces what otherwise would be murder under section 1(1) of this chapter to voluntary manslaughter.

The statute specifies that sudden heat is a mitigating factor to Murder, as opposed to an element of Voluntary Manslaughter. Although Voluntary Manslaughter is a lesser-included offense of Murder, it is an atypical example of a lesser-included offense. Sudden heat must be separately proved and, therefore, if there is no serious evidentiary dispute over sudden heat, it is error for a trial court to instruct a jury on voluntary manslaughter in addition to murder.

"Sudden heat" is characterized as anger, rage, resentment, or terror sufficient to obscure the reason of an ordinary person, preventing deliberation and premeditation, excluding malice, and rendering a person incapable of cool reflection. Anger alone is not sufficient to support an instruction on sudden heat. Nor will words alone "constitute sufficient provocation to warrant a jury instruction on voluntary manslaughter," and this is "especially true" when the words at issue are not intentionally designed to provoke the defendant, such as fighting words.

In addition to the requirement of something more than "mere words," the provocation must be "sufficient to obscure the reason of an ordinary man," an objective as opposed to subjective standard. Finally, Voluntary Manslaughter involves an "impetus to kill" which arises "suddenly."

The trial court refused to instruct the jury on Voluntary Manslaughter, concluding that Bruckman's words to Suprenant were insufficient provocation for sudden heat. Where the trial court rejects a Voluntary Manslaughter instruction based on a lack of evidence of sudden heat, we review the trial court's decision for an abuse of discretion.

The parties agree that the record discloses evidence that Suprenant became enraged; they disagree as to the existence of a serious evidentiary dispute such that the jury could conclude that the lesser offense was committed but the greater was not. In arguing that sufficient evidence existed to support the giving of a Voluntary Manslaughter instruction, Suprenant claims that he "lost it" when Bruckman failed to deny that she had been unfaithful to him and was gathering things to move out of the residence with their children. He argues that the act of gathering belongings went beyond mere words. In response, the State points to the legal insufficiency of mere words and also to evidence that shows deliberation and cool reflection inconsistent with sudden heat.

Perigo v. State, 541 N.E.2d 936, 938 (Ind.1989) involved the killing of a woman and her fetus after she admitted to the defendant that "their relationship was finished," she had engaged in sexual intercourse with another man, and did not know by whom she was pregnant. The defendant had unsuccessfully argued to the trial court that confessions of illicit sex are sufficient provocation for a Voluntary Manslaughter verdict. On appeal, the Court reiterated the principle that "words alone are not sufficient provocation to reduce murder to manslaughter", but nonetheless recognized, "[i]n some circumstances, words may be combined with actions engendering sufficient provocation to reduce an offense from murder to manslaughter."

Subsequently, the Court has recognized that discovery of alleged infidelity can "introduce the element of sudden heat." *Evans v. State*, 727 N.E.2d 1072, 1077 (Ind.2000). In *Evans*, the defendant had witnessed his recent girlfriend having sexual intercourse with another man, placing "sudden heat" in issue; yet the State had negated the presence of sudden heat by showing that the defendant had, after witnessing the tryst, gone downstairs, armed himself with knives, cut the telephone line, gone back upstairs, stood outside the bedroom for over a minute, and then struggled with and killed the man. *See also Ford v. State*, 704 N.E.2d 457, 460 (Ind.1998) (observing that there was substantial evidence that a husband was not acting under sudden heat when, three days after discovering his wife's affair, he took a pistol and shot her twice at close range); *Horan v. State*, 682 N.E.2d 502, 507 (Ind.1997) (there was no serious evidentiary dispute as to whether husband was acting in sudden heat when he beat his wife's lover to death after an earlier confrontation and beating).

Here, the alleged provocation was comprised of words ending a relationship accompanied by preparations to leave. Although there was some non-verbal action by the victim, we do not find that the lawful conduct of gathering ones belongings goes so far beyond "mere words" as to constitute "sudden heat" justifying a Voluntary Manslaughter instruction.

Furthermore, the record is replete with evidence that the impetus to kill did not "suddenly" arise in response to a contemporaneous event. The couple had been arguing at length. Earlier on the day of Bruckman's death, Suprenant had told his mother that Bruckman planned to leave and take the children. During that conversation, he was alternately calm and angry. He had also told his father of Bruckman's alleged infidelity.

Most compelling, Suprenant stopped his attack on Bruckman when confronted by the children, forced each of them into their rooms, and returned to resume stabbing his victim. [When] Suprenant's screaming children confronted him, he had ample time to reflect upon the heinousness of his actions and seek help for the children's mother. He chose not to do so. We find no abuse of discretion in the trial court's rejection of a Voluntary Manslaughter instruction.

Affirmed.

POINTS FOR DISCUSSION

a. Proving Lack of Provocation

As a matter of due process, the prosecution has the burden of proving the existence of all of the elements of a crime beyond a reasonable doubt. *In re Winship*, 397 U.S. 358, 90 S.Ct. 1068, 25 L.Ed.2d 368 (1970). As a result, because the traditional provocation defense to a murder charge has been viewed as serving to negative the element of malice aforethought that is requisite for a murder conviction (thus mitigating the offense to voluntary manslaughter), in jurisdictions that use this traditional defense, the Supreme Court has held that—when provocation is offered as a (mitigating) defense—the burden of proof is upon the prosecution to prove beyond a reasonable doubt that the defendant was not provoked. *Mullaney v. Wilbur*, 421 U.S. 684, 95 S.Ct. 1881, 44 L.Ed.2d 508 (1975).

b. Extreme Emotional Disturbance

In jurisdictions where a version of the provocation defense has been enacted in such a way that it does *not* serve to mitigate a finding of malice necessary to establish murder, the burden of proof of establishing provocation may be placed upon the defendant. *Patterson v. New York*, 432 U.S. 197, 97 S.Ct. 2319, 53 L.Ed.2d 281 (1977) (upholding a New York "extreme emotional disturbance" mitigating defense which placed the burden of proof on the defendant where that defense served to mitigate second-degree murder which did not have malice aforethought as an element).

c. Imperfect Defense

An "imperfect defense" arises when a defendant commits an intentional murder, but does so under circumstances in which he or she honestly believes—unreasonably—fit within the parameters of a legal defense, usually self-defense. Most, but not all, jurisdictions recognize the existence of imperfect defenses. In those that do, when a complete defense is imperfectly established, i.e. every element is met except reasonableness, the crime is mitigated from murder to voluntary manslaughter.

C. UNINTENTIONAL KILLINGS

The typical set of unintentional killings found in an American jurisdiction's crimes code consists of second-degree murder, felony-murder, and involuntary or reckless manslaughter.

Again, as mentioned previously, it is important to be aware that there is great variability in each state's homicide provisions. In some states, for example, the residual category of murder (sometimes called second-degree or, in some states, third-degree murder) is treated as the equivalent of an intentional killing, albeit as a lesser included offense of first-degree murder. In some states, there is no felony-murder offense at all. And in some states, there are additional homicide offenses which are deemed to be equivalent or less serious in moral culpability to involuntary manslaughter, *e.g.*, negligent homicide or homicide by vehicle.

1. Unpremeditated Murder

At common law, as previously noted, the crime of murder involved a homicide committed with "malice aforethought." Malice could be express or implied. When implied, often these crimes involved unintentional killings that were committed by someone whose conduct manifested gross recklessness or an extreme indifference to the value of human life.

This type of murder is called different things in different jurisdictions. Most often, it is deemed "second-degree murder." In common law terms, it is referred to as "depraved heart murder"; in Model Penal Code terms, § 210.2, the crime is reckless murder committed "under circumstances manifesting extreme indifference to the value of human life." Sometimes, it is simply denominated "murder" (implying the absence of premeditation or the specific intent to kill found in "first-degree" or "premeditated" murder definitions).

STATE V. BURLEY
137 N.H. 286, 627 A.2d 98 (1993).

BATCHELDER, JUSTICE.

On January 7, 1989, the defendant was at home with his ex-wife, Debbie Glines, with whom he had reconciled. He drank at least six beers between noon and 6:00 p.m. At approximately 6:30 p.m., he telephoned 911 requesting an ambulance for a gunshot wound. The police and ambulance crews arrived to find Ms. Glines lying on the kitchen floor with a gunshot wound on the right side of her head, from which she eventually died.

The defendant told the officers on the scene that he had been cleaning a .22 caliber semi-automatic handgun when it accidentally discharged. At the station the defendant explained that he had been keeping the handgun and a .22 caliber rifle for a friend. He stated that he retrieved the gun and a loaded clip of ammunition from a closet, placed them on tables in the living room, went to the kitchen for a beer, and took a cotton swab from the bathroom to clean the gun, which he admitted he had cleaned two weeks before. He loaded the gun, knowing he had made it ready to fire, before getting the beer. After watching television for twenty minutes, he picked up the gun and went to sit on the living room floor at the entryway to the kitchen. He knew that his ex-wife was in the kitchen. The gun went off, he stated, as he was cleaning excess oil from it, with the gun in his left hand and a finger in the trigger housing. He acknowledged familiarity with the operation of a .45 caliber semi-automatic, which is functionally similar to a .22.

A search of the defendant's apartment revealed two spent bullet casings in a garbage bag. No cotton swabs were found in the living room or kitchen. The defendant agreed to re-enact the shooting at his apartment. Although at first stating that he did not know what had happened to the empty casing, when the officers told him it had been found in the trash, he admitted that he must have thrown it away. He admitted that he had occasionally "dry-fired" the gun by aiming the unloaded weapon at articles around the room. He was unable to tell the officers where they might find the clip to the .22, which they had been unsuccessful in locating.

Several days later the defendant returned to the police station after locating the clip. It had apparently been in his jacket pocket and had fallen out at his mother's house later on the night of the shooting. At that time, he admitted, after being told of a bullet found lodged in his wall, that the second shell found in the trash came from his having fired the rifle in the apartment two days before shooting his ex-wife. He had been "joking around with it and it discharged." Ultimately, the defendant admitted he had not been cleaning the handgun when he shot his ex-wife, although he denied he had been dry-firing it. He stated that he "was fooling around with it on the floor and it went off." In all, he gave the police three different versions of how he had been holding the gun that night.

The defendant was tried on the charge of second degree murder. He requested and was granted a lesser included offense instruction for manslaughter and for negligent homicide.

The indictment charged that the "defendant committed the crime of second degree murder by causing the death of his wife under circumstances manifesting an extreme indifference to the value of human life, by shooting her in the head with a pistol." The defendant argues that, as extreme indifference represents a greater degree of culpability than recklessness, additional factual allegations must appear in the indictment. The indictment informed the defendant that he was charged with recklessly, under circumstances manifesting extreme indifference to the value of human life, causing his ex-wife's death on a specific date by shooting her in the head. This was constitutionally sufficient.

The defendant next argues that the evidence was insufficient to prove the element of extreme indifference. We will uphold the verdict unless, viewing the evidence and all reasonable inferences in the light most favorable to the State, no reasonable trier of fact could have found guilt beyond a reasonable doubt. In a prosecution for second degree murder charging extreme indifference to the value of human life, "the existence and extent of disregard manifested" are for the jury to determine on the facts of the case.

The evidence here showed, *inter alia*, that the defendant was familiar with the operation of a semi-automatic handgun, that he knew he had loaded the .22, and that he knew his ex-wife was in the next room. He had been drinking beer all afternoon and his blood alcohol content nearly five hours after the shooting was .15. At the time of the shooting, he was sitting with his elbows resting on raised knees with the barrel of a gun he knew to be loaded pointing into the kitchen where his ex-wife was located. The gun was cocked and ready to fire, and the defendant's finger was in the trigger housing. A firearms expert testified that due to its safety features the gun could not have fired without simultaneously gripping the safety on the back of the handle and squeezing the trigger. The defendant, who had told the police he knew not to point a gun at anyone, finally admitted that he had been "fooling around" with it after consistently lying by saying he had been cleaning it. On all the evidence the jury was warranted in finding that the defendant's conduct occurred under circumstances manifesting extreme indifference to the value of human life and in thereby finding him guilty of second degree murder.

Affirmed.

2. Felony-Murder

At common law, one of the ways in which murder could be established was to demonstrate that the accused committed a homicide in the process of committing or attempting to commit a felonious act. Today, most (but not all) jurisdictions continue to recognize felony-murder as a distinct homicide offense, either as a separate component of first-degree murder, or as an entirely distinct crime.

Although felony-murder can be proved by establishing an unintended killing in the course of the commission of certain specified felonies, in another sense, felony-murder is actually an intentional killing in which the intent to kill is imputed (or "transferred") from the accused's intent to commit the dangerous felony at issue.

POINTS FOR DISCUSSION

a. Model Penal Code

Although the Model Penal Code nominally rejects the felony-murder rule, it does contain the following provision concerning homicides that occur in the course of the commission of seven specified felonies:

§ 210.2. Murder.

(1) Except as provided in Section 210.3(1)(b), criminal homicide constitutes murder when . . . it is committed recklessly under circumstances manifesting extreme indifference to the value of human life. Such recklessness and indifference are presumed if the actor is engaged or is an accomplice in the commission of, or an attempt to commit, or flight after committing or attempting to commit robbery, rape or deviate sexual intercourse by force or threat of force, arson, burglary, kidnapping or felonious escape.

b. Independent Felony Required

In many jurisdictions, the triggering felony for felony murder cannot be an offense that is inherent in the act of killing itself, like assault or battery or discharging a firearm. In other words, the triggering felony must be independent of the killing itself. *See, e.g., People v. Rosenthal*, 394 Ill. App. 3d 499, 914 N.E.2d 694, 333 Ill. Dec. 275 (2009).

c. Triggering Felonies

Some states do not enumerate an exclusive list of triggering felonies for application of the felony-murder rule (or to establish murder, as in the MPC), but instead apply the rule to in any situation where the facts are deemed sufficiently dangerous to human life to justify application of the doctrine. Using this latter approach, would a defendant be guilty of felony murder where he and three of his friends chased their victim, tripped and kicked him, and dropped a boulder on his head, thus committing an aggravated assault that resulted in the victim's unintended death? Or would the defendant only be guilty of reckless or negligent homicide? *See Roary v. State*, 385 Md. 217, 867 A.2d 1095 (2005*).*

Does it make sense to apply the felony-murder doctrine to *all* felonies? For example, under federal law, it is a felony to file a false tax return. On the way to the post office to file a fraudulent return, A's brakes fail without warning and despite regular and diligent maintenance. Unable to stop, A hits and kills a pedestrian. Should this be treated as felony murder?

d. Acquittal of Underlying Felony

In Pennsylvania, as in many other states, a defendant may only be convicted of felony murder if the victim's death occurred during the commission of or an attempt to commit (or flight after committing or attempting to commit) enumerated, serious felonies, which include in Pennsylvania, "robbery, rape, or deviate sexual intercourse by force or threat of force, arson, burglary or kidnapping." Pa. Cons. Stat. § 2502(b) & (d). If a defendant is charged with *both* robbery and felony murder based upon the death of a frightened robbery victim from a heart attack, should a felony-murder conviction stand if the jury finds the defendant innocent of the robbery? Should a robbery verdict stand if the jury finds the defendant innocent of felony-murder during the commission of the robbery?

e. Misdemeanor Manslaughter

At common law, a misdemeanor-manslaughter rule also existed, imputing the offense of manslaughter to actors who committed an unlawful act not amounting to a felony which nonetheless resulted in the death of a victim. This rule was rejected by the draftsmen of the Model Penal Code as "objectionable on the same ground as the felony-murder rule." It has also been abolished in most states. Moreover, in those states that still retain a version of the rule, either by common law or by statute, typically the unlawful act needs to be *"malum in se"* (inherently wrong and immoral in nature in contrast to *"malum prohibitum"* offenses that are wrong simply because a legislature says so) in order to suffice to establish manslaughter. Do you think there is a place in modern American penal codes for some version of this common-law rule?

f. *Faulkner's* Logic

Is the felony murder doctrine consistent with *Regina v. Faulkner* (in Chapter 3 on *Mens Rea*), in which a sailor went down in the hold of a ship to steal some rum and accidentally burned the ship? The English court concluded that Faulkner could not be convicted of "maliciously" burning a ship. If A intends to rob a convenience store and a customer is accidentally killed when B drops his gun, is it fair or appropriate to convict A of murder? Is a murder conviction consistent with the justifications for punishment?

3. Involuntary Manslaughter

The crime of involuntary manslaughter is, as the name implies, an unintentional killing. It is distinguished from unintentional murder, however, by the absence of the element of malice.

The *mens rea* showing actually required to establish the existence of involuntary manslaughter varies widely by jurisdiction. In most jurisdictions, involuntary manslaughter is established when it is proved that the accused has acted with gross negligence (sometimes, in circular fashion, deemed "criminal negligence"), resulting in someone's death. In other jurisdictions (and the Model Penal Code), however, involuntary manslaughter is not established absent the higher showing of recklessness; rarely, a lesser showing of ordinary negligence (sometimes, again, in circular fashion, called "civil negligence") is all that is required to establish this offense.

NOAKES V. VIRGINIA
280 Va. 338, 699 S.E.2d 284 (2010).

Opinion by JUSTICE CYNTHIA D. KINSER.

In this appeal, a defendant challenges the sufficiency of the evidence to support her conviction for involuntary manslaughter, specifically contesting the findings that she was criminally negligent and that her acts were a proximate cause of a toddler's death. Because there is sufficient evidence to support both findings, we will affirm the judgment of conviction.

The relevant facts are undisputed. The defendant, Elizabeth Pollard Noakes, provided child care services in her home, and on the day in question, October 18, 2006, had in her care Noah Alexander Colassaco, a fifteen-month-old child, and two other children. Noakes had been caring for Noah for approximately three weeks and, throughout that time, had experienced difficulty in getting Noah to lie down and sleep during "nap time." Instead, he usually would stand in the crib and cry. Noakes had tried "traditional means" to help Noah sleep, which included "rocking him to sleep" and "patting his back," without success.

Around noon on the day in question, Noakes put Noah and another toddler she was caring for in their cribs for an afternoon nap. The cribs were located in an upstairs, "loft" bedroom that was partially visible from Noakes' bedroom. The cribs, however, were not visible from Noakes' bedroom. Noah's crib, as viewed from the loft's entrance, was positioned lengthwise against the back wall of the room, in the far right corner. The rectangular crib was abutted on the right by one wall, on the rear with another, and on the left by another crib, with only the front, lengthwise portion unobstructed. A third crib, in which Noakes placed the other toddler that day, was positioned a few feet from Noah's crib, nearer the entrance of the loft and also on the right wall. When Noakes left the loft, Noah was standing "facing the front of the crib" and crying.

At approximately 12:30 p.m., Noakes returned to the loft to "check on" Noah, who was still standing in the crib and crying. Knowing that when Noah stood in his crib, his chin was above the crib's sides, and also that Noah would fall asleep if he were lying or sitting in the crib instead of standing, Noakes decided to place a make-shift covering over the crib to prevent Noah from standing. After removing Noah from his crib, Noakes placed a thirty-three and one-quarter pound, collapsed "dog crate," which ran the length of the crib but was substantially narrower, on top of the crib. Noakes reasoned that the crate's weight would prevent Noah from standing up in the crib.

Noakes tested the stability of her contraption by shaking the crib with the crate on top to determine if the crate could fall into the crib and injure Noah. Satisfied that the crate could not fall into the crib, Noakes removed the crate, put Noah back into the crib, and placed a fabric-covered piece of approximately one-inch thick cardboard on top of the crib. The cardboard was added, in part, to cushion the force of any impact between Noah's head and the crate if Noah attempted to stand. Although the cardboard would cover the entirety of the crib's top, Noakes positioned it so the cardboard extended out over the front of the crib, where Noah often stood, thus leaving a small "gap" in the rear between the crib's side and the cardboard. Noakes then placed the dog crate on top of the cardboard, towards the front side of the crib, where it covered a little more than one-half of the crib's width. Noakes examined the covering to ensure that Noah would not be able to reach into the dog crate and injure his fingers.

With Noah in his now-covered crib, Noakes remained in the loft for a short while to determine if the enclosure was causing any distress to Noah and if he was attempting to stand up in the crib despite the covering. Observing no problems, Noakes left the loft. Sometime before 1:00 p.m., Noakes, however, heard a noise from the loft and returned to find Noah sitting in his crib but not sleeping, with his face pressed against crib's front, mesh side. Concluding that Noah would not fall asleep if he were able to look for her, Noakes placed a toy in front of the crib to obstruct Noah's view "so that he would not be looking for Noakes but would just get bored and go to sleep."

Noakes again left the loft at about 1:00 p.m. and did not return until 3:15 p.m., when she came to wake the other toddler from his nap. Noakes testified, however, that she monitored the toddlers audibly from her bedroom during that time and heard no noise from either of them. Noakes testified that when she returned to wake the other child, she did not look at Noah's crib, which was several feet to the left of the other crib, but "within her peripheral vision of the room." She believed, however, that Noah was asleep since she did not hear any sounds from him when she awakened the other toddler.

Shortly after 4:00 p.m., Noakes returned to the loft to wake Noah and found him unconscious. He was standing with his chin resting on the side of the crib, one or both of his hands gripping the crib's side, and his head and neck wedged between the cardboard and the crib. His lips were blue and his skin was cold to Noakes' touch. Noakes surmised that Noah had attempted to stand, had pushed up against the cardboard causing the dog crate to slide a few inches thereby creating a space between the covering on top of the crib and the crib's wall. Noah then had moved his head toward the crib's center, where he normally stood, trapping himself in a space between the side of the crib and the cardboard, which was held in place by the weight of the dog crate. Despite Noakes' efforts to revive Noah and the intervention of emergency medical personnel, Noah was pronounced dead at Noakes' home.

Noakes was subsequently convicted in a bench trial in the Circuit Court of the County of Chesterfield of involuntary manslaughter. The trial court sentenced Noakes to five years of incarceration, with four years suspended on the condition that she "be of good behavior upon her release from confinement" for a period of twenty years.

On appeal to the Court of Appeals of Virginia, a divided panel affirmed the trial court's judgment. Upon rehearing en banc, the Court of Appeals found that the "trial court could reasonably have concluded that Noakes recklessly disregarded Noah's safety by proceeding with her plan to prevent Noah from standing up by placing the dog crate on his crib." Noakes now appeals to this Court. In a single assignment of error, she asserts the evidence was insufficient as a matter of law to sustain her conviction, claiming that "her acts did not rise to the level of criminal negligence nor could she have anticipated the unforeseeable acts that would be performed by the child while inside the crib."

When the sufficiency of the evidence is challenged on appeal, we review "the evidence in the light most favorable to the Commonwealth, the prevailing party in the trial court" and "accord the Commonwealth the benefit of all reasonable inferences deducible from the evidence." We give the trial court's judgment sitting as the factfinder "the same weight as a jury verdict," and we will affirm that judgment unless it "is plainly wrong or without evidence to support it."

We have defined the common law crime of involuntary manslaughter as "the killing of one accidentally, contrary to the intention of the parties, in the prosecution of some unlawful, but not felonious, act; or in the improper performance of a lawful act." To convict a person for involuntary manslaughter caused by the improper performance of a lawful act, the Commonwealth must show that the improper performance of the lawful act "amounted to an unlawful performance of such lawful act, not merely a negligent performance; that is, the lawful act must have been done in a way so grossly negligent and culpable as to indicate an indifference to consequences or an absence of decent regard for human life." "The accidental killing must be the proximate result of a lawful act performed in a manner 'so gross, wanton, and culpable as to show a reckless disregard of human life.'"

"In this context, the terms 'gross, wanton, and culpable' describe conduct. The word 'gross' means 'aggravated or increased negligence' while the word 'culpable' means 'deserving of blame or censure.'" Gross negligence amounts to criminal negligence "when acts of a wanton or willful character, committed or omitted, show 'a reckless or indifferent disregard of the rights of others, under circumstances reasonably calculated to produce injury, or which make it not improbable that injury will be occasioned, and the offender knows, or is charged with the knowledge of, the probable result of his or her acts.'" While the improper performance of a lawful act must be "'so gross and culpable as to indicate a callous disregard of human life,'" it need "'not be so gross as to raise the presumption of malice.'"

In determining whether conduct rises to the level of criminal negligence, an "objective standard" applies, and criminal negligence may be found to exist when the defendant "either knew or should have known the probable results of his/her acts." Thus, the Commonwealth did not need to prove that Noakes actually knew or intended that her conduct would cause, or would likely cause, Noah's death, but rather that Noakes should have known her acts created a substantial risk of harm to Noah.

Noakes concedes on brief "that it is not necessary for a defendant to foresee the specific manner in which injury occurred." Noakes, nevertheless, argues that in evaluating the foreseeability of death or serious injury to Noah, attention must be given to the measures she "took to insure that death or serious injury would not occur." Noakes points to her purpose for covering the crib-"to assist the child in sleeping"-and the "painstaking lengths [taken by her] to anticipate possible dangers and prevent them," as well her "regular" returns "to the adjoining bedroom so that she could monitor the child as she did housework." Noakes claims, "each of these measures reduced the probability of harm to the child to the point that no reasonably intelligent person, using an objective standard, could be charged with the knowledge that the child probably would be harmed by the object." In summary, Noakes claims that "it was her inability to predict any and all possible dangers that failed her."

Upon review of the evidence, we conclude that Noakes' conduct in placing cardboard and a thirty-three and one-quarter pound, collapsed dog crate atop Noah's crib and failing to visually check on him for about three hours was wanton and willful, "showing a reckless or indifferent disregard of Noah's rights, under circumstances that made it not improbable that injury would be occasioned, and Noakes is charged with the knowledge of the probable result of her acts." Noakes knew that Noah would attempt to stand in his crib and also that when doing so, Noah's head and chin rose above the height of the crib's sides. While she obviously took steps to prevent the crate's falling upon Noah and his reaching into the crate, Noakes should have known that a toddler, used to standing but constrained against his will, might attempt to free himself, thereby dislodging the makeshift covering and sustaining serious injury. The measures that Noakes undertook to prevent the crate from falling upon Noah demonstrate her actual knowledge of the inherent danger of the contraption she placed atop the crib. And, because Noakes knew that she had placed Noah in an inherently dangerous situation that could cause serious injury, she certainly should not have left Noah unattended for approximately three hours.

In sum, we agree with the Court of Appeals' conclusion:

> The act of attempting to limit Noah's ability to stand in his crib was not inherently unlawful; however, a rational factfinder could indeed determine that the placing of a thirty-three-pound dog crate on Noah's crib, combined with Noakes' inattentiveness in the face of this experimental and dangerous set-up and with Noah's conceded determination to stand up in his crib, constituted reckless and unlawful conduct in utter disregard of Noah's safety.

Affirmed.

STATE V. BROOKS
163 Vt. 245, 658 A.2d 22 (1995).

ALLEN, CHIEF JUSTICE.

Defendant purchased a home that was equipped with a driveway heater. Hot water, heated by gas in the unit's boiler, flowed through a system of pipes beneath the driveway to melt snow and ice. Exhaust fumes from the system were supposed to exit through a vent located on the backside of the garage. Defendant turned on the driveway heater before running an errand. While he was gone, another occupant, Jill McDermott, and her infant became ill from noxious fumes that had emanated from the garage. When defendant returned home, McDermott asked him to take her and the baby to the hospital. Defendant took them to the emergency room where they were examined and released.

Defendant thought the fumes were caused by a plumbing problem and called C & L Plumbing and Heating. C & L sent an employee to inspect the heater who determined that a dislodged flap was preventing proper exhaust. He explained the malfunction to defendant and told him that repairs should be made and safety features added. A Vermont Gas Systems (VGS) employee also examined the system. Both servicemen decided the gas should remain off until repairs were made. The VGS employee told McDermott the system was not safe to operate and that she was lucky to be alive, "because it was carbon monoxide." McDermott relayed these comments to defendant. That night, the owner of C & L called defendant and told him that the heater had been improperly installed. A VGS supervisor also called and explained the dangers of the condition and agreed that it should be repaired.

In May 1988, defendant hired a real estate agent to sell his home. Defendant did not mention the heater's history to the agent. Instead, defendant instructed the agent to turn the heater on, then off, when demonstrating it to prospective buyers. The heater was a highlighted feature in agent's marketing materials. In July 1988, the agent showed the house to Linda Cifarelli. The agent explained and demonstrated the driveway heating system by turning it on for approximately five minutes. During their second showing, defendant, who was present to answer questions, explained and demonstrated the driveway heater again, but did not mention its prior problem or faulty condition. Cifarelli purchased the house. During a professional home inspection, defendant demonstrated the heater, but did not explain how it worked or mention its history. At the closing, defendant insisted that the Cifarellis return to the house with him for a more detailed showing because "he knew things the inspector wouldn't know." Defendant showed Linda Cifarelli and her parents the central vacuum system, the drainage system, and the driveway heater. When showing the heater, he told them it was not necessary to run it for more than two hours.

On the evening of December 9, 1988, Linda Cifarelli and her husband, John, turned on the driveway heater because it was snowing. They put their two young daughters to bed upstairs and followed shortly after. A house guest, Andrew Csermak, stayed awake to watch television. After a while, Csermak became dizzy and nauseous, and eventually vomited. Csermak cracked a window and fell asleep on the downstairs couch. When Csermak awoke at noon, he was concerned because the Cifarellis were not yet awake. He went upstairs and discovered that only the infant daughter was still breathing. Csermak called 911.

Upon arrival, the police and firemen discovered the bodies of John and Linda Cifarelli and their four year old daughter. The police also found the garage door dripping with condensation and the driveway heater running. Autopsies revealed that Linda and John Cifarelli and their daughter died of carbon monoxide poisoning.

Defendant was convicted of involuntary manslaughter by reckless endangerment. Because the underlying unlawful act charged was reckless endangerment, defendant's conviction could only be sustained upon finding reckless intent. Defendant argues that the instruction defining recklessness was flawed because it incorporated both the criminal negligence and recklessness standards but did not distinguish between the two. Defendant maintains that while recklessness requires an actual awareness of the risk and of the resulting harm, criminal negligence requires a less stringent showing that the actor should have known of the risk and harm. According to defendant, the failure to distinguish between the two levels of intent amounted to plain error, because the jury could have convicted him if it found only that he should have known either that the heater was not repaired, or that the heater posed a risk.

We have endorsed the Model Penal Code's definition of recklessness, MPC § 2.02(2)(c), which explains:

> A person acts recklessly with respect to a material element of an offense when he consciously disregards a substantial and unjustifiable risk that the material element exists or will result from his conduct. The risk must be of such a nature and degree that, considering the nature and purpose of the actor's conduct and the circumstances known to him, its disregard involves a gross deviation from the standard of conduct that a law-abiding person would observe in the actor's situation.

In contrast, criminal negligence occurs when the actor should be aware that a substantial and unjustifiable risk exists or will result from his conduct. Disregarding the risk amounts to a gross deviation from the standard of care that a reasonable person would observe in the actor's situation.

Contrary to defendant's suggestion, both recklessness and criminal negligence require an objective view of the risk; the difference is one of degree. The more critical distinction between recklessness and criminal negligence is the actor's subjective awareness of the risk. Recklessness requires a conscious disregard of the risk. In contrast, criminal negligence results when an actor is unaware of the risk which the actor should have perceived.

The court properly instructed the jury to objectively assess the risk and to determine whether defendant consciously disregarded that risk. For further clarification, it referred the jury to the reckless endangerment instruction, which expressly required a finding that defendant "actually knew from the circumstances then existing that the heater had not properly been repaired." If there was any flaw in the instruction, it stemmed from the court's use of the term "reasonable-person" instead of "law-abiding person" when describing the standard for objectively assessing the nature of the risk. This does not amount to plain error.

Defendant challenges the court's denial of his motion for acquittal, claiming there was insufficient evidence to convict on the essential elements of recklessness and a legal duty. We consider whether the evidence, taken in a light most favorable to the State and excluding modifying evidence, is sufficient to fairly and reasonably support a finding of guilt beyond a reasonable doubt. Defendant contends that proof of both recklessness and the existence of a legal duty hinged on finding that he actually knew the driveway heater had not been repaired. Defendant argues that there was insufficient evidence to prove beyond a reasonable doubt that he knew the driveway heating unit had not been repaired. We disagree.

Defendant knew the heater was malfunctioning and emitting fumes when he took McDermott and her infant child to the hospital in November 1987. Representatives from C & L and VGS testified that they explained the exhaust problem to defendant and told him that the system was dangerous and needed repairs. Although there was conflicting testimony about who was responsible for the repairs, resolving this confusion was less important than determining when, and if, defendant thought the repairs were completed.

Defendant's position was that he thought the heater was fixed by VGS shortly after, if not immediately following, the November 1987 accident. Other witnesses, however, testified to conversations with defendant about repairing the heater which refute defendant's position. The C & L employee, Linden, testified that one month after the accident, defendant told him the heater was still unrepaired. Linden then told defendant he was "playing Russian roulette." Defendant suggests that he construed Linden's conversation with him to mean that Linden had fixed the problem. Linden testified, however, that a reasonable person would not have thought the problem was fixed. In sum, there was sufficient evidence fairly and reasonably supporting a finding that defendant actually knew the heater had not been repaired when he sold his home to the

Cifarellis. With this critical finding and other supporting evidence, the jury could reasonably conclude that defendant had the requisite reckless intent. There was sufficient evidence to support a finding that defendant's failure to disclose the existence of the malfunctioning heater before selling his home amounted to a conscious disregard of a substantial and unjustifiable risk.

There was also sufficient evidence that defendant breached his legal duty to disclose the heater's defect. " 'Where material facts are accessible to the vendor only, and he knows them not to be within the reach of the diligent attention, observation and judgment of the purchaser, the vendor [of real estate] is bound to disclose such facts.' " Defendant knew that the heater could emit noxious fumes into the home, if unattended, and that it was unrepaired when his home was on the market. Defendant also accompanied both Linda Cifarelli and the home inspector on their tours of the home. In each instance, he demonstrated the heater, but did not mention its history. The jury could reasonably conclude that defendant knew that the Cifarellis, despite two walk-throughs and a home inspection, were unaware of the heater's dangerous condition. Thus, there was sufficient evidence upon which the jury could find that defendant failed to disclose a material defect when he had a duty to disclose them.

Defendant also argues that the scope of involuntary manslaughter predicated on reckless endangerment is prone to arbitrary and discriminatory enforcement. Although we cannot specify every set of facts which constitute reckless conduct, the recklessness standard is sufficiently precise to prevent it from being arbitrarily applied. The scope of conduct which may be deemed reckless is sufficiently narrowed by the requirement that the risk, when objectively viewed, amounts to a gross deviation from the standard of conduct that a law-abiding person would observe in the actor's situation. The statute is not unconstitutionally vague.

Affirmed.

POINT FOR DISCUSSION

Model Penal Code

The Model Penal Code contains the following provisions defining manslaughter and negligent homicide. Note the difference in the applicable *mens rea* elements:

§ 210.3. Manslaughter.

(1) Criminal homicide constitutes manslaughter when:

(a) it is committed recklessly; or

(b) a homicide which would otherwise be murder is committed under the influence of extreme mental or emotional disturbance for which there is reasonable explanation or excuse. The reasonableness of such explanation or excuse shall be determined from the viewpoint of a person in the actor's situation under the circumstances as he believes them to be.

(2) Manslaughter is a felony of the second degree.

§ 210.4. Negligent Homicide.

(1) Criminal homicide constitutes negligent homicide when it is committed negligently.

(2) Negligent homicide is a felony of the third degree.

STATE V. POWELL
336 N.C. 762, 446 S.E.2d 26 (1994).

FRYE, JUSTICE.

Hoke Lane Prevette, a five-foot, one and one-half inch, ninety-four pound jogger, was attacked by defendant's dogs and died as a result of multiple dog bites. The dogs were away from defendant's property and had been loose earlier that day.

Defendant owned two Rottweilers, "Bruno" and "Woody." Each dog was a little over one year old. Bruno weighed eighty pounds and Woody weighed one hundred pounds. At approximately 9:00 p.m., Hoke Prevette, who was five-foot, one and one-half inches tall and weighed ninety-four pounds, left his home to go jogging. At about 11:00 p.m., James Fainter and his wife returned [home,] discovered Prevette's body in their front yard, and notified the police. Prevette did not have a pulse. Dr. John Butts, Chief Medical Examiner for the State of North Carolina, concluded that Prevette died as the result of multiple dog bites. Prevette's external injuries included shallow scrapes, deeper puncture wounds that extended down into tissue, evulsing skin, and skin torn away creating large holes in some places. His internal injuries included broken ribs on the left side and collapsed lungs. The cause of death was determined to be collapsed lungs, loss of blood, and choking.

David Moore, who lived nearby, testified that he saw defendant's dogs when he arrived home at about 9:30 p.m. One of the dogs growled but both dogs relented when Moore stamped his foot. Another neighbor [encountered] two Rottweilers he recognized as defendant's dogs earlier that evening when he drove his sister and sister-in-law home. He held the dogs at bay while the women entered the house.

After the discovery of Prevette's body, Police Officer Jason Swaim went to defendant's house to investigate a report that defendant's dogs had been out that evening. When Swaim advised defendant that he wanted to see his dogs, defendant responded, "Oh my God, what have they done now?" Defendant admitted that his dogs had been out twice that day and that he picked the dogs up in his automobile at approximately 9:00 p.m. at the intersection of Cascade Avenue and Dinmont Street.

Robert Neill of the State Bureau of Investigation Crime Laboratory testified that six hairs removed from Prevette's clothing were canine; however, he could not match the hairs to a particular dog. An SBI forensic serologist found human blood on Woody's collar, on a sample of Woody's hair, on the dog dish, on a portion of the wall from defendant's home, and on defendant's car seat. A forensic odontologist testified that dental impressions taken from Bruno and Woody were compatible with some of the lacerations in the wounds pictured in scale photographs of Prevette's body.

Several witnesses testified to seeing Bruno and Woody running loose in the neighborhood prior to 20 October 1989 and to their aggressive behavior. Defendant's former girlfriend testified that defendant abused the dogs by kicking and hitting them. Animal Psychologist Donna Brown testified regarding an evaluation for aggressive propensities that she performed on Bruno and Woody in November 1989. She videotaped her testing and showed the videotape to the jury. Dr. Brown concluded that both dogs showed dominance and predatory aggression. She opined that an attack on a person would be consistent with her observations of Bruno's and Woody's behavior.

Animal Behavioralist Peter Borthelt testified for the defense that, although he had not evaluated the dogs, he had reviewed Dr. Brown's videotape and her results which he found to be ambiguous. He testified that aggressiveness was only one possible interpretation of the dogs' behavior and that some of it could be labeled "play."

Defendant presented several witnesses who testified that Bruno and Woody were friendly and playful and responded to his commands to get down or sit.

Other defense witnesses testified that the dogs were not aggressive when they were loose in the neighborhood. Powell was convicted of involuntary manslaughter.

Defendant contends that there was insufficient evidence to establish the essential elements of involuntary manslaughter; thus, the trial court erred in denying his motion to dismiss at the close of all the evidence. Involuntary manslaughter is the unlawful killing of a human being without malice, without premeditation and deliberation, and without intention to kill or inflict serious bodily injury. Involuntary manslaughter may also be defined as the unintentional killing of a human being without malice, proximately caused by (1) an unlawful act not amounting to a felony nor naturally dangerous to human life, or (2) a culpably negligent act or omission. "An intentional, willful or wanton violation of a statute or ordinance, designed for the protection of human life or limb, which proximately results in injury or death, is culpable negligence." A death which is proximately caused by culpable negligence is involuntary manslaughter.

At the time of the attack on Prevette, a Winston-Salem ordinance provided:

> No dog shall be left unattended outdoors unless it is restrained and restricted to the owner's property by a tether, rope, chain, fence or other device. Fencing, as required herein, shall be adequate in height, construction and placement to keep resident dogs on the lot, and keep other dogs and children from accessing the lot. One (1) or more secured gates to the lot shall be provided.

A safety statute or ordinance is one designed for the protection of life or limb and which imposes a duty upon members of society to uphold that protection. According to the Court of Appeals and the State, this section of the Winston-Salem Code "was designed to protect both the persons of Winston-Salem and their property, and thus is a safety ordinance." Defendant contends that the ordinance is merely a nuisance law "designed to prevent roaming dogs from trespassing, damaging property, leaving waste in neighbors' yards and interfering with traffic."

After a careful reading of the ordinance, we conclude that it is designed to protect persons as well as property. Although it is silent as to its purpose, a logical reading of the ordinance leads us to conclude that it promotes the safety of persons as well as property. It is without question that the ordinance has the effect of protecting property from damage by roaming dogs. However, the life and limb of pedestrians, joggers, and the public at large are protected by this ordinance as well. The ordinance protects people generally by confining the dogs to the owner's property while providing, in some cases, an adequate fence to keep animals and children from accessing the lot and being exposed to the dogs. The fact that the ordinance serves a dual purpose does not make it any less a safety ordinance.

The evidence that defendant intentionally, willfully, or wantonly violated the safety ordinance was aptly set out by the Court of Appeals.

> Bruno and Woody had been picked up by animal control officers on at least three occasions prior to the fatal attack. The dogs had been taken by animal control officers to the animal shelter as recently as August, 1989, two months prior to the death of Prevette. Defendant admitted that his dogs had been out twice on the day of Prevette's death. On one occasion in July, 1989, after the dogs escaped by digging out from underneath the fence, defendant simply covered the escape hole with a cooler after returning the dogs to the fence. Defendant's next-door neighbor testified that the dogs were allowed to run loose "on a regular basis," day and night, and that defendant would often "just open the door and let the dogs out." Defendant's ex-girlfriend testified that defendant let the dogs run free both day and night.

The trial judge instructed the jury that "the violation of a statute or ordinance governing the care of dogs which results in injury or death will constitute culpable negligence if the violation is willful, wanton, or intentional." Viewed in the light most favorable to the State, as we must on a motion to dismiss, we find that the State presented sufficient evidence that defendant intentionally, willfully, or wantonly violated the ordinance.

The decision of the Court of Appeals is affirmed.

POINT FOR DISCUSSION

Vehicular Homicide Offenses

In a number of jurisdictions, separate vehicular homicide offenses exist (distinct from involuntary manslaughter) which apply to deaths resulting from negligent operation of a motor vehicle. Typically, these specific forms of negligent homicide statutes provide for lower levels of punishment than involuntary manslaughter statutes, but are established with a lesser showing of culpability.

Why do you suppose jurisdictions might prefer to enact *separate* criminal offenses to apply to vehicular homicide? Why not cover this activity under the standard involuntary manslaughter offense or under a *general* negligent homicide statute?

> **Hypo 1: *Perils of Criminal Defense***
>
> Defendant became upset with his defense counsel after a jury found him guilty of the charged offenses and, while the prosecutor was making his sentencing arguments to the court, defendant abruptly struck his attorney on the side of the head with his fist with such force that counsel was immediately knocked unconscious and fell to the floor. Defendant continued to punch and kick him until being tackled by sheriff's deputies. After he was subdued, defendant also attempted to bite his then-unconscious attorney as the two men lay on the courtroom floor. The audio recording device used by the court reporter captured several statements defendant made during and immediately after the incident, including the following:
>
>> "I would try to kill. I hope he's dead! I tried to kill him, he tried, he just took my life. I hope you die ------ f-----! I told you you was f------ with the wrong one! Oh jack ass leg [sic] lawyer. They found me guilty. I hope you die George! You took my life, I'm gonna to take yours. I hope the bastard die. You done f----- the last ----- you gonna f--- in your lifetime."
>
> Counsel was badly injured and had to be hospitalized in intensive care. Was this act premeditated sufficiently to support conviction of defendant for attempted murder? (Does this case give you any second thoughts about a career as criminal defense counsel?) *See State v. Forrest*, 609 S.E.2d 241 (N.C. Ct. App. 2005).

> **Hypo 2: *Homicidal Dream***
>
> Defendant forcibly entered a mobile home while the residents were asleep. He removed his clothes, pulled four large steak knives from a knife block, walked to the bedroom where the residents were sleeping, and stabbed both of them in the chest. He then fled, leaving his clothing behind, and took refuge in his own nearby trailer. One victim died. The other called the police who found evidence linking defendant to the scene, including his wallet and the keys to his car and trailer house, all of which he had left behind in the kitchen when he fled the murder scene naked. When the police awakened defendant, he agreed to accompany them to the police station. On the way to the station, he told them that he knew why they wanted to talk with him. He said he had had a dream in which he "knifed" a couple of people and he was afraid they were dead. Defendant asked the police if this incident really happened. When told

that it had, he started to cry. He said he had spent the evening drinking and that he did not remember everything that happened. He did remember entering the trailer, grabbing knives, entering a bedroom, and making a swinging motion at two people. He also remembered running naked back to his trailer. He previously had fantasized about killing people whom he did not know, "like a spy" would do. Also, months before the killing, defendant had wondered aloud in the presence of friends what it would be like to kill someone and had asked them if they ever had thought about killing anyone. Was this killing "premeditated?" *See State v. Netland*, 535 N.W.2d 328 (Minn. 1995).

Hypo 3: *Shooting While High on Meth*

Crystal Brady, Andrea Larez, Kaprice Conde, and Julian Tafoya had been up for five days partying. They got into a car and began cruising around Roswell, New Mexico, where they lived, listening to loud music, smoking meth and marijuana, and drinking alcohol. Brady was driving the car, which belonged to Larez. The car had a standard transmission, which was unfamiliar to Brady, and at one point the occupants heard a loud sound, and the car stalled out. Right after the car stalled, Tafoya shot Larez repeatedly in the back of the head. Conde and Brady both testified that there was a sudden gunshot followed by more shots. A police officer in the area described the gunfire as multiple shots in fairly rapid succession, possibly with a short pause between the fourth and fifth shot. After the first shot, Brady observed that Larez had been shot and appeared to have died instantly from the wound. When asked what Brady was thinking after she saw that Larez had been shot, she testified that "she didn't think—it was all so sudden." Brady further testified that upon seeing that Larez had been shot, she turned toward the back of the car screaming and saw Tafoya's face. She did not remember him saying anything, but added that "he looked like a scared little punk," and that she thought he was really high. After being shot, Brady was able to exit the car and crawl away for help. Was Tafoya's killing of Larez "premeditated?" *See State v. Tafoya*, 285 P.3d 604, 2012–NMSC–030 (N.M. 2012).

Hypo 4: *Firing at Police*

Uniformed police officers were executing a no-knock search warrant at Paul Lyons' apartment. The officers yelled "Police search" outside the apartment and, at the very same moment, broke down the front door with a battering ram. Lyons fired at the entering officers, killing one of them only a few feet inside his apartment. Is Lyons guilty of premeditated murder? *See State v. Lyons*, 340 N.C. 646, 459 S.E.2d 770 (1995).

Hypo 5: *Provocation Without Passion*

Alice learns that her husband is having an adulterous relationship with Lorena. A reasonable person would have been outraged by the news, but Alice was not outraged. However, because she hates Lorena, Alice used the news as an opportunity to kill her. Is Alice entitled to a mitigation of her crime to manslaughter?

Hypo 6: *Reasonable Impotent?*

Bedder, who was sexually impotent, tried in vain to have sex with a prostitute. She jeered at him and attempted to get away. Defendant tried to prevent her from leaving, but she slapped him in the face and punched him in the stomach. At this point, defendant took out a knife and stabbed the prostitute to her to death. Is Bedder entitled to a voluntary manslaughter instruction if he is tried for murder? *See Bedder v. DPP*, [1954] 2 All E.R. 801, [1954] 1 W.L.R. 1119, 38 Cr.App. 133.

Hypo 7: *The Klansman*

During the Summer of 2005, a former Ku Klux Klan member, Edgar Ray Killen, was convicted of killing three civil rights workers in 1964. The evidence showed that the victims were brutally beaten and shot, and that their bodies were buried in an earthen dam. The case was complicated by the age of the evidence, fading witness recollections, and by the fact that no witness was able to positively place Killen at the scene of the crime. The trial ended with a conviction of manslaughter as a lesser included offense of murder, rather than murder itself. Given the nature of the killings, how do you explain a conviction for manslaughter instead of murder? *See Killen v. State*, 958 So.2d 172 (Miss. 2007).

Hypo 8: *Imperfect Battered Spouse Defense?*

Defendant Karla Porter contracted with a third-party to kill her abusive husband. Convicted of first degree murder, she claims on appeal that because she believed she was in imminent danger from her husband even though she felt no such fear on the day of the murder, she was entitled to an imperfect self-defense jury instruction at trial. Does this argument make sense? *See Porter v. State*, 455 Md. 220, 166 A.3d 1044 (2017).

Hypo 9: *Russian Roulette*

Three teenage boys are playing Russian Roulette. They insert a single bullet in a gun that can be loaded with six bullets. One boy spins the cylinder, places the gun to another boy's head, and pulls the trigger. The gun discharges, killing the boy. The remaining two boys, who never intended to kill their friend, are horrified. Is it possible to say that they have committed murder in the "purposeful" or "knowing" sense? Have they committed reckless murder as in *Burley*? Argue the case for the prosecution. How might the defense respond? What facts makes this a "murder case?" Is it the way the gun was loaded? The way the "game" was played? Something else? *See Commonwealth v. Malone*, 354 Pa. 180, 47 A.2d 445, 447 (1946).

Hypo 10: *Shooting to Scare*

Burkman had a stormy relationship with the victim, Kathryn Burns. On the day in question, Burkman argued with her about whether she was having an affair with a co-worker. At some point, Burkman retrieved a gun from the linen closet and threw it on the bed in front of Burns who picked up the gun, looked at it, and pulled back the hammer. Burkman asked her why she pulled the hammer back—did she want to kill herself? Burns simply shrugged. Burkman then waved the gun in front of her face and yelled at her that she should kill herself. Intending to scare Burns, Burkman aimed the gun at a pillow behind her and fired. The bullet accidentally struck and killed her. Is Burkman guilty of murder? *See Cook v. Maryland*, 118 Md. App. 404, 702 A.2d 971 (Ct. Spec. App. 1997).

Hypo 11: *Homicidal Child Neglect*

The police, investigating allegations of child abuse, found Malone sitting with five of her children in the living room of her house. In a second floor bedroom, they found her seven-month-old twin daughters dead from starvation. The facts revealed that Malone was a cocaine addict who neglected her children. Neither the prosecution nor the defense denies that she neglected a "duty" to her children. The only question was whether she committed the crime of manslaughter or reckless murder. Is your answer to this question affected by the fact that Malone's drug addiction rendered her unaware of her children's needs and therefore of the risk of death? *See Commonwealth v. Miller*, 426 Pa. Super. 410, 627 A.2d 741 (1993).

Hypo 12: *High Speed Chase*

Defendant Jason McKinley was found guilty of second degree murder due to the fact that he had run a red light while being chased by a police car for speeding, smashing head on into another car at between 93 and 100 miles per hour, killing the driver. McKinley argues that while he was "admittedly reckless," the evidence did not support a murder conviction, only an involuntary manslaughter conviction. Is he right? *See McKinley v. State*, 945 A.2d 1158 (Del. 2008).

Hypo 13: *Bombing Buildings*

Would an individual who placed and exploded a bomb in a building which she believed was unoccupied, but which resulted in the unintended death of someone who was (unbeknownst to the bomber) trespassing in that building, be guilty of felony murder? Why or why not? How about second-degree (reckless) murder?

Hypo 14: *Guns for Intimidation*

A & B decide to rob a convenience store. Both are carrying guns, but they explicitly agree that neither is to shoot anyone else. The weapons are being carried simply for the purpose of intimidation. Consider the following scenarios and decide whether A is guilty of felony murder if the following events occur during the robbery:

a. becomes enraged at a recalcitrant clerk and kills him in cold blood;

b. accidentally drops his gun, and it discharges killing a customer;

c. The clerk pulls out a weapon and shoots and kills B;

d. As A & B are trying to escape, a police officer arrives and shoots and kills B; and

e. On the way to commit the robbery, A fails to see a red light and smashes into another car and kills a passenger.

Hypo 15: *Next Day Chase*

Suppose that the police are looking for A, a robbery suspect, the robbery having occurred the previous day. Suddenly a police officer sees A's car on the highway, and during the high-speed car chase that follows, A runs into and kills, B, a pedestrian. Is A guilty of felony murder under the California approach described in *Portillo*? If these events occurred in Pennsylvania with a felony murder statute as described in Point for Discussion d., *supra*, would that make a difference in your analysis?

Hypo 16: *Horsing Around*

A horse escaped from a fenced enclosure at the Sea Horse Ranch. The fence was weather-worn, rotting, and dilapidated. The horse strayed onto an adjacent coastal highway, and while running free after dark one evening, collided with a car, killing the passenger when the impact of the collision crushed the roof of the passenger compartment. Assuming that the owners knew of the dilapidated condition of the fence and that horses had escaped from there previously (eight horses were found wandering free on the road that night), could they be prosecuted successfully for involuntary manslaughter? How about negligent homicide under the Model Penal Code formulation above? See *Sea Horse Ranch, Inc. v. Superior Court*, 24 Cal. App. 4th 446, 30 Cal. Rptr. 2d 681 (1994).

> **Hypo 17: *Spousal Psychosis***
>
> Andrea Yates was convicted of murder for drowning her five children. The evidence revealed that, following her second pregnancy and with every pregnancy thereafter, she suffered post-partum psychosis. At the time of the murders, she claimed that she believed that the only way to get her children to heaven (and thereby escape the devil), was to kill them. Suppose that Andrea's husband, Rusty, was aware that she suffered post-partum psychosis after each pregnancy, but continued having children with her. Suppose further that, at the time of the killings, it was clear that she was suffering mental problems in conjunction with post-partum psychosis following the birth of her fifth child. Nevertheless, each morning, Rusty went to work and left Andrea alone with their children. Rusty's mother came to help Andrea later in the day, but there was a two-hour gap during which Andrea was alone with the children. If the preceding suppositions are treated as fact, did Rusty commit either involuntary manslaughter or negligent homicide (as defined by the MPC)?

CHAPTER 8

Assault & Battery

Early state criminal codes often did not define the elements of the crimes of "battery" or "assault" because judges were expected to use English precedents to identify and interpret these elements. These precedents recognized two definitions of the battery crime and one definition of the assault crime. Over time, the elements of these definitions were codified in most states, but even today, some codes leave the terms "battery" and "assault" undefined.

The common law battery crimes were broadly defined under English law. One type required proof that the defendant's conduct caused "bodily injury" to the victim, and the other type required proof of an "offensive touching" of the victim. By contrast, the only type of "assault" crime under English law was the attempt to commit a battery, and it was defined narrowly to cover only defendants who had the actual ability to commit a battery and came very close to doing so. Over time, many state courts and legislatures decided to recognize a second type of "frightening" assault crime, requiring evidence that the defendant engaged in frightening conduct with the intent to cause the victim to fear bodily injury. Most states also require the result element of a frightened victim.

Today the bodily injury type of battery crime, and both types of assault crimes, are defined by statute in most states. The offensive touching battery crime has been preserved by only a minority of states, either through codification or through precedents interpreting the undefined term "battery" in a statute.

The MPC drafters endorsed the trend toward abandoning the offensive-touching battery crime by leaving this crime out of the MPC. They also followed the longstanding tradition established by state legislatures for distinguishing between "aggravated" and "simple" categories of battery and assault crimes. However, the MPC drafters used the name "Assault" for all versions of these crimes. In order to avoid confusion, the term "battery" will be used in this chapter as the name for *any* crime that derives from one of the two types of common law battery. The term "assault" will be used only for crimes that derive either from the attempted battery assault crime or the frightening assault crime.

In this chapter, the evolution of the elements of common law battery and assault will be studied, as the foundation for understanding the origins of such modern offenses as exposure to HIV, reckless endangerment, stalking, and domestic violence crimes. Domestic violence in American Indian communities is now recognized to be a modern public policy crisis.

A. OVERVIEW OF THE LAW

Offensive Touching Battery. This common law crime required the *actus reus* of offensive touching and the *mens rea* of criminal negligence. The MPC and most states have abolished this crime.

Bodily Injury Battery. This common law crime required the *actus reus* of causing bodily injury and the *mens rea* of criminal negligence. The MPC and many states use the MPC mental states for this crime, along with broad definitions of bodily injury.

Exposure to Life-Threatening Disease. Many states have enacted statutes to define this crime, some of which are focused specifically on intentional exposure to the HIV infection. Some states have amended their battery statutes to achieve the same purpose.

Attempted Battery Assault. This common law crime required the *actus reus* of an attempt, meaning "coming close" to the completion of the battery crime, by such means as "an offer of violence." The *mens rea* for attempt is the intent to achieve the result of the completed crime, and typically this is the intent to commit bodily injury battery. Legislatures and courts are divided regarding the preservation of the common law requirement that a defendant must have the actual ability to commit a battery.

Frightening Assault. This crime was adopted originally through judicial recognition by state courts. The elements of this crime resemble those of assault in tort law, including the *actus reus* of frightening conduct and the *mens rea* of the intent to put the victim in fear of receiving bodily injury. Most states also require the result element of a frightened victim.

Reckless Endangerment. This crime was proposed in the MPC and is used in many states. The *actus reus* is conduct that may place another person in danger of serious bodily injury and the *mens rea* is recklessness.

Stalking. This crime has been enacted in many states since 1990. A typical modern statute includes the elements of recklessly engaging in a course of conduct, targeted at a specific person, which would cause a reasonable person to fear for his or her personal safety or to suffer emotional distress.

Domestic Violence. This crime has been enacted in many states since 1977, and its names include "domestic assault," "domestic battery," and "domestic violence." A typical statute includes the elements of causing specified harms, such as those prescribed in battery and assault statutes, against a family or household member.

Civil Rights. Both federal and state hate-crime laws punish the commission of bodily injury batteries (and attempted batteries) motivated by the "actual or perceived" identity of the victim.

> **Major Themes**
>
> **a. Battery**—Today most states codes and courts recognize the validity of the common law bodily injury battery crime, whereas the offensive touching crime is recognized only by a minority. Both types of battery are treated as simple battery, and most states use additional elements to punish aggravated battery. The need for a crime to punish the intentional exposure to HIV has inspired the enactment of new statutory provisions as well as amendments to expand battery crimes to cover this conduct.
>
> **b. Assault**—The crime of assault has expanded over time. The common law provided only for the crime of attempted battery assault, which has been expanded in some states to cover defendants who lack the actual ability but have the apparent ability to commit a battery. The trend toward expansion was also expressed through the judicial recognition of the frightening assault crime. Legislatures have recognized the need for enacting new assault-like crimes, including reckless endangerment, stalking, and domestic violence crimes.

B. BATTERY

1. Offensive Touching Battery

It is useful to focus on the differences between the elements of the two common law battery crimes, in order to understand the reasons that most states now punish only the more serious type, which is bodily injury battery.

The *Adams* case illustrates the decision of one state court to expand the scope of offensive touching battery through judicial interpretation of its original common law elements. The *Adams* majority opinion and the *Adams* dissent implicitly disagree about the meaning of the legality principle, in the context of interpreting a common law battery crime that is not defined by statute. The *Adams* dissent reflects the view that legislatures, not courts, should invent new crimes such as "laser battery." The *Adams* majority assumes that the court has the authority to rely on the common law tradition of reasoning by analogy to expand an old legal concept to fit a new harm like an offensive touching with an "intangible substance."

ADAMS V. COMMONWEALTH
33 Va. App. 463, 534 S.E.2d 347 (2000).

[Before] WILLIS, LEMONS and FRANK, JJ.

FRANK, JUDGE.

[On] appeal, [Adams] contends the evidence was insufficient to prove: (1) a touching and (2) that he had the requisite intent to commit the offense [of battery]. We disagree and affirm the conviction.

I. BACKGROUND

[On] September 22, 1998, while on duty at the Gloucester County High School, Sergeant Steven Giles of the Gloucester County Sheriff's Department was struck in his right eye by a laser light owned by [Adams], who was a twelfth-grade student at the school. Giles had been talking with another [sheriff's officer] and the school nurse when he felt a "stinging sensation" in his eye. [The other officer] told Giles that [Adams] had "just lit [him] up," as there was "a red dot" on him.

Giles approached [Adams] and asked what he had. [Adams] said, "It can't hurt you," and handed over the laser light, which was attached to his key chain. Giles gave the laser light to the assistant principal and told [Adams] he could retrieve it later.

Giles said he "felt a burning sensation" in his eye and "saw red" before looking away, but he did not know how long the laser had been pointed at him. Giles had his eye checked the next morning by a local doctor who found "heavy irritation" but no other injury.

[The other officer] testified that [Adams] was approximately 150 feet from Giles and the laser light had "jump[ed] all around his upper torso and head." [The other officer] did not "actually see the thing strike [Giles'] eye," but he saw Giles flinch when he was hit. [Two students] testified that they did not see the laser strike Giles in the face or eyes. They also said they had not been hurt when similarly hit in the eye with a laser light.

[Adams] testified that he purchased the laser light for six dollars at a convenience store two days before the offense. He said it had no warning on it regarding use and that he had not been hurt when hit in the eye by the light. [Adams] denied hitting Giles in the face or eye and claimed he had not intended to strike Giles with the light but, instead, was "just goofing off" to get [the] attention [of the other officer] by waving the laser around. [Adams] had a friendly relationship with [the other officer.] [Adams], however, did not get along well with Sergeant Giles. He stated that Giles had previously given him a hard time. . . .

[After a bench trial, the trial judge convicted Adams of the crime of "[battery] against another [person,] knowing or having reason to know that such other person is a law-enforcement officer . . . engaged in the performance of his public duties." Conviction for this felony requires that a person "shall be sentenced to a mandatory, minimum term of six months in jail." VA. CODE ANN. § 18.2–57(C).]

II. ANALYSIS

In reviewing the sufficiency of the evidence on appeal, "[we] may not disturb the trial court's judgment unless it is 'plainly wrong or without evidence to support it.'" *Barlow v. Commonwealth*, 26 Va. App. 421, 429, 494 S.E.2d 901 (1998). . . . ["]Battery is [the] least touching of another's person[,] willfully or in anger, whether by the party's own hand, or by some means set in motion by him." *Seegars v. Commonwealth*, 18 Va. App. 641, 644, 445 S.E.2d 720, 722 (1994).

A battery is an unlawful touching of another. It is not necessary that the touching result in injury to the person. Whether a touching is a battery depends on the intent of the actor, not on the force applied. See *Wood v. Commonwealth*, 149 Va. 401, 140 S.E. 114, 115 (1927). . . .

A. Touching

Adams contends that shining the laser on Sergeant Giles was insufficient to constitute a touching for the purposes of *assault and battery*. Touch is defined as to be in contact or to cause to be in contact. *See Merriam-Webster's Desk Dictionary* 573 (1995).

In Virginia, it is abundantly clear that a perpetrator need not inflict a physical injury to commit a battery. *See, e.g., Lynch v. Commonwealth*, 131 Va. 762, 765, 109 S.E. 427 (1921). The cases that guide our analysis, however, have not addressed circumstances where contact with the corporeal person was accomplished by directing a beam of light at the victim. Because substances such as light or sound become elusive when considered in terms of battery, contact by means of such substances must be examined further in determining whether a touching has occurred. Such a test is necessary due to the intangible nature of those substances and the need to limit application of such a principle (touching by intangible substances) to reasonable cases. Because the underlying concerns of battery law are breach of the peace and sacredness of the person, the dignity of the victim is implicated and the reasonableness and offensiveness of the contact must be considered. Otherwise, criminal convictions could result from the routine and insignificant exposure to concentrated energy that inevitably results from living in populated society.

Accordingly, we hold that for purposes of determining whether a battery has occurred, contact by an intangible substance such as light must be considered in terms of its effect on the victim. There need be no actual injury for a touching to have occurred. However, to prove a touching, the evidence must prove that the substance made objectively offensive or forcible contact with the victim's person resulting in some manifestation of a physical consequence or corporeal hurt. . . .

[Adams], by aiming the laser at the officers, effected a contact that caused bodily harm to Sergeant Giles. [Adams] argued there was no touching because the laser has no mass and, therefore, cannot physically touch Sergeant Giles. This argument is misplaced. The laser, directed by [Adams], came into contact with Sergeant Giles' eye and, as a result, there was an unlawful touching.

B. Intent

Proving intent by direct evidence often is impossible. Like any other element of a crime, it may be proved by circumstantial evidence, as long as such evidence excludes all reasonable hypotheses of innocence flowing from it. Circumstantial evidence of intent may include the conduct and statements of the alleged offender, and "[t]he finder of fact may infer that [he] intends the natural and probable consequences of his acts." *Campbell v. Commonwealth*, 12 Va. App. 476, 484, 405 S.E.2d 1, 4 (1991) (en banc).

The trial court, sitting as the fact finder, was entitled to reject [the] testimony [of Adams] that he was "just goofing off" to attract [the] attention of [the officer standing next to Giles]. The court specifically found that [Adams] intended to hit Giles with the laser and that [a] battery occurred. That decision is not plainly wrong or without supporting evidence and must be upheld on appeal.

For the reasons stated, we affirm the judgment of the trial court.

LEMONS, JUDGE, dissenting.

[Whether] a touching is a battery depends upon the intent of the actor, not upon the force applied. Here, the evidence does not support beyond a reasonable doubt that Adams had the intent to offensively touch Sergeant Giles. In order to have such intent, Adams would have to know or be reasonably charged with

Assault & Battery

knowledge that a six-dollar novelty item attached to his key chain had the potential for offensive touching. It is not within common knowledge that such a device has such capacity. There is no evidence that Adams had specific knowledge of such capacity. That Adams had a bad relationship with Giles may explain his motive, but it does not prove intent to offensively touch. A finder of fact may infer that an actor intends the natural and probable consequences of his acts. In the absence of common knowledge of the capacity of this device, no inference may be drawn. Without inference or specific knowledge, there is no proof that Adams intended to offensively touch Giles.

Additionally, the majority redefines "touching" for the purpose of common law battery. Although the reasoning is logical, it is unwise, because the unintended consequences may reach too far. Will the next prosecution for battery be based upon failure to dim high beams in traffic, flash photography too close to the subject, high intensity flashlight beams or sonic waves from a teenager's car stereo? Rather than stretch the boundaries of the common law understanding of what is necessary for a "touching" to occur, criminalizing conduct that involves intangible objects put in motion should be left to specific legislative action rather than generalized redefinition that may sweep into the ambit of criminal behavior conduct that is not intended. *See, e.g.*, 720 Ill. Comp. Stat. 5/2–10.2, 2–10.3, 5/12–2, 12–4 (West 2000) (shining or flashing a laser gunsight near or on a person constitutes aggravated assault or aggravated battery); 720 Ill. Comp. Stat. 5/24.6/20 (West 2000) (aiming a laser pointer at a police officer is a misdemeanor); Wash. Rev. Code § 9A–49.020 (1999) (felony to discharge a laser beam at various peace officers or pilots, bus drivers or transit operators in the commission of their respective duties).

I respectfully dissent.

POINTS FOR DISCUSSION

a. *Actus Reus* for Offensive Touching Battery

The *Adams* majority opinion relies on state precedents in criminal cases that quote approvingly from Blackstone's broad definition of the battery tort:

> The least touching of another's person wilfully, or in anger, is a battery; for the law cannot draw the line between different degrees of violence, and therefore totally prohibits the first and lowest stage of it: every man's person being sacred, and no other having a right to meddle with it, in any the slightest manner.

3 WILLIAM BLACKSTONE, COMMENTARIES ON THE LAWS OF ENGLAND *120. The *Adams* majority also echoes Blackstone's thinking in reasoning that "the underlying concerns of battery law" include "the sacredness" and "dignity" of the victim, as well as the need to deter breaches of the peace.

Implicitly, the *Adams* majority finds these policy concerns to be so strong that they require the judicial expansion of the *actus reus* element of "battery" to include offensive touching by "intangible substances." More specifically, the *Adams* majority endorses the need for a battery conviction when "the evidence prove[s] that [an intangible] substance made objectively offensive or forcible contact with the victim's person resulting in some manifestation of a physical consequence or corporeal hurt."

Should other state courts adopt the *Adams* majority's definition of battery? Does the *Adams* majority's definition of battery encompass even "offensive contacts" that are trivial or harmless? Assume, for example, that the laser beam had touched Sergeant Giles on the back of his hand, without causing pain, irritation, or even a red mark on his skin. Would this touching satisfy the *Adams* Court's definition of battery? How will a judge or jury draw the line between "offensive" touchings with intangible substances and inoffensive touching after *Adams*?

b. *Mens Rea* for Offensive Touching Battery

The *mens rea* element required for the offensive touching battery by the *Adams* Court is described as "the intent to touch offensively," but common law authorities and most states recognize that mere criminal negligence is sufficient for any type of battery conviction.

The contrasting opinions in *Adams* illustrate how the "intent to touch offensively" is an ambiguous concept. It is useful to compare the mental state analysis offered by Judge Frank and Judge Lemons with the four MPC mental states. This comparison makes it more obvious that the *Adams* majority does *not* require evidence of recklessness: that the defendant consciously disregarded the substantial risk that his conduct of "waving around the laser" would cause the result of an "offensive touching." What evidence of a criminal negligence mental state would Judge Lemons require, and what policy reasons support his view?

What reasons may explain why most states and the MPC have abolished offensive touching battery? What other reasons may explain why some states have preserved it?

c. New Crimes for Harms to Law Enforcement Officers

When a legislature fails to enact new crimes to define newly-recognized harms that pose a danger other than "bodily injury" to law enforcement officers, then a prosecutor must rely on the old common law crime of "offensive touching" battery if that crime continues to be recognized in state precedents. For example, Virginia prosecutors relied on that crime to convict a defendant who spat on an officer during an arrest, and to convict a defendant who left a deputy's hand covered in blood during a handshake. *See Gilbert v. Commonwealth*, 45 Va. App. 67, 608 S.E.2d 509 (2005); *Harman v. Commonwealth*, 2009 WL 362126 (Va. App.) (Feb. 17, 2009).

A more tailored way to punish such conduct is illustrated by the Indiana legislature's enactment of the crime of "battery by body waste" to cover persons who "knowingly or intentionally in a rude, insolent, or angry manner plac[e] blood or another body fluid or waste on a law enforcement officer . . . identified as such and while engaged in the performance of official duties." A higher penalty is imposed if the defendant "knew or recklessly failed to know that [he or she] was infected with: (a) hepatitis B; (b) HIV; or (c) tuberculosis." *See Newman v. State*, 677 N.E.2d 590 (Ind. App. 1997). How many policy decisions about the elements of a body-waste type of battery crime are reflected in this Indiana statute?

As of 2012, HIV-specific laws in thirteen states punished the conduct of spitting or biting. Most of the prosecutions for these HIV-specific charges involve defendants who spit at or bite a police officer or corrections personnel. However, "there are no known cases of a law enforcement officer getting infected with HIV in the line of duty through these kinds of events." Nor are there any documented cases of HIV transmission "caused by contact with vomit, urine, or feces." *See* http://www.hivlawandpolicy.org/resources/view/834.

2. Bodily Injury Battery

POINTS FOR DISCUSSION

a. *Actus Reus* & *Mens Rea* of Bodily Injury Battery

The same mental state of criminal negligence was used for both types of common law battery crimes—causing offensive touching and causing bodily injury. For the bodily injury crime, the MPC uses "recklessness", while saving the "negligence" mental state for the crime of causing bodily injury with a deadly weapon.

The broad scope of the *actus reus* element of "bodily injury" at common law is reflected in the similar Model Penal Code definition of this term that was borrowed and adopted in many states, namely, "physical pain, illness, or any impairment of physical condition." The MPC does not define "impairment" but courts can point to the definition of that term in legal dictionaries, namely, "any deviation from normal health." What are the policy reasons that may explain the unwillingness of courts and legislatures to define "bodily injury" more narrowly, especially in the majority of states that have abolished the "offensive touching" battery crime?

b. Aggravated vs. Simple Battery

The crime of battery was only a misdemeanor at common law, and the corresponding felony crime was mayhem, which was defined narrowly to punish those who caused bodily injuries that affected a victim's ability to fight in battle. As the mayhem crime became obsolete in England and America, state legislatures replaced it with felony crime definitions of "aggravated battery," an American invention. Today the "simple battery" crime in most state codes resembles the English misdemeanor crime of bodily injury battery, whereas "aggravated battery" is likely to require one of these extra elements: 1) the result of "serious bodily injury" instead of mere "bodily injury"; 2) the use of a "deadly or dangerous weapon"; 3) the mental state for a violent felony crime, such as the intent to kill or the intent to rob; or 4) the fact that the victim was a member of a specified class, such as law enforcement officers.

c. Model Penal Code Approach

The MPC drafters followed the tradition of using the serious injury and deadly weapon elements to make distinctions between higher-penalty and lower-penalty battery crimes. They defined the MPC versions of battery using the MPC mental states, and they did not use any status-of-victim elements for their higher-penalty crimes. *See* Model Penal Code § 211.1, Comment 2 at 185 (1980). Thus, the MPC equivalent of "aggravated battery" includes only the crimes of knowingly causing bodily injury with a deadly weapon and recklessly causing serious bodily injury under circumstances manifesting extreme indifference to the value of human life. The MPC equivalent of "simple battery" includes only the crimes of recklessly causing bodily injury and negligently causing bodily injury with a deadly weapon. However, many state statutes continue to use the four traditional elements to define the aggravated versions of battery crimes today, and some state codes use a wide variety of other elements as well.

d. Rare Consent Defense

Consent is rarely a defense to crimes that result in bodily injury, and one reason is because "society has an interest in punishing [such crimes] as breaches of the public peace and order so that an individual cannot consent to a wrong that is committed against the public peace." *State v. Shelley*, 85 Wash. App. 24, 29, 929 P.2d 489, 491–492 (1997). Another reason is that consent cannot be a defense to activities that are "against public policy"; thus, "a child cannot consent to hazing [and] a gang member cannot consent to an initiation beating." *State v. Hiott*, 97 Wash. App. 825, 828, 987 P.2d 135, 136–137 (1999). However, some states have codified MPC § 211(2)(b) that recognizes the consent defense when "the conduct and the injury are reasonably foreseeable hazards of joint participation in a lawful athletic contest or competitive sport." The *Hiott* Court emphasized that the consent defense must be limited to games that are "accepted by society as lawful athletic contests" or "competitive sports," which games "carry with them generally accepted rules, at least some of which are intended to prevent or minimize injuries," and which "commonly prescribe the use of protective devices or clothing to prevent injuries."

3. Exposure to Life-Threatening Disease

The common law extended the bodily injury battery crime to acts that indirectly inflict physical harm, such as causing a victim to ingest poison or to become infected with a sexually-transmitted disease, such as syphilis. See *State v. Lankford*, 29 Del. 594, 102 A. 63 (1917). As of 2019, 34 state codes included provisions that establish criminal liability for engaging in acts that create a risk of exposure or transmission of HIV or the AIDS virus. The next case provides one example of a legislative decision to enact a statute tailored specifically to sexual acts by persons who know that they are infected with a life-threatening communicable disease.

STATE V. RICHARDSON
289 Kan. 118, 209 P.3d 696 (2009).

The opinion of the court was delivered by JOHNSON, J.

[Richardson] appeals his convictions and sentences for two counts of exposing another to a life-threatening communicable disease. [He first] claims that the statute defining the crime is unconstitutionally *vague* [and also claims] that the district court erred in failing to treat K.S.A. 21-3435 as a specific intent crime[.]

For more than a decade, Richardson has known that he is infected with [HIV]. . . . [The] State charged Richardson with violating K.S.A. 21–3435 for having sexual intercourse with M.K. and E.Z. [Richardson] waived his right to a jury trial and proceeded to a bench trial, which included the parties' stipulations that Richardson knew he was infected with HIV; that he engaged in sexual intercourse with [M.K. on] October 17, 2005, and [with E.Z.] between October 1 [and] 30, 2005[.] Other than the parties' stipulations, the evidence submitted during Richardson's bench trial consisted entirely of the testimony of two medical doctors[.] [Their testimony concerned the circumstances when HIV may be transmitted.]

Richardson defended on the basis that the State had failed to establish that HIV is always a life-threatening disease; that he had actually exposed the victims to the disease because of the lack of evidence that bodily fluids were exchanged during intercourse; [and that] he had the specific intent to expose his sexual partners to HIV. The District Court found Richardson guilty on both counts and sentenced him to consecutive prison terms[.]

[We first consider] whether K.S.A. 21–3435 is a specific intent crime. The district court did not specifically say that it was interpreting [the statute] as only requiring a general criminal intent. However, Richardson insists that the district court must have applied that interpretation because it found Richardson guilty without the State presenting any evidence of a specific intent to expose the victims to HIV. The State counters that, despite the language of the applicable statute, the legislature intended to create a general intent crime. . . .

[In] relevant part, the statute provides:

"(a) It is unlawful for an individual who knows oneself to be infected with a life threatening communicable disease knowingly:

(1) To engage in sexual intercourse or sodomy with another individual with the intent to expose that individual to that life threatening communicable disease."

[The] statute requires the defendant to "knowingly" engage in that prohibited conduct. Therefore, [the] crime-defining statute does not criminalize reckless conduct. Just as clearly, [the statute] "identifies or requires a further particular intent which must accompany the prohibited acts," *i.e.*, the intent to expose the sex partner to the life-threatening communicable disease. See [*State v.*] *Cantrell*, 234 Kan. 426, 673 P.2d 1147 [(1983)].

The State acknowledges that, on its face, [the statute] purports to be a specific intent crime. However, the State does not acknowledge that this State's appellate courts have consistently interpreted statutes that define a crime by using the phrase "with intent to" as requiring a specific intent element.

Instead, without proffering any authority, the State contends that giving effect to the statute's plain specific intent language would actually thwart the legislature's intended purpose of preventing the intentional exposure of others to HIV. The State argues that any act of sexual intercourse or sodomy by an HIV positive person, even utilizing a condom, creates some element of risk that the virus will be transmitted to the sex partner, so that total abstinence is the only means by which an infected person may avoid exposing another to HIV. Accordingly, the State suggests that the specific intent to expose another to HIV is inherently included in the defendant's general intent to engage in sexual intercourse.

Under the State's interpretation, a person infected with HIV must be totally abstinent or risk being prosecuted for a felony each and every time he or she engages in sexual intercourse or sodomy, regardless of whether the act is between two consenting (perhaps married) adults with full knowledge of the virus and utilizing prophylactic measures. We disagree.

[The] State's public policy arguments cannot be reconciled with the plain language of [the statute] and we find that the statute creates a specific intent crime. The State was required to prove that Richardson, knowing he was infected with HIV[,] engaged in sexual intercourse with M.K. and E.Z. with the specific intent to expose them to HIV.

[Second,] a claim that a statute is void for vagueness necessarily requires a court to interpret the language of the statute in question to determine whether it gives adequate warning as to the prescribed conduct. . . . [Moreover,] the need for clarity of definition and the prevention of arbitrary and discriminatory enforcement is heightened for criminal statutes because criminal violations result in the loss of liberty[.]

Richardson [argues] that the term "expose" [in the "intent to expose" element] is [unconstitutionally vague] as to the conduct which is prohibited. He suggests that it could mean engaging in conduct which might present any risk of transmission of HIV or it could mean that the prohibited conduct must involve causing bodily fluids to actually come into contact with the other person. He also suggests that a person infected with HIV must speculate on what viral load level might be sufficient to trigger a criminally prohibited exposure[.]

The flaw in those arguments is that the statute does not define the prohibited conduct as exposing another to the life-threatening disease, but rather it criminalizes sexual intercourse or sodomy with the *specific intent* to expose the sex partner to the known life-threatening communicable disease. One need not ruminate on exactly how the act must be performed to meet the legal definition of "expose" or even know that a transmittal of the disease is possible. It is enough that the defendant *intended* to expose his or her sex partner to the disease. That state of mind is certainly a matter well within the common understanding of a defendant. . . .

[Richardson] also complains that [the statute] does not specifically define the term "life threatening." Ironically, however, he states in his brief that "[t]he common sense definition of the term 'life threatening' is 'something that poses a threat to life.'" We wholeheartedly agree with that assessment and believe that it effectively refutes the [vagueness argument]. A person of ordinary intelligence would understand what the statute means by the term "life threatening."

Moreover, Richardson's example that such common diseases as influenza can be threatening does not support his argument. If, during a swine flue pandemic, a person knowingly has sexual intercourse or sodomy with another with the intent to expose the sex partner to the life-threatening influenza, then the offender has subjected himself or herself to prosecution under [the statute]. [The] prosecutor's burden may be more difficult to carry. Nevertheless, that does not make the fact that influenza may be a life-threatening communicable disease any less amenable to common understanding. . . . [The] statute is not unconstitutionally vague.

[Third,] Richardson argues that the evidence was insufficient to support his convictions because the State presented no evidence on the requisite element of specific intent[.] . . . [The State argues that the mere fact that Richardson engaged in sexual intercourse while knowing that he was infected with HIV was enough to prove that he intended to expose M.K. and E.Z. to the virus. According to the State, "there is no conceivable means by which the State could prove, apart from the act of sexual intercourse itself, that an HIV positive individual who knowingly engages in sexual intercourse with another acts with 'intent to expose' the other to the virus." We disagree. Prosecutors are routinely called upon to prove a defendant's specific intent in committing a prohibited act and normally must carry that burden with circumstantial evidence. Here the State simply made no attempt to prove the requisite circumstances.

Interestingly, at the preliminary hearing, the State presented evidence that M.K. and E.Z did not know that Richardson had HIV when they had sex with him; that Richardson did not use a condom; and that Richardson had falsely represented to E.Z. that he was free from sexually transmitted diseases. These are prime examples of proven circumstances that could support an inference that Richardson intended to expose M.K. and E.Z. to HIV. Inexplicably the State chose not to present any of this information at trial, and those facts were not included in the parties' stipulation. . . .

[In] conclusion, the record reveals that, at trial, the State failed to prove circumstances from which a rational factfinder could reasonably infer that the defendant had the specific intent to expose either M.K. or E.Z. to HIV. Instead, the State has asked us to infer or presume the requisite circumstantial evidence of specific intent from other circumstances or inferences. Such a presumption upon a presumption is insufficient to carry the State's burden. Accordingly, we find the evidence was insufficient to support the convictions and reverse[.]

C. ASSAULT

1. Attempted Battery Assault

Under English law, assault was the name given to the attempted battery crime. The strict proof requirements of this crime inspired state courts to recognize the frightening assault crime, drawing from elements of the frightening assault tort. The *Henson* case explores the reasons for the development of the trend in favor of replacing the attempted battery requirement of "actual ability" with "apparent ability" to commit battery.

COMMONWEALTH V. HENSON
357 Mass. 686, 259 N.E.2d 769 (1970).

QUIRICO, JUSTICE.

[This is an appeal from conviction for the crime of assault by means of a dangerous weapon, to wit, a revolver.] The only issue before us is whether there was error in denying a motion by the defendant for a directed verdict.

The evidence would permit the jury to find the following facts. On December 24, 1968, Theodore Finochio, an off-duty police officer[,] was at a gasoline station in Boston. He was not in uniform, but he had his service revolver in a holster under his coat. Another man and woman also were in the station at that time. The defendant and a female companion entered the station and the female [companion] used profane language. Finochio asked the defendant to keep [his companion] quiet. The defendant reached in his pocket, pulled out a revolver, aimed it at Finochio's stomach and said[,] "Why should I?" Finochio put up his hands and said[,] "No reason at all." He described his state of mind at that time by saying[,] "I thought I was done for." The defendant then turned to go out of the station, holding the revolver at his side. Finochio took out his revolver, pointed it at the defendant and said, "Hold it there, buddy, I am a police officer." The defendant [turned] and fired two shots at Finochio at a distance of about five feet. They exchanged further shots in that chase which lasted about twenty to thirty seconds until the defendant was captured, subdued and handcuffed, and his revolver taken from his hand. The defendant fired a total of five or more shots, and Finochio fired six, one of which struck the defendant. Finochio was not struck by any projectile, and he received no injuries or powder burns in the incident. No projectiles were recovered at the scene. The defendant had taken the revolver from his female companion before going to the gasoline station. Before the shooting he noticed that it was loaded. [He had examined the shells and recognized them as blanks.]

On this evidence the jury could find that the defendant . . . intended to create, and did create, the impression on the persons present that he had a loaded revolver which was capable of shooting Finochio, and that until the defendant's running gun battle with Finochio was over and he was subdued, no one present except the defendant knew that [his] revolver was loaded with blanks. Finally, [the jury] could find that all persons present, except the defendant, reasonably believed that the defendant's revolver was loaded with live bullets which he was firing at Finochio.

Despite this factual situation, the defendant contends that [his] conduct could not [constitute] the aggravated offence of assault by means of a dangerous weapon since the shells in the revolver at the time were blanks. [Basically,] he argues that because the revolver was not loaded with live ammunition, he did not have the ability to accomplish a battery by means of the revolver, and thus cannot be convicted of assault by means of the revolver. . . .

[But] the defendant's secret intent not to shoot Finochio based on his undisclosed inability to do so with the blank shells is not material. The defendant's acts, judged without the benefit of his secret knowledge that he was firing blanks, constituted a reasonably obvious case of an assault by means of a loaded revolver, involving a violent breach of the public order and setting in motion the normal reaction thereto by Finochio. The issue before us is[,] [S]hould the defendant now be allowed to avoid criminal responsibility for his conduct on the ground that he had only blank shells in his [revolver]?

[An] examination of decisions on this question in other jurisdictions shows a considerable conflict of authority, but it may be accurate to state that a majority [have] concluded that the crime of aggravated assault by means of a firearm [is] not made out by evidence of the pointing of an unloaded firearm. *See* Annotation, 79 A.L.R.2d 1412. That [conclusion] applies whether the case is one where it was established that the firearm was not loaded at the time of the alleged assault, or one where was there was no proof that the firearm was loaded[.]

[In *Commonwealth v. White*, 110 Mass. 407, 409 (1872), a conviction for simple assault was upheld because, "It is not the secret intent of the assaulting party, nor the undisclosed fact of his ability or inability to commit a battery, that is material; but what his conduct and the attending circumstances denote at the time to the [victim] assaulted. . . . It is the outward demonstration that constitutes the mischief which is punished as a breach of the peace."]

[This reasoning] applies with even greater force to a case of apparent ability to accomplish a battery attempted or threatened by means of a firearm. The threat to the public peace and order is greater, and natural reactions thereto by the intended victim and others may be more sudden and violent than in cases where no weapon is involved. There is no reason why the rule of apparent ability should not apply to charges of aggravated assaults by means of weapons[.] Thus, the mere fact that a firearm brandished by an assailant is known by him to be unloaded, or to be loaded with blank cartridges, does not entitle him to an acquittal on a charge of assault by means of a dangerous weapon.

POINTS FOR DISCUSSION

a. *Actus Reus* & *Mens Rea* of Attempted Battery Assault

It is difficult to determine precisely "how close" a defendant must come to committing a battery, in order to be guilty of the attempted battery crime known as assault. Common law authorities distinguished between the phase of "violence menaced", which was not close enough to the completion of a battery to be punishable, and the phase of "violence begun to be executed," which *did* qualify as assault. Acts that fell short of an "offer of violence" did not satisfy the *actus reus* for an "attempt."

The crime of attempted battery assault requires neither the result of the victim's fear of bodily injury nor the intent to create such fear. Instead, the crime requires the intent to achieve the result of a battery, and acts that come "sufficiently near" to that result. Thus, an insensible victim is no obstacle to prosecution. However, most attempted battery assaults involve a victim who is aware of the assailant's conduct.

The momentum for the judicial recognition of the frightening assault crime was fueled by the restrictions of attempted battery assault, which also required "a present ability to commit a violent injury." As the MPC Commentaries observed, this element "imported into the offense an even stricter notion of proximity to the completed act than characterized the law of criminal attempt." Model Penal Code § 211.1, Comment 1 at 177 (1980). Even acts that qualified as an "offer of violence," coupled with the intent to achieve the result of a battery, would not fit into the attempted battery assault category when the weapon involved was an unloaded gun.

The Model Penal Code drafters chose to redefine the attempted battery type of assault in accordance with the *actus reus* and *mens rea* requirements used for any attempt crime in the MPC. Thus, the term "attempt" incorporates these two elements within it: 1) the mental state of an affirmative "desire to cause the result" of either bodily injury or serious bodily injury; and 2) an act of preparation that takes a "substantial step in a course of conduct planned to culminate in [the] commission of the crime." *See* Model Penal Code § 5.01, Comment 2 at 301 (1980); Model Penal Code § 5.01(1)(c).

There are three types of "attempts" in MPC § 211.1; 1) an attempt to cause bodily injury; 2) an attempt to cause serious bodily injury; and 3) an attempt to cause serious bodily injury with a deadly weapon. Did the *Henson* defendant commit any of these crimes?

b. Actual or Apparent Ability to Commit Battery

In reflecting upon the significance of the landmark Massachusetts decision in *Commonwealth v. White*, the *Henson* Court characterized the *White* holding as the "modern rule" of assault, and quoted this description of *White*'s implications, which serves equally well to describe *Henson*'s ruling:

> Where an assault may be committed[,] [t]here must be some power, actual or apparent, for doing bodily harm, but apparent power is sufficient[.] Hence in jurisdictions giving full scope to the modern rule of criminal assault, this offense may be committed where the battery itself is actually impossible, if it reasonably seems possible either to the assailant or to his victim[,] [assuming that] the assailant could place the [victim] in apprehension of an immediate battery by means that appeared to be effective although the assailant himself knew otherwise.

[In these] jurisdictions [it] is possible to commit [assault] by pointing an unloaded weapon at another within normal range.

Henson, 259 N.E.2d at 774 (quoting ROLLIN M. PERKINS, CRIMINAL LAW 91–93 (1957)).

Consider the possible reasons that led the majority of state courts and legislatures, at the time of the *Henson* decision, to retain the common law requirement of "actual ability" for attempted battery assault. Would the widespread recognition of the frightening assault crime make it more or less likely for courts to abandon the "actual ability" requirement and endorse the "apparent ability" requirement instead?

One important aspect of a court's decision to endorse the "apparent ability" concept is the impact of this decision on the mental state definition for the attempted battery crime. For example, a person like the *Henson* defendant, who knows that his weapon lacks the "present ability" to cause bodily injury, does not possess the necessary "intent to accomplish a battery." How does the *Henson* Court describe the defendant's mental state? Why does the court find this mental state to be the equivalent of the intent to accomplish battery?

2. Frightening Assault

The following case illustrates how statutes that punished only "assault" came to be interpreted by nineteenth century state court judges to include both the original attempted battery crime and a tort type of frightening assault crime. Yet the tort model was only a starting point for judges engaged in the task of defining the elements of the frightening assault crime. That task proved to be a difficult one, and modern cases have provided the occasion for judicial disputes about whether particular elements should be required, and why legislative definitions are preferable.

CARTER V. COMMONWEALTH
42 Va. App. 681, 594 S.E.2d 284 (2004) (en banc).

JEAN HARRISON CLEMENTS, JUDGE:

[On] December 29, 1998, around 11:00 p.m., Officer B.N. O'Donnell of the City of Charlottesville Police Department observed a speeding car and, activating his vehicle's overhead flashing blue emergency lights, initiated a traffic stop. O'Donnell, who was on routine patrol at the time in a high crime area of the city, was driving a marked police vehicle and wearing his police uniform and badge.

After the car pulled over, O'Donnell shone his vehicle's "take down" lights and spotlight onto the car and approached on foot.

Two people were inside the car, the driver and Carter, who was seated in the front passenger seat. O'Donnell initiated a conversation with the driver, asking for his driver's license and registration and informing him why he had been stopped. The driver responded to O'Donnell in a "hostile" tone of voice. While conversing with the driver, O'Donnell used his flashlight to conduct a "plain view search" of the car to make sure there were no visible weapons or drugs in it. O'Donnell noticed that Carter had his right hand out of sight "down by his right leg." Carter then suddenly brought his right hand up and across his body. Extending the index finger on his right hand straight out and the thumb straight up, he pointed his index finger at the officer and said, "Pow." Thinking Carter "had a weapon and was going to shoot" him, O'Donnell "began to move backwards" and went for his weapon. A "split second" later, O'Donnell realized "it was only [Carter's] finger." O'Donnell testified: "The first thing I thought was that I was going to get shot. [It's] a terrifying experience, and if I could have gotten my weapon, I would have shot him. [O'Donnell testified that Carter then "started laughing."] [O'Donnell] asked Carter "if he thought it was funny," and Carter responded, "Yes, I think it is funny."

[Initially, O'Donnell did not arrest Carter because O'Donnell did not know whether he could charge Carter with any crime. A few days later, O'Donnell obtained a warrant for Carter's arrest for assaulting a police officer under VA. CODE ANN. § 18.2–57(C), which provides that "any person [who] commits an assault . . . against . . . a law-enforcement officer . . . engaged in the performance of his public duties as such . . . shall be guilty of a Class 6 felony."]

On appeal, Carter asserts the Commonwealth failed to prove his conduct constituted an assault of a law-enforcement officer because [in pointing his finger,] he did not have the present ability to inflict harm on the officer. [The] Commonwealth contends that, under long-established Virginia case law, a defendant need not have had the present ability to inflict harm at the time of the offense to be guilty of assault. It is enough [that] the defendant's conduct created in the mind of the victim a reasonable fear of apprehension of bodily harm[,] [and] the trial court properly found the evidence sufficient[.]

[At] common law, the term "assault" originally had two distinct meanings, one when used in the context of criminal law and another when used in the context of torts law. A criminal assault was "an attempt to commit a battery." Under this definition of assault, it did not matter "whether the victim was put in

Assault & Battery

fear or was even aware of the assault." ROGER D. GROOT, CRIMINAL OFFENSES AND DEFENSES IN VIRGINIA 48 (2004). It mattered only that the accused had the specific intent and present ability to commit the battery and "performed some direct [act] towards its commission."

Conversely, a tortious assault was an overt intentional act that placed another in reasonable apprehension of immediate bodily harm. [Additionally,] absent an intention to batter, there must have been "an actual intention to cause apprehension[,] [which must have been] one which normally [would] be aroused in the mind of a reasonable person." [W. PAGE KEETON et al, KEETON & PROSSER ON THE LAW OF TORTS § 10 (5th ed. 1984).] In time, however, the tort type of assault [became] recognized, "in addition to (not as an alternative to) the attempted-battery type of assault." [WAYNE R. LAFAVE, CRIMINAL LAW § 7.16, at 746 (3d ed. 2000).] In Virginia, our Supreme Court has long recognized the existence of both concepts of assault in the criminal-law context. [See] Berkeley v. Commonwealth, 88 Va. 1017, 14 S.E. 916 (1892)[.]

[Although the phrase] "coupled with a present ability" [appeared] in the common law definition of assault in Harper v. Commonwealth, 196 Va. 723, 733, 85 S.E.2d 249, 255 (1955), [that definition] was not intended to be an all-inclusive definition of assault in Virginia[.] [Harper was] a case requiring determination of whether an attempted-battery type of criminal assault occurred.

[For] these reasons, we hold that one need not, in cases such as this [one], have a present ability to inflict imminent bodily harm at the time of the alleged offense to be guilty of assault. It is enough that one's conduct created at the time of the alleged offense a reasonable apprehension of bodily harm in the mind of the victim. Thus, an apparent present ability to inflict imminent bodily harm is sufficient to support a conviction for assault.

In this case, the trial court found that Carter's "act of pointing what the officer believed at the time to be a weapon at him" did, "in fact, place Officer O'Donnell in reasonable apprehension or fear." The evidence in the record abundantly supports this finding, and the finding is not plainly wrong. [That] the officer's terror was brief does not alter the fact, as found by the trial court, that the officer believed for a moment that Carter had the intention and present ability to kill him. Moreover, under the circumstances surrounding the incident, we cannot say, as a matter of law, that such a belief was unreasonable. Thus, although Carter did not have a weapon, the trial court could properly conclude from the evidence presented that Carter had an apparent present ability to inflict imminent bodily harm and that his conduct placed Officer O'Donnell in reasonable apprehension of such harm." [Accordingly,] we affirm Carter's conviction.

Affirmed.

BENTON, J., with whom FITZPATRICK, C.M., joins, dissenting.

The common law definition of "assault" [did] not encompass this type of intentional conduct, which is intended to startle but is performed without a present ability to produce the end if carried out. Because of the definitional limitations of this common law rule, other states have addressed this type of conduct by statutory enactments. "[M]ost modern codes either include physical menacing in the crime of assault or else create a separate crime of 'menacing' or 'threatening' covering such conduct." WAYNE R. LAFAVE, *Criminal Law* § 16.3(b), at 825 n.21 (4th ed. 2003). When legislatures statutorily define a crime in this manner "[f]or this type of assault, a present ability to inflict injury is clearly unnecessary." *Id.*

For these reasons, I disagree with the majority opinion's holding that a conviction for criminal assault can be sustained [even] though the evidence failed to prove the accused had a present ability to harm the officer. I would hold that Carter committed an "act accompanied with circumstances denoting an intention" to menace but it was not "coupled with a present ability . . . to use actual violence" or "calculated to produce the end if carried into execution." *See, e.g., People v. Vaiza*, 244 Cal. App. 2d 121, 52 Cal. Rptr. 733 (1966) (holding that "[i]f a person threatens to shoot another with . . . a chocolate candy pistol, there is no ability to commit . . . any injury with it on the person of another"); *Johnson v. State*, 158 Ga. App. 432, 280 S.E.2d 856, 857 (1981) (holding that the evidence failed to establish "the present ability to inflict a violent injury" where the evidence proved the accused shook his finger while making a threat at persons in a car).

[Accordingly,] I would reverse the conviction for assault.

POINTS FOR DISCUSSION

a. Attempt Crime or Result Crime

By the time the Model Penal Code was proposed, most state courts had given judicial recognition to the frightening assault crime, and had articulated the definition of its elements in precedents interpreting the undefined statutory term "assault" in state criminal codes. For some courts, the elements of the attempted battery assault crime provided a model that could be imitated by defining the elements of the frightening assault crime to require: 1) a menacing threat of injury,

Assault & Battery

or "conduct as could induce in a victim a well-founded apprehension of peril" of such injury; 2) the actual or apparent ability to injure the victim; and 3) the intent to frighten the victim. The *Carter* case illustrates a debate over the definition of the second element.

When state courts used the "attempt crime" model as the template for the elements of the frightening assault crime, there was no reason to require the result element that the victim was frightened. Necessarily, an "attempt crime" is not a "result crime." The MPC drafters approved of the element choices made by courts that adopted the "attempt crime" model for defining frightening assault. For example, the mental state element is the affirmative "desire to cause the result" of putting a victim in fear, which resembles the "intent to frighten." *Compare* Model Penal Code § 5.01. Similarly, the MPC conduct element of "physical menace" resembles the case law element of "menacing threat of injury." Moreover, the MPC implicitly creates liability for defendants who have the *apparent* ability to carry out their threats of "physical menace," which rule is endorsed in the case law definitions of the frightening assault crime.

However, most state courts adopted a definition of frightening assault that is based on the "result model," not on the "attempt model." As *Carter* explains, tort law was the source from which judges borrowed the policy justification for expanding criminal assault liability. The tort of assault covered civil defendants whose threats of bodily harm were accompanied with the intent to frighten rather than the intent to injure. These defendants could not be prosecuted criminally for attempted battery assault, and judges invoked the existence of tort liability as a reason for expanding the assault crime to encompass their behavior, which "is so likely to result in a breach of the peace that it should be a punishable offense." For those judges who preferred to define the frightening assault crime with the same elements as the corresponding tort, only the "result model" could accomplish that goal, because the tort of frightening assault did not exist in the absence of a victim who suffered fear. By contrast, the "attempt model" appealed to judges who did not view the suffering of a frightened victim as the *sine qua non* of the criminal harm to be punished with the frightening assault crime.

The limits of the "result model" for the frightening assault crime may be circumvented if the prosecutor can charge the attempted battery assault crime instead. For example, in *United States v. Bell*, 505 F.2d 539 (7th Cir. 1974), the defendant was convicted of "assault" based on his conduct toward a victim who suffered from a mental condition that made her unable to comprehend what was going on around her. The "assault" statute did not define the elements of the crime. According to case law, the frightening assault crime required "an act putting another in reasonable apprehension of bodily harm." Therefore, given the victim's lack of capacity to be frightened by the defendant's conduct, the court upheld the conviction on the theory that the defendant committed attempted battery assault, which may be committed upon a victim without his or her knowledge.

The usefulness of the frightening assault crime is illustrated by the court's analysis in *Robinson v. United States*, 506 A.2d 572 (D.C. App. 1986), where the defendant pointed a gun at a police officer and then put the gun down as ordered. He was charged with "assault" under a statute that did not define the elements of the crime, and the court observed that it was fortunate that the trial judge instructed the jury using case law definitions that covered both types of assault crime. The defendant could not have been convicted of attempted battery assault in the absence of demanding "proximity" evidence that he either fired the gun at the officer or attempted to fire it. However, the evidence was sufficient to show a frightening assault because the act of pointing the gun constituted a menacing threat and the "intent to frighten" the officer could be inferred from that conduct. The result of a frightened victim was not required by case law, and so the court ignored the defendant's argument that the victim's training as a police officer "might have made him resistant to such threats of danger," because the officer's reaction to the defendant's frightening conduct was irrelevant.

Two limitations upon the frightening assault crime may be found in case law and codes. The first is the exclusion of merely verbal threats, unless accompanied by some show of physical force, which is described in the MPC as "physical menace." A second typical limit is the requirement noted in *Carter*, that such conduct must be of the kind to cause "reasonable" apprehension, and in states where actual fear is required it must be "reasonable." The MPC does not use the term "reasonable." A third limit is codified in only a few states, which is the MPC requirement that the attempt must be to put another in "fear of imminent *serious* bodily injury." Most state codes extend the crime to include "fear of immediate bodily injury."

b. Proof Requirements

In a state where the "attempt model" of the elements is used, the mental state will be the "purpose" or "intent" to accomplish the result, namely, the result of causing apprehension of bodily injury. In a state where the "result model" of the elements is used, the same mental state will be required, presumably because it was borrowed from the assault tort mental state of the intent to frighten. Thus, the mental states of recklessly or negligently causing another person to be frightened will not establish the frightening assault crime.

What implicit policy reasons may explain Justice Benton's disagreement, as expressed in his dissenting opinion, with the majority opinion in *Carter*? Does Justice Benton's dissent in *Carter* implicitly echo any of the concerns of the dissent by Justice Lemons in *Adams*?

c. Aggravated vs. Simple Assault

Just as the English misdemeanor battery crime evolved into the state crimes of simple battery and aggravated battery, so did the original English assault crime of attempted battery evolve into simple and aggravated forms, as did the tort type of frightening assault crime that was recognized by many state courts, starting in the nineteenth century. The attempted battery assault crime in the *Henson* statute is categorized as aggravated because of the extra element of using a dangerous weapon. The assault crime in *Carter* is an aggravated type because of the extra element of a law enforcement officer victim. For an example of a wide variety of elements that can be used in an aggravated assault statute, see the Illinois statute, 720 ILCS 5/10–5.5, at http://www.ilga.gov/legislation/ilcs/fulltext.asp?DocName=072000050K12-2.

D. MODERN CRIMES BEYOND ASSAULT & BATTERY

1. Reckless Endangerment

The MPC drafters proposed the creation of the new crime of "recklessly endangering another person," in order to fill liability gaps that existed because of the limitations of the battery and assault crimes. The drafters recognized that many states had enacted crimes for particular types of endangerment, and they proposed instead to "replace the haphazard coverage of prior law with one comprehensive provision" to reach "any kind of [reckless] conduct" that places other people in danger. Model Penal Code § 211.2, Comment 1 at 196 (1980). This crime is defined as follows:

> A person commits a misdemeanor if he recklessly engages in conduct which places or may place another person in danger of death or serious bodily injury. Recklessness and danger shall be *presumed* where a person knowingly points a firearm at or in the direction of another, whether or not the actor believes the firearm to be loaded.

More specifically, the presumption means that jurors may be instructed that "they may regard knowingly pointing a firearm at another as sufficient evidence of the dangerousness of the actor's conduct and of his recklessness with respect to risk of death or serious bodily injury." Model Penal Code § 211.2, Comment 3 at 204 (1980).

Although the reckless endangerment crime has been enacted in many states, some courts have interpreted its scope in restrictive ways. Moreover, in the decades since the MPC was proposed, courts have recognized that the MPC definition of the crime was not drafted with particular kinds of modern dangers in mind.

2. Stalking

The first stalking statute was enacted in 1990 and today the stalking crime is included in all state codes and in the federal code. The *Simone* case illustrates the difficulties involved in defining the elements of the crime, in obtaining evidence for conviction, and in ensuring the enforcement of stalking laws generally.

STATE V. SIMONE
152 N.H. 755, 887 A.2d 135 (2005).

DALIANIS, J.

[In] 2001, Coral Olson was employed by the U.S. Census Bureau as a field service representative. Olson traveled door-to-door to conduct census surveys. She would then re-contact the same respondents by telephone and by personal visit until she had obtained sufficient survey information. In January 2001, Olson went to the [Simone's] home to conduct a census survey. Olson gave [Simone] her business card with her home phone number, and conducted several follow-up telephone calls and one follow-up personal visit to complete the census survey. After [Simone] completed his census survey, however, he continued to call Olson. The defendant told Olson that he was interested in her; Olson responded that she was married and not interested in him. Nevertheless [he] persisted in calling her. [She] did not initiate any of these personal telephone calls. [She] told him not to contact her. If she did not answer the telephone, [Simone] would call repeatedly and leave messages each time until she finally answered. . . .

In August 2001, Olson contacted the Temple Police Department[,] met with Officer Steven Duval [and] expressed her desire that [Simone] cease contact. On August 18, 2001, Officer Duval spoke with [Simone] about the situation. Nonetheless, [Simone] continued to pursue Olson [and so] Olson obtained a protective order prohibiting [Simone] from contacting her. Notwithstanding the protective order, [Simone] continued to call her. Olson testified that between the fall of 2001 and June 2003, [Simone] placed more unwanted calls to her than she could estimate [and] also sent [her] packages, which she did not open. As a result, Olson frequently contacted the Temple police.

On June 11, 2003, [Simone] called Olson [and] she again told [him] not to contact her [but] he called back and left [three] lengthy messages on Olson's answering machine. [In his first message, he said,] "that he had a lot of anger towards [her]." [In his second message, he] admitted that he had previously misrepresented himself to Olson's husband in order to obtain personal information about her and about her marriage. [Then he] said, "I don't care if the police come and arrest me. I don't care if I go to court. And I don't care if I get seven years or 70 years. This means so much to me to tell you that I'm terribly sorry and remorseful and I don't care if I rot in hell. And I know I will die in, in jail[.]" [In his third message, he said:]

> [I] honestly don't care and I've made the decision now. I know this is very severe and even stupid of me to call you, but I basically don't care because I, I consider on August the 13th of 2001 when you broke up with me, that my life had changed drastically. It's not gotten any better and I realize that was like, you know, that was like the nail in the coffin for me. I, I'm already dead and jail is just a place to finalize that act.

[Simone's message also said that even though] he "was terribly, terribly sorry over the bad things that he did[,] it was worth rotting in jail for, and [he] would do it again in a heartbeat." He said that "he had a lot of demons inside" but that . . . [he] "never entertained the thoughts of hurting [Olson]." He also admitted that he was stopped [by the police] while traveling to her home late at night.

After listening to these messages, Olson called the police department and Officer Duval came to her home. Olson received another call from [Simone] just as Officer Duval arrived. Officer Duval took the telephone and spoke with [Simone] for about 20 minutes [and then Simone] called again and left a fourth message . . . . [stating] that he would be "prosecuted and face a felony charge" and [that] he would pray for Olson every night. Officer Duval left [and] returned [30 minutes later] to respond to a 911 call made by Olson. . . .

Olson arrived home on June 17, 2003 to find twenty new messages [left by Simone during a two-hour period] on her answering machine. [In his messages, Simone said that] he was "sorry it had come to this"[,] . . . implored Olson "not to return the things that are coming in the mail [and said] that he was sorry that he did not have her anymore [and] that he lost everything that he loved. . . . [In sixteen of the calls, Simone repeatedly asked Olson if she was present in her home and begged her to answer the telephone.] [Olson] immediately called the police department and Officer Duval came to her home. [On June 18,] Olson called Officer Duval to report that she had received two packages from [Simone]. On June 24, Olson reported to Officer Duval that she had received yet another package and a letter from [Simone, who] continued to call . . . .

In October 2003, a [county grand jury] indicted [Simone] on one count of stalking under [a New Hampshire statute] which criminalizes "knowingly . . . engag[ing] in a course of conduct targeted at a specific person which would cause a reasonable person to fear for his or her personal safety . . . and the person is actually placed in such fear." [On] appeal, [Simone] argues [that] the State failed to present sufficient evidence to support the jury's verdict [that] his conduct: (1) would cause a reasonable person to fear for his or her personal safety; and (2) actually placed Olson in fear for her personal safety[.] . . .

[Simone] argues that we must interpret the phrase, "fear for his or her personal safety," as used in the stalking statute, to require a fear of physical violence. We need not reach [this] argument, however, because even if [this is so,] the evidence was sufficient to [satisfy the elements of the statute].

[Simone] contends that his conduct would not cause a reasonable person to fear physical violence because he never assaulted Olson or explicitly threatened her with violence, and he "mostly apologized and expressed his continuing love" in his repeated telephone calls to her. We disagree. . . . [A] reasonable person could view [Simone's] unrelenting telephone calls and gifts to Olson, especially in light of [Simone's] emotional instability, as evidence that [he] was obsessed with Olson and posed a threat of physical violence to her. [He told Olson that he had "serious personal problems" and felt suicidal and out of control.] [Simone] and Olson never had a personal relationship. . . . [In light of all the evidence,] we conclude that there was sufficient evidence to prove beyond a reasonable doubt that [Simone's] conduct would cause a reasonable person to fear for his or her personal safety.

Next, [Simone] argues the State failed to prove that his conduct caused Olson actually to fear for her personal safety. At trial, the State asked Olson about the impact of [Simone's] conduct upon her. Olson answered, "I live in fear every day. I don't know—I don't know what's going to happen next, or what [the defendant is] going to do." Both Olson and Officer Duval testified that Olson frequently contacted the police between August 2001 and June 2003 as a result of [Simone's] conduct. [The] trial court twice noted that Olson's testimony and demeanor on the witness stand . . . gave rise to a reasonable inference that Olson actually feared the defendant. [In light of all the evidence, we conclude] that there was sufficient evidence beyond a reasonable doubt that [Simone's] conduct actually caused Olson to fear for her personal safety. Accordingly, the jury properly convicted the defendant of stalking . . . .

POINTS FOR DISCUSSION

a. Original Elements of Stalking Crime

The first stalking statute was enacted in California in 1990 after five women were murdered by their stalkers. The goal of stalking statutes is to address the harmful features of stalking behavior that are not addressed by assault and related crimes. Such crimes are concerned with single incidents whereas a stalking statute focuses on repeated behavior that causes fear of bodily injury, in the absence of oral or written threats and where evidence of the intention to cause fear may be lacking. In theory, a stalking statute makes it possible for police to intervene before a stalker takes violent action, and imposes serious penalties that may serve as a greater deterrent to stalking behavior. Legislatures have continued to amend their stalking statutes in order to take account of criticisms and enforcement problems with the earliest versions of these laws.

In 1993, the National Institute of Justice developed a "Model Anti-Stalking Code" which has been influential in some states. There are several points of consensus displayed by most stalking statutes, but a variety of legislative preferences are exhibited with regard to particular elements. The typical stalking statute requires that the defendant's "course of conduct" must be "directed at a specific person," and must be "repeated" at least twice. Some statutes require that the conduct must create actual fear in the victim, and some statutes require that the conduct would cause fear in a reasonable person. Other statutes follow the approach in the New Hampshire statute in *Simone*, which requires both of the latter elements. Like the Model Code and most statutes, the *Simone* statute applies to conduct that causes the victim either to fear for her own physical safety or for the physical safety of an immediate family member.

One influential aspect of the 1993 Model Code is the conduct element, which is defined so as to create two independent bases for prosecution. One type of prohibited conduct is the act of maintaining "a visual or physical proximity to a person," and most state statutes now include the acts of following a person or placing a person under surveillance. The second type of prohibited conduct is the conveyance of "threats" that may be oral, written, or implied by conduct.

Most states followed the broad approach of the Model Code in not providing specific examples of acts that qualify as part of a "course of conduct." But some statutes include such examples, while noting that a "course of conduct" may "include but not be limited to" such acts. The *Simone* statute uses a list that includes these and other examples: 1) appearing in close proximity to or entering the victim's (or immediate family member's) residence, place of employment, school, or other place where the person may be found; 2) causing damage to the victim's (or immediate family member's) residence or property; and 3) any act of communication by any method of transmission (including electronic transmission) after being notified that the victim does not desire further communication. Why would a legislature choose to include such a list? What additional examples would be useful to include?

b. Modern Trends

In 2007, the National Center for Victims of Crime proposed revisions for the Model Code based on empirical research about stalking behavior and victim experiences, which research revealed the need for broader definitions of the crime, especially given the many ways in which "affordable technology has fundamentally and profoundly changed the way stalkers monitor and initiate contact with their victims." The new proposed definition of stalking applies to:

> Any person who purposefully engages in a course of conduct directed at a specific person and knows or should know that the course of conduct would cause a reasonable person to: (a) fear for his or her safety or the safety of a third person; or (b) suffer other emotional distress.

Note that the updated definition does not require the "actual fear" element, in accordance with the judgment of 14 states in 2007. This definition also makes it unnecessary to show, as required by the *Simone* statute, that the victim suffered "fear for her safety," because proof of the alternate element of "emotional distress" is sufficient. In 2007, "roughly half the states include[d] 'emotional distress' or something similar in their stalking laws." The latter concept is defined as "significant mental suffering or distress that may, but does not necessarily, require medical or other professional treatment or counseling." A "reasonable person" is defined as a "reasonable person in the victim's circumstances." The term "course of conduct" has been expanded to include "two or more acts, including, but not limited to," the following:

> acts in which the stalker directly, indirectly, or through third parties, through any action, method, device, or means, follows, monitors,

Assault & Battery

observes, surveils, threatens, or communicates to or about a person, or interferes with a person's property.

Finally, unlike the 1993 Model Code, the 2007 Code includes an illustrative, non-exhaustive, list of 19 examples of stalking behaviors that all state laws should cover. Here are a few examples of the technology-related behaviors: 1) using the internet or a computer "to steal a victim's identity or to interfere with a victim's credit;" 2) using surveillance either in person, or "through technology," or "through third parties"; 3) "posting pictures of a victim on the internet," or "disseminating embarrassing or inaccurate information about a victim"; 4) "impersonating a victim through technology or other means"; and 5) sending "flowers, cards, or e-mail messages to a victim's home or workplace." *See* National Center for the Victims of Crime, The Model Stalking Code Revisited: Responding to the New Realities of Stalking (2007), http://djcs.wv.gov/grant-programs/all-general-programs/STOP%20VAWA/Documents/Publications/Model%20Stalking%20Code.pdf.

From a prosecutor's point of view, what are the potential effects of each of the changes in the 2007 model definition of the elements of the stalking crime? How are the experiences of stalking victims, like Coral Olson in the *Simone* case, reflected in each of the changes? Assuming that a state legislature enacts the proposed 2007 definition of the stalking crime, what barriers to effective enforcement of the crime may remain?

c. Enforcement of Stalking Laws

The *Simone* case illustrates how a variety of factors may impede the enforcement of the stalking laws. Notably, the problem of enforcement in *Simone* cannot be attributed to a lack of legislation. First, each of the defendant's telephone calls and deliveries of packages to the victim could have been prosecuted under the state statute defining the crime of "harassment." Second, each time the defendant engaged in two of these communications, they could have been prosecuted as a "course of conduct" under the stalking statute, because that term is defined as including two or more acts "over a period of time, however brief," which evidence "a continuity of purpose." Third, after the victim in *Simone* obtained the protective order that prohibited the defendant from contacting her, the defendant could have been prosecuted under the stalking statute for each time that he recklessly engaged in a single act that violated the order. *See* N.H. REV. STAT. §§ 633:3–a, 644:4 (West 2006). Yet the *Simone* opinion describes a prosecution for a single count of stalking that began with an indictment obtained more than two years after the victim first contacted the police department, seeking assistance in putting an end to the communications from the defendant.

In retrospect, one factor that may have delayed the stalking prosecution was the need for evidence that the defendant's conduct would cause a "reasonable person" to fear for his or her physical safety. What evidence did the *Simone* Court rely on to support its conclusions that there was sufficient fear of each kind to justify conviction? Aside from concern about the adequacy of the fear evidence, what other factors could explain the delay in prosecution?

One hypothetical at the end of this chapter provides the opportunity for making arguments about the interpretation of "fear for personal safety," which is used in most stalking statutes, and about the need for legislatures to redefine and expand this concept.

3. Domestic Violence

a. State Crimes

There are many crimes that may be committed during the course of abusive behavior by a person who fits a modern definition of a "family or household member of the victim," which could include "a spouse, a person living as a spouse, or a former spouse" or other relationships. These crimes include murder or manslaughter, negligent homicide, rape or sexual assault, assault and battery (possibly with a dangerous weapon), burglary or breaking and entering, criminal trespass, disorderly conduct, disturbing the peace, willful and malicious destruction of property, harassment (including harassing phone calls), violation of a restraining order, intimidation of a witness, and a variety of attempt crimes. *See* ELIZABETH M. SCHNEIDER *ET AL*, DOMESTIC VIOLENCE AND THE LAW: THEORY AND PRACTICE, 275–276 (2d ed. 2008).

In 1977 the California legislature enacted the felony crime of "domestic violence" to cover "the infliction of injury on [the] spouse, cohabitee or parent of a child" of the defendant. Many state codes now include such crimes and define them in a variety of ways. For example, the Vermont legislature enacted a Domestic Assault statute in 1993 with three degrees of the crime. The lowest degree of the crime imposes a maximum punishment of one year in jail for attempting to cause or recklessly causing bodily injury to a family or household member, or for willfully causing such a victim to fear imminent serious bodily injury. The aggravated second degree crime allows for a five-year prison sentence for committing a second domestic assault offense or for committing a first offense that violates a restraining order issued by the criminal court. The aggravated first degree crime applies when a person commits domestic assault while armed with a deadly weapon, or after having been convicted of this crime, or attempts to cause or recklessly causes serious bodily injury to the victim. *See* 33 Vt. Stat. Ann. 13 §§ 1042, 1043, 1044 (1993).

b. Federal Crimes

When Congress enacted the Violent Crime Control and Law Enforcement Act of 1994, this statute included the Violence Against Women Act of 1994 (VAWA), which "federalized the enforcement of restraining orders by requiring that states provide full faith and credit to orders issued by sister states [and] also criminalized interstate violations of restraining orders." *See* Schneider at 355. The VAWA also made "interstate domestic violence" a federal crime that encompasses all "intimate partners", and interstate stalking was added to the list of crimes in this provision in 1996. The statutory definition of interstate domestic violence in 18 U.S.C. § 2261 provides as follows:

> (1) Crossing a State line—A person who travels across a State line [with] the intent to injure, harass, or intimidate that person's spouse or intimate partner, and who, in the course of or as a result of such travel, intentionally commits a crime of violence and thereby causes bodily injury to such spouse or intimate partner, shall be punished [as provided].

> (2) Causing the crossing of a State line—A person who causes a spouse or intimate partner to cross a State line [by] force, coercion, duress, or fraud and, in the course or as a result of that conduct, intentionally commits a crime of violence and thereby causes bodily injury to the person's spouse or intimate partner, shall be punished [as provided].

The penalty for the § 2261 crime depends on the injuries to the victim. A sentence of life or any term of years may be imposed if the victim dies; a maximum sentence of 20 years is allowed if the victim suffers permanent disfigurement or life-threatening bodily injury. A maximum sentence of 10 years applies if a dangerous weapon is used or if the victim suffers serious bodily injury. Otherwise, the maximum sentence is five years. *See* Michelle Easterling, *For Better or Worse: The Federalization of Domestic Violence*, 98 W. Va. L. Rev. 933 (1996).

c. Domestic Violence in Indian Country

The following excerpt provides an analysis of the impact of the 2013 Amendment to the Violence Against Women Act that established new tools for Indian tribes to combat widespread domestic violence:

As a result of changes in federal law, domestic violence offenders and their defense attorneys are more likely to find themselves or their clients appearing in American Indian tribal courts. In 2013 President Obama signed into law the reauthorization of the Violence Against Women Act (VAWA), a federal statute that addresses domestic violence and other crimes against women, Pub. L. No. 113-4 (2013). When originally enacted in 1994 VAWA created new federal offenses and sanctions, provided training for federal, state, and local law enforcement and courts to address these crimes, and funded a variety of community services to protect and support victims. Most significantly, the amended version of VAWA recognizes that tribal courts have jurisdiction over criminal cases brought by tribes against non-members, including non-Indians that arise under VAWA.

Significantly, this is the first time since the Supreme Court's decision in *Oliphant v. Suquamish Indian Tribe,* 435 U.S. 191 (1978), that Congress recognized tribal courts' criminal jurisdiction over non-Indians. This change in the law represents a major change for native communities and especially native women. Native American and Alaska Native women experience sexual violence at a rate two and a half times higher than other women in the United States. [*See* U.S. Dep't of Justice, National Institute of Justice, Public Law 280 and Law Enforcement in Indian Country: Research Priorities (Dec. 2005), https://www.ncjrs.gov/pdffiles1/nij/209839.pdf.]

The special domestic violence criminal jurisdiction conferred under the VAWA reauthorization not only provides an additional tool to address violence in Indian country, but also strengthens tribal courts and tribal sovereignty. Congress' recognition of tribal criminal jurisdiction comes with limitations and places obligations on tribes. Tribes wishing to take advantage of VAWA's jurisdictional provisions may need to amend tribal law and hire new judges and public defenders. Further, there remain significant limitations on who can be prosecuted in tribal courts.

VAWA pilot programs and prosecutions of non-Indians in domestic violence cases have commenced in select tribal courts in the following states: Arizona, Michigan, Montana, North Dakota, North Carolina, Louisiana, Oklahoma, Oregon, South Dakota, and Washington and it is extremely likely that many more will follow.

Here is a summary of the new law's requirements and limitations:

Types of Offenses. Under the amended statute, P.L. 113–4 (2013), tribes can prosecute any type of violence committed by a person who is or has been in a "dating or domestic relationship" with the victim. Tribes can also prosecute violations of protection orders that occur in Indian country (see, definition below) as long as those protection orders were issued to prevent (a) violent or threatening acts, or (b) contact, communication, or physical proximity with or to the victim.

Types of Defendants. Tribes can only prosecute VAWA cases against a non-Indian defendant if he or she has one of the following connections to the tribe's reservation or lands: (a) resides in Indian country (b) is employed in Indian country, or (c) is the spouse, intimate partner, or dating partner of an Indian living in Indian country or a Tribal member. The last category includes former spouses, individuals who share a child in common, and individuals in social relationships of a romantic or intimate nature. These new jurisdictional rules have very limited impact with non-recognized tribes.

Types of Victims. Tribes can only use the jurisdictional provisions of VAWA to prosecute crimes against Indian victims. This new law does not recognize tribal authority to prosecute non-Indians for violent acts against non-Indian victims.

Procedural Safeguards. Tribes will need to guarantee that their criminal codes and rules of criminal procedure provide defendants with certain procedural safeguards. These include the right to a trial by an impartial jury of members of the community, and the tribes cannot exclude non-Indians. Whenever a tribe intends to impose imprisonment, it must provide counsel/public defenders for indigent defendants. It must guarantee that proceedings are presided over by a law-trained judge. It must make publicly available the tribal criminal statutes and rules of procedure and the criminal proceedings must be recorded. Defendants ordered detained under VAWA must be informed by the tribal court of their right to file federal habeas corpus petitions. Tribes must comply with all provisions of the ICRA and guarantee "all other rights whose protection is required under the US Constitution" in order to exercise this criminal jurisdiction, 25 U.S.C.A. § 1302. It has not yet been established precisely what "other rights" this refers to. The guarantee of these fundamental rights are something which may very well end up becoming the topic of future legal challenges.

Pilot Programs. As a result of the new federal legislation, in February 2013 the Justice Department announced a pilot program with three initial tribes, giving them jurisdiction over non-Indians in domestic violence cases on their reservations. In 2014, the tribal courts in those three jurisdictions began to exert their newly enhanced jurisdiction and in 2015 two additional tribes were approved to begin exercising special domestic violence jurisdiction as part of the pilot program. After 2015 more than eleven tribes were approved to exercise the special domestic violence jurisdiction. The tribal courts in those jurisdictions are at varying stages of exercising the approved jurisdiction. It is likely they will all begin prosecuting cases shortly, if they have not already done so.

Diamond, James, *An Overview of Practicing American Indian Criminal Law in Federal, State, and Tribal Courts, and an Update About Recent Expansion of Criminal Jurisdiction Over Non-Indians* (May 14, 2018). FEDERAL LAWYER, April 2018, at 18.

4. Civil Rights

Some criminal civil rights laws serve to punish bodily injury battery crimes (and attempted battery crimes) that are motivated by the victim's identity. For example, the Matthew Shepard and James Byrd, Jr., Hate Crimes Prevention Act of 2009, 18 U.S.C. § 249, applies to a person who "willfully causes bodily injury [or death] to any person," or who "attempts to cause bodily injury" "through the use of fire, a firearm, a dangerous weapon, or an explosive or incendiary device," either (1) "because of the actual or perceived race, color, religion, or national origin of any person"; or (2) "because of the actual or perceived religion, national origin, gender, sexual orientation, gender identity, or disability of any person" when the crime affected interstate and foreign commerce.

Although this statute does not apply to identity-motivated threats of injury, such acts may be prosecuted under other federal criminal laws, such as the Civil Rights Act of 1968, 18 U.S.C. § 249, or the federal statute that punishes the interstate communication of threats. *See* http://www.justice.gov/crt/about/crm/

Assault & Battery

matthewshepard.php. Almost all state criminal codes include hate crime laws that apply to identity-motivated acts of violence or frightening crimes.

> **Hypo 1: *Disarming Officer***
>
> Assume that a state legislature has abolished the "offensive touching" type of battery, but that the legislature is concerned about the need to punish a particular type of conduct that does not qualify for the "bodily injury" type of battery. This conduct is the act of "disarming" a police officer, which may occur during an arrest when a person manages to catch an officer by surprise and remove the officer's gun from its holster. What elements should the legislature consider using to define this special kind of "touching" crime, and what policy decisions are involved in choosing each of these elements? *Compare* Wash. Rev. Code § 9A.76.023 (1998).

> **Hypo 2: *MPC Choices***
>
> There are four different crimes in Model Penal Code § 211.1 that are derived from the common law crime of bodily injury battery. The provisions labeled here as (1) and (2) are the equivalent of crimes punished as simple battery, whereas (3) and (4) are the equivalent of crimes punished as aggravated battery:
>
> (1) purposely, knowingly or recklessly causes *bodily injury* to another; or
>
> (2) negligently causes *bodily injury* to another with a *deadly weapon*;
>
> (3) causes *serious bodily injury* to another purposely, knowingly or recklessly under circumstances manifesting extreme indifference to the value of human life;
>
> (4) purposely or knowingly causes *bodily injury* to another with a *deadly weapon*.
>
> Identify any variations of bodily injury battery that you notice are missing from this list, and consider the reasons that the MPC drafters may have rejected them. Then explain whether the defendant in *Adams* could be convicted using any of these MPC crimes.

> ### Hypo 3: *HIV Statutes*
>
> These hypotheticals focus on arguments that may be made for choosing particular elements to define the HIV exposure crime.
>
> a. *Conduct Element.* If a defendant is convicted based on the same evidence that was available to the *Richardson* prosecutor concerning victim E.Z., would it be more difficult for the prosecutor to persuade the appellate court to affirm a conviction under the Washington statute or under the Tennessee statute? Explain. *Compare State v. Whitfield*, 132 Wash. App. 878, 134 P.3d 1203 (2006); *State v. Bonds*, 189 S.W.3d 249 (Tenn. 2006).
>
> b. *Mental State Element.* Most statutes require the prosecutor to prove that the defendant knows of his or her HIV-positive status. Consider the implications of a statute that used the recklessly mental state for this element. What are the pros and cons of using "recklessly" instead of "knowingly"?
>
> c. *Consent Defense.* Assume that a legislature decides that it is a good idea to make some version of a consent defense available to the HIV exposure crime like the one committed by the *Richardson* defendant. What elements should be used to define this defense? *Compare* IOWA CODE ANN. § 709C.1.

> ### Hypo 4 *MPC Choice*
>
> There is only one assault crime in Model Penal Code § 211.1 that is derived from the crime of frightening assault. There is no aggravated MPC version of the crime, and the crime of "simple assault" establishes liability for:
>
> (1) attempts by physical menace to put another in fear of imminent serious bodily injury.
>
> Recall that the MPC defines the mental state of an "attempt" as "the desire to cause the result" and defines the conduct as an act of preparation that takes a "substantial step in a course of conduct planned to culminate in [the] commission of a crime."
>
> Now identify the possible elements of the frightening assault crime that you notice are missing from the MPC definition, and consider the possible reasons that the MPC drafters may have rejected them. Then explain whether the defendant in *Carter* could be convicted under this MPC definition of assault.

> ### Hypo 5: *Lying in Wait*
>
> When Sergeant Judy arrived at Tad's home in Gallup, New Mexico, with a warrant to arrest him for possession of an illegal handgun, Tad ran out the back door and down the street. Then with Judy chasing him on foot, Tad ran around the front end of a house trailer that was 20 feet long. Instead of following him, Judy stopped to listen for any indication that Tad was still running. When she heard no footsteps, Judy assumed that Tad might be lying in wait for her on the other side of the trailer. So Judy went the other way and tiptoed around the back end of the trailer. She carefully peered around the corner and saw that Tad was, indeed, facing toward the front end of the trailer with the gun in his right hand, extended forward and pointing toward the space where he expected Judy to appear. Therefore, Judy trained her gun on Tad and approached him quietly from behind. Then she shouted, "Drop the gun, now!" and Tad dropped his gun immediately. Tad was arrested and charged with the crime of "aggravated assault with a firearm on a law enforcement officer." The New Mexico statute that defines Tad's crime does not specify the elements of "assault," and the statute was enacted in 1912 when New Mexico became a state. Tad's defense counsel filed a pre-trial motion to dismiss the charge on the grounds that Tad "did not have the present ability to commit an injury," because Tad's gun did not have a bullet in the firing chamber when he dropped it. However, the gun was loaded and all Tad needed to do was to pull back a slide mechanism, in order to "chamber" the bullet so he could shoot it. Also, Tad had already taken off the safety catch when he was pointing the gun at the space where he expected Judy to appear, while he was lying in wait.
>
> You are the assistant prosecutor in Tad's case, and you recognize that the term "assault" in the statute can be interpreted in two different ways. First, what are the elements of each type of assault crime that is encompassed in the statute? Second, for each type of assault crime, explain how the facts provide sufficient evidence of all the elements of that crime. Third, assuming that defense counsel argues that there is insufficient evidence for particular element(s), explain why the defense argument(s) are unpersuasive. *Compare People v. Chance*, 44 Cal. 4th 1164, 189 P.3d 971, 81 Cal. Rptr. 3d 723 (2008).

> ### Hypo 6: *Cocaine During Pregnancy*
>
> Assume that when baby Ron is born in the county hospital, he has cocaine in his bloodstream. His mother Regina admits that she used cocaine during her pregnancy. The prosecutor charges her with the crime of reckless endangerment as defined in MPC § 211.2. Regina is convicted. On appeal, her defense counsel argues that the crime of reckless endangerment was not intended to encompass the conduct of a mother in using cocaine during her pregnancy. What arguments can be made in favor of this position? Can the prosecutor make any counter-arguments in reply? *Compare Kilmon v. State*, 394 Md. 168, 905 A.2d 306 (2006); *Whitner v. State*, 328 S.C. 1, 492 S.E.2d 777 (1997).

> ### Hypo 7: *Gym Class*
>
> Kia was married when she sought counseling from Joe, a counselor employed by her church in Nashua, New Hampshire. After some months, their relationship became "intimate." Kia recognized that it was "unhealthy" and told other church members, so Joe was fired by church officials, who told him to cut off contact with Kia. During the year that followed, Kia obtained a divorce, met and dated a new acquaintance, and then remarried. Six months later, when Kia was driving to her husband's office with her four-year-old daughter in the car, she realized that Joe was following her in his car. She pulled over and when Joe approached the vehicle to talk to her, she spoke to him through a crack in the window. When Joe asked for her address so that he could send her a "wedding card," Kia refused to give it to him and told him to stop all contact with her. Joe agreed. The next week, Joe started showing up at the gym where Kia exercised, and he began to attend the weekly yoga class that she attended. Kia was "very alarmed" by Joe's presence in the class, and she tried to ignore it for two weeks. Once when Joe tried to talk to her during the class, Kia told him to stop all contact with her. Again, Joe agreed. But he kept attending the yoga class. Finally, Kia stopped going because Joe's presence in the class "felt so threatening."
>
> One month later, Joe started calling Kia's house. When Kia or her husband would answer the phone, Joe would hang up without saying anything. Then after a few weeks, Joe called and told Kia's husband that he (Joe) "had some unfinished business with her." At this point, Kia and her husband called the police, and Joe was arrested for the stalking crime. Assume that the stalking

Assault & Battery

statute in *Simone* applies to this case. How will the prosecutor argue at trial that the evidence shows that all the elements of the statute are satisfied? If the New Hampshire legislature enacted the updated 2007 model definition of the stalking crime, and if that statute applied to this case, what difference would that make? *Compare Sparks v. Deveny*, 189 P.3d 1268 (Ore. App. 2008).

Hypo 8: *Bullying*

In 2011, the stalking statute in the State of Victoria, Australia, was amended in an effort to expand criminal liability to cover the conduct known as "bullying." The amendment is known as "Brodie's Law," in honor of a nineteen-year-old woman, Brodie Panlock, who committed suicide after being bullied by four male co-workers. Conviction under the amended statute may result in a prison sentence of up to ten years. Under the old statute, the "behaviors" element was defined to include traditional acts of stalking, such as following a victim or keeping a victim under surveillance. The amendment expanded the list of "behaviors" to include:

(1) making threats to the victim;

(2) using abusive or offensive words to, or in the presence of, the victim;

(3) performing abusive or offensive acts in the presence of the victim;

(4) directing abusive or offensive acts towards the victim; or

(5) acting in any other way that could reasonably be expected to cause a victim to engage in self-harm.

The 2011 amendment also added the following italicized language to the mental state for the stalking crime: "the intention of causing physical or mental harm to the victim, *including self-harm*, or of arousing apprehension or fear in the victim for his or her own safety or that of any other person." The definition of "mental harm" was amended to include "psychological harm" and "suicidal thoughts." *See* http://www.justice.vic.gov.au/home/safer+communities/crime+prevention/bullying+-+brodies+law.

Assume that a state legislature in the U.S. is considering the question whether to enact similar amendments to a stalking statute. What are the pro and con arguments that would be made in the legislative debate?

> **Hypo 9: *Policies and Impact***
>
> Describe the various policy reasons that may explain why state legislatures have enacted "domestic assault" crimes like those in Vermont, and the impact that such crimes could have on the criminal justice system.

CHAPTER 9

Rape & Sexual Assault

The common law crime of rape was a capital offense and it was defined as an act of genital penetration through sexual intercourse, by a man with a woman not his wife, through the use of force or by threat of force, without the consent of the victim. This definition was reflected in the case law and statutes of most states until the 1970s. Courts required a prosecutor to prove that the victim resisted the defendant "to the utmost" and reported the crime promptly. Corroborating evidence was required to support the victim's testimony, and jurors were instructed in the words of Lord Hale that they should give special scrutiny to the victim's testimony because rape "is an accusation easily to be made and hard to be proved, and harder to be defended by the party accused." Evidence of the victim's sexual reputation and prior sexual experiences could be offered by the defendant to show that her "lack of chastity" demonstrated that she was more likely to fabricate a claim of rape or to consent to forcible sex.

In 1975 the Michigan legislature enacted the first "rape reform" statute and thereby launched a widespread movement for change in the statutory definitions of the elements of rape crimes and the evidentiary rules governing rape trials. The new statutes typically redefined the rape crime as gender neutral, and expanded the scope of the crime to include acts of sexual penetration by fingers or objects, as well as oral or anal sexual conduct. Some statutes eliminated the "resistance" and "lack of consent" elements and allowed conviction when sexual intercourse was accomplished by "fear" in lieu of "force" or "threat of force." Courts and legislatures abolished the utmost resistance requirement, the corroboration requirement, the prompt report requirement, and the Lord Hale instruction. Even the marital rape exemption was abandoned or limited. Many states enacted new crimes to allow convictions for lesser degrees of rape, thus expanding the scope of criminal sexual conduct. States also adopted "rape shield" provisions in evidence codes which regulate the admissibility of evidence of the victim's prior sexual conduct. The large variety of statutory changes required courts to revise their interpretations of rape crime elements and defenses, to design new jury instructions, and to modify "sufficiency of the evidence" standards for conviction. Some statutes renamed the rape crime as "sexual assault", and in this chapter, these terms will be used synonymously unless otherwise indicated.

There are two other areas of rapid change in state sexual assault statutes: expanding the statute of limitations for commencement of prosecution and mandatory minimum sentences in offenses where children are victims. As new elements were added to the emerging rape definitions in statutes, courts took on the task of redefining the concepts of force, threat, fear, resistance, and consent. Their decisions often evidenced sharp disagreements, and the subsequent codifications of contested holdings have provided a continuing supply of controversies that illustrate the evolving cultural and legal definitions of rape.

A. OVERVIEW OF THE LAW

Force, Threat, or Fear. Modern statutes and decisions recognize that force or threat of force are unnecessary for conviction, because rape may be committed when accomplished by conduct creating fear of bodily injury when there is evidence that the victim's fear is genuine and reasonable.

Lack of Consent. When lack of consent is an element of rape, modern courts recognize that it may be expressed through the victim's words or conduct, and that evidence of verbal resistance may be sufficient. Where consent is defined as freely given and affirmative agreement, the absence of such agreement is evidence of lack of consent.

Affirmative Defense of Consent. Even when the lack of consent element is not present in a rape statute, courts may recognize the affirmative defense of consent. The defendant must have a reasonable belief in such consent and may bear the burden of persuasion because this affirmative defense does not negate an element of the crime.

***Mens Rea* and Mistake of Fact.** When lack of consent is an element of the rape crime, the "mistake of fact as to consent" defense may be recognized in statute or case law. Courts require the defendant's mistake to be reasonable and based on good faith, which means that the mental state of negligence is required for the lack of consent element. The prosecution bears the burden of persuasion and must rebut the mistake defense beyond a reasonable doubt because this defense seeks to negate an element of the crime.

Rape by Deception. Some states have enacted statutory definitions of this crime. But courts continue to define it narrowly to include only cases where the defendant's "fraud" caused the victim to be ignorant of the fact that the defendant performed sexual intercourse upon the victim.

Rape of Drugged or Intoxicated Victim. Both the common law and modern statutes define rape to include sexual intercourse with a sleeping, unconscious, or drugged victim, who necessarily lacks the capacity to consent. A defendant can be convicted when he administered drugs to an unknowing victim that caused the lack of capacity to consent.

Statutory Rape. Most states use gender neutral statutes with age-gap provisions to confer immunity on teenagers who are close in age and engage in consensual sex. Some states recognize the "mistake of fact as to age" defense.

Rape Trauma Syndrome. An expert witness may provide testimony to describe the behavior of rape victims in order to dispel the misconceptions of jurors about such behavior, and in order to rehabilitate a rape victim's credibility when defense counsel argues that the victim's behavior is not consistent with the claim of rape.

Rape Shield Laws. These laws create general prohibitions on the admission of evidence regarding prior sexual conduct of the victim in rape prosecutions, with

---

Major Themes

a. Common Law Rape Crime— Before the rape reform era, most state codes and case law used definitions of rape that included the conduct of sexual intercourse by genital penetration by a man with a woman not his wife, through the use of force or by threat of force, without the consent of the victim. The victim's "utmost resistance" to this act was required. It was difficult to obtain convictions because of special evidence rules, jury attitudes toward victims and defendants, and appellate court reversals of convictions based on sufficiency-of-the-evidence formulas that reflected lack of deference to jury fact-finding concerning the credibility of victims and defendants.

b. Rape Reforms— The rape reform era began in 1975 with the enactment of the Michigan rape statute. In the ensuing decades, there were widespread changes in the law of rape, including the relabeling of the crime as sexual assault, the redefinition of the elements of the forcible rape crime, the enactment of crimes involving additional types of sexual conduct, the enactment of gender neutral statutes, the abolition of the marital rape exemption, and the abandonment of special evidence rules that created barriers to conviction. Appellate courts began to defer to jury fact-finding on credibility issues, and to affirm convictions in cases that could not have been prosecuted in the pre-reform era.

exceptions made for particular types of evidence that is deemed to be probative concerning the elements of the crime.

B. FORCIBLE RAPE

The two most important elements for the common law crime of forcible rape were "force" and "lack of consent." While it is useful to study these elements separately, it is important to understand the historical connections between them that continue to influence modern judicial interpretations of their meaning. Some modern statutes define these elements as separate and independent requirements for conviction, whereas other statutes treat them as being intertwined, as when the term "force" is described as "force used to overcome the victim's will." Today most statutes define rape with reference to "force," "threat of force," and "fear," rather than "lack of consent." Even statutes that rely on "lack of consent" as the key element of rape may define that term so as to equate it with "force" or "compulsion."

The common law definition of rape did not include an explicit *mens rea*, and rape was viewed as a general intent crime. A prosecutor was required to prove that a defendant engaged intentionally in sexual intercourse, and intended to use force or threat of force to accomplish that act. But a prosecutor did not need to prove that a defendant intended to engage in nonconsensual intercourse.

1. Force, Threat, or Fear

During the pre-reform era, courts looked to the victim to supply evidence of the defendant's use of unlawful "force," as illustrated by the "utmost resistance" requirement. The function of this extreme type of resistance evidence was to persuade judges that a defendant's use of "force" was sufficiently harmful to justify conviction, and that a victim's claim of rape was credible. Without such proof of resistance, judges could view the use of "force" to accomplish sexual intercourse as an ambiguous event that could be characterized as "seduction" rather than "rape."

Over time, some courts replaced the "utmost resistance" requirement with that of "sufficient" resistance under the circumstances, depending on the character of the "force" or "threat of force" used by the defendant. As judges began to recognize that a threat of violence could explain a victim's submission to sexual intercourse without resistance, the "force" and "threat" concepts began to expand. Ultimately, statutes and judicial decisions came to endorse the view that a defendant's provocation of a victim's "reasonable fear" could justify conviction in the absence of a victim's physical resistance. In this way, "fear" caused by an implicit threat came to serve as a substitute for actual "force" or an explicit "threat of force." However, during the pre-reform era, courts and legislatures usually required fear of imminent death or serious bodily injury.

At the outset of the rape reform era, some judges began to question the need for any type of resistance requirement on policy grounds, arguing that women should not be forced to risk death or injury in order to provide the prosecutor with evidence that a rape occurred. Courts began to accept proof of verbal resistance as a substitute for physical resistance, and to look more closely at a defendant's actions, rather than a victim's actions, in assessing the existence of "force" and "fear." Legislatures began to enact new statutes that codified "fear" as a prohibited means for accomplishing rape, and some statutes required only fear of "immediate and unlawful bodily injury." Such reform statutes, like that in the *Iniguez* case, required courts to rethink their prior interpretations of the evolving elements of the rape crime.

PEOPLE V. INIGUEZ

7 Cal. 4th 847, 872 P.2d 1183, 30 Cal. Rptr. 2d 258 (1994) (In Bank).

ARABIAN, J.

[The] Court of Appeal reversed the defendant's conviction for rape on the grounds that the evidence of force or fear of immediate and unlawful bodily injury was insufficient. We granted review to determine whether there was sufficient evidence to support the verdict, and to delineate the relationship between evidence of fear and the requirement under Penal Code [§] 261(a)(2) that the sexual intercourse be "accomplished against a person's will" in a case where lack of consent is not disputed. We reverse the Court of Appeal.

On June 15, 1990, the eve of her wedding, at approximately 8:30 p.m., 22 year-old Mercy P. arrived at the home of Sandra S., a close family friend [who] was to stand in at the wedding the next day for Mercy's mother[.] Mercy was planning to spend the night at [Sandra's] home [and Mercy] met defendant, Sandra's fiancé, for the first time that evening. Defendant was scheduled to stand in for Mercy's father during the wedding. Mercy noticed that defendant was somewhat "tipsy" when he arrived. He had consumed a couple of beers and a pint of Southern Comfort[.] Mercy, Sandra, and defendant celebrated Mercy's impending wedding by having dinner and drinking some wine. There was no flirtation or any remarks of a sexual nature between defendant and Mercy at any time during the evening. Around 11:30 p.m., Mercy went to bed in the living room.

She slept on top of her sleeping bag. She was wearing pants with an attached skirt, and a shirt. She fell asleep at approximately midnight.

Mercy was awakened between 1:00 and 2:00 a.m. when she heard some movements behind her. She was lying on her stomach, and saw defendant, who was naked, approach her from behind. Without saying anything, defendant pulled down her pants, fondled her buttocks, and inserted his penis inside her. Mercy weighed 105 pounds. Defendant weighed approximately 205 pounds[.] Less than a minute later, defendant ejaculated, got off her, and walked back to the bedroom[.]

Officer Fragoso, who interviewed Mercy several days after the attack, testified that she told him she had not resisted defendant's sexual assault because, "She said she knew that the man had been drinking. She hadn't met him before; he was a complete stranger to her. When she realized what was going on, she said she panicked, she froze. She was afraid that if she said or did anything, his reaction could be of a violent nature. So she decided just to lay still, wait until it was over with and then get out of the house as quickly as she could and get to her [fiancé] *and tell him what happened.*"

Mercy immediately telephoned her fiancé Gary and left a message for him. She then telephoned her best friend Pam, who testified that Mercy was so distraught she was barely comprehensible. Mercy asked Pam to pick her up, grabbed her purse and shoes, and ran out of the apartment. Mercy hid in the bushes outside [for] approximately half an hour while waiting for Pam because she was terrified defendant would look for her.

Pam arrived about 30 minutes later, and drove Mercy to Pam's house. Mercy sat on Pam's kitchen floor, her back to the wall, and asked Pam, "Do I look like the word 'rape' [is] written on [my] face?" Mercy wanted to take a shower because she "felt dirty," but was dissuaded by Pam. Pam telephoned Gary, who called the police. Gary and his best man then drove Mercy to the hospital, where a "rape examination" was performed. [Blood and semen were found in Mercy's vagina and on her underpants.]

The following day, Mercy and Gary married[.] Neither Sandra nor defendant participated in the wedding. [The defendant] was arrested the same day. When asked by the arresting officer if he had had sexual intercourse with Mercy, defendant replied, "I guess I did, yes."

Dr. Charles Nelson, a psychologist, testified as an expert on "rape trauma syndrome." He stated that victims respond in a variety of ways to the trauma of being raped. Some try to flee, and others are paralyzed by fear. This latter response he termed "frozen fright."

Defendant conceded at trial that the sexual intercourse was nonconsensual. However, defense counsel argued that the element of force or fear was absent. "So if he was doing anything, it's not force or fear[.] It's a situation where it looks to him like he can get away with it and a situation where his judgment [has] flown out the window[.] He keeps doing it, probably without giving much thought to it, but certainly there is nothing there to indicate using fear ever entered his mind. What he was doing was taking advantage, in a drunken way, of a situation where somebody appeared to be out of it." [Author's Note: The California rape statute also applied to a defendant who engaged in sexual intercourse with a person whom the defendant knew was 'unconscious of the act" because the person was asleep.]

[Rape is defined under Penal Code § 261(a)(2) as "an act of sexual intercourse accomplished with a person not the spouse of the perpetrator, [w]here it is accomplished against a person's will by means of force, violence, or fear of immediate and unlawful bodily injury on the person of another."] [The trial] court [also] instructed in relevant part[,] "Verbal threats are not critical to a finding of fear of unlawful injury, threats can be implied from the circumstances or inferred from the assailant's conduct. A victim may entertain a reasonable fear even where the assailant does not threaten by words or deed." The jury found defendant guilty of rape. He was sentenced to state prison [for] six years.

The Court of Appeal reversed [in an unpublished opinion], concluding that there was insufficient evidence that the act of sexual intercourse was accomplished by means of force or fear of immediate and unlawful bodily injury. On the issue of fear, the court stated: "While the [defendant] was admittedly much larger than the small victim, he did nothing to suggest that he intended to injure her. No coarse or sexually suggestive conversation had taken place. Nothing of an abusive or threatening nature had occurred. The victim was sleeping in her aunt's house, in which screams presumably would have raised the aunt and interrupted the intercourse. Although the assailant was a stranger to the victim, she knew nothing about him which would suggest that he was violent. [The] event of intercourse [was] singularly unusual in terms of its ease of facilitation, causing no struggle, no injury, no abrasions or other marks, and lasting, as the victim testified, 'maybe a minute.' " . . .

The test on appeal for determining if substantial evidence supports a conviction is whether "a reasonable trier of fact could have found the prosecution sustained its burden of proving the defendant guilty beyond a reasonable doubt."

In making this determination, we " 'must view the evidence in a light most favorable to [the State] and presume in support of the judgment the existence of every fact the trier could reasonably deduce from the evidence.' " [*People v. Johnson*, 26 Cal. 3d 557, 576 (1980).]

Prior to 1980, section 261 "defined rape as an act of sexual intercourse under circumstances where the person resists, but where 'resistance is overcome by force or violence' or where 'a person is prevented from resisting by threats of great and immediate bodily harm, accompanied by apparent power of execution[.]' " *People v. Barnes*, 42 Cal. 3d 284, 292 (1986). Under the former law, a person was required to either resist or be prevented from resisting because of threats. *Id.* at 295.

Section 261 was amended in 1980 to eliminate both the resistance requirement and the requirement that the threat of immediate bodily harm be accompanied by an apparent power to inflict the harm. As the legislative history explains, "threat is eliminated and the victim need only fear harm. The standard for injury is reduced from great and immediate bodily harm to immediate and unlawful bodily injury."

In discussing the significance of the 1980 amendments in *Barnes*, we noted that "studies have demonstrated that while some women respond to sexual assault with active resistance, others 'freeze,' " and "become helpless from panic and numbing fear." *Barnes, supra*, 42 Cal.3d at 299. In response to this information, "For the first time, the Legislature has assigned the decision as to whether a sexual assault should be resisted to the realm of personal choice." "By removing resistance as a prerequisite to a rape conviction, the Legislature has brought the law of rape into conformity with other crimes such as robbery, kidnapping and assault, which require force, fear, and nonconsent to convict. In these crimes, the law does not expect falsity from the complainant who alleges their commission and thus demand resistance as a corroboration and predicate to conviction." *Id.* at 301.

[The] deletion of the resistance language from section 261 by the 1980 amendments thus effected a change in the purpose of evidence of fear of immediate and unlawful injury. Prior to 1980, evidence of fear was directly linked to resistance; the prosecution was required to demonstrate that a person's *resistance* had been overcome by force, or that a person was prevented from resisting by threats of great and immediate bodily harm. As a result of the amendments, evidence of fear is now directly linked to the overbearing of a victim's will; the prosecution is required to demonstrate that the act of sexual intercourse was

Rape & Sexual Assault

accomplished against the person's *will* by means of force, violence, or fear of immediate and unlawful bodily injury.

In *Barnes*, [we] addressed the question of the role of force or fear of immediate and unlawful bodily injury in the absence of a resistance requirement. We stated that "[a]lthough resistance is no longer the touchstone of the element of force, the reviewing court still looks to the circumstances of the case, including the presence of verbal or nonverbal threats, or the kind of force that might reasonably induce fear in the mind of the victim, to ascertain sufficiency of the evidence of a conviction under § 261(2)." "Additionally, the [victim's] conduct must be measured against the degree of force manifested or in light of whether her fears were genuine and reasonably grounded." "In some circumstances, even a [victim's] unreasonable fear of immediate and unlawful bodily injury may suffice to sustain a conviction under § 261(2) if the accused knowingly takes advantage of that fear in order to accomplish sexual intercourse." [*Id.* at 304.]

Thus, the element of fear of immediate and unlawful bodily injury has two components, one subjective and one objective. The subjective component asks whether a victim genuinely entertained a fear of immediate and unlawful bodily injury sufficient to induce her to submit to sexual intercourse against her will. In order to satisfy this component, the extent or seriousness of the injury feared is immaterial.

In addition, the prosecution must satisfy the objective component, which asks whether the victim's fear was reasonable under the circumstances, or, if unreasonable, whether the perpetrator knew of the victim's subjective fear and took advantage of it. The particular means by which fear is imparted is not an element of rape.

Applying these principles, we conclude that the evidence that the sexual intercourse was accomplished against Mercy's will by means of fear of immediate and unlawful bodily injury was sufficient to support the verdict in this case. First, there was substantial evidence that Mercy genuinely feared immediate and unlawful bodily injury. Mercy testified that she froze because she was afraid, and the investigating police officer testified that she told him she did not move because she feared defendant would do something violent.

The Court of Appeal stated, however, "But most importantly, the victim was unable to articulate an experience of fear of immediate and unlawful bodily injury." This statement ignores the officer's testimony as to Mercy's state of mind. Moreover, even absent the officer's testimony, the prosecution was not required to elicit from Mercy testimony regarding what precisely she feared. "Fear" may be inferred from the circumstances despite even superficially *contrary* testimony of the victim. See *People v. Renteria*, 61 Cal.2d 497, 499 (1964); *People v. Borra*, 123 Cal.App. 482, 484–85 (1932) [robbery cases]. In addition, immediately after the attack, Mercy was so distraught her friend Pam could barely understand her. Mercy hid in the bushes outside the house waiting for Pam to pick her up because she was terrified defendant would find her; she subsequently asked Pam if the word "rape" was written on her forehead, and had to be dissuaded from bathing prior to going to the hospital.

Second, there was substantial evidence that Mercy's fear of immediate and unlawful bodily injury was reasonable. The Court of Appeal's statements[—]that defendant "did nothing to suggest that he intended to injure" Mercy, and that "[a]lthough the assailant was a stranger to the victim, she knew nothing about him which would suggest that he was violent"[—]ignor[e] the import of the undisputed facts. Defendant, who weighed twice as much as Mercy, accosted her while she slept in the home of a close friend, thus violating the victim's enhanced level of security and privacy.

Defendant, who was naked, then removed Mercy's pants, fondled her buttocks, and inserted his penis into her vagina for approximately one minute, without warning, without her consent, and without a reasonable belief of consent. Any man or woman awakening to find himself or herself in this situation could reasonably react with fear of immediate and unlawful bodily injury. Sudden, unconsented-to groping, disrobing, and ensuing sexual intercourse while one appears to lie sleeping is an appalling and intolerable invasion of one's personal autonomy that, in and of itself, would reasonably cause one to react with fear.

The Court of Appeal's suggestion that Mercy could have stopped the sexual assault by screaming and thus eliciting Sandra S.'s help, disregards both the Legislature's 1980 elimination of the resistance requirement and our express language in *Barnes* upholding that amendment. It effectively guarantees an attacker freedom to intimidate his victim and exploit any resulting reasonable fear so long as she neither struggles nor cries out. Moreover, it is sheer speculation that Mercy's assailant would have responded to screams by desisting the attack, and not by causing her further injury or death.

The jury could reasonably have concluded that under the totality of the circumstances, this scenario, instigated and choreographed by defendant, created a situation in which Mercy genuinely and reasonably responded with fear of immediate and unlawful bodily injury, and that such fear allowed him to accomplish sexual intercourse with Mercy against her will.

The judgment of the Court of Appeal is reversed, and the case is remanded to that court for further proceedings consistent with this opinion.

POINTS FOR DISCUSSION

a. Reasons for Rape Law Reforms

The 1980 reform statute in *Iniguez* is one example of a nationwide pattern of legislative action that emerged after the enactment of the 1975 Michigan reform statute. The 1980 Revised Comments to the republished Model Penal Code of 1962 explain some of the reasons that rape law reforms were viewed as necessary:

> [T]here is reason to suppose that rape is the most dramatically underreported of all violent crimes and that the incidence of rape far exceeds the number of reported crimes. This assumption certainly seems plausible in light of the ordeal that a rape victim may face upon public disclosure of the event.
>
> There are at least two other factors that may contribute to the present sense [that rape law revision is necessary]. The first is that the probability of apprehension of a suspect is not good even when the police are called. Among the factors that contribute to this result are conclusions by the police that the rape complaint is unfounded and the relatively high frequency of cases where the offender and the victim are strangers and where there is consequent difficulty in identifying the offender. Second, arrest for rape is unlikely to result in conviction. Contributing factors to this result include the unwitting destruction of evidence by victims, special evidentiary rules relating to rape, and the difficulty of tying the offender to the crime by evidence other than the testimony of a victim who, because of the emotions surrounding the event and testimony about it, may prove especially vulnerable to disbelief.
>
> Cumulatively, these bits of data suggest that the criminal justice system actually identifies and punishes a small fraction of the total population of rape offenders. [Rape law reform] has also been a special target of feminist reform. There have been accusations that the law of rape reflects sexist assumptions about appropriate behavior of men and women, as well [as] insensitivity to the plight of rape victims.

Model Penal Code § 213.1, Comment (3), at 283–286 (1980). For a study of the history of the enactment and impact of the Michigan rape reform statute, see JEANNE C. MARSH, ALISON GEIST & NATHAN CAPLAN, RAPE AND THE LIMITS OF

LAW REFORM (1982). Note that the American Law Institute has been embarked upon a project to update the 1962 MPC provisions on the rape crime since 2012.

b. Jury Attitudes

Courts have noted the persistence of false and biased juror perceptions of rape complainants, some which are described in *Commonwealth v. King*, 445 Mass. 217, 238–39, 834 N.E.2d 1175, 1194–95 (2005), as follows:

> [T]he research and scholarship of which we are aware suggests that damaging stereotypes persist. Some jurors may continue to believe incorrectly that "real" victims will *promptly* disclose a sexual attack. Some jurors may continue to harbor prejudicial misperceptions about the nature of rape and rape allegations, including that complainants who wear revealing clothing, consume drugs or alcohol, or have unorthodox or promiscuous lifestyles cannot be "real" victims of rape; that forced sex by a spouse or a past partner does not constitute "real" rape; and that false accusations of sexual assault are more frequent than those of other violent crimes.

The sources cited in the *King* opinion included "empirical research on juries' decision-making behavior in rape cases," which revealed that jurors "may rely on rape 'scripts' which they bring with them into the jury room," and that jurors "come to the rape judgment situation with preconceptions and attitudes that lead them to entertain particular stories about what may have happened [and] these stories are then used to arrive at a legal decision or verdict." *Id.* at 239 n.20, 834 N.E.2d at 1195 n.20.

c. Model Penal Code Proposals

The American Law Institute published the final draft of the MPC in 1962, and the drafters did much of their work on prior drafts during the 1950s. Their proposals reflect the law and legal thinking of their times. In MPC § 213.1(1)(a), they defined the rape crime as the conduct of "A male who has sexual intercourse with a female not his wife [if] he compels her to submit by force or by threat of imminent death, serious bodily injury, extreme pain or kidnapping, to be inflicted on anyone."

The MPC definition of rape is not gender neutral, and the MPC also retains the marital rape exemption, the corroboration requirement, and a version of the Lord Hale instruction. *See* Model Penal Code §§ 213.6(2), (4) & (5). The MPC included no proposal for a "rape shield" evidence rule, which first appeared in the 1975 Michigan reform statute. The term compulsion "plainly implies nonconsent," and the absence of a resistance element does not mean that "inquiry into the level of resistance by the victim cannot or should not be made." Model Penal Code § 213.1, Comment (4)(a), at 306–307 (1980). Notably, the 1980 Commentary criticized the 1975 Michigan reform statute as an "unacceptable" "overreaction" to the concerns of reformers. In hindsight, however, the Michigan statute provided a more enduring legacy than the 1962 MPC rape definition, because the MPC drafters did not anticipate the imminent widespread abandonment or modification of the various common law concepts and evidence rules embedded in their definition of rape. *Compare id.*, Comment (3)(b)(ii), at 288–89 (1980). New prosecutions became possible in the 1990s because of reform-oriented statutes and case law. What types of rape prosecutions would have been impossible under the MPC—which became possible under *Iniguez*?

d. Definitions of Force

The *Iniguez* Court did not address the sufficiency of the evidence of the "force" element because there was sufficient evidence of the "fear" element. Even though the element of "force" may operate in a variety of ways, statutes that use this element typically do not specify the nature or amount of the force required. Here are three different case law definitions of "force," which illustrate a wide range of meanings for this ambiguous concept.

i. Force as Threat That Overcomes Will to Resist

The term "force" has been defined as including threats that create fear. When the element of "force" appears in a rape statute, then "[f]orce is an essential element of the crime [but] no particular amount of force, either actual or constructive, is required to constitute rape. [Force] may exist without violence. If the acts and threats of the defendant were reasonably calculated to create in the mind of the victim—having regard to the circumstances in which she was placed—a real apprehension, due to fear, of imminent bodily harm, serious enough to impair or overcome her will to resist, then such acts and threats are the equivalent of force." *State v. Baby*, 404 Md. 220, 260, 946 A.2d 463, 486–87 (2008) (relying on *Hazel v. State*, 221 Md. 464, 469, 157 A.2d 922, 925 (1960)).

ii. Force as Psychological Pressure

The term "force" has been defined to include the imposition of psychological pressure. Where the statutory definition of "force" includes an act that "coerces the victim to submit by threatening to use force or violence on the victim," then "force" may include a threat that "may be implied as well as express," and "force" may "consist of the imposition of psychological pressure upon a person who, under all of the circumstances, is vulnerable and susceptible to such pressure." *State v. DiPetrillo*, 922 A.2d 124, 134 (R.I. 2007).

iii. Force as the Act of Penetration

One broad definition of "force" equates it with the type of force required for a battery. Where the crime of sexual assault is defined by statute as the commission of "an act of sexual penetration with another person [where] the actor uses physical force," the term "physical force" should be interpreted as "any amount of force" that results in "offensive touching." The term "physical force" should *not* be interpreted as requiring "the application of some amount of force in addition to the act of penetration," or as "force used to overcome lack of consent." *State of New Jersey in the Interest of M.T.S.*, 129 N.J. 422, 443, 609 A.2d 1266, 1277 (1992).

Two hypotheticals at the end of the chapter present the opportunity to apply the analysis of the "fear" element in the *Iniguez* opinion to different facts, and to compare the applications of different interpretations of the ambiguous "force" element.

e. Non-Consensual Sex Without Force

In a majority of states, as one scholar notes, "it is finally true that non-consent alone" without force may establish criminal liability. But "reform still faces formidable opposition" regarding two issues: 1) "What is the minimum requirement?" meaning "what counts as consent?"; and 2) "what circumstances nullify [apparent] consent?" meaning "[w]hen does yes not mean yes?" Stephen J. Schulhofer, *Reforming the Law of Rape*, 35 L. & INEQUALITY 335, 343 (2017).

2. Lack of Consent

The importance of a victim's "lack of consent" casts a long shadow over modern rape law. At common law, defendants could attempt to raise a reasonable doubt about the "lack of consent" element by arguing that a victim's consent could be inferred from submission or lack of resistance. Some drafters of rape reform statutes singled out this element for elimination in the hope of making it easier to obtain convictions, by making it unnecessary to prove lack of consent beyond a reasonable doubt.

Almost half the states continue to use the "lack of consent" element in rape statutes. Some of these states use this element exclusively, but more states use it together with the "force, threat, or fear" elements. When the "lack of consent" element does not appear in a statute, this does not mean that consent is irrelevant to conviction. For example, the element of "force" or "compulsion" may be interpreted as incorporating the "lack of consent" concept into the meaning of that term.

POINTS FOR DISCUSSION

a. Reforms Regarding Lack of Consent Element

The original functions of the "lack of consent" element in common law definitions of rape are summarized in *State of New Jersey in the Interest of M.T.S.*, 129 N.J. 422, 432–39, 609 A.2d 1266, 1271–74 (1992):

> Under traditional rape law[,] the state had to show both that force had been used and that the penetration had been against the woman's will. Force was identified and determined not as an independent factor but in relation to the response of the victim, which in turn implicated the victim's own state of mind[.] Although the terms "non-consent" and "against her will" were often treated as equivalent under the traditional definition of rape, both formulations squarely placed on the victim the burden of proof and of action. Effectively, a woman who was above the age of consent had [to] actively and affirmatively withdraw that consent for the intercourse to be against her will[.]
>
> The presence or absence of consent often turned on credibility[.] According to the oft quoted Lord Hale, to be deemed a credible witness, a woman had to be of good fame, disclose the injury immediately, suffer signs of injury, and cry out for help. Courts and commentators historically distrusted the testimony of victims, "assuming that women lie about their lack of consent for various reasons: to blackmail men, to explain the discovery of a consensual affair, or because of psychological illness." [Note, 56 GEO. WASH. L. REV. 399, 403 (1988).] Evidence of resistance was viewed as a solution to the credibility problem; it was the "outward manifestation of nonconsent, [a] device for determining whether a woman actually gave consent." [Note, 18 STAN. L. REV. 680, 689 (1966).]
>
> [To] refute the misguided belief that rape was not real unless the victim fought back, reformers emphasized empirical research indicating that women who resisted forcible intercourse often suffered far more serious injury as a result. [Reformers also] emphasized that rape had its legal origins in laws designed to protect the property rights of men to their

wives and daughters. [They] argued that vestiges of the old law remained, particularly in the understanding of rape as a crime against the purity or chastity of a woman. The burden of protecting that chastity fell on the woman, with the state offering its protection only after the woman demonstrated that she had resisted sufficiently[.]

Critics of rape law agreed that the focus of the crime should be shifted from the victim's behavior to the defendant's [conduct]. [There] were, however, differences over the best way to redefine the crime. Some reformers advocated a standard that [did not use the "force, threat or fear" elements and instead] defined rape as unconsented-to sexual intercourse; others urged the elimination of any reference to consent from the definition of rape. Nonetheless, all proponents of reform shared a central premise: that the burden of showing non-consent should not fall on the victim of the crime. In dealing with the problem of consent the reform goal was not so much to purge the entire concept of consent from the law as to eliminate the burden that had been placed on victims to prove they had not consented.

b. Definitions of Lack of Consent

During the reform era, some legislatures and courts adopted definitions of lack of consent that made it easier for prosecutors to obtain convictions in cases where the evidence showed verbal resistance by the victim or passive submission as in *Iniguez*. In the pre-reform era, defense counsel could attempt to raise a reasonable doubt about the "lack of consent" element by arguing that consent was implied by the victim's ultimate submission and failure to demonstrate sufficient resistance. But when "consent" was redefined to require evidence of "affirmative agreement," for example, the prosecutor could show "lack of consent" by pointing to an absence of "agreement evidence," and defense counsel presumably would need some agreement evidence to raise a reasonable doubt about the lack of consent element.

Here are three different definitions of "lack of consent" that illustrate the modern range of its meanings.

i. Lack of Consent as Resistance

One statute defines the lack of consent element as including: "a) the victim expressed a lack of consent through words; or b) the victim expressed a lack of consent through conduct." The statute also provides: "c) the victim need only resist, either verbally or physically, so as to make the victim's refusal to consent genuine and real and so as to reasonably make known to the actor the victim's refusal to consent; and d) a victim need not resist verbally or physically where it would be useless or futile to do so." *See* Neb. Rev. Stat. § 28–318 (1995).

ii. Lack of Consent as Manifested Unwillingness

The lack of consent element has been defined by one court as communication from the victim to the defendant, in which "the victim must manifest her unwillingness objectively." "If [the] victim objectively communicates lack of consent and the defendant subjectively fails to receive the message, he is guilty. The appropriate inquiry is whether a reasonable person in the circumstances would have understood that the victim did not consent." *State v. Ayer*, 136 N.H. 191, 195–96, 612 A.2d 923, 926 (1992).

iii. Lack of Consent as Absence of Affirmative Agreement

The lack of consent element may be defined through definitions of "consent," as in a statute that defines this term as "words or overt actions" "indicating freely given agreement to have sexual intercourse." *See* Wisc. Stat. Ann. § 940.225(3) (1979). This definition "demonstrates that failure to resist is not consent." *State v. Lederer*, 99 Wis. 2d 430, 299 N.W.2d 457 (Ct. App. 1980). Another court's interpretation of "freely given agreement" is that "permission to engage in sexual penetration must be affirmative and it must be given freely, but that permission may be inferred either from acts or statements reasonably viewed in light of the surrounding circumstances. Persons need not, of course, expressly announce their consent to engage in intercourse for there to be affirmative permission. Permission . . . can be and indeed often is indicated through physical actions rather than words. Permission is demonstrated when the evidence, in whatever form, is sufficient to demonstrate that a reasonable person would have believed that the [victim] had affirmatively and freely given authorization to the act." *State of New Jersey in the Interest of M.T.S.*, 129 N.J. 422, 432–39, 609 A.2d 1266, 1271–74 (1992).

c. Uses of Resistance Evidence

During the pre-reform era, courts recognized that resistance evidence could serve as "force" or "fear" elements as well as the "lack of consent" element. In the modern era, some judges have objected this idea. For example, in *State v. Borthwick*, 255 Kan. 899, 880 P.2d 1261 (1994), the court was unanimous in ruling that the victim's testimony concerning her verbal and physical resistance provided sufficient evidence of the element of lack of consent. This evidence included the victim's testimony that she tried to keep her legs together and said "stop" repeatedly. The *Borthwick* majority also relied on this evidence, as well as other testimony of the victim, to affirm the reasonableness of the jury's finding that the victim was "overcome by force or fear." But the *Borthwick* dissenters argued that the "lack of consent" evidence could not be used in this way. What reasons may explain the conflicting views on this point?

d. Withdrawal of Consent

Most courts hold that the withdrawal of a victim's consent after the commencement of sexual intercourse may lead to conviction for the rape crime. What arguments can explain this result?

3. Consent as an Affirmative Defense

When the legislature removes the lack of consent element from a modern rape statute, a court may decide that this policy decision was not intended to preclude judicial recognition of the defendant's ability to raise "consent" as an affirmative defense. The *Koperski* opinion describes the reasons why courts recognize that defense, and thereby establish the opportunity for acquittal that exists when a defendant can supply sufficient evidence of a victim's "consent."

STATE V. KOPERSKI
254 Neb. 624, 578 N.W.2d 837 (1998).

GERRARD, JUSTICE.

David Koperski was convicted by a jury of first degree sexual assault and sentenced [to] 4 years probation and 60 days in jail. The [court of appeals] affirmed the district court's judgment. [We] reverse [and] remand this [case] to the district court for a new trial. . . .

The testimony of K.O., the victim, showed the following facts. She and her friend Marti went to a nightclub. They planned to stay at a friend's apartment afterwards, but when they arrived at 2:00 a.m., the friend was not home. Marti called her friend Koperski, and he said they could spend the night at his apartment. When K.O. and Marti arrived, the house was full of party guests. K.O. felt sick and fell asleep on the couch in the living room. After the guests left, Marti and Koperski's three roommates retired for the night.

Koperski decided to check on K.O. He woke her up and kissed her. She kissed him back. Then Koperski jumped over the back of the couch, landed on top of K.O., and simulated intercourse by grinding his hips. K.O.'s response was to stop kissing Koperski. She repeatedly told him no, and attempted to push him away. Instead of stopping, Koperski got to his knees and pulled down K.O.'s pants and underwear. She tried to pull them back up, but Koperski pulled them back down again. He was kneeling on her pants and K.O. was unable to get up off the couch. Koperski did not need to use his arms to hold K.O. down. It was his body weight that did so. He is 6 feet tall and weighs 185 pounds, and K.O. is 5 feet 1 inch tall and weighs 130 pounds. When Koperski lay back down on K.O., his penis was exposed and erect. With Koperski back on top of her, K.O. again told him to stop, but he continued to lie on top of K.O., begging for sex. K.O. thought that she could push Koperski away and that he would listen to her. When Koperski penetrated her, K.O. began crying. Then Koperski stopped, got up, and said, "I'm sorry, I don't know what came over me."

At the close of the evidence, Koperski's counsel asked the trial court to instruct the jury with respect to the issue of consent. The trial court refused because [under the statute] the lack of consent was not an element to be proved by the State. The court thought that allowing each side an opportunity to argue the issue of consent would be adequate[.] . . .

[Koperski] was charged under § 28–319(1)(a), which provides: "(1) Any person who subjects another person to sexual penetration and (a) overcomes the victim by force, threat of force, express or implied, [or] coercion . . . is guilty of sexual assault in the first degree." Noticeably absent from the statutory text is the word "consent." . . . [The] trial court is required to give an instruction where there is any evidence, which could be believed by the trier of fact, in support of a legally cognizable theory of defense[.]

Accordingly, the issues before this court are whether consent is a defense to a charge of first degree sexual assault[,] and if so, whether any evidence was adduced in support of a legally cognizable theory of defense regarding consent. If such evidence was adduced, then the jury instructions given must . . . adequately cover [the] theory [of] defense[.] . . .

Although lack of consent is not an element of § 28–319(1)(a), it can hardly be said that consent is not an issue in regard to a charge of first degree sexual assault. Generally, the law may only proscribe nonconsensual sexual conduct, in other words, sexual conduct which is forced upon a person by another without the consent of such person, or where one person is incapable of consenting, or where, although there is consent, such consent is invalid due to, for example, the victim's minority or diminished mental capacity. However, it is evident that consent may well be an issue in a prosecution for first degree sexual assault even though lack of consent is not an express, substantive element of the crime. . . .

It is true that consent is not a statutorily defined affirmative defense[.] Nonetheless, consent can operate as a defense to a charge of first degree sexual assault under § 28–319(1)(a) [because] [c]onsent may operate as a failure of proof in regard to the essential element of the use of force, or in regard to the essential element that the victim must be overcome[.] Accordingly, we conclude that consent may be a defense to a charge of first degree sexual assault[.] The next step in our inquiry is to determine whether any evidence was adduced [in] support of [the] consent theory of defense. . . .

[Because] consensual sexual intercourse is not a harm proscribed by legislative enactment, if, by examining the facts and circumstances of the accused's conduct, it is objectively reasonable to conclude that the alleged victim consented to sexual penetration, then the accused should be free from criminal culpability. The [court] reached a similar conclusion in *State v. Smith*, 210 Conn. 132, 554 A.2d 713 (1989). Like § 28–319(1)(a), the Connecticut statute . . . did not expressly make lack of consent an element of the crime of first degree sexual assault. Nevertheless, the court held that consent was a defense because it negated the statutory element of force. The court went on to explain how the defense of consent operates:

> While the word "consent" is commonly regarded as referring to the state of mind of the complainant in a sexual assault case, it cannot be viewed as a wholly subjective concept. Although the actual state of mind of the actor in a criminal case may in many instances be the issue upon which culpability depends, a defendant is not chargeable with knowledge of the internal workings of the minds of others except to the extent that he should reasonably have gained such knowledge from his observations of their [conduct]. [W]hether a complainant has consented to intercourse depends upon her manifestations of such consent as reasonably construed. . . .

[In] this regard, we agree with the reasoning of the Connecticut [court]. Accordingly, for criminal prosecutions brought under § 28–319(1)(a), we hold that the trial court must instruct the jury on the defense of consent when evidence is produced which, under all of the circumstances, could reasonably be viewed by the jury as an indication of affirmative and freely given consent to sexual penetration by the alleged victim. The focus remains on the accused's conduct in determining whether or not the accused has overcome the alleged victim, resulting in sexual penetration against his or her will[.] [Because] enough evidence had been produced in support of [Koperski's] theory of defense [based on his testimony], we determine that the issue of consent should have been submitted to the jury. . . .

[In] refusing Koperski's proffered jury instructions regarding consent, the trial court expressed the view that making consent a separate element or aspect of the case was confusing. Instead of an instruction regarding Koperski's theory of defense, the trial court thought it sufficient to simply not prohibit Koperski from arguing the issue of consent in his closing statement to the jury. Contrary to the trial court's intuition, failing to instruct the jury regarding Koperski's consent theory of defense was in fact a source of confusion as evidenced by the jury's question to the court during deliberations asking whether it could even consider the issue of consent[.] . . .

We cannot agree with the State than an instruction regarding the substantive elements of the offense subsumes an instruction regarding Koperski's consent theory of defense. An instruction regarding [those] elements alone fails to apprise the jury that an alleged victim's consent must be affirmatively and freely given, that such consent may be manifested by words or conduct, and that from the facts and circumstances in regard to the accused's conduct, it must be objectively reasonable to conclude that consent was given by the alleged victim. Thus, we determine that the trial court erred in not submitting the issue of consent to the jury and that such error was prejudicial to Koperski[.]

Reversed and remanded with directions.

POINTS FOR DISCUSSION

a. Recognition of the Consent Defense

The *Koperski* decision illustrates how the goal of reformers "was not so much to purge the entire concept of consent from the law as to eliminate the burden that had been placed on victims to prove they had not consented," as noted earlier in the excerpt from the *M.T.S.* opinion. The *Koperski* Court assumed that the Nebraska legislature, in removing the lack of consent element from the statute, sought only to achieve this limited goal. There would seem to be no danger that the statute would punish consensual sexual conduct, given the fact that criminal liability is limited to a person who "overcomes the victim by force, [or] threat of force, express or implied, [or by] coercion." Yet the court reasoned that the concept of "consent" cannot be disentangled from these other elements and made irrelevant to conviction, even after the removal of the "lack of consent" element.

Like other courts that recognize the affirmative defense of consent, the *Koperski* Court required that "it must be objectively reasonable" for the defendant "to conclude that consent was given by [the] victim." The defendant's proposed jury instruction echoed this requirement in requiring "a reasonable and good faith belief" in consent. This concept should not be confused with the "reasonable *mistake of fact* as to consent," which concept is explored in the next topic in this chapter. The function of the *Koperski* holding is to allow the "affirmative defense of consent" to be raised when the rape statute includes *no* reference to a "lack of consent" element. By contrast, the function of the "reasonable mistake of fact defense" is to attach the *de facto* mental state of "negligence" to the element of the "lack of consent," when that element is required either by statute or by case law.

Finally, the *Koperski* judges were aware of the fact that after the events in *Koperski*, the legislature had amended the rape statute to make the lack of consent an element of the crime again. This amendment could not be applied retroactively to Koperski's conduct, but it could be applied to the conduct of future defendants. Hoe might the existence of this amendment have influenced the judges in *Koperski?*

b. Consent Evidence Needed for Acquittal

The *Koperski* Court observed that the trial judge was obliged to give an instruction for a cognizable defense when there is "*any* evidence" in support that "could be believed by the trier of fact." The testimony of the defendant and victim conflicted, but the Court ruled that the defendant had satisfied the burden of producing "enough" evidence to obtain an instruction on the consent defense. However, the court did not describe the defendant's burden of persuasion that would be required to obtain an acquittal based on the consent defense.

When an affirmative defense does not negate an element of a crime, as was true in *Koperski,* the burden of persuasion may be placed upon the defendant. So the *Koperski* defendant presumably could be required to prove "consent" by at least a preponderance of the evidence (51%) to obtain an acquittal at his new trial. Then the prosecutor would argue that the jurors should convict the defendant if they viewed the evidence concerning "consent" as 50/50 at best, assuming that all the elements of the crime had been proved beyond a reasonable doubt.

4. *Mens Rea* & Mistake of Fact

a. General Intent

At common law, rape was a "general intent" crime, which meant that courts required a prosecutor to prove only that the defendant intentionally engaged in the prohibited conduct of sexual intercourse. There was no need for proof of the defendant's mental state concerning the element of "lack of consent." This view was consistent with the common law assumption that each crime has essentially one mental state, which contrasts with the modern view that a particular mental state must be identified for every element of a crime. Statutes that codified the elements of the common law rape crime typically made no mention of mental state. This silence was interpreted by courts as evidence that legislatures did not intend to require any proof of mental state, aside from the same "general intent" required by the common law. As long as this status quo prevailed, the defense of "mistake of fact as to consent" was not relevant to the rape crime, for the recognition of such a defense would have required the existence of a mental state that may be negated by the mistake.

b. Recognition of Mistake of Fact Defense

The first case to establish a different approach to the mental state for rape was *People v. Mayberry*, 15 Cal. 3d 143, 125 Cal. Rptr. 745, 542 P.2d 1337 (1975), which was decided the same year that the first rape reform statute was enacted in Michigan. However, the *Mayberry* rule did not reflect the emerging "reform" policies of the new era. On the contrary, the *Mayberry* rule created a new *mens rea* defense to the rape crime.

The rape crime in *Mayberry* was defined in the pre-1980 statute described in *Iniguez*, which covered cases where the victim "resists, but her resistance is overcome by force or violence," or where the victim "is prevented from resisting by threats of great and immediate bodily harm, accompanied by apparent power of execution." The prosecutor was required to show that the victim's resistance demonstrated her lack of consent. So the "resistance" element operated as the equivalent of a "lack of consent" element, according to case law.

The *Mayberry* Court held that the trial judge erred in refusing the defendant's request for an instruction on "a mistake of fact as to consent." The court reasoned broadly that the mistake of fact defense should be recognized for rape because of the existence of two statutes that prescribed general rules for the entire criminal code: 1) that "in every crime . . . there must exist a union, or joint operation of act and intent, or criminal negligence," which "intent" means a "wrongful intent"; and 2) that a person is incapable of committing a crime who commits an act under a mistake of fact disproving any criminal intent. According to the court, the potential life sentence for rape made it "extremely unlikely that the Legislature intended to exclude the rape crime from the requirement of "wrongful intent." Therefore, if the victim did not consent but the defendant made a good faith, reasonable mistake about that "fact," then he could not possess the wrongful intent about consent that should be required for a rape conviction.

However, the *Mayberry* Court limited the circumstances in which the mistake of fact jury instruction would be available, in observing that two aspects of the trial record justified the mistake instruction. First, the defendant's own testimony "could be viewed" as demonstrating his reasonable and good faith mistaken belief in the victim's consent. Second, the victim's testimony was "equivocal." The court explained this characterization as follows: "Although she did not want the defendant to think she was consenting, her 'act' and admitted failure physically to resist him after the initial encounter or to attempt to escape or obtain help might have misled him as to whether she was consenting." *Id.* at 1344-46.

The court's recognition of the defendant's right to a mistake of fact instruction imposed a new burden on the prosecutor at the new trial in *Mayberry*. When a defendant *does* seek to negate an element of a crime, such as the mental state of "wrongful intent," the burden of persuasion may *not* be placed upon the defendant. Therefore, it would be the prosecutor's burden to prove beyond a reasonable doubt that the *Mayberry* defendant did *not* have a good faith, reasonable mistaken belief in consent. In other words, the defendant would obtain an acquittal if he raised a reasonable doubt as to whether he had such a belief. In effect, the *Mayberry* Court redefined the rape crime to require proof of the common law mental state of "criminal negligence" concerning the "lack of consent" element.

c. Refusal to Recognize Mistake of Fact Defense

When the "lack of consent" element is removed from a reform statute defining the rape crime, a court may decide to reject a defendant's argument that the *Mayberry* "mistake of fact as to consent" defense should be given judicial recognition. For example, the Nebraska Supreme Court was willing to recognize the "affirmative defense of consent," but not the "mistake of fact as to consent" defense in *State v. Koperski*, 254 Neb. 624, 578 N.W.2d 837, 845 (1998). A minority of state courts similarly do not recognize the latter defense on the ground that it is up to the legislature to create it. What policy arguments may be used by the courts that take this position?

POINT FOR DISCUSSION

Limitations on Mistake Instruction

The mistake of fact defense is now recognized in a majority of states, usually based on legislation rather than judicial recognition. But courts in these states have established a variety of limitations upon the right to obtain a jury instruction on the mistake of fact defense. Some courts require that a defendant must testify, and some will not allow an instruction where there is evidence of force or of actual consent. In some states, there is a heightened evidence requirement for the defendant's burden of production. For example, the California Supreme Court decided after *Mayberry* that "some evidence" of the defense was not enough, and that a trial court must give a requested instruction "only when the defense is supported" by "substantial evidence." *People v. Flannel*, 25 Cal.3d 668, 684–85, 160 Cal.Rptr. 84, 603 P.2d 1 (1979).

Some courts follow *Mayberry* in requiring evidence that the victim's conduct as to consent was "equivocal," and this concept was given further elaboration in *People v. Williams*, 4 Cal. 4th 354, 841 P.2d 961, 966, 14 Cal. Rptr. 2d 441 (1992) (In Bank). The *Williams* Court affirmed the trial court's rejection of the defendant's request for a *Mayberry* instruction, reasoning that, "[A] mistake of fact occurs when one perceives facts differently from how they actually exist. [Here] the testimony [of the defendant], if believed, established actual consent[.] [The] testimony [of the victim], if believed, would preclude any reasonable belief of consent. These wholly divergent accounts create no middle ground from which [the defendant] could argue he reasonably misinterpreted [the victim's] conduct. There was no substantial evidence of equivocal conduct warranting an instruction as to reasonable and good faith, but mistaken, belief of consent to intercourse."

5. Marital Rape Exemption

Today all the states have abolished the marital rape exemption, but some allow lesser punishment for spousal rape. The earliest justifications for the exemption included the idea that wives had no legal identity that was independent from their husbands, and that consent to matrimony operated to establish a wife's consent to intercourse with her husband in all circumstances. Even before the rape reform era, however, these justifications had become outmoded, and courts endorsed additional rationales to explain the need for the marital rape exemption. What rationales could have been used for this purpose, and why would judicial support for those rationales lose ground during the rape reform era?

The MPC drafters proposed that the marital rape exemption should be retained and should be extended to apply to unmarried persons living together as spouses. *See* Model Penal Code 213.1, Comment (8)(c), at 345–346 (1980). The reasons for the MPC position are as follows:

> [In] the case of intercourse coerced by force or threat of physical harm [the] law already authorizes a penalty for assault. [The] issue is whether

the still more drastic sanctions of rape should apply. The answer depends on whether the injury caused by forcible intercourse by a husband is equivalent to that inflicted by someone else. The gravity of the crime of forcible rape derives not merely from its violent character but also from its achievement of a particularly degrading kind of unwanted intimacy. Where the attacker stands in an ongoing relation of sexual intimacy, that evil, as distinct from the force used to compel submission, may well be thought qualitatively different. [That], in any event, is the conclusion long endorsed by the law of rape and carried forward in the Model Penal Code provision.

During the early years of the rape reform era, when 40 states still retained some form of the marital rape exemption, one court famously invalidated it on Equal Protection grounds as gender-based discrimination in *People v. Liberta*, 64 N.Y.2d 152, 166–167, 474 N.E.2d 567, 575, 485 N.Y.S.2d 207, 215 (1984). The *Liberta* Court criticized the MPC defense of the exemption as follows:

> The fact that rape statutes exist [is] a recognition that the harm caused by a forcible rape is different, and more severe, than the harm caused by an ordinary assault. [There] is no evidence to support the argument that marital rape has less severe consequences than other rape. On the contrary, numerous studies have shown that marital rape is frequently quite violent and generally has *more* severe, traumatic effects on the victim than other rape. [We] agree with the other courts which have analyzed the [marital rape] exemption, which have been unable to find any present justification for it.

Some other courts have followed *Liberta*'s approach and invalidated the marital rape exemption. But usually the abolition of the exemption has occurred through legislation rather than through judicial decisions. *See* WAYNE R. LAFAVE, CRIMINAL LAW § 17.4(d).

6. Death Penalty for Rape

In the 1960s, civil rights litigation was undertaken in a number of states in order to challenge the constitutionality of the death penalty for rape on Equal Protection grounds. *See* MICHAEL MELTSNER, CRUEL AND UNUSUAL: THE SUPREME COURT AND CAPITAL PUNISHMENT, 73–105 (1973). This litigation relied on empirical evidence concerning race discrimination. *See* Model Penal Code § 213.1, Comment (3)(a), at 281–282 n. 27 (1980). The MPC Commentary summarized the history of race discrimination and the rape crime as follows:

White [men's sexual] imposition upon black women may have been common in the old South. It is the reverse case that tended to dominate the public mind and that assumed a distinctive role in the regional consciousness. [This] reaction also explains the disproportionate tendency of Southern and Border states to punish rape as a capital offense. In 1925, the following states authorized the death penalty for rape: Alabama, Arkansas, Delaware, Florida, Georgia, Kentucky, Louisiana, Maryland, Mississippi, Missouri, Nevada, North Carolina, Oklahoma, South Carolina, Tennessee, Texas, Virginia, West Virginia. There has also been a long history in those jurisdictions of a *de jure* or *de facto* limitation of the death penalty for rape to black offenders. The Georgia Penal Code of 1811 set the penalty for rape at 16 years imprisonment, but the Code applied only to free whites. Blacks were subject to punishment of death under Georgia [statutes]. Even [after] *de jure* discrimination in rape penalties was [abolished], blacks continued to be subject disproportionately to the death penalty for rape. [The Wolfgang and Reidel study published in 1973 showed that] in a 20-year period in 11 southern states, seven times as many blacks were sentenced to death as [whites]. [The Justice Department statistics of 1971 showed that] 89.9 per cent of those executed for rape since 1930 have been non-white, almost double the percentage of blacks among those persons executed for [murder].

The Equal Protection litigation of the 1960s was followed by the Supreme Court's invalidation of death penalty statutes under the Eighth Amendment in *Furman v. Georgia*, 408 U.S. 238 (1972). At the time, statutes in 17 jurisdictions allowed capital punishment for rape. After *Furman*, 35 states enacted new capital homicide statues, but only six Southern states enacted new capital rape statutes. In *Gregg v. Georgia*, 428 U.S. 153, 179 (1976), the Court validated the post-*Furman* homicide statutes with procedural safeguards that complied with the Eighth Amendment's prohibition on "arbitrary" capital sentencing procedures. But in *Coker v. Georgia*, 433 U.S. 584 (1977), the Court invalidated a death sentence for rape on Eighth Amendment grounds, without reference to the pre-*Furman* Equal Protection challenges or the empirical evidence of race discrimination. The *Coker* defendant received a death sentence for the rape of an "adult" woman, and the Court limited its holding to this crime. But the Court also reasoned more broadly that rape cannot be compared to murder "in terms of moral depravity and of the injury to the person and to the public," and concluded that it is "disproportionate" and "excessive" to impose the death penalty, "which 'is unique in its severity and irrevocability,' [upon] the rapist who, as such, does not take human life." *Id.* at 598.

In *Kennedy v. Louisiana*, 554 U.S. 407 (2008), the Court addressed the issue left open in *Coker* and held that the death penalty is "disproportionate" and "excessive" for the crime of child rape. The Court's narrow reasoning emphasized that the Eighth Amendment's "evolving standards of decency" required this determination, as evidenced by the consensus of 44 state legislatures and Congress, which did not make child rape a capital crime as of 2008. More broadly, the *Kennedy* Court expanded upon *Coker*'s logic, and ruled that any "nonhomicide crimes against individual persons" cannot be punished with the severe and irrevocable penalty of death, because such crimes "cannot be compared" in their "severity and irrevocability" with "intentional first degree murder." *Id.* at 2660.

C. RAPE BY DECEPTION

When state courts encountered the idea of "rape by deception" in the nineteenth century, this occurred in cases where prosecutors sought to persuade judges to adopt the fiction that the common law element of "force" could be interpreted to include a defendant's misrepresentations or "fraud" upon the victim. Modern courts have hesitated to go beyond the nineteenth century solutions to the problem of fraud in the absence of a statute that expressly prohibits sex acts "accomplished by fraud."

D. RAPE OF DRUGGED OR INTOXICATED VICTIM

At common law, the crime of rape included the act of sexual intercourse with a sleeping, unconscious, or drugged woman, because such victims are incapable of giving consent or resisting unwanted sexual acts. Most state codes include a definition of rape that either requires the defendant to administer drugs to the victim or requires that the victim should be in an impaired state because of drugs when the rape occurred. For example, the California rape statute applies where sexual intercourse occurs and "where a person is prevented from resisting by any intoxicating or anaesthetic substance, or any controlled substance, and this condition was known, or reasonably should have been known by the accused" or "where a person is unconscious or asleep [and this is known by the accused]." *See* Cal. Pen. Code § 261(a)(3) (2002). It is also common for rape statutes to apply where a victim is incapable of giving consent because of physical or mental helplessness.

Some drugs can cause a victim to become unconscious and then, after a rape occurs, to have amnesia about what happened before the victim became unconscious. These circumstances may make it difficult for a prosecutor to obtain sufficient evidence for a rape conviction. However, in *Sera v. Norris*, 400 F.3d 538 (8th Cir. 2005), the victim could not testify that an act of sexual intercourse occurred, but the court upheld the defendant's convictions for multiple rapes of the victim based on unusual circumstantial evidence. The defendant was found to be in possession of a bottle of Rohypnol in his suitcase, "a so-called 'date rape drug'" that can cause "hypnosis, total muscle relaxation, and loss of memory" in the form of "anterograde amnesia." A person who has taken the drug "can be talking and functioning yet still not be able to remember what is happening" and alcohol magnifies the effects of the drug, causing a deeper state of unconsciousness. The victim testified that she took three trips with the defendant, and that he gave her two alcoholic drinks during each trip, just before she lost her memory of what happened next. There was sufficient evidence for a jury to find that the defendant raped the victim after putting Rohypnol in her drinks during each of the three trips, based on the similarity of her symptoms, the defendant's access to the drug, and a videotape which showed the defendant raping the unconscious victim during the first trip.

Even though a victim was not unconscious, the prosecutor may seek to prove that the victim was "sufficiently" impaired to lack "the capacity" for consent. Assume, for example, that the legislature decides to define rape to include "an act of sexual penetration accomplished with any person" when "the victim is incapable of giving consent because of any intoxicating agent." Notice that this statute does not require the prosecutor to prove the element of the victim's "lack of consent." Also, the statute implicitly provides that the affirmative defense of consent is not available when the victim is "incapable of giving consent" for the reason described. Notably, the prosecution must show, beyond a reasonable doubt, that the victim did lack "the capacity to consent" because of the consumption of alcohol, for example. Then defense counsel presumably would attempt to raise a reasonable doubt about this element. One important question is whether the prosecutor also should be required to prove that the defendant possessed a particular mental state regarding the victim's lack of capacity to consent due to intoxication.

The Model Penal Code drafters endorsed several other rape definitions in addition to forcible rape. They included sexual intercourse with an "unconscious" female or with a female "whose power to appraise or control her conduct has been substantially impaired by administering or employing without her knowledge drugs, intoxicants or other means for the purpose of preventing resistance." Each of these two crimes required the elements of sexual intercourse by a male with a female not his wife. *See* MPC 213/1(1)(b0 and (c).

E. STATUTORY RAPE

When the American common law absorbed the English statutory crime of sexual intercourse with a female under the age of 10, the term "statutory rape" became the name of the crime. Consent was no defense because a child victim was presumed to be incapable of consent. Mistake as to the victim's age was no defense because strict liability was allowed for this key element of the crime. By the 1950s, most statutes had raised the age of the victim to 16 or 17, or even to 18 in a few states. This development was troubling for judges who did not want to impose harsh penalties for the crime of consensual sex *between* underage teenagers, especially when only boys were subject to prosecution. By 1980 the crime covered only victims under 16 in most states. During the rape reform era, most states adopted gender-neutral statutory rape provisions

---

POINTS FOR DISCUSSION

a.   **Evolution of "Romeo and Juliet" Statutes**

During the rape reform era, states adopted "age gap" provisions conferring immunity from prosecution for statutory rape where both "victims" and "defendants" are teenagers. These provisions resemble the MPC proposal of a four-year-age-gap immunity, which was "chosen to reflect the prevailing pattern of secondary education" so that "felony sanctions for mutually consensual behavior" would not apply to school "romancers." *See* Model Penal Code § 213.3(1)(a), Comment (2), at 386. These age-gap immunity provisions are sometimes called "Romeo and Juliet" statutes. In a few states, age-gap statutes that are not gender neutral have been challenged on equal protection grounds. *See, e.g., State v. Limon*, 280 Kan. 275, 122 P.3d 22 (2005) (invalidating opposite-sex clause in Romeo and Juliet statute).

b.   **Reasonable Mistake of Fact as to Age**

State courts continue to debate the question whether to recognize the "mistake of fact as to age" defense for statutory rape. The common law definition of the crime treated the age element as having a strict liability mental state. The trend toward recognizing the mistake of fact defense began with *People v. Hernandez*, 61 Cal. 2d 529, 39 Cal. Rptr. 361, 393 P.2d 673 (1964), which precedent was relied on in *Mayberry* when the same court recognized the "mistake of fact as to consent" defense to forcible rape. However, the trend developed slowly after *Hernandez*, and over 40 years passed before one third of the states endorsed the defense of mistake of fact as to age.

Like the *Mayberry* mistake defense, courts usually require the mistake about age to be reasonable, thereby requiring a mental state of negligence for the age element. Only a few states require recklessness. In defending a strict liability interpretation for statutes that apply only to younger victims, such as those under age 14, some courts have emphasized the need to protect from them the severe physical and psychological consequences of sexual acts. *See, e.g., People v. Douglas*, 381 Ill. App.3d 1067, 886 N.E.2d 1232 (2008); WAYNE R. LAFAVE, CRIMINAL LAW, § 17.4(C) (5th ed. 2010).

F. INTERNET CRIMES

Modern sexual assault statutes include enactments that seek to protect victims, including minors, from dangers related to sexual activity that is facilitated by internet communications. One example is provided by a statute enacted by the New Hampshire legislature in 1998, which defines the prohibited "use of computer services" crime as follows: "No person shall knowingly utilize a computer on-line service, internet service, or local bulletin board service to solicit, lure, or entice a child [defined as a person under age 18] to commit acts described in any offense under [a provision that includes a long list of sex crimes]." The legislative history indicates that the "overarching purpose" of the enactment of the statute was to "deter sexual offenses against juveniles." New Hampshire precedents have construed the term "utilize" to establish criminal liability for defendants who "enlist computer technology" in some way other than communicating with a victim. Such defendants have included a stepfather who used a laptop computer to show his stepdaughter a pornographic video during a weekend visit in order to "lure or entice" her into the future commission of a sexual act, which was an enumerated crime. Another enumerated crime is the solicitation of sex acts, which means that prohibited communications under the "uses of computer services" statute may include emails and Facebook messages sent to victims by defendants. The legislative history of the New Hampshire statute illustrates the traditional purposes of such enactments, which include the need for new and broader statutes to "deter sexual offenses against juveniles" and to "assist law enforcement in the protection of [juveniles] from the types of dangers presented by the computer and the internet."

G. EVIDENCE RULES FOR RAPE PROSECUTIONS

1. Rape Trauma Syndrome Evidence

During the 1980s, prosecutors started to use the testimony of expert witnesses concerning "rape trauma syndrome." This evidence is widely used in rape trials today, and its relevance is based on its potential usefulness to explain post-rape victim behavior that may seem otherwise inexplicable to jurors. However, courts continue to confront the need to identify limits on expert testimony, in order to avoid the presentation of unreliable evidence and the danger that jurors will abandon their fact-finding responsibility by deferring to expert testimony.

POINT FOR DISCUSSION

"Syndrome" Evidence

State evidence codes allow expert testimony to be admissible on any subject "sufficiently beyond common experience that the opinion of an expert would assist the trier of fact." This evidence rule may be used by courts to justify the admission of expert testimony concerning the behavior of rape victims, both to dispel common misconceptions about how they behave and to allow the prosecutor to rehabilitate a rape victim's credibility if defense counsel argues that the victim's conduct is inconsistent with the claim of rape. However, such testimony may not be used by a prosecutor to prove the elements of the crime. The purpose of the expert's testimony is to provide information about the potential effects of trauma that may be experienced by victims generally, so that informed jurors may evaluate the victim's behavior based on that information. Given the fact that the purpose of expert testimony is *not* to provide a diagnosis of the victim, some courts have recognized that the admissibility of such testimony "does not depend on a showing based on a recognized 'syndrome.'" *See People v. Brown*, 33 Cal. 4th 892, 905–06, 16 Cal.Rptr.3d 447, 94 P.3d 574 (2004).

2. Rape Shield Laws

The first rape shield statute was part of the 1975 Michigan rape reform statute; within three years of its enactment, 30 states had adopted such laws and Congress adopted Federal Rule 412. All states now use some type of rape shield law, and many of them based on the Michigan model. Rape shield laws eliminate the common law presumption that a victim's prior sexual conduct is relevant to prove her lack of credibility and willingness to consent to forcible sex. The opposite presumption, that such evidence is not generally relevant in a rape trial, is expressed in rape shield laws, either through a statutory list of exclusions and exceptions or through the delegation of case-by-case determinations of relevancy to the discretion of trial judges. Both types of rape shield laws require that even non-excluded evidence will not be admissible unless its probative value outweighs its potential prejudicial effect. When defendants challenge the exclusion of rape-shield evidence as a violation of their Sixth Amendment rights to fair trial and confrontation of witnesses, courts will apply specific interpretations of these rights that have been established in the rape-shield context. The complexity and variety of state and federal rape shield rules has spawned a constant stream of litigation and continuing legislative change.

a. Goals of Rape Shield Laws

The main goal of rape shield laws is "to prevent a sexual assault trial from degenerating into an attack upon the [victim's] reputation rather than focusing on the relevant legal issues[.]" *Commonwealth v. Jones*, 826 A.2d 900 (Pa. Super. 2003). In *State v. Sheline*, 955 S.W.2d 42, 44–45 (Tenn. 1997), the court summarized the relevant policy concerns as follows:

> Rape shield laws were adopted in response to anachronistic and sexist views that a woman who had sexual relations in the past was more likely to have consented to sexual relations with a specific criminal defendant. Those attitudes resulted in two rape trials at the same time—the trial of the defendant and the trial of the rape victim based on her past sexual conduct. It has been said that the victim of a sexual assault is assaulted twice—once by the criminal justice system. The protections in rape shield laws recognized that intrusions into the irrelevant sexual history of a victim were not only prejudicial and embarrassing but also a practical barrier to many victims reporting sexual crimes.

The presumption that sexual history evidence will cause the jury to be unfairly prejudiced against the victim and the prosecution derives from the experience of prosecutors in the pre-reform era. Studies of rape reforms report judges, prosecutors, and defense attorneys typically view rape shield laws as the reform with the most significant impact, in terms of enhancing the prosecutor's opportunity to obtain rape convictions. *See, e.g.*, JEANNE C. MARSH, ALISON GEIST, & NATHAN CAPLAN, RAPE AND THE LIMITS OF LAW REFORM. 59–65 (1982);

CASSIA SPOHN & JULIE HORNEY, RAPE LAW REFORM: A GRASSROOTS REVOLUTION AND ITS IMPACT (1992).

b. Exclusions & Exceptions

The "exclusions and exceptions" model of rape shield laws is illustrated by Federal Rule of Evidence 412. The Rule defines "generally inadmissible evidence" to include: (1) evidence offered to prove that any alleged victim engaged in any sexual behavior; and (2) evidence offered to prove any alleged victim's sexual disposition. The Rule also provides for these exceptions: A) a "specific instance of sexual behavior" by the victim to prove that a person other than the accused was the source of semen, injury, or other physical evidence; B) a "specific instance of sexual behavior" by the victim with respect to the person accused of the sexual misconduct, offered by the accused to prove consent or by the prosecution; C) evidence the exclusion of which would violate the constitutional rights of the defendant. Almost half the states use a similar model, but a substantial minority use a case-by-case approach that requires trial judges to weigh the probative value of the evidence against the prejudicial impact of the evidence on the jury.

c. Prior Sexual Conduct

In 1994, the term "prior sexual conduct" in Federal Rule 412 was amended to replace the word "conduct" with "behavior." According to the Advisory Committee Notes, "prior sexual behavior" of the victim "connotes all activities that involve actual physical conduct" and "the word 'behavior' should be construed to include activities of the mind, such as fantasies or dreams." In arguing that the term "prior sexual conduct" in a statute should be interpreted to emulate the federal definition of "prior sexual behavior," one judge reasoned as follows:

> As recently as 1970, *Wigmore on Evidence* suggested that every woman who claimed she had been raped should be subjected to a psychological evaluation. The reason for this claim was, "The unchaste (let us call it) mentality finds incidental but direct expression in the narration of imaginary sex incidents of which the narrator is the heroine or victim." [This] language suggests the attitude that some women accuse men of rape because they have conflated sexual fantasy with criminal violence.
>
> The Rape Shield Statute represents an express rejection of such attitudes. We now recognize the scarring effects of sexual assault, and the burden placed on victims by testifying about such a deeply personal

invasion. [E]vidence of past sexual acts with others has little probative value of whether a victim consented to have sex with a defendant in the present [and] this lack of probative force extends to evidence about a victim's sexual fantasies. Requiring a victim to testify about sexual fantasies can be as intrusive as testifying about prior sexual acts.

People v. Garcia, 179 P.3d 250, 261 (Colo. App. 2007) (Bernard, J., specially concurring). However, the *Garcia* majority rejected this argument because "[the] fantasy could be established without revealing whether the victim had ever acted it out" and so inquiry into such statements would not subject the victim "to a fishing expedition into her past sexual conduct." State courts remain divided as to whether prior sexual "conduct" or "behavior" should include oral or written statements about previous sexual activity, sexual thoughts or sexual fantasies.

In *Michigan v. Lucas*, 500 U.S. 145 (1991), the Court determined that case-by-case determinations are required to decide whether the exclusion of evidence under a rape shield statute violates the Sixth Amendment.

Hypo 1: *Taking Car Keys*

Pat met Rusk at a bar where she went with a woman friend after a high school reunion. Pat testified that she told Rusk that she was a single mother and had to be home soon to take care of her child. Rusk asked her for a ride home and she agreed, telling him it was "just a ride." When they arrived at his rooming house, Pat parked but did not turn off the ignition. Rusk asked her to come up to his room and she refused. Rusk then took the car keys out of the ignition, walked over to Pat's side of the car, opened the door and said, "Now will you come up?" Pat was stranded in an unfamiliar neighborhood, and so she followed Rusk up to his room. She begged Rusk to return her keys and to let her leave his room. He kept saying, "No." Pat was scared because of what he said and because of the look in his eyes. She asked him, "If I do what you want, will you let me go without killing me?" She started to cry and he put his hands on her throat. Pat described this act as a "light choking" but acknowledged that it could have been a "heavy caress." Pat asked Rusk, "If I do what you want, will you let me go?" Rusk said, "Yes," and sexual intercourse followed. Pat got dressed, left the rooming house, and then reported the rape to the police. Is there sufficient evidence to convict Rusk under the "fear" element in the *Iniguez* statute, or any of the three definitions of "force" described in point d. after *Iniguez*? Compare *Rusk v. State*, 43 Md. App. 476, 406 A.2d 624 (1979) *rev'd*, *State v. Rusk*, 289 Md. 230, 424 A.2d 720 (1981).

> ### Hypo 2: *Dorm Room*
>
> Berkowitz and Kia are college sophomores. Berkowitz was in his dorm room when Kia came looking for his roommate. He invited her to "hang out for a while" and offered to give her a back rub. She declined the back rub but sat down on his floor. Berkowitz moved down to the floor and "kind of pushed" Kia with his body, straddled her and kissed her. Kia could not move because his weight was over her body. She said she had to go and meet her boyfriend and Berkowitz lifted up her shirt and bra and fondled her. Kia said, "No." He undid his pants while she said, "No." When Berkowitz tried to put his penis in her mouth, she said, "No, I gotta go, let me go." Berkowitz got up and locked the door so that people outside could not enter but a person inside could leave. When Kia rose to her feet, Berkowitz put Kia down on the bed, straddled her and removed her sweatpants and underwear. Kia could not move because Berkowitz was on top of her. Berkowitz put his penis in her vagina, and she muttered, "No, no, no" because, as she testified later, "It was just so scary." After 30 seconds, Berkowitz pulled out his penis, ejaculated on Kia's stomach, and got off her. She got up, dressed quickly, grabbed her books, and ran downstairs to her boyfriend. Kia was crying and her boyfriend called the police to report the rape. Is there sufficient evidence to convict Berkowitz under the "fear" element in the *Iniguez* statute, or any of the three definitions of "force" described in point d. after *Iniguez*? Compare *Commonwealth v. Berkowitz*, 415 Pa. Super. 505, 522–523, 609 A.2d 1338, 1346–1347 (1992), aff'd, 537 Pa. 143, 641 A.2d 1161 (1994).

> ### Hypo 3: *Intoxicated Victim*
>
> Inga went to a bar on Hilton Head Island at 9:00 p.m. with her friend Abby to celebrate Abby's birthday. By midnight, Inga had consumed four beers and several shots of hard liquor. Then Abby's boyfriend Al arrived at the bar, accompanied by his friend Derk, whom Inga did not know. The four agreed to go to Al's house, where Inga consumed two more beers. Abby and Al noticed that Inga seemed incoherent when she lay down on the living room couch around 1:00 a.m., which is when Abby and Al retired for the night. At the time, Derk was lying down on the floor. Inga testified that she does not remember what happened from the time that she arrived at Al's house until the time when she noticed that she was lying on the floor with Derk on top of her, engaging in sexual intercourse. Inga pushed Derk off and screamed for Abby and Al,

who took Inga to the hospital. The police arrested Derk for rape. Derk testified at his trial that, "I don't know how intoxicated Inga was that night. I only saw her drink two beers at Al's house. Then after Abby and Al went to bed, Inga rolled off the couch and found me on the floor. She said that she wanted to have sex, and so we did."

The trial judge must decide between two competing jury instructions. Assume that the relevant definition of rape in South Carolina is "an act of sexual penetration accomplished with any person" when "the victim is incapable of giving consent because of any intoxicating agent." The prosecutor argues that this instruction should be given: "Consent is not a defense to the crime of rape defined as sexual penetration where the victim is incapable of giving consent because of intoxication. In determining whether the victim was incapable of giving consent because of intoxication, you must consider all the circumstances in determining whether the victim's intoxication rendered her unable to exercise reasonable judgment."

The defense counsel argues that this instruction should be given: "Consent is not a defense to the crime of rape defined as sexual penetration where the victim is incapable of giving consent because of intoxication, if the victim was incapable of giving consent because intoxication rendered her unable to exercise reasonable judgment, and if the Defendant knew that the victim was unable to exercise reasonable judgment because of her intoxication." What arguments will be made by each side to support these competing instructions? How should the court rule, in light of all the rape reform policies that are illustrated in this chapter? *Compare State v. Jones*, 804 N.W.2d 409 (S.D. 2011).

Hypo 4: *Rape Myths*

Scholars have noted that, "Rape myths vary among societies and cultures," "consistently following a patten whereby they blame the victim for their rape, express a disbelief in claims of rape, exonerate the perpetrator, and allude that only certain types of women are raped." The same scholars observed that "rape myths, like all myths, are designed to serve up psychological comfort, not hard facts," because believing "that rape victims are innocent and not deserving of their fate is incongruous with the general belief in a just world." Thus, "in order to avoid cognitive dissonance, rape myths serve to protect" that belief. What rape myths can be identified as influencing the pre-reform legal doctrines and the later reforms concerning the forcible rape crime? In addition to the avoidance of cognitive dissonance, what other factors may explain the persistence of rape myths? What additional legal reforms could be adopted to decrease their influence? *See* Kate Harding, ASKING FOR IT: THE ALARMING RISE OF RAPE CULTURE—AND WHAT WE CAN DO ABOUT IT at 22 (2015) citing Amy Grubb & Emily Turner, *Attribution of Blame in Rape Cases: A Review of the Impact of Rape Myth Acceptance, Gender Role Conformity and Substance Use on Victim Blaming*, 17 AGGRESSION AND VIOLENT BEHAVIOR 443–453 (2012).

Hypo 5: *Arranging a Rendezvous*

Assume that an eighteen-year-old male student sends Facebook messages to a fifteen-year-old female student at the same residential prep school. These messages convey the offer to meet the female in a "hidden location" on campus where, the message implies, sexual activity of some kind may ensue. Later the male student is convicted of a variety of misdemeanor sexual offenses, as well as the "use of computer services" crime, which is a felony and requires him to register as a sex offender. The computer services crime requires the prosecutor to prove that the defendant "utilized a computer online service, and/or internet service to seduce, solicit, lure, or entice another person to engage in an act of sexual penetration;" that he "actually believed that the person he was attempting to seduce, solicit, lure, or entice, was under the age of 16"; and that the defendant "acted knowingly."

The defense counsel concedes on appeal that the literal meaning of the text of the computer statute is clear, and that on the facts, the defendant is guilty of the computer crime. Even so, the defense counsel argues that if the literal meaning of the statute is applied by the court, then there will be "absurd results" that could not have been intended by the legislature. Therefore, the statute should not be enforced against the defendant and his conviction should be reversed. More specifically, defense counsel argues that: 1) the legislature must have been concerned primarily with the use of the computer and the internet by "adult pedophile strangers" who prey upon juveniles, not with 18-year-old students who solicit 15-year-old schoolmates; and 2) no conviction would have occurred if the defendant had solicited the same sex acts with the victim in a note or conversation, so it would be "absurd" for the legislature to criminalize only the use of emails and Facebook messages and not other methods of solicitation. What arguments can the prosecutor make to rebut these "absurd results" arguments?

CHAPTER 10

Property Crimes

The roots of the modern law of property crimes lie in the fifteenth century when English judges invented the crimes of larceny and larceny by trick. Although the judges were willing to use legal fictions to expand the original larceny crime to some degree, it required legislation by Parliament to create the crimes of embezzlement and false pretenses in the late eighteenth century. These four crimes were codified only by name in early state criminal codes and their elements were defined by precedents; the same was true for other English property crimes, including receiving stolen property, robbery, and burglary. Today most states use some version of the Model Penal Code (MPC) provisions on "theft" crimes, which are widely regarded as one of the most significant and successful MPC reforms. Yet some state codes retain the definitions of common law property crimes, and some codes blend these old definitions together with MPC elements.

The broad goals of the MPC drafters mirror those of the English judges whose opinions helped to expand the scope of larceny to encompass new harms that came to be recognized by society. The most significant revisions of the common law crimes occurred in the MPC's merger of larceny, larceny by trick, and embezzlement into the new crime of "theft by unlawful taking or disposition," and in the revision of the false pretenses crime into the new crime of "theft by deception." These innovative crimes abandoned many of the common law elements that had become anachronistic technicalities, thereby both simplifying and broadening the modern definitions of "theft." The same goals also characterize the MPC's expanded versions of the crimes of receiving stolen goods and robbery. By contrast, the MPC version of burglary crime is exceptional in embodying the goal of staying closer to the original common law definition.

In this chapter, the evolution of the elements of the seven most important common law property crimes will be studied in order to show how the original definitions influenced the elements of their modern descendants. In addition, the modern crime of carjacking will be examined as an illustration of the evolution of the robbery crime. The chapter begins with a case involving the federal crime of interstate transportation of stolen property in order to illustrate the difficulties inherent in defining the taking of "property" that may be the subject of a criminal prosecution.

A. OVERVIEW OF THE LAW

Defining "Property." Modern statutes often follow the approach of the MPC in defining "property" as "anything of value," but more limited definitions may be used to serve a particular purpose.

Larceny. This crime was designed by English judges and requires a trespassory taking and carrying away of property from the possession of another, without consent, with the intent to steal, which means the intent to deprive the owner permanently of the property.

Larceny by Trick. This version of larceny applies where the trespassory taking occurs by means of false representations that lead the owner to pass only possession of the property, not title. Both the larceny and larceny by trick crimes were redefined in the Model Penal Code as "theft by unlawful taking or disposition."

Embezzlement. This crime was designed by Parliament and requires the fraudulent conversion of the property of another by an entrusted person in lawful possession who has the intent to steal and the intent to convert the property to his or her own benefit. The embezzlement crime was redefined in the Model Penal Code as "theft by unlawful taking or disposition."

False Pretenses. This crime was designed by Parliament and requires the owner to pass title to property through reliance on false representations. The false pretenses crime was redefined in the Model Penal Code as "theft by deception."

Receiving Stolen Property. This crime was designed by Parliament and requires the act of receiving property which is stolen, knowing that it is stolen, with the intent to deprive the owner of it. The Model Penal Code expanded the mental state of this crime to include the belief that the property probably was stolen.

Robbery & Carjacking. This crime was designed by English judges and requires all the elements of larceny, plus two more, namely taking from the person or presence of the victim, by means of force or putting in fear of violence. The federal carjacking statute uses robbery elements plus the intent to cause serious bodily harm. The Model Penal Code eliminated the element of "person or presence" from the robbery crime, and expanded robbery to include an intentional threat to cause bodily harm on the victim, during the course of committing a property crime.

Burglary. This crime was designed by English judges and requires the breaking and entering of a dwelling at night time with the intent to commit a felony therein. Modern burglary statutes have expanded the crime to include the act of entering or remaining in an occupied structure with the intent to commit a crime at the time of entry.

> **Major Themes**
>
> **a. Influence of MPC**—The MPC has had a major influence on the law of property crimes. Most state codes use MPC "theft" crimes. Others use common law property crimes.
>
> **b. Mens Rea & Actus Reus**—Virtually all definitions of property crimes require specific intent, such as the intent or purpose to deprive another of his or her property. The concept of possession is a key element of defining the *actus reus* for all property crimes except burglary.

B. DEFINING "PROPERTY"

Definitions of criminal takings of "property" have changed over time as new forms of property have been recognized by legislatures and courts. Yet the unpredictable evolution of technology has created an endless stream of issues for courts charged with the task of interpreting the meaning of "property" in particular statutory contexts. The *Farraj* case illustrates how it is necessary for courts to interpret legislative intent when determining whether to apply the term "goods" to intangible property, such as a stolen document sent via email or stolen computer source code.

UNITED STATES V. FARRAJ
142 F. Supp. 2d 484 (S.D.N.Y. 2001).

MARRERO, DISTRICT JUDGE.

[Said Farraj is charged with crimes including one count of] interstate transportation of stolen property in violation of 18 U.S.C. § 2314[.] [He] now moves [to] dismiss [the count charging this crime] on the ground that the allegedly stolen property does not fall within the scope of § 2314[.] For the reasons discussed below, the [motion is] denied.

In [the] summer of 2000, Said Farraj was a paralegal with the [Manhattan] law firm of Orrick, Harrington & Sutcliffe LLP. At the time, Orrick represented plaintiffs in a *class action tobacco case*[.] [*See Falise v. American Tobacco Co.*, 94 F. Supp. 2d 316 (E.D.N.Y. 2000).] In preparation for the *Falise* trial, the attorneys and paralegals at Orrick created a trial plan ["Trial Plan"], "exceed[ing] 400 pages and includ[ing], among other things, trial strategy, deposition excerpts and summaries, and references to anticipated trial exhibits." Only Orrick employees assigned to *Falise* were permitted access to the Trial Plan. [Farraj was included among such employees].

The Government charges that [Farraj], using the moniker "FlyGuyNYt," e-mailed an 80-page excerpt of the Trial Plan [on June 17, 2000] to the *Falise* defendants' attorneys [located in five states] and offered to sell them the entire Plan. An FBI agent posing as one of the *Falise* defendants' attorneys negotiated with [Farraj] via email and ultimately agreed to purchase the Trial Plan for $2 million. On July 21, 2000, [the defendant's brother] met with a second undercover FBI agent at a McDonald's restaurant in lower Manhattan to receive payment. [The brother] was arrested then and gave a statement to the FBI implicating [the defendant].

The Government charges [that] by e-mailing the Trial Plan excerpt across state lines, [Farraj] violated [the National Stolen Property Act], which provides [that] "[w]hoever transports, transmits, or transfers in interstate or foreign commerce any goods, wares, merchandise, securities, or money, of the value of $5,000 or more, knowing the same to have been stolen, converted, or taken by fraud ... shall be fined under this title or imprisoned [up to ten years]." [Farraj] moves to dismiss, arguing that § 2314 applies only to the physical asportation of tangible goods or currency, not to "information" stored and transmitted electronically, such as the Trial Plan excerpt e-mailed here. Neither the Supreme Court nor the Second Circuit has addressed this question directly, and this appears to be an issue of first impression in this District.

[The] Second Circuit has held that the phrase "goods, wares, or merchandise" is "a general and comprehensive designation of such personal property or chattels as are ordinarily a subject of commerce." *In re Vericker*, 446 F.2d 244, 248 (2d Cir. 1971) (Friendly, J.). The Second Circuit has at times determined that [paper] documents fall outside the scope of § 2314. At other times, however, the Second Circuit and other courts have held that documents may be considered "goods, wares, [or] merchandise" under § 2314. *See, e.g., United States v. Greenwald*, 479 F.2d 320 (6th Cir. 1973) (documents containing secret chemical formulae); *United States v. Bottone*, 365 F.2d 389 (2d Cir. 1966) (drug manufacturing processes); *United States v. Seagraves*, 265 F.2d 876 (3d Cir. 1966) (geophysical maps).

The FBI documents at issue in *Vericker* detailed the criminal activity of certain individuals. Judge Friendly reasoned that the FBI documents were not "goods, wares, [or] merchandise" within the meaning of [§ 2314] because the substance contained in the documents was not ordinarily the subject of commerce. The Trial Plan at issue here, however, [was] the work product of a business relationship between client and attorney, and may thus be viewed as an ordinary subject of commerce, created for a commercial purpose and carrying inherent commercial value at least as to the persons directly interested in the matter.

[Farraj] argues that even if trial plans generally may be viewed as goods under § 2314, he is accused of transmitting an "intangible," an electronic form of the document, and therefore that it was not a good, but merely "information."

The text of § 2314 makes no distinction between tangible and intangible property, or between electronic and other manner of transfer across state lines. Indeed, in 1988, Congress amended § 2314 to include the term[s] "transmits" [or "transfers"] to reflect its agreement with the Second Circuit and other courts which had held that § 2314 applied to money wire transfers, where the only interstate transportation took place electronically and where there was no transportation of any physical item. *See* Anti-Drug Abuse Act of 1988, § 7507(a), 134 Cong. Reg. S17367, S17370 (statement of Sen. Biden) (citing *United States v. Gilboe*, 684 F.2d 235 (2d Cir. 1982)[.]) In *Gilboe*, the Second Circuit addressed the issue of electronic transfer for the first time and recognized that

> the manner in which funds were moved does not affect the ability to obtain tangible paper dollars or a bank check from the receiving account. . . . Indeed, we suspect that actual dollars rarely move between banks, particularly in international transactions. . . . The primary element of this offense, transportation, "does not require proof that any specific means of transporting were used."

684 F.2d at 238 (quoting *Pereira v. United States*, 347 U.S. 1, 9, 74 S. Ct. 358, 98 L.Ed. 435 (1954)).

The Second Circuit has also held that § 2314 was violated when the defendants stole documents containing some drug manufacturing process, copied and returned them, and then sent the copies abroad. The court noted that it did not matter that the item stolen was not the same as that transported. Rather, as observed by Judge Friendly [in *Bottone*, 365 F.2d at 394]:

> where the physical form of the stolen goods is secondary in every respect to the matter recorded in them, the transformation of the information in the stolen papers into a tangible object never possessed by the original

owner should be deemed immaterial. It would offend common sense to hold that these defendants fall outside the statute simply because, in efforts to avoid detection, their confederates were at pains to restore the original papers to [the employer] and transport only copies or notes[.]

Relying in part on the Second Circuit's decisions in *Gilboe* and *Bottone*, the court in *United States v. Riggs*, 739 F. Supp. 414 (N.D.Ill. 1990), held that the defendant violated § 2314 when he downloaded a text file containing proprietary information onto a home computer [and] transferred it over a computer network to his co-defendant in another state, who then uploaded it onto a computer bulletin board. The court reasoned that just because the defendant stored the information on a computer, rather than printing it on paper, his acts were not removed from the purview of the statute:

> [I]n the instant case, if the information in [the] text file had been affixed to a floppy disk, or printed out on a computer printer, then [the defendant's] transfer of that information across state lines would clearly constitute the transfer of "goods, wares, or merchandise" within the meaning of § 2314. This court sees no reason to hold differently simply because [the defendant] stored the information inside a computer instead of printing it out on paper. In either case, the information is in a transferable, accessible, even salable form.

Id. at 421. The court noted that "[r]eading a tangibility requirement into the definition of 'goods, wares, or merchandise' might unduly restrict the scope of § 2314, especially in this modern technological age," and recognized that although not tangible in a conventional sense, the stolen property was physically stored on a computer hard drive and could be viewed and printed out with the push of a button. *See id.* at 422[.]

[Weighing] the scant authority at hand, the Court is persuaded that the view most closely analogous to Second Circuit doctrine is that which holds that the transfer of electronic documents via the internet across state lines does fall within the purview of § 2314. The indictment is therefore upheld and the motion to dismiss [the count charged under § 2314] is denied.

POINTS FOR DISCUSSION

a. **Common Law Limitations on "Property"**

In the fifteenth century, English judges took on the task of defining the elements of the earliest property crime, which they called "larceny." Their view was that only "tangible" personal property ("personalty") needed to be protected by the criminal law, such as livestock, harvested crops, and weapons of war. This is why they defined the larceny crime to punish the act of "taking and carrying away" such property. The judges did not define larceny to cover the taking of property that they viewed as having little or no value, such as wild and domesticated animals. They also decided that land ("realty") could "safely be excluded" from the larceny crime because it was "immovable," "fairly indestructible," and difficult to take and carry away. The judges also excluded things attached to land, such as growing crops and "fixtures." *See* Model Penal Code § 223.2, Comment 3, at 166–167 (1980). During the ensuing centuries, Parliament enacted statutes that defined specific types of "property" as being subject to larceny prosecutions. Some of these things had been excluded by earlier judicial decisions, whereas other things represented new forms of wealth. The early American state larceny statutes imitated the English statutes, and preserved the tradition of creating miscellaneous collections of "property" examples.

b. Updating "Property" Definitions

When a statutory definition of "property" consists of an exclusive list of examples, it is necessary for the legislature to keep adding examples to protect new forms of property. Here is an example of an evolving list in a Massachusetts statute (Mass. Gen. Laws. Ann. Ch. 266, § 30(2)):

> The term "property" . . . shall include money, personal chattels, a bank note, bond, promissory note, bill of exchange or other bill, order or certificate, a book of accounts for or concerning money or goods due or to become due or to be delivered, a deed or writing containing a conveyance of land, any valuable contract in force, a receipt, release or defeasance, a writ, process, certificate of title or duplicate certificate [issued under ch. 185], a public record, anything which is of the realty or is annexed thereto, a security deposit received [pursuant to § 15B, ch. 196], electronically processed or stored data, either tangible or intangible, data while in transit, telecommunications services, and any domesticated animal, including dogs, or a beast or bird which is ordinarily kept in confinement.

Two of these statutory examples of "property"—"domesticated animals" and "anything which is of the realty or is annexed thereto"—are derived from an earlier Massachusetts statute that expanded the English judge-made definition of "property." Yet it was not until 1987 that the legislature amended the statute to add the phrase "including dogs." Before 1987, the statute only described the "beast or bird" category. More predictably, the terms "electronically processed or stored data" were added in 1983 and "telecommunications services" was added in 1995.

Whenever a court identifies a gap in a statutory list of property examples, it is traditional for the court to dismiss a prosecution involving the omitted type of property and declare that the legislature should decide whether or not to amend the statute to fill that gap. Note that a court identified the "release of the right to money" as not covered by the Massachusetts statute in *Commonwealth v. Mills*, 51 Mass. App. Ct. 366, 371–372, 745 N.E.2d 981, 987 (2001). But the legislature has not yet amended the statute to add that type of property.

The National Stolen Property Act (NSPA) in *Farraj* describes an exclusive list of property examples: "goods, wares, merchandise, securities, or money." One solution for the statutory interpretation problem in *Farraj* was for the trial judge to dismiss the prosecution and declare that Congress should decide whether to amend the statute to add the words, "tangible or intangible" before the term "goods." What reasons may explain why other courts might prefer to adopt this solution instead of endorsing the *Farraj* interpretation of the statute?

c.   **Model Penal Code Approach**

The MPC defines "property" in § 223.0(6) as "anything of value." This phrase is followed by a list of illustrative (not exclusive) examples, in order to make it clear that particular types of property, which were excluded under English law, qualify as a thing of value. This illustrative list includes: "real estate, tangible and intangible personal property, contract rights, choses-in-action and other interests in or claims to wealth, admission or transportation tickets, captured or domestic animals, food and drink, [and] electric or other power." Note that in 1962, the term "intangible personal property" meant a legally enforceable property right, which might or might not be expressed in a document. The term "thing of value" had been used in some federal and state statutes that recognized a broad definition of property in the pre-MPC era. What does the absence of this term in the NSPA suggest regarding the likely Congressional intent concerning its application to the *Farraj* defendant's conduct?

d.   **Intangible Information as "Goods"**

The National Stolen Property Act was enacted in 1934 as an "extension of the National Motor Vehicle Theft Act," which was enacted in 1919. That earlier statute "was an attempt to supplement the efforts of the States to combat automobile thefts," "[p]articularly in areas close to state lines, [where] state law enforcement authorities were seriously hampered by car thieves' ability to transport stolen vehicles beyond the jurisdiction in which the theft occurred." *Dowling v. United States*, 473 U.S. 207, 218–219 (1986). The NSPA does not define the terms "goods," "wares," "merchandise," or "money," but the statute does use a list of more than 25 exclusive examples to define the term "security." The *Farraj* case did not make new law in holding that a paper copy of the Trial Plan would qualify as "ordinarily the subject of commerce." This is because other federal precedents recognized that stolen documents containing confidential business information may qualify as "goods," as long as "a market, legal or otherwise, exists" for that information. But the *Farraj* case did make new law in holding that the NSPA could be applied to intangible information.

How does the trial judge in *Farraj* use the existing federal precedents and the legislative history of the 1988 amendment to support the expansion of the term "goods" to include information conveyed in an electronic format? What reasons may explain why virtually no other federal court after *Farraj* approved the extension of the NSPA to stolen intangible information? *See United States v. Aleynikov*, 676 F.3d 71 (2d Cir. 2012) (implicitly rejecting *Farraj* ruling). The *Farraj* defendant faced an additional charge under the federal Computer Fraud and Abuse Act (CFAA), 8 U.S.C. § 1030(a). There are seven CFAA crimes, and ultimately the defendant pled guilty to one of them, "unauthorized computer access" under § 1030(a)(3).

C. LARCENY & EMBEZZLEMENT (THEFT BY UNLAWFUL TAKING OR DISPOSITION)

Many modern "theft" statutes emulate the MPC's merger of the crimes of larceny and embezzlement in the "theft by unlawful taking or disposition" crime. An understanding of the reasons that underlie this merger may be obtained from the cases that illustrate the anachronistic distinctions between these crimes, which are still used in some state codes, and which depend upon the meaning of the complex and fictionalized concept of a "trespassory taking from possession."

1. Larceny

The original crime of larceny required a "trespassory taking" of property from the "possession" of the owner, without the consent of the owner. There was also an "asportation" requirement, which meant that the property was supposed to be "carried away." Even a small movement might satisfy this element. The crime required the "intent to steal," meaning an intent to deprive the owner permanently of the property. The federal criminal code and some state codes continue to use this definition, but most states have replaced it with some version of the MPC crime of "theft by unlawful taking or disposition." The *Mafnas* case illustrates how some courts must rely on 500-year-old larceny fictions invented by English judges in order to interpret the scope of a modern federal statute.

UNITED STATES V. MAFNAS
701 F.2d 83 (9th Cir. 1983).

Before ELY, and KENNEDY, CIRCUIT JUDGES, and NIELSEN, DISTRICT JUDGE.

PER CURIAM:

Appellant (Mafnas) was convicted in the U.S. District Court of Guam of stealing money from two federally insured banks in violation of 18 U.S.C. § 2113(b) which [applies to] "[whoever] take[s] [and carries away,] with intent to steal [or purloin, any property or] money belonging to . . . any bank[.]"

Mafnas was employed by the Guam Armored Car Service (Service), which was hired by the Bank of Hawaii and the Bank of America to deliver bags of money. On three occasions Mafnas opened the bags and removed money. As a result he was convicted of three counts of stealing money from the banks.

This Circuit has held that § 2113(b) applies only to common law larceny which requires a trespassory taking. *Bennett v. United States*, 399 F.2d 740 (9th Cir. 1968). Mafnas argues his taking was embezzlement rather than larceny as he had lawful possession of the bags, with the consent of the banks, when he took the money. [If Mafnas is correct, his conviction must be reversed, and then presumably he may be indicted for committing the embezzlement crime.]

This problem arose centuries ago, and common law has evolved to handle it. The law distinguishes between possession and custody. [As explained in 3 WHARTON'S CRIMINAL LAW 353 (1980):]

> Ordinarily, . . . if a person receives property for a limited or temporary purpose, he is only acquiring custody. Thus, if a person receives property from the owner with instructions to deliver it to the owner's house, he is only acquiring custody; therefore, his subsequent decision to keep the property for himself would constitute larceny.

The District Court concluded that Mafnas was given temporary custody only, to deliver the money bags to their various destinations. The later decision to take the money was larceny, because it was beyond the consent of the owner, who retained constructive possession until the custodian's task was completed. This rationale was used in *United States v. Pruitt*, 446 F.2d 513, 515 (6th Cir. 1971). There, Pruitt was employed by a bank as a messenger. He devised a plan with another person to stage a fake robbery and split the money which Pruitt was delivering for the bank. The Sixth Circuit found that Pruitt had mere custody for the purpose of delivering the money, and that his wrongful conversion constituted larceny.

Mafnas distinguishes *Pruitt* because the common law sometimes differentiates between employees, who generally obtain custody only, and others[,] who acquire [lawful] possession. Although not spelled out, Mafnas essentially claims that he was a bailee, and that the contract between the banks and Service resulted in Service having lawful possession, and not mere custody over the bags. ["]A bailment situation is said to arise where an owner, while retaining title, delivers [property] to another for some particular purpose upon an express or implied contract.["] [*See Lionberger v. United States*, 371 F.2d 831, 840 (Ct.Cl. 1967).]

The common law also found an answer to this situation[:]

[When] the bailee-carrier was given possession of a bale, but not its contents[,] [and] pilfered the entire bale, he was not guilty of larceny; but when he broke open the bale and took a portion or all of the contents, he was guilty of larceny because his taking was trespassory and it was from the constructive possession of another.

3 WHARTON'S CRIMINAL LAW 353-354. Either way, Mafnas has committed the common law crime of larceny, replete with trespassory taking.

Mafnas also cannot profit from an argument that any theft on his part was from [the] Service and not from the banks. Case law is clear that since what was taken was property belonging to the banks, it was property or money "in the care, custody, control, management, or possession of any bank" within the meaning of 18 U.S.C. § 2113(b), notwithstanding the fact that it may have been in the possession of an armored car service serving as a bailee for hire. *See United States v. Jakalski*, 237 F.2d 503 (7th Cir. 1956).

Therefore, his conviction is affirmed.

POINTS FOR DISCUSSION

a. Origins of Trespass Element in Larceny

In the fifteenth century and earlier, the meaning of a "taking" as an element of the judge-made crime of larceny "had no artificial meaning." As one scholar explains:

Trespass as an essential element of larceny simply meant taking a chattel from one who had possession of it. [Anglo-Saxon] and early Norman economic conditions limited both the objects and the methods of theft. Movable property consisted of cattle, farm products, and furniture. [Since] theft of cattle by armed bands was by far the most important crime against property, it requires no stretch of imagination to see what was meant by "trespass" in the early law.

JEROME HALL, THEFT, LAW AND SOCIETY 6 (2d ed. 1952). When the judicial definition of larceny expanded, on a case-by-case basis, to cover any "trespassory" taking from the owner's "constructive possession," the common law meaning of this element of larceny became highly fictionalized.

b. Taking & "Carrying Away"

By the time Blackstone described the asportation or "carrying away" element of larceny in the 1783 edition of his treatise, its meaning had become fictionalized, as evidenced by these examples of sufficient proof of asportation: 1) if a person "leads another man's horse out of a close and is apprehended in the fact"; 2) if a guest, "stealing goods out of an inn, removes them from his chamber"; 3) if a thief, "intending to steal plate, takes it out of a chest and lays it down upon the floor, but is surprised before he can make his escape with it." 4 WILLIAM BLACKSTONE, COMMENTARIES ON THE LAWS OF ENGLAND, *200. Ultimately, American courts held that a "slight movement" was sufficient to show asportation.

c. "Trespassory Taking from Possession"

A classic scenario for larceny in the early English law was the stealth crime of taking a horse away from the owner's barn. In this case, the owner's rightful possession of the horse was obvious, and the trespass was synonymous with the act of taking without the consent of the owner. But in situations in which property came into the hands of the thief through some action of the owner, the English judges invented the concept of mere "custody" to describe the thief's relationship to the property. Such "custody" meant, first, that the property remained in the "constructive possession" of the rightful owner, and second, that when the thief absconded with the property, that act constituted a "trespassory taking" from the "possession" of the owner.

The *Mafnas* Court's analysis illustrate several examples of "constructive possession" rules. First, consider the conviction of the *Pruitt* defendant, as described in *Mafnas*. As a bank messenger, he was an employee of the bank, whose job was to transport and deliver money to branch banks. The English judges created a larceny rule for employees, namely "servants" whose job was to take orders from their "masters," and whose relationship to a master's property was deemed to be that of mere "custody." So when the servant-employee in *Pruitt* ignored the master-bank's instructions, and gave the bank's money to an accomplice instead, that act constituted a trespassory taking of the money from the bank's constructive possession.

One obstacle that confronted the English judges was that a contract of bailment created lawful possession of goods in the "bailee," who held the bailor-owner's property for some purpose, such as transportation and delivery, and who typically received compensation for carrying out that purpose. Therefore, the judges created two larceny rules to deal with thieving bailees. When goods were shipped together in bulk without being packaged, taking any part of the shipment constituted the trespassory taking of "breaking bulk." When goods were shipped in packaging, the package was the "bale", and opening the packaging to remove the contents constituted the trespassory taking of "breaking bale." Taking an entire bale without breaking it open would not constitute larceny. These larceny fictions emerged from the *Carrier's Case* (1473), where the defendant was hired to deliver bales but never did so, breaking open the bales instead, and taking the contents. He was guilty of larceny because the owner was deemed to have retained lawful possession of the contents inside the bale. *See generally* WAYNE R. LAFAVE, CRIMINAL LAW §§ 19.2, 19.8, 974–976, 1026 (5th ed. 2010).

How does the *Mafnas* Court apply these larceny fictions to the facts of *Mafnas*? What reasons may explain the failure of the English judges to abandon the "trespassory taking" requirement entirely, and their preference for stretching its meaning through a variety of larceny fictions instead? What reasons may explain the failure of Congress to replace the larceny crime in the *Mafnas* statute with a modern definition of the crime?

d. Larceny by Trick

The crime of larceny by trick enabled prosecutors to convict defendants who "trespassed against possession" by telling lies to obtain possession of property, instead of taking it by stealth. The crime is illustrated by the English decision in *Pear's Case* (1779), where the defendant hired a horse with the understanding that the horse would be returned to the owner. But the defendant actually intended to sell the horse at the time of the hire and he sold the horse and kept the proceeds. The defendant was not a servant, employee, bailee or other agent, and so he claimed that he had obtained temporary lawful possession of the horse. But the English judges decided to call this conduct "larceny," based on the reasoning that the defendant's false promise to return the horse was a "trick" that could be treated as a "trespass," thus making the defendant's conduct a "taking from the owner's possession." Given the fact that the owner's act of parting with possession was based on fraud, this act could not create lawful possession in the thief.

The larceny by trick crime requires proof of all the elements of larceny, as well as the trick element of false representation, which can be a false promise about the future or a false statement about past or present facts. The element of "conversion" of the property also is necessary for a conviction for larceny by trick, and the owner must be tricked into parting with possession of property, not into parting with title. Like the larceny crime, larceny by trick is a crime designed to protect actual or constructive possession of property.

e. **Gaps in the Larceny Rules**

The willingness of English judges to construct larceny fictions had two important limits, which explains why Parliament enacted statutes to define the crimes of embezzlement and false pretenses. The scenario that required the enactment of the embezzlement crime was the decision in *Bazeley's Case* (1799), where property was transmitted from a third party to the master's servant, with instructions to deliver it to the master. The English judges held that no larceny occurred when the servant misappropriated the property by converting it for his own benefit. In their view, the servant had acquired lawful "possession" of the property from the third party, and could not be guilty of a "trespassory taking" from the possession of the master.

Similarly, the English judges were not willing to expand larceny by trick to encompass the case where a thief obtained *title* to property by means of false statements. They limited the scope of the larceny by trick crime to a scenario where the owner's apparent passing of possession was nullified because of the trick, so that possession remained with the owner, as occurs in all larceny fictions. In their view, this fiction could not be maintained when the owner passed title because of the trick. Therefore, the judges interpreted Parliament's "false pretenses" crime as covering this liability gap. Notably, the MPC Commentaries attribute the reluctance of English judges to expand the larceny fictions to a "combination of circumstances," with the "most direct influence" being "a revulsion against capital punishment, which was the penalty for all theft offenses except petty larceny during much of the 18th century." *See* Model Penal Code § 223.2, Comment (1)(a), at 128–129 (1980).

f. Claim of Right Defense

It is common for states to endorse the "claim of right" defense to property crimes, either in statutes or in case law. Almost all states require only an honest belief in a claim of right, and do not require that this honest belief also should be "reasonable." In effect, an honest belief in a claim of right operates as a total defense because it negates the *mens rea* of the "intent" or "purpose" to deprive another person of his or her property. By codifying the "honest claim of right" as an affirmative defense, a legislature can make it clear "that recklessness or negligence should not serve as a basis for theft liability." *See* Model Penal Code § 223.1(3), Comment 4, at 152 (1980).

2. Embezzlement

The crime of embezzlement was established by the inventive action of Parliament in 1799 when English judges refused to stretch the larceny crime to cover the conduct of embezzlers. Early American statutes followed Parliament's example in limiting the categories of entrusted persons whose conduct was subject to prosecution for embezzlement. Later statutes expanded the concept of entrustment to cover a wide variety of defendants. The traditional elements of embezzlement include the fraudulent conversion of the property of another by an entrusted person in lawful possession who had the intent to convert the property for his or her own use. These elements are simplified in the modern MPC crime of "theft by unlawful taking or disposition," which applies to a person who "unlawfully takes or *exercises unlawful control over*" property, and who has either the "purpose to deprive" or the purpose "to benefit himself or another not entitled thereto." The *Batin* case illustrates how it may be difficult for a prosecutor to persuade a court that an employee was entrusted with the kind of "constructive possession" of property that makes an embezzlement conviction possible.

BATIN V. STATE
118 Nev. 61, 38 P.3d 880 (2002) (en banc).

LEAVITT, J.:

Appellant Marlon Javar Batin was convicted [of] embezzlement for stealing money from his employer, [the] Nugget Hotel and Casino. [W]e now conclude that Batin did not commit embezzlement as a matter of law because there was no evidence presented of the entrustment element of that crime. [We] reverse the judgment of conviction.

In 1993, Batin moved [to Nevada] from the Philippines and began working as a dishwasher at the Nugget. After several years at the Nugget, Batin became a slot mechanic. Batin's job duties [included] fixing jammed coins and refilling the "hopper." Warren Reid Anderson, Batin's supervisor, explained [in his testimony] that the "hopper" is the part of the slot machine that pays the coins back, and is separate from the "bill validator" component of the slot machine where the paper currency is kept. Anderson further testified that Batin had no duties with respect to the paper currency in the bill validator, except to safeguard the funds, and that the cash in the bill validator "wasn't to be touched." Likewise, Anderson testified that if a customer had a problem with a machine that required a cash refund, "it would require supervisory backup in order to take any money out of a slot machine and pass it back to a customer." Batin also testified about his job duties as a slot mechanic. Like Anderson, Batin testified that he was prohibited from handling the paper currency inside the bill validator.

As a slot mechanic, Batin was given an "SDS" card that was used to both access the inside of the slot machine and identify him as the employee that was opening the slot machine door. The computerized SDS system is physically connected to each slot machine and counts the paper currency placed into each machine's bill validator. The SDS actually records the different denominations of bills and runs numerous reports concerning the currency. The SDS also registers every time that the slot machine door is open or closed. If the power is turned off to a particular slot machine, the SDS system will only record the opening and closing of the door; it cannot track what happens inside the machine.

Lori Barrington, soft count supervisor, explained that after the money is counted by SDS, it is then counted three more times by a minimum of three Nugget employees. Barrington further testified that there was not much variance between the amount of money SDS recorded that the casino was supposed to have and the amount of money the casino actually had. In fact, out of 1100 slot machines, there were perhaps three errors per month totaling approximately $100.00 in variance.

In March and early June 1999, however, there were larger discrepancies discovered between the amount of money that the SDS recorded had been put into the slot machines and the amount of money the slot machine actually contained. Kathleen Plamabeck, the Nugget's Internal Auditor, testified to several shortages from four different slot machines, totaling approximately $40,000.00.

In reviewing the SDS reports, Plambeck testified that she found a pattern of conduct. Namely, prior to the time that a shortage had been detected on a slot machine, Batin inserted his SDS card into the slot machine, opened the door, turned off the power, and thereafter closed the door on the machine. Plambeck found this pattern of conduct unusual because it was not necessary to turn off the slot machine for most repairs, and no one other than Batin had been turning off the power on the slot machines with the shortages. Batin testified at trial, however, that he turned off the power on the slot machines so that he would not be electrocuted and that he had always turned off the power prior to working on the slot machines.

James Carlisle, an agent with the Nevada Gaming Control Board, investigated Batin and discovered that he gambled regularly at three local casinos, and that he lost tens of thousands of dollars. When Carlisle questioned Batin about how he was able to afford to gamble such large sums of money, Batin could not or did not answer. At trial, however, Batin testified that he was able to afford to gamble large sums of money because he won often.

Although Batin adamantly denied taking the money, Batin was arrested and charged [with] embezzlement. The information alleged that Batin had been entrusted with money by his employer and converted the money for a purpose other than that for which it was entrusted. After a jury trial, Batin was convicted [of] embezzlement.

Batin contends that his [conviction] for embezzlement should be reversed because there was insufficient evidence of an essential element of the crime. We agree.

[To] prove that a defendant committed the crime of embezzlement, the State must demonstrate [that] the defendant was a *"person with whom any money, property or effects ha[d] been deposited or entrusted,"* and that the defendant "use[d] or appropriate[d] the money, property, or effects . . . in any manner or for any other purpose than that for which [it was] deposited or entrusted." [Nev. Rev. Stat. § 205.300(1).]

The key distinguishing element of the crime of embezzlement is the element of entrustment. In order to be guilty of embezzlement, a defendant must have been entrusted with lawful possession of the property prior to its conversion. For purposes of proving embezzlement, the lawful possession need not be actual; rather, the State may show that a defendant had constructive possession of the property converted. This court has defined constructive possession as " 'both the power and the intention at a given time to exercise dominion or control over a thing, either directly or through another person or persons.' " [*Palmer v. State*, 112

Nev. 763, 768, 920 P.2d 112, 115 (1996) (quoting *Black's Law Dictionary* 1163 (6th ed. 1990)).]

In proving constructive possession, a showing that a defendant was given mere access to the property converted is insufficient. Often, an individual is entrusted with access to a particular place or thing without being given dominion and control over the property therein. This is particularly true in instances, like the present one, where the individual is expressly told that he is not allowed to touch the property in the place to which access is granted.

[Here] the record reveals that Batin was not entrusted with lawful possession, constructive or otherwise, of the currency he allegedly took from the bill validators. In fact, both Batin and his supervisor testified that Batin had no job duties whatsoever involving this currency and that it "wasn't to be touched." Further, Batin had absolutely no power to exercise control over this currency, as Batin was required to contact his supervisor for any job task involving possession of the currency inside the bill validator, such as a cash refund to a customer. [We] cannot say that an individual exercises control over property when he is prohibited from touching it.

In light of the foregoing, we are compelled to reverse Batin's conviction. The State failed to prove the entrustment element of the crime of embezzlement beyond a reasonable doubt[.] [The court observed in a footnote that the evidence at trial would have supported a conviction for larceny and that the prosecutor can retry the defendant on that charge.]

MAUPIN, C.J., with whom BECKER, J., agrees, dissenting.

In viewing the evidence in a light most favorable to the State, we conclude that there is ample evidence to support the jury's verdict that Batin had constructive possession of the paper currency inside the bill validator. The State proffered evidence that Batin's employer entrusted him with an SDS card, which allowed Batin to access the bill validator inside the slot machine where the currency was kept. Moreover, Batin's job, as prescribed by his employer, included safeguarding the funds contained inside the bill validator when he made a slot machine repair and when supervising non-employee slot machine repairmen. In safeguarding the currency inside the bill validator, Batin was entrusted with dominion and control over that currency in a manner sufficient to support the jury's finding that Batin had constructive possession over the funds that he converted.

Accordingly, because we conclude that there was sufficient evidence of the crime of embezzlement, we would affirm the judgment of conviction.

Property Crimes

POINTS FOR DISCUSSION

a. Charging the Wrong Crime

It may be difficult for a prosecutor to charge a defendant with the "right" property crime without knowing how an appellate court will define embezzlement and larceny in the context of particular facts. What are the reasons that explain why defense counsel will argue on appeal that their clients were convicted of the wrong property crime, even when counsel recognize that these clients could be charged and later convicted for a different property crime?

b. Entrustment

The *Batin* prosecutor lost because of a failure of proof concerning the "entrustment" of the defendant's by his employer with the "possession" of the paper currency in the form of "control" over it. As the court explained, "We cannot say that an individual exercises control over property when he is prohibited from touching it." At the charging stage of a case, however, it may be difficult for a prosecutor to anticipate what the testimony of all the witnesses will show at trial. The concept of "constructive possession" of property by an "entrusted" employee is a legal fiction, and so it is not surprising to discover that the inherent ambiguity of this concept led to disagreement about its meaning in *Batin*. What new evidence might have persuaded the *Batin* court that the crime was embezzlement? What are the possible reasons that the dissenters were less demanding than the *Batin* majority about the sufficiency of the entrustment evidence in the record.

c. MPC Fusion of Larceny & Embezzlement Crimes

The MPC drafters proposed that a single crime, "theft by unlawful taking or disposition" (TUTD) under § 223.2(1), should be created to replace the English common law crimes of larceny, larceny by trick, and embezzlement. This MPC crime applies to "movable" property, namely "anything of value," the location of which can be moved. The use of new vocabulary, both for the name of the crime and for its elements, signaled the intent of the MPC drafters to abandon the legal fictions and technical distinctions that characterized the old common law crimes. The MPC crime is a much simpler and broader version of its predecessors. In only one sentence the Code combines the larceny 'taking" crime with the embezzlement "control" crime by defining the new crime as applying to "a person who unlawfully *takes or exercises control* over movable property of another with purpose to deprive" the other thereof.

D. FALSE PRETENSES (THEFT BY DECEPTION)

After English judges expanded the larceny concept to include "larceny by trick," they refused to expand this crime to cover defendants who used deception to obtain title to property, and Parliament's "false pretenses" crime was used to fill that liability gap. Many legislatures enacted this crime in early state criminal codes. The MPC created the "theft by deception" crime as a substitute in § 223.3.

E. RECEIVING STOLEN PROPERTY

In late seventeenth century England, a person who received stolen goods could be prosecuted only as an accessory after the fact to the property crime committed by the thief, and only if the thief was convicted first. Not until the early nineteenth century was the conduct of "receiving stolen goods" recognized by Parliament as a separate and independent crime. State codes originally defined the crime to cover defendants who "receive" property, "knowing" the property is "stolen," with the "intent to deprive the owner." Modern statutes typically use some expanded version of these elements for the crime of "Receiving Stolen Property" (RSP).

POINT FOR DISCUSSION

Elements of Receiving Stolen Property

Originally the crime of receiving stolen property applied to property that was stolen through larceny. But gradually it came to apply to the receipt of goods stolen by any means, and most modern statutes use that broad definition, even when the larceny term "stolen" appears in the title of the crime. Most states also have abandoned the common law element that required the goods to be "stolen," so that it is possible to prosecute defendants who have been caught in a sting operation, even when the goods may have lost their stolen character. *See* Model Penal Code § 223.6, Comments 4(b), 4(c), at 239–240 (1980).

Most states use the MPC mental state that allows conviction upon proof that the defendant believed that the property "probably has been stolen." Even in states where the mental state element is "knowledge" that property was stolen, the consensus in case law is that proof of positive knowledge is not required. Evidence of suspicious circumstances or suspicious comments and behavior by the defendant may supply the necessary inference of knowledge. Most states also require that a defendant possess the "intent to deprive the owner" of the property, whereas the MPC requires that the prosecutor prove only that the defendant did not possess the intent to restore the property. *See* Model Penal Code § 223.6, Comment 4(a), at 237 (1980). The concept of "possession" is vital for the definition of the crime of receiving stolen property because courts and legislatures equate that concept with the element of "receiving."

F. ROBBERY & CARJACKING

Robbery is the oldest common law property crime and predates larceny. The MPC Commentary describes robbery as "the theft of property under circumstances calculated to terrorize the victim." *See* Model Penal Code § 222.1, Comment 1, at 96 (1980). The earliest common law version of the robbery crime required a taking of property by means of actual physical violence committed upon the person. Later it was expanded to punish a taking by the "constructive violence" of putting the victim in fear. Initially, this fear included either fear of bodily injury or fear of violence to "habitation or property." *See* WAYNE R. LAFAVE, CRIMINAL LAW, § 20.3, at 1046, n.1 (5th ed. 2010). Later this element evolved into fear of violence to the victim, and the robbery crime took on its most familiar English common law form, which required all the same elements as larceny, plus two additional elements: 1) the taking of property "from the person or presence of the victim"; 2) by means of force or by putting the victim in fear of violence.

In the early 1990s, Congress and many state legislatures decided to enact "carjacking" statutes in order to punish one type of robbery with more severe penalties, namely the violent taking of an automobile. Some carjacking statutes, including the federal statute in *Lake*, were modeled on the elements of the common law robbery crime, and therefore included the requirement that the car must be taken "from the person or presence of the victim." The *Lake* case illustrates how courts have sought to achieve the purposes of both the robbery and the carjacking crimes by using an expansive definition of "presence."

UNITED STATES V. LAKE
150 F.3d 269 (3d Cir. 1998).

ALITO, CIRCUIT JUDGE.

[Lake] was convicted under 18 U.S.C. § 924(c)(1) of using or carrying a firearm during and in relation to a crime of violence, namely, a carjacking [under] 18 U.S.C. § 2119[.] Lake challenges his conviction on [the] grounds [that] he did not take the motor vehicle in question "from the person or presence" of the victim. We reject this [argument,] and we therefore affirm.

The events that led to Lake's prosecution occurred at Little Magen's Bay in St. Thomas, United States Virgin Islands. The road to the beach at Little Magen's Bay ends at the top of a hill [where a parking area is located]. There is a steep path bordered by vegetation and rocks that leads from the [parking area] down to the beach, and the [parking area] cannot be seen from the beach.

On the day in question, Lake hitchhiked to Little Magen's Bay and encountered Milton Clarke, who was sitting on the beach reading a newspaper. Lake asked whether Clarke owned a white car parked up on the road [at the parking area]. Clarke said that he did, and Lake initially walked away. However, Lake returned a few moments later and asked to borrow the car. When Clarke refused, Lake stated that it was an emergency. Clarke again refused and Lake walked off. When Lake returned yet again, Clarke said: ["L]isten, think about it. If I walked up to you and asked you, can I borrow your car[,] [a]re you going to lend it to me? Of course not. So why don't you leave me the hell alone. I'm here to have a nice time. Just chill. Go someplace else.["]

Lake walked off and sat on a rock, while Clarke anxiously watched him out of the corner of his eye, but Lake soon returned with the same request. When Clarke swore again, Lake asked if he could have a drink from Clarke's cooler. Clarke said: "[D]on't you get it? Leave me alone." Lake then lifted up his shirt, showed Clarke the handle of a gun, and said: "[Y]ou know what that is?" Clarke stood up and started backing away, but Lake pulled the gun from his waist band, put it against Clarke's face, and demanded the car keys. Clarke said that he did not have the keys and started walking toward the water with Lake following. Clarke waded into waist-deep water, and Lake walked out onto a promontory overlooking the water.

While Clarke was in the water, his friend, Pamela Croaker, appeared on the beach. Clarke shouted a warning, prompting Lake to approach Croaker. Lake demanded that Croaker surrender her car keys, and Croaker said: "I don't even know you. Why would I give you the keys to the car?" Lake then grabbed the keys, and the two wrestled for possession of the keys. [Lake placed the gun close to her head and again told her to surrender the keys.] [Croaker] surrendered the keys but asked to keep her house keys. Lake went up the steep path to the parking area where Croaker had parked her car out of sight of the beach. Lake then drove away in Croaker's car after leaving her house keys on the hood of Clarke's car. [B]oth Croaker and Clarke followed [Lake] up the path, but when they arrived [at the parking area], [Lake] was driving away. [Later] that day, the police apprehended Lake in the stolen car[.] The gun was never recovered. . . .

[Under] the carjacking statute, the prosecution must prove that the defendant (1) "with intent to cause death or serious bodily harm" (2) took a motor vehicle (3) that had been "transported, shipped, or received in interstate or foreign commerce" (4) "from the person or presence of another" (5) "by force and violence or by intimidation." . . . [Lake] maintains [that] he took [Croaker's] keys, not her car, from her person or presence and that the car was not in Croaker's presence when he took it because she could not see or touch the car at that moment.

The carjacking statute's requirement that the vehicle be taken "from the person or presence of the victim" "tracks the language used in other federal robbery statutes," such as 18 U.S.C. §§ 2111, 2113, and 2118. [H.R.Rep. No. 102–851(I), at 5 (1992).] Under these statutes, "property is in the presence of a person if it is 'so within his reach, observation or control, that he could if not overcome by violence or prevented by fear, retain his possession of it.'" *United States v. Burns*, 701 F.2d 840, 843 (9th Cir. 1983). *See also* LAFAVE & SCOTT, SUBSTANTIVE CRIMINAL LAW § 8.11 at 443 (1986) (" 'Presence' in this connection is not so much a matter of eyesight as it is one of proximity and control[.]")

Here [Lake] took Croaker's car keys at gunpoint on the beach and then ran up the path and drove away in her car. Croaker pursued Lake but did not reach the parking area in time to stop him. Applying the definition of "presence" [used in *Burns*,] we conclude that a rational jury could have found that Croaker could have prevented the taking of her car if she had not been fearful that Lake would shoot or otherwise harm her. Croaker testified that the sight of Lake's gun caused her great fear. She stated that when she first saw the gun she "felt like [she] was going [to] faint." Although Croaker did not say in so many words that she hesitated for some time before pursuing Lake up the path, the sequence of events laid out in her testimony supports the inference that this is what occurred. Croaker stated that at the point when she surrendered the keys, Clarke "was struggling back through the water to come back," but that she did not start to run up the path until Clarke emerged from the water[.] Clarke testified that, when Lake ran up the path, Croaker was "pulling herself together[,]" that he "caught up to [Croaker] at the bottom of the paved driveway" and that the two of them proceeded up the path together. They reached the parking area in time for Croaker to see Lake driving away in her car but not in time to stop him. Both Croaker and Clarke stated that at this point they were very scared. Based on this testimony, a rational jury could infer that Croaker hesitated before pursuing Lake due to fear and that if she had not hesitated she could have reached the parking area in time to prevent Lake from taking her car without employing further force, violence, or intimidation. We do not suggest this inference was compelled, but because such an inference was rational, we hold that the evidence was sufficient. . . .

In sum, we hold that the evidence was sufficient to establish all of the elements of the carjacking statute[.]

For these reasons, we affirm the judgment of the district court.

BECKER, CHIEF JUDGE, dissenting.

When the defendant took the car keys from his victim, Pamela Croaker, Ms. Croaker's car was, in city terms, a block away, up the hill, out of sight. Under these circumstances, I would join an opinion upholding Lake's conviction for "keyjacking," or for both key robbery [and key] larceny. I cannot, however, agree that he is guilty of carjacking. The majority draws upon federal robbery statutes to explicate how the vehicle (as opposed to its keys) may be considered to have been taken from the "person or presence of the victim." Disciples of the jurisprudence of pure reason may, in analytic terms, find this approach convincing. As I will explain[,] I do not. At all events, my polestar is the plain meaning of words, and in my lexicon, Ms. Croaker's car cannot fairly be said to have been taken from her person or presence, hence I respectfully dissent.

The robbery statutes upon which the carjacking statute is based do not themselves define the phrase "from the person or presence of the victim." Webster's New International Dictionary defines presence as "the vicinity of, or area immediately near one." However, rather than relying on the plain meaning, the majority turns to a construction of the phrase "person or presence" adopted by the Ninth Circuit in *United States v. Burns*, 701 F.2d 840 (9th Cir. 1983), where, in construing a federal robbery statute, that court reasoned that "property is in the presence of a person if it is 'so within his reach, inspection, observation or control, that he could if not overcome by violence or prevented by fear, retain his possession of it.' " Based on this definition, the majority concludes that a rational jury "could infer that Croaker hesitated before pursuing Lake due to fear and that if she had not hesitated she could have reached the parking area in time to prevent Lake from taking her car without employing further force, violence, or intimidation." This proves too much. If it is true that had Croaker not hesitated out of fear she could have followed Lake up the steep path leading from the secluded beach to the road, then it is equally true (barring physical limitations) that she could have followed him up that path and then halfway across St. Thomas. The fact that Croaker's car was nearby is thus not relevant; if she could have followed Lake up the hill, she could have followed him anywhere. I am aware, of course, that the craft of judging requires line-drawing, but I simply do not see how that endeavor can be principled when it is predicated on open-ended definitions of key statutory terms, especially where those terms admit of plain meaning.

POINTS FOR DISCUSSION

a. Elements of Carjacking

In 1991, the conduct that became known as "carjacking" attracted public attention when one victim died after being dragged for two miles during a violent seizure of a car in Maryland. This event inspired the widespread enactment of carjacking statutes, including the federal Anti Car Theft Act of 1992 and similar state statutes, even though the conduct of carjackers was covered by the robbery crime. The federal statute was amended in 1994 to require "the intent to cause death or serious bodily harm." State statutes exhibit a variety of mental state choices.

Even when a legislature borrows the elements of a state's common law robbery statute in order to define the carjacking crime, it is common for a legislature to add extra elements to a carjacking statute. For example, a California carjacking statute applies to cases where the defendant has only the intent to "temporarily deprive" the person in possession of a motor vehicle, and to cases where the defendant takes the motor vehicle from the "person or presence" of a passenger who is *not* in possession of it, including children. Moreover, a court will interpret the elements of a carjacking crime based on policy concerns relating to the unique dangers to which carjacking victims are subjected. For example, carjacking victims may be run over, abducted in their vehicles, driven at high speeds by captors who are chased by police, and killed or injured in car crashes. *See People v. Lopez*, 31 Cal. 4th 1051, 79 P.3d 548, 6 Cal. Rptr. 3d 432 (2003).

By the time that carjacking statutes were enacted, however, most states no longer defined robbery using all the elements of larceny plus the elements of a forcible taking from the "person or presence" of the victim. Instead, most states endorsed the MPC view that the "person or presence" element is unnecessary in a modern robbery statute. A typical modern robbery crime only requires the defendant to intentionally threaten the victim with bodily harm during the course of committing a theft. *Compare* Model Penal Code § 222.1, Comment (3)(d), at 112 (1980). This is why many state carjacking statutes do not reflect the borrowing of all the common law elements of robbery. For example, the Maryland statute requires only the intent to do the prohibited act of "obtaining unauthorized possession" of a motor vehicle "from another individual in actual possession" by "putting that individual in fear" through "intimidation"[.]" *See Harris v. State*, 353 Md. 596, 728 A.2d 180 (1999). What are the possible reasons that most state codes today do not include the "person or presence" element in the robbery crime? Do those reasons apply equally well to the carjacking crime?

b. Defining Presence

The *Lake* majority takes a conventional approach to the interpretation of the federal carjacking statute by identifying the federal robbery statutes as the source of the "person or presence" element, and relying on robbery precedents to interpret the meaning of that element. The *Lake* dissent rejects this approach and prefers to rely on the dictionary meaning of "presence." Similarly, each opinion goes in opposite directions in explaining why the defendant's conduct does or does not fit the harm that Congress intended to punish in the carjacking statute.

Why is the dissent's argument about the applicability of the dictionary definition of "presence" unpersuasive in light of the language of the carjacking statute and its legislative history? Although the *Burns* interpretation of the term "presence" may be "open-ended" to some degree, is the dissent correct to say that the *Lake* majority's reasoning would require the affirmance of the conviction if the victim's car had been located "halfway across St. Thomas"? Should the carjacking crime apply to a case in which the defendant, after robbing a bank, tied up the bank manager in her office, ordered her (at gunpoint) to turn over her car keys and reveal the location of her car, and then used the bank manager's car to flee the scene? *Compare United States v. Moore*, 198 F.3d 793 (10th Cir. 1999).

c. Other Elements

The *Lake* defendant also argued that the evidence was insufficient to show either the element that he had the mental state for carjacking or the element that Croaker's car had been transported in interstate or foreign commerce. Why would the *Lake* Court reject each argument? What scenarios would not qualify for carjacking liability under Chief Judge Becker's narrow definition of the "purpose or presence" element, but would qualify for liability under the *Lake* majority's definition?

G. BURGLARY

The crime of common law burglary was defined by English judges as required the breaking and entering of a dwelling at night time with the intent to commit a felony therein. That felony crime might be stealing in many cases, but burglary encompassed the intent to commit any felony. Modern burglary statutes have broadened the crime to cover daytime intrusions into structures or vehicles. The *T.J.E.* case illustrates how a court may decide to interpret a modern burglary statute narrowly, in order to make it inapplicable to mere shoplifters. The subsequent redefinitions of burglary by the state legislature, which implicitly rejected the *T.J.E.* interpretation, reveal how difficult it may be to achieve the same result in other ways.

IN THE MATTER OF T.J.E.
426 N.W.2d 23 (S.D. 1988).

WUEST, CHIEF JUSTICE.

T.J.E. appeals her adjudication and disposition as a *juvenile delinquent*. We reverse.

T.J.E., age 11, entered a retail store during business hours with her aunt. While in the store, T.J.E. took and ate a piece of candy from a display and left with her aunt without paying for the candy. T.J.E. was stopped outside of the store by the manager and ultimately admitted to him that she had eaten a piece of candy without paying for it. [Her aunt offered to pay for it but the manager called the police.]

[The] State subsequently filed a petition in the circuit court alleging T.J.E. to be a delinquent child [because she allegedly committed] second degree burglary. After an adjudicatory hearing the circuit court sustained the allegations of second degree burglary.

We find that the evidence presented by [the] state during T.J.E.'s adjudicatory hearing was insufficient to sustain the allegations in its petition [that] T.J.E. committed the offense of second degree burglary in violation of SDCL [§] 22–32–3: ["]Any person who *enters* or *remains* in an occupied structure with intent to commit any crime therein[.]"

[First,] [w]e find no proof in the record that at the time T.J.E. entered the store with her aunt she had the intent to commit a crime inside. We decline to interpret the impulsive act of this 11 year old child in taking candy after entering the store as evincing an intent *at the time of her entry* to commit theft. This clearly distinguishes this case from our affirmance of a burglary conviction in *State v. Shult*, 380 N.W.2d 352 (S.D. 1986), where the defendant took an item of merchandise [a frozen pizza] from a convenience store [at a time when it was open to the public]. In *Shult* there was an admission by him that at the time he entered the store he had the specific intent to commit theft therein. There is no such evidence in the present case.

[Second,] [t]he circuit court [found] that T.J.E. *remained* in the store with the intent to commit theft, thereby committing second degree burglary by *remaining* in an occupied structure with the intent to commit a crime therein. A literal reading of the word "remains" in the statute would support this finding and would end the need for further inquiry. However, where the literal meaning of a statute leads to absurd or unreasonable conclusions, ambiguity exists. To interpret the word "remains" in [§] 22–32–3 to hold [that] a person commits second degree burglary whenever he is present in an occupied structure with the intent to commit a crime therein would make every shoplifter a burglar. It would make the commission of any crime indoors, no matter how severe, subject to a felony burglary charge. We do not believe the legislature intended such absurd results when it amended the burglary statutes in 1976.

Because the history of our state burglary statutes makes reference to the state of California, we have previously looked to that state for guidance in interpretation of our own burglary provisions[.] The statute defining the offense of burglary in California, unlike [§] 22–32–3, does not contain the word "remains." Nevertheless, the [S]upreme [C]ourt of [California] has discussed the type of presence in a building or structure necessary for commission of burglary. [That] court has interpreted the law of burglary in that state as retaining the principle that burglary must be committed by a person who has no right to be in the building or structure burglarized. [*People v.*] *Gauze*, 125 Cal. Rptr. [773,] 775, 542 P.2d [1365,] 1367 [(1975)].

To read the word "remains" in [§ 22–32–3] to mean that a person can commit burglary when he is lawfully present in an occupied structure ... contravenes the principle [that] burglary must be committed by a person who has no right to be in the structure. However, if we were to read the word "remains" as it is qualified in the statutes of eleven other states to mean that a person can commit second degree burglary when he is *unlawfully* present or present *without authority* in an occupied structure, [then this interpretation] would avoid the possibility for absurdity and retain the principle that burglary must be committed by a person with no right to be in the structure. . . .

[Where] a person enters a business place open to the general public with the intent to commit a crime therein, he enters without invitation and is not one of the public invited or entitled to enter the structure. *People v. Barry*, 94 Cal. 481, 29 P. 1026, 1027 (1892). Relying on this premise, the California Supreme Court has reasoned that holding such a person subject to prosecution for burglary does not reflect abandonment of the principle that burglary must be committed by a person who has no right to be in the structure. We find this reasoning persuasive[.]

[We] conclude, therefore, that the word "remains" in the second degree burglary statute means to *unlawfully* remain in a structure. Therefore, second degree burglary was not committed in this case where T.J.E. entered an occupied structure and *after* entry, while *lawfully* remaining in the structure, formed the intent to commit an offense therein[.]

We find that state failed to establish that T.J.E. either entered or *unlawfully* remained in an occupied structure with the intent to commit a crime therein. Therefore, the evidence was insufficient to sustain the allegations in [the] state's delinquency petition. Accordingly, we reverse the circuit court's adjudication and disposition of T.J.E. as a juvenile delinquent.

HENDERSON, JUSTICE (specially concurring).

[Under § 22–30A–17,] [p]etty theft of less than $100 is [a] Class 2 misdemeanor [punishable by no more than 30 days jail and/or a fine of no more than $100]. Here, obviously, the shoplifting is a petty theft offense[.]

[If] an eleven year old takes a chocolate Easter egg, a few days before Easter, and without paying for it, eats it, and walks out of the store, has he/she committed second-degree burglary under the statutes of South Dakota? [The shoplifting charge] was not considered by the State. [Instead,] the State and trial court seized upon, and employed, a second-degree burglary charge. [The] preposterous result witnessed in Tripp County by the prosecution of this little girl, was a type of horror/nonsensical situation envisioned in my dissent [in] *Schult*[,] 380 N.W.2d at 358:

> "This second-degree burglary statute has a sweep whereby any and all crimes in occupied structures are amalgamated together by the same punishment depending upon the whim of the prosecutor. Prosecutors must have some channels of discretion and restraint."

[The] prosecutor [here] chose to prosecute under a felony, the child having eaten a chocolate Easter egg, rather than prosecuting for a Class 2 misdemeanor[.] No child should suffer such an adjudication upon his/her record for second-degree burglary by virtue of snitching a chocolate Easter egg and eating it without paying for it; nor, for that matter, be put under the mandate of a court with five conditions which govern the child's conduct for a period of three months. [The] child was determined, as a matter of law, to be a burglar. [The] penalty [for an adult defendant] for second-degree burglary in South Dakota is a maximum sentence of 15 years and a $15,000 fine. [The] adjudication [of delinquency] afflicts a harm upon the child which is needless and disproportionate to the act[.] For a child to go through this type of proceeding and counseling and trips to a court services officer, can be humiliating, degrading, and self-defeating. In common language, a little girl should not have been treated this way. This was a de minimis act. This case should not have reached the circuit court and Supreme Court levels. It could have been treated in an informal setting.

This prosecution creates [an] opportunity of political advantage for the prosecutor to be known as a tough prosecutor to enhance his image of convictions in the community. [But] [h]ow harmful is it to society to remove a candy chocolate egg from a store? . . .

[T.J.E.] should have, initially, been treated as a possible shoplifter with store manager and parent(s) having a conference[.] Prosecutors should use a prosecutorial function to a better advantage than displayed here. [T.J.E's] adult relative offered to pay for the chocolate egg which T.J.E. consumed before the forces of the law were set in motion. It is difficult not to scoff at this type of justice and not to feel sorry for the little girl and her aunt who were caught up in the capricious law enforcement on a given day in Tripp County. Law, in the end, does have to make sense.

POINTS FOR DISCUSSION

a. **Burglary in the Colonies**

As an offense inherited by the Colonies from British judges, the common law offense of burglary was well suited to protect colonial values. Early Americans treasured their possessions and their privacy, values still guarded today. As the Colonies became more heavily populated, urban burglary became a common problem and was treated seriously and brutally. For example, in 1647 a first-time burglar in the Massachusetts Bay Colony had the letter "B" branded on their forehead. Public shaming and humiliation were important elements of seventeenth century colonial punishment. A second offender in Massachusetts received branding and a public whipping and a third offense was a capital crime. Repeat burglars were executed in other Colonies as well, such as Maryland and Pennsylvania. In fact, it was not until 1786 that Pennsylvania reclassified burglary as a non-capital offense, something not done in Massachusetts until 1839. Why do you think burglary was treated with such severity in the seventeenth and early eighteenth centuries?

b. **Who Is a Burglar?**

The starting point for the *T.J.E.* Court's analysis is the observation that the burglary crime is meant to punish people who have "no right to be in the building or structure burglarized." The need for identifying this class of appropriate defendants is a result of the 1976 repeal of the longstanding statutory definition of burglary, rooted in the 1862 Dakota Territory Statute: "If a person break and enter the dwelling house of another in the night time, with intent to commit larceny, he shall be deemed guilty of burglary[.]" The "distinctive situation" for which this crime "was originally devised" was the "invasion of premises under circumstances that are likely to terrorize occupants." *See* Model Penal Code § 222.1, Comment (2), at 67 (1980). Proof of the breaking and entering elements usually supplied evidence of the *mens rea*, namely the intent at the time of entry to commit the requisite crime inside the dwelling. In the absence of a violent type of entry to confirm the defendant's criminal purpose for entry, the defendant was *not* a burglar and would be prosecuted instead for trespass or whatever crimes were committed inside the dwelling, such as larceny or attempted larceny.

By contrast, the broad scope of the new 1976 burglary definition in the *T.J.E.* statute requires only the act of entering *or* remaining in an occupied structure, and a literal reading implies that the timing of the formation of the requisite "intent to commit a crime therein" is irrelevant. Therefore, this statute creates two distinct problems. First, it makes it possible for a prosecutor to charge all shoplifters with burglary. Second, it provides no means for limiting the status of "burglar" to the category of target defendants who "have no right to be in the building or structure burglarized."

The task of the *T.J.E.* Court is to remedy both of these problems, through the strategy of first declaring the 1976 statute to be "ambiguous" because of the "absurd" breadth of its literal interpretation, and then finding a narrowing construction that will provide a workable formula to answer the question, Who is a burglar? As it turns out, this task implicitly requires the court to answer the more specific question, Who is a *mere* shoplifter and *not* a burglar?

It is evident that the *T.J.E* Court views the candy-eating juvenile as an impulsive shoplifter who does *not* belong in the burglary category. How does the court's narrowing interpretation of the word "remains" to mean "unlawfully remains" allow the juvenile defendant to escape liability for burglary? Note that the *T.J.E.* Court refers approvingly to the burglary conviction of the *Shult* defendant, who was caught taking a frozen pizza from a convenience store and later admitted to the police that he intended to take it when he entered the store. Why is the *Shult* defendant both a shoplifter *and* a burglar under the *T.J.E.* Court's reasoning? Would it be possible to interpret the "unlawfully-remains" concept so as to treat the *Shult* defendant as being *merely* a shoplifter and not a burglar?

c. Limiting the Expansion of Burglary

The MPC drafters viewed modern burglary statutes as too broad, recognizing that "a greatly expanded burglary statute authorizes the prosecutor and the courts to treat as burglary behavior that is distinguishable from theft [only] on purely artificial grounds." This is why the MPC burglary definition preserves the common law requirement that the *mens rea* must coincide with the act of *entry*: "A person is guilty of burglary if he enters a building or occupied structure . . . with purpose to commit a crime therein." The definition of "occupied" structure is limited to any "place adapted for overnight accommodation of persons, or for carrying on business therein, whether or not a person is actually present." *See* Model Penal Code §§ 221.0, 221.1. This restriction preserves the common law's concern with the protection of places where people might normally be present, and excludes many of the places covered by modern burglary statutes, such as aircraft, watercraft, land vehicles, and buildings of any kind. *See* Model Penal Code § 221.1, Comment 3, at 72. Although some states emulate these limitations, most state codes continue to rely on elements that resemble the contemporary statutes described in the *T.J.E.* opinion.

d. Legislative Exemptions

The problems addressed by the *T.J.E.* Court are solved in the MPC burglary definition by including two exemptions used in many states. A burglary does not occur either when "the premises are at the time [of the entry] open to the public" *or* when the defendant "is licensed or privileged to enter." The second exemption is meant to cover cases where a person's "ownership or employment interest in the premises warrant his entry" or "where there are other circumstances where a privilege to enter should be inferred." *See* Model Penal Code § 221.1, Comment 3, at 68.

e. Responses to *T.J.E.* Decision

In response to the *T.J.E.* decision, the South Dakota legislature enacted similar amendments to the definitions of second degree burglary (for occupied structures) and third degree burglary (for unoccupied structures) in 1989. The revised version of the second degree burglary statute applied to:

> Any person who enters an occupied structure with intent to commit any crime other than the act of *shoplifting*[,] or [who] remains in an occupied structure after forming the intent to commit any crime other than *shoplifting*[.]

Note that the shoplifting statute applied at the time to "any person who takes merchandise displayed for sale in a store without the consent of the owner and with the intention of converting it to the person's use without paying the purchase price for the merchandise." *See* SDCL § 22–30A.–19.1.

Even though the 1989 statute did not codify the *T.J.E.* interpretation of the 1976 statute, the South Dakota Supreme Court continued to require this interpretation until 2006. Then the court reversed its position and overruled *T.J.E.* on the theory that the legislature's failure to codify the *T.J.E.* holding in the 1989 statute constituted an implicit rejection of it. *See State v. Burdick*, 712 N.W.2d 5 (S.D. 2006). By this time, however, the South Dakota legislature had amended the burglary statutes again in 2005. A few years later, the court ruled that the legislature's failure to codify the *T.J.E.* holding in the 2005 statute implied the intent to reject that holding again. *See State v. Miranda*, 776 N.W.2d 77 (S.D. 2009). The amended 2005 statute is still in force, and the second degree burglary statute now emulates the exemptions in the MPC, because it applies to:

> Any person who enters or remains in an occupied structure with intent to commit any crime, unless the premises are, at the at the time, open to the public or the person is licensed or privileged to enter or remain[.]

Hypo 1: *The Florida "Superthief"*

It is estimated that John Arthur MacLean, the self-styled "Superthief," committed more than 2,000 Florida burglaries of Florida homes in the 1970s, netting an estimated $133 million in jewels and cash. His burglaries were meticulously done with a bit of humor thrown in for his own entertainment. Whether it was gluing dentures to doorknobs, eating and drinking food he found, or forgoing "unworthy" gems for the control panel of his victim's alarm, MacLean left his mark, along with a used Milky Way candy wrapper, which was his signature calling card. After MacLean was finally caught and convicted, just $1 million of his profits were recovered, leaving several million dollars of the fruits of his heists unaccounted for.

Consider MacClean's success in eluding the police and committing so many burglary crimes fifty years ago. What factors may have contributed to his success—and to his ultimate capture? What does MacClean's success suggest regarding the enforcement priorities and investigative capacities of the Florida police forces in the 1970s? If MacClean had engaged in stealing cars instead of burglarizing homes, would he have been as successful in the 1970s or in the present day? What changes in the priorities and investigative capacities of police forces today might make it easier to capture a burglar like MacClean? Aside from burglary, what other unsolved crimes might MacClean have committed in the 1970s, which crimes could now be prosecuted with evidence sufficient to convict him—and why?

Hypo 2: *Leaving Store*

A security officer in a J.C. Penney's store was behind an observation window when he saw Ellis concealing sportswear items under her clothing and in her purse. The officer, who was holding his walkie-talkie radio transmitter, followed her out of the store. When Ellis was 10 feet outside the store, she turned around and saw the officer directly approaching her, radio in hand. Ellis then ran back into the store and threw the sportswear items under a rack displaying other clothing. Does this evidence prove all the elements of larceny? *Compare State v. Ellis*, 618 So.2d 616 (La. App. 1993).

Hypo 3: *Snatching Property*

Assume that a Florida statute defines robbery as the "taking of property from the person of another" when "in the course of the taking there is the use of force or putting in fear." However, the term "force" is not defined in the statute, and it is unclear whether the crime applies to the snatching of property, out of the hands of a victim or from the victim's person, before the victim realizes what happened. Should the snatching of property, by no more force than is necessary to remove the property from an unresisting victim, qualify as robbery under the Florida statutes? Explain the pro and con arguments here. *Compare Robinson v. State*, 692 So.2d 883 (Fla. 1997).

Hypo 4 *Handing over the Cashier's Drawer*

Bob walked into the Jiffy Lube Automobile Service Center at 3:00 pm and approached the cashier, Tina, who was standing alone at the cash register. Only a few customers were in the store at the time. When Bob was charged with robbery, Tina testified at his trial, stating that, "I got robbed." When asked for details, Tina said that she did not know Bob and assumed that he was a customer with a question. Then Bob said, "Don't say anything." Bob did not point anything at her. Then Tina handed Bob the cash register drawer. He walked away with the drawer, which was full of cash, and he left the store. When Tina was asked whether she believed that Bob had a weapon, she testified that, "I wasn't taking any chances.' When asked to describe Bob's appearance, Tina stated that he had a tear drop tattoo under one eye. When asked what this tattoo meant to her, Tina testified that, "One of my friends got the same tattoo when one of his relatives died. But I've heard that sometimes people get that tattoo in prison." Bob was convicted of robbery and sentenced to 15 years. The maximum larceny sentence would have been two years but Bob was not charged with larceny. The only issue raised by Bob's defense counsel on appeal is the sufficiency of the evidence that Bob "took property either by means of force or by putting the other person in fear of violence." What pro and con arguments will be made by the prosecution and defense regarding the evidence on this issue?

Hypo 5: *Who Is a Burglar?*

Millie is a truck driver who delivers milk to stores on her route. She has keys that allow her to enter each store through the back door so that she can put the milk containers into the refrigerators located in the storeroom areas. One evening at midnight, Millie is putting away the milk at a store in Bismarck, South Dakota, when she happens to notice that the refrigerator contains two six-packs of her favorite root beer. So she takes one of the six-packs with her when she drives away. A few minutes later, Rick emerges from the restroom inside the store. Rick had entered the store at 10:55 p.m. and purchased a candy bar. Then he went to the restroom. The clerk locked up the store at 11:00 p.m. and failed to notice that Rick never left the restroom. Rick peeks into the refrigerator, notices the remaining six-pack of root beer, picks it up, and leaves the store with it. The next morning, Palmer arrives at the store after it opens, picks up a carton of eggs, and pays for it at the cash register. As he walks toward the exit door, Palmer notices a display of root beer for sale inside the store. He picks up one can of root beer and palms it, dropping it into his pocket as he leaves. Are any of these three people guilty of burglary? Explain whether the prosecutor can obtain convictions against Millie, Rick, and Palmer, under each of these statutes: 1) the 1976 burglary statute as construed in the *T.J.E.* opinion; 2) the amended 1989 burglary statute; 3) the amended 2005 burglary statute. *Compare State v. Burdick*, 712 N.W.2d 5 (S.D. 2006); *State v. Miranda*, 776 N.W.2d 77 (S.D. 2009).

> **Hypo 6: *Defining Structure***
>
> Vic is an artist and he uses the back room of his house as a workshop. He has built a "lean-to" structure to provide sheltered parking for people who visit his workshop and he parks his own truck inside the lean-to. The outside wall of the workshop provides one wall for the lean-to, and Vic constructs two more walls and puts a roof on top. But one side of the lean-to is left completely open, so that cars can be parked inside. Vic also installs a door in the wall of his workshop to permit entry into the lean-to from the house. Vic has installed motion detectors with an alarm system all around the lean-to structure. One night when the alarm goes off, Vic finds Sara inside the lean-to, holding Vic's property that she has taken from a shelf on the wall. Sara is convicted of burglary under a Kansas statute that provides: "Burglary is entering into any building, manufactured home, mobile home, tent or other structure which is not a dwelling, with intent to commit a felony therein." On appeal, what reasoning could the court use to support the ruling that Vic's lean-to is not a "structure" within the meaning of the burglary statute? *Compare State v. Moler*, 269 Kan. 362, 2 P.3d 773 (2000).

CHAPTER 11

Justification Defenses

The defenses that are commonly known as "justification" defenses include self-defense, defense of others, defense of property and of dwelling, the law enforcement defense, and the necessity or choice of evils defense. Each defense has a different common law history, but most of these defenses share a special concern with the use of deadly force which a defendant seeks to justify on the basis of a belief in some perceived danger to human life. Most of the limitations on these defenses, which are imposed by statutes and case law, concern the meaning of the requirements as "necessity," "imminence," and the "reasonableness" of the defendant's belief in that prospect of danger.

A. OVERVIEW OF THE LAW

Self-Defense. This defense requires a person to have a reasonable belief that the use of deadly force is necessary in order to avoid the imminent threat of deadly force from another person. An aggressor who is the first to use deadly force against another person will lose the right of self-defense unless the aggressor withdraws from the conflict. Most states require the duty to retreat in public spaces, and the castle doctrine protects a person from the need to retreat in his or her dwelling from an intruder—and sometimes from a cohabitant.

Imperfect Self-Defense. Some courts define this defense as being applicable to a case where a defendant is unreasonable in his or her perception of imminent danger, or in his or her belief that deadly force is necessary to respond to the danger, or both.

Defense of Dwelling. This defense traditionally required a reasonable belief that an intruder threatened harm to the occupants of a dwelling, but new statutory rights to use deadly force have modified or eliminated this requirement.

Necessity or Choice of Evils. The all-purpose MPC definition of this defense requires that a person must believe that their violation of a law is required

> **Major Themes**
>
> **a. Influence of the MPC**—The MPC made a significant contribution in clarifying the elements of the justification defenses and in influencing the codification of those elements. The MPC endorsed some rules that continue to attract support from a majority of states, such as the duty to retreat.
>
> **b. Modern Expansion of Defenses**—There has been notable legislative expansion of the right to use deadly force in situations where self-defense would not be justified, specifically concerning the right to use such force against intruders into a dwelling or a vehicle. The use of expert testimony concerning the effects of battering has become a widespread norm for trials of battered criminal defendants, and self-defense claims by such defendants continues to test the limitations imposed by the traditional requirements of self-defense.

in order to avoid a greater evil, assuming that the evil avoided is greater than the one sought to be prevented by the enforcement of the law. Courts sometimes rely on "factor tests" to delineate the scope of a necessity defense for a particular category of recurring claims.

B. SELF-DEFENSE

The English common law interpretation of self-defense allowed a person to use deadly force against an aggressor who threatened deadly force, as long as the defensive use of such force was necessary because of the imminent threat of death or great bodily harm that was posed by the aggressor's conduct. What was essential, however, was not the factual reality of these conditions, but the requirement of a reasonable belief in both the imminence and deadly character of the threat, and in the necessity of using deadly force for self-protection from that threat. Modern statutory definitions of self-defense usually reflect some versions of these elements.

1. Necessity & Duty to Retreat

The English common law required a reasonable belief in the necessity of using deadly force in self-defense, and one hallmark of this necessity was the defender's compliance with the duty to retreat before resorting to deadly force. The state courts recognized this requirement until the 1870s, when one court declared that a "true man" should not be "obliged to fly" from an attacker, but should be able to stand his ground without retreating, in order to use deadly force in self-defense. The *Brown* case illustrates the influence of "no duty to retreat" rule some 50 years later in federal court, by which time this position had gained the support of many state courts.

BROWN V. UNITED STATES
256 U.S. 335 (1921).

MR. JUSTICE HOLMES delivered the opinion of the Court.

The petitioner was convicted of murder in the second degree committed upon one Hermis at a place in Texas within the exclusive jurisdiction of the United States, and the judgment was affirmed by the Circuit Court of Appeals[.] A writ of certiorari was granted by this Court[.] . . .

[One] question [that is raised] concerns the instructions at the trial. There had been trouble between Hermis and the defendant for a long time. There was evidence that Hermis had twice assaulted the defendant with a knife and had made threats communicated to the defendant that the next time, one of them would go off in a black box. On the day in question the defendant [was on federal property,] superintending excavation work for a post office [in Beeville, Texas]. In view of Hermis's threats[,] [the defendant] had taken a pistol with him and had laid it in his coat upon a dump. Hermis was driven up by a witness, in a cart to be loaded, and the defendant said that certain earth was not to be removed, whereupon Hermis came toward him, the defendant says, with a knife. The defendant retreated some twenty or twenty-five feet to where his coat was and got his pistol. Hermis was striking at him and the defendant fired four shots and killed [Hermis]. The judge instructed the jury among other things that "it is necessary to remember, in considering the question of self defence, that the party assaulted is always under the obligation to retreat so long as retreat is open to him, provided that he can do so without subjecting himself to the danger of death or great bodily harm." The instruction was reinforced by the further intimation that unless "retreat would have appeared to a man of reasonable prudence, in the position of the defendant, as involving danger of death or serious bodily harm[,]" the defendant was not entitled to stand his ground. An instruction to the effect that if the defendant had reasonable grounds of apprehension that he was in danger of losing his life or of suffering serious bodily harm from Hermis he was not bound to retreat was refused. So the question is brought out with sufficient clearness whether the formula laid down by the Court and often repeated by the ancient law is adequate to the protection of the defendant's rights.

[Concrete] cases or illustrations stated in the early law in conditions very different from the present[,] like the reference to retreat in Coke['s] [Third Institute (1669)], have had a tendency to ossify into specific rules without much regard for reason. Rationally the failure to retreat is a circumstance to be considered with all the others in order to determine whether the defendant went farther than he was justified in doing[,] not a categorical proof of guilt. The law has grown, and even if historical mistakes have contributed to its growth it has tended in the direction of rules consistent with human nature. Many respectable writers agree that if a man reasonably believes that he is in immediate danger of death or grievous bodily harm from his assailant he may stand his ground and that if he kills him he has not [exceeded] the bounds of lawful self defence[.] Detached reflection cannot be demanded in the presence of an uplifted knife. Therefore in this Court, at least, it is not a condition of immunity that one in that situation should pause to consider whether a reasonable man might not think it possible to fly with safety or to disable his assailant rather than to kill him[.] The law of Texas very strongly adopts these views as is shown by many cases[.]

[There] was evidence that the last shot was fired after Hermis was down. The jury might not believe the defendant's testimony that it was an accidental discharge[.] [But even] if the last shot was intentional and may seem to have been unnecessary[,] the defendant would not necessarily lose his immunity if it followed close upon the others while the heat of the conflict was on, and if the defendant believed that he was fighting for his life.

The Government presents a different case. It denies that Hermis had a knife and even that Brown was acting in self defence. Notwithstanding the repeated threats of Hermis and intimations that one of the two would die at the next encounter, which seem hardly to be denied, of course it was possible for the jury to find that Brown had not sufficient reason to think that his life was in danger at that time, that he exceeded the limits of reasonable self defence or even that he was the attacking party. But upon the hypothesis to which the evidence gave much color, that Hermis began the attack, the instruction [on the duty to retreat] was wrong.

Judgment reversed.

POINTS FOR DISCUSSION

a. Rejection of the Duty to Retreat

Soon after the Ohio Supreme Court opined in 1876 that a "true man" should not be bound by the duty to retreat, the Indiana Supreme Court endorsed this position in 1877, reasoning that the right of self-defense is "founded on the law of nature[,] and is not, nor can be, superseded by any law of society." The court declared that, "[T]he tendency of the American mind seems to be very strongly against the enforcement of any rule which requires a person to flee when assailed[.]" The Texas Supreme Court decided in 1885 that although the common law required "the assailed party to 'retreat to the wall' ", it was unnecessary to maintain that doctrine because the Texas Penal Code had abandoned it. Therefore, defendants should have the right to obtain a jury instruction that there was no duty to retreat required to invoke the defense of self-defense. One scholar describes the spread of the "no duty to retreat" doctrine as "[f]ollowing the westward movement of settlers from the Appalachians to the Pacific Coast," and notes that the rule "became so deeply entrenched" in Texas "as to be referred to by legal scholars generally as the 'Texas rule.' " *See* RICHARD MAXWELL BROWN, NO DUTY TO RETREAT: VIOLENCE AND VALUES IN AMERICAN HISTORY AND SOCIETY 8, 26 (1991).

b. Preservation of the Duty to Retreat

The MPC Commentary observes that Justice Holmes did not advocate in *Brown* that a rigid "no duty to retreat" rule should be adopted as a rule for the federal criminal law. Instead, he advanced "what seems to be a median position," which is expressed in his statement that, "rationally the failure to retreat is a circumstance to be considered with all the others in order to determine whether the defendant went farther than he was justified in doing[,] not a categorical proof of guilt." This Commentary also describes the duty to retreat rule as a "logical derivative of the underlying justifying principle of self-defense: belief in the necessity of the protective action." The MPC position is that the duty to retreat only arises when a person needs to use deadly force, "and even then retreat is only a requisite if the actor knows that [he or she] can avoid the need to use such force *with complete safety* by retreating." This standard is supported by the assumption that "it is to be expected that all doubts will be resolved in the actor's favor, and that such moral claim as there is to standing one's ground can easily be recognized in the doubtful cases." The MPC drafters placed "a high value on the preservation of life." Therefore, they were not willing to recognize the "moral claim to exoneration" of an actor who "kills when [he or she] clearly need not do so" for self-protection—"when, in other words, [the actor] knows that he can avoid the need to kill at no risk to [self]." *See* Model Penal Code § 3.04, Comment (4)(c), at 52–55. Today many states continue to endorse some version of the duty to retreat, although many others now support limitations upon its enforcement.

c. Defense of Others

The elements of the "defense of others" are similar to the elements of self-defense. One important requirement for the defense of others is that a person must reasonably believe that the other person is being subjected to an unlawful use of force. Only if such force is deadly may a person resort to deadly force in an attempt to defend the other. If it turns out that, unbeknownst to the rescuer, the force used against the other person was lawful, as when an undercover officer uses force to arrest the other person, the older view was that the defense of others would be unavailable because the other had no right to defend himself or herself. However, this "alter ego" rule is not endorsed in more recent statutes and case law that protect a defendant who reasonably believes that another person is being unlawfully attacked.

d. Original Castle Doctrine

The English common law's commitment to the duty to retreat was limited to the sphere of public spaces and did not apply to a defendant's dwelling. Instead, judges viewed a person's home as that person's "castle," where retreat was never required before resorting to the use of deadly force in self-defense. Some state courts applied this "no duty to retreat in the castle" doctrine to cases involving the use of deadly force against both intruders and cohabitants of the dwelling. Other state courts, however, limited this doctrine to invocations of the right to self-defense against an intruder, and rejected the right of cohabitants to invoke the castle doctrine against each other.

e. Aggressor Rule

An aggressor is a person who cannot invoke self-defense at common law because the aggressor was the first person to threaten the use of deadly force. The defender who responds to an aggressor justifiably with deadly force is the person who is entitled to claim self-defense. However, an aggressor who threatens non-deadly force may become a person who is then threatened unjustifiably with deadly force in response. In this case, the initial aggressor will be entitled to claim self-defense when responding in kind with deadly force. Notably, an aggressor who is the first to threaten deadly force, and thereby loses the right to self-defense, will be able to regain that right as long as the aggressor takes steps to make it clear to the defender that the aggressor is withdrawing from the conflict in good faith.

What are the differences between the duty to retreat instruction rejected by Justice Holmes and the MPC definition of the duty to retreat? How would the MPC drafters explain why the MPC definition is preferable to the "median position" taken by Holmes? How would the defendant in *Brown* argue for self-defense under the MPC version of the duty to retreat? *See* point f. *infra* for MPC language.

f. Model Penal Code Approach

The MPC § 3.04(2)(b) states that the use of *deadly* force is not justifiable unless a person *believes* that such force is *necessary* for self-protection against death or serious bodily injury. A person *also* must *believe* that such force is *immediately* necessary for that purpose against the use of unlawful force by another person *on the present occasion* under MPC § 3.04(1).

The MPC § 3.04(2)(b)(ii)(A) defines the duty to retreat as follows: "The use of deadly force is not justifiable if . . . the person knows that [he or she] can avoid the necessity of using such force with complete safety by retreating . . . except that the person is not obliged to retreat from his dwelling or place of work, unless [he or she] was the initial aggressor[.]"

The MPC § 3.04(2)(b)(i) defines an aggressor who loses the right to use deadly force self-defense as a person, who "with the purpose of causing death or serious bodily injury, provoked the use of force against [himself or herself] in the same encounter." The right to self-defense may be regained "by so far breaking off the struggle that any renewal by the other party can be viewed as a distinct engagement." Model Penal Code § 3.04, Comment 4(b), at 52.

2. Reasonable Belief & Imperfect Self-Defense

The common law required an objectively reasonable belief in the elements of self-defense. But the Model Penal Code drafters describe this defense as applying to any person who "believes" in the existence of the relevant elements, in order to make it clear that only a subjective belief is necessary, not an objectively "reasonable" belief. Most states use a hybrid standard. It may be difficult to define and apply such a standard, when the difference between acquittal and conviction for homicide crimes depends on the jury's assessment of a defendant's beliefs.

POINTS FOR DISCUSSION

a. Comparing Mistake & Imperfect Self-Defense

Courts are called upon to limit the benefit of acquittal to defendants with worthy self-defense claims, while according some lesser benefit to defendants with less worthy self-defense claims and implicitly greater culpability. The MPC drafters preferred to label the latter class of defendants as people who had made a "mistake" about the necessity for using deadly force. Although they may have "believed" in this necessity. But if they were reckless or negligent in forming that belief under the circumstances, then they could be convicted of recklessness or negligence crimes. Even so, they could not be convicted of crimes with purposely or knowingly mental states, because an honest, good faith, subjective yet mistaken belief in self-defense will disable a prosecutor from proving such mental states.

b. Objections to the Subjective Standard

Courts have criticized the MPC's reliance on a subjective standard that is expressed through conferring the right to self-defense on any person who "believes" in the existence of the relevant elements of the defense. For example, in the *Goetz* case, the court reasoned that interpreting the statutory definition of self-defense "to require only that the defendant's belief was 'reasonable to *him*'" would be to allow "the defendant's own perceptions" to "completely exonerate him from any criminal liability." In the court's view, "[t]o completely exonerate such an individual, no matter how aberrational or bizarre his thought patterns, would allow citizens to set their own standards for the permissible use of force." *See People v. Goetz*, 68 N.Y.2d 96, 497 N.E.2d 41, 506 N.Y.S.2d 18 (1986).

c. Measuring Reasonableness

By contrast, the *Goetz* Court's endorsement of the so-called hybrid standard may help to explain the continued adherence of a majority of states to the requirement of an objectively "reasonable" belief in all the elements of self-defense. The measure of such "reasonableness," according to the *Goetz* Court, should take into account "the 'circumstances' facing a defendant [in] his 'situation.'" These circumstances include "the physical movements of the potential assailant," "any relevant knowledge the defendant had about that person," "the physical attributes of all persons involved, including the defendant," and "any prior experiences" the defendant had which could provide a "reasonable basis" for the belief that a threat of deadly force was to be expected from the potential assailant, and thus, that the use of deadly force was needed for self-protection.

3. Battered Defendants

In the early 1980s, defense counsel began to seek admission of expert testimony concerning the battering experiences of defendants who killed their batterers and were charged with murder or manslaughter crimes. These defense counsel also requested jury instructions on self-defense that would allow a jury to consider how the battering experience could inform the reasonableness of a battered defendant's belief in the necessity of using deadly force for self-protection against the imminent threat of death or great bodily harm posed by a batterer. For the first decade of the era when these claims by battered defendants came to the attention of the courts, it was difficult for their counsel to achieve either of these goals. The following case illustrates the responses of one court that ultimately became the norm in the case law of many states.

BECHTEL V. STATE
840 P.2d 1 (Okla. Crim. App. 1992).

JOHNSON, JUDGE:

[Donna Lee Brechtel was convicted of first degree murder for the killing of her husband, Ken Brechtel, and sentenced by the jury to life imprisonment. On appeal she argued that the trial judge erred in refusing to allow expert testimony on the battered women syndrome. The court concluded that the trial court's failure to allow this testimony amounted to reversible error requiring a new trial.]

The following facts are primarily from the testimony of the Appellant[.] Although there was great conflict between her testimony and that as presented by the State, [we] are presenting her testimony to show facts necessary to meet the first prong of our guidelines under the Battered Woman Syndrome.

[Appellant married the victim, Ken Brechtel, on August 25, 1982.] She recalled that the first incidence of violence perpetrated by the victim upon her was on July 4, 1982, when around midnight, he began crying about his deceased son and, in a drunken rage, grabbed her by the head and threw her into the windshield of his boat. As she tried to get to the telephone, he started to throw canned goods out of the closet at her. She left but was caught and put in a car by Ken; while they were stopped at a stop sign, she jumped out of the car. Mr. Bechtel came around the side of the car, threw her back in, and told her not to ever do that again. Inside the car, he grabbed her head by the hair and slammed her into the window and again, told her not to get out of the car. When they arrived at her home, Appellant jumped out of the car, ran into her house and locked the doors. When Ken Bechtel threatened to kick the "m ... f ..." door in, Appellant responded by telling him that she had guns in her home. Mr. Bechtel eventually left. This was the first of approximately 23 battering incidents leading to the fatal shooting on September 23, 1984.

Testimony at trial revealed that the deceased committed the batterings when intoxicated and without provocation. The batterings consisted of the deceased grabbing Appellant by either her ears or hair and pounding her head on the ground, wall, door, cabinet or other available object. During many of the episodes he would sob profusely and ramble about his deceased son who was born retarded. During all of the episodes, the deceased threatened or otherwise intimidated Appellant.

On three occasions, Appellant was treated in the Emergency Room. On each of the occasions, the deceased provided the information as to the cause of the injury. On one occasion, Appellant was treated for neck injury and provided with a neck collar. On the other occasions, she was treated for cuts to her hand and feet. On five occasions, Appellant sought police help. Each time the police arrived at her home, the deceased was made to leave. On one occasion, Appellant stopped at the scene of an accident and asked the policeman at the scene to remove the deceased who, in a drunken rage, was kicking the windshield and beating on the dashboard. The deceased was removed and taken to the residence and was there when Appellant arrived. Appellant was subsequently beaten by the deceased.

On several occasions, Appellant was able to escape her residence and stay overnight at various hotels. Appellant related the incidents to some of her close friends and the deceased's family. However, though some of the abuse occurred on business trips, she never told the deceased's business associates. Appellant also sought help from the deceased's family as to his alcohol problem. She made inquiries of several treatment facilities and made appointments for the deceased, who promised after later incidents to undergo treatment, but never did.

On September 23, 1984, the day of his death, the deceased returned home unexpectedly at approximately 5:30 a.m. from a hunting trip, highly intoxicated. He awakened Appellant and ordered her to get out of the bed so they could have a drink. He ordered her out on the patio where the deceased related to her and her friend, [Ms.] Billy Bender, who was visiting from out of state, that he had been picked up for driving under the influence by the Nichols Hills Police. Ken Bechtel continued to drink coffee with liquor. He became angry when Appellant kept turning down the jukebox whenever he would turn it up.

After about three or four hours, Appellant decided to go back to bed. Once in her bedroom, she could hear Mr. Bechtel crying. She became afraid. Aware that Ms. Bender might be in difficulty, she went to the doors of the patio to try to get Ms. Bender's attention. Finally, Ms. Bender came inside to get some cigarettes. When she tried to return to the patio, Appellant admonished her not to go back but to leave Mr. Bechtel alone to sleep it off and for her to go to bed immediately. The next thing Appellant remembered was hearing the night table drawer opening and seeing the deceased with the .25 gun in his hand. He told Appellant that she would not need that G. D. gun anymore.

As he walked towards the door leading to the backyard, Appellant jumped up and ran to the closet where she frantically looked for her purse and keys. After retrieving her purse, she turned to go to the kitchen when a naked Ken Bechtel pulled her by the hair and threw her back on the bed. He was rambling and crying about his son Kenny and questioning her about why she was not at home when he tried to call her earlier. He held his arm against her throat. Appellant raised her leg to free herself when they both fell onto the floor. The deceased threatened to "f—k you and kill your ass." He began pounding her head into the floor. He picked her up by the head and pulled her back on the bed. He pulled her gown off and rammed his fingers into her vagina. He then climbed on top of her, held her down by placing his knees on her arms and banged her head against the headboard. He ejaculated on her face and stomach, after which he slumped on top of her. She eased from under him and went to the bathroom to wash herself.

While in the bathroom, the deceased came up behind her, grabbed the back of her head, threw her down on the floor, bit her on the left breast and finally lay his head on her lower body. During this time, Appellant tried to calm him down by repeating it's okay, it's all right. Then the telephone rang. It was a friend inquiring about his luggage. During this time, Appellant vomited. As she was trying to put on some clothes, Ken returned, accusing her of taking the friend's luggage and betting that she thought it was her "G.D." kids. He put her arm behind her back and his arm against her throat and forced her back onto the bed. At this point his eyes were glazed over and he was crying and rambling as he continued to beat her head against the headboard. He slumped on top of her.

Appellant tried to get from under him, but he would mumble whenever she made an effort. Finally, she eased herself from under him. As she sat on her knees on the floor beside the bed, she lit a cigarette, held it in one hand and her head with the other hand. As she got ready to smoke the cigarette, she heard a gurgling sound, looked up and saw the contorted look and glazed eyes of the deceased with his arms raised. Appellant reached for the gun under the bed and shot the deceased as she tried to get up and run.

Appellant defended this case on the theory of self-defense. In Oklahoma, self-defense is the subject of statutory and case law. The relevant portions of [the self-defense statute provide]:

> Homicide is also justifiable when committed by any person ... in the lawful defense of such person ... when there is a reasonable ground to apprehend a design to commit a felony, or to do some great personal injury, and imminent danger of such design being accomplished[.]

This Court has held that the bare belief that one is about to suffer death or great personal injury will not, in itself, justify taking the life of his adversary. There must exist *reasonable* grounds for such belief at the time of the killing. Further, the right to take another's life in self-defense is not to be tested by the honesty or good faith of the defendant's belief in the necessity of the killing, but by the fact whether he had *reasonable* grounds for such belief. Fear alone never justifies one person to take the life of another. Such fear must have been induced by some overt act, gesture or word spoken by the deceased at the time the homicide occurred which would form a *reasonable* ground for the belief that the accused is about to suffer death or great bodily harm.

For the purposes of deciding this appeal, we analyze two of the requirements of self-defense: (1) *reasonableness* and (2) *imminence*. These two requirements, as applied to this case, can be understood only within the framework of the Battered Woman Syndrome.

1. *Admissibility of Testimony as It Relates to the Battered Woman Syndrome*

On appeal, Appellant contends that the trial court erred in refusing to allow expert testimony on the battered woman syndrome as such testimony would aid the trier of fact in assessing how her experiences as a battered woman affected her state of mind at the time of the killing. This, she argues, goes to the *reasonableness* of her belief that she was in *imminent* danger. We agree.

An offer of proof concerning the admissibility of testimony on the Battered Woman Syndrome was made in-camera where the trial judge heard testimony from Dr. Lenore Walker, a licensed, practicing psychologist and diplomate in clinical psychology who pioneered the research on the Battered Woman Syndrome, and the State's witness, Dr. Herbert C. Modlin, a licensed, practicing psychiatrist. Dr. Walker discussed the methodology used by her in diagnosing such syndrome and related that this is taught in the graduate schools and accepted in the entire scientific community of research. On refusing to allow the testimony, the trial judge offered [these] reasons: 1) The lack of general acceptance of the theory in the psychological community based on the fact that the syndrome is not listed in the *Diagnostic and Statistical Manual of Mental Disorders-3-R* (DMS-3R), a publication of the American Psychiatric Association; and 2) The testimony did not appear to be necessary or helpful to the jury since the jury was capable of making a decision based on all of the evidence.

We find no support for the trial court's first reason. The relevant scientific community in this case is the psychological community and not the psychiatric community. Moreover, both experts acknowledged that the syndrome is considered a sub-category of Post-traumatic Stress Disorder, which is generally accepted and is listed in the DSM-3R. Based upon our independent review of the available sources on the subject, we believe that the syndrome is a mixture of both psychological and physiological symptoms but is not a mental disease in the context of insanity. Further, we believe that because psychologists see more battered women than psychiatrists, the psychological community has had the opportunity to be and, indeed, have been more responsive to the problems or symptoms experienced by those suffering from the syndrome.

Other courts have accepted the syndrome as a scientifically recognized theory. To date, thirty-one (31) states and the District of Columbia allow the use of expert testimony on the subject. Five (5) states acknowledged its validity, but held the testimony inadmissible based on the facts of the particular case. In addition, hundreds of books, articles and commentaries have been written and numerous studies have been done on the subject. Based on the aforesaid, we find that the Battered Woman Syndrome is a substantially scientifically accepted theory.

We next address the trial court's ruling that expert testimony does not appear to be necessary or helpful to the jury since Appellant's testimony [describes] numerous drunken assaults and threats, including the vicious assault and threat to kill her on the night of the homicide, [which] are, in the trial court's opinion, "easily within the common understanding of all the jurors and easily come within the legal definition of self-defense. The jury may consider all the rest of the evidence offered and yet to be offered in conjunction with the Defendant's statement of the incident, and they can make the decision." We do not agree, especially in light of the two inquiries submitted by the jury during its deliberation. These inquiries demonstrate the lack of common understanding of the elements of self-defense, particularly where the defendant is a battered woman.

Expert testimony in Oklahoma is admissible if it will assist the trier of fact in search of the truth and augment the normal experience of the juror by helping him or her draw proper conclusions concerning particular behavior of a victim in a particular circumstance or circumstances. [The evidence rule in 12 O.S.1981 § 2702] provides: "If scientific, technical or *other specialized knowledge* will assist the trier of fact to understand the evidence or to determine a fact in issue, a witness qualified as an expert by knowledge, skill, experience, training or education may testify in the form of an opinion or otherwise." (Emphasis added).

Appellant argues that expert testimony regarding the syndrome is admissible to help the jury understand the battered woman, and, why Appellant acted out of a reasonable belief that she was in imminent danger when considering the issue of self-defense. We agree.

While the Court does not, as a matter of law, adopt the definition of a "Battered Woman", it was first defined by Dr. Lenore Walker in her book, THE BATTERED WOMAN SYNDROME (1979), as follows:

> The battered woman is a woman who is repeatedly subjected to any forceful, physical or psychological behavior by a man in order to coerce her to do something he wants her to do without any concern for her rights. Battered women include wives or women in any form of intimate relationship with men. Furthermore, in order to be classified as a battered woman, the couple must go through the battering cycle at least twice. Any woman may find herself in an abusive relationship with a man once. If it occurs a second time, and she remains in the situation, she is defined as a battered woman. *Id.* at XV.

Misconceptions regarding battered women abound, making it more likely than not that the average juror will draw from his or her own experience or common myths, which may lead to a wholly incorrect conclusion. Thus, we believe that expert testimony on the syndrome is necessary to counter these misconceptions. . . .

We believe that the Battered Woman Syndrome has gained substantial scientific acceptance and will aid the trier of fact in determining facts in issue, i.e., *reasonableness* and *imminence* (discussed below), when testimony on the same is offered in cases of self-defense[.] Thus, we conclude that the trial court erred in not allowing testimony on the syndrome. We find the trial court's failure to allow said testimony amounts to reversible error requiring a new trial.

2. *Reasonableness and the Battered Woman Syndrome*

The key to the defense of self-defense is reasonableness. A defendant must show that she had a *reasonable* belief as to the *imminence* of great bodily harm or death and as to the force necessary to compel it. Several of the psychological symptoms that develop in one suffering from the syndrome are particularly relevant to the standard of *reasonableness* in self-defense. One such symptom is a greater sensitivity to danger which has come about because of the intimacy and history of the relationship. Dr. Walker, in her offer of proof below, explained that the abuse occurs in a cycle (The Cycle Theory), which consists of three phases. The first phase is the "tension-building" period. The second stage is the "acute-explosion" period, where the abuse takes place. The third stage is the "loving, contrition" period.

It is during the tension-building period that the battered woman develops a heightened sensitivity to any kinds of cues of distress. Thus, because of her intimate knowledge of her batterer, the battered woman perceives danger faster and more accurately as she is more acutely aware that a new or escalated violent episode is about to occur.

> What is or is not an overt demonstration of violence varies with the circumstances. Under some circumstances a slight movement may justify instant action because of reasonable apprehension of danger, under other circumstances this would not be so. And it is for the jury, and not for the judge passing upon the weight and effect of the evidence, to determine how this may be.

Indeed, considering her particular circumstances, the battered woman's perception of the situation and her belief as to the *imminence* of great bodily harm or death may be deemed *reasonable*.

During the loving, contrition period, the abuser makes amends by being loving, making promises to change and avowing that the abuse will never happen again. It is during this stage that the battered woman is being positively reinforced by her abuser. In most battering cases, this period is of the longest duration. The cultural characteristics of women influence the battered woman's belief that if she could only do something to help her abuser, then the bad part of him will go away. Thus, the battered woman learns to develop coping skills rather than escape skills and develops a "psychological paralysis" and "learned helplessness."

Thus, Dr. Walker's testimony as to how Appellant's particular experiences as a battered woman suffering from the Battered Woman Syndrome affected her perceptions of danger, its imminence, what actions were necessary to protect herself and the reasonableness of those perceptions are relevant and necessary to prove Appellant's defense of self-defense. However, it now becomes necessary to determine the standard of reasonableness against which the finder of fact must measure the accused's belief.

Standards of reasonableness has been traditionally characterized as either "objective" or "subjective." Under the objective standard of reasonableness, the trier of fact is required to view the circumstances, surrounding the accused at the time of the use of force, from the standpoint of hypothetical reasonable person. Under the subjective standard of reasonableness, the fact finder is required to determine whether the circumstances, surrounding the accused at the time of the use of force, are sufficient to induce in the accused an honest and reasonable belief that he/she must use force to defend himself/herself against imminent harm.

Oklahoma's standard of reasonableness may be gleaned from past decisions of this Court and is set forth in [jury instruction 743], which reads as follows:

> A person is justified in using deadly force in self-defense if that person reasonably believed that use of deadly force was necessary to protect herself from imminent danger of death or great bodily harm. Self-defense is a defense although the danger to life or personal security may not have been real, if a reasonable person, in the circumstances and from the viewpoint of the defendant, would reasonably have believed that she was in imminent danger of death or great bodily harm.

The aforesaid instruction was given in this case. While the instruction explicitly states that the fact finder should assume the viewpoint and circumstances of the defendant in assessing the reasonableness of his or her belief, i.e. subjective, it also requires the defendant's viewpoint to be that of a reasonable person, in similar circumstances and with the same perceptions, i.e., objective. Thus, Oklahoma's standard is a hybrid, combining both the objective and subjective standards[.] . . .

However, in light of the jury's inquiry and our decision today to allow testimony on the Battered Woman Syndrome in appropriate cases, we deem it necessary to modify [jury instruction] 743 by striking the words "reasonably" and "reasonable" from such instruction. We hereby adopt a new [743A] instruction that will be given in all Battered Woman Syndrome cases. Such modified instruction shall read as follows:

> A person is justified in using deadly force in self-defense if that person believed that use of deadly force was necessary to protect herself from imminent danger of death or great bodily harm. Self-defense is a defense although the danger to life or personal security may not have been real, if a person, in the circumstances and from the viewpoint of the defendant, would reasonably have believed that she was in imminent danger of death or great bodily harm.

3. *Imminence and the Battered Woman Syndrome*

In addition to the reasonableness standard, Oklahoma's law of self-defense also imposes the temporal requirement of *imminence*. The thinking is that it is unreasonable to be provoked to the point of killing well after the provocative or assertive conduct has occurred.

Furthermore, the syndrome has been analogized to the classic hostage situation in that the battered woman lives under long-term, life-threatening conditions in constant fear of another eruption of violence. *See* W. LaFave & A. Scott, Criminal Law 458 (2d ed. 1986), and P. Robinson, 2 Criminal Law Defenses (1984). Robinson gives the example where the captor tells the hostage that he intends to kill him in three days. If on the first day, the hostage sees an opportunity to kill the captor and avoid the threat of his own death, a literal application of the requirement that the threat be "imminent" would prevent the hostage from using deadly force until the captor is standing over him with a knife. For the battered woman, if there is no escape or sense of safety, then the next attack, which could be fatal or cause serious bodily harm, is imminent. Based on the traditionally accepted definition of imminent and its functional derivatives, a battered woman, to whom the threat of serious bodily harm or death is always imminent, would be precluded from asserting the defense of self-defense.

Under our "hybrid" reasonableness standard, the meaning of *imminent* must necessarily envelope the battered woman's perceptions based on all the facts and circumstances of his or her relationship with the victim. In *Women's Self-Defense Cases: Theory and Practice* (1981), Elizabeth Bochnak writes:

> The battered woman learns to recognize the small signs that precede periods of escalated violence. She learns to distinguish subtle changes in tone of voice, facial expression, and levels of danger. She is in a position to know, perhaps with greater certainty than someone attacked by a stranger, that the batterer's threat is real and will be acted upon.

Thus, according to the author, an abused woman may kill her mate during the period of threat that precedes a violent incident, right before the violence escalates to the more dangerous levels of an acute battering episode. Or, she may take action against him during a lull in an assaultive incident, or after it has culminated, in an effort to prevent a recurrence of the violence. And so, the issue is not whether the danger was in *fact* imminent, but whether, given the circumstances as she perceived them, the defendant's *belief was reasonable that the danger was imminent.*

Because there is the presumption in *imminence* that the defender may find an alternative to the use of deadly force, we find it necessary to address the duty to retreat, which duty is implicit in said presumption. Additionally, Appellant complained that the trial court refused to give her requested instructions on "no duty to retreat" but gave instead [the pattern instruction 748]. [That instruction provides: "A person who was not the aggressor or who did not provoke another with intent to cause an altercation has no duty to retreat, but may stand firm and use the right of self-defense."] [We] find that [the instruction given by the trial judge] adequately states the law in Oklahoma and the trial court did not err in refusing to give Appellant's requested instruction[.]

For the foregoing reasons, this case is Reversed and Remanded for a new trial, consistent with this opinion.

PARKS, J., concurring in result:

I find that evidence concerning Battered Woman Syndrome was relevant to the jury's assessment of appellant's theory of the case—self defense. While I conclude that the syndrome should have been presented to the jury in this case, I disagree with the majority's decision to radically overhaul the laws pertaining to self defense. The facts asserted by appellant, that the victim made a threatening movement and she shot him, constitute classic self defense and do not necessitate the sweeping changes imposed by the majority. Our inquiry should be limited to an assessment of the syndrome's reliability and its relevance to the facts presented. . . .

Currently, the jury is asked to view the circumstances as they appeared to the defendant and then is asked to determine whether a reasonable person, caught in the dynamics of those identical circumstances, would respond as the defendant did. I find that the syndrome should have been admitted as it sheds light on the circumstances surrounding the altercation *as they appeared to the appellant*. The facts before us require us to decide nothing more. . . .

LUMPKIN, VICE-PRESIDING JUDGE, dissenting:

[Appellant's] evidence does not reveal the "Battered Woman Syndrome" was implicated on the night of September 23, 1984. The facts related by Appellant only raise a case of traditional self defense based on the right of self defense to resist any attempt to murder or commit a felony upon her, or the imminent threat as perceived by Appellant due to the victim's threats and actions committed that night. The "Cycle Theory" is not relevant based on the evidence. However, I recognize evidence regarding the victim's past trait of character for violence [is] relevant [and admissible] as it goes to Appellant's perception as a reasonable person regarding the imminence of danger of death or great bodily harm. The admissibility of this evidence does not require the adoption of the "Battered Woman Syndrome". . . .

[The] Court seems to disregard the evidence of the case in a reaching attempt to adopt a syndrome which is not applicable to the facts and does not comport with the requirements of being generally accepted in the scientific/medical community. While I agree that evidence of the Post-traumatic Stress Disorder, which is accepted as a standard for diagnosis in the medical community, would be relevant evidence in a proper case to provide a jury with the medical and psychological diagnostic criteria required to determine the reasonableness of a defendant's actions, it is not relevant here. The appropriate resolution of the ills of society should be left to the Legislative and Executive branches of our government. This Court should restrict itself to the application of the law to the facts presented in the record. I therefore must dissent [from] the Court's actions in this case.

POINTS FOR DISCUSSION

a. Evidence of Battering "Effects" & "Experiences"

The *Bechtel* opinion illustrates the controversies that occupied the attention of courts in self-defense cases with battered defendants during the first fifteen years after the publication of Lenore Walker's study in 1979. That era was followed by a period of revisionism, illustrated by the California legislature's enactment in 2004 of a statute that deleted all statutory references to "Battered Women's Syndrome" and replaced them with references to "intimate partner battering and its effects." Similarly, it is common for courts today to avoid references to the "syndrome" and to make references instead to "expert testimony on domestic violence," for example. Notably, in a case in which the prosecutor sought to introduce expert testimony about battering when prosecuting the batterer, the evidence was deemed admissible even though the battering episode that led to the criminal charges was the first episode of physical violence in the relationship between the battered victim and the defendant. *See People v. Brown*, 33 Cal. 4th 892, 16 Cal. Rptr. 3d 447, 94 P.3d 574 (Cal. 2004).

b. Retreat from Batterer's Castle

The trial judge in *Bechtel* rejected the defendant's proposed instruction on the duty to retreat, which read as follows: "If [the defendant] actually believed and had reasonable grounds to believe that she was in imminent danger of death or serious bodily harm and that deadly force was necessary to repel such danger, she was not required to retreat or consider whether she could retreat safely. No woman is required to leave her home to avoid an attack, even if the attacker is another member of the same household. A woman is entitled to stand her ground and use such force as is reasonably necessary under the circumstances to protect herself from serious bodily harm." The *Bechtel* Court approved the trial judge's instruction instead, which contained no reference to retreat from a batterer in the home, as an accurate statement of the law, and thereby ignored the value of informing jurors of the more particular right of a battered cohabitant wife to stand her ground when attacked by a battering cohabitant husband.

However, the *Bechtel* defendant's proposed jury instruction foreshadowed the increasing judicial approval during the 1990s of the "no duty to retreat from an attacking cohabitant in the castle" rule. This development may be attributed to the increased familiarity of appellate court judges with expert witness testimony concerning domestic violence, and their increased sensitivity to the impact of the older rules in some states that limited the protection of the castle doctrine to the inhabitants of the castle who need to use deadly force in self-defense against intruders.

c. **Reconsideration of Judgments**

During the pre-*Bechtel* era, many battered women defendants were convicted and sentenced to prison without jury consideration of the history of their battering by their intimate partner. Some states have enacted laws that allow courts to reconsider the judgments in some of these cases. For an example of a case seeking this remedy under the California statute, *see* https://www.pbs.org/newshour/show/crime-after-crime-examines-battered-woman-s-struggle-to-leave-prison.

C. DEFENSE OF DWELLING

Assuming that the requirements for self-defense cannot be met, when can a person use deadly force in relation to property, and more specifically, in relation to a dwelling? In the case of defense of property that is not a dwelling, even if a person reasonably believes that there is a threat of trespass or theft, this would not justify the use of deadly force. In the case of defense of a dwelling against entry by an intruder, statutes and courts allow the use of deadly force but place limitations upon that use. The most demanding limitations require that the defending person must reasonably believe that an intruder posed "a substantial danger of serious bodily harm" to the defending person or others, or that the intruder actually "threatened deadly force" against the defending person. But some courts and statutes impose less stringent conditions, requiring only that the defending person reasonably believes that the intruder will commit a felony or seek to harm a person in the dwelling. During recent decades, legislatures have enacted new defense-of-dwelling statutes that establish even more generous rights to use deadly force.

D. EXPANDING THE RIGHT TO USE DEADLY FORCE

The "Make My Day" laws of the 1980s and 1990s can be viewed as the "first wave" of statutes that expanded the common law requirements for the "defense of dwelling." For example, an Oklahoma statute allowed an occupant of a dwelling, including people other than the owner or resident, to use deadly force against a person who made an unlawful entry, when the occupant reasonably believes that person might use physical force against any occupant. The "second wave" of such statutes include the new "castle" laws related to dwellings and the "stand your ground" laws. All of these laws expand the right to use deadly force, and in each state where they have been enacted, the legislative history typically shows that the National Rifle Association drafted and lobbied for these statutes.

POINTS FOR DISCUSSION

a. New "Castle" Laws

The common law "castle doctrine" held that there was no "duty to retreat" inside one's dwelling when relying upon the affirmative defense of self-defense. That defense was limited as described in topic B in this chapter, *supra*. The new "castle" laws, however, do not require a defendant who uses deadly force inside a dwelling against an intruder to satisfy the traditional self-defense requirements (or the common law "defense of dwelling" requirements). The first castle law was enacted in Florida in 2005. Today such laws have been enacted in 22 states. A "castle" law authorizes the use of deadly force when a dwelling occupant has "reason to believe" that an "unlawful and forcible" entry is occurring. The occupant is *presumed* to have the reasonable fear of imminent peril of great bodily harm or death that would be needed to raise the affirmative defense of self-defense at trial. The intruder is also *presumed* to be entering the dwelling with the intent to commit an unlawful act involving force or violence. The law confers immunity from prosecution and civil liability on the occupant, and also protects the occupant who uses deadly force from arrest unless "there is probable cause that the force that was used was unlawful." Finally, a court must award "reasonable attorneys fees, court costs, compensation for loss of income, and all expenses incurred by the defendant of any civil action if the court finds that the defendant is immune from prosecution." *See* Fla. Stat. Ann. § 776.013 (2005).

b. "Stand Your Ground" Laws

The term "stand your ground law" sometimes may be used to refer to the "no-duty-to-retreat" doctrine discussed in *Brown*, which is also codified in some state statutes that define the elements of self-defense. However, the term "stand your ground law" has now become associated with a law that incorporates all the facets of the expanded right to use deadly force established in the 2005 Florida statute. Today there are 35 states with either statutes or case law declaring that there is no duty to retreat from another in a place in which one is lawfully present and not engaged in criminal activity.

E. LAW ENFORCEMENT DEFENSE

On the rare occasions when a police officer is prosecuted for their use of deadly force to kill during an arrest, the law enforcement defense may be invoked. The MPC allows such force to prevent the commission of a felony if the officer believes there is a substantial risk that the suspect will cause serious bodily injury to another and the force is immediately necessary to effect an arrest. See MPC § 3.07. The Supreme Court has held that under the Fourth Amendment, the police use of deadly force to arrest a fleeing felon creates § 1983 liability "[w]here the suspect poses no immediate threat to the officer and no threat to others, the harm resulting from failing to apprehend him does not justify the use of deadly force to do so." *Tennessee v. Garner*, 471 U.S. 1 (1985). In *Graham v. Connor*, 490 U.S. 386 (1989), the Court held that the use of deadly force is not "excessive" in a § 1983 suit if it is "objectively reasonable" from the perspective of a "reasonable police officer" on the scene and under the circumstances. Relevant factors include the severity of the crime, whether the suspect poses a threat to the safety of the officer or others, and whether the suspect is actively resisting arrest or attempting to flee. For example, the Court upheld the reasonableness of the police use of force in the form of a high speed car chase of a suspect that led to a crash in which the suspect suffered injuries that made him a quadriplegic. The Court reasoned that the extremely reckless driving of the suspect created a deadly threat to the public, including police officers and motorists, and so the harm of failing to apprehend him did justify the dangerous pursuit. *See Scott v. Harris*, 550 U.S. 372 (2007).

F. NECESSITY OR CHOICE OF EVILS DEFENSE

The necessity defense arises when an individual is faced with a choice of two evils, and one is the commission of an illegal act. [The] justification for the necessity defense is not that a person faced with a choice of two evils lacks the *mens rea* for the crime in question, but that the law promotes the achievement of

Justification Defenses

higher values at the expense of lower ones and that " 'sometimes the greater good for society will be accomplished by violating the literal language of the criminal law.' " W. LaFave & A. Scott, Jr., Criminal Law § 50 (1972).

POINTS FOR DISCUSSION

a. Model Penal Code Approach

The MPC "choice of evils" defense under § 3.02(1) applies when a person believes conduct is necessary to avoid a harm or evil to oneself or another provided that the harm or evil is greater than the one sought to be prevented by the law defining the crime.

b. Factor Tests for Necessity

By contrast with the MPC's all-purpose definition of necessity, "factor tests" may be created by courts to define specialized parameters for necessity defense claims that fall into particular categories. For example, one such category is that of prisoner escape cases, and courts continue to debate whether one of the required factors for such cases should be an attempt to surrender to the authorities after the escape from dangerous prison conditions has been accomplished. *See, e.g., People v. Lovercamp*, 43 Cal. App. 3d 823, 118 Cal. Rptr. 110 (1975) (requiring this factor); *Spakes v. State*, 913 S.W.2d 597 (Tex. Crim. App. 1996) (en banc) (not requiring this factor). The popularity of "factor tests" suggests that courts may be willing to treat the necessity defense as an opportunity to construct policy-based criteria for the enforcement of particular laws.

c. Rarely Successful Defense

Although it is the rare defendant who succeeds in obtaining a necessity instruction, there are a wide variety of circumstances in which defendants seek to raise the necessity defense. Courts traditionally reject requested instructions on the necessity defense when sought by defendants who commit acts of civil disobedience that violate trespass laws during political protests, who violate drunk driving laws in order to achieve important purposes, and who violate "contraband" laws concerning the regulation of drugs and weapons. Yet the door of the necessity defense remains open, even if the opening is necessarily narrow because of judicial recognition of the need to enforce the legislature's definitions of the criminal law.

> ### Hypo 1: *Broken Bottle*
>
> Ron pulls into a gas station in the heart of Los Angeles. While he is pumping gas, he is approached by an impoverished man wearing very old and dirty clothes, who is begging for money. The man says, very politely, "Gee mister, is there any chance that you could spare some money for some food. If so, I'd really appreciate it. Thank you." However, the man is carrying a broken whiskey bottle in his hand and the bottle is pointed toward Ron. Can Ron respond by using deadly force? If California law imposes the duty to retreat as long as such retreat can occur in complete safety, does Ron have the duty to retreat? If so, what must Ron do on these facts?

> ### Hypo 2: *Subway Shootings*
>
> Assume that Goetz is a white passenger on the downtown IRT express subway train in New York City. He is carrying a loaded .38 caliber pistol inside his coat, in violation of the prohibition against possession of unlicensed weapons. Goetz had been mugged on a prior occasion on the streets of the city, and this is why he carries the pistol. When Goetz enters the subway car, he notices four "noisy and boisterous" Black youths, who are sitting together at one end of the car. The other 20 passengers are sitting at the other end of the car. Two of the youths are carrying screwdrivers inside their coats so that they can break into video game coin boxes. But Goetz cannot see the screwdrivers. Goetz sits down near the four youths. Two of the youths stand up and approach Goetz, and one youth asks for five dollars. Goetz asks him to repeat his question. This time the youth says, "Give me five dollars."
>
> a. *Shooting at Youths.* Assume that the sound of shots rings out in the subway car. Goetz has taken aim at each of the four youths and fired a shot at each one. Goetz is charged with attempted murder. How can his defense counsel argue self-defense?
>
> b. *Backs Turned.* Assume that before Goetz fired any shots, he said, "I have no money." Then the two youths turned their backs to Goetz and moved a few feet away from him, which is as far as they could move because they were at the end of the car already. If Goetz takes aim at each youth and fires at their backs, how can his defense counsel argue for self-defense if Goetz is charged with attempted murder?

c. *Flashing Gun.* Assume that instead of firing any shots, Goetz shows the handle of the gun to the four youths, and that he "flashes" it in a threatening manner that suggests he will use it if he is not left alone. Assume that one of the youths does have a gun concealed in his jacket, and that in response to Goetz's "flashing" of the gun, the youth pulls out his weapon and points it at Goetz. If Goetz draws and fires at this youth, how can his defense counsel argue self-defense in a trial for attempted murder?

Compare People v. Goetz, 68 N.Y.2d 96, 497 N.E.2d 41, 506 N.Y.S.2d 18 (1986).

Hypo 3: *The Death of Trayvon Martin*

Zimmerman was charged with second degree murder but did not testify at his trial. Assume that when the jury heard his recorded statements to police, the following details emerged. Zimmerman, age 28, acknowledged that he had been following Martin, age 17, as Martin walked through a housing complex on his way to a condo where he was staying as a guest. Zimmerman was a neighborhood watch volunteer at the complex. He did not recognize Martin and thought he might be a burglar. While Zimmerman was in his car and on the phone with a police dispatcher to report Martin's presence, Martin circled the car, reached for his waistband, and then walked off. Zimmerman got out of his car and walked in the same direction as Martin, in order to look at a street sign to relay the street name to the dispatcher. The dispatcher told Zimmerman to wait for the police and not approach Martin.

When he was on his way back to his car, Martin appeared out of nowhere and asked Zimmerman, "Do you have a problem?" Zimmerman answered "No," and Martin said, "You do now," attacking Zimmerman as he tried to use his cell phone to call 911. Martin knocked him to the ground with a punch. Martin also screamed, "You're going to die tonight," and put his hand over Zimmerman's nose and mouth so that he could not breathe. Martin was on top of Zimmerman, pummeling him and slamming his head repeatedly into the pavement, so that it felt like Zimmerman's "head was going to explode." When Zimmerman felt Martin's hand "go down" his side, Zimmerman thought Martin was reaching for Zimmerman's gun. So Zimmerman grabbed it, pulled it out, and shot Martin. During the struggle, Zimmerman said that he repeatedly screamed for help, and witnesses saw Martin on top of Zimmerman.

The police who came to the scene also noticed that Zimmerman had a broken nose and injuries on the back of his head.

If these facts are believed by the jury, is there sufficient evidence to show by a preponderance that Zimmerman established these common law elements of self-defense: 1) that he had a reasonable belief that Martin posed an imminent threat of great bodily harm or death; and 2) that he had a reasonable belief that it was necessary to use deadly force in order to avoid that threat? Could the prosecutor have persuaded a reasonable jury, beyond a reasonable doubt, that the evidence did not support Zimmerman's self-defense claim? Or at least that Zimmerman's beliefs in imminence and necessity were unreasonable so that a reckless manslaughter conviction was appropriate?

Note: In the actual *Zimmerman* case, the defendant advanced a traditional self-defense claim based on his statements to police and public interviews. He did not testify at trial. If he had invoked the Florida stand your ground law to seek immunity from prosecution and civil liability, presumably it would have been necessary for him to testify at the hearing on these issues under Florida law.

Hypo 4: *Sensitive to Threats*

Assume that Jack has been an inmate at a state prison in Illinois for several decades. Now he is an old man, and the day comes when he is finally released from prison. His prison experience has made him very sensitive to potential threats when others get close to him. So when Jack is standing at a bus stop outside the prison walls, Jack notices immediately when the man standing next to him reaches into a raincoat pocket. Jack's perception at that moment is that the man intends to kill Jack with a weapon that is concealed in the pocket. As it happens, Jack managed to leave the prison with a homemade knife or "shiv" concealed in his sock.

So just as the man pulls his hand out of the pocket, Jack reaches down quickly, pulls out the shiv, and stabs the man in the chest. The man dies and Jack is charged with murder. Assume that self-defense is defined in Illinois using the MPC provision, and so Jack must *believe* that deadly force is *necessary* for self-protection against death or serious bodily injury, and *also* must *believe* that such force is *immediately* necessary for that purpose against the use of unlawful force by another person *on the present occasion*. How can Jack's defense counsel argue for acquittal based on "perfect" self-defense? How can the prosecutor argue that Jack must be convicted of murder or manslaughter?

Hypo 5: *Stand Your Ground Laws*

What are the pro and con arguments concerning the enactment of the MPC rule that imposes a duty to retreat outside of one's dwelling (but only when it is possible to retreat in "complete safety") upon a person who otherwise qualifies for the traditional requirements of self-defense? What are the pro and con arguments concerning the enactment of a law that reflects all the elements of the 2005 Florida statute?

CHAPTER 12

Excuses

Like justification defenses, excuses are general defenses applicable to all offenses and available even though the person satisfies the offense's elements. However, excuse defenses concentrate on the person's lack of subjective blameworthiness, while justification defenses focus on the person's conduct. Excuses admit that the act may cause or threaten a harm the criminal law normally disallows, but excuse the person because his characteristics or situation suggest that he does not merit criminal liability.

A. OVERVIEW OF THE LAW

Justification Versus Excuse. Like justification defenses, excuses are general defenses applicable to all offenses and available even though the person's conduct satisfies the elements of an offense. However, excuse defenses focus on the person's lack of subjective blameworthiness. Even though an act may cause or threaten a harm the criminal law normally would punish, an excuse defense applies when a person's characteristics or situation suggest that he or she does not merit criminal liability.

Defense of Duress. The defense of duress arises when an individual is faced with a threat of death or serious bodily injury, and chooses to commit a crime rather than suffer the threatened consequences. *See United States v. Contento-Pachon*, 723 F.2d 691 (9th Cir. 1984). In general, the individual must have a reasonable belief that the threat is serious, and there must be no reasonable means of escape. As a general rule, duress is not a defense to an intentional murder. However, the Model Penal Code permits the defense in any situation when an individual is faced with threat "which a person of reasonable firmness in his situation would have been unable to resist."

Insanity. There is little justification for punishing those who commit crimes while insane. As the Second Circuit stated in *United States v. Freeman*, 357 F.2d 606,

615 (2d Cir. 1966): "Those who are substantially unable to restrain their conduct are, by definition, undeterrable and their 'punishment' is no example for others; those who are unaware of or do not appreciate the nature and quality of their actions can hardly be expected rationally to weigh the consequences of their conduct. Finally, what segment of society can feel its desire for retribution satisfied when it wreaks vengeance upon the incompetent? Although an understandable emotion, a need for retribution can never be permitted in a civilized society to degenerate into a sadistic form of revenge."

Test for Insanity. Although there is general agreement that the insane should not be held criminally responsible for their conduct, few agree about how to define insanity. For many years, U.S. courts applied the insanity test articulated by the House of Lords in the nineteenth century in *M'Naghten's Case*. Because of dissatisfaction with the *M'Naghten* and irresistible impulse tests, the courts and the American Law Institute developed alternative tests. In *United States v. Freeman*, 357 F.2d 606 (2d Cir. 1966), the Court applied a test focusing on whether the unlawful act "was the product of mental disease or mental defect." Section 4.01 of the Model Penal Code provides that "A person is not responsible for criminal conduct if at the time of such conduct as a result of mental disease or defect he lacks substantial capacity either to appreciate the wrongfulness of his conduct or to conform his conduct to the requirements of law."

Insanity and the Criminal Process. Insanity can be relevant at three different points in the criminal process. First, as in *M'Naghten*, individuals who commit criminal acts while insane cannot be convicted of those acts. Second, defendants who are insane at the time of their trials cannot be tried, and will be committed until they are sane enough to proceed. The defendant must "have sufficient present ability to consult with his lawyer with a reasonable degree of rational understanding—and have a rational as well as factual understanding of the proceedings against him." *Dusky v. United States*, 362 U.S. 402 (1960). Finally, defendants sentenced to capital punishment cannot be executed until they regain their sanity. *See Ford v. Wainwright*, 477 U.S. 399 (1986).

Infancy and Capacity. The question, in some cases, is whether the age of a juvenile affects his capacity to commit a crime. At one point, the law relied on age-based assumptions regarding capacity. Later decisions applied the *M'Naghten* test. Some modern decisions rely on circumstantial factors which suggest that the defendant does, or does not, have capacity.

Excuses

> **Major Themes**
>
> **a. Duress**—The duress defense recognizes the non-blameworthy character of a person's criminal act when that act is coerced by a threat of immediate serious bodily harm. The common law requires that an immediate and inescapable threat, typically of serious bodily harm, must have provided the source of the duress that led to the commission of the crime.
>
> **b. Insanity**—All but a very few states define legal insanity as a condition that exists when, because of a mental disease or defect, a person lacks the capacity to know that his conduct was wrong. Ever since the *M'Naghten* decision in 1847, there has been continual judicial and legislative debate over the question whether additional definitions of insanity are needed. Today a large minority of states define insanity to include a person who lacks the capacity to conform his or her conduct to the requirements of the law. An even larger minority of states make the defense available to a person who does not know the nature and quality of his or her conduct.
>
> **c. Infancy**—Infancy can also be a defense to criminal conduct. Some courts apply the *M'Naghten* rule to determine whether a minor has sufficient mental capacity to be criminally responsible.

B. DURESS

The defense of duress arises when an individual is faced with a threat of death or serious bodily injury, and chooses to commit a crime rather than suffer the threatened consequences. *See United States v. Contento-Pachon*, 723 F.2d 691 (9th Cir. 1984). In general, the individual must have a reasonable belief that the threat is serious, and there must be no reasonable means of escape.

Although it may be theoretically possible for a defendant to assert that he is innocent of the underlying offense, and that he committed it because of duress, there is a logical inconsistency between the two positions. The defense of duress assumes that defendant committed the crime, and that the ordinary requirements for conviction are present, but allows defendant to argue that the commission should be excused because of the duress. *See Dixon v. United States*, 548 U.S. 1 (2006); *United States v. Bailey*, 444 U.S. 394 (1980).

POINT FOR DISCUSSION

Model Penal Code

Consider the MPC's approach to the defense of duress:

§ 2.09. Duress.

(1) It is an affirmative defense that the actor engaged in the conduct charged to constitute an offense because he was coerced to do so by the use of, or a threat to use, unlawful force against his person or the person of another, which a person of reasonable firmness in his situation would have been unable to resist.

(2) The defense provided by this Section is unavailable if the actor recklessly placed himself in a situation in which it was probable that he would be subjected to duress. The defense is also unavailable if he was negligent in placing himself in such a situation, whenever negligence suffices to establish culpability for the offense charged.

(3) It is not a defense that a woman acted on the command of her husband, unless she acted under such coercion as would establish a defense under this Section. [The presumption that a woman, acting in the presence of her husband, is coerced is abolished.

(4) When the conduct of the actor would otherwise be justifiable under Section 3.02, choice of evils, this Section does not preclude such defense.

C. INSANITY

There is little justification for punishing those who commit crimes while insane. As the Second Circuit stated in *United States v. Freeman*, 357 F.2d 606, 615 (2d Cir. 1966):

Those who are substantially unable to restrain their conduct are, by definition, undeterrable and their "punishment" is no example for others. Indeed, those who are unaware of or do not appreciate the nature and quality of their actions can hardly be expected rationally to weigh the consequences of their conduct. Finally, what segment of society can feel its desire for retribution satisfied when it wreaks vengeance upon the incompetent? Although an understandable emotion, a need for retribution can never be permitted in a civilized society to degenerate into a sadistic form of revenge.

1. *M'Naghten* & Irresistible Impulse Tests

Although there is general agreement that the insane should not be held criminally responsible for their conduct, few agree about how to define insanity. For many years, U.S. courts applied the insanity test articulated by the House of Lords in the nineteenth century in *M'Naghten's Case*.

M'NAGHTEN'S CASE
10 Cl. & F. 200, 8 Eng. Rep. 718 (House of Lords 1843).

LORD CHIEF JUSTICE TINDAL:

[Daniel M'Naghten shot at Sir Robert Peel's carriage intending to kill Peel. M'Naghten actually shot Edward Drummond, Peel's private secretary, who was the only person inside the carriage. At his trial, M'Naghten claimed that he killed Drummond under the influence of insane delusions, and the jury found him not guilty by reason of insanity. Because the verdict was unpopular, the House of Lords debated the decision and appended conclusions to the report of the original case.]

The first question proposed by your Lordships is this: "What is the law respecting alleged crimes committed by persons afflicted with insane delusion in respect of one or more particular subjects or personas, for instance, where at the time of commission of the alleged crime the accused knew he was acting contrary to law, but did the act complained of with a view, under the influence of insane delusion, of redressing or revenging some supposed grievance or injury, or of producing some supposed public benefit?"

In answer to which question, assuming that your Lordships' inquiries are confined to those persons who labour under such partial delusions only, and are not in other respects insane, we are of opinion that, notwithstanding the party accused did the act complained of with a view, under the influence of redressing or revenging some supposed grievance or injury, or of producing some public benefit, he is nevertheless punishable according to the nature of the crime committed, if he knew at the time of committing such crime that he was acting contrary to law; by which expression we understand your Lordships to mean the law of the land.

Your Lordships are pleased to inquire of us, secondly, "What are the proper questions to be submitted to the jury, where a person alleged to be afflicted with insane delusion respecting one or more subjects or persons, is charged with the commission of a crime (murder, for example), and insanity is set up as a defence?"

And, thirdly, "In what terms ought the question to be left to the jury as to the prisoner's state of mind at the time when the act was committed?" As these two questions appear to us to be more conveniently answered together, we have to submit our opinion to be, that the jurors ought to be told in all cases that every man is to be presumed to be sane, and to possess a sufficient degree of reason to be responsible for his crimes, until the contrary be proved to their satisfaction; and that to establish a defence on the ground of insanity, it must be clearly proved that, at the time of the committing of the act, the party accused was labouring under such a defect of reason, from disease of the mind, as not to know the nature and quality of the act he was doing; or, if he did know it, that he did not know he was doing what was wrong. The mode of putting the latter part of the question to the jury on these occasions has generally been, whether the accused at the time of doing the act knew the difference between right and wrong. If the accused was conscious that the act was one which he ought not to do, and if that act was at the same time contrary to the law of the land, he is punishable; and the usual course therefore has been to leave the question to the jury, whether the party accused had a sufficient degree of reason to know that he was doing an act that was wrong.

The fourth question which your Lordships have proposed to us is this:—"If a person under an insane delusion as to existing facts, commits an offence in consequence thereof, is he thereby excused? To which question the answer must of course depend on the nature of the delusion: but, making the same assumption as we did before, namely, that he labours under such partial delusion only, and is not in other respects insane, we think he must be considered in the same situation as to responsibility as if the facts with respect to which the delusion exists were real. For example, if under the influence of his delusion, he supposes another man to be in the act of attempting to take away his life, and he kills that man, as he supposes, in self-defense, he would be exempt from punishment. If his delusion was that the deceased has inflicted a serious injury to his character and fortune, and he killed him in revenge for such supposed injury, he would be liable to punishment.

The question lastly proposed by your Lordships is—"Can a medical man conversant with the disease of insanity, who never saw the prisoner previously to the trial, but who was present during the whole trial and the examination of all the witnesses, be asked his opinion as to the state of the prisoner's mind at the time of the commission of the alleged crime, or his opinion whether the prisoner was conscious at the time of doing the act that he was acting contrary to law, or whether he was labouring under any and what delusion at the time? In answer thereto, we state to your Lordships, that we think the medical man, under the circumstances supposed, cannot in strictness be asked his opinion in the terms above stated, because each of those questions involves the determination of the truth of the facts deposed to, which it is for the jury to decide, and the questions are not mere questions upon a matter of science, in which case such evidence is admissible. But where the facts are admitted or not disputed, and the question becomes substantially one of science only, it may be convenient to allow the question to be put in that general form, though the same cannot be insisted on as a matter of right.

POINTS FOR DISCUSSION

a. *M'Naghten* & Insane Delusions

Because of the House of Lords' answer to the fourth question, some jurisdictions interpreted *M'Naghten* to apply to insane delusions only when "the imaginary state of facts would, if real, justify or excuse the act." These jurisdictions held that defendant "must be considered in the same situation as to responsibility as if the facts with respect to which the delusion exists were real." *See Parsons v. State*, 81 Ala. 577, 2 So. 854 (1887).

b. Irresistible Impulse Test

Some jurisdictions supplemented the *M'Naghten* test with the "irresistible impulse" test which provided that, even if defendant knew the difference between right and wrong and knew that his act was wrong, defendant cannot be convicted if he acted under an "irresistible impulse." *Parsons v. State*, 81 Ala. 577, 2 So. 854 (1887), is the leading case: "We think it sufficient if the insane delusion so subverts his will as to destroy his free agency by rendering him powerless to resist by reason of the duress of the disease."

Take Note

In addition to the insanity defense, a defendant might also raise a "diminished capacity" defense. This defense questions whether defendant had the capacity to form the *mens rea* of the crime. In *United States v. Brawner*, 471 F.2d 969, 153 U.S. App. D.C. 1 (D.C.Cir. 1972), the court summarized this defense: "Expert testimony as to a defendant's abnormal mental condition may be received and considered, as tending to show that defendant did not have the specific mental state required for a particular crime or degree of crime-even though he was aware that his act was wrongful and was able to control it, and hence was not entitled to complete exoneration."

CLARK V. ARIZONA
548 U.S. 735 (2006).

JUSTICE SOUTER delivered the opinion of the Court.

The case presents two questions: whether due process prohibits Arizona's use of an insanity test stated solely in terms of the capacity to tell whether an act charged as a crime was right or wrong; and whether Arizona violates due process in restricting consideration of defense evidence of mental illness and incapacity to its bearing on a claim of insanity, thus eliminating its significance directly on the issue of the mental element of the crime charged (known in legal shorthand as the *mens rea*, or guilty mind). We hold that there is no violation of due process in either instance.

On June 21, 2000, Officer Jeffrey Moritz of the Flagstaff Police responded to complaints that a pickup truck with loud music blaring was circling a residential block. The officer turned on the emergency lights and siren of his marked patrol car and pulled Clark over. Less than a minute later, Clark shot the officer, who died soon after. Clark was charged with first-degree murder for intentionally or knowingly killing a law enforcement officer in the line of duty. At trial, Clark did not contest the shooting and death, but relied on his undisputed paranoid schizophrenia at the time of the incident in denying that he had the specific intent to shoot a law enforcement officer or knowledge that he was doing so, as required by the statute. Accordingly, the prosecutor offered circumstantial evidence that Clark knew Officer Moritz was a law enforcement officer. The testimony for the prosecution indicated that Clark had intentionally lured an officer to the scene to kill him, having told some people a few weeks before the incident that he wanted to shoot police officers.

In presenting the defense case, Clark claimed mental illness, which he sought to introduce for two purposes. First, he raised the affirmative defense of insanity, putting the burden on himself to prove by clear and convincing evidence, that "at the time of the commission of the criminal act he was afflicted with a mental disease or defect of such severity that he did not know the criminal act was wrong." Second, he aimed to rebut the prosecution's evidence of the requisite *mens rea*, that he had acted intentionally or knowingly to kill a law enforcement officer. The trial court ruled that Clark could not rely on evidence bearing on insanity to dispute the *mens rea*. The court cited *State* v. *Mott*, 187 Ariz. 536, 931 P.2d 1046 (en banc) (1997), which "refused to allow psychiatric testimony to negate specific intent," and held that "Arizona does not allow evidence of a defendant's mental disorder short of insanity to negate the *mens rea* element of a crime."

As to his insanity, Clark presented testimony from classmates, school officials, and his family describing his increasingly bizarre behavior over the year before the shooting. Witnesses testified, for example, that paranoid delusions led Clark to rig a fishing line with beads and wind chimes at home to alert him to intrusion by invaders, and to keep a bird in his automobile to warn of airborne poison. There was lay and expert testimony that Clark thought Flagstaff was populated with "aliens" (some impersonating government agents), the "aliens" were trying to kill him, and bullets were the only way to stop them. A psychiatrist testified that Clark was suffering from paranoid schizophrenia with delusions about "aliens" when he killed Officer Moritz, and he concluded that Clark was incapable of luring the officer or understanding right from wrong and that he was thus insane at the time of the killing. In rebuttal, a psychiatrist for the State gave his opinion that Clark's paranoid schizophrenia did not keep him from appreciating the wrongfulness of his conduct, as shown by his actions before and after the shooting (such as circling the residential block with music blaring as if to lure the police to intervene, evading the police after the shooting, and hiding the gun). The judge then issued a special verdict of first-degree murder, expressly finding that Clark shot and caused the death of Officer Moritz beyond a reasonable doubt and that Clark had not shown that he was insane at the time. The judge noted that though Clark was indisputably afflicted with paranoid schizophrenia at the time of the shooting, the mental illness "did not distort his perception of reality so severely that he did not know his actions were wrong." For this conclusion, the judge expressly relied on "the facts of the crime, the evaluations of the experts, Clark's actions and behavior both before and after the shooting, and the observations of those that knew Clark." The sentence was life imprisonment without the possibility of release for 25 years. The Court of Appeals affirmed the conviction and the Supreme Court of Arizona denied review. We affirm.

Clark first says that Arizona's definition of insanity, being only a fragment of the Victorian standard from which it derives, violates due process. The landmark English rule in *M'Naghten's Case*, 10 Cl. & Fin. 200, 8 Eng. Rep. 718 (1843). When the Arizona Legislature first codified an insanity rule, it adopted the full *M'Naghten* test. In 1993, the legislature dropped the cognitive incapacity part, leaving only moral incapacity as the nub of the stated definition. Under current Arizona law, a defendant will not be adjudged insane unless he demonstrates that "at the time of the commission of the criminal act he was afflicted with a mental disease or defect of such severity that he did not know the criminal act was wrong."

Clark challenges the 1993 amendment excising the express reference to the cognitive incapacity element. He argues that elimination of the *M'Naghten* reference to nature and quality "offends a principle of justice so rooted in the traditions and conscience of our people as to be ranked as fundamental," *Patterson v. New York,* 432 U. S. 197, 202 (1977). History shows no deference to *M'Naghten* that could elevate its formula to the level of fundamental principle, so as to limit the traditional recognition of a State's capacity to define crimes and defenses. Even a cursory examination of the traditional Anglo-American approaches to insanity reveals significant differences among them, with four traditional strains variously combined to yield a diversity of American standards. The main variants are the cognitive incapacity, the moral incapacity, the volitional incapacity, and the product-of-mental-illness tests. The first two emanate from the alternatives stated in the *M'Naghten* rule. The volitional incapacity or irresistible-impulse test, which surfaced over two centuries ago (first in England, then in this country, asks whether a person was so lacking in volition due to a mental defect or illness that he could not have controlled his actions. And the product-of-mental-illness test was used as early as 1870, and simply asks whether a person's action was a product of a mental disease or defect.

Seventeen States and the Federal Government have adopted a recognizable version of the *M'Naghten* test with both its cognitive incapacity and moral incapacity components. One State has adopted only *M'Naghten*'s cognitive incapacity test, and 10 (including Arizona) have adopted the moral incapacity test alone. Fourteen jurisdictions, inspired by the Model Penal Code, have in place an amalgam of the volitional incapacity test and some variant of the moral incapacity test, satisfaction of either (generally by showing a defendant's substantial lack of capacity) being enough to excuse. Three States combine a full *M'Naghten* test with a volitional incapacity formula. New Hampshire alone stands by the product-of-mental-illness test. The alternatives are multiplied further by variations in the prescribed insanity verdict: a significant number of these jurisdictions supplement the traditional "not guilty by reason of insanity" verdict with an alternative of "guilty but mentally ill." Finally, four States have no affirmative insanity defense, though one provides for a "guilty and mentally ill" verdict. These four, like a number of others that recognize an affirmative insanity defense, allow consideration of evidence of mental illness directly on the element of *mens rea* defining the offense.

With this varied background, it is clear that no particular formulation has evolved into a baseline for due process, and that the insanity rule, like the conceptualization of criminal offenses, is substantially open to state choice. Indeed, the legitimacy of such choice is the more obvious when one considers the interplay of legal concepts of mental illness or deficiency required for an insanity defense, with the medical concepts of mental abnormality that influence the expert opinion testimony by psychologists and psychiatrists commonly introduced to support or contest insanity claims. For medical definitions devised to justify treatment, like legal ones devised to excuse from conventional criminal responsibility, are subject to flux and disagreement. There being such fodder for reasonable debate about what the cognate legal and medical tests should be, due process imposes no single canonical formulation of legal insanity.

Though Clark is correct that the application of the moral incapacity test (telling right from wrong) does not necessarily require evaluation of a defendant's cognitive capacity to appreciate the nature and quality of the acts charged against him, his argument fails to recognize that cognitive incapacity is itself enough to demonstrate moral incapacity. Cognitive incapacity, in other words, is a sufficient condition for establishing a defense of insanity, albeit not a necessary one. As a defendant can therefore make out moral incapacity by demonstrating cognitive incapacity, evidence bearing on whether the defendant knew the nature and quality of his actions is both relevant and admissible. In practical terms, if a defendant did not know what he was doing when he acted, he could not have known that he was performing the wrongful act charged as a crime. Indeed, when the two-part rule was still in effect, the Supreme Court of Arizona held that a jury instruction on insanity containing the moral incapacity part but not a full recitation of the cognitive incapacity part was fine, as the cognitive incapacity part might be "treated as adding nothing to the requirement that the accused know his act was wrong.'" *State v. Chavez*, 143 Ariz. 238, 239, 693 P.2d 893, 894 (1984). We are satisfied that neither in theory nor in practice did Arizona's 1993 abridgment of the insanity formulation deprive Clark of due process.

Clark's second claim of a due process violation challenges the rule adopted by *Mott*. This case ruled on the admissibility of testimony from a psychologist offered to show that the defendant suffered from battered women's syndrome and therefore lacked the capacity to form the *mens rea* of the crime charged against her. The state court held that testimony of a professional psychologist or psychiatrist about a defendant's mental incapacity owing to mental disease or defect was admissible, and could be considered, only for its bearing on an insanity defense; such evidence could not be considered on the element of *mens rea*, that is, what the State must show about a defendant's mental state (such as intent or understanding) when he performed the act charged against him.

Understanding Clark's claim requires attention to the categories of evidence with a potential bearing on *mens rea*. First, there is "observation evidence" in the everyday sense, testimony from those who observed what Clark did and heard what he said; this category would also include testimony that an expert witness might give about Clark's tendency to think in a certain way and his behavioral characteristics. This evidence may support a professional diagnosis of mental disease and in any event is the kind of evidence that can be relevant to show what in fact was on Clark's mind when he fired the gun. Observation evidence in the record covers Clark's behavior at home and with friends, his expressions of belief around the time of the killing that "aliens" were inhabiting the bodies of local people (including government agents), his driving around the neighborhood before the police arrived, and so on. Contrary to the dissent's characterization, observation evidence can be presented by either lay or expert witnesses.

Second, there is "mental-disease evidence" in the form of opinion testimony that Clark suffered from a mental disease with features described by the witness. This evidence characteristically but not always comes from professional psychologists or psychiatrists who testify as expert witnesses and base their opinions in part on examination of a defendant, usually conducted after the events in question. The thrust of this evidence was that, based on factual reports, professional observations, and tests, Clark was psychotic at the time in question, with a condition that fell within the category of schizophrenia.

Third, there is evidence we will refer to as "capacity evidence" about a defendant's capacity for cognition and moral judgment (and ultimately also his capacity to form *mens rea*). This, too, is opinion evidence. Here, as it usually does, this testimony came from the same experts and concentrated on those specific details of the mental condition that make the difference between sanity and insanity under the Arizona definition. In their respective testimony on these details the experts disagreed: the defense expert gave his opinion that the symptoms or effects of the disease in Clark's case included inability to appreciate the nature of his action and to tell that it was wrong, whereas the State's psychiatrist was of the view that Clark was a schizophrenic who was still sufficiently able to appreciate the reality of shooting the officer and to know that it was wrong to do that.

Mott itself imposed no restriction on considering evidence of the first sort, the observation evidence. We read the *Mott* restriction to apply, rather, to evidence addressing the two issues in testimony that characteristically comes only from psychologists or psychiatrists qualified to give opinions as expert witnesses: mental-disease evidence (whether at the time of the crime a defendant suffered from a mental disease or defect, such as schizophrenia) and capacity evidence (whether the disease or defect left him incapable of performing or experiencing a mental process defined as necessary for sanity such as appreciating the nature and quality of his act and knowing that it was wrong). *Mott* was careful to distinguish this kind of opinion evidence from observation evidence generally and even from observation evidence that an expert witness might offer, such as descriptions of a defendant's tendency to think in a certain way or his behavioral characteristics; the Arizona court made it clear that this sort of testimony was perfectly admissible to rebut the prosecution's evidence of *mens rea*. Thus, only opinion testimony going to mental defect or disease, and its effect on the cognitive or moral capacities on which sanity depends under the Arizona rule, is restricted.

In this case, the trial court seems to have applied the *Mott* restriction to all evidence offered by Clark for the purpose of showing what he called his inability to form the required *mens rea*. Thus, the trial court's restriction may have covered not only mental-disease and capacity evidence as just defined, but also observation evidence offered by lay (and expert) witnesses who described Clark's unusual behavior. Clark's objection to the application of the *Mott* rule does not, however, turn on the distinction between lay and expert witnesses or the kinds of testimony they were competent to present. All Members of the Court agree that Clark's general attack on the *Mott* rule covers its application in confining consideration of capacity evidence to the insanity defense. The only issue properly before us is the challenge to *Mott* on due process grounds, comprising objections to limits on the use of mental-disease and capacity evidence. We consider the claim, as Clark otherwise puts it, that "Arizona's prohibition of 'diminished capacity' evidence by criminal defendants violates" due process.

Clark claims a right to require the fact finder in this case to consider testimony about his mental illness and his incapacity directly, when weighing the persuasiveness of other evidence tending to show *mens rea*, which the prosecution has the burden to prove. As Clark recognizes, however, the right to introduce relevant evidence can be curtailed if there is a good reason for doing that. *Holmes v. South Carolina*, 547 U. S. 319 (2006). If evidence may be kept out entirely, its consideration may be subject to limitation, which Arizona claims the power to impose here. State law says that evidence of mental disease and incapacity may be introduced and considered, and if sufficiently forceful to satisfy the defendant's burden of proof under the insanity rule it will displace the presumption of sanity and excuse from criminal responsibility. But mental-disease and capacity evidence may be considered only for its bearing on the insanity defense, and it will avail a defendant only if it is persuasive enough to satisfy the defendant's burden as defined by the terms of that defense. The mental-disease and capacity evidence is thus being channeled or restricted to one issue and given effect only if the defendant carries the burden to convince the fact finder of insanity; the evidence is not being excluded entirely, and the question is whether reasons for requiring it to be channeled and restricted are good enough to satisfy the standard of fundamental fairness that due process requires. We think they are.

The first reason supporting the *Mott* rule is Arizona's authority to define its presumption of sanity (or capacity or responsibility) by choosing an insanity definition, and by placing the burden of persuasion on defendants who claim incapacity as an excuse from customary criminal responsibility. No one denies that a State may place a burden of persuasion on a defendant claiming insanity. But if a State is to have this authority in practice as well as in theory, it must be able to deny a defendant the opportunity to displace the presumption of sanity more easily when addressing a different issue in the course of the criminal trial. Yet, just such an opportunity would be available if expert testimony of mental disease and incapacity could be considered for whatever a fact finder might think it was worth on the issue of *mens rea*. Now, a State is of course free to accept such a possibility in its law. After all, it is free to define the insanity defense by treating the presumption of sanity as a bursting bubble, whose disappearance shifts the burden to the prosecution to prove sanity whenever a defendant presents any credible evidence of mental disease or incapacity. In States with this kind of insanity rule, the legislature may well be willing to allow such evidence to be considered on the *mens rea* element for whatever the fact finder thinks it is worth. What counts for due process, however, is simply that a State that wishes to avoid a second avenue for exploring capacity, less stringent for a defendant, has a good reason for confining the consideration of evidence of mental disease and incapacity to the insanity defense. It is obvious that Arizona's *Mott* rule reflects such a choice.

A State's insistence on preserving its chosen standard of legal insanity cannot be the sole reason for a rule like *Mott*. An insanity rule gives a defendant already found guilty the opportunity to excuse his conduct by showing he was insane when he acted, that is, that he did not have the mental capacity for conventional guilt and criminal responsibility. But, if the same evidence that affirmatively shows he was not guilty by reason of insanity (or "guilty except insane") under Arizona law also shows it was at least doubtful that he could form *mens rea*, then he should not be found guilty in the first place; it thus violates due process when the State impedes him from using mental-disease and capacity evidence directly to rebut the prosecution's evidence that he did form *mens rea*.

Are there, then, characteristics of mental-disease and capacity evidence giving rise to risks that may reasonably be hedged by channeling the consideration of such evidence to the insanity issue on which, in States like Arizona, a defendant has the burden of persuasion? We think there are: in the controversial character of some categories of mental disease, in the potential of mental-disease evidence to mislead, and in the danger of according greater certainty to capacity evidence than experts claim for it.

To begin with, the diagnosis may mask vigorous debate within the profession about the very contours of the mental disease itself. See, *e.g.*, American Psychiatric Association, Diagnostic and Statistical Manual of Mental Disorders xxxiii (4th ed. text rev. 2000) (hereinafter DSM-IV-TR). Members of this Court have previously recognized that the end of such debate is not imminent. The consequence of this professional ferment is a general caution in treating psychological classifications as predicates for excusing otherwise criminal conduct. Next, there is the potential of mental-disease evidence to mislead jurors (when they are the fact finders) through the power of this kind of evidence to suggest that a defendant suffering from a recognized mental disease lacks cognitive, moral, volitional, or other capacity, when that may not be a sound conclusion at all. Even when a category of mental disease is broadly accepted and the assignment of a defendant's behavior to that category is uncontroversial, the classification may suggest something very significant about a defendant's capacity, when in fact the classification tells us little or nothing about the ability of the defendant to form *mens rea* or to exercise the cognitive, moral, or volitional capacities that define legal sanity. The limits of the utility of a professional disease diagnosis are evident in the dispute between the two testifying experts in this case; they agree that Clark was schizophrenic, but they come to opposite conclusions on whether the mental disease in his particular case left him bereft of cognitive or moral capacity. Evidence of mental disease, then, can easily mislead; it is very easy to slide from evidence that an individual with a professionally recognized mental disease is very different, into doubting that he has the capacity to form *mens rea*, whereas that doubt may not be justified. Of course, in the cases mentioned before, in which the categorization is doubtful or the category of mental disease is itself subject to controversy, the risks are even greater that opinions about mental disease may confuse a jury into thinking the opinions show more than they do. Because allowing mental-disease evidence on *mens rea* can thus easily mislead, it is not unreasonable to address that tendency by confining consideration of this kind of evidence to insanity, on which a defendant may be assigned the burden of persuasion.

There are, finally, particular risks inherent in the opinions of the experts who supplement the mental-disease classifications with opinions on incapacity: on whether the mental disease rendered a particular defendant incapable of the cognition necessary for moral judgment or *mens rea* or otherwise incapable of understanding the wrongfulness of the conduct charged. Unlike observational evidence bearing on *mens rea*, capacity evidence consists of judgment, and judgment fraught with multiple perils: a defendant's state of mind at the crucial moment can be elusive no matter how conscientious the enquiry, and the law's categories that set the terms of the capacity judgment are not the categories of psychology that govern the expert's professional thinking. Even when an expert is confident that his understanding of the mind is reliable, judgment addressing the basic categories of capacity requires a leap from the concepts of psychology, which are devised for thinking about treatment, to the concepts of legal sanity, which are devised for thinking about criminal responsibility. In sum, these empirical and conceptual problems add up to a real risk that an expert's judgment in giving capacity evidence will come with an apparent authority that psychologists and psychiatrists do not claim to have. We think that this risk, like the difficulty in assessing the significance of mental-disease evidence, supports the State's decision to channel such expert testimony to consideration on the insanity defense, on which the party seeking the benefit of this evidence has the burden of persuasion.

It bears repeating that not every State will find it worthwhile to make the judgment Arizona has made, and the choices the States do make about dealing with the risks posed by mental-disease and capacity evidence will reflect their varying assessments about the presumption of sanity as expressed in choices of insanity rules. The point here simply is that Arizona has sensible reasons to assign the risks as it has done by channeling the evidence.

Arizona's rule serves to preserve the State's chosen standard for recognizing insanity as a defense and to avoid confusion and misunderstanding on the part of jurors. For these reasons, there is no violation of due process under *Chambers* and its progeny, and no cause to claim that channeling evidence on mental disease and capacity offends any "principle of justice so rooted in the traditions and conscience of our people as to be ranked as fundamental," *Patterson*, 432 U. S, at 202.

The judgment of the Court of Appeals of Arizona is, accordingly, affirmed.

It is so ordered.

[Justice Breyer concurred in part and dissented in part; he would have remanded the case to determine whether the Arizona law is consistent with the distinctions drawn by the majority.]

JUSTICE KENNEDY, with whom JUSTICE STEVENS and JUSTICE GINSBURG join, dissenting.

The central theory of Clark's defense was that his schizophrenia made him delusional. He lived in a universe where the delusions were so dominant, the theory was, that he had no intent to shoot a police officer or knowledge he was doing so. It is one thing to say he acted with intent or knowledge to pull the trigger. It is quite another to say he pulled the trigger to kill someone he knew to be a human being and a police officer. If the trier of fact were to find Clark's evidence sufficient to discount the case made by the State, which has the burden to prove knowledge or intent as an element of the offense, Clark would not be guilty of first-degree murder under Arizona law.

The trial court's exclusion was all the more severe because it barred from consideration on the issue of *mens rea* all this evidence, from any source, thus preventing Clark from showing he did not commit the crime as defined by Arizona law. Arizona's rule is problematic because it excludes evidence no matter how credible and material it may be in disproving an element of the offense. The Court's cases have noted the potential arbitrariness of *per se* exclusions and, on this rationale, have invalidated various state prohibitions. If the rule does not substantially burden the defense, then it is likely permissible. Where, however, the burden is substantial, the State must present a valid reason for its *per se* evidentiary rule.

In the instant case Arizona's proposed reasons are insufficient to support its categorical exclusion. While the State contends that testimony regarding mental illness may be too incredible or speculative for the jury to consider, this does not explain why the exclusion applies in all cases to all evidence of mental illness. "A State's legitimate interest in barring unreliable evidence does not extend to *per se* exclusions that may be reliable in an individual case." States have discretion to bar unreliable or speculative testimony and to adopt rules to ensure the reliability of expert testimony. Arizona has done so, and there is no reason to believe its rules are insufficient to avoid speculative evidence of mental illness. The risk of jury confusion also fails to justify the rule. The State defends its rule as a means to avoid the complexities of determining how and to what degree a mental illness affects a person's mental state. The difficulty of resolving a factual issue, though, does not present a sufficient reason to take evidence away from the jury when it is crucial for the defense. Even were the risk of jury confusion real enough to justify excluding evidence in most cases, this would provide little basis for prohibiting all evidence of mental illness without any inquiry into its likely effect on the jury or its role in deciding the linchpin issue of knowledge and intent. Indeed, Arizona has a rule in place to serve this very purpose.

Even assuming the reliability and jury-confusion justifications were persuasive in some cases, they would not suffice here. It does not overcome the constitutional objection to say that an evidentiary rule that is reasonable on its face can be applied to bar significant defense evidence without any rational basis for doing so. The reliability rationale has minimal applicability here. Many mental diseases are difficult to define and the subject of great debate. Schizophrenia, however, is a well-documented mental illness, and no one seriously disputes either its definition or its most prominent clinical manifestations. The State's own expert conceded that Clark had paranoid schizophrenia and was actively psychotic at the time of the killing. The jury-confusion rationale, if applicable here, is the result of the Court's own insistence on conflating the insanity defense and the question of intent. Considered on its own terms, the issue of intent and knowledge is a straightforward factual question. A trier of fact is quite capable of weighing defense testimony and then determining whether the accused did or did not intend to kill or knowingly kill a human being who was a police officer. The issue can be difficult to decide in particular instances, but no more so than many matters juries must confront.

The Court says mental-illness evidence "can easily mislead." and may "tell us little or nothing about the ability of the defendant to form *mens rea*." These generalities do not, however, show how relevant or misleading the evidence in this case would be. Evidence of Clark's mental illness bears directly on *mens rea*, for it suggests Clark may not have known he was killing a human being. While the Court discusses at length the likelihood of misjudgment from placing too much emphasis on evidence of mental illness, it ignores the risk of misjudging an innocent man guilty from refusing to consider this highly relevant evidence at all. This testimony was relevant to determining whether Clark knew he was killing a human being.

The fact that mental-illness evidence may be considered in deciding criminal responsibility does not compensate for its exclusion from consideration on the *mens rea* elements of the crime. While 13 States still impose significant restrictions on the use of mental-illness evidence to negate *mens rea*, a substantial majority of the States currently allow it. The fact that a reasonable number of States restrict this evidence weighs into the analysis, but applying the rule as a *per se* bar, as Arizona does, is so plainly unreasonable that it cannot be sustained. While defining mental illness is a difficult matter, the State seems to exclude the evidence one would think most reliable by allowing unexplained and uncategorized tendencies to be introduced while excluding relatively well-understood psychiatric testimony regarding well-documented mental illnesses. It is unclear, moreover, what would have happened in this case had the defendant wanted to testify that he thought Officer Moritz was an alien. If disallowed, it would be tantamount to barring Clark from testifying on his behalf to explain his own actions. If allowed, Arizona's rule would simply prohibit the corroboration necessary to make sense of Clark's explanation. In sum, the rule forces the jury to decide guilt in a fictional world with undefined and unexplained behaviors but without mental illness. This rule has no rational justification and imposes a significant burden upon a straightforward defense: He did not commit the crime with which he was charged.

POINTS FOR DISCUSSION

a. Indefinite Commitment

In *Jackson v. Indiana*, 406 U.S. 715 (1972), defendant was unable to understand the nature of the charges against him or to participate in his defense, and the court ordered him committed until he "is sane." Jackson's counsel claimed that the commitment amounted to a "life sentence" without conviction. The Court agreed, noting that Jackson was subjected "to a more lenient commitment standard and to a more stringent standard of release" which condemned him "in effect to permanent institutionalization without the showing required for commitment or the opportunity for release." The Court found violations of equal protection and due process.

b. Pleading Insanity

In order to invoke the sanity issue, defendant must plead the defense. Consider the requirements of the Federal Rules of Criminal Procedure:

Rule 12.2. Notice of Insanity Defense or Expert Testimony of Defendant's Mental Condition

(a) Defense of Insanity. If a defendant intends to rely upon the defense of insanity at the time of the alleged offense, the defendant shall, within the time provided for the filing of pretrial motions or at such later time as the court may direct, notify the attorney for the government in writing of such intention and file a copy of such notice with the clerk. If there is a failure to comply with the requirements of this subdivision, insanity may not be raised as a defense. The court may for cause shown allow late filing of the notice or grant additional time to the parties to prepare for trial or make such other order as may be appropriate.

(b) Expert Testimony of Defendant's Mental Condition. If a defendant intends to introduce expert testimony relating to a mental disease or defect or any other mental condition of the defendant bearing upon the issue of guilt, the defendant shall, within the time provided for the filing of pretrial motions or at such later time as the court may direct, notify the attorney for the government in writing of such intention and file a copy of such notice with the clerk. The court may for cause shown allow late filing of the notice or grant additional time to the parties to prepare for trial or make such other order as may be appropriate.

(c) Mental Examination of Defendant. In an appropriate case the court may, upon motion of the attorney for the government, order the defendant to submit to an examination pursuant to 18 U.S.C. § 4241 or 4242. No statement made by the defendant in the course of any examination provided for by this rule, whether the examination be with or without the consent of the defendant, no testimony by the expert based upon such statement, and no other fruits of the statement shall be admitted in evidence against the defendant in any criminal proceeding except on an issue respecting mental condition on which the defendant has introduced testimony.

(d) Failure to Comply. If there is a failure to give notice when required by subdivision (b) of this rule or to submit to an examination when ordered under subdivision (c) of this rule, the court may exclude the testimony of any expert witness offered by the defendant on the issue of the defendant's guilt.

c. **Imposing the Defense**

In *State v. Jones*, 99 Wash. 2d 735, 664 P.2d 1216 (En Banc 1983), the court held that an insanity plea could be imposed over the defendant's objection. However, in *Frendak v. United States*, 408 A.2d 364 (D.C. App. 1979), where the court also imposed an insanity plea over the defendant's objection, it was held that "the trial judge may not force an insanity defense on a defendant found competent to stand trial if the individual intelligently and voluntarily decides to forego that defense":

> A defendant may fear that an insanity acquittal will lead to confinement in a mental institution for a period longer than the potential jail sentence. Second, defendant may object to the quality of treatment or the type of

> confinement to which he may be subject in an institution for the mentally ill. Third, a defendant may choose to avoid the stigma of insanity. Fourth, in some states, an adjudication of insanity may affect a person's legal rights, for example, the right to vote or serve on a federal jury, and may even restrict his or her ability to obtain a driver's license. Finally, a defendant may oppose the imposition of an insanity defense because he or she views the crime as a political or religious protest which a finding of insanity would denigrate. In any event, a defendant may forego the defense because of a feeling that he or she is not insane, or that raising the defense would be equivalent to an admission of guilt. These reasons substantially outweigh the goal of ensuring that some abstract concept of justice is satisfied by protecting one who may be morally blameless from a conviction and punishment which he or she might choose to accept. Because the defendant must bear the ultimate consequences of any decision, if a defendant has acted intelligently and voluntarily, a trial court must defer to his or her decision to waive the insanity defense.

The court held that "the trial court still must have the discretion to raise an insanity defense, *sua sponte*, when a defendant does not have the capacity to reject the defense." When a defendant refuses to plead insanity, and the judge interposes the defense against his wishes, defendant is not automatically committed under federal law. *Lynch v. Overholser*, 369 U.S. 705 (1962).

d. Drugs & Competency

In *Sell v. United States*, 539 U.S. 166 (2003), the Court held that the Constitution allows the government to administer antipsychotic drugs involuntarily to a mentally ill criminal defendant—in order to render that defendant competent to stand trial for serious, but nonviolent, crimes—in limited circumstances. Relying on its prior decisions in *Washington v. Harper*, 494 U.S. 210 (1990), and *Riggins v. Nevada*, 504 U.S. 127 (1992), the Court stated that "the Constitution permits the Government involuntarily to administer antipsychotic drugs to a mentally ill defendant facing serious criminal charges in order to render that defendant competent to stand trial, but only if the treatment is medically appropriate, is substantially unlikely to have side effects that may undermine the fairness of the trial, and, taking account of less intrusive alternatives, is necessary significantly to further important governmental trial-related interests." The Court emphasized the important governmental interest in bringing a defendant charged with a serious crime to trial. However, the Court held that, "In order to make this evaluation, the court should focus upon such questions as: Why is it medically appropriate forcibly to administer antipsychotic drugs to an individual who (1) is *not* dangerous *and* (2) *is* competent to make up his own mind about treatment? Can bringing such an individual to trial *alone* justify in whole (or at least in significant part) administration of a drug that may have adverse side effects, including side effects that may to some extent impair a defense at trial? Courts must also consider whether a particular drug will tend to sedate a defendant, interfere with communication with counsel, prevent rapid reaction to trial developments, or diminish the ability to express emotions are matters important in determining the permissibility of medication to restore competence, but not necessarily relevant when dangerousness is primarily at issue. We cannot tell whether the side effects of antipsychotic medication were likely to undermine the fairness of a trial in Sell's case."

Because of dissatisfaction with the *M'Naghten* and irresistible impulse tests, the courts and the American Law Institute developed alternative tests.

e. Evaluation by State Psychiatrists

In *State v. Richardson*, 276 Or. 325, 555 P.2d 202 (In Banc 1976), the court held that "when a defendant pleads not guilty by reason of insanity the state is entitled to a mental examination," and the privilege against self-incrimination does not protect a defendant against that examination: "if he refuses, his affirmative defense of mental defect will be stricken." However, in *Motes v. State*, 256 Ga. 831, 353 S.E.2d 348 (1987), the court held that defendant was not required to submit to an examination if he proceeds without an expert: "If the defendant wants to introduce expert testimony, then the state must be allowed the same privilege and the defendant must cooperate."

f. Consequences of NGI Verdict

In *State v. Karstetter*, 110 Ariz. 539, 521 P.2d 626 (In Banc 1974), defendant was convicted of murder after the prosecutor stated in closing argument that the court appointed psychologist did not recommend hospitalization and psychiatric care. The court concluded that the prosecutor did not commit reversible error even though a majority of the states preclude the jury from receiving this information. See *Erdman v. State*, 315 Md. 46, 553 A.2d 244, 249–50 (1989). However, in *Shannon v. United States*, 512 U.S. 573 (1994), the U.S. Supreme Court held that a federal district court is not required to inform the jury of the consequences of rendering a "not guilty by reason of insanity" (NGI) verdict: "The principle that juries are not to consider the consequences of their verdicts is a reflection of the basic division of labor in our legal system between judge and jury. The jury's function is to find the facts and to decide whether, on those facts, the defendant is guilty of the crime charged. The judge, by contrast, imposes sentence on the defendant after the jury has arrived at a guilty verdict. Information regarding the consequences of a verdict is therefore irrelevant to the jury's task. Moreover, providing jurors sentencing information invites them to ponder matters that are not within their province, distracts them from their fact-finding responsibilities, and creates a strong possibility of confusion. An instruction of some form may be necessary under certain limited circumstances. If, for example, a witness or prosecutor states in the presence of the jury that a particular defendant would 'go free' if found NGI, it may be necessary for the district court to intervene with an instruction to counter such a misstatement."

In *Cordova v. People*, 817 P.2d 66 (Colo., 1991), the trial court overruled defendant's request for an informational instruction advising the jury of the consequences of a NGI verdict (that defendant would be committed). The court reversed: "In light of the manifest risk of the jury's mistaken belief that a verdict of not guilty by reason of impaired mental condition might result in the defendant's return to the community—a risk which the defendant's requested instruction was calculated to negate—the fairness of the trial was detrimentally affected by the trial court's erroneous ruling on the defendant's request for the informational instruction." See also *State v. Shickles*, 760 P.2d 291 (Utah 1988); *State v. Hamann*, 285 N.W.2d 180 (Iowa 1979).

g. Jury's Awareness of Drugs

In *In re Pray*, 133 Vt. 253, 336 A.2d 174 (1975), defendant, while in state custody for trial purposes, was given thorazine four times a day, and tofranil and phenobarbital twice a day, and an occasional dosage of chlorohydrate. Absent the medicine, he was not competent to stand trial. With the medicine, he was quiet, tractable, rational, well oriented, answered questions clearly, cooperatively, and knew what was going on. He showed no effects of the depression on which his insanity defense was based. The U.S. Supreme Court reversed the conviction: "At the very least, the jury should have been informed that he was under heavy, sedative medication, that his behavior in their presence was strongly conditioned by drugs administered to him at the direction of the State, and that his defense of insanity was to be applied to a basic behavior pattern that was not the one they were observing. In fact, it may well have been necessary, in view of the critical nature of the issue, to expose the jury to the undrugged, unsedated Gary Pray, insofar as safety and trial progress might permit. A life sentence ought not to rest on the shaky premise that an undisclosed behavioral alteration, brought about by the State, did not affect the jury's resolution of the issue of insanity. The matter must be retried."

h. Bifurcation of Guilt & Sanity

In some states, the insanity issue is bifurcated from guilt issues. In *Vardas v. Estelle*, 715 F.2d 206 (5th Cir. 1983), defendant claimed that his due process rights were violated by the established Texas procedure allowing the issue of sanity to be tried contemporaneously with the issue of guilt or innocence. He claimed that he should have been granted a separate trial on the issue of insanity. The court rejected the argument.

i. Guilty but Mentally Ill

John Hinckley attempted to assassinate President Ronald Reagan outside a hotel in Washington, D.C., and was acquitted on the grounds of insanity. *See United States v. Hinckley*, 525 F. Supp. 1342 (D.D.C. 1981), *aff'd*, 672 F.2d 115 (D.C.Cir. 1982). The verdict provoked a strong adverse public reaction. Following the Hinckley verdict, a number of states made it more difficult to assert the insanity defense and others abolished the defense altogether. The verdict also led to creation of the so-called "guilty but mentally ill" verdict. Essentially, under this approach, defendant is convicted of the crime but declared to be mentally ill. In theory, this verdict requires the state to determine whether psychiatric treatment is necessary or warranted, and (hopefully) to provide treatment. At the end of the sentence, defendant must be released—unless the state is able to satisfy the standards for commitment. Led also to 18 U.S.C. § 20(a).

j. Lay Witnesses

In *United States v. Milne*, 487 F.2d 1232 (5th Cir. 1973), defendant sought to offer the testimony of three lay witnesses who described their interactions with defendant, his heavy drug use and his bizarre behavior. All of the witnesses had known defendant for a year or more and had seen him nearly every day. The court overruled the trial court's decision to exclude the evidence: "The lay opinion of a witness who is sufficiently acquainted with the person involved and has observed his conduct is admissible as to the sanity of such individual." "Insanity is a variance from usual or normal conduct. For that reason a lay witness should be required to testify as to unusual, abnormal or bizarre conduct before being permitted to express an opinion as to insanity. The trial judge must exercise a sound discretion in concluding whether or not a particular witness is qualified."

k. *Yates* Case

In 2006, the murder conviction of Andrea Yates was reversed on appeal because of false testimony given by the State's expert witness at trial. Yates is a woman who murdered her five children in 2001 by drowning them in a bathtub.

See Deborah W. Denno, *Who Is Andrea Yates? A Short Story About Insanity*, 10 DUKE J. GENDER L. & POLICY 1–139 (2003). On July 26, 2006 at her retrial, Andrea Yates was acquitted by reason of insanity under the *M'Naghten* test, based on evidence of her post-partum depression and psychosis. Under Texas law, she must be institutionalized until a court decides that she is no longer deemed to be a threat to herself or to others. She was sent to a prison-like maximum security facility and she was later moved to a low security mental hospital.

> **Take Note**
>
> Insanity can be relevant at three different points in the criminal process. First, as in *M'Naghten*, individuals who commit criminal acts while insane cannot be convicted of those acts. Second, defendants who are insane at the time of their trials cannot be tried, and will be committed until they are sane enough to proceed. The defendant must "have sufficient present ability to consult with his lawyer with a reasonable degree of rational understanding—and have a rational as well as factual understanding of the proceedings against him." *Dusky v. United States*, 362 U.S. 402 (1960). Finally, defendants sentenced to capital punishment cannot be executed until they regain their sanity. *See Ford v. Wainwright*, 477 U.S. 399 (1986); *Panetti v. Quarterman*, 551 U.S. 930 (2007).

1. Multiple Personalities and the Billy Milligan Case

Within the already controversial subject of the insanity defense exists a defense that is challenging for criminal courts and forensic psychiatrists: the multiple personality disorder, known now as the Dissociative Identity Disorder. The disorder, recognized by the Diagnostic and Statistical Manual of Mental Disorders, is characterized by a person whose psychiatric examination reveals two or more distinct personalities, and who possess legitimate gaps in recalling events like personal information or traumatic events. The Ohio case of William (Billy) Milligan is the first case where the Disorder was successfully raised by a criminal defendant. In 1975 Milligan was first arrested for armed robbery and rape. Two years later he was arrested again, this time for the rape of three women on the Ohio State University campus. Milligan's lawyers argued that Milligan possessed twenty-four distinct personalities and that two of the personalities, "Ragan" (a twenty-three-year-old Yugoslavian male) and "Adalana" (a nineteen-year-old lesbian female) committed the offenses. A team of several psychiatrists confirmed Milligan's diagnoses for the disorder. Ultimately, Milligan was found not guilty by reason of insanity by the Ohio State Court and hospitalized in a state mental hospital. He was released in 1991 and died in 2014. As might be expected, Milligan's successful defense drew considerable public interest.

Do you think a person legitimately diagnosed with a Dissociative Identity Disorder and having multiple personalities can form the requisite *mens rea* to be held accountable for their crimes?

2. Effect of Insanity Acquittal

What happens to a defendant who has been acquitted by reason of insanity? In some jurisdictions, the defendant is automatically committed to an insane asylum. In most jurisdictions, the decision to commit is discretionary. At the federal level, an acquittee may be held for up to 40 days. 18 U.S.C. § 4243. In *In re Rosenfield*, 157 F. Supp. 18 (D.D.C. 1957), defendant was found not guilty by reason of insanity and was committed to Saint Elizabeth's Hospital for the mentally ill under a statute requiring mandatory commitment of those acquitted on insanity grounds. Later, defendant was conditionally released. The Court upheld the statute.

JONES V. UNITED STATES
463 U.S. 354 (1983).

JUSTICE POWELL delivered the opinion of the Court.

The question is whether petitioner, who was committed to a mental hospital upon being acquitted of a criminal offense by reason of insanity, must be released because he has been hospitalized for a period longer than he might have served in prison had he been convicted.

In the District of Columbia a criminal defendant who successfully invokes the insanity defense is committed to a mental hospital. The statute provides several ways of obtaining release. Within 50 days of commitment the acquittee is entitled to a judicial hearing to determine his eligibility for release, at which he has the burden of proving by a preponderance of the evidence that he is no longer mentally ill or dangerous. If he fails to meet this burden, the committed acquittee subsequently may be released, with court approval, upon certification of his recovery by the hospital chief of service. Alternatively, the acquittee is entitled to a judicial hearing every six months at which he may establish by a preponderance of the evidence that he is entitled to release.

Independent of its provision for the commitment of insanity acquittees, the District of Columbia also has adopted a civil-commitment procedure, under which an individual may be committed upon clear and convincing proof by the Government that he is mentally ill and likely to injure himself or others. The individual may demand a jury in the civil-commitment proceeding. Once committed, a patient may be released at any time upon certification of recovery by the hospital chief of service. Alternatively, the patient is entitled after the first 90 days, and subsequently at 6-month intervals, to request a judicial hearing at which he may gain his release by proving by a preponderance of the evidence that he is no longer mentally ill or dangerous.

On September 19, 1975, petitioner was arrested for attempting to steal a jacket from a department store and charged with attempted petit larceny, a misdemeanor punishable by a maximum prison sentence of one year. The court ordered petitioner committed to St. Elizabeth's, a public hospital for the mentally ill, for a determination of his competency to stand trial. On March 2, 1976, a hospital psychologist submitted a report to the court stating that petitioner was competent to stand trial, that petitioner suffered from "Schizophrenia, paranoid type," and that petitioner's alleged offense was "the product of his mental disease." Petitioner subsequently pleaded not guilty by reason of insanity. The Government did not contest the plea. The court found petitioner not guilty by reason of insanity and committed him to St. Elizabeth's pursuant to § 24–301(d)(1).

On May 25, 1976, the court held the 50-day hearing required by § 24–301(d)(2)(A). A psychologist from St. Elizabeth's testified that, in the opinion of the staff, petitioner continued to suffer from paranoid schizophrenia and that "because his illness is still quite active, he is still a danger to himself and to others." Petitioner's counsel presented no evidence. The court then found that "defendant-patient is mentally ill and as a result of his mental illness, at this time, he constitutes a danger to himself or others." Petitioner was returned to St. Elizabeth's. Petitioner obtained new counsel and a second release hearing was held on February 22, 1977. By that date, petitioner had been hospitalized for more than one year, the maximum period he could have spent in prison if he had been convicted. On that basis, he demanded that he be released unconditionally or recommitted pursuant to the civil-commitment standards in § 21–545(b), including a jury trial and proof by clear and convincing evidence of his mental illness and dangerousness. The Superior Court denied petitioner's request for a civil-commitment hearing, reaffirmed the findings made at the May 25, 1976, hearing, and continued petitioner's commitment to St. Elizabeth's. The District of Columbia Court of Appeals affirmed the judgment. We granted certiorari and affirm.

It is clear that "commitment for any purpose constitutes a significant deprivation of liberty that requires due process protection." A State must have "a constitutionally adequate purpose for the confinement." Congress has determined that a criminal defendant found not guilty by reason of insanity in the District of Columbia should be committed indefinitely to a mental institution for treatment and the protection of society. Petitioner does not contest the Government's authority to commit a mentally ill and dangerous person indefinitely to a mental institution, but rather contends that "the petitioner's trial was not a constitutionally adequate hearing to justify an indefinite commitment."

Petitioner's argument rests principally on *Addington v. Texas*, 441 U.S. 418 (1979), in which the Court held that the Due Process Clause requires the Government in a civil-commitment proceeding to demonstrate by clear and convincing evidence that the individual is mentally ill and dangerous. Petitioner contends that these due process standards were not met in his case because the judgment of not guilty by reason of insanity did not constitute a finding of present mental illness and dangerousness and because it was established only by a preponderance of the evidence. Petitioner concludes that the Government's only conceivably legitimate justification for automatic commitment is to ensure that insanity acquittees do not escape confinement entirely, and that this interest can justify commitment at most for a period equal to the maximum prison sentence the acquittee could have received if convicted. Because petitioner has been hospitalized for longer than the one year he might have served in prison, he asserts that he should be released unconditionally or recommitted under the District's civil-commitment procedures.

We turn first to whether the finding of insanity at the criminal trial is sufficiently probative of mental illness and dangerousness to justify commitment. A verdict of not guilty by reason of insanity establishes two facts: (I) defendant committed an act that constitutes a criminal offense, and (ii) he committed the act because of mental illness. Congress has determined that these findings constitute an adequate basis for hospitalizing the acquittee as a dangerous and mentally ill person. We cannot say that it was unreasonable and therefore unconstitutional for Congress to make this determination.

The fact that a person has been found, beyond a reasonable doubt, to have committed a criminal act certainly indicates dangerousness. Indeed, this concrete evidence generally may be at least as persuasive as any predictions about dangerousness that might be made in a civil-commitment proceeding. We do not agree with petitioner's suggestion that the requisite dangerousness is not established by proof that a person committed a non-violent crime against property. This Court never has held that "violence," however that term might be defined, is a prerequisite for a constitutional commitment.

Nor can we say that it was unreasonable for Congress to determine that the insanity acquittal supports an inference of continuing mental illness. It comports with common sense to conclude that someone whose mental illness was sufficient to lead him to commit a criminal act is likely to remain ill and in need of treatment. The precise evidentiary force of the insanity acquittal, of course, may vary from case to case, but the Due Process Clause does not require Congress to make classifications that fit every individual with the same degree of relevance. Because a hearing is provided within 50 days of the commitment, there is assurance that every acquittee has prompt opportunity to obtain release if he has recovered.

Petitioner also argues that, whatever the evidentiary value of the insanity acquittal, the Government lacks a legitimate reason for committing insanity acquittees automatically because it can introduce the insanity acquittal as evidence in a subsequent civil proceeding. This argument fails to consider the Government's strong interest in avoiding the need to conduct a *de novo* commitment hearing following every insanity acquittal—a hearing at which a jury trial may be demanded, and at which the Government bears the burden of proof by clear and convincing evidence. Instead of focusing on the critical question whether the acquittee has recovered, the new proceeding likely would have to relitigate much of the criminal trial. These problems accent the Government's important interest in automatic commitment. We therefore conclude that a finding of not guilty by reason of insanity is a sufficient foundation for commitment of an insanity acquittee for the purposes of treatment and the protection of society.

Petitioner next contends that his indefinite commitment is unconstitutional because the proof of his insanity was based only on a preponderance of the evidence, as compared to *Addington's* civil-commitment requirement of proof by clear and convincing evidence. Petitioner ignores important differences between the class of potential civil-commitment candidates and the class of insanity acquittees that justify differing standards of proof. The *Addington* Court expressed particular concern that members of the public could be confined on the basis of "some abnormal behavior which might be perceived by some as symptomatic of a mental or emotional disorder, but which is in fact within a range of conduct that is generally acceptable." In view of this concern, the Court deemed it inappropriate to ask the individual "to share equally with society the risk of error." But since automatic commitment under § 24–301(d) (1) follows only if the acquittee himself advances insanity as a defense and proves that his criminal act was a product of his mental illness, there is good reason for diminished concern as to the risk of error. The proof that he committed a criminal act as a result of mental illness eliminates the risk that he is being committed for mere "idiosyncratic behavior." A criminal act by definition is not "within a range of conduct that is generally acceptable."

We conclude that concerns critical to our decision in *Addington* are diminished or absent in the case of insanity acquittees. Accordingly, there is no reason for adopting the same standard of proof in both cases. "Due process is flexible and calls for such procedural protections as the particular situation demands." The preponderance of the evidence standard comports with due process for commitment of insanity acquittees.[17]

The remaining question is whether petitioner nonetheless is entitled to his release because he has been hospitalized for a period longer than he could have been incarcerated if convicted. The Due Process Clause "requires that the nature and duration of commitment bear some reasonable relation to the purpose for which the individual is committed." The purpose of commitment following an insanity acquittal, like that of civil commitment, is to treat the individual's mental illness and protect him and society from his potential dangerousness. The committed acquittee is entitled to release when he has recovered his sanity or is no longer dangerous. Because it is impossible to predict how long it will take for any given individual to recover—or indeed whether he ever will recover—Congress has chosen, as it has with respect to civil commitment, to leave the length of commitment indeterminate, subject to periodic review of the patient's suitability for release.

In light of the congressional purposes underlying commitment of insanity acquittees, we think petitioner clearly errs in contending that an acquittee's hypothetical maximum sentence provides the constitutional limit for his commitment. A particular sentence of incarceration is chosen to reflect society's view of the proper response to commission of a particular criminal offense, based on a variety of considerations such as retribution, deterrence, and rehabilitation. The State may punish a person convicted of a crime even if satisfied that he is unlikely to commit further crimes.

Different considerations underlie commitment of an insanity acquittee. As he was not convicted, he may not be punished. His confinement rests on his continuing illness and dangerousness. Thus, under the District of Columbia statute, no matter how serious the act committed by the acquittee, he may be released within 50 days of his acquittal if he has recovered. In contrast, one who

---

[17] A defendant could be required to prove his insanity by a higher standard than a preponderance of the evidence.

committed a less serious act may be confined for a longer period if he remains ill and dangerous. There simply is no necessary correlation between severity of the offense and length of time necessary for recovery. The length of the acquittee's hypothetical criminal sentence therefore is irrelevant to the purposes of his commitment.

We hold that when a criminal defendant establishes by a preponderance of the evidence that he is not guilty of a crime by reason of insanity, the Constitution permits the Government, on the basis of the insanity judgment, to confine him to a mental institution until such time as he has regained his sanity or is no longer a danger to himself or society. This holding accords with the widely and reasonably held view that insanity acquittees constitute a special class that should be treated differently from other candidates for commitment. We have observed before that "when Congress undertakes to act in areas fraught with medical and scientific uncertainties, legislative options must be especially broad and courts should be cautious not to rewrite legislation." This admonition has particular force in the context of legislative efforts to deal with the special problems raised by the insanity defense.

The judgment of the District of Columbia Court of Appeals is

Affirmed.

JUSTICE BRENNAN, with whom JUSTICE MARSHALL and JUSTICE BLACKMUN join, dissenting.

The Government's interests in committing petitioner are the isolation, protection, and treatment of a person who may, through no fault of his own, cause harm to others or to himself. Whenever involuntary commitment is a possibility, the Government has a strong interest in accurate, efficient commitment decisions. Nevertheless, *Addington* held both that the Government's interest in accuracy was not impaired by a requirement that it bear the burden of persuasion by clear and convincing evidence, and that the individual's interests in liberty and autonomy required the Government to bear at least that burden. An acquittal by reason of insanity of a single, nonviolent misdemeanor is not a constitutionally adequate substitute for the due process protections of proof by clear and convincing evidence of present mental illness or dangerousness, with the Government bearing the burden of persuasion. I cannot agree that the Government should be excused from the burden that *Addington* held was required by due process.

JUSTICE STEVENS, dissenting.

A plea of guilty, may provide a sufficient basis for confinement for the period fixed by the legislature as punishment for the acknowledged conduct, provided of course that the acquittee is given a fair opportunity to prove that he has recovered from his illness. But surely if he is to be confined for a longer period, the State must shoulder the burden of proving by clear and convincing evidence that such additional confinement is appropriate.

Take Note

In *Jones v. State*, 289 So.2d 725 (Fla. 1974), defendant offered the testimony of two psychiatrists and a psychologist based on a history testified to by them. The State objected to the testimony on the basis that defendant had not testified as to the history. The court concluded that a "qualified expert may testify to his opinion concerning the defendant's mental condition based either upon (1) personal examination of the defendant made by the witness, or (2) the testimony in the case, if he has been in court and heard it all. (3) He may also give his opinion upon hypothetical questions propounded by counsel." In addition, "it is not necessary that the expert state the detailed circumstances of the examination before giving his finding. The facts and symptoms which he observed, and on which he bases his opinion, may be brought out on cross-examination." "The court below should have allowed the psychiatrists to testify as to their opinions without relating what the defendant told concerning the alleged facts of the case." "Unless a person is a raving maniac or complete imbecile, a jury can hardly be deemed competent to reach a satisfactory decision on the question of his mental condition without the aid of expert witnesses."

Food for Thought

Prior to *Jones*, in order to civilly commit someone to a mental institution, the state was required to prove by clear and convincing evidence that he was presently mentally ill and dangerous to himself or to others. *Jones* suggests that such proof is not required when a defendant is found not guilty by reason of insanity. Was *Jones* correctly decided? *See State ex rel Collins v. Superior Court*, 150 Ariz. 295, 723 P.2d 644 (1986).

Food for Thought

How does an attorney go about proving that a client was insane at the time of the alleged offense? In other words, what types of evidence might be offered in support of a plea of insanity?

POINTS FOR DISCUSSION

a. Civil Commitment

In *Baxstrom v. Herold*, 383 U.S. 107 (1966), when petitioner's prison term ended, he was committed to a hospital for the criminally ill. The Court held that petitioner had not been committed pursuant to proper procedures: "Petitioner was denied equal protection by the statutory procedure under which a person may be civilly committed at the expiration of his penal sentence without the jury review available to all other persons civilly committed. Petitioner was further denied equal protection by his civil commitment to an institution maintained by the Department of Correction beyond the expiration of his prison term without a judicial determination that he is dangerously mentally ill."

b. Medical Treatment

In *Rouse v. Cameron*, 373 F.2d 451, 125 U.S. App. D.C. 366 (D.C.Cir. 1966), defendant was acquitted on the grounds of insanity and confined to Saint Elizabeth's Hospital. When he received no psychiatric treatment, defendant sought habeas corpus. The court held that defendant was entitled to treatment, but not necessarily to release: "The purpose of involuntary hospitalization is treatment, not punishment. Commitment rests upon the 'necessity for treatment of the mental condition which led to the acquittal by reason of insanity.' Absent treatment, the hospital is 'a penitentiary where one could be held indefinitely for no convicted offense even though the offense of which he was previously acquitted might not have been a serious felony or might have been a misdemeanor.'" The court's holding was based on a statute which provided that a "person hospitalized for a mental illness shall be entitled to medical and psychiatric care and treatment." Some studies show that most insanity acquittees spend more time in mental hospitals than they would have spent in prison had they been convicted of the crime of which they were acquitted.

D. INFANCY & MENTAL RETARDATION

Mental capacity issues can arise when a child or a mentally retarded adult commits a crime. In these cases, there will be questions about whether such a person has the criminal capacity to be held responsible for the crime. Consider the following case.

IN RE DEVON T.
85 Md. App. 674, 584 A.2d 1287 (1991).

MOYLAN, JUDGE.

In a world dizzy with change, it is reassuring to find Daniel *M'Naghten* alive and well in juvenile court. It was, of course, *M'Naghten*'s bungled attempt to assassinate Prime Minister Sir Robert Peel, killing by mistake Sir Robert's private secretary Edward Drummond, that led to his prosecution for murder and the assertion of his now eponymic insanity defense. When the House of Lords placed its imprimatur upon the jury's acquittal by reason of insanity, "the *M'Naghten* test" was impressed indelibly upon the Common Law of Anglo-America. *Regina v. M'Naghten,* 10 Cl. and Fin. 200, 8 Eng. Rep. 718 (1843).

The cognitive capacity to distinguish right from wrong in the language of *M'Naghten* was not a characteristic of the insanity defense exclusively. It has traditionally been the common denominator criterion for a whole family of defenses based upon mental incapacity—insanity, infancy, mental retardation, intoxication (at least of the involuntary variety). The cause of the mental incapacity might vary from one such defense to the next but the ultimate nature of the resulting incapacity was a constant. In any of its manifestations, criminal responsibility traditionally turned and largely still turns upon the difference between a mind *doli capax* (capable of malice or criminal intent) and a mind *doli incapax* (incapable of malice or criminal intent). Capability or capacity might be eroded in various ways but the ultimate quality of the required mental capacity itself was unchanging. Hence, we tentatively use the traditional *M'Naghten* test in our review of an adjudication of juvenile delinquency in the Circuit Court for Baltimore City. For the moment, however, let Daniel M'Naghten retire to the wings as we bring onto the stage the contemporary players.

The juvenile appellant, Devon T., was charged with committing an act which, if committed by an adult, would have constituted the crime of possession of heroin with intent to distribute. The trial court concluded that Devon was delinquent. The case arose when Devon was directed to empty his pockets by the security guard at the Booker T. Washington Middle School, under the watchful eye of the Assistant Principal, the search produced a brown bag containing twenty zip-lock pink plastic bags that contained heroin. Devon contends that the State did not offer legally sufficient evidence to rebut his presumptive incapacity because of infancy. At the time of the offense, Devon was 13 years, 10 months, and 2 weeks of age.

The case law and the academic literature alike conceptualize the infancy defense as but an instance of the broader phenomenon of a defense based upon lack of moral responsibility or capacity. The criminal law generally will only impose its retributive or deterrent sanctions upon those who are morally blameworthy—those who know they are doing wrong but nonetheless persist in their wrongdoing.

After several centuries of pondering the criminal capacity of children and experimenting with various cut-off ages, the Common Law settled upon its current resolution of the problem by late Tudor and early Stuart times. As explained by LaFave & Scott, *Criminal Law*, (2d ed. 1986), at 398, the resolution was fairly simple:

"At common law, children under the age of seven are conclusively presumed to be without criminal capacity, those who have reached the age of fourteen are treated as fully responsible, while as to those between the ages of seven and fourteen there is a rebuttable presumption of criminal incapacity."

The authors make clear that infancy was an instance of criminal capacity generally: "The early common law infancy defense was based upon an unwillingness to punish those thought to be incapable of forming criminal intent and not of an age where the threat of punishment could serve as a deterrent." *See also* Walkover, *The Infancy Defense in the New Juvenile Court*, 31 UCLA L. REV. 503, 507 (1984). In *Adams v. State*, 8 Md. App. 684, 262 A.2d 69 (1970), *cert. denied*, 400 U.S. 928 (1970), we recognized for the first time this venerable common law defense as part of the inherent law of Maryland.

With the creation shortly after the turn of the present century of juvenile courts in America, diverting many youthful offenders from criminal courts into equity and other civil courts, the question arose as to whether the infancy defense had any pertinence to a juvenile delinquency adjudication. Under the initially prevailing philosophy that the State was acting in delinquency cases as *parens patriae* (sovereign parent of the country), the State was perceived to be not the retributive punisher of the child for its misdeeds but the paternalistic guardian of the child for its own best interests. Under such a regime, the moral responsibility or blameworthiness of the child was of no consequence. Morally responsible or not, the child was in apparent need of the State's rehabilitative intervention and the delinquency adjudication was but the avenue for such intervention. This was the philosophy that persuaded this Court in *Matter of Davis* to forbear from extending the defense of infancy to juvenile court proceedings.

Over the course of the century, however, buffeted by unanticipated urban deterioration and staggering case loads, the reforming vision faded. Although continuing to stress rehabilitation over retribution more heavily than did the adult criminal courts, delinquency adjudications nonetheless took on, in practice if not in theory, many of the attributes of junior varsity criminal trials. The Supreme Court, in *In re Gault*, 387 U.S. 1 (1967), and *In re Winship*, 397 U.S. 358 (1970), acknowledged this slow but inexorable transformation of the juvenile court apparatus into one with increasingly penal overtones. It ultimately guaranteed, therefore, a juvenile charged with delinquency most of the due process protections afforded an adult charged with crime. *Mullaney v. Wilbur*, 421 U.S. 684 (1975), soon made explicit what was implicit in *Winship* that among the elements of a crime that the State is constitutionally obligated to prove beyond a reasonable doubt are mental elements as well as physical elements. A crime, by definition, consists of guilty mind as well as a guilty act—the *mens rea* as well as the *actus reus*. It follows ineluctably that if the State, when the issue is properly generated, is required to prove beyond a reasonable doubt the existence of a criminally responsible *mens rea* when proceeding against an adult, it cannot be relieved of that burden when proceeding in a quasi-penal fashion against a juvenile.

In terms of the applicability of the infancy defense to delinquency proceedings, the implications of the new dispensation are clear. A finding of delinquency, unlike other proceedings in a juvenile court, unmistakably connotes some degree of blameworthiness and unmistakably exposes the delinquent to, whatever the gloss, the possibility of unpleasant sanctions. Clearly, the juvenile would have as an available defense to the delinquency charge 1) the fact that he was too criminally insane to have known that what he did was wrong, 2) that he was too mentally retarded to have known that what he did was wrong, or 3) that he was too involuntarily intoxicated through no fault of his own to have known that what he did was wrong. It would be inconceivable that he could be found blameworthy and suffer sanctions, notwithstanding precisely the same lack of understanding and absence of moral accountability, simply because the cognitive defect was caused by infancy.

The infancy defense was not applied to all juvenile court proceedings but only to delinquency adjudications, where moral blameworthiness is an integral part of the wrongdoing. Where the conduct itself of the juvenile, irrespective of moral accountability, calls for some rehabilitative intervention on the part of the State, Judge Eldridge carefully pointed out that the State may still file a petition alleging a Child in Need of Supervision (CINS) or a Child in Need of Assistance

(CINA). "As these proceedings are not necessarily based on the commission of acts constituting crimes, the infancy defense obviously has no relevance to them."

In a juvenile delinquency adjudication, however, the defense of infancy is now indisputably available in precisely the same manner as it is available in a criminal trial. The availability of such a defense raises several subsidiary questions. What precisely is the *probandum*—the quality of mind that has to be proved? To whom are allocated the burdens of proof (production and persuasion) with respect to that *probandum*? What are the standards or levels of proof necessary to carry those burdens?

With respect to the allocation of both burdens, the answer is clear. Once the question of criminal incapacity because of infancy is legitimately in the case, the unequivocal command of the due process clause is that the burdens of proof (assuming the proper generation of the issue) are allocated to the State. *In re Winship*, 397 U.S. 358, 364 (1970). It is equally clear, under *Winship*, that the State's constitutionally mandated standard of persuasion is that of beyond a reasonable doubt.

Those questions do not concern us here. Our attention, rather, turns to the two remaining questions: 1) what precisely is that quality of mind that constitutes criminal capacity in an infant? and 2) was the State's evidence in this case legally sufficient to satisfy its burden of production that the infant here possessed such mental capacity?

Before the juvenile master, the appellant timely raised the infancy defense. One party or the other introduced the undisputed fact that at the time of the allegedly delinquent act, Devon was 13 years, 10 months, and 2 weeks of age. Thus, the issue of mental incapacity due to infancy was properly before the court.

On that issue, Devon initially had the benefit of presumptive incapacity. The presumption having been generated, the State had the burdens (of both production and persuasion) of rebutting that presumption. Assuming that it met its burden of production, an issue we shall turn to in the next section of this opinion, the State successfully carried its burden of persuasion. The fact finder was persuaded. Since the weighing of evidence (that admissible data which may persuade one fact finder not at all or only a little bit may persuade another fact finder a lot) is the exclusive prerogative of the fact finder, there is nothing before us with respect to the burden of persuasion.

To overcome the presumption of incapacity, what precisely was that quality of Devon's mind as to which the State was required to produce legally sufficient evidence? It was required to produce evidence permitting the reasonable inference that Devon—the Ghost of *M'Naghten* speaks:—"at the time of doing the act knew the difference between right and wrong."

We resort to the analogy between this particular incapacity and other incapacities as a precedential "backup" because the Maryland case law bearing directly upon this particular instance of the larger phenomenon is so scant. The first of our analogues is incapacity due to involuntary intoxication. Although as a policy matter, general mental incapacity (even when, in fact, present) may never be predicated upon *voluntary* intoxication, involuntary intoxication may give rise to a defense of mental incapacity in much the same way that insanity traditionally did. The authorities generally analyzed the intoxication (provided it was involuntary) in terms of its corrosive effect upon the cognitive ability of the mind to discriminate between right and wrong.

The second of our analogues is incapacity due to mental retardation. The Common Law always treated mental retardation as a separate category of mental incapacity, although it analogized it to both infancy and lunacy as an effective cause of the inability to know right from wrong, to distinguish between good and evil. Maryland has recently merged two of these traditionally distinguishable incapacity defenses into one, broadening its test for "insanity" or "criminal responsibility" to include as an effective cause thereof not only "mental disorder" but also "mental retardation." Health-Gen. Art., § 12–108(a) (1982, 1990 Repl. Vol).

The third and final analogue is the thoroughly litigated defense of incapacity due to criminal insanity during the approximate century and a quarter when that defense was analyzed exclusively in terms of cognitive capacity under the *M'Naghten* test.

The analogy between incapacity due to infancy and incapacity due to insanity, mental retardation, or involuntary intoxication has lost some of its original symmetry to the extent that those latter incapacities have been broadened (directly or indirectly) to include a volitional as well as a cognitive component. The infancy defense retains its exclusive concern with the cognitive element.

When *Adams v. State* first incorporated the infancy defense into Maryland law, the opinion of Judge Morton made it very clear that the pivotal mental quality being examined was *M'Naghten*'s classic cognitive appreciation of the difference between right and wrong:

"It was, therefore, incumbent upon the State to produce sufficient evidence to overcome the presumption that the appellant was *doli incapax,* an expression ordinarily employed by the text writers. The proof necessary to meet this burden has been variously phrased: It must be shown that the individual 'had discretion to judge between good and evil;' 'knew right from wrong;' had 'a guilty knowledge of wrong-doing;' was 'competent to know the nature and consequences of his conduct and to appreciate that it was wrong.' Perhaps the most modern definition of the test is simply that the surrounding circumstances must demonstrate, beyond a reasonable doubt, that the individual knew what he was doing and that it was wrong."

In *In re William A.*, 313 Md. 690, 548 A.2d 130 (1988), Judge Eldridge perceptively stressed that the critical mental faculty for rendering an infant morally responsible for his otherwise delinquent actions was that same cognitive or intellectual capacity that would enable an adult to entertain a criminal *mens rea*:

"As previously discussed, Maryland law defines a 'delinquent act' as 'an act which would be a crime if committed by an adult.' Most crimes require some *mens rea* characteristics; they are elements of the crimes. If, when one commits an act, the requisite *mens rea* for a crime does not exist, the act does not constitute a crime. The defense of infancy relates to the presence or absence of the *mens rea*. Consequently, the infancy defense relates to whether the act committed by a juvenile "would be a crime if committed by an adult." In short, when Devon walked around the Booker T. Washington Middle School with twenty zip-lock bags of heroin, apparently for sale or other distribution, could Devon pass the *M'Naghten* test? Was there legally sufficient data before him to permit Judge Brown to infer that Devon knew the difference between right and wrong and knew, moreover, that what he was doing was wrong?

As we turn to the legal sufficiency of the evidence, it is important to know that the only mental quality we are probing is the cognitive capacity to distinguish right from wrong. Other aspects of Devon's mental and psychological make-up, such as his scholastic attainments, his I.Q., his social maturity, his societal adjustment, his basic personality, etc., might well require evidentiary input from psychologists, from parents, from teachers or other school authorities, etc. On knowledge of the difference between right and wrong, however, the general case law, as well as the inherent logic of the situation, has established that that particular psychic phenomenon may sometimes permissibly be inferred from the very circumstances of the criminal or delinquent act itself. Indeed, *Adams v. State* spoke of the fact that "the surrounding circumstances must demonstrate that the individual knew what he was doing and that it was wrong."

Before looking at the circumstances of the delinquent act in this case, a word is in order about the quantity of proof required. *In re William A.* quotes with approval from *Adams v. State*, 8 Md. App. at 688–689, 262 A.2d 69, in pointing out:

> "It is generally held that the presumption of *doli incapax* is 'extremely strong at the age of seven and diminishes gradually until it disappears entirely at the age of fourteen.' Since the strength of the presumption of incapacity decreases with the increase in the years of the accused, the quantum of proof necessary to overcome the presumption would diminish in substantially the same ratio."

See also R. Boyce & R. Perkins, *Criminal Law,* (3d ed. 1983), at 936.

That kind of a sliding standard of proof or inverse proportion is relatively rare in law. Because the weighing of evidence (if the case law really means what it says) is in the *unfettered* discretion of the fact finder, that sliding standard of proof cannot, as a matter of pure logic, affect the literal issue of the legal sufficiency of the evidence, that is, the burden of production. It speaks volumes, however, about the burden of persuasion. It thereby casts at least reflected light on the issue before us, as it communicates a strong sense of precisely what it is that is being adjudicated. Some analysis may be helpful as to how a presumption "diminishes gradually until it disappears entirely," as to how "incapacity decreases" as age increases, and as to how "the quantum of proof diminishes in substantially the same ratio."

On the issue of Devon's knowledge of the difference between right and wrong, if all we knew were that Devon's age was at some indeterminate point between his seventh birthday and his fourteenth birthday, the State's case would be substantially weaker than it is now. The evidence before Judge Brown that Devon, at the time of the allegedly delinquent act, was 13 years, 10 months, and 2 weeks of age was substantial, although not quite sufficient, proof of his cognitive capacity.

The applicable common law on *doli incapax* with relation to the infancy defense establishes that on the day before their seventh birthday, no persons possess cognitive capacity. (0 per cent). It also establishes that on the day of their fourteenth birthday, all persons (at least as far as age is concerned) possess cognitive capacity. (100 per cent). On the time scale between the day of the seventh birthday and the day before the fourteenth birthday, the percentage of persons possessing such capacity steadily increases. The statistical probability is that on the day of the seventh birthday, at most a tiny fraction of one per cent will possess cognitive capacity. Conversely, on the day before the fourteenth birthday, only a tiny fraction of one per cent will lack such cognitive capacity. Assuming a steady rate of climb, the mid-point where fifty per cent of persons will lack cognitive capacity and fifty per cent will possess it would be at 10 years and 6 months of age. That is the scale on which we must place Devon.

We stress that the burden in that regard, notwithstanding the probabilities, was nonetheless on the State. The impact of the allocation of the burden of proof to the State is that the infant will enjoy the benefit of the doubt. The fact that the quantum of proof necessary to overcome presumptive incapacity diminishes in substantially the same ratio as the infant's age increases only serves to lessen the State's burden, not to eliminate it. The State's burden is still an affirmative one. It may not, therefore, passively rely upon the mere absence of evidence to the contrary.

We hold that the State successfully carried that burden. A minor factor, albeit of some weight, was that Devon was essentially at or near grade level in school. The report of the master, received and reviewed by Judge Brown, established that at the time of the offense, Devon was in middle school, embracing grades 6, 7, and 8. The report of the master, indeed, revealed that Devon had flunked the sixth grade twice, with truancy and lack of motivation as apparent causes. That fact nonetheless revealed that Devon had initially reached the sixth grade while still eleven years of age. That would tend to support his probable inclusion in the large majority of his age group rather than in a small and subnormal minority of it.

The juvenile master was in a position to observe first-hand Devon's receiving of legal advice from his lawyer, his acknowledgment of his understanding of it, and his acting upon it. His lawyer explained that he had a right to remain silent and that the master would not infer guilt from his exercise of that right. He acknowledged understanding that right. His lawyer also advised him of his right to testify but informed him that both the assistant state's attorney and the judge might question him about the delinquent act. Devon indicated that he wished to remain silent and say nothing. Although reduced to relatively simple language, the exchange with respect to the risk of self-incrimination and the privilege against self-incrimination forms a predicate from which an observer might infer some knowledge on Devon's part of the significance of incrimination.

The exchange, moreover, might have significance in two distinct evidentiary regards. It suggests that Devon's lawyer, who presumably had significant opportunity to talk to him before the hearing, concluded that Devon understood the significance of criminality and incrimination. Under the classic case in all of the evidence textbooks of *Wright v. Tatham*, 5 Cl. & Fin. 670 (1838), this belief on the part of a close observer is relevant evidence for the proposition that the thing believed is true.

The significance of the colloquy in this case is far more direct. Here, the master was in a position to observe Devon closely throughout the exchange. It does require us to extrapolate that Devon's mental capacity on the day of the hearing, July 20, reflected his mental capacity two months earlier on May 25. That precise situation was before the Court in *Adams v. State*. The appellant Adams there was 13 years, 9 months, and 2 weeks old at the time of the alleged murder; one month younger than Devon here at the time of his alleged delinquency. Adams there, as Devon here, "did not testify in his own defense at the guilt or innocence stage of the trial." Adams nonetheless received legal advice from his lawyer under the watchful eye of the judge. We found that fact very significant in holding that the evidence there was legally sufficient to overcome the presumption of incapacity due to infancy.

8 Md.App. at 689, 262 A.2d 69. The transcript revealed a further exchange between the juvenile master and Devon, also not without some significance. After Devon and his companion Edward had already been adjudicated delinquent and when no further risk of incrimination inhered, the master asked each of the two what, if anything, he would like to say and was met by "stonewalling." This inferable allegiance to the Underworld's "Code of Silence" suggests that Devon and Edward were no mere babies caught up in a web they did not comprehend. The permitted inference, rather, was that they were fully conscious of the ongoing war between lawful authority and those who flout it and had deliberately chosen to adhere to the latter camp.

We turn, most significantly, to the circumstances of the criminal act itself. We note the relevance of such circumstances to the issue at hand.

The most significant circumstance was the very nature of the criminal activity in which Devon engaged. It was not mere possession of heroin. It was possession of twenty packets of heroin with the intent to distribute. There were no needle marks or other indications of personal use on Devon's body. There is no evidence suggesting that this sixth grader, directly or indirectly, had the affluence to purchase drugs for himself in that amount. Indeed, he acknowledged that he had been selling drugs for two days when the current offense occurred. His motivation was "that he just wanted something to do."

The evidence indicated that Devon and Edward and several other students had been regularly using the absent grandmother's home as a base of operations for selling drugs. Devon and his companions were not innocent children unaware of the difference between games and crimes but "street wise" young delinquents knowingly involved in illicit activities. Realistically, one cannot engage in the business of selling drugs without some knowledge as to sources of supply, some pattern for receiving and passing on the money, some network of potential customers, and some *modus operandi* to avoid the eye of the police and of school authorities. It is almost inconceivable that such a crime could be engaged in without the drug pusher's being aware that it was against the law. That is, by definition, criminal capacity.

> **Make the Connection**
>
> Criminal liability arises in part from the choice a person makes to engage in conduct that constitutes a criminal harm. Without sufficient capacity to choose, blame is improper. An excuse defense represents a legal conclusion that even though a person's conduct is wrong, liability is inappropriate because some characteristic of the person or his situation vitiates the person's blameworthiness.

We hold that the surrounding circumstances here were legally sufficient to overcome the slight residual weight of the presumption of incapacity due to infancy.

Judgment affirmed; costs to be paid by appellant.

> ### Hypo 1: *The Bank Robbery*
>
> Defendant Gaylord Anguish, who was charged with robbery, admitted that he committed the crime, but claimed that he acted under duress. The evidence showed that Anguish stole a van from a child care center, drove the van to a drive-through bank window where he threatened to blow up the bank unless they gave him money, and escaped with $15,000. Anguish claimed that these events transpired after he learned that a Federal Bureau of Investigation (FBI) agent was having an extra-marital affair, and that the FBI agent and his lover had conspired to kill the lover's husband. After defendant attempted to confront the FBI agent with his knowledge, his house was burglarized and he began receiving threatening telephone calls. He reported these incidents to the police and the FBI, but neither agency took any action. Subsequently, but prior to the robbery, two men accosted him in his car (they were waiting in the back seat), put a gun to his head, and told him to rob a bank. The men told him that

if he did not rob the bank, he and his family would be harmed. To add credibility to the threat, the men showed defendant a copy of a picture of his wife and daughter. In order to facilitate the robbery, defendant decided to steal the van. Was the threat sufficiently imminent? Was defendant required to go to the police rather than comply with the threat? Can the defense also be used to excuse the theft of the van? *See Anguish v. State*, 991 S.W.2d 883 (Tex. App. 1999).

Does the MPC require that the threat be imminent or immediate? How would this Hypo be resolved under the MPC?

Hypo 2: *Duress and the Crime of Murder*

Jonathan, with a cocked gun pointed at his head, is ordered by his archenemy to kill another person "or die." The other person is lying helpless on the floor, and Jonathan takes a knife (given to him by the threatener) and slits the victim's throat. Should the defense of duress apply to an intentional murder? Can the law hope to deter Jonathan from committing a murder under such circumstances? *See United States v. LaFleur*, 971 F.2d 200 (9th Cir. 1992). Since the threatener provided Jonathan with a knife, did he have a sufficient and adequate means of escape so that the defense should not apply? How would this problem be resolved under the Model Penal Code?

Food for Thought

Delbert is forced to participated in a bank robbery (by wearing a mask and acting like he is holding a gun) by a man who threatens to shoot him if he does not. During the robbery, the threatener shoots and kills a bank guard. At his trial, Delbert tries to offer proof of duress, but the state objects that the defense cannot be invoked as a defense to murder. Should a charge of felony murder be handled differently (in terms of whether the defense applies) than an intentional murder? *See State v. Hunter*, 241 Kan. 629, 740 P.2d 559 (1987).

Food for Thought

Rios, who said some offensive things in a bar, was chased to his car by an angry mob. Rios managed to get into the car and lock the doors, but some members of the mob began beating on his car. In fear for his life, Rios starts the car and begins inching forward. When the police arrive, they realize that Rios is legally drunk and charge him with driving under the influence. Can Rios assert the defense of duress to the strict liability offense of driving under the influence of alcohol? *See State v. Rios*, 127 N.M. 334, 980 P.2d 1068 (Ct. App. 1999).

Hypo 3: *Making Grapefruit Juice*

Defendant squeezes Johnson's head until Johnson dies. At trial, the evidence shows that defendant was so mentally ill that he perceived that Johnson was a grapefruit rather than a person. In squeezing Johnson's head, defendant believed that he was creating grapefruit juice. Under *M'Naghten*, is defendant insane?

Hypo 4: *God's Representative*

Defendant entered a church with a shotgun and tried to kill a minister. At the time, defendant suffered from paranoid schizophrenia, which caused him to hear voices and to be preoccupied with ideas that were quite real for him. Defendant had a feeling of being God or a representative of God, who was present at the Last Supper, and who had at various times been threatened or attacked by others who did not give him credit for his rightful position. At the time of the shooting, defendant felt that he was being "threatened" and he responded violently in order to protect himself. Defendant believed that his actions were totally justified. He "sensed" that other persons were in his body displacing him. Defendant found the situation intolerable and felt that he had to defend himself from what he described as "salvation level attacks." In shooting the minister, defendant believed that he rightfully deserved money and respect from the church that he was not getting. Therefore, defendant needed to eliminate this "sermon giver" (the minister) so that he could arrange for another who would respond and give defendant the money to which he was entitled. Was defendant insane under the *M'Naghten* test? How would you argue the case for the defendant? How might the State respond? *See State v. Boan*, 235 Kan. 800, 686 P.2d 160 (1984).

Food for Thought

Defendant, who possessed an extra male (Y) chromosome, was charged with attempted murder. Studies have shown that males who possess this extra Y chromosome, referred to as "47 XYY individuals" exhibit aggressive behavior as a result of this chromosomal abnormality. However, not all XYY individuals are by nature involuntarily aggressive. Some identified XYY individuals have not exhibited such behavior. Given this evidence, is defendant insane under the M'Naghten or MPC tests? *See People v. Tanner*, 13 Cal. App. 3d 596, 91 Cal. Rptr. 656 (1970).

Hypo 5: *Multiple Personalities*

Defendant was charged with kidnapping a baby. She suffered from multiple personality disorder resulting from childhood physical and sexual abuse and two rapes. At the time of the kidnapping, defendant wanted to convince a former boyfriend that she was pregnant with his child. She had photographs made which made her appear pregnant. Later, she abducted a baby from a hospital nursery. One of defendant's alter personalities, "Rina," perhaps with another alter personality, "Bridget," controlled defendant's conduct at the time of the kidnapping. Her host or dominant personality, "Gidget," did not consciously participate in the abduction. Psychiatric experts could not establish that the alter personality in control at the time of the offense ("Rina") was legally insane, *i.e.*, "unable to appreciate the nature and quality or the wrongfulness of [defendant's] acts." The experts also testified that "each of the personalities taken alone knew, or was very capable of knowing, what she was doing and of making moral judgments." Under the circumstances, was defendant insane and not criminally responsible for the abduction? How would you argue the case for the defendant? How would you argue the case for the State? *See United States v. Denny-Shaffer*, 2 F.3d 999 (10th Cir. 1993). *See also State v. Wheaton*, 121 Wash. 2d 347, 850 P.2d 507 (En Banc 1993).

Hypo 6: *Pathological Gambling Disorder*

A jewelry store manager was indicted for stealing jewelry from his employer. Defendant contends that a compulsion to gamble rendered him unable to resist becoming a thief and stealing to support his habit. The American Psychiatric Association's Diagnostic and Statistical Manual of Mental Disorders § 312.31 (3d ed. 1980) contains the following description of pathological gambling:

> The essential features are a chronic and progressive failure to resist impulses to gamble and gambling behavior that compromises, disrupts, or damages personal, family, or vocational pursuits. The gambling preoccupation, urge, and activity increase during periods of stress. As the gambling increases, the individual is usually forced to lie in order to obtain money and to continue gambling, but hides the extent of the gambling. There is no serious attempt to budget or save money. When borrowing resources are strained, antisocial behavior in order to obtain money for more gambling is likely. Any criminal

behavior—*e.g.*, forgery, embezzlement, or fraud—is typically nonviolent. There is a conscious intent to return or repay the money.

Was defendant "insane" under the MPC test? How would defense counsel argue the case? How might the State respond? *See United States v. Runnells*, 985 F.2d 554 (4th Cir. 1993); *United States v. Gould*, 741 F.2d 45 (4th Cir. 1984); *United States v. Torniero*, 735 F.2d 725 (2d Cir. 1984); *United States v. Lewellyn*, 723 F.2d 615 (8th Cir. 1983).

Food for Thought

At the time he committed a double homicide, defendant believed he was in a combat situation during the Vietnam War. Psychiatric evidence revealed that defendant was suffering a dissociative flashback episode related to his Vietnam experience. He perceived himself as searching a suspected enemy, such as Viet Cong guerrillas, rather than robbing a tavern. Is defendant insane under the *M'Naghten* or MPC tests? *See State v. Coogan*, 154 Wis. 2d 387, 391–92, 453 N.W.2d 186, 187 (Ct.App. 1990).

Hypo 7: *More on PTSD*

Defendant was suffering from PTSD at the time of a homicide. A psychologist testified that children who grow up in war-torn and other violent areas can suffer PTSD. Defendant offered seventeen examples of violent events during her childhood that allegedly caused the onset of PTSD. These included the fact that: defendant saw a friend shoot his gun in a drug house and was terrified; a man pulled a gun on defendant and her mother, and defendant stepped into the path of the gun; gang members shot at a friend while in defendant's presence; defendant's sister's boyfriend, a father-figure to defendant, was shot and paralyzed; defendant was robbed of her coat at gunpoint; defendant's cousin was killed in a drive-by shooting; defendant's uncle, a close friend, was shot and killed; defendant was robbed of jewelry at gunpoint; defendant was tied up and raped when she was fourteen years old; defendant's cousin was shot in a street fight and lost the use of her arm; defendant stepped in front of a man with a gun to protect her aunt; defendant was severely beaten and robbed by a group of girls; defendant's mother shot a man, in front of defendant, because he was molesting defendant while giving her a bath; defendant was regularly beaten by her mother and father; defendant's father shot at her mother "because there was too much salt in the gravy"; and defendant, from age four to six, saw her mother and father "regularly dine with loaded revolvers at their sides during family dinners" to protect them from the violent outbursts of the other. Defendant argues that she was unable to appreciate the wrongfulness of her conduct or conform her conduct to the requirements of law. Can defendant argue that she was insane under the MPC test?" *See State v. Morgan*, 195 Wis. 2d 388, 536 N.W.2d 425 (1995).

Food for Thought

A mother called 911 just after midnight and stated that "I've just killed my boys." She also stated that God ordered her to do it. When they arrived at the scene, police officers found a six-year-old and eight-year-old in the front yard with their skulls smashed. They also found a 14-month-old baby alive in his crib with a fractured skull. The evidence revealed that the mother had suffered from delusional psychotic disorder and had been through three major psychotic episodes over the prior three years. Does the fact that the mother was sufficiently "aware" of reality to contact police after the killings suggest that she was not insane?

CHAPTER 13

Sentencing

Every jurisdiction has its own sentencing provisions and its own sentencing procedures. As with the issues of whether and how to criminalize any particular conduct, the legislature in each jurisdiction has the power and the discretion essentially to enact whatever punishments for whatever criminal conduct it desires. In general, it can be said that crimes designated as felonies are more heinous and punished more severely—both in potential incarceration periods and/or fines—than those denominated misdemeanors. But even that basic rule of thumb is not always true. Again, what to punish and how much to punish it are decisions for the legislature, and there is a great deal of variation between different jurisdictions.

That said, however, there are some very limited but very important constitutional limits on this power, involving the Sixth and Eighth Amendments. Those limitations are the subject of this chapter.

> **FYI**
>
> The Sixth and Eighth Amendments to the United States Constitution (part of the Bill of Rights) provide as follows:
>
> Amendment VI
>
> In all criminal prosecutions, the accused shall enjoy the right to a speedy and public trial, by an impartial jury of the state and district wherein the crime shall have been committed, which district shall have been previously ascertained by law, and to be informed of the nature and cause of the accusation; to be confronted with the witnesses against him; to have compulsory process for obtaining witnesses in his favor, and to have the assistance of counsel for his defense.
>
> Amendment VIII
>
> Excessive bail shall not be required, nor excessive fines imposed, nor cruel and unusual punishments inflicted.

A. OVERVIEW OF THE LAW

Sentencing Fact-Finding. Any fact (other than a prior conviction) which is necessary to support a sentence exceeding the maximum authorized by the facts established by a plea of guilty or a jury verdict must be admitted by the defendant or proved to a jury beyond a reasonable doubt.

Judges' Sentencing Discretion. Trial judges still retain their traditional discretion to consider sentencing factors in determining an appropriate sentence as long as they do not engage in fact-finding with respect to an element of the crime in jury trials.

Capital Punishment Permissible. The Supreme Court has concluded that jurisdictions may punish heinous homicidal acts by imposition of the death penalty. Legislatures may reasonably conclude that capital punishment is justified on the basis of retribution and/or deterrence. There is a recent trend, however, toward legislative repeal of state death penalty statutes.

Capital-Sentencing Proceedings. Sentences of death must be individualized; they cannot be mandatory. The sentencing jury (or judge in a bench trial) must find the existence of at least one aggravating circumstance that has been narrowly and precisely defined by statute. But all relevant mitigating evidence of any kind may be introduced at a capital-sentencing hearing on the convicted defendant's behalf.

Life Sentence Without Parole Unconstitutional for Juveniles. The Supreme Court has recently held that imposition of a life without parole sentence on a juvenile offender who did not commit homicide is unconstitutional under the Eighth Amendment.

Some Death Sentences Cruel & Unusual. The Supreme Court has concluded that capital punishment is categorically unconstitutional for: rape and other non-homicide crimes committed against individuals; crimes committed before the accused reached the age of 18; and for defendants whose intellectual functioning is in a low range

B. JUDGE VS. JURY

In recent years, the Supreme Court, interpreting the Sixth Amendment, has made it clear that sentencing judges may not engage in fact-finding relevant to an increase in sentencing where that is the province of the jury. When precisely is that the province of the jury? *Booker* is the leading case on that point.

UNITED STATES V. BOOKER
543 U.S. 220 (2005).

JUSTICE STEVENS delivered the opinion of the Court in part.*

The question presented in each of these cases is whether an application of the Federal Sentencing Guidelines violated the Sixth Amendment. In each case, the courts below held that binding rules set forth in the Guidelines limited the severity of the sentence that the judge could lawfully impose on the defendant based on the facts found by the jury at his trial. We hold that both courts correctly concluded that the Sixth Amendment does apply to the Sentencing Guidelines. In a separate opinion authored by Justice BREYER, the Court concludes that in light of this holding, two provisions of the Sentencing Reform Act of 1984 (SRA) that have the effect of making the Guidelines mandatory must be invalidated in order to allow the statute to operate in a manner consistent with congressional intent.

> **Hear It**
>
> You can listen to the oral argument in this case at http://www.oyez.org/cases/2000-2009/2004/2004_04_104/.

Respondent Booker was charged with possession with intent to distribute at least 50 grams of cocaine base (crack). Having heard evidence that he had 92.5 grams in his duffel bag, the jury found him guilty of violating 21 U.S.C. § 841(a)(1). That statute prescribes a minimum sentence of 10 years in prison and a maximum sentence of life for that offense. § 841(b)(1)(A)(iii).

Based upon Booker's criminal history and the quantity of drugs found by the jury, the Sentencing Guidelines required the District Court Judge to select a "base" sentence of not less than 210 nor more than 262 months in prison. The judge, however, held a post-trial sentencing proceeding and concluded by a preponderance of the evidence that Booker had possessed an additional 566 grams of crack and that he was guilty of obstructing justice. Those findings mandated that the judge select a sentence between 360 months and life imprisonment; the judge imposed a sentence at the low end of the range. Thus, instead of the sentence of 21 years and 10 months that the judge could have imposed on the basis of the facts proved to the jury beyond a reasonable doubt, Booker received a 30-year sentence.

Respondent Fanfan was charged with conspiracy to distribute and to possess with intent to distribute at least 500 grams of cocaine in violation of 21 U.S.C.

---

* JUSTICE SCALIA, JUSTICE SOUTER, JUSTICE THOMAS, and JUSTICE GINSBURG join this opinion.

§§ 846, 841(a)(1), and 841(b)(1)(B)(ii). He was convicted by the jury after it answered "Yes" to the question "Was the amount of cocaine 500 or more grams?" Under the Guidelines, without additional findings of fact, the maximum sentence authorized by the jury verdict was imprisonment for 78 months. The trial judge conducted a sentencing hearing at which he found additional facts that, under the Guidelines, would have authorized a sentence in the 188-to-235-month range. Specifically, he found that respondent Fanfan was responsible for 2.5 kilograms of cocaine powder, and 261.6 grams of crack. He also concluded that respondent had been an organizer, leader, manager, or supervisor in the criminal activity. Both findings were made by a preponderance of the evidence. Under the Guidelines, these additional findings would have required an enhanced sentence of 15 or 16 years instead of the 5 or 6 years authorized by the jury verdict alone. The judge followed the provisions of the Guidelines that did not implicate the Sixth Amendment by imposing a sentence on respondent "based solely upon the jury verdict in this case."

It has been settled throughout our history that the Constitution protects every criminal defendant "against conviction except upon proof beyond a reasonable doubt of every fact necessary to constitute the crime with which he is charged." *In re Winship*, 397 U.S. 358, 364, 90 S.Ct. 1068, 25 L.Ed.2d 368 (1970). It is equally clear that the "Constitution gives a criminal defendant the right to demand that a jury find him guilty of all the elements of the crime with which he is charged." These basic precepts, firmly rooted in the common law, have provided the basis for recent decisions interpreting modern criminal statutes and sentencing procedures.

In *Apprendi v. New Jersey*, 530 U.S. 466, 120 S.Ct. 2348, 147 L.Ed.2d 435 (2000), the defendant pleaded guilty to second-degree possession of a firearm for an unlawful purpose, which carried a prison term of 5-to-10 years. Thereafter, the trial court found that his conduct had violated New Jersey's "hate crime" law because it was racially motivated, and imposed a 12-year sentence. This Court set aside the enhanced sentence. We held: "Other than the fact of a prior conviction, any fact that increases the penalty for a crime beyond the prescribed statutory maximum must be submitted to a jury, and proved beyond a reasonable doubt."

The fact that New Jersey labeled the hate crime a "sentence enhancement" rather than a separate criminal act was irrelevant for constitutional purposes. As a matter of simple justice, it seemed obvious that the procedural safeguards designed to protect Apprendi from punishment for the possession of a firearm should apply equally to his violation of the hate crime statute. Merely using the label "sentence enhancement" to describe the latter did not provide a principled basis for treating the two crimes differently.

In *Blakely v. Washington*, 542 U.S. 296, 124 S.Ct. 2531, 159 L.Ed.2d 403 (2004), we dealt with a determinate sentencing scheme similar to the Federal Sentencing Guidelines. There the defendant pleaded guilty to kidnaping, a class B felony punishable by a term of not more than 10 years. Other provisions of Washington law, comparable to the Federal Sentencing Guidelines, mandated a "standard" sentence of 49-to-53 months, unless the judge found aggravating facts justifying an exceptional sentence. Although the prosecutor recommended a sentence in the standard range, the judge found that the defendant had acted with " 'deliberate cruelty' " and sentenced him to 90 months.

The requirements of the Sixth Amendment were clear. The application of Washington's sentencing scheme violated the defendant's right to have the jury find the existence of " 'any particular fact' " that the law makes essential to his punishment. That right is implicated whenever a judge seeks to impose a sentence that is not solely based on "facts reflected in the jury verdict or admitted by the defendant." We rejected the State's argument that the jury verdict was sufficient to authorize a sentence within the general 10-year sentence for class B felonies, noting that under Washington law, the judge was required to find additional facts in order to impose the greater 90-month sentence.

If the Guidelines as currently written could be read as merely advisory provisions that recommended, rather than required, the selection of particular sentences in response to differing sets of facts, their use would not implicate the Sixth Amendment. We have never doubted the authority of a judge to exercise broad discretion in imposing a sentence within a statutory range. Indeed, everyone agrees that the constitutional issues presented by these cases would have been avoided entirely if Congress had omitted from the SRA the provisions that make the Guidelines binding on district judges. For when a trial judge exercises his discretion to select a specific sentence within a defined range, the defendant has no right to a jury determination of the facts that the judge deems relevant.

The Guidelines as written, however, are not advisory; they are mandatory and binding on all judges. The availability of a departure in specified circumstances does not avoid the constitutional issue, just as it did not in *Blakely* itself. The Guidelines permit departures from the prescribed sentencing range in cases in which the judge "finds that there exists an aggravating or mitigating circumstance of a kind, or to a degree, not adequately taken into consideration by the Sentencing Commission in formulating the guidelines that should result in a sentence different from that described." At first glance, one might believe that the ability of a district judge to depart from the Guidelines means that she is bound only by the statutory maximum. Were this the case, there would be no *Apprendi* problem. Importantly, however, departures are not available in every case, and in fact are unavailable in most. In most cases, as a matter of law, the Commission will have adequately taken all relevant factors into account, and no departure will be legally permissible. In those instances, the judge is bound to impose a sentence within the Guidelines range. It was for this reason that we rejected a similar argument in *Blakely*, holding that although the Washington statute allowed the judge to impose a sentence outside the sentencing range for " 'substantial and compelling reasons,' " that exception was not available for Blakely himself. The sentencing judge would have been reversed had he invoked the departure section to justify the sentence.

Booker's case illustrates the mandatory nature of the Guidelines. The jury convicted him of possessing at least 50 grams of crack in violation of 21 U.S.C. § 841(b)(1)(A)(iii) based on evidence that he had 92.5 grams of crack in his duffel bag. Under these facts, the Guidelines specified an offense level of 32, which, given the defendant's criminal history category, authorized a sentence of 210-to-262 months. Booker's is a run-of-the-mill drug case, and does not present any factors that were inadequately considered by the Commission. The sentencing judge would therefore have been reversed had he not imposed a sentence within the level 32 Guidelines range.

Booker's actual sentence, however, was 360 months, almost 10 years longer than the Guidelines range supported by the jury verdict alone. To reach this sentence, the judge found facts beyond those found by the jury: namely, that Booker possessed 566 grams of crack in addition to the 92.5 grams in his duffel bag. The jury never heard any evidence of the additional drug quantity, and the judge found it true by a preponderance of the evidence. Thus, just as in *Blakely*, "the jury's verdict alone does not authorize the sentence. The judge acquires that authority only upon finding some additional fact." There is no relevant distinction between the sentence imposed pursuant to the Washington statutes in *Blakely* and the sentences imposed pursuant to the Federal Sentencing Guidelines in these cases.

Traditional judicial authority [existed] to increase sentences to take account of any unusual blameworthiness in the manner employed in committing a crime, an authority that the Guidelines require to be exercised consistently throughout the system. This tradition, however, does not provide a sound guide to enforcement of the Sixth Amendment's guarantee of a jury trial in today's world.

It is quite true that once determinate sentencing had fallen from favor, American judges commonly determined facts justifying a choice of a heavier sentence on account of the manner in which particular defendants acted. The effect of the increasing emphasis on facts that enhanced sentencing ranges, however, was to increase the judge's power and diminish that of the jury. It became the judge, not the jury, who determined the upper limits of sentencing, and the facts determined were not required to be raised before trial or proved by more than a preponderance.

As the enhancements became greater, the jury's finding of the underlying crime became less significant. And the enhancements became very serious indeed.

As it thus became clear that sentencing was no longer taking place in this tradition, the Court was faced with the issue of preserving an ancient guarantee under a new set of circumstances. The new sentencing practice forced the Court to address the question how the right of jury trial could be preserved, in a meaningful way guaranteeing that the jury would still stand between the individual and the power of the government under the new sentencing regime. And it is the new circumstances, not a tradition or practice that the new circumstances have superseded, that have led us to the answer developed in *Apprendi* and subsequent cases culminating with this one. It is an answer not motivated by Sixth Amendment formalism, but by the need to preserve Sixth Amendment substance.

All of the foregoing supports our conclusion that our holding in *Blakely* applies to the Sentencing Guidelines. We recognize, as we did in *Apprendi*, and *Blakely*, that in some cases jury factfinding may impair the most expedient and efficient sentencing of defendants. But the interest in fairness and reliability protected by the right to a jury trial-a common-law right that defendants enjoyed for centuries and that is now enshrined in the Sixth Amendment-has always outweighed the interest in concluding trials swiftly. As Blackstone put it:

> "However convenient these new methods of trial may appear at first, (as doubtless all arbitrary powers, well executed, are the most convenient) yet let it be again remembered, that delays, and little inconveniences in the forms of justice, are the price that all free nations must pay for their liberty in more substantial matters; that these inroads upon this sacred bulwark of the nation are fundamentally opposite to the spirit of our constitution; and that, though begun in trifles, the precedent may gradually increase and spread, to the utter disuse of juries in questions of the most momentous concerns."

Accordingly, we reaffirm our holding in *Apprendi*: Any fact (other than a prior conviction) which is necessary to support a sentence exceeding the maximum authorized by the facts established by a plea of guilty or a jury verdict must be admitted by the defendant or proved to a jury beyond a reasonable doubt.

POINTS FOR DISCUSSION

a. Guilty Pleas

Note that when the *Booker* Court, in the Stevens majority opinion, concluded that "any fact (other than a prior conviction) which is necessary to support a sentence exceeding the maximum authorized by the facts established by a plea of guilty or a jury verdict *must be admitted by the defendant* or proved to a jury beyond a reasonable doubt" (emphasis added), it anticipated that when a criminal defendant pleaded guilty—often as a result of a plea bargain—he or she would also have to admit every fact leading to a sentence above the statutory maximum in a guilty plea colloquy. Why would a defendant ever do that?

b. "Sentencing Factors"

The Court in *Booker* made it clear that trial judges continue to retain discretion to consider traditional sentencing factors in determining an appropriate sentence. But what is a "sentencing factor" and what is, instead, an element of the crime (whether explicitly or implicitly)?

The Supreme Court was faced with this very question in *United States v. O'Brien*, 560 U.S. 218, 130 S.Ct. 2169, 176 L.Ed.2d 979 (2010). In *O'Brien*, the Court had to interpret 18 U.S.C. § 924(c), which prohibits the use or carrying of a firearm in relation to a crime of violence or drug trafficking crime, or the possession of a firearm in furtherance of such crimes. A violation of that statute carries a mandatory minimum term of five years' imprisonment, but if the firearm is a "machinegun," the statute requires a 30-year mandatory minimum sentence. Whether a firearm was used, carried, or possessed was, the Government and the defendant conceded, an element of the crime. What was at issue was the question whether the fact that the firearm was a machinegun was an element to be proved to the jury beyond a reasonable doubt or a sentencing factor to be proved to the judge at sentencing.

The *O'Brien* Court then assessed the applicable Congressional intent by looking in detail at five factors: (1) the language and structure of the statute; (2) tradition; (3) the risk of unfairness; (4) the severity of the sentence; and (5) the legislative history. After this review, the Court concluded that whether a firearm was a machinegun or not is an element of the crime, not a sentencing factor.

What does that holding mean for a U.S. Attorney's office today that wants to prosecute someone under 18 U.S.C. § 924(c)?

c. Mandatory Minimum Sentences

The Supreme Court has ruled that "facts that increase a mandatory minimum sentence are elements and must be submitted to the jury and found beyond a reasonable doubt," overruling its earlier decision directly to the contrary. *Alleyne v. United States*, 570 U.S. 99, 133 S.Ct. 2151, 186 L.Ed.2d 314 (2013). In *Alleyne*, the sentencing range supported by the jury's verdict was five years' imprisonment to life. The sentencing court, however, imposed a 7-year mandatory minimum sentence based on its finding by a preponderance of evidence that the firearm used in the commission of the crime was "brandished." Because the finding of brandishing increased the penalty to which the defendant was subjected, it was held to be an element of the crime which had to be found by the jury beyond a reasonable doubt. Since the judge, rather than the jury, found brandishing, the defendant's Sixth Amendment rights were violated.

d. Aggravating Circumstances for Death Penalty

The Supreme Court has made clear that an advisory jury's *recommendation* to a sentencing judge that aggravating circumstances exist supporting imposition of the death penalty does not comport with the Sixth Amendment where the court still had to independently find and weigh the aggravating and mitigating circumstances before entering a sentence of life or death: "The maximum punishment Timothy Hurst could have received without any judge-made findings was life in prison without parole. A judge increased Hurst's authorized punishment based on her own factfinding. We hold that Hurst's sentence violates the Sixth Amendment." *Hurst v. Florida*, 577 U.S. 92, 136 S.Ct. 616, 193 L.Ed.2d 504 (2016).

C. CAPITAL PUNISHMENT

In 2008, the Supreme Court found that "[t]hirty-seven jurisdictions—36 States plus the Federal Government—have the death penalty." *Kennedy v. Louisiana*, 554 U.S. 407, 128 S.Ct. 2641, 2653, 171 L.Ed.2d 525 (2008). Since 2008, five more states have abolished the death penalty: Maryland (2013); Connecticut (2012 & 2016); Illinois (2011); New Mexico (2009), and Washington (2018). (The Nebraska Legislature also abolished capital punishment in 2015, but it was reinstated by a statewide vote in 2016.) The constitutionality of capital punishment was established in *Gregg v. Georgia*, 428 U.S. 153, 96 S.Ct. 2909, 49 L.Ed.2d 859 (1976). Justices Stewart, Powell, and Stevens concluded that it is not necessarily wrong for a legislature to conclude that the death penalty "serve[s] two principal social purposes: retribution and deterrence of capital crimes by prospective offenders." *Id.* at 182, 96 S.Ct. at 2929. Justice White, Chief Justice Burger, Justice Rehnquist, and Justice Blackmun concurred.

CALIFORNIA V. BROWN
479 U.S. 538 (1987).

CHIEF JUSTICE REHNQUIST delivered the opinion of the Court.

The question presented for review in this case is whether an instruction informing jurors that they "must not be swayed by mere sentiment, conjecture, sympathy, passion, prejudice, public opinion or public feeling" during the penalty phase of a capital murder trial violates the Eighth and Fourteenth Amendments to the United States Constitution. We hold that it does not.

Respondent Albert Brown was found guilty by a jury of forcible rape and first-degree murder in the death of 15-year-old Susan J. At the penalty phase, the State presented evidence that respondent had raped another young girl some years prior to his attack on Susan J. Respondent presented the testimony of several family members, who recounted respondent's peaceful nature and expressed disbelief that respondent was capable of such a brutal crime. Respondent also presented the testimony of a psychiatrist, who stated that Brown killed his victim because of his shame and fear over sexual dysfunction. Brown himself testified, stating that he was ashamed of his prior criminal conduct and asking for mercy from the jury.

California Penal Code Ann. § 190.3 provides that capital defendants may introduce at the penalty phase any evidence "as to any matter relevant to mitigation including, but not limited to, the nature and circumstances of the present offense, and the defendant's character, background, history, mental condition and physical condition." The trial court instructed the jury to consider the aggravating and mitigating circumstances and to weigh them in determining the appropriate penalty. But the court cautioned the jury that it "must not be swayed by mere sentiment, conjecture, sympathy, passion, prejudice, public opinion or public feeling." Respondent was sentenced to death.

On automatic appeal, the Supreme Court of California reversed the sentence of death. Over two dissents on this point, the majority opinion found that the instruction at issue here violates the Federal Constitution: " 'federal constitutional law forbids an instruction which denies a capital defendant the right to have the jury consider any "sympathy factor" raised by the evidence when determining the appropriate penalty.'" We granted certiorari to resolve whether such an instruction violates the United States Constitution.

The Eighth Amendment jurisprudence of this Court establishes two separate prerequisites to a valid death sentence. First, sentencers may not be given unbridled discretion in determining the fates of those charged with capital offenses. The Constitution instead requires that death penalty statutes be structured so as to prevent the penalty from being administered in an arbitrary and unpredictable fashion. *Gregg v. Georgia*, 428 U.S. 153, 96 S.Ct. 2909, 49 L.Ed.2d 859 (1976); *Furman v. Georgia*, 408 U.S. 238, 92 S.Ct. 2726, 33 L.Ed.2d 346 (1972). Second, even though the sentencer's discretion must be restricted, the capital defendant generally must be allowed to introduce any relevant mitigating evidence regarding his " 'character or record and any of the circumstances of the offense.' " Consideration of such evidence is a "constitutionally indispensable part of the process of inflicting the penalty of death." The instruction given by the trial court in this case violates neither of these constitutional principles.

We think that the California Supreme Court improperly focused solely on the word "sympathy" to determine that the instruction interferes with the jury's consideration of mitigating evidence. "The question, however, is not what the State Supreme Court declares the meaning of the charge to be, but rather what a reasonable juror could have understood the charge as meaning." To determine how a reasonable juror could interpret an instruction, we "must focus initially on the specific language challenged." If the specific instruction fails constitutional muster, we then review the instructions as a whole to see if the entire charge delivered a correct interpretation of the law. In this case, we need not reach the second step of analysis because we hold that a reasonable juror would not interpret the challenged instruction in a manner that would render it unconstitutional.

The jury was told not to be swayed by "mere sentiment, conjecture, sympathy, passion, prejudice, public opinion or public feeling." Respondent does not contend, and the Supreme Court of California did not hold, that conjecture, passion, prejudice, public opinion, or public feeling should properly play any role in the jury's sentencing determination, even if such factors might weigh in the defendant's favor. Rather, respondent reads the instruction as if it solely cautioned the jury not to be swayed by "sympathy." Even if we were to agree that a rational juror could parse the instruction in such a hypertechnical manner, we would disagree with both respondent's interpretation of the instruction and his conclusion that the instruction is unconstitutional.

By concentrating on the noun "sympathy," respondent ignores the crucial fact that the jury was instructed to avoid basing its decision on mere sympathy. Even a juror who insisted on focusing on this one phrase in the instruction would likely interpret the phrase as an admonition to ignore emotional responses that are not rooted in the aggravating and mitigating evidence introduced during the penalty phase. While strained in the abstract, respondent's interpretation is simply untenable when viewed in light of the surrounding circumstances. This instruction was given at the end of the penalty phase, only after respondent had produced 13 witnesses in his favor. Yet respondent's interpretation would have these two words transform three days of favorable testimony into a virtual charade. We think a reasonable juror would reject that interpretation, and instead understand the instruction not to rely on "mere sympathy" as a directive to ignore only the sort of sympathy that would be totally divorced from the evidence adduced during the penalty phase.

We also think it highly unlikely that any reasonable juror would almost perversely single out the word "sympathy" from the other nouns which accompany it in the instruction: conjecture, passion, prejudice, public opinion, and public feeling. Reading the instruction as a whole, as we must, it is no more than a catalog of the kind of factors that could improperly influence a juror's decision to vote for or against the death penalty. The doctrine of *noscitur a sociis* is based on common sense, and a rational juror could hardly hear this instruction without concluding that it was meant to confine the jury's deliberations to considerations arising from the evidence presented, both aggravating and mitigating.

An instruction prohibiting juries from basing their sentencing decisions on factors not presented at the trial, and irrelevant to the issues at the trial, does not violate the United States Constitution. It serves the useful purpose of confining the jury's imposition of the death sentence by cautioning it against reliance on extraneous emotional factors, which, we think, would be far more likely to turn the jury against a capital defendant than for him. And to the extent that the instruction helps to limit the jury's consideration to matters introduced in evidence before it, it fosters the Eighth Amendment's "need for reliability in the determination that death is the appropriate punishment in a specific case." Indeed, by limiting the jury's sentencing considerations to record evidence, the State also ensures the availability of meaningful judicial review, another safeguard that improves the reliability of the sentencing process.

We hold that the instruction challenged in this case does not violate the provisions of the Eighth and Fourteenth Amendments to the United States Constitution.

JUSTICE BRENNAN, with whom JUSTICE MARSHALL joins, and with whom JUSTICE STEVENS joins in part, dissenting.

Adhering to my view that the death penalty is in all circumstances cruel and unusual punishment forbidden by the Eighth and Fourteenth Amendments, I dissent from the Court's opinion to the extent that it would result in the imposition of the death penalty upon respondent. *Gregg v. Georgia*, 428 U.S. 153, 227, 96 S.Ct. 2909, 2950, 49 L.Ed.2d 859 (1976). However, even if I believed that the death penalty could be imposed constitutionally under certain circumstances, I would affirm the California Supreme Court, for that court has reasonably interpreted the jury instruction at issue to divert the jury from its constitutional duty to consider all mitigating evidence introduced by a defendant at the sentencing phase of trial.

A sentencing instruction is invalid if it precludes the sentencer from "considering, as a mitigating factor, any aspect of a defendant's character or record that the defendant proffers as a basis for a sentence less than death." Furthermore, an instruction cannot stand if it leaves the jury unclear as to whether it may consider such evidence. "We may not speculate as to whether the sentencer actually considered all of the mitigating factors and found them insufficient to offset the aggravating circumstances," since our case law "requires us to remove any legitimate basis for finding ambiguity concerning the factors actually considered."

The issue in this case is whether a jury might reasonably interpret the California jury instruction in either of these two ways. The facial language of the instruction, the manner in which it has been construed in trials in California, and experience with other provisions of the state sentencing scheme all buttress California's interpretation of its own jury instruction. In light of this evidence, there is simply no warrant for this Court to override the state court's assessment of how a jury in California might reasonably interpret the instruction before us.

The instruction at issue informed the jury: "You must not be swayed by mere sentiment, conjecture, sympathy, passion, prejudice, public opinion or public feeling." In forbidding the sentencer to take sympathy into account, this language on its face precludes precisely the response that a defendant's evidence of character and background is designed to elicit, thus effectively negating the intended effect of the Court's requirement that all mitigating evidence be considered.

The State acknowledges that sympathy for the defendant is appropriate, but contends that the antisympathy instruction simply prevents the jury from relying on "untethered sympathy" unrelated to the circumstances of the offense or the defendant. Yet, as the California court has noted on other occasions, the instruction gives no indication whatsoever that the jury is to distinguish between "tethered" and "untethered" sympathy. The Court nonetheless accepts the notion that a jury would interpret the instruction to require such a distinction. None of the reasons it offers for accepting this implausible construction are persuasive. The vast majority of jurors can be expected to interpret "sympathy" to mean "sympathy," not to engage in the tortuous reasoning process necessary to construe it as "untethered sympathy."

This Court has proclaimed that in capital cases "the fundamental respect for humanity underlying the Eighth Amendment requires consideration of the character and record of the individual offender and the circumstances of the particular offense as a constitutionally indispensable part of the process of inflicting the penalty of death." Because of the qualitatively different nature of the death penalty, "there is a corresponding difference in the need for reliability in the determination that death is the appropriate punishment in a specific case." Even construed in its most favorable light, the jury instruction at issue in this case did not come close to providing the requisite assurance that the jury in this case was fully aware of the scope of its sentencing duties. Since Brown's mitigating evidence was composed totally of information on his character and background intended to elicit sympathy, it is highly likely that the instruction eliminated his only hope of gaining mercy from the sentencer. Given our particular concern for the reliability of the procedures used to impose the death penalty, as well as the considerable support for the California court's interpretation, it is baffling that this Court strains to find a way to override the state court's construction of its own jury instruction. I cannot acquiesce in such a course of action, and therefore dissent.

JUSTICE BLACKMUN, with whom JUSTICE MARSHALL joins, dissenting.

The defense's goal in the penalty phase of a capital trial is, of course, to receive a life sentence. While the sentencer's decision to accord life to a defendant at times might be a rational or moral one, it also may arise from the defendant's appeal to the sentencer's sympathy or mercy, human qualities that are undeniably emotional in nature.

In a capital sentencing proceeding, the sentencer's discretion must be guided to avoid arbitrary or irrational decisions. When a jury serves as the sentencing authority, such guidance is provided, in part, through jury instructions. This Court, however, has recognized and even safeguarded the sentencer's power to exercise its mercy to spare the defendant's life.

The sentencer's ability to respond with mercy towards a defendant has always struck me as a particularly valuable aspect of the capital sentencing procedure. Long ago, when, in dissent, I expressed my fear of legislation that would make the death penalty mandatory, and thus remove all discretion from the sentencer, I observed that such legislation would be "regressive, for it would eliminate the element of mercy in the imposition of punishment." In my view, we adhere so strongly to our belief that sentencers should have the opportunity to spare a capital defendant's life on account of compassion for the individual because, recognizing that the capital sentencing decision must be made in the context of "contemporary values" we see in the sentencer's expression of mercy a distinctive feature of our society that we deeply value.

In the real world, as in this case, it perhaps is unlikely that one word in an instruction would cause a jury totally to disregard mitigating factors that the defendant has presented through specific testimony. When, however, a jury member is moved to be merciful to the defendant, an instruction telling the juror that he or she cannot be "swayed" by sympathy well may arrest or restrain this humane response, with truly fatal consequences for the defendant. This possibility I cannot accept, in light of the special role of mercy in capital sentencing and the stark finality of the death sentence.

POINTS FOR DISCUSSION

a. Mandatory Death Sentences

As intimated in *Brown*, the Supreme Court has made it clear that jurisdictions may not enact capital sentencing schemes that make imposition of capital punishment mandatory, rather than based upon an individualized consideration of the convicted defendant. *See, e.g., Woodson v. North Carolina*, 428 U.S. 280, 305, 96 S.Ct. 2978, 2991, 49 L.Ed.2d 944 (1976) (plurality opinion) ("we conclude that the death sentences imposed upon the petitioners under North Carolina's mandatory death sentence statute violated the Eighth and Fourteenth Amendments and therefore must be set aside"); *Roberts v. Louisiana*, 428 U.S. 325, 333, 96 S.Ct. 3001, 3006, 49 L.Ed.2d 974 (1976) ("The constitutional vice of mandatory death sentence statutes lack of focus on the circumstances of the particular offense and the character and propensities of the offender is not resolved by Louisiana's limitation of first-degree murder to various categories of killings.").

b. Aggravating & Mitigating Circumstances

The Supreme Court has *not* required that capital-punishment jurisdictions use any particular, specific, prescribed capital-sentencing scheme. *See, e.g., Kansas v. Marsh*, 548 U.S. 163, 173–75, 126 S.Ct. 2516, 165 L.Ed.2d 429 (2006); *Franklin v. Lynaugh*, 487 U.S. 164, 178, 108 S.Ct. 2320, 101 L.Ed.2d 155 (1988) (plurality).

But the Supreme Court *has required* that a convicted defendant in a homicide case cannot be sentenced to death unless the sentencing jury (or judge in a bench trial) finds at least one "aggravating circumstance" to exist beyond a reasonable doubt at either the guilt or penalty phase. *See, e.g., Tuilaepa v. California*, 512 U.S. 967, 971–72, 114 S.Ct. 2630, 129 L.Ed.2d 750 (1994) ("To render a defendant eligible for the death penalty in a homicide case, we have indicated that the trier of fact must convict the defendant of murder and find one 'aggravating circumstance' (or its equivalent) at either the guilt or penalty phase.").

These aggravating circumstances (sometimes called "special circumstances") must be narrowly and precisely defined by statute. Moreover, they must not apply to every defendant convicted of a capital offense (otherwise there would be an unconstitutional mandatory death sentence, as discussed above), and they must not be unconstitutionally vague.

In contrast, as discussed in *Brown*, *all* relevant mitigating evidence of any kind—whether cumulative or not—may be introduced at a capital-sentencing hearing on the convicted defendant's behalf. *See also, e.g., Roper v. Simmons*, 543 U.S. 551, 568, 125 S.Ct. 1183, 161 L.Ed.2d 1 (2005) ("In any capital case a defendant has wide latitude to raise as a mitigating factor 'any aspect of [his or her] character or record and any of the circumstances of the offense that the defendant proffers as a basis for a sentence less than death.' "); *Johnson v. Texas*, 509 U.S. 350, 361–62, 113 S.Ct. 2658, 125 L.Ed.2d 290 (1993); *Lockett v. Ohio*, 438 U.S. 586, 604, 98 S.Ct. 2954, 57 L.Ed.2d 973 (1978) ("[W]e conclude that the Eighth and Fourteenth Amendments require that the sentencer, in all but the rarest kind of capital case, not be precluded from considering, as a mitigating factor, any aspect of a defendant's character or record and any of the circumstances of the offense that the defendant proffers as a basis for a sentence less than death.").

c. Discriminatory Application

Whether or not capital punishment is constitutional, there is significant public debate about whether it is applied in a racially discriminatory fashion. In *McCleskey v. Kemp*, 481 U.S. 279, 107 S.Ct. 1756, 95 L.Ed.2d 262 (1987), a 5-to-4 majority of the Court rejected a challenge to Georgia's capital punishment procedures as racially discriminatory. *See, e.g., id.* at 313, 107 S.Ct. at 1778 ("In light of the safeguards designed to minimize racial bias in the process, the fundamental value of jury trial in our criminal justice system, and the benefits that discretion provides to criminal defendants, we hold that [the study alleging racial disparity in capital sentences put forward by defendant McCleskey] does not demonstrate a constitutionally significant risk of racial bias affecting the Georgia capital sentencing process.").

Based, however, on the belief that the death penalty is applied unfairly throughout the United States, the American Bar Association has, since 1997, called for "capital jurisdictions to impose a moratorium on all executions until they can (1) ensure that death penalty cases are administered fairly and impartially, in accordance with due process, and (2) minimize the risk that innocent persons may be executed." See American Bar Association Death Penalty Moratorium Implementation Project, https://www.americanbar.org/groups/crsj/projects/death_penalty_due_process_review_project/about_us/history.html.

d. Method of Execution

Some prisoners sentenced to death in Oklahoma filed an action in federal court contending that the method of execution used by the State violated the Eighth Amendment because it created an unacceptable risk of severe pain. They argued that midazolam, the first drug employed in the State's three-drug protocol, failed to render a person insensate to pain. The Supreme Court, in a 5-to-4 decision, disagreed, holding that "first, the prisoners failed to identify a known and available alternative method of execution that entails a lesser risk of pain, a requirement of all Eighth Amendment method-of-execution claims. Second, the District Court did not commit clear error when it found that the prisoners failed to establish that Oklahoma's use of a massive dose of midazolam in its execution protocol entails a substantial risk of severe pain." *Glossip v. Gross*, 576 U.S. 863, 135 S.Ct. 2726, 192 L.Ed.2d 761 (2015). Justice Sotomayor, dissenting with three other Justices, argued that the majority reached this result "by misconstruing and ignoring the record evidence regarding the constitutional insufficiency of midazolam as a sedative in a three-drug lethal injection cocktail, and by imposing a wholly unprecedented obligation on the condemned inmate to identify an available means for his or her own execution. The contortions necessary to save this particular lethal injection protocol are not worth the price."

D. PROPORTIONALITY

The Supreme Court has held that punishments for criminal offenses violate the Cruel and Unusual Punishments Clause of the Eighth Amendment when they are disproportionate to the proscribed crime. When exactly is that the case? The Court has given this question a lot of thought the last few years in a variety of different settings.

GRAHAM V. FLORIDA
560 U.S. 48 (2010).

JUSTICE KENNEDY delivered the opinion of the Court.

> **Hear It**
>
> You can listen to the oral argument in this case at http://oyez.org/cases/2000-2009/2009/2009_08_7412.

Petitioner is Terrance Jamar Graham. He was born on January 6, 1987. Graham's parents were addicted to crack cocaine, and their drug use persisted in his early years. Graham was diagnosed with attention deficit hyperactivity disorder in elementary school. He began drinking alcohol and using tobacco at age 9 and smoked marijuana at age 13.

In July 2003, when Graham was age 16, he and three other school-age youths attempted to rob a barbeque restaurant in Jacksonville, Florida. One youth, who worked at the restaurant, left the back door unlocked just before closing time. Graham and another youth, wearing masks, entered through the unlocked door. Graham's masked accomplice twice struck the restaurant manager in the back of the head with a metal bar. When the manager started yelling at the assailant and Graham, the two youths ran out and escaped in a car driven by the third accomplice. The restaurant manager required stitches for his head injury. No money was taken.

Graham was arrested for the robbery attempt. Under Florida law, it is within a prosecutor's discretion whether to charge 16- and 17-year-olds as adults or juveniles for most felony crimes. Graham's prosecutor elected to charge Graham as an adult. The charges against Graham were armed burglary with assault or battery, a first-degree felony carrying a maximum penalty of life imprisonment without the possibility of parole; and attempted armed-robbery, a second-degree felony carrying a maximum penalty of 15 years' imprisonment.

On December 18, 2003, Graham pleaded guilty to both charges under a plea agreement. Graham wrote a letter to the trial court. After reciting "this is my first and last time getting in trouble," he continued "I've decided to turn my life around." Graham said "I made a promise to God and myself that if I get a second chance, I'm going to do whatever it takes to get to the National Football League."

The trial court accepted the plea agreement. The court withheld adjudication of guilt as to both charges and sentenced Graham to concurrent 3-year terms of probation.

Less than 6 months later, on the night of December 2, 2004, Graham again was arrested. The State's case was as follows: Earlier that evening, Graham participated in a home invasion robbery. His two accomplices were Meigo Bailey and Kirkland Lawrence, both 20-year-old men. According to the State, at 7 p.m. that night, Graham, Bailey, and Lawrence knocked on the door of the home where Carlos Rodriguez lived. Graham, followed by Bailey and Lawrence, forcibly entered the home and held a pistol to Rodriguez's chest. For the next 30 minutes, the three held Rodriguez and another man, a friend of Rodriguez, at gunpoint while they ransacked the home searching for money. Before leaving, Graham and his accomplices barricaded Rodriguez and his friend inside a closet.

The State further alleged that Graham, Bailey, and Lawrence, later the same evening, attempted a second robbery, during which Bailey was shot. When detectives interviewed Graham, he denied involvement in the crimes. He said he encountered Bailey and Lawrence only after Bailey had been shot. One of the detectives told Graham that the victims of the home invasion had identified him. He asked Graham, "Aside from the two robberies tonight how many more were you involved in?" Graham responded, "Two to three before tonight." The night that Graham allegedly committed the robbery, he was 34 days short of his 18th birthday.

The trial court held hearings on Graham's probation violations about a year later, in December 2005 and January 2006. The judge who presided was not the same judge who had accepted Graham's guilty plea to the earlier offenses.

Graham maintained that he had no involvement in the home invasion robbery; but, even after the court underscored that the admission could expose him to a life sentence on the earlier charges, he admitted violating probation conditions by fleeing. The State presented evidence related to the home invasion, including testimony from the victims. The trial court noted that Graham, in admitting his attempt to avoid arrest, had acknowledged violating his probation. The court further found that Graham had violated his probation by committing a home invasion robbery, by possessing a firearm, and by associating with persons engaged in criminal activity.

The trial court held a sentencing hearing. Under Florida law the minimum sentence Graham could receive absent a downward departure by the judge was 5 years' imprisonment. The maximum was life imprisonment. Graham's attorney requested the minimum nondeparture sentence of 5 years. A presentence report prepared by the Florida Department of Corrections recommended that Graham receive an even lower sentence-at most 4 years' imprisonment. The State recommended that Graham receive 30 years on the armed burglary count and 15 years on the attempted armed robbery count.

After hearing Graham's testimony, the trial court explained the sentence it was about to pronounce:

"Mr. Graham, as I look back on your case, yours is really candidly a sad situation. You had, as far as I can tell, you have quite a family structure. You had a lot of people who wanted to try and help you get your life turned around including the court system, and you had a judge who took the step to try and give you direction through his probation order to give you a chance to get back onto track. And at the time you seemed through your letters that that is exactly what you wanted to do. And I don't know why it is that you threw your life away. I don't know why.

"But you did, and that is what is so sad about this today is that you have actually been given a chance to get through this, the original charge, which were very serious charges to begin with. The attempted robbery with a weapon was a very serious charge.

"In a very short period of time you were back before the Court on a violation of this probation, and then here you are two years later standing before me, literally the-facing a life sentence as to-up to life as to count 1 and up to 15 years as to count 2.

"And I don't understand why you would be given such a great opportunity to do something with your life and why you would throw it away. The only thing that I can rationalize is that you decided that this is how you were going to lead your life and that there is nothing that we can do for you. And as the state pointed out, that this is an escalating pattern of criminal conduct on your part and that we can't help you any further. We can't do anything to deter you. This is the way you are going to lead your life, and I don't know why you are going to. You've made that decision. I have no idea. But, evidently, that is what you decided to do.

"So then it becomes a focus, if I can't do anything to help you, if I can't do anything to get you back on the right path, then I have to start focusing on the community and trying to protect the community from your actions. And, unfortunately, that is where we are today is I don't see where I can do anything to help you any further. You've evidently decided this is the direction you're going to take in life, and it's unfortunate that you made that choice.

"I have reviewed the statute. I don't see where any further juvenile sanctions would be appropriate. I don't see where any youthful offender sanctions would be appropriate. Given your escalating pattern of criminal conduct, it is apparent to the Court that you have decided that this is the way you are going to live your life and that the only thing I can do now is to try and protect the community from your actions."

The trial court found Graham guilty of the earlier armed burglary and attempted armed robbery charges. It sentenced him to the maximum sentence authorized by law on each charge: life imprisonment for the armed burglary and 15 years for the attempted armed robbery. Because Florida has abolished its parole system, a life sentence gives a defendant no possibility of release unless he is granted executive clemency.

Graham challenged his sentence under the Eighth Amendment. The First District Court of Appeal of Florida affirmed, concluding that Graham's sentence was not grossly disproportionate to his crimes. The Florida Supreme Court denied review.

The Eighth Amendment states: "Excessive bail shall not be required, nor excessive fines imposed, nor cruel and unusual punishments inflicted." To determine whether a punishment is cruel and unusual, courts must look beyond historical conceptions to " 'the evolving standards of decency that mark the progress of a maturing society.' " "This is because 'the standard of extreme cruelty is not merely descriptive, but necessarily embodies a moral judgment. The standard itself remains the same, but its applicability must change as the basic mores of society change.' "

The Cruel and Unusual Punishments Clause prohibits the imposition of inherently barbaric punishments under all circumstances. "Punishments of torture," for example, "are forbidden." These cases underscore the essential principle that, under the Eighth Amendment, the State must respect the human attributes even of those who have committed serious crimes.

For the most part, however, the Court's precedents consider punishments challenged not as inherently barbaric but as disproportionate to the crime. The concept of proportionality is central to the Eighth Amendment. Embodied in the Constitution's ban on cruel and unusual punishments is the "precept of justice that punishment for crime should be graduated and proportioned to the offense."

The Court's cases addressing the proportionality of sentences fall within two general classifications. The first involves challenges to the length of term-of-years sentences given all the circumstances in a particular case. The second comprises cases in which the Court implements the proportionality standard by certain categorical restrictions on the death penalty.

In the first classification the Court considers all of the circumstances of the case to determine whether the sentence is unconstitutionally excessive. Under this approach, the Court has held unconstitutional a life without parole sentence for the defendant's seventh nonviolent felony, the crime of passing a worthless check. *Solem v. Helm*, 463 U.S. 277, 103 S.Ct. 3001, 77 L.Ed.2d 637 (1983). In other cases, however, it has been difficult for the challenger to establish a lack of proportionality. A leading case is *Harmelin v. Michigan*, 501 U.S. 957, 111 S.Ct. 2680, 115 L.Ed.2d 836 (1991), in which the offender was sentenced under state law to life without parole for possessing a large quantity of cocaine. A closely divided Court upheld the sentence. The controlling opinion concluded that the Eighth Amendment contains a "narrow proportionality principle," that "does not require strict proportionality between crime and sentence" but rather "forbids only extreme sentences that are 'grossly disproportionate' to the crime." Again closely divided, the Court rejected a challenge to a sentence of 25 years to life for the theft of a few golf clubs under California's so-called three-strikes recidivist sentencing scheme. *Ewing v. California*, 538 U.S. 11, 123 S.Ct. 1179, 155 L.Ed.2d 108 (2003). The Court has also upheld a sentence of life with the possibility of parole for a defendant's third nonviolent felony, the crime of obtaining money by false pretenses, *Rummel v. Estelle*, 445 U.S. 263, 100 S.Ct. 1133, 63 L.Ed.2d 382 (1980), and a sentence of 40 years for possession of marijuana with intent to distribute and distribution of marijuana, *Hutto v. Davis*, 454 U.S. 370, 102 S.Ct. 703, 70 L.Ed.2d 556 (1982).

The second classification of cases has used categorical rules to define Eighth Amendment standards. The previous cases in this classification involved the death penalty. The classification in turn consists of two subsets, one considering the nature of the offense, the other considering the characteristics of the offender. With respect to the nature of the offense, the Court has concluded that capital punishment is impermissible for nonhomicide crimes against individuals. *Kennedy v. Louisiana*, 554 U.S. 407, 128 S.Ct. 2641, 171 L.Ed.2d 525 (2008). In cases turning on the characteristics of the offender, the Court has adopted categorical rules prohibiting the death penalty for defendants who committed their crimes before the age of 18, *Roper v. Simmons*, 543 U.S. 551, 125 S.Ct. 1183, 161 L.Ed.2d 1 (2005), or whose intellectual functioning is in a low range, *Atkins v. Virginia*, 536 U.S. 304, 122 S.Ct. 2242, 153 L.Ed.2d 335 (2002).

In the cases adopting categorical rules the Court has taken the following approach. The Court first considers "objective indicia of society's standards, as expressed in legislative enactments and state practice" to determine whether there is a national consensus against the sentencing practice at issue. Next, guided by "the standards elaborated by controlling precedents and by the Court's own understanding and interpretation of the Eighth Amendment's text, history, meaning, and purpose," the Court must determine in the exercise of its own independent judgment whether the punishment in question violates the Constitution.

The present case involves an issue the Court has not considered previously: a categorical challenge to a term-of-years sentence. The approach in cases such as *Harmelin* and *Ewing* is suited for considering a gross proportionality challenge to a particular defendant's sentence, but here a sentencing practice itself is in question. This case implicates a particular type of sentence as it applies to an entire class of offenders who have committed a range of crimes. As a result, a threshold comparison between the severity of the penalty and the gravity of the crime does not advance the analysis. Here, in addressing the question presented, the appropriate analysis is the one used in cases that involved the categorical approach, specifically *Atkins*, *Roper*, and *Kennedy*.

The analysis begins with objective indicia of national consensus. "The 'clearest and most reliable objective evidence of contemporary values is the legislation enacted by the country's legislatures.'" Six jurisdictions do not allow life without parole sentences for any juvenile offenders. Seven jurisdictions permit life without parole for juvenile offenders, but only for homicide crimes. Thirty-seven States as well as the District of Columbia permit sentences of life without parole for a juvenile nonhomicide offender in some circumstances. Federal law also allows for the possibility of life without parole for offenders as young as 13. Relying on this metric, the State and its amici argue that there is no national consensus against the sentencing practice at issue.

This argument is incomplete and unavailing. "There are measures of consensus other than legislation." Actual sentencing practices are an important part of the Court's inquiry into consensus. Here, an examination of actual sentencing practices in jurisdictions where the sentence in question is permitted by statute discloses a consensus against its use. Although these statutory schemes contain no explicit prohibition on sentences of life without parole for juvenile nonhomicide offenders, those sentences are most infrequent. According to a recent study, nationwide there are only 109 juvenile offenders serving sentences of life without parole for nonhomicide offenses.

Many States have chosen to move away from juvenile court systems and to allow juveniles to be transferred to, or charged directly in, adult court under certain circumstances. Once in adult court, a juvenile offender may receive the same sentence as would be given to an adult offender, including a life without parole sentence. But the fact that transfer and direct charging laws make life without parole possible for some juvenile nonhomicide offenders does not justify a judgment that many States intended to subject such offenders to life without parole sentences.

For example, under Florida law a child of any age can be prosecuted as an adult for certain crimes and can be sentenced to life without parole. The State acknowledged at oral argument that even a 5-year-old, theoretically, could receive such a sentence under the letter of the law. All would concede this to be unrealistic, but the example underscores that the statutory eligibility of a juvenile offender for life without parole does not indicate that the penalty has been endorsed through deliberate, express, and full legislative consideration. Similarly, the many States that allow life without parole for juvenile nonhomicide offenders but do not impose the punishment should not be treated as if they have expressed the view that the sentence is appropriate. The sentencing practice now under consideration is exceedingly rare. And "it is fair to say that a national consensus has developed against it."

Community consensus, while "entitled to great weight," is not itself determinative of whether a punishment is cruel and unusual. In accordance with the constitutional design, "the task of interpreting the Eighth Amendment remains our responsibility."

Roper established that because juveniles have lessened culpability they are less deserving of the most severe punishments. As compared to adults, juveniles have a " 'lack of maturity and an underdeveloped sense of responsibility' "; they "are more vulnerable or susceptible to negative influences and outside pressures, including peer pressure"; and their characters are "not as well formed." These salient characteristics mean that "it is difficult even for expert psychologists to differentiate between the juvenile offender whose crime reflects unfortunate yet transient immaturity, and the rare juvenile offender whose crime reflects irreparable corruption." Accordingly, "juvenile offenders cannot with reliability be classified among the worst offenders." A juvenile is not absolved of responsibility for his actions, but his transgression "is not as morally reprehensible as that of an adult."

No recent data provide reason to reconsider the Court's observations in *Roper* about the nature of juveniles. As petitioner's amici point out, developments in psychology and brain science continue to show fundamental differences between juvenile and adult minds. For example, parts of the brain involved in behavior control continue to mature through late adolescence. Juveniles are more capable of change than are adults, and their actions are less likely to be evidence of "irretrievably depraved character" than are the actions of adults. It remains true that "from a moral standpoint it would be misguided to equate the failings of a minor with those of an adult, for a greater possibility exists that a minor's character deficiencies will be reformed."

The Court has recognized that defendants who do not kill, intend to kill, or foresee that life will be taken are categorically less deserving of the most serious forms of punishment than are murderers. There is a line "between homicide and other serious violent offenses against the individual." Serious nonhomicide crimes "may be devastating in their harm but 'in terms of moral depravity and of the injury to the person and to the public,' they cannot be compared to murder in their 'severity and irrevocability.'" This is because "life is over for the victim of the murderer," but for the victim of even a very serious nonhomicide crime, "life is not over and normally is not beyond repair." Although an offense like robbery or rape is "a serious crime deserving serious punishment," it follows that, when compared to an adult murderer, a juvenile offender who did not kill or intend to kill has a twice diminished moral culpability. The age of the offender and the nature of the crime each bear on the analysis.

As for the punishment, life without parole is "the second most severe penalty permitted by law." It is true that a death sentence is "unique in its severity and irrevocability"; yet life without parole sentences share some characteristics with death sentences that are shared by no other sentences. The State does not execute the offender sentenced to life without parole, but the sentence alters the offender's life by a forfeiture that is irrevocable. It deprives the convict of the most basic liberties without giving hope of restoration, except perhaps by executive clemency-the remote possibility of which does not mitigate the harshness of the sentence.

Life without parole is an especially harsh punishment for a juvenile. Under this sentence a juvenile offender will on average serve more years and a greater percentage of his life in prison than an adult offender. A 16-year-old and a 75-

year-old each sentenced to life without parole receive the same punishment in name only. This reality cannot be ignored.

The penological justifications for the sentencing practice are also relevant to the analysis. Criminal punishment can have different goals, and choosing among them is within a legislature's discretion. It does not follow, however, that the purposes and effects of penal sanctions are irrelevant to the determination of Eighth Amendment restrictions. A sentence lacking any legitimate penological justification is by its nature disproportionate to the offense. With respect to life without parole for juvenile nonhomicide offenders, none of the goals of penal sanctions that have been recognized as legitimate—retribution, deterrence, incapacitation, and rehabilitation—provides an adequate justification.

Retribution is a legitimate reason to punish, but it cannot support the sentence at issue here. Society is entitled to impose severe sanctions on a juvenile nonhomicide offender to express its condemnation of the crime and to seek restoration of the moral imbalance caused by the offense. But "the heart of the retribution rationale is that a criminal sentence must be directly related to the personal culpability of the criminal offender." And as *Roper* observed, "whether viewed as an attempt to express the community's moral outrage or as an attempt to right the balance for the wrong to the victim, the case for retribution is not as strong with a minor as with an adult." The case becomes even weaker with respect to a juvenile who did not commit homicide. *Roper* found that "retribution is not proportional if the law's most severe penalty is imposed" on the juvenile murderer. The considerations underlying that holding support as well the conclusion that retribution does not justify imposing the second most severe penalty on the less culpable juvenile nonhomicide offender.

Deterrence does not suffice to justify the sentence either. *Roper* noted that "the same characteristics that render juveniles less culpable than adults suggest that juveniles will be less susceptible to deterrence." Because juveniles' "lack of maturity and underdeveloped sense of responsibility often result in impetuous and ill-considered actions and decisions," they are less likely to take a possible punishment into consideration when making decisions. This is particularly so when that punishment is rarely imposed. That the sentence deters in a few cases is perhaps plausible, but "this argument does not overcome other objections." Even if the punishment has some connection to a valid penological goal, it must be shown that the punishment is not grossly disproportionate in light of the justification offered. Here, in light of juvenile nonhomicide offenders' diminished moral responsibility, any limited deterrent effect provided by life without parole is not enough to justify the sentence.

Incapacitation, a third legitimate reason for imprisonment, does not justify the life without parole sentence in question here. Recidivism is a serious risk to public safety, and so incapacitation is an important goal. But while incapacitation may be a legitimate penological goal sufficient to justify life without parole in other contexts, it is inadequate to justify that punishment for juveniles who did not commit homicide. To justify life without parole on the assumption that the juvenile offender forever will be a danger to society requires the sentencer to make a judgment that the juvenile is incorrigible. The characteristics of juveniles make that judgment questionable. "It is difficult even for expert psychologists to differentiate between the juvenile offender whose crime reflects unfortunate yet transient immaturity, and the rare juvenile offender whose crime reflects irreparable corruption."

Here one cannot dispute that this defendant posed an immediate risk, for he had committed, we can assume, serious crimes early in his term of supervised release and despite his own assurances of reform.

> **Food for Thought**
>
> Do you agree? Is a 16-year old *always* different from an 18-year old in this respect, i.e. whether the former is "incorrigible" is "questionable," but whether the latter is "incorrigible" is not?

Graham deserved to be separated from society for some time in order to prevent what the trial court described as an "escalating pattern of criminal conduct," but it does not follow that he would be a risk to society for the rest of his life. Incapacitation cannot override all other considerations, lest the Eighth Amendment's rule against disproportionate sentences be a nullity.

Finally there is rehabilitation, a penological goal that forms the basis of parole systems. The concept of rehabilitation is imprecise; and its utility and proper implementation are the subject of a substantial, dynamic field of inquiry and dialogue. It is for legislatures to determine what rehabilitative techniques are appropriate and effective.

A sentence of life imprisonment without parole, however, cannot be justified by the goal of rehabilitation. The penalty forswears altogether the rehabilitative ideal. By denying the defendant the right to reenter the community, the State makes an irrevocable judgment about that person's value and place in society. This judgment is not appropriate in light of a juvenile nonhomicide offender's capacity for change and limited moral culpability.

In sum, penological theory is not adequate to justify life without parole for juvenile nonhomicide offenders. This determination; the limited culpability of juvenile nonhomicide offenders; and the severity of life without parole sentences all lead to the conclusion that the sentencing practice under consideration is cruel and unusual. This Court now holds that for a juvenile offender who did not commit homicide the Eighth Amendment forbids the sentence of life without parole. This clear line is necessary to prevent the possibility that life without parole sentences will be imposed on juvenile nonhomicide offenders who are not sufficiently culpable to merit that punishment. Because "the age of 18 is the point where society draws the line for many purposes between childhood and adulthood," those who were below that age when the offense was committed may not be sentenced to life without parole for a nonhomicide crime.

There is support for our conclusion in the fact that, in continuing to impose life without parole sentences on juveniles who did not commit homicide, the United States adheres to a sentencing practice rejected the world over. This observation does not control our decision. The judgments of other nations and the international community are not dispositive as to the meaning of the Eighth Amendment. But " '[t]he climate of international opinion concerning the acceptability of a particular punishment' " is also " 'not irrelevant.' " The Court has looked beyond our Nation's borders for support for its independent conclusion that a particular punishment is cruel and unusual.

As petitioner contends and respondent does not contest, the United States is the only Nation that imposes life without parole sentences on juvenile nonhomicide offenders. We also note, as petitioner and his amici emphasize, that Article 37(a) of the United Nations Convention on the Rights of the Child, ratified by every nation except the United States and Somalia, prohibits the imposition of "life imprisonment without possibility of release for offences committed by persons below eighteen years of age." As we concluded in *Roper* with respect to the juvenile death penalty, "the United States now stands alone in a world that has turned its face against" life without parole for juvenile nonhomicide offenders.

The Constitution prohibits the imposition of a life without parole sentence on a juvenile offender who did not commit homicide. A State need not guarantee the offender eventual release, but if it imposes a sentence of life it must provide him or her with some realistic opportunity to obtain release before the end of that term. The judgment of the First District Court of Appeal of Florida is reversed, and the case is remanded for further proceedings not inconsistent with this opinion.

JUSTICE THOMAS, with whom JUSTICE SCALIA joins, and with whom JUSTICE ALITO joins in part, dissenting.

The Court holds today that it is "grossly disproportionate" and hence unconstitutional for any judge or jury to impose a sentence of life without parole on an offender less than 18 years old, unless he has committed a homicide. Although the text of the Constitution is silent regarding the permissibility of this sentencing practice, and although it would not have offended the standards that prevailed at the founding, the Court insists that the standards of American society have evolved such that the Constitution now requires its prohibition.

The Court does not conclude that life without parole itself is a cruel and unusual punishment. It instead rejects the judgments of those legislatures, judges, and juries regarding what the Court describes as the "moral" question of whether this sentence can ever be "proportionate" when applied to the category of offenders at issue here.

I am unwilling to assume that we, as members of this Court, are any more capable of making such moral judgments than our fellow citizens. Nothing in our training as judges qualifies us for that task, and nothing in Article III gives us that authority.

Until today, the Court has based its categorical proportionality rulings on the notion that the Constitution gives special protection to capital defendants because the death penalty is a uniquely severe punishment that must be reserved for only those who are "most deserving of execution." Of course, the Eighth Amendment itself makes no distinction between capital and noncapital sentencing, but the " 'bright line' " the Court drew between the two penalties has for many years served as the principal justification for the Court's willingness to reject democratic choices regarding the death penalty.

Today's decision eviscerates that distinction. "Death is different" no longer. The Court now claims not only the power categorically to reserve the "most severe punishment" for those the Court thinks are " 'the most deserving of execution,' " but also to declare that "less culpable" persons are categorically exempt from the "second most severe penalty." No reliable limiting principle remains to prevent the Court from immunizing any class of offenders from the law's third, fourth, fifth, or fiftieth most severe penalties as well.

Lacking any plausible claim to consensus, the Court shifts to the heart of its argument: its "independent judgment" that this sentencing practice does not "serv[e] legitimate penological goals." The Court begins that analysis with the obligatory preamble that " 'the Eighth Amendment does not mandate adoption of any one penological theory,' " then promptly mandates the adoption of the theories the Court deems best.

The Court acknowledges that, at a minimum, the imposition of life-without-parole sentences on juvenile nonhomicide offenders serves two "legitimate" penological goals: incapacitation and deterrence. That should settle the matter, since the Court acknowledges that incapacitation is an "important" penological goal. Yet, the Court finds this goal "inadequate" to justify the life-without-parole sentences here. A similar fate befalls deterrence. The Court acknowledges that such sentences will deter future juvenile offenders, at least to some degree, but rejects that penological goal, not as illegitimate, but as insufficient.

Ultimately, however, the Court's "independent judgment" and the proportionality rule itself center on retribution—the notion that a criminal sentence should be proportioned to " 'the personal culpability of the criminal offender.' " Our society tends to treat the average juvenile as less culpable than the average adult. But the question here does not involve the average juvenile. The question, instead, is whether the Constitution prohibits judges and juries from ever concluding that an offender under the age of 18 has demonstrated sufficient depravity and incorrigibility to warrant his permanent incarceration.

In holding that the Constitution imposes such a ban, the Court cites "developments in psychology and brain science" indicating that juvenile minds "continue to mature through late adolescence," and that juveniles are "more likely than adults to engage in risky behaviors." But even if such generalizations from social science were relevant to constitutional rulemaking, the Court misstates the data on which it relies.

The Court equates the propensity of a fairly substantial number of youths to engage in "risky" or antisocial behaviors with the propensity of a much smaller group to commit violent crimes. But research relied upon by the amici cited in the Court's opinion differentiates between adolescents for whom antisocial behavior is a fleeting symptom and those for whom it is a lifelong pattern. That research further suggests that the pattern of behavior in the latter group often sets in before 18. And, notably, it suggests that violence itself is evidence that an adolescent offender's antisocial behavior is not transient.

In sum, even if it were relevant, none of this psychological or sociological data is sufficient to support the Court's " 'moral' " conclusion that youth defeats culpability in every case. The integrity of our criminal justice system depends on the ability of citizens to stand between the defendant and an outraged public and dispassionately determine his guilt and the proper amount of punishment based on the evidence presented. That process necessarily admits of human error. But so does the process of judging in which we engage. As between the two, I find far more "unacceptable" that this Court, swayed by studies reflecting the general tendencies of youth, decree that the people of this country are not fit to decide for themselves when the rare case requires different treatment.

POINT FOR DISCUSSION

Geriatric Release

The Supreme Court has found that Virginia's decision to review the sentences of minors previously sentenced to life imprisonment under a "geriatric release program," applying only after they are over 65 years old and using normal parole consideration factors for assessment for release, was a reasonable application of *Graham*, providing a meaningful opportunity to obtain release. *Virginia v. LeBlanc*, 137 S.Ct. 1726, 198 L.Ed.2d 186 (2017). What do you think? Is this too long to wait—until he or she is 65—for a first meaningful review of the appropriateness of a minor's life sentence?

MILLER V. ALABAMA
567 U.S. 460 (2012).

JUSTICE KAGAN delivered the opinion of the Court.

The two 14-year-old offenders in these cases were convicted of murder and sentenced to life imprisonment without the possibility of parole. In neither case did the sentencing authority have any discretion to impose a different punishment. State law mandated that each juvenile die in prison even if a judge or jury would have thought that his youth and its attendant characteristics, along with the nature of his crime, made a lesser sentence (for example, life with the possibility of parole) more appropriate. Such a scheme prevents those meting out punishment from considering a juvenile's "lessened culpability" and greater "capacity for change," *Graham v. Florida*, 560 U.S. 48, 130 S.Ct. 2011, 2026–2027, 2029–2030 (2010), and runs afoul of our cases' requirement of individualized sentencing for defendants facing the most serious penalties. We therefore hold that mandatory life without parole for those under the age of 18 at the time of their crimes violates the Eighth Amendment's prohibition on "cruel and unusual punishments."

The Eighth Amendment's prohibition of cruel and unusual punishment "guarantees individuals the right not to be subjected to excessive sanctions." That right, we have explained, "flows from the basic 'precept of justice that punishment for crime should be graduated and proportioned' " to both the offender and the offense. As we noted the last time we considered life-without-parole sentences imposed on juveniles, "the concept of proportionality is central to the Eighth Amendment." *Graham*, 130 S.Ct., at 2021. And we view that concept less through a historical prism than according to " 'the evolving standards of decency that mark the progress of a maturing society.' "

> **Hear It**
>
> The oral argument in *Miller* is particularly interesting. You can listen to it here: http://www.oyez.org/cases/2010-2019/2011/2011_10_9646. If you had been listening to this argument when it was made, how accurately do you think you would have been able to predict the positions that were ultimately taken by each of the justices?

The cases before us implicate two strands of precedent reflecting our concern with proportionate punishment. The first has adopted categorical bans on sentencing practices based on mismatches between the culpability of a class of offenders and the severity of a penalty. So, for example, we have held that imposing the death penalty for nonhomicide crimes against individuals, or imposing it on mentally retarded defendants, violates the Eighth Amendment. Several of the cases in this group have specially focused on juvenile offenders, because of their lesser culpability. *Graham* further likened life without parole for juveniles to the death penalty itself, thereby evoking a second line of our precedents. In those cases, we have prohibited mandatory imposition of capital punishment, requiring that sentencing authorities consider the characteristics of a defendant and the details of his offense before sentencing him to death. Here, the confluence of these two lines of precedent leads to the conclusion that mandatory life-without-parole sentences for juveniles violate the Eighth Amendment.

Children are constitutionally different from adults for purposes of sentencing. Because juveniles have diminished culpability and greater prospects for reform, we explained, "they are less deserving of the most severe punishments." There are three significant gaps between juveniles and adults. First, children have a " 'lack of maturity and an underdeveloped sense of responsibility,' " leading to recklessness, impulsivity, and heedless risk-taking. Second, children "are more vulnerable to negative influences and outside pressures," including from their family and peers; they have limited "control over their own environment" and lack the ability to extricate themselves from horrific, crime-producing settings. And third, a child's character is not as "well formed" as an adult's; his traits are "less fixed" and his actions less likely to be "evidence of irretrievable depravity."

Our decisions in this regard rest not only on common sense—on what "any parent knows"—but on science and social science as well. In *Roper v. Simmons*, 543 U.S. 551, 570 (2005), we cited studies showing that " 'only a relatively small proportion of adolescents' " who engage in illegal activity " 'develop entrenched patterns of problem behavior.' " And in *Graham*, we noted that "developments in psychology and brain science continue to show fundamental differences between juvenile and adult minds"—for example, in "parts of the brain involved in behavior control." We reasoned that those findings—of transient rashness, proclivity for risk, and inability to assess consequences—both lessened a child's "moral culpability" and enhanced the prospect that, as the years go by and neurological development occurs, his " 'deficiencies will be reformed.' "

Roper and *Graham* emphasized that the distinctive attributes of youth diminish the penological justifications for imposing the harshest sentences on juvenile offenders, even when they commit terrible crimes. Because " 'the heart of the retribution rationale' " relates to an offender's blameworthiness, " 'the case for retribution is not as strong with a minor as with an adult.' " Nor can deterrence do the work in this context, because " 'the same characteristics that render juveniles less culpable than adults' "—their immaturity, recklessness, and impetuosity—make them less likely to consider potential punishment. Similarly, incapacitation could not support the life-without-parole sentence in *Graham*. Deciding that a "juvenile offender forever will be a danger to society" would require "making a judgment that [he] is incorrigible"—but " 'incorrigibility is inconsistent with youth.' " And for the same reason, rehabilitation could not justify that sentence. Life without parole "forswears altogether the rehabilitative ideal." It reflects "an irrevocable judgment about an offender's value and place in society," at odds with a child's capacity for change.

Graham concluded from this analysis that life-without-parole sentences, like capital punishment, may violate the Eighth Amendment when imposed on children. To be sure, *Graham's* flat ban on life without parole applied only to nonhomicide crimes, and the Court took care to distinguish those offenses from murder, based on both moral culpability and consequential harm. But none of what it said about children—about their distinctive (and transitory) mental traits and environmental vulnerabilities—is crime-specific. Those features are evident in the same way, and to the same degree, when (as in both cases here) a botched robbery turns into a killing. So *Graham's* reasoning implicates any life-without-parole sentence imposed on a juvenile, even as its categorical bar relates only to nonhomicide offenses.

Most fundamentally, *Graham* insists that youth matters in determining the appropriateness of a lifetime of incarceration without the possibility of parole. In the circumstances there, juvenile status precluded a life-without-parole sentence, even though an adult could receive it for a similar crime.

But the mandatory penalty schemes at issue here prevent the sentencer from taking account of these central considerations. By removing youth from the balance—by subjecting a juvenile to the same life-without-parole sentence applicable to an adult—these laws prohibit a sentencing authority from assessing whether the law's harshest term of imprisonment proportionately punishes a juvenile offender. That contravenes *Graham's* (and also *Roper's*) foundational principle: that imposition of a State's most severe penalties on juvenile offenders cannot proceed as though they were not children.

And *Graham* makes plain these mandatory schemes' defects in another way: by likening life-without-parole sentences imposed on juveniles to the death penalty itself. Life-without-parole terms, the Court wrote, "share some characteristics with death sentences that are shared by no other sentences." Imprisoning an offender until he dies alters the remainder of his life "by a forfeiture that is irrevocable." And this lengthiest possible incarceration is an "especially harsh punishment for a juvenile," because he will almost inevitably serve "more years and a greater percentage of his life in prison than an adult offender." The penalty when imposed on a teenager, as compared with an older person, is therefore "the same . . . in name only." All of that suggested a distinctive set of legal rules: In part because we viewed this ultimate penalty for juveniles as akin to the death penalty, we treated it similarly to that most severe punishment. We imposed a categorical ban on the sentence's use, in a way unprecedented for a term of imprisonment. And the bar we adopted mirrored a proscription first established in the death penalty context—that the punishment cannot be imposed for any nonhomicide crimes against individuals.

That correspondence—*Graham's* "treatment of juvenile life sentences as analogous to capital punishment"—makes relevant here a second line of our precedents, demanding individualized sentencing when imposing the death penalty. Of special pertinence here, we insisted in these rulings that a sentencer have the ability to consider the "mitigating qualities of youth." So *Graham* and *Roper* and our individualized sentencing cases alike teach that in imposing a State's harshest penalties, a sentencer misses too much if he treats every child as an adult. To recap: Mandatory life without parole for a juvenile precludes consideration of his chronological age and its hallmark features—among them, immaturity, impetuosity, and failure to appreciate risks and consequences. It prevents taking into account the family and home environment that surrounds him—and from which he cannot usually extricate himself—no matter how brutal or dysfunctional. It neglects the circumstances of the homicide offense, including the extent of his participation in the conduct and the way familial and peer pressures may have affected him. Indeed, it ignores that he might have been charged and convicted of a lesser offense if not for incompetencies associated with youth—for example, his inability to deal with police officers or prosecutors (including on a plea agreement) or his incapacity to assist his own attorneys. And finally, this mandatory punishment disregards the possibility of rehabilitation even when the circumstances most suggest it.

We therefore hold that the Eighth Amendment forbids a sentencing scheme that mandates life in prison without possibility of parole for juvenile offenders. By making youth (and all that accompanies it) irrelevant to imposition of that harshest prison sentence, such a scheme poses too great a risk of disproportionate punishment. Because that holding is sufficient to decide these cases, we do not consider Jackson's and Miller's alternative argument that the Eighth Amendment requires a categorical bar on life without parole for juveniles, or at least for those 14 and younger. But given all we have said in *Roper, Graham,* and this decision about children's diminished culpability and heightened capacity for change, we think appropriate occasions for sentencing juveniles to this harshest possible penalty will be uncommon. That is especially so because of the great difficulty we noted in *Roper* and *Graham* of distinguishing at this early age between "the juvenile offender whose crime reflects unfortunate yet transient immaturity, and the rare juvenile offender whose crime reflects irreparable corruption." Although we do not foreclose a sentencer's ability to make that judgment in homicide cases, we require it to take into account how children are different, and how those differences counsel against irrevocably sentencing them to a lifetime in prison. We accordingly reverse the judgments of the Arkansas Supreme Court and Alabama Court of Criminal Appeals and remand the cases for further proceedings not inconsistent with this opinion.

CHIEF JUSTICE ROBERTS, with whom JUSTICE SCALIA, JUSTICE THOMAS, and JUSTICE ALITO join, dissenting.

Determining the appropriate sentence for a teenager convicted of murder presents grave and challenging questions of morality and social policy. Our role, however, is to apply the law, not to answer such questions. The pertinent law here is the Eighth Amendment to the Constitution, which prohibits "cruel and unusual punishments." Today, the Court invokes that Amendment to ban a punishment that the Court does not itself characterize as unusual, and that could not plausibly be described as such. I therefore dissent.

The parties agree that nearly 2,500 prisoners are presently serving life sentences without the possibility of parole for murders they committed before the age of 18. The Court accepts that over 2,000 of those prisoners received that sentence because it was mandated by a legislature. And it recognizes that the Federal Government and most States impose such mandatory sentences. Put simply, if a 17-year-old is convicted of deliberately murdering an innocent victim, it is not "unusual" for the murderer to receive a mandatory sentence of life without parole. That reality should preclude finding that mandatory life imprisonment for juvenile killers violates the Eighth Amendment.

In any event, the Court's holding does not follow from *Roper* and *Graham*. Those cases undoubtedly stand for the proposition that teenagers are less mature, less responsible, and less fixed in their ways than adults—not that a Supreme Court case was needed to establish that. What they do not stand for, and do not even suggest, is that legislators—who also know that teenagers are different from adults—may not require life without parole for juveniles who commit the worst types of murder.

It is a great tragedy when a juvenile commits murder—most of all for the innocent victims. But also for the murderer, whose life has gone so wrong so early. And for society as well, which has lost one or more of its members to deliberate violence, and must harshly punish another. In recent years, our society has moved toward requiring that the murderer, his age notwithstanding, be imprisoned for the remainder of his life. Members of this Court may disagree with that choice. Perhaps science and policy suggest society should show greater mercy to young killers, giving them a greater chance to reform themselves at the risk that they will kill again. But that is not our decision to make. Neither the text of the Constitution nor our precedent prohibits legislatures from requiring that juvenile murderers be sentenced to life without parole. I respectfully dissent.

JUSTICE THOMAS, with whom JUSTICE SCALIA joins, dissenting.

Today's decision invalidates a constitutionally permissible sentencing system based on nothing more than the Court's belief that "its own sense of morality preempts that of the people and their representatives." Because nothing in the Constitution grants the Court the authority it exercises today, I respectfully dissent.

JUSTICE ALITO, with whom JUSTICE SCALIA joins, dissenting.

The Court now holds that Congress and the legislatures of the 50 States are prohibited by the Constitution from identifying any category of murderers under the age of 18 who must be sentenced to life imprisonment without parole. Even a 17 ½-year-old who sets off a bomb in a crowded mall or guns down a dozen students and teachers is a "child" and must be given a chance to persuade a judge to permit his release into society. Nothing in the Constitution supports this arrogation of legislative authority.

What today's decision shows is that our Eighth Amendment cases are no longer tied to any objective indicia of society's standards. Our Eighth Amendment case law is now entirely inward looking. Future cases may extrapolate from today's holding, and this process may continue until the majority brings sentencing practices into line with whatever the majority views as truly evolved standards of decency. The Constitution does not authorize us to take the country on this journey.

Index

ABANDONMENT
Attempt, this index

ACCESSORIES
Accomplice Liability, this index

ACCOMPLICE LIABILITY
    Generally, 107–129
Acquittal of principal, 111
Aiding or encouraging
    Generally, 111–113
    Convicted accomplice, 115
    Mere presence, 111, 115
    Model Penal Code, 113–115
Common law, 107
Conspiracy and accomplice liability, 108
Mens rea, 108
Merger of principals and accessories, 108–111
Model Penal Code
    Generally, 108
    Aiding or encouraging, 113–115
    Corporate liability, 109, 124–126
Promoting or facilitating crime
    Generally, 115–120
    Specific intent, 120

ACTUS REUS
Attempt, this index
Attempted battery assault, 251, 252
Battery, this index
Conspiracy, this index

AIDING OR ENCOURAGING
Accomplice Liability, this index

AMNESIA
Traumatic amnesia, 29, 30

ASSAULT
    Generally, 235–237, 249–259
    See also Battery, this index
Actual or apparent ability to commit battery, 252, 253
Actus reus and *mens rea*, attempted battery assault, 251, 252
Aggravated *vs.* simple assault, 259
Attempt crime or result crime, 256–258
Attempted battery assault
    Generally, 236, 249–253
    Actual or apparent ability to commit battery, 252, 253
    Actus reus and *mens rea*, 251, 252
Frightening assault
    Generally, 236, 253–259
    Aggravated *vs.* simple assault, 259
    Attempt crime or result crime, 256–258
    Proof requirements, 258, 259
Sexual assault. Rape and Sexual Assault, this index

ATTEMPT
    Generally, 131–155
Abandonment
    Generally, 132, 143–145
    Model Penal Code, 145
Actus reus
    Generally, 132, 137–143
    Common law definitions, 139, 140
    Model Penal Code, 140, 141
Impossibility
    Generally, 133, 145–150
    Jaffe Rule, 147
Mens rea, 131, 135–137
Model Penal Code
    Generally, 137
    Abandonment, 145
    Actus reus, 132, 140
    Mens rea, 131, 137
Other crimes, relationship to, 131
Theory, 131

BATTERED DEFENDANTS
    Generally, 358–370
Evidence of battering effects and experiences, 369
Reconsideration of judgments, 370
Retreat from batterer's castle, 369, 370

BATTERY
Generally, 235–249
See also Assault, this index
Actus reus
    Bodily injury battery, 243, 244
    Offensive touching battery, 241, 242
Aggravated *vs.* simply battery, 244
Bodily injury battery
    Generally, 243–245
    Actus reus and *mens rea*, 243, 244
    Aggravated *vs.* simply battery, 244
    Consent as rare defense, 245
    Model Penal Code approach, 244
Law enforcement officers, new crimes for harms to, 243
Life threatening disease, exposure to, 245–249
Mens rea
    Bodily injury battery, 243, 244
    Offensive touching battery, 242
Offensive touching battery
    Generally, 237–243
    Actus reus, 241, 242
    Law enforcement officers, new crimes for harms to, 243
    Mens rea, 242

BURGLARY
Generally, 340–347
Colonies, burglary in, 344
Legislative exemptions, 346
Limiting expansion of burglary, 346
Responses to T.J.E. decision, 346, 347
Who is a burglar, 344, 345

CAPACITY TO COMMIT CRIME
Infancy and mental retardation, 402, 411–421

CAPITAL PUNISHMENT
Generally, 204
Rape, 302–304
Sentencing, this index

CARJACKING
Robbery and Carjacking, this index

CAUSATION
Generally, 81–105
Actual or legal cause, 82
But for test, 86
Intervening causes, 82
Model Penal Code, 81, 82, 85
Participation, causation and, 86
Proof of causation, 81
Suicide and causation, 98 et seq.
Year and a day rule, 81, 84

CHOICE OF EVILS
Necessity Defense, this index

CIVIL RIGHTS
Hate crimes, 237, 270, 271

COMMUNICABLE DISEASES
Exposure to, 245–249

COMPLICITY
Accomplice Liability, this index
Vicarious liability, 109–126

CONSPIRACY
Generally, 155–196
Accomplice liability, conspiracy and, 108
Actus reus (agreement)
    Generally, 165–171
    Co-conspirator hearsay exception, 173
    Scouts and steerers, 173
    Wheels and chains, 173
Bilateral. Unilateral/bilateral jurisdictions, below
Charging conspiracy *vs.* substantive offenses, 165
Co-conspirators
    Culpability, 133, 186–196
    Hearsay exception, 173
Knowledge *vs.* intent, 165
Mens rea
    Generally, 133, 160–165
    Charging conspiracy *vs.* substantive offenses, 165
    Knowledge *vs.* intent, 165
    Negligent crimes, conspiracy to commit, 165
    Other conspiracies, 164
Merger
    Generally, 179–186
    Multiple inchoate offenses, 186
Negligent crimes, conspiracy to commit, 165
Overt act
    Generally, 133, 174–178
    How much is enough, 177
    Venue, 177
Renunciation, 178, 179

Index

Scouts and steerers, 173
Undercover agents, use of, 160
Unilateral/bilateral jurisdictions
    Generally, 133, 155–160
    Coverage, 160
    New legislation, 160
    Undercover agents, use of, 160
Venue, 177
Wheels and chains, 173
Withdrawal, 178, 179

CONTROLLED SUBSTANCES
Drugs and Narcotics, this index

DEADLY FORCE, USE OF
Expansion of right to use, 371, 372

DEATH PENALTY
Capital Punishment, this index

DEFENSES
Battered Defendants, this index
Battery, consent as rare defense, 245
Deadly force, expansion of right to use, 371, 372
Dwelling, defense of, 351, 370, 371
Intoxication or drugged condition, 50, 68
Involuntary act defenses, 21, 22
Justification Defenses, this index
Larceny, claim of right defense, 329
Law enforcement defense, 372
Necessity Defense, this index
Others, defense of, 355, 356
Rape and Sexual Assault, this index
Self-Defense, this index
Stand your ground laws, 372
Unconsciousness defense, 21

DOMESTIC VIOLENCE
    Generally, 237, 266–270
Battered Defendants, this index
Federal crimes, 267
Indian Country, 268–270
State crimes, 266, 267

DRUGS AND NARCOTICS
Insanity, this index
Mens rea, drugged condition, 50, 68
Rape of drugged victim, 279, 304–306

DURESS
    Generally, 379, 381
Model Penal Code, 382

DUTY TO RETREAT
Self-Defense, this index

DWELLING, DEFENSE OF
Generally, 351, 370, 371

EMBEZZLEMENT
    Generally, 316, 329–334
Charging wrong crime, 333
Entrustment, 333
Model Penal Code fusion of larceny and embezzlement crimes, 333

EVIDENCE
Battered defendants, evidence of effects and experiences, 369
Conspiracy, hearsay exception, 173
Rape and Sexual Assault, this index

EXCUSES
    Generally, 379–426
Duress
    Generally, 379, 381
    Model Penal Code, 382
Infancy and mental retardation, 411–421
Insanity, this index
Justification *vs.* excuse, 379

FALSE PRETENSES
Generally, 316, 334

FELONS AND FELONIES
Felon registration statutes, 38, 39
Felony-murder. Homicide, this index

GUILTY PLEAS
Sentencing, 434

HATE CRIMES
Generally, 237, 270, 271

HOMICIDE
    Generally, 197–234
Capital punishment
    Generally, 204
    Sentencing, this index
Defenses. Manslaughter (voluntary), below
Deterrence and premeditation, 198, 204
Extreme emotional disturbance, 209
Felony-murder
    Generally, 198, 212–214
    Acquittal of underlying felony, 214
    Faulkner's logic, 214
    Independent felony requirement, 213
    Misdemeanor manslaughter, 214

Model Penal Code, 213
Triggering felonies, 213
Heat of passion defense, 205–208
Imperfect defense, 209
Malice, 198
Manslaughter (involuntary)
    Generally, 198, 214–227
    Mens rea, 215
    Model Penal Code, 223, 224
    Vehicular homicide offenses, 227
Manslaughter (voluntary)
    Generally, 198, 205–209
    Extreme emotional disturbance, 209
    Heat of passion defense, 205–208
    Imperfect defense, 209
    Model Penal Code, 205
    Provocation defense
        Generally, 205–208
        Lack of provocation, proving, 208, 209
Misdemeanor manslaughter, 214
Model Penal Code
    Felony-murder, 213
    Heat of passion, 205
    Manslaughter (involuntary), 223, 224
    Manslaughter (voluntary), 205
    Murder, 203, 204
Murder
    Generally, 199–205
    Capital punishment, 204
    Degrees, 199–205
    Deliberation, 198
    Deterrence and premeditation, 198, 204
    Felony-murder, above
    Malice, 198
    Model Penal Code, 203
    Unpremeditated, 210–212
Negligent homicide, 198, 224
Premeditation, 198, 204
Provocation. Manslaughter (voluntary), above
Unpremeditated murder, 210–212
Vehicular homicide offenses, 227

IMPOSSIBILITY
Attempt, this index

INCHOATE OFFENSES
Attempt, this index
Conspiracy, this index

INFANCY
Capacity, infancy and, 402, 411–421

INSANITY
    Generally, 379, 380, 382–411
Acquittal, effect of
    Generally, 404–411
    Civil commitment, 411
    Medical treatment, 411
Bifurcation of guilt and sanity, 402
Civil commitment, 411
Criminal process, 380
Drugs
    Competency and drugs, 399, 400
    Jury's awareness of drugs, 401
Evaluation by state psychiatrists, 400
Expert testimony, defendant's mental condition, 398
Guilty but mentally ill, 402
Imposing the defense, 398, 399
Indefinite commitment, 397
Insane delusions, 385
Irresistible impulse test, 385
Lay witnesses, 402
M'Naghten
    Generally, 383–385
    Insane delusions, 385
Medical treatment, 411
Mental examination of defendant, 398
Multiple personalities, 403, 404
Pleading insanity, 397, 398
State psychiatrists, evaluation by, 400
Test for insanity, 380
Verdict of NGI, consequences of, 400, 401
Yates case, 402, 403

INTENT
Conspiracy, knowledge *vs.* intent, 165
Mens Rea, this index

INTOXICATION
Mens rea, 50, 68–74
Public drunkenness, 36–38
Rape of intoxicated victim, 279, 304–306

JUSTIFICATION DEFENSES
    Generally, 351–377
Battered Defendants, this index
Deadly force, expansion of right to use
    Generally, 371
    New "castle" laws, 371
    Stand your ground laws, 372

Index

Dwelling, defense of, 351, 370, 371
Law enforcement defense, 372
Necessity Defense, this index
Others, defense of, 355, 356
Self-Defense, this index
Stand your ground laws, 372

LARCENY
Generally, 316, 323–329
Claim of right defense, 329
Gaps in larceny rules, 328
Larceny by trick, 327, 328
Model Penal Code fusion of larceny and embezzlement crimes, 333, 334
Taking and "carrying away," 326
Trespass element, origins of, 325, 326
Trespassory taking from possession, 326, 327

LAW ENFORCEMENT OFFICERS
Battery, new crimes for harms to, 243

LIFE SUPPORT
Termination of, 43, 44

LIFE THREATENING DISEASE
Exposure to, 245–249

MANSLAUGHTER
Homicide, this index

MEDICAL CARE
Prayer without medical care, 44

MENS REA
Generally, 49–79
Accomplice liability, 108
Attempt, 135–137
Attempted battery assault, 251
Conspiracy, this index
Criminal intention, levels of, 50–58
Drugged condition, 50, 68–74
Ignorance of law, 79
Intent and motive, difference between, 56–58
Intoxication, 50, 68–74
Involuntary manslaughter, 215
Jurisdictional variations in definitions, 55
Levels of criminal intention, 50–58
Mistake of fact, 50, 74–76
Mistake of law
    Generally, 50, 76–79
    Exceptions, 79
    Ignorance of law, 79

Model Penal Code, 53–55
Proof of specific *mens rea*, 49
Rape and Sexual Assault, this index
Strict liability, 49, 58–68

MENTAL RETARDATION
Capacity to commit crime, 411–421

MERGER
Conspiracy, 179–186

MISTAKE
Imperfect self-defense and mistake, comparing, 357, 358
Mens Rea, this index
Rape and Sexual Assault, this index

MOTIVE
Intent and motive, difference between, 56–58

MURDER
Homicide, this index

NECESSITY DEFENSE
Generally, 2, 351, 352, 372, 373
Factor tests for necessity, 373
Model Penal Code approach, 373
Necessity and duty to retreat. Self-Defense, this index
Rarely successful defense, 373

OMISSIONS
Generally, 22, 39–48
Life support, termination of, 43, 44
Prayer without medical care, 44
Taking responsibility, 42, 43

PRINCIPALS AND ACCESSORIES
Accomplice Liability, this index

PROMOTING OR FACILITATING CRIME
Accomplice Liability, this index

PROPERTY CRIMES
Generally, 315–350
Burglary, this index
Common law limitations on "property," 320, 321
Defining property
    Generally, 317–323
    Common law limitations, 320, 321
    Intangible information as "goods," 322, 323

Model Penal Code approach, 322
Updating definitions, 321, 322
Embezzlement, this index
False pretenses, 334
Intangible information as "goods," 322, 323
Larceny, this index
Overview, 316, 317
Receiving stolen property, 334, 335
Robbery and Carjacking, this index

PUNISHMENT
Purposes of Criminal Law, this index
Sentencing, this index

PURPOSES OF CRIMINAL LAW
Generally, 1–19
Customs and public opinion, 7
Imposing punishment, 6, 7
Punishment, purposes of
Generally, 8–17
Deterrence, 1, 15, 16
Economic efficiency, 16, 17
Rehabilitation, 1, 15
Restraint, 1, 16
Retribution, 2, 15
Social condemnation, 14, 15
Selection of victim, 7

RAPE AND SEXUAL ASSAULT
Generally, 277–314
Affirmative agreement, absence of as lack of consent, 293
Age, reasonable mistake of fact as to, 307
Consent as affirmative defense
Generally, 278, 294–298
Acquittal, consent evidence needed, 298
Recognition of consent defense, 297, 298
Consent, lack of
Generally, 278, 290–294
Affirmative agreement, absence of, 293
Manifested unwillingness, 293
Non-consensual sex without force, 290
Reforms, 291, 292
Resistance as lack of consent, 292, 293
Resistance evidence, use of, 293, 294
Withdrawal of consent, 294
Death penalty for rape, 302–304

Deception, rape by, 279, 304
Defenses
Consent as affirmative defense, above
Mens rea and mistake of fact defense, below
Drugged victim, rape of, 279, 304–306
Evidence
Acquittal, consent evidence needed, 298
Rape trauma syndrome, 279, 308
Resistance evidence, use of, 293, 294
Forcible rape
Generally, 280–304
Consent as affirmative defense, above
Consent, lack of, above
Death penalty, 302
Definitions of force, 289, 290
Force, threat, or fear, 278, 280–290
Jury attitudes, 288
Law reform, reasons for, 287, 288
Marital rape exemption, 301, 302
Mens rea and mistake of fact defense, below
Model Penal Code proposals, 288, 289
Non-consensual sex without force, 290
Penetration, force as act of, 290
Psychological pressure, force as, 289, 290
Will to resist, force as threat that overcomes, 289
Internet crimes, 307
Intoxicated victim, rape of, 279, 304–306
Jury attitudes, 288
Law reform, reasons for, 287, 288
Manifested unwillingness, lack of consent as, 293
Marital rape exemption, 301, 302
Mens rea and mistake of fact defense
Generally, 278, 298–301
General intent, 298, 299
Mistake instructions, limitations on, 300, 301
Recognition or refusal to recognize defense, 299, 300
Mistake of fact
Mens rea and mistake of fact defense, above
Statutory rape, reasonable mistake as to age, 306, 307

Index

Model Penal Code proposals, 288, 289
Non-consensual sex without force, 290
Overview, 278–280
Penetration, force as act of, 290
Prior sexual conduct and rape shield laws, 310, 311
Psychological pressure, force as, 289, 290
Rape shield laws
    Generally, 279, 308–310
    Exclusions and exceptions, 310
    Goals, 309, 310
    Prior sexual conduct, 310, 311
Rape trauma syndrome evidence, 279, 308
Resistance as lack of consent, 292, 293
Resistance evidence, use of, 293, 294
Shield laws. Rape shield laws, above
Statutory rape
    Generally, 279, 306, 307
    Age, reasonable mistake of fact as to, 306, 307
    Romeo and Juliet statutes, evolution of, 306
Will to resist, force as threat that overcomes, 289
Withdrawal of consent, 294

RECEIVING STOLEN PROPERTY
Generally, 316, 334, 335

RECKLESS ENDANGERMENT
Generally, 236, 259, 260

RESCUE
Duty to rescue, 22

ROBBERY AND CARJACKING
    Generally, 316, 317, 335–340
Defining presence, 340
Elements of carjacking, 339, 340

SELF-DEFENSE
    Generally, 351–370
Aggressor rule, 356
Battered Defendants, this index
Duty to retreat. Necessity and duty to retreat, above
Imperfect self-defense. Reasonable belief and imperfect self-defense, below
Mistake and imperfect self-defense, comparing, 357, 358
Necessity and duty to retreat
    Generally, 352–357
    Aggressor rule, 356

Model Penal Code approach, 357
Original castle doctrine, 356
Others, defense of, 355, 356
Preservation of duty to retreat, 355
Rejection of duty to retreat, 354, 355
Original castle doctrine, 356
Others, defense of, 355, 356
Reasonable belief and imperfect self-defense
    Generally, 357
    Measuring reasonableness, 358
    Mistake and imperfect self-defense, comparing, 357, 358
    Subjective standard, objections to, 358
Retreat. Necessity and duty to retreat, above

SENTENCING
    Generally, 427–463
Capital punishment
    Generally, 428, 435–443
    Aggravating and mitigating circumstances, 435, 442
    Cruel and unusual punishment, 428
    Discriminatory application, 442, 443
    Mandatory death sentences, 441
    Method of execution, 443
Factors, 434, 435
Geriatric release, 457–463
Guilty pleas, 434
Judge *vs.* jury
    Generally, 428–435
    Aggravating circumstances for death penalty, 435
    Factors, 434, 435
    Guilty pleas, 434
    Mandatory minimum sentences, 435
Judicial discretion, 428
Juveniles, life sentence without parole, 428
Mandatory minimum sentences, 435
Overview, 428
Proportionality
    Generally, 443–463
    Geriatric release, 457–463

SEXUAL ASSAULT
Rape and Sexual Assault, this index

STALKING
    Generally, 237, 260–266
Enforcement of laws, 265, 266

Modern trends, 264, 265
Original elements of crime, 263, 264

STATUTORY RAPE
Rape and Sexual Assault, this index

STRICT LIABILITY
Generally, 49, 58–68

SUICIDE
Causation, 98 et seq.

VENUE
Conspiracy, 177

VICARIOUS LIABILITY
  Generally, 109–126
Corporate liability, 109, 124–126

VOLUNTARY ACT
  Generally, 21–48
Brake failure, 24
Carried away, 24
Drunkenness in public, 36–38
Felon registration statutes, 38, 39
Involuntary act defenses, 21, 22
Legal duty to act, 22
Model Penal Code, 23
Omissions, this index
Possession as voluntary act, 24
Reflex shock reaction, 30
Status crimes, 22
Traumatic amnesia, 29, 30
Unconsciousness defense, 21